THE INTERNATIONAL WORLD OF ELECTRONIC MEDIA

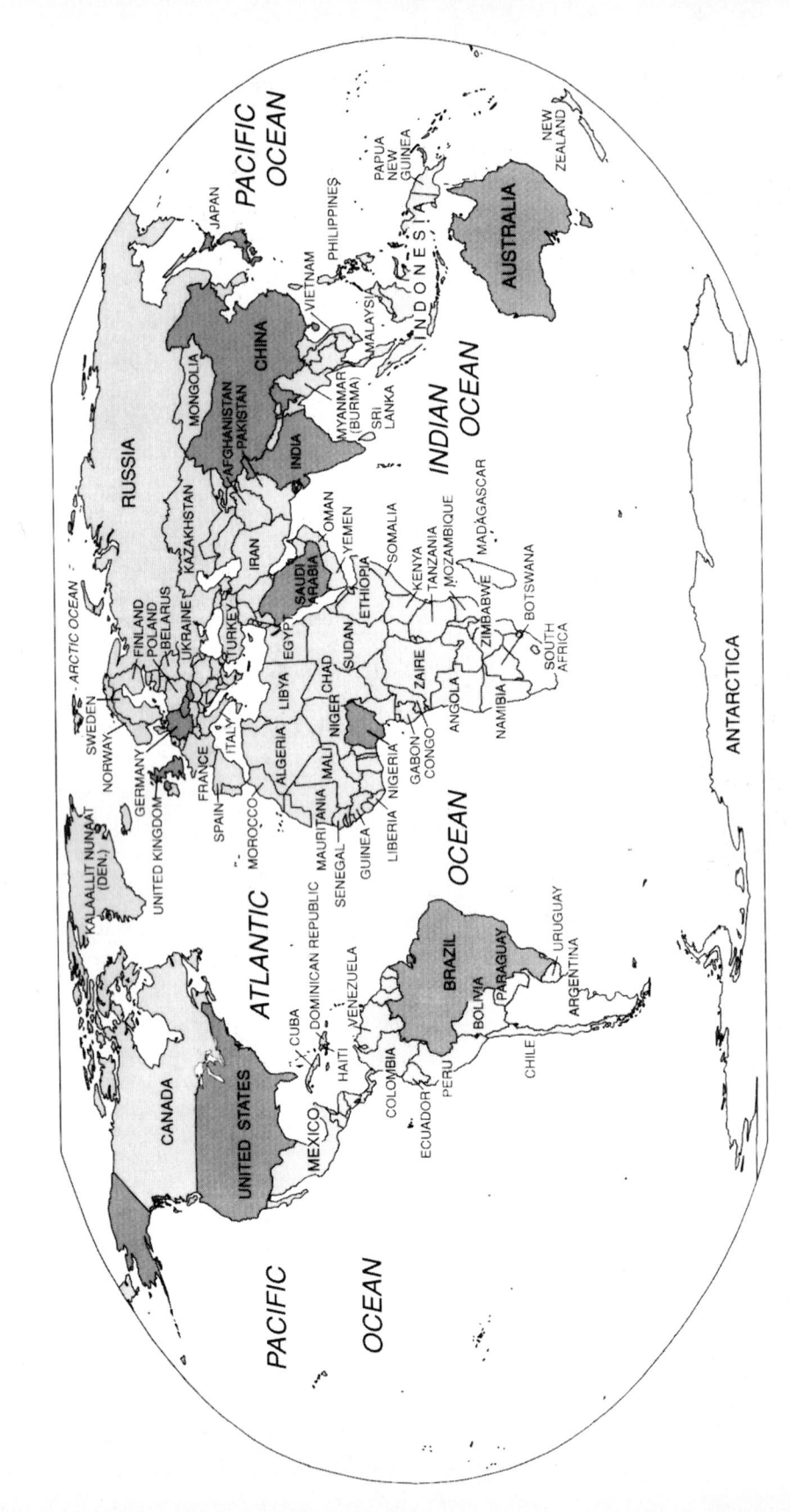

THE INTERNATIONAL WORLD OF ELECTRONIC MEDIA

EDITED BY

Lynne Schafer Gross
California State University, Fullerton

McGraw-Hill, Inc.

New York St. Louis San Francisco Auckland Bogotá Caracas
Lisbon London Madrid Mexico City Milan Montreal New Delhi
San Juan Singapore Sydney Tokyo Toronto

McGraw-Hill Series in Mass Communication

CONSULTING EDITOR

Barry L. Sherman

Anderson: *Communication Research: Issues and Methods*

Carroll and Davis: *Electronic Media Programming: Strategies and Decision Making*

Dominick: *The Dynamics of Mass Communication*

Dominick, Sherman, and Copeland: *Broadcasting/Cable and Beyond: An Introduction to Modern Electronic Media*

Dordick: *Understanding Modern Telecommunications*

Gross: *The International World of Electronic Media*

Hickman: *Television Directing*

Holsinger and Dilts: *Media Law*

Richardson: *Corporate and Organizational Video*

Sherman: *Telecommunications Management: Broadcasting/Cable and the New Technologies*

Walters: *Broadcast Writing: Principles and Practice*

Whetmore: *American Electric: Introduction to Telecommunications and Electronic Media*

Wilson: *Mass Media/Mass Culture: An Introduction*

Wurtzel and Rosenbaum: *Television Production*

This book was set in Times Roman by Better Graphics, Inc.
The editors were Hilary Jackson, Fran Marino, and David A. Damstra;
the production supervisor was Cynthia Regan.
The cover was designed by Carla Bauer.
R. R. Donnelley & Sons Company was printer and binder.

THE INTERNATIONAL WORLD OF ELECTRONIC MEDIA

Copyright © 1995 by McGraw-Hill, Inc. All rights reserved. Printed in the United States of America. Except as permitted under the United States Copyright Act of 1976, no part of this publication may be reproduced or distributed in any form or by any means, or stored in a data base or retrieval system, without the prior written permission of the publisher.

 This book is printed on recycled, acid-free paper containing 10% postconsumer waste.

1 2 3 4 5 6 7 8 9 0 DOH DOH 9 0 9 8 7 6 5 4

ISBN 0-07-025142-8

Library of Congress Cataloging-in-Publication Data

The International world of electronic media / edited by Lynne Schafer Gross.
    p.   cm.
    Includes bibliographical references and index.
    ISBN 0-07-025142-8
    1. Broadcasting.   2. Mass media.   I. Gross, Lynne S.
HE8689.4.I58   1995
384.54—dc20   94-28055

*To Kendall and Tilda:
May they someday visit
many of these countries.*

CONTENTS

Preface ix

1. **THE IMPORTANCE OF ELECTRONIC MEDIA THROUGHOUT THE WORLD** 1

PART I

North America

Overview of North America 22

2. **UNITED STATES OF AMERICA, BY LYNNE SCHAFER GROSS** 29

PART II

South America

Overview of Central and South America 54

3. **BRAZIL, BY JOSEPH STRAUBHAAR** 61

PART III

Western Europe

Overview of Western Europe 88

4. **UNITED KINGDOM OF GREAT BRITAIN, BY BRIAN T. EVANS** 99

5. **GERMANY, BY WOLFGANG HASTERT** 123

PART IV

Eastern Europe

Overview of Eastern Europe 148

6. **THE SLOVAK REPUBLIC AND THE CZECH REPUBLIC (FORMERLY CZECHOSLOVAKIA), BY IVAN STADTRUCKER** 157

7. **RUSSIA, BY SERGEI V. EROFEEV** 175

PART V

The Middle East

Overview of the Middle East   194

8. SAUDI ARABIA, BY DOUGLAS A. BOYD   203

PART VI

Africa

Overview of Africa   224

9. NIGERIA, BY LOUISE M. BOURGAULT   233

PART VII

Asia

Overview of Asia   254

10. INDIA, BY LALIT AND SUREKHA ACHARYA   261

11. CHINA, BY JOSEPH S. JOHNSON WITH OBSERVATIONS BY DU RUIQING   277

12. JAPAN, BY NOBUO OTSUKA   299

PART VIII

Australasia

Overview of Australasia   320

13. AUSTRALIA, BY BRUCE MOLLOY AND DEREK WILDING   325

EPILOGUE   348

Index   351

PREFACE

This book was born through a union of a love of travel and of radio and television. As I have worked in various countries, I have been struck by the similarities and differences in media around the world and by the rapidly changing nature of the electronic media.

Although I have wanted to write a book about the international electronic media scene for some time, I knew I could never catch the moving target and write something that was up-to-date about a large number of countries. I decided instead to ask experts in the media of particular countries to write chapters for the book.

As the chapters came in and I began perusing them, I was very happy with my decision to involve all of these writers. To me, the introspection they have brought to the chapters is fascinating. I hope you agree. Because most of the authors are natives of the countries about which they write, they convey not only the facts about their electronic media systems but also the attitudes and subtle pressures. How something is said is often as revealing as what is said.

This book is a kaleidoscope of information about various countries, but it is also a snapshot in time. With a topic such as this, it is difficult to keep up-to-date, but the authors and I tried to update material as close to deadline as possible. Between the date the chapters were originally due and the date of publication, one of the countries selected was divided into two and a number of the organizations referred to went bankrupt, merged, or expanded into forms very unlike their former selves. However, the information is as up-to-date as possible and the political ramifications discussed point the way toward the changes that have occurred and are likely to continue to occur.

FEATURES OF THE BOOK

Several special features set this book apart from others that cover international electronic media. Some of these features are the following:

- Each section of the world is introduced with a brief overview that indicates the general traits and trends in that part of the world. This enables readers to place the material of the individual chapters into a regional context.
- Each overview includes a map of the section of the world being considered, with details shown for each country that is discussed. A country's media attitude is influenced by its relationship with its neighbors.
- At the beginning of each chapter is a list of some basic statistics about the country—geographic area, capital, population, religions, languages, type of government, gross domestic product, literacy. The statistics are the same for each country, allowing for ease of comparison. This background is needed in order to understand the media structure. For example, the amount of wealth a country has determines what type of radio and TV facilities it can afford; the form of government influences the amount of control the state has over the press and the type of news that is broadcast.
- The chapters are written by authors with outstanding credentials. They have lived in, worked in, and/or taught courses on the media in the countries about which they write.
- Information about some of the countries has not been previously published. This is particularly true of the Eastern European countries that recently emerged from years of censorship and totalitarian control. The authors now feel free to tell what actually happened in the past.
- The chapter organization allows for easy comparison of the various countries because all chapters contain the same overriding topics. This lends itself well to compare-and-contrast discussions and essay questions.
- The book includes a map of the world that highlights the countries that are discussed in detail in the text. This will help students pinpoint the location of each country in relationship to the rest of the world.
- Photographs and tables illustrate points discussed in the text and allow readers to obtain more of a sense of the physical environment of each country.
- Each chapter includes a selected bibliography for those who wish to read further.

ORGANIZATION OF THE BOOK

The book begins with an introductory chapter that covers the importance of media on the international scene and the importance of the world community in the development of electronic media. It lays the groundwork for many of the issues discussed in succeeding chapters.

After that, the organization is according to areas of the world—North America, South America, Western Europe, Eastern Europe, the Middle East, Africa, Asia, and Australasia. For each area, I have written an overview that includes philosophical underpinnings, generalizations, and a number of specifics for countries not covered in detail. This is followed by information about one or more representative countries from the area, discussed thoroughly by the author of each chapter.

All of the chapters are organized under the same major headings: general characteristics of the country; the development of electronic media in the particular country; organization and financing; programming; laws and regulations; the audience; technology; external services; the importance in the world media community; and the major electronic media issues facing the country. The inclusion of these topics should enable readers to compare and contrast the electronic media characteristics of the various countries.

At the end of the book there is a short epilogue that ties together various points brought out in the chapters and raises issues for the future.

ACKNOWLEDGMENTS

I am indebted not only to all the chapter authors but also to many others who have given me guidance and information, particularly Richard Barton, Pennsylvania State University; Clay Carter, California Polytechnic University, San Luis Obispo; Prudence Faxon, California Polytechnic University, Pomona; Joe Foote, Southern Illinois University; John Gregory, Pasadena City College; Nishan Havandjian, California Polytechnic University, San Luis Obispo; Brian Litman; George Mastroianni, California State University, Fullerton; Brian Pauling, New Zealand Broadcasting School in Christchurch; Paul Prince, Kansas State University; Paul Smeyak, University of Florida; George Whitehouse, University of South Dakota; Manfred Wolfram, University of Cincinnati; and Fran Marino and Hilary Jackson of McGraw-Hill. I would also like to thank my husband for his help and patience as he has accompanied me on some of my information-gathering trips.

Lynne Schafer Gross

THE
INTERNATIONAL
WORLD OF
ELECTRONIC
MEDIA

CHAPTER 1

The Importance of Electronic Media Throughout the World

A FEW RADIO AND TELEVISION TALES

When Polish leader Lech Walesa was asked what had caused the collapse of communism in Eastern Europe, he pointed to a TV set and said, "It all came from there."

In largely Islamic Turkey, two Muslim parents locked their daughter in the house because she had appeared on the TV program *Saklambac* without their permission. *Saklambac* is a local version of *The Dating Game* produced under a licensing agreement with the show's U.S. creator, Chuck Barris. The parents objected to the fact that their daughter had talked to strange men.

For several years during the 1980s, British viewer polls found that Steven Spielberg's 1983 film *E.T.* was consistently voted the most popular videocassette. Not an unusual finding, except that *E.T.* had not yet been legally released on videocassette in England. The viewers were seeing pirated tapes.

A Chinese intellectual imprisoned in China in 1989 made a list of complaints about his captors. One was that he hadn't been read his rights the way they do it on the television show *Hunter*.

The disc jockey banters in English and takes telephone requests for Madonna, Michael Jackson, and other top-40 artists. Then comes the traffic report that gives away the location. It's not the Hollywood Freeway that's backed up; it's Chien-Kuo Road in Taipei, Taiwan.

At the Vatican, Archbishop John Foley rises by 6 A.M. to watch CNN so that he knows what to pray for.

These stories, and many others like them, point out the ramifications of the global flow of information and the importance placed upon electronic media in all countries.

Back in the 1960s, a Canadian professor, Marshall McLuhan, predicted that television would create a "global village." In his words, " 'Time' has ceased, 'space' has vanished. We now live in . . . a simultaneous happening." McLuhan's prophesies are becoming more and more true each day.

But all is not perfect within this simultaneous happening. The proliferation and importance of the electronic media has its downsides and its controversies. The bulk of this book will discuss individual countries and how they organize and operate radio and TV and deal with the issues they face in relation to media interactions with the rest of the world. This chapter will look at issues from a global point of view, discussing the background information, pros, cons, and gray areas that color the effectiveness and acceptance of the media.

Major among the issues are the free flow of information versus the need for national identity, the effects of global journalism, the ramifications of entertainment program exchange, the impact of satellites, the influence of the videocassette recorder (VCR), the growth of global advertising, the power of multinational media companies, and the problems related to technical standards.

THE FREE FLOW OF INFORMATION VERSUS THE NEED FOR NATIONAL IDENTITY

The issue of free flow of information versus national identity is one that encompasses virtually all other issues related to the globalization of radio and TV. On the free-flow side are those who feel that any country or media organization that wants to should be able to send media information to the people of any other country. On the national identity side are those who feel that each country should decide for itself what information should be allowed to enter its borders.

The Basis of the Arguments Not surprisingly, the main advocate of free flow is the United States, followed by the countries of Western Europe. The feeling among these countries is that when unimpeded communications traffic is allowed, people everywhere benefit. Not so, say the advocates for national identity. What happens when free flow is allowed, they claim, is that the rich industrial countries do all the sending and the poor developing countries do all the receiving. This gives people in the have-not countries a slanted view and tends to make their national cultural, psychological, and political values irrelevant. It also corrupts people in poorer countries and makes them want products and services they don't need and can't afford. "Nonsense," counter the free-flow advocates. "People are not that gullible and passive. They don't just sit there and absorb through osmosis everything they see and hear from the media. The power of the sender is not nearly as potent as the power of the receiver. In fact, when there are attempts by the industrial powers to influence other countries, these attempts often backfire. People are much more influenced by those around them than they are by the media."

Of course, where a nation stands on the issue of free flow depends largely on where it sits. The countries in what is often referred to as the Third World have distinctly different ideas than countries in the First World. (Until the breakup of communism, politicians and the media often referred to the First, Second, and Third Worlds. The First World consisted of the industrialized capitalistic countries such as the United States, England, and Japan. The Second World was the Soviet Union and its Eastern European satellite countries such as Poland and Czechoslovakia. The Third World consisted of poorer, developing countries such as Nigeria and Pakistan that the First and Second World countries often tried to court into their political camps. With the downfall of communism in Eastern Europe, the Second World really no longer exists. The term "First World" is not used much any more, but the term "Third World" is still used to describe nations with relatively low living standards.)

Most of these Third World nations threw off their colonial status in the 1950s and 1960s and are now in the process of trying to develop their own unique political and economic systems. They worry that their native customs, which they value, will be destroyed if young people from Afghanistan to Zimbabwe become Madonna wanna-bes. They feel the power of the media and contend that it strengthens the strong and weakens the weak. All nations, even the ones that cannot afford it, feel the need to develop a national broadcasting system, much as they feel the need to have a national airline (be it only one airplane) or a national army.

The industrialized nations, particularly the United States, have a history of free flow within their own borders. The First Amendment of the U.S. Constitution guarantees freedom of the press. Americans are used to advocacy journalism on the part of their reporters and often value the rights of the communicator more than the rights of those being communicated about—political campaigns where reporters try to uncover every flaw in a candidate are a case in point. It is difficult for people raised in the United States to imagine that anyone, anywhere else in the world, wouldn't want freedom of expression. Other industrial nations, although they do not share the degree of democracy present in the United States, still feel that they are doing Third World nations a favor by helping them obtain culture and information. Western Europeans, with their colonial history, and Japanese, with their work ethic, feel the need for and the appropriateness of influencing others.

The argument of free flow versus national identity is not new. When the telegraph was introduced in the late 1800s, some people feared that national sovereignty would be threatened and European versions of news would dominate. And history has shown that the growth of radio and television has strengthened the demand for democracy and spread popular (American and Western European) culture.

A major platform for the free flow versus national identity debate was created by the United Nations Educational, Scientific, and Cultural Organization (UNESCO) during the 1970s. Most of the Third World countries had emerged from colonialism and were being courted by the First and Second Worlds. Although they were receptive to financial help from either of the powerful sides, these countries wanted their own autonomy and the potential to develop into powerful entities. During the late 1960s and early 1970s several statements had been issued calling for world equity, sovereign equality, interdependence, common interest, and cooperation among states regardless of their economic and social structures. High among the desires of Third World leaders was access to communication technologies. They were opposed to the idea of free flow because they felt it brought a new type of colonization—electronic colonization.

The New World Information Order
UNESCO set up an International Commission for the Study of Communication Problems made up of representatives of the First, Second, and Third Worlds in an attempt to create a New World Information Order (NWIO). It tackled the complexities, changing realities, dilemmas, contradictions, and possible solutions concerning the world's communication structure. The commission's report (often referred to as the MacBride report because Sean MacBride of Ireland was the chairman) was issued early in 1980 and formally titled *Many Voices, One World: Communication and Society Today and Tomorrow*.

The report favored free flow but softened the concept by calling for free flow with a wider, more balanced dissemination. It strongly suggested that the Third World be provided with the means to contribute as well as to receive. It addressed new technologies such as computers, satellites, and data banks and recommended that have-nots should have access to these technologies but needed to proceed carefully so that negative effects were not experienced. It advocated training programs for Third World journalists and supported the idea of grassroots citizen groups involved in media. The commission came out against the general concept of censorship but was opposed to a journalistic code for the entire world that would incorporate anticensorship provisions.

The MacBride report was hailed as the first international document that provided a truly global view of the world's communication problems. But of course it was also criticized by both sides. Those on the Third World side felt the document didn't go far enough in supporting developing countries. They also feared that the recommendations for training and new technologies would lead to greater dependency of the weak on the strong and would strengthen transnational corporations. Others, particularly U.S. journalists, were upset about the weakness of the free-flow compromise and issued a dissenting document, the Declaration of Talloires (drawn up in Talloires, France) that asserted the importance of advertising and took out the word "balanced" in discussing the dissemination of information. It stated instead that everyone had a universal right to be freely informed.

The issues related to the NWIO have never been resolved and are still being debated more than 10 years after the MacBride report was issued. They relate to a great deal of what has transpired regarding technology, advertising, international media corporations, and programming in both the journalism and the entertainment categories.

THE EFFECTS OF GLOBAL JOURNALISM

Modern television has changed the way that politics and world affairs are conducted. To the extent that the free-flow argument has won (and it seems to have the upper hand), nations now find it much harder to keep their people in the dark about news—even about events occurring in their own country. National leaders find they must be responsive to world opinion, not just feedback from their own constituents.

The Shrinking of Time One of the major media factors that affects the conduct of politics is the shrinking of time. As recently as the 1960s, President John F. Kennedy had 6 days to ponder what to do before going public about the Cuban missile crisis. In 1991 during the Persian Gulf conflict, President George Bush was lucky to have 6 hours before having to make a major decision. Vietnamese war news, as powerful as it appeared, was actually several days late because film had to be flown out of Vietnam before it could be transmitted. Now, in the age of satellites and miniature TV cameras, the remotest of riots, floods, and famines can be viewed worldwide while they are happening.

This places great responsibility upon reporters to be accurate and thorough, which is difficult to accomplish when everything is happening quickly. Although pictures usually don't lie, very often a journalist's interpretation or selection of video events can jell worldwide public opinion. And these opinions jell sooner than they would otherwise because of the speed of modern electronic media. TV has managed to shorten the time between action and thought and between thought and action. Reporters attempting to obtain a "scoop" and gather information faster and better than reporters in another country or in another organization within their own country have an ethical responsibility to make sure they are reporting in a responsible manner that will not inflame international tensions.

Terrorism Journalists are also faced with ethical dilemmas in relation to international terrorism. Terrorism is legitimate news; it is rare, unexpected, violent, and intense. However, because of the media, terrorism has often become theater—played out on an international stage. Terrorists seek out the media and rely on the coverage and the resulting publicity. As the media broadcast the events, the world learns what the terrorists want and what is important to them. Journalists pursue a multitude of angles and often wind up explaining the terrorists' demands and issues more fully than any of these outlaws could have hoped.

Occasionally this leads to world understanding, but often it simply encourages other terrorists to undertake crimes, hoping for the same media exposure. When perpetrators of terror demand time on the airwaves, journalists are caught in a tight bind. Giving time encourages the crime and others similar to it; refusing to give time usually endangers innocent people who are being held hostage. In these cases, the media become part of the event, not just the reporters of it.

News Providers A large number of organizations provide news to the international community. Individual countries or regions have their own news services that emphasize national and international events that are most likely to be of interest to them. The Africa News Service, British Information Service, and Xinhua News Agency (China) are examples.

Several truly international television news services exist, primarily VisNews (often referred to as Reuters Television) and World Television News. The former is owned by Reuters (a British company), NBC, and the British Broadcasting Corporation (BBC), and the latter by Capital Cities/ABC, Nine Network in Australia, and ITN (a British news service). Although these companies have multinational owners, they are all from well-developed industrial countries, a fact that is not lost on lesser-developed nations.

In addition, regularly scheduled newscasts of one country often appear in another country. Mexican newscasts are shown on Spanish-language stations in a variety of countries. CBS, NBC, and ABC evening newscasts are broadcast in many countries (with subtitles in non-English-speaking nations.) These newscasts are not shown in national prime-time periods (in fact, they are often shown in the middle of the night), but people in other countries who want to hear the U.S. version of news can do so. The same is true for BBC news.

A large number of the world's nations operate government-run external services (to be discussed in greater detail in the following chapters) with the specific mission of broadcasting news and information, intertwined with entertainment, in such a way that it presents the host country in a good light to other specifically targeted countries and delivers to these countries information they are probably not getting from their own governments. The radio service Voice of America and the television service Worldnet are U.S. examples. Other countries with extensive external broadcasting include Britain and China.

Cable News Network The titan in supplying news to the entire world, however, is Cable News Network (CNN). Formed in 1980 by U.S. entrepreneur Ted Turner, its concept of 24-hour news was considered harebrained by most of the news establishment. However, 10 years later Turner was laughing all the way to the bank as his brainchild's profits soared to $134 million. Although CNN started as a cable TV network for viewers in the United States, Turner had internationalism in mind from the beginning. When the service went worldwide in the mid-1980s, entities in various countries slowly but surely subscribed to (or bootlegged) the satellite feeds until today close to 150 countries air CNN. When major news events occur, CNN's subscriber list increases dramatically. For example, after the 1987 stock market crash, numerous banks and security firms around the world bought the service.

Although in some countries CNN is available to the general public through broadcast or cable TV (this accounts for the taxi driver in Poland who claims he learned English from anchor Bobbie Battista), in other countries it is seen only by national leaders who have satellite dishes or by people staying in hotel rooms that are wired to receive it. And this popularity with the movers and shakers of the world has made it all the more powerful.

It has been watched regularly by Fidel Castro, Margaret Thatcher, Muammar Kaddafi, King Fahd of Saudi Arabia when he has insomnia, and George Bush, who, while he was president, once quipped, "I learn more from CNN than I do from the CIA."

Because of its continuous coverage, it is always at or close to the scene of news. While most news services are shutting down international bureaus and laying off people, CNN is opening new bureaus and increasing its staff, which is presently over 1700. Where it does not have its own correspondents, it has developed relationships with local stations that feed reports to CNN. As a result, it has become known for being first with breaking news and, much to its credit, is watched by other journalistic organizations (ABC, CBS, NBC, BBC), which get leads for their own stories from it.

One of CNN's most intriguing concepts is *CNN World Report*, a truly international newscast. Each of about 100 contributing news disseminators sends in a weekly piece about its country, which then entitles it to use anything submitted about other countries. These can be major national stories such as the merger of South Yemen and North Yemen, or softer feature material such as a change in perfume manufacturing.

Another of CNN's contributions to international journalism has been U.S.-style reporting. Newscasts from many nations consisted of long (and boring, by American standards) stories about events such as the prime minister's wife giving toys to children in hospitals or factory workers receiving awards for high productivity. The footage was largely unedited and often contained talking-head speeches—the minister of transportation with a 10-minute justification for lowering the speed limit, for example. Now that the world's journalists have seen zippy U.S. newscasts, the "sound bite" and flashy editing have been added to evening newscasts around the world.

Of course, something as omnipotent as CNN is not without its detractors. Who is to say that short, snappy stories are superior to long, complete ones. Like other news networks, it has

CNN newscasts are seen throughout the world. Shown here is news anchor Susan Rook. (© *1994 Cable News Network, Inc. All rights reserved*)

been criticized for its coverage of terrorism and its occasional tendency to hype the importance of rather minor occurrences. But the most vociferous criticisms have revolved around its Americanism, or lack thereof. People in other countries tend to think it is too American and accuse it of practicing cultural imperialism. Some say that although it is a channel that claims to have a global vocation, it views the world through an American prism. A number of U.S. organizations, on the other hand, feel that it is too internationalized and often neglects to give the American point of view. In fact, during the Persian Gulf conflict, CNN correspondent Peter Arnett, the only Western news reporter permitted to stay in Baghdad, was accused of becoming a messenger for the Iraqi point of view.

Something as successful as CNN is not likely to go unchallenged. The BBC has already started World Service Television as a competitor to CNN, and other would-be 24-hour worldwide news services are in the planning stages. However, CNN has an undisputed spot in history. It more than any other single entity has brought the world closer to Marshall McLuhan's "global village."

THE RAMIFICATIONS OF ENTERTAINMENT PROGRAM EXCHANGE

Most countries, since the inception of their television systems, have aired entertainment programs produced in other countries. The granddaddy of program suppliers has been the United States, which during the early days of television sold more programming overseas than all other countries combined.

Early Television The reasons for programming dominance by the United States are multitudinous. The major growth of television occurred after World War II. The United States, which had not been physically attacked during the war, did not have to devote itself to reconstructing its cities as much of Europe did. As a result, it was free to pursue other endeavors—one of which was the development of television programming. When other countries got around to building TV systems, they found that purchasing programs from the United States was much cheaper than producing them themselves. They could produce a few of their own information programs and fill the rest of the schedule with American entertainment shows. The United States, being a wealthy country, could also afford to keep cranking out new programming year after year, for itself and for the rest of the world.

U.S. producers were accommodating. During the early days of TV, shows broke even or made money simply by being shown on ABC, CBS, or NBC. Foreign sales were pure gravy. Therefore programmers were willing to sell their programs for whatever foreign countries could pay. A wealthy European country such as France might pay $50,000 for the same programming material that was sold to a poor country such as India for $500. *I Love Lucy* was so popular in India that many of that generation's baby girls were named Lucy.

Another reason for U.S. success was that the type of entertainment programming Americans produced was popular with people around the world. The fun, danger, and challenge built into this programming had universal appeal.

Other countries were also involved in international entertainment programming distribution during the early days. The Soviet Union sent programming to the Eastern European Communist countries, most of which did not partake at all of American programming. Shows from the BBC were presented in many countries, and Brazilian soap operas were particularly popular in Latin countries, but the domination of the United States was unsurpassed.

Early Radio Radio programming has had a different evolution. The technology is relatively inexpensive, and so most nations could afford to

The claim has been made that *I Love Lucy* is being shown somewhere in the world every minute of every day. (© *Viacom*)

supply their own programming. Also, the language problem is more acute with radio than with TV. While TV programs can be subtitled or dubbed into a foreign language, audio-only in a foreign language is unintelligible. Most of early radio was nation-specific.

The element of radio that eventually became internationalized was music. Because of modern music's emphasis on beat and emotion and its deemphasis on complicated lyrics, music has become an international form of communication. Once again, it is music from the United States (followed closely by British music) that can be heard pouring from radios in Algeria, Bangladesh, China, Djibouti, and most of the rest of the world.

Radio programs in their entirety are not sold on a large scale internationally, and no country's radio industry profits greatly from international distribution. It is the recording industry that sees that the musical content of the programs is well internationalized.

Opposition to U.S. Entertainment The influx of Western (particularly American) music and entertainment TV programming was not overwhelmingly appreciated by the establishments of other nations. As in the case of news programming, cries of electronic colonialism arose, but this time it had more to do with customs than with information. The U.S. lifestyle portrayed in westerns, sitcoms, and dramas was not one that governments wanted their people to emulate. The degree of sex was abhorrent to Muslim and other religious countries, the materialism was inconsistent with the resources of Third World countries, and the violence was distasteful to most countries. Although the economic price of the programs was acceptable, the acculturation "price" was suspect.

Yet the programming was popular with most of the worldwide audience members. Countries that purchased programming from the United States found that it motivated people to obtain TV sets and watch them, something that did not happen in response to the generally stodgy programming produced locally.

In order to limit the infiltration of American ideas, a number of governments placed quotas on how much internationally produced programming could be shown on their national television systems. Generally these quotas called for about 50 percent national programming and 50 percent foreign, although they varied greatly from place to place and year to year. Canada, which feels particularly inundated with U.S. culture, has proposed quotas for Canadian-produced programming that are as high as 90 percent.

Structural Changes Gradually the world has changed. Although the United States is still the dominant exporter of entertainment programming, the ground rules have shifted. On the one hand, most nations of the world have added numerous channels of programming during the last 10 years. Originally, most countries had only one or two noncommercial government-run radio networks and TV channels. But deregulation and privatization have been the order of the past decade, even in the newly liberated ex-Communist countries, creating commercially based, independently operated outlets for programming.

The old-fashioned station-network broadcasting structure has been supplemented primarily with cable TV and direct broadcast satellite (DBS). Other forms, however, such as multichannel multipoint distribution service (MMDS), a local over-the-air service consisting of several channels that operates at higher frequencies than broadcast TV and therefore requires a special converter to be seen, and satellite master antenna television (SMATV), a system that distributes television signals by wire to apartment complexes, hotels, condominiums, and other multiple-unit buildings, have added to the number of available channels. All of this has increased the demand for programming produced in the United States and for that produced by other industrialized countries such as Britain and Australia.

On the other hand, many of the countries that originally depended on relatively cheap American programming to fill their channel time have developed professional programming skills and are now producing a greater proportion of their own material. Indigenous programming is on the rise, and foreign programming is on the decline. The countries producing their own programming (Italy, France, Germany, Hong Kong, Japan, and others) are placing it on the marketplace hoping to profit from exports. Countries establish quotas not just to keep out undesirable social ideas but also to provide TV production jobs for their own citizens.

Several program fairs are held each year where countries sell shows to other countries, the most famous of which is MIP-TV, held each spring in Cannes, France. Many of the countries that used to attend only as buyers now wear both buyers' and sellers' hats.

New Programming Strategies Meanwhile, back in the United States, program producers have become dependent upon foreign sales and the $2.3 billion they bring in annually. No longer does an airing on NBC guarantee a profit. Syndication (national and international) is needed before most series can erase the red ink.

Also, the United States has created more competition for itself, thus reducing the amount of money that can be received for any one program. Previously, only programs that aired on the three major networks were for sale, but now a vast array of cable TV programming is also available. The Disney Channel and Playboy (and many services in between) do well on the international market.

As a result, many programs produced in various countries take international possibilities into consideration during the preproduction stage. The ideas that actually make it into production are those that have mass appeal, can be broadcast in many areas of the world, and can be shown as reruns many times. Music, on both radio and TV, fits the bill. MTV is the second most popular American cable service overseas after CNN. (East German youths raised MTV flags over the Berlin Wall as it was being torn down.) Sports events, although they generally cannot be shown over and over, are also a very popular form of international programming.

Franchising A rather new form of programming exchange involves franchised imitations. Companies that develop a successful concept license the idea to other countries. The shows are produced locally with local crews and talent, but the company that supplied the idea receives money. Game shows and soap operas are genres that lend themselves particularly well to franchising.

Not surprisingly the hit *Wheel of Fortune* has been particularly successful using this strategy. King World, the distributor of this Merv Griffin Productions show, sends a "bible" and several consulting executives to each country that wants to air the program. It requires that the format be essentially the same as that of the show aired in the United States, but the "Vanna Whites" and "Pat Sajaks" are local, as are all the contestants. "The show will last longer than would a purely American import," observes King World's co-owner Michael King. "People in other countries are more interested in seeing how people like themselves fare with the questions. What they have is an imported idea that looks very local."

America's Funniest Home Videos, based on an idea brought to the United States from Japan, has been another successful franchise. The Germans have *Smile, Please*, and the British, Australians, Dutch, and others produce localized clones.

Consultants In a slightly different vein, foreign countries often hire American producers, directors, and writers as consultants to help them develop programming that will have worldwide appeal. The French soap opera *Riviera* has a distinctly U.S. feel because the executive producer and creative director are American. The French producer of *Marc et Sophie*, a sitcom about a psychiatrist and his confused wife, acknowledges that the themes are straight out of American TV. "TV is an art form," she says. "In France, there's still the sense that there is no difference between poetry and a 60-minute television program. With sitcoms, they must learn to tell a story. For Europe, television is a new language. The United States has the most experience in that language. To succeed in the new television environment, you must understand what the rules are."

The importing of consultants is also occurring in radio, where people from the United States are brought in to help develop various music formats.

Coproduction Probably the biggest programming trend of all worldwide is coproduction. Various companies from different countries invest money in a show concept and provide creative input. When the show is finished, they air it in their respective countries and gain financially from sales to other countries.

Although this sounds delightfully simple, many problems arise. Changing currency rates cause havoc with deals that take months, or even years, to consummate. If Germans offer to put up 30 percent, they want to keep the figure in marks and not be subjected to the fluctuations of the dollar, pound, or yen. Some countries tie strings to their money, insisting that a certain percentage of crew members be from that country or that a certain percentage of shooting take place there. Other countries don't want to supply cash but ask for distribution rights in exchange for providing crew members—who may or may not be competent.

But the monetary problems are dwarfed by the creative ones. U.S. companies have engaged in coproductions for several decades, often because using foreign locations or crews enabled them to circumvent the quota problem; in some countries a program produced in the country is considered to be part of the local quota even though the original idea and many of the elements have come from another country. However, Americans, with their supposed expertise in television production, easily mustered creative control. No more. People from other countries are now demanding, as part of the legal production deal, that their ideas and concepts be included. Often this creates cultural clashes. For example, in TV in the United States the producer has the final say, whereas in France the director exerts the primary control. If a U.S. producer and a French director must work together, sparks can fly.

Nevertheless, a large number of coproductions have been successfully completed. The U.S. company Rysher Entertainment is coproducing the series *Thunder in Paradise* with Germany's RTL Plus. A twenty-six-part half-hour documentary series, *Spies,* has as producing partners CBS, Tokyo Broadcasting System (TBS), Arts and Entertainment, and Columbia House, a video mail-order club. CBS has distribution rights everywhere except in Japan, where TBS owns the rights, A&E's realm is U.S. cable rights, and Columbia House owns home video rights. In a similar manner a French broadcaster, TF1, is coproducing with American Saban International and a Korean network, MBC.

United States Imports One of the reasons companies in various countries are interested in coproducing with U.S. companies is that they hope this will gain them entry into the vast American television market. Historically, although the United States has exported the most programming, it has imported the least.

For many years no more than 2 percent of what was shown on U.S. television came from another country, and most of that was BBC productions shown on PBS. When in 1987 the BBC sold its weekly chart show *Top of the Pops* to CBS, it was the first deal it had made with a U.S. commercial network since 1971.

For the United States, homegrown programming was the best, and Americans had little tolerance for subtitles or foreign accents. However, the economic downsizing of commercial broadcasting has made networks and stations consider the possibility of airing shows from other countries, mainly because it is cheaper to purchase them than to produce new shows. Cable TV networks, most of which must be very cost-conscious, have from the beginning been more receptive than their commercial kin to programming from other lands. As a result, a few shows, such as England's *A Fine Romance* and Australia's *Neighbours,* have been shown on U.S. commercial and cable TV.

A number of American independent stations have been successful programming nothing but material from foreign countries to cater to people who speak foreign languages—Japanese, Spanish, Korean. They make good customers for other countries.

So many changes are occurring in worldwide telecommunications that the future of entertainment program exchange is uncertain. Most countries air considerably less entertainment fare than the United States, but the percentages are increasing and the sources are multiplying.

THE IMPACT OF SATELLITES

When the first communications satellite, Telstar I, was launched in 1962, few predicted the major impact that satellite technology would have on telecommunications. The satellite, more than any other single device, has shrunk communication time and space. Satellites transmit instantaneously around the globe so that the entire world population has the potential to watch an astronaut launching or landing, a coronation, a royal wedding, a papal visit, a war, the Olympics, an Oscar telecast, or any other of a myriad of events.

Satellite Issues But satellites have created a number of problems that are closely related to the issue of free flow versus national identity. Satellite signals cross national boundaries without having to show a passport. Their footprints cover large areas with divergent political, economic, and social standards, circumventing the establishment. There is nothing to stop a Syrian Muslim with a satellite dish from viewing the Italian striptease show *Tutti Frutti*. European satellite owners can watch anything from highbrow French talk shows to Dutch pornography. News from any area of the world can be seen, instantaneously and uncensored, in virtually any other part of the world.

Governments have made attempts to prevent their people from obtaining satellite dishes, but they have been largely unsuccessful because a gray market for dishes exists in most countries. As dishes become smaller and smaller, they become harder to regulate. For example, the Colombian government, which estimated that 300,000 people owned satellite receivers, asked these owners to register the dishes. Only 50 did.

In some instances governments are slow to act regarding satellites, and satellite programming simply takes over. This has happened in India, where programing from the Hong Kong–based STAR satellite service has quickly become the most viewed programming. Innumerable Indian entrepreneurs set up satellite dishes and ran the signal, by wire, to people's living quarters. This "cable TV" has not been sanctioned by the government, and politicians have not enacted any laws to curtail or even regulate it. STAR has been quickly accepted in much of Asia and has brought about phenomenal viewing and social changes that authorities have not been able to control.

The other major problem brought about by satellite technology was that it further fanned the flames between have and have-not countries. Only a limited number of satellites can be placed in the sky where they appear to hang motionless, beaming a signal to a particular part of the earth. Satellites are expensive to build and launch, and Third World countries feared that the industrial nations would occupy all the good orbital slots, leaving none for them when they were ready, technically and economically, to enter the modern communications era.

ITU and Intelsat Two organizations have dealt with international problems related to satellites, and both had aided developing nations, at least to some extent.

One is a branch of the United Nations called the International Telecommunications Union (ITU). Its basic mission is to reconcile radio wave problems and to make sure transmitting and receiving equipment meets established technical standards. It mediates spectrum disputes when one nation claims that another is in some way interfering with its radio signals. For example, Mexican stations sometimes broadcast with higher power than that assigned to them and cause static and loss of signal for stations in the United States. Similarly, countries that feel their programs are being jammed by another nation can register complaints with the ITU. The ITU undertakes much of its business through World Radiocommunication Conferences (WRCs) [until 1993 these were called World Administrative Radio Conferences (WARCs) and Regional Radiocommunication Conferences (RRCs)]. Most of the countries in the world send engineers to these meetings where as a group they make technical recommendations.

One of the issues to come before a number of conferences was the allocation of satellite orbital slots. The ITU worked out a compromise between the have and have-not countries wherein each country would be guaranteed one orbital slot but the rest would be distributed on a first-come, first-served basis. This compromise has allowed developing nations to orbit satellites but most of the slots are being utilized by industrial countries.

The other international organization dealing with satellites is the International Telecommunications Satellite Organization (Intelsat). Formed in 1964 at the urging of the United States, Intelsat was to launch satellites and handle international communications for all the nations of the world. At first the organization was managed by the United States, but in 1973 it became an independent organization owned by a consortium of countries, all of which paid a yearly fee. In addition, they paid Intelsat rent for satellite time whenever they wanted to use one of the birds for an event such as the Olympics or a world soccer championship. The idea was that any nation, no matter how large or how small, could have access to satellite technology by paying moderate fees to Intelsat.

For a number of years Intelsat had a virtual monopoly on international satellite traffic, not only for radio and television but also for telephones. As often happens with monopolies, Intelsat became irresponsible toward its constituents. It overcharged countries and used its proceeds to build a lavish building in Washington, D.C., where oak-paneled rooms awaited worldwide delegates who hardly ever came to Washington. Eventually the member countries realized what was happening, and Intelsat changed its ways. However, a number of entrepreneurs (both individuals and countries) wanted to set up satellite systems to compete with Intelsat. The matter was debated at both national and international forums, and eventually other companies were allowed into the arena.

Most of these systems serve regional or national needs—Asiasat, Turksat, Thaicom, Arabsat, Insat (India), Hispansat, PanAmSat, Intersputnik (Eastern Europe), Eutelsat (Western Europe), Telsat (Canada), Satcom (United States). Intelsat still carries 80 percent of transoceanic TV, but the other satellite systems are available to provide competition for Intelsat and to provide prestige and power to the countries and organizations that own them.

THE INFLUENCE OF THE VIDEOCASSETTE RECORDER

The videocassette recorder has been a great democratizer of electronic media. It has placed media control in the hands of the viewers rather than the authorities, and it has changed passive consumers into active producers.

Consumer Empowerment VCRs are relatively small, cheap, and accessible. They do not present transmission hassles, and they are not subject to government quotas. As a result, the establishment (be it government, a corporation, or parents) finds it difficult to control what is seen by way of videotape. Muslims in Saudi Arabia can smuggle in pornographic programs, or a U.S. viewer can tape *Nightline* while watching *The Tonight Show*, thus circumventing the networks' carefully planned scheduling strategies.

The camcorder has turned consumers into producers through such popular programs as *America's Funniest Home Videos* wherein people submit their "home movies" for telecast. Footage shot by ordinary people has also been used for news programs. Someone in the right place and at the right time armed with a camcorder can shoot earthquake, flood, or police brutality footage that can be sold to media organizations and distributed worldwide.

The real lure of the VCR is American movies. These are relished throughout the world and are the main reason that people purchase recorders. Even in areas where individuals cannot afford VCRs, citizens band together to buy one VCR for a community hall. Eighty to a hundred people will crowd around a single TV set to watch *Rocky IV, Close Encounters of the Third Kind,* or *Friday the Thirteenth.* Some countries have even established mobile video parlors that travel from village to village showing both educational and entertainment material. These can prove more technically reliable than state-run broadcast systems.

Piracy Because videocassettes are relatively small, cheap, and accessible, they are subject to a particular type of theft known as piracy. Someone obtains a legal (or illegal) videotape of a movie, copies it onto a multitude of videocassettes, and sells it inexpensively. The "pirate" does not pay royalty fees to the copyright holder.

Piracy is a thorny problem, not only because it is hard to apprehend the perpetrators but also because people in many countries do not understand the concept of copyright. In a country such as Malaysia, where very few movies are produced and where hardly anyone gets paid for any type of artistic work, people do not understand why writers should be paid *again* after they have already been paid to write a script.

Even after a populace has been educated about copyright, it often remains insensitive to it. In the Third World, government officials frequently view U.S. film studios as wealthy, evil capitalists and their own pirates as resourceful entrepreneurs trying to aid the poor local economy. When pirates are brought to trial in their own countries, local juries usually side with them against the big film companies.

But piracy has been a problem not only in poor, unsympathetic countries. Pirates abound in the United States, Britain, Germany, and other well-developed countries. That's how *E.T.* could be the top-rated video in England even though it had not yet been officially released there. A number of illegal videocassettes have been made by people who go into a movie theater with a camcorder, tape the movie off the screen, and sell copies of the (very grainy) film for a tidy profit. On a grander scale is the example of a Panamanian who became a flashy millionaire with a gold Cadillac by selling pirated copies of U.S. films in bulk to freighters going through the duty-free zone of the Panama Canal. American film projectionists have been known to "borrow" movies from theaters during sneak previews, dub them in their apartment on a rented film chain, and then sell these master videocassettes for between $800 and $1800, from which they are further dubbed for worldwide distribution.

Soliciting the aid of the Federal Bureau of Investigation (FBI) has been the main method the motion picture industry has used in trying to control piracy—a practice that means a loss of billions of dollars per year for the studios. In addition, the Motion Picture Association of America has formed a Film Security Office that hires ex–FBI agents and other law enforcement–type employees to track down pirate rings. Electronic signals (copyguards) placed on videotapes to prevent them from being copied have also helped, but clever technical wizards can circumvent these devices.

Piracy remains a major problem for the film industry, but the legitimate uses of the VCR outweigh the illegitimate ones. Ownership of VCRs is growing at a rapid rate worldwide and definitely affects the overall structure of international communication if for no other reason than that it gives people one more alternative to traditional broadcast fare.

THE GROWTH OF GLOBAL ADVERTISING

Several executives of Saatchi and Saatchi, an international advertising agency, predict a consumer convergence where cultural differences will depend more on the kind of shoes people wear than on where they live. Of course, they base this prediction on the fact that goods advertised in an international market will find their target group among people with similar personalities, needs, and interests rather than among people in a particular country.

Such may become the case. Advertising is now multicultural, aided in great part by radio and television. In fact, some advertising agencies are putting together global buys. Ad agency BBDO, for example, decided Gillette should buy time or space in three continents' worth of media all owned by the same company. By doing so, Gillette was able to receive a reduced rate from the organization.

In most countries the original broadcasting systems were government-run and commercial-free. Money was obtained through general taxes or license fees on radios and TV sets. This worked well for radio, a relatively inexpensive medium that could live on limited resources, but television was another matter. Its costs often exceeded its government expense account, and countries began to look for other ways to pay the bills.

The U.S. broadcasting model, which had been advertising-based from almost the beginning, was not considered one to emulate. Europeans, Asians, and Africans did not want screaming commercials luring them into buying things they did not need. But since more money was needed, advertising crept in cautiously and politely. Ads were low-key and clustered together. They did not interrupt programming; they appeared only at the beginning or end of a show and in some instances only once a day. In many countries, ads are still rather low-key and infrequent, but other countries have succumbed to more hard-sell, strategically placed commercials. Some have even surpassed the United States in quantity and brashness. Merchandising, wherein products related to particular programs—*Alf* dolls, *Incredible Hulk* lunchboxes—are offered for sale, is also becoming commonplace around the world.

Not surprisingly, this commercialism has been highly criticized. Some media practitioners feel that the United States lured other countries into accepting advertising so that American goods could be sold worldwide, thereby increasing the coffers. Industrialized companies looking for new markets were happy to sell baby formula to Third World mothers who didn't need it and actually harmed their babies by bottle-feeding rather than breastfeeding them. As a side effect, they point out that advertising increased the need for U.S. programming—another social negative. The reasoning is that American programming guarantees ratings, and ratings are becoming more important now that radio and television are so dependent on advertising.

The international debate over advertising that centers around economic need versus social good will probably never end; it never has in the United States. In the meantime, Chinese parents complain that their children are humming tunes from Coca-Cola commercials, and Argentine parents try to cope with their children's desires for *Simpsons* tee shirts.

THE POWER OF MULTINATIONAL MEDIA COMPANIES

Because radio and television have become so internationally oriented, companies in the media business which were once content with national distribution are now spreading their wings. They want to cash in on opportunities that might be available worldwide. Many of these organizations are headed by media barons who can gain not only money, but also power and prestige, by swallowing fish from many countries.

A good example is Rupert Murdoch, Australia-born media mogul who leveraged two small Australian newspapers into an $8 billion empire, News Corporation, that includes 20th Century Fox films, the Fox TV network, a number of U.S. TV stations, 50 percent ownership in the BSkyB British-French satellite service, majority interest in the Asian satellite service STAR, a minority stake in a Spanish TV station, the *London Sun*, *The Times* of London, and book publisher HarperCollins. Calling himself an "opportunist," Murdoch isn't afraid to gamble. He has made a great deal of money but has also accumulated a large debt.

Silvio Berlusconi was "Mr. Television" within his home country, Italy, where his company, Fininvest, owned the two most popular national television channels. He then spread out into part-ownership deals in Spain and Germany and for a while tried running the now bankrupt French Channel 5. He was able to parlay his media fame and fortune into politics and is now prime minister of Italy.

Mexico's Emilio Azcarraga owns Televisa, Mexico's four-channel television network, as well as other television properties that extend from Chile to the United States. In addition, he owns a Miami-based Spanish-language magazine distributor and a Mexican newspaper.

These three men have great power over what is seen, heard, and read throughout the world. So does the head of Matsushita, the Japanese company that now owns MCA-Universal, and the head of Sony, which has bought Columbia Pictures. A British company purchased the U.S. production company MTM, and a French company did likewise with Filmation. TV Globo of Brazil owns Tele-Monte Carlo.

Should these companies be allowed to extend so far beyond their national borders? Supporters say yes because they bring welcome capital that can improve the companies they buy. Detractors say no because they have a tendency to exploit the foreign companies they buy and they bring with them unwelcome cultural modes. (The lighthearted fear at Universal Studios when Matsushita purchased it was that only sushi would be served in the cafeteria.)

Different countries have rules regarding what foreigners may or may not buy. For example, in the United States only American citizens can own radio or TV stations—so Rupert Murdoch gave up his Australian citizenship and became naturalized in the United States so that he could buy a group of stations. In New Zealand there are no ownership restrictions, which is why a Canadian company now owns the commercial TV network.

Whether international ownership is good or bad, it is probably here to stay. The stakes are so high that multinational companies will not back off gracefully.

PROBLEMS RELATED TO TECHNICAL STANDARDS

One of the problems inhibiting the exchange of programming material is that various nations have differing technical standards for the transmission and reception of television signals. Although innumerable attempts have been made to resolve these discrepancies, engineers throughout the world have not been able to agree (or convince their governments to agree) on very many worldwide standards. The difficulty with varying standards is that tapes produced in one country cannot be run on equipment in another country. They must first be dubbed from one format to another, and the duplication process lowers the technical quality of the reproduced image.

NTSC, SECAM, and PAL One example of standards incompatibility revolves around the number of lines of information created on a TV screen. In some countries it is 525 lines created every $\frac{1}{30}$ second, and in others it is 625 lines every $\frac{1}{25}$ second.

The way that color is encoded in the signal also varies. The first color system was the product of an American committee called the National Television Systems Committee (NTSC). The Europeans took a look at this system and dubbed it "Never Twice the Same Color." The French then developed another color-encoding system called Séquence Couleur à Mémoire (SECAM), which the Americans referred to as "Something Essentially Contrary to the American Method." The Germans invented Phase Alternate Line (PAL) to bring "Peace at Last," but it didn't, and all three systems exist, each being used in different countries.

HDTV A chance to develop worldwide standards presented itself when a whole new standard that essentially doubled the number of lines on a TV screen was proposed. First developed by the Japanese in the late 1970s, high-definition television (HDTV) scanned at 1125 lines every $\frac{1}{30}$ second and changed the height and width of the TV set from a ratio of 3 to 4 to a ratio of 5.33 to 3. In other words, it made TV sets wider than the ones presently in use; the ratio is similar to that of wide-screen movies.

The Japanese HDTV system was demonstrated in various places around the world and received positive reviews. In the mid-1980s, the system was discussed at a WARC (the same United Nations conference that discussed satellite orbital slots) and came close to being accepted as a world standard. But the Europeans balked because the system scanned at $\frac{1}{30}$ second, a time rate that was not compatible with the European electric current system, which operates at 50 cycles per second. The technical difficulties could have been resolved, but politics also intervened. By the mid-1980s, various nations were becoming leery of Japan's electronic dominance and did not want to relegate to them the power and money that would come from having their HDTV standard accepted worldwide. At any rate, in 1986 Western European countries refused to accept the Japanese system, and the whole idea of one international standard broke down.

The Japanese began transmitting internally using their system, and the Europeans developed another system that scanned at 1250 lines every $\frac{1}{25}$ second. The United States, now far behind both Europe and Japan, began to play catch-up. Along the way some U.S. companies developed a new digitally based concept called compression that enabled more video information to be placed in less space. This means high-definition pictures can be transmitted using less of the electronic spectrum than originally planned. A consortium of American companies is now in the process of developing this digitally based system, and the United States should have HDTV sometime in the near future. However, the superiority of the compression technology has thrown the Japanese and European technologies into somewhat of a tailspin. The outcome is anyone's guess, but it probably will not be a unified worldwide standard.

Any solution to the HDTV technical dilemma will not be a permanent solution to program distribution. New technological ideas arise on the horizon almost daily. There are those who feel we are headed toward a "digital pail" wherein all sorts of information and entertainment sources—television, radio, magazines, telephones, video games, data banks, books—will be dumped into computers and outputted to tiny, flat, portable screens. Such a process would require a myriad of new standards.

Despite the many problems inherent in the internationalization of electronic media, opportunities abound. Those who are willing to adapt to cultures unlike their own and develop a sensi-

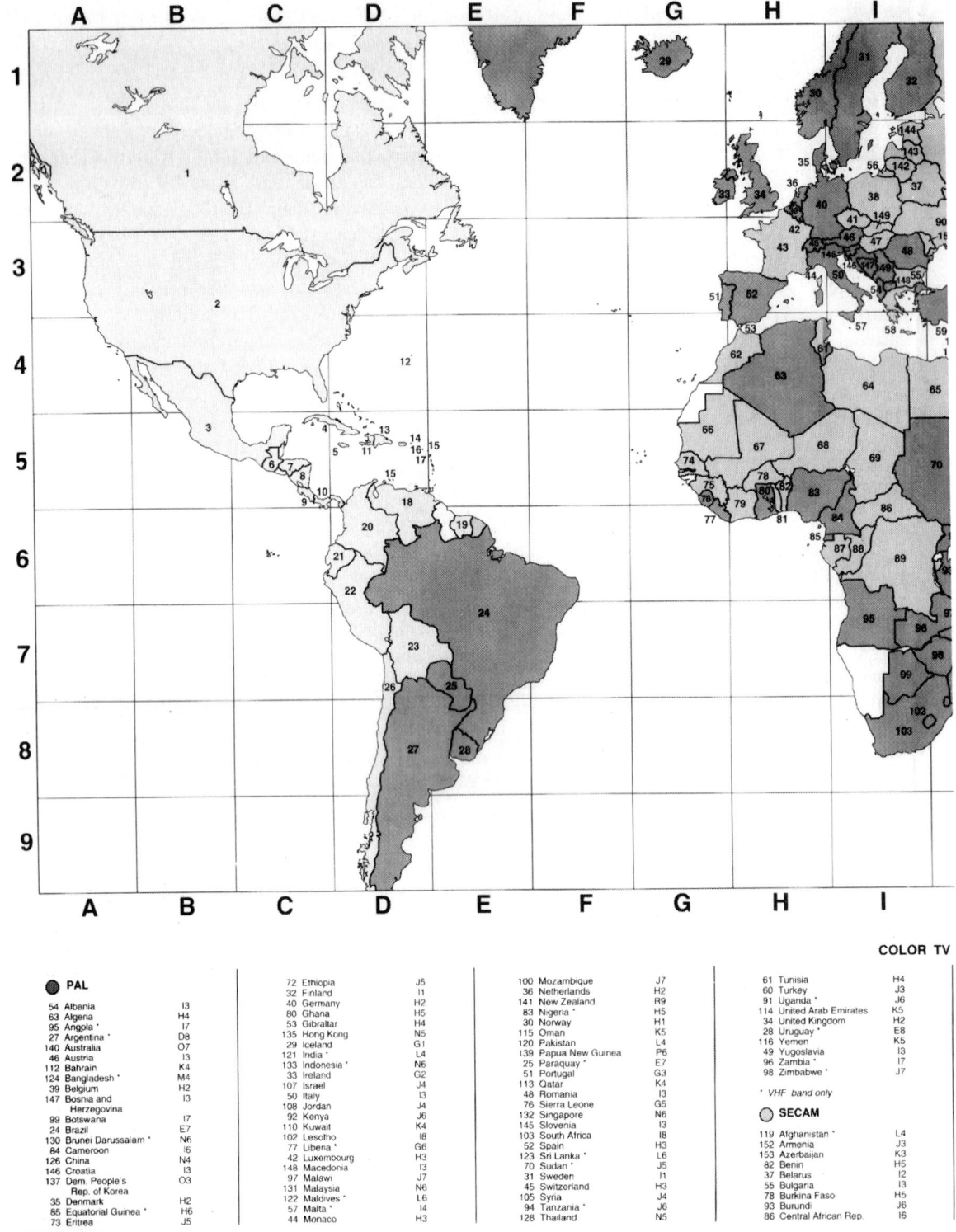

FIGURE 1-1
Countries that use NTSC, PAL, and SECAM.

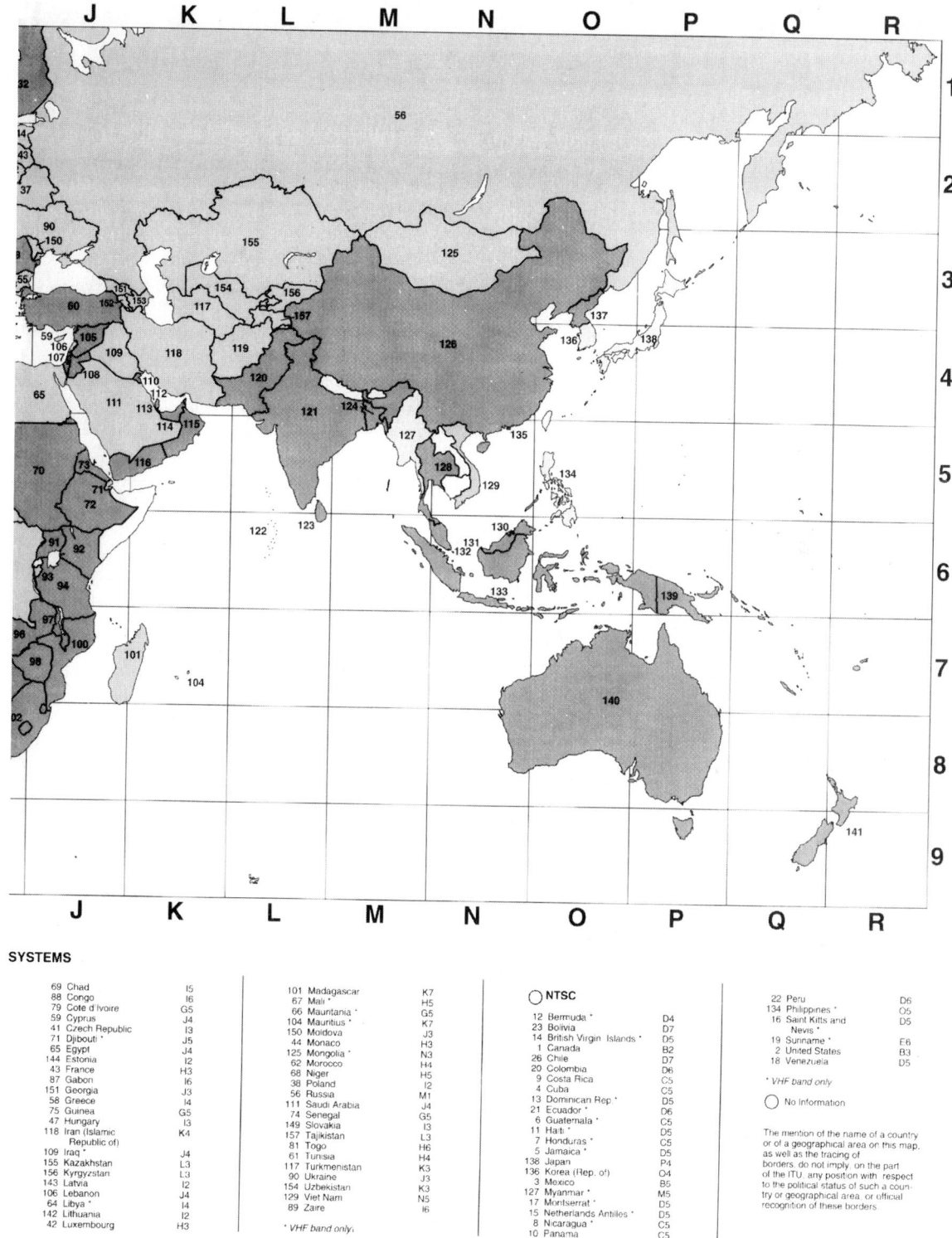

tivity toward ideas and behavior modes that may seem archaic or incorrect will be able to have rewarding careers helping to further develop the global village.

SELECTED BIBLIOGRAPHY

Bollier, David. "At War with the Pirates," *Channels*, March 1987, pp. 29–35.

Boyd, Douglas, Joseph Straubhaar, and John Lent. *The Videocassette Revolution*. New York: Longman, 1989.

Browne, Donald R. "International Commercial Radio Broadcasting: Nation Shall Speak Profit unto Nation," *Journal of Broadcasting and Electronic Media*, Spring 1986, pp. 195–212.

Foisie, Geoffrey, "Hollywood Heads for Europe, Hat in Hand," *Broadcasting*, 15 November 1993, p. 70.

Ganley, Gladys, and Oswald Ganley. *Global Political Fallout: The VCR's First Decade*. Norwood, NJ: Ablex, 1987.

Gelman, Morrie. "Special Report: CNN and the Gulf War," *Variety*, 22 March 1991, pp. 19–26.

Gerbner, George, and Marsha Siefert, eds. *World Communications: A Handbook*. New York: Longman, 1984.

Head, Sydney W. *World Broadcasting Systems*. Belmont, CA: Wadsworth, 1985.

Howell, W. J. *World Broadcasting in the Age of the Satellite*. Norwood, NJ: Ablex, 1986.

International Radio Consultative Committee. *Television Systems Used around the World*. Geneva, Switzerland: International Telecommunications Union, 1992.

Lippman, John. "Tuning in the Global Village," *Los Angeles Times*, 20 October 1992, pp. H-1–H-12.

MacBride Commission. *Communications and Society Today and Tomorrow*. Paris: UNESCO, 1980.

Margolis, Irwin. "Agencies Face Up to Challenge Posed by Global Buying," *Television/Radio Age*, 2 February 1987, pp. 54–55.

McPhail, Thomas L. *Electronic Colonialism: The Future of International Broadcasting and Communication*. Beverly Hills, CA: Sage, 1981.

Merrill, John C., ed. *Global Journalism: A Survey of the World's Mass Media*. New York: Longman, 1991.

Patterson, Richard, ed. *The International TV and Video Guide*. London: Tantivy Press, 1986.

Singh, Kusum, and Bertram Gross. "'MacBride': The Report and the Response," *Journal of Communication*, Autumn 1981, pp. 104–117.

Weimann, Gabriel. "Media Events: The Case of International Terrorism," *Journal of Broadcasting and Electronic Media*, Winter 1987, pp. 21–39.

Wells, Ken. "All the World Loves a Good Game Show, Even a Bad One," *Wall Street Journal*, 8 December 1992, p. 1.

World Guide to Television and Programming. Philadelphia: North American, 1993.

PART ONE

NORTH AMERICA

Overview of North America

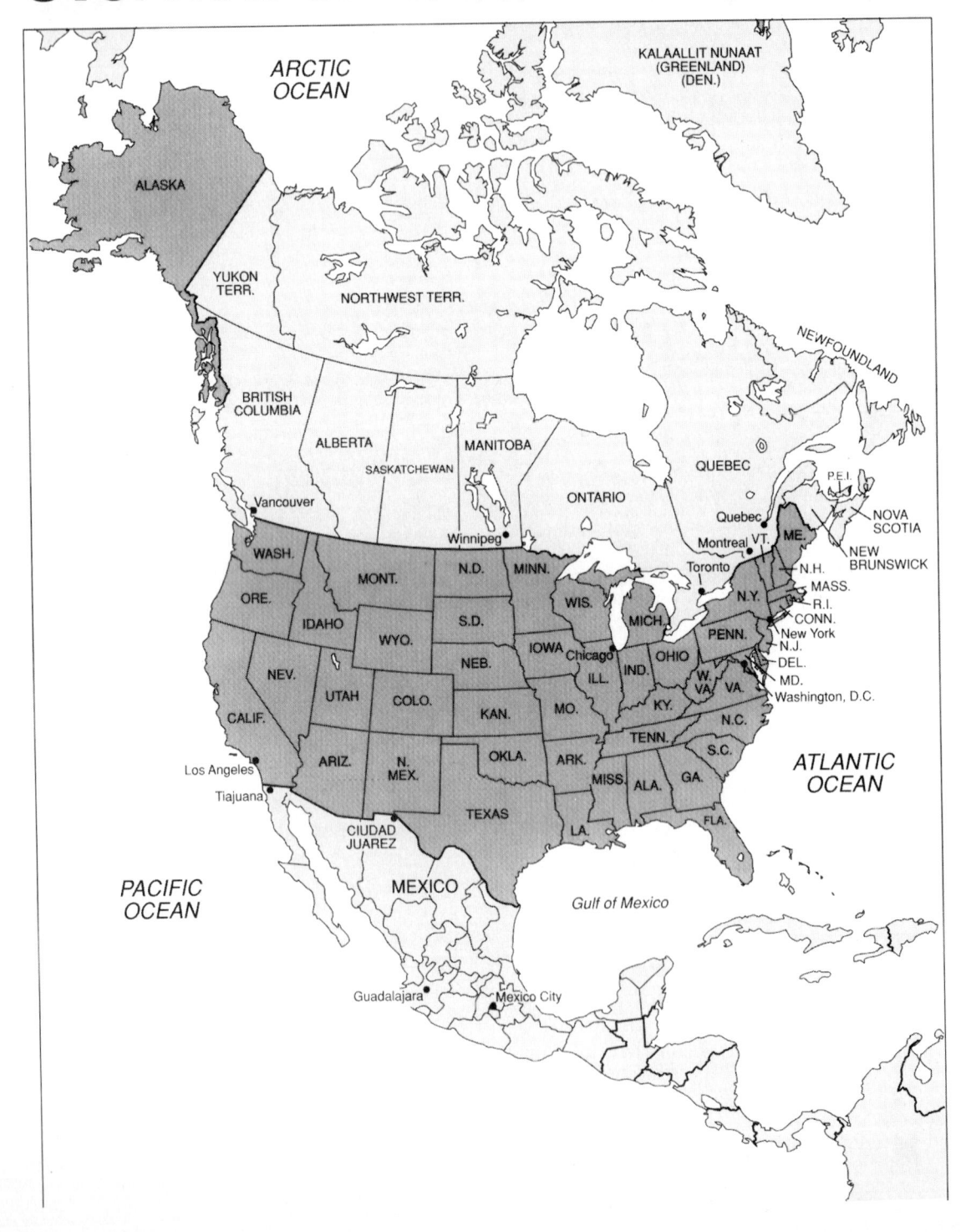

The three North American countries—Canada, the United States, and Mexico—have many similarities in their electronic media structures. For example, all three countries share a strong emphasis on privatization. Private ownership and control of the media have been characteristic of the United States since its very early days. Freedom of the press from governmental influence reflects and enhances the democratic form of government. Private ownership is also dominant in both Canada and Mexico. In line with this, all three countries, unlike countries in many parts of the world, have had a long-term acceptance of the concept of commercialism. Advertising has been a way of life for the electronic media since their early days.

North America also claims many "firsts" in electronic media. People in the United States like to think they were the first in the world to develop radio stations in the early 1920s, but Canada can one-up them because in 1919 it had a radio station in Montreal built by Guglielmo Marconi, the Italian who invented radio. Mexico is usually considered the first of the Third World countries to develop both viable radio and reliable television. Canada and the United States were pioneers in cable TV. These two countries had earlier, stronger systems than other sections of the world.

The following chapter is devoted to the United States and, for readers who live there, will be the most familiar of all countries discussed in this book. (Those knowledegable about the U.S. electronic media structure are certainly free to skip the chapter.) For those readers who are not from the United States or who have never studied U.S. media, this chapter can serve as a comparative takeoff point for the other chapters of this book. The United States has also been selected to represent North America because of its importance in the worldwide electronic media field. However, Canada and Mexico have interesting and important systems that deserve an overview.

CANADA

Canada's geography has played a very important part in the development of its electronic media. The country is vast and sparsely populated. Its 26,835,000 inhabitants live on 3,849,000 square miles, which is less than 7 people per square mile. Of course, the people are not spread out 7 per square mile; most of them live very near the U.S. border, so close in fact that 50 percent of the Canadian population can receive television from TV stations located in the northern United States.

The "invasion" of U.S. programming has presented a major problem for the Canadian electronic media because, on the whole, the Canadian people prefer programming from across the border to what is produced in their own country. Despite quotas restricting imported programming and government subsidies for Canadian-produced material, Canadians watch their own homegrown product only 29 percent of the time. Most of the rest of what they watch is U.S. programming—and a bit from Britain.

People in Canada watch a great deal of TV, as evidenced by the fact that the TV set is on about 6 hours a day in the average Canadian household. Radio is also very popular. Canada is one of the few countries where there are more radios than people.

Geography also plays a part in Canada's media structure in that people in the northern remote areas are few and far between and hard to serve. Privately owned commercial stations cannot make money serving these areas, and so the government must help. This is largely why a mixed system of electronic media has arisen in Canada. Here a government-run public broadcasting system (modeled after the British Broadcasting Corporation—see Chapter 4) exists side by side with a private broadcasting system (similar in structure to the U.S. commercial broadcasting system—see Chapter 2) and a very healthy cable TV structure.

Public Broadcasting The government-run public system is called the Canadian Broadcasting Corporation (CBC), and it covers 99 percent of the country with radio and TV. Both the radio and TV services have two networks, one broadcasting in English and one broadcasting in French. The CBC provides a French service throughout the country, even though 80 percent of French-speaking people live in Quebec. The degree and type of service offered in French have been a contentious issue, like many of the other issues related to French culture versus Anglo culture.

The CBC also has the mission of serving the outlying areas that commercial television would not find economically viable. Much of this broadcasting is done through Canadian-owned satellites.

CBC radio is noncommercial, but television networks carry commercials. Canada used to collect annual license fees from all households that owned a radio, but it has discontinued this practice. Now all of the CBC's radio budget and 75 percent of the CBC's TV budget come from general government funding. Despite this, CBC programming is amazingly free of government interference.

One of the unusual aspects of public broadcasting in Canada is that the CBC uses privately owned stations as outlets. In other words, private stations affiliate with a government-run network.

Private Broadcasting The main private network system is CTV, although there are other networks such as Global TV, which covers only Ontario, and TV Ontario. CTV, which broadcasts only in English, is cooperatively owned by twenty stations. A few other stations do not participate in its ownership but receive programming from it in a manner similar to U.S. network-affiliated stations. As previously mentioned, some private stations affiliate with the CBC; in addition, some affiliate with both CTV and the CBC, selecting the programs from each that they wish to air. There are also a few independent stations that do not affiliate with any network, but buy or produce their own programming, and a few that affiliate with the other smaller networks.

Private radio is station-oriented, with independent individual stations programming their own material. As in the case of TV, a number of private radio stations affiliate with the CBC.

Cable Television Canada started cable TV in 1950, 2 years before it had its own broadcast TV network. There were 140,000 TV receivers in Canada before it officially started television broadcasting. Of course, what was happening was that cable TV systems were bringing in U.S. stations and placing them on cable channels for subscribers to watch.

Today over 75 percent of Canadians subscribe to cable TV, compared to 60 percent in the United States. Cable still brings them a great deal of U.S. programming—the commercial networks, a number of stations, and cable network services. Of course, Canadian stations are also shown on cable TV, and Canadian companies have developed cable networks such as News World, Youth Television, The Sports Network, and Much Music. Cable systems must give precedence to Canadian cable networks over U.S. networks, but most of the systems have enough channels to offer both.

The Canadian government delayed the introduction of pay-cable for several years because it was wary of domination by U.S. programming, but in 1982 it licensed six pay-cable companies. At first it had very strong quotas against U.S. programming on pay-cable networks, but it lightened them because it became evident that Canadians could buy their own satellite dishes to receive U.S. programming. More recently, Canadians have added pay-per-view services to their cable menu.

Dealing with U.S. Programming The abundance and popularity of U.S. programming cause problems not only for those in Canada who are involved in electronic media but also for politicians who are constantly trying to stem the tide of the U.S. cultural invasion. Panels, commissions, and committees constantly study the effects of U.S. television on Canada, and new rules and quotas are enacted, changed, opposed, and proposed, all in an attempt to enable Canada to express its own cultural identity. Quotas and other restrictions for the CBC are usually more stringent than they are for private networks.

Most of the time about 60 percent of TV programming is supposed to be Canadian. But that means Canadians must have the resources to produce this programming. The government helps with a matching grant fund for Canadian producers. Some of this money comes from a tax on the profits of pay-cable operations. In addition, the government often allows productions to be considered "Canadian" if they have enough Canadian elements. The rules regarding this change frequently, but often they are based on a point system. For example, a production receives two points if the writer or director is Canadian, and one point if an actor, editor, or cinematographer is Canadian. In order to be considered Canadian, the production elements must add up to a certain number of points.

Regulations other than those affecting quotas and pay also affect the situation regarding U.S. programming. For example, in 1993, the Canadian Radio and Television Commission (the organization that oversees Canadian electronic media in a manner similar to the U.S. Federal Communications Commission) enacted a very stringent antiviolence code for broadcasters. It bans gratuitous violence, which is defined as anything that does not play an integral role in developing the plot, character, or theme of the material as a whole. Adult-oriented violence is restricted to 9:00 P.M. to 6:00 A.M. Children's programming cannot show violence in a way that minimizes its effects, encourages violence, or invites dangerous imitation. What some Canadian broadcasters fear is that nearby U.S. stations or U.S. stations shown on cable systems, which do not have to abide by these rules, will siphon off even more audience members than they presently do.

Of course, there is another side to the U.S-Canadian media debate. Canada, in part because of its government subsidies, has become an inexpensive, attractive country for the production of U.S.-produced programs. This "runaway production," as U.S. media practitioners call it, is taking jobs from U.S. cinematographers, makeup artists, sound operators, and others trying to make a living in the film and video business. When U.S. companies shoot video programs, as many of them do, in Vancouver or Toronto, they are taking money out of the United States and placing it in Canada.

In addition, Canadian advertisers receive a tax deduction for placing commercials on Canadian stations but not on U.S. stations across the border. This irritates stations in cities like Buffalo and Detroit that would like to avail themselves of Canadian advertising money. In addition, despite all the complaining, much of the programming produced in Canada is quite good and garners money through its sale to other countries, especially to other English-speaking countries such as Australia and New Zealand.

The feud between U.S. and Canadian electronic media practitioners and politicians sometimes seems to loom large, but in contrast to some other parts of the world, the two countries coexist in quite a civil manner.

MEXICO

At present, Mexico has both government and private broadcasting, but the government is planning to sell most of its broadcasting interests to private companies. Government broadcasting has never been a strong force, capturing only about 5 percent of the audience. Most of the rest tune into the virtual monopoly, Televisa.

Televisa The media structure of most of Central and South America is dominated by generations of media barons (see the overview of South America and Chapter 3). Mexico also follows this pattern. In this case the baron is Emilio Azcárraga, whose father started a company with a chain of radio stations. The father introduced trumpets into the classic Mexican mariachi band in the 1930s so that the music would be livelier on radio, and today all mariachis have horns.

During the 1950s the Azcárraga family expanded into television networking. At the time there were three private television channels which competed with one another, bidding outlandish prices for popular stars and outdoing one another with sensationalized programming. The government threatened to intervene in order to stop the abuses, and so the networks merged and Azcárraga rose to the top. He named the company Televisa in 1973, shortly after his father died. Azcárraga maintained the three channels and added a fourth.

All of these channels operate out of Mexico City. Three are national networks, and the fourth, which is now more like a station broadcasting only in Mexico City, is planning to become national. They program different material and do not compete with each other. Channel 1 programs telenovelas, Spanish-language soap operas, a genre that is very popular throughout South America. Channel 2 is devoted to foreign-produced shows, mostly from the United States. Channel 3 delivers news; and Channel 4, the one that is not national, reruns programs from the first network.

In addition, Azcárraga operates what is at present Mexico's only cable TV system, and he has interests in many other media and nonmedia organizations including two soccer teams and a Cultural Center for Contemporary Art.

He is very cozy with Mexican politicians to the extent that some cynics refer to Televisa as the "Ministry of Communication." Azcárraga decides what is and is not news in Mexico. He has been an unswerving ally of President Carlos Salinas and the other members of what has been essentially a one-party government. His news service reports in a very positively biased manner regarding government activities. During election campaigns, Televisa is unabashedly in favor of Salinas and the others in his party, and Azcárraga freely admits to Televisa's bias. He considers his company to be part of the government system and as such supports government candidates.

In return, the government favors Televisa. For example, although Mexican law allows no more than 8 minutes per hour of commercials, the secretary of communications and transportation grants Televisa the right to air 20 minutes of commercials an hour. A law passed in 1960 imposed a 25 percent tax on television earnings, but Televisa was able to negotiate so that half of the taxes are paid in airtime. Televisa gives 30 minutes a day to public service announcements for government agencies and makes its facilities available for important messages from the president's office. In addition it makes 12.5 percent of its time available for government programming such as education and culture. The government uses some, but not all, of this time. The result of this "taxation" is that government officials are on Televisa a great deal in addition to the progovernment news coverage.

Sometimes friction arises between Azcárraga and the government, however. When Azcárraga wanted the cellular phone concession in Mexico and the government didn't give it to him, he had a program produced that attacked the secretary of communications and transportation.

Televisa also figures heavily in the lives of advertisers and actors. It captures 70 percent of all Mexican advertising, and sponsors are largely at Televisa's mercy. Either they buy with Azcárraga or their products aren't advertised. Televisa dictates the terms and decides what ads will be aired and when. The monopoly can also make or break actors' careers. For example, Televisa soap opera actress Maria Rubio accepted an opportunity to be on a 12-hour series for a Puerto Rico channel. When she returned to Mexico, Televisa's doors were closed to her. She also could not work in theaters because Televisa would then not accept the theaters' advertising.

Other organizations have attempted to break Televisa's monopoly any number of times. There have been attempts to establish other cable TV systems, new broadcast channels, satellite TV, and MMDS, but all of them have in one way or another failed, often because of strict requirements imposed by the government.

Azcárraga has made inroads into other countries, most notably the United States, but here he is unable to be cozy with the government and has not had long-term success. During the 1960s and 1970s he owned a twelve-station Spanish-language network, Univision. The United States found him in violation of U.S. laws stating that no foreigners can own TV stations, and so in 1986 he had to sell the properties. Hallmark bought the network and most of the stations. He has tried other ventures in the United States but with little success. One was a nationwide sports daily newspaper that folded in less than a year.

He is very successful, however, at selling Televisa's programming abroad, including sales to Spanish-language services in the United States. Televisa receives 10 percent of its revenues from selling to other countries. Mexico's telenovelas are popular worldwide. The Russians in Siberia rank the fate of Marianna, the heroine of the Mexican telenovela *The Rich Also Cry,* as their third greatest worry in life after obtaining weapons for self-defense and raising their children.

Government Broadcasting Government broadcasting started in 1923 in Mexico, but it has never been a dominant force. In 1972 the government took over Channel 13 in Mexico City because it had gone bankrupt. It then went on to buy sixteen other stations and form the advertising-based Mexican Television Cultural Network. This, several radio stations, and an educational TV network represent the government's forays into electronic media.

However, these government channels do for Mexico what government radio and TV do in many countries—supply services to remote areas not served by private broadcasting and broaden program options to include culture and education.

The government has now decided to sell its stations and networks to private interests, which could create competition for Televisa. The government also seems to be looking favorably upon the importation of foreign Spanish-language program services such as Spanish versions of some of the U.S. cable channels.

Televisa does not appear to feel challenged by either of these potential competitors. It has the world's largest library of Spanish-language programming, and given its history of avoiding competition, it may be able to keep its dominance. Then again, times are changing and media are becoming more internationalized everywhere. The tight-knit structure of one country is no longer impervious to outside forces.

CHAPTER 2

United States of America

Lynne Schafer Gross

Lynne Gross has published eleven books that deal with radio and television in the United States. She has also taught the subject at a number of universities including California State University, Fullerton; Pepperdine University; UCLA; and Loyola Marymount University. In addition, she has taught radio and television production in Malaysia, Guyana, Swaziland, and Australia. She is currently chair of the Broadcast Education Association and is a past board member of the Academy of Television Arts and Sciences. She has also worked in the electronic media industry as a producer and director of programming for a cable TV system.

Lynne Gross.

STATISTICS

Geographic Area: 3,618,770 square miles
Capital: Washington, D.C.
Population: 248,709,873
Religions: Protestant, Catholic, Jewish
Language: English
Type of Government: Federal republic with strong democratic tradition headed by a president
Gross Domestic Product: $5.4 trillion
Literacy: 97 percent

GENERAL CHARACTERISTICS

The United States is awash in electronic media. As already discussed in Chapter 1, it produces a vast amount of programming, much of which is seen throughout the world. But programming is even more abundant in the United States itself. The production and consumption of radio and television material have produced a major industry and become a major social preoccupation. Part of this affluence of media has to do with the overall wealth of the United States, part is related to geography, and part can be attributed to the U.S. political system of democracy and its economic system of capitalism.

Overall Wealth Although the United States has very definite pockets of poverty, the country as a whole and the people within it are well off. The country's gross domestic product is the highest in the world, as is its per capita income. This, combined with a 40-hour workweek, gives people both the time and money to indulge in electronic media.

And indulge they do. Watching TV is the major leisure-time preoccupation of people in the United States. Almost every household has a TV set; and over 60 percent have two or more. In addition, over 60 percent of homes subscribe to cable TV, and 75 percent own at least one videocassette recorder. Since the advent of cable TV in the late 1970s, the number of programming choices has grown exponentially. In 1980 the average home could receive eight channels of different programming; now the average is twenty-eight channels. And people do watch these program services. The home TV set is on an average of 7 hours a day, with the typical viewer watching about 4 hours of that time.

Radio, too, is abundant. Again, almost all homes have at least one radio set; the average home owns five, including the omnipresent radios installed in automobiles. People listen to radio about 3 hours a day—in their cars, in their homes, at the beach, while jogging, while studying, while attending parties. The number of radio stations that can be received by any one person varies widely depending on geographic location and atmospheric conditions, but there are some places in the United States where over 100 radio stations can be tuned in.

Telephones are in 93 percent of households, and at present they are used primarily for person-to-person voice communication and the transmission of data through fax and computer modems. Telephone companies, however, have expressed great interest in entering the TV program distribution business and are making plans to undertake television services.

The one area of the electronic media that is more predominant in some other areas of the world than it is in the United States is direct broadcast satellite (DBS). Although Americans have the money to enter the DBS world, this media form has not met with any degree of success. However, a few companies are working hard to make DBS a reality, so it may become a U.S. electronic media player in the near future.

Americans love gadgets. Most TV sets and VCRs have remote controls, and a sizable number of U.S. homes have remote controls for their remote controls. Over 30 percent of homes contain computers, and over 10 percent of families own camcorders. Recessionary conditions have leveled off purchases of consumer electronics, but as long as people in the United States have money, they are likely to continue to be awash in the latest in electronic media.

Geographic Influence The United States is the fourth largest country in the world, encompassing over 3.6 million square miles (9 million square kilometers). The continental United States, consisting of forty-eight states, stretches almost 3000 miles (4500 kilometers) from the Atlantic Ocean to the Pacific Ocean. Alaska to the north and Hawaii to the west are also part of the country. This vast expanse has been responsible in part for the creation of an extensive distribution system consisting of about 10,700 radio stations, 1400 TV stations, and 11,000 cable TV systems.

Almost from its beginning, broadcasting has included both national and local elements. Starting in the late 1920s, national radio networks programmed entertainment and information intended to be of interest to everyone. They sent this programming by wire to local stations situated throughout the country; individual homes could not receive the feeds because the wires went only from the network headquarters in New York to the various stations. Local stations picked up network programs and retransmitted them through the airwaves to homes in the local area. The stations also broadcast material that was intended to be of interest to the local area, not to the nation as a whole.

When TV started in the late 1940s, it adopted a similar pattern, except that signals were sent by microwave instead of by wire. But again, the individual homeowner could not intercept the microwave signal because it was sent on a narrow beam from one microwave dish to another, starting in New York and traveling to stations throughout the country.

When cable TV became popular in the late 1970s, it too adopted a national-local distribution system. National networks sent programming by satellite to local cable TV systems that distributed this programming by wire to individual homes in a particular neighborhood. When satellite technology became a reality, the traditional radio and TV networks converted from their old wire and microwave systems to satellite distribution.

Of course, as already pointed out in Chapter 1, development of the satellite made it much easier for programming to be distributed just about anywhere. If a person or company in Guatemala could buy a satellite dish to receive CNN, MTV, and other U.S. programming, so could a person in Dallas, Texas. But this has not happened to any great degree. Only about 4 percent of people in the United States (primarily hard-core gadget lovers and people in rural areas without cable TV service) have bought satellite dishes to increase their programming options.

Although satellites have rendered the geographic need for the national-local system obsolete, it still exists. In fact, part of the reason DBS has not succeeded in the United States is that it has not been welcomed by the established electronic media structure. If programming were distributed nationally from satellite to home, the viability of local stations could disappear; they would have no reason for being except to supply programming about the local community, and that type of programming takes a definite backseat with audience members when compared to the more glamorous national programming. But the local-national arrangement also has a political base, as will be seen in the next section.

Democracy's Influence The electronic media have been highly influenced by the United States' political anchorage in democracy. Under this form of government, individuals are expected to participate in the governing of the country. In order to allow for this involvement, many decisions are made at the local level, including decisions related to electronic media. For example, cable TV systems have been regulated by local city governments. When the U.S. Congress was setting up the overall organization for radio in the 1920s, it considered having only a national system but opted instead for local stations that would be responsive to local communities. So the national-local structure that has grown up in the United States is a result not only of geography but also of political philosophy.

Another element of democracy centers around the belief that the life and opinions of each individual are highly valued. The people, directly or indirectly, have a great say concerning what happens in the country. Within the radio and television industry, the response of citizens is of prime importance. If people do not like particular programs, they are taken off the air. The networks and stations are not paternalistic—they strive to give the people what they want and rarely make decisions based on what they think is good for the populace. For example, very few instructional programs are aired by commercial stations because when they are shown, not many people watch them. Entertainment programming is what people watch, so that is primarily what they get.

Capitalism's Influence The U.S. economic system of capitalism is based on private property and a free market. The assumption is that private companies will survive if they supply something that is in demand. In a free market, companies are able to try to sell virtually anything, and individuals are free to choose what they want to buy and what they prefer to reject. The government does very little to intervene in this supply-demand cycle. U.S. broadcasting is regulated by the government, but overall it feels the hand of state to a much lesser extent than is common in most countries.

The companies involved with electronic media definitely rely on the theory of supply and demand. They respond to the demands of the people by supplying programs that will attract an audience. However, they are also responsive to the demands of advertisers because most media forms in the United States are supported by advertising. If a station or network cannot pay its bills through the advertising money it collects, it cannot stay in business. Of course, what advertisers want is a large number of people listening or watching who might be interested in buying their products. Hence there is a vicious circle involving programming to attract an audience to attract advertisers so that programs can be made to attract an audience that will attract advertisers, and so on.

THE DEVELOPMENT OF ELECTRONIC MEDIA IN THE UNITED STATES

The main elements that figure into the U.S. electronic media scene today are commercial radio and TV networks and stations, public radio and TV networks and stations, cable TV networks and systems, and the videocassette recorder. Each of these has had its own particular development.

Commercial Broadcasting Americans like to claim that they were the first to introduce radio broadcasting—but so do the British, the Germans, the Italians, the Russians, and many others. The beginnings are actually obscured because the first uses of radio were not within the realm of electronic media as we know it today. In the early 1900s, radio technology was used for ship-to-shore communications, but the concept of using the airwaves to provide entertainment and information for the masses (*broad*casting) did not arise to any degree until the 1920s.

Lee DeForest, a somewhat egomaniacal U.S. inventor who dubbed himself "the father of radio," claims he was the first to envision radio as an entertainment form when in 1910 he broadcast Enrico Caruso singing from the Metropolitan Opera House in New York. Within the United States, there are conflicting claims as to which station was first on the air, but the most commonly accepted "winner" is KDKA in Pittsburgh, Pennsylvania, because in 1920 it became the first station to apply to the government for a license to begin a regular broadcasting service. By 1923 there were over 600 stations throughout the country. Most of them programmed phonograph music and any amateur singing or speaking acts that wandered in the door and performed for free.

Almost from the beginning commercials were used to provide the money needed to operate the stations. But this advertising-based concept came about largely by accident. American Telephone and Telegraph (AT&T), a company whose primary business was telephones, owned a radio station in New York. It operated this station as a "toll station." The idea was that people who wanted to say something to a large audience could do so by paying a toll in the same way that they put money into the telephone to say something to one person. Individuals weren't very much interested in this concept, but in 1922 a real estate company paid to broadcast a message over the AT&T station, and various other companies followed suit. Within a few years ads were fairly plentiful, but they were primarily factual and low-key, especially in comparison to today's commercials.

With money coming in, programming changed and grew. Stations did not need to depend on free talent wandering in; they could pay for top talent and set definite schedules. But individual radio stations had trouble filling all their airtime, and so they started joining together to share programming. Eventually three major networks—National Broadcasting Company (NBC), Columbia Broadcasting System (CBS), and American Broadcasting Company (ABC)—were formed to provide programming that would be sent, through wires, to stations all over the country. The networks provided the bulk of the station programming, but, as previously mentioned, some of the airtime was filled with local programming produced by the stations themselves. The stations became known as affiliates of the network, and this network-affiliate relationship still exists today. Only one station per city could affiliate with each network, and so some stations, called independents, created and obtained all their own programming.

As radio became increasingly popular, more and more stations went on the air. However, the airwaves themselves were not very well controlled, and stations interfered with one another technically. By 1926 the airwaves were in a state of chaos, and the U.S. Congress passed a law to establish a body to bring order from chaos by redesigning the allocation of frequencies and the overall structure of radio. A few years later, Congress passed a new but similar law, the Communications Act of 1934. This set up the Federal Communications Commission (FCC) to oversee not only radio but also telephone communications and any future types of telecommunications. The Communications Act of 1934 still governs communication today.

Radio was very successful and profitable during the 1930s and 1940s. Programs such as *Amos 'n' Andy*, *The Jack Benny Show*, and *Fib-*

The Jack Benny Show, with Jack Benny, Mary Livingstone, and guests Charlie McCarthy and Edgar Bergen. *(NBC TV)*

ber McGee and Molly were anxiously awaited by millions of Americans who listened, usually as a family group, to huge consoles in their living rooms. Advertisers produced and controlled most of the programs that were then scheduled by the networks and sent to stations that broadcast them to local communities.

A new medium, television, came to the fore in the 1940s. TV's genesis, like radio's, is obscured in nationalistic claims, but most historians credit its U.S. evolution largely to David Sarnoff, president of the Radio Corporation of America, who pushed for its development and who arranged for TV to be demonstrated at the New York World's Fair in 1939.

Commercial television was broadcast experimentally before World War II but emerged as a full-fledged, FCC-approved medium during the late 1940s. Its popularity caught on quickly, fanned by ex–vaudeville comedian Milton Berle, who starred each Tuesday night in *Texaco Star Theater*, a program that featured slapstick skits, outrageous costumes, and a host of guest performers. In short order, 108 stations went on the air.

The FCC, mindful of the interference mess of

NBC's Milton Berle, the first major entertainer to have his own TV show (1948). He was promptly acclaimed "Mr. Television" and caused Tuesday night to be known as "Berle Night." *(NBC TV)*

the early days of radio, imposed a "freeze" on TV station allocations from 1948 to 1952 so that it could work out a reasonable system for providing TV service to the nation. It came up with a formal allocation of frequencies, designating exactly which channels would be available for broadcast in each U.S. city. During the freeze, one of the country's classic programs, *I Love Lucy*, was born. Milton Berle's show, and most of everything on TV at that time, aired live, but *I Love Lucy* was filmed and therefore available to be run over and over and over—as it still is all over the world.

TV adopted the same structure as radio. Advertisers supplied programs that were sent by the three networks to local affiliated stations. Independent stations created their own programming or bought it from syndicators who peddled movies, reruns of network shows, and programs made especially for the independents. Affiliates also bought some of this syndicated programming for the hours that were not filled with network shows or with their own locally produced shows.

However, the cost of producing television programs was much greater than that of producing radio, and sponsors found they could not bear all these expenses. As a result, multiple advertisers began paying for shows, and the networks took more control over program content. Sometimes the networks produced the shows themselves, but mostly they paid Hollywood production companies to produce for them. The networks recouped their costs by charging advertisers money to have their commercials aired between programs or as interruptions within them.

The success of TV greatly altered radio because radio's top talent (and its top advertisers) fled to the medium with both sight and sound. During the 1950s, radio underwent hard times. What finally emerged to put radio back on its feet was the locally based disc jockey show—local personalities chattering and playing records. Most stations feature a specific format of music, such as the newest rock, country-western, or music from the 1960s, that appeals to a particular segment of the population. Some stations program all-news or all-talk, the latter featuring call-in shows in which members of the audience phone in to ask questions or express opinions. Radio networks, robbed of their entertainment programming, began concentrating on supplying news and features. Most networks developed several different services to go along with the formats that stations were airing, for example, fast-paced short newscasts for rock stations and longer, more in-depth news for easy listening stations.

All of the early stations were amplitude-modulated (AM). Frequency-modulated (FM) radio was technically developed in the 1930s but did not received widespread political or popular support. During the late 1940s, when the FCC was determining the fate of TV, it also set aside frequencies for FM radio. With FM's "legitimization," it began a long, slow growth. At first FM radio stations had trouble recruiting an audience, largely because old radio sets could not receive FM frequencies. But as newer AM-FM sets became available, the superior sound quality of FM started to be appreciated, especially by those who valued their music. Now in the United States the FMs are the healthy stations and the AMs, which have poorer technical quality, garner lower audience numbers.

Radio today is a fragmented industry with most stations attracting small audiences. Most people have several favorite stations that they listen to, often as background for other activities such as driving a car or studying. Most radio networks are not high-profile, although a few of them have talk show or disc jockey personalities who are well known throughout the country. Most, however, supply news, features, and music that blends in with the local station format. NBC has sold its radio services, but ABC and CBS still own some. In addition, many other companies have entered the network business, each trying to develop programming that will appeal to enough stations so that advertisers will be interested in buying enough commercial time to allow the network to make a profit—the free market in action.

Within the last few years the TV operations of NBC, CBS, and ABC have undergone financial stress. Buffeted by an increasing number of independent stations, a plethora of cable TV services, and the videocassette recorder, these networks no longer claim the large audiences they once had. They have also been hurt by the 1986 establishment of a new network, Fox Broadcasting, founded by Australian-born Rupert Murdoch. Fox's inventive, rather off-the-wall programming (*The Simpsons* features a cartoon family of self-proclaimed losers; the leads of *Married . . . with Children* act disparagingly toward the institution of marriage and throw stinging sexual barbs at each other) has attracted many young viewers away from the three older networks. In the 1970s, over 90 percent of the people watching TV in the evening were watching either NBC, CBS, or ABC. By the 1990s, the number had dropped to about 60 percent.

Public Broadcasting Some of the very early radio stations in the United States were educational in nature in that they were owned by universities and used primarily to broadcast home study courses to people in the local area. However, with all the technical interference early stations received from one another, the courses often couldn't be heard, and both students and faculty became jaundiced about the effectiveness of educational radio. In addition, wealthy companies that wanted to get into the radio business offered universities large sums of money to turn their stations over to commercial interests. The universities, disillusioned with the airwaves and tempted by the money, sold the stations to profit-oriented companies that programmed primarily entertainment.

When the FCC was establishing both FM radio and TV, several organizations asked that some stations be reserved for educators so that commercial interests couldn't buy them out. As a result, the FCC set aside some FM and some TV stations in each city for a type of broadcasting that would not air any advertisements and would program material of a cultural nature. During the 1950s and 1960s, these educational stations (as they were then called) limped along. The FM radio stations were hindered by the same lack of FM radio sets that kept FM commercial stations from developing. TV stations created inexpensive, rather dull programming primarily with money they received from charitable organizations and from audience members who sent in checks.

Then in 1967, Congress passed the Public Broadcasting Act, which changed the name of these stations from "educational" to "public" to rid them of their stodgy image, approved government funding for public broadcasting, and established an operational structure for the new system. A TV network, Public Broadcasting Service (PBS), and a radio network, National Public Radio (NPR), were established. The Corporation for Public Broadcasting (CPB) was set up to receive the money from the government and then distribute it to PBC, NPR, and local public stations. In this way CPB served as a buffer so that the government would not influence the programming policies of the networks or stations.

The money the government gives CPB comes from the general tax money. In this way, public broadcasting is funded similarly to the government-run broadcasting systems of many other nations.

U.S. public broadcasting is a minor player in a broadcasting structure dominated by commercial interests. Rarely do more than 3 percent of viewers watch public TV, but these people are among the better educated and most influential.

PBS does not produce any programs itself. Some of what it shows it buys from foreign countries, primarily Britain. But the bulk of what it airs comes from public television stations throughout the country. For example,

WETA in Washington, D.C., produces a nightly news program called *The MacNeil/Lehrer Newshour* that it makes available to PBS. PBS then distributes the program by satellite so that all public TV stations in the country can air it. PBS does not broadcast all day long, and so individual public TV stations must produce some of their own material (usually local public affairs programs) or buy programming from various private companies that produce educationally oriented material.

NPR produces much of its own programming and also airs some programs that have been developed at local stations. In 1982 a separate public radio network, American Public Radio (APR), was formed by several public radio stations. It does not produce any programming but airs material sent to it by public radio stations. Stations can pick and choose whatever programming they want from NPR and APR (now called Public Radio International). In addition, they program some of their own material, particularly classical music.

Both public TV and public radio have improved program quality greatly now that they receive government funding and have an established organizational structure.

Cable Television Cable television existed in the United States as far back as the 1940s. It was located primarily in areas that had poor TV reception or none at all. A group of neighbors would join together, place an antenna on a hilltop to receive the over-the-air signal of the nearest TV station, transfer that signal to a wire, and then run the wire (often by looping it from tree to tree) into each of the neighborhood homes. During the 1950s, 1960s, and 1970s, the business became a little more sophisticated in that companies (rather than individuals) strung the cable on telephone poles (rather than trees). These companies charged their subscribers a modest amount (several dollars a month) for providing this cable TV service. But overall, cable TV was a sleepy business that simply extended the reach of local stations by placing the signal in a wire and taking it to places that could not receive it through a regular TV antenna.

Then in the late 1970s a service owned by Time Inc. (now Time Warner, Inc.), Home Box Office (HBO), decided to use satellite technology to show a championship boxing match to subscribers in two cable TV systems that it owned. This experiment was so successful that HBO began using satellites to distribute more programming, not just to its own systems but also to cable operations throughout the country. HBO charged the cable systems, and the cable systems in exchange charged the cable subscribers a little more than they had been paying. Soon other companies decided to cash in on this bonanza, and a host of cable networks (ESPN, CNN, MTV, Showtime) joined HBO on the satellite. Cities with good TV reception that had found no need for cable TV in the past began wiring so that homes could receive these new services. In 1975 only 12 percent of American households had cable TV; but by the 1990s over 60 percent were subscribers.

Not all cable systems have the same number of channels, but the average system allows about forty channels of different programming to enter each home, and plans are in the making that will include hundreds of channels. Because each system can choose which services it wishes to place on its channels, people in the same city do not necessarily receive the same program services. A system on the east side of town might offer The Weather Channel, while a system on the west side would not have that channel among its offerings.

Cable services have been divided into several different categories. A majority of the cable networks (ESPN, MTV, CNN, USA) are referred to as basic services. They carry advertisements and are offered to the subscriber for a small monthly fee. Most of these services, unlike broadcast networks, tend to be narrow in scope. They do not program for a broad audience; rather they narrowcast—Nickelodeon targets children, ESPN is meant for sports fans, MTV is aimed at teenagers, Lifetime gears programming toward women. Another category of networks, called pay services, are commercial-free but charge a higher monthly fee. Most of them (HBO, Showtime, The Movie Channel, The Disney Channel) program movies and special events. Pay-per-view services (Playboy, Request TV) are the most expensive of all, but customers pay only for what they actually watch. Generally pay-per-view needs an interactive wire that goes from the subscriber's home to the cable system to let the cable system's computer know that someone is watching. The customer is then billed for the cost of that program at the end of the month. The primary fare on pay-per-view is movies, concerts, and high-profile sports events.

In addition to the cable networks, some local cable systems also set aside one or more of their channels for locally produced programming. They may run a local origination channel that provides news and features, or they may turn one or more channels over to local citizens who then program it. The cable systems also retransmit programs from local area commercial and public TV stations and sometimes from local radio stations.

The cable TV industry has been very successful in the United States. Its profitability has tapered down from the rather wild days of the late 1970s, but it is still one of the country's top-earning businesses.

Videocassette Recorders The first videotape recorders were introduced in the United States by Ampex in 1956. However, they were very bulky and expensive and meant to be used only by professional broadcasters. Recorders gradually decreased in size, technical complexity, and cost, and by the late 1970s, videocassette recorders meant to be used in homes were introduced by Sony and Matsushita.

Since their introduction, VCRs have taken the United States by storm. They are used primarily to play back movies rented from local video stores, which seem to have sprung up on just about every city street. They are also used to tape programs broadcast by commercial, public, or cable TV facilities so that these programs can be watched at a time other than when they were originally shown on TV.

ORGANIZATION AND FINANCING

Almost all of the organizations that own electronic media entities in the United States are privately owned (not government-owned). This type of ownership applies to most U.S. industries—automobile, food, clothing, computer software. These private companies obtain money from investors (individuals or other private companies) who hope they will earn a return on their investment. The company uses the money for such things as starting up new activities and buying expensive equipment. Companies also obtain money by selling their products or services at a price that brings in more money than the amount needed to produce and sell the product. In other words, the company makes a profit. Part of this profit is paid to the investors as the return on their investment. Profit is a very important driving force in U.S. economics. Broadcasting companies make a profit by bringing in more money (mainly in the form of advertising dollars) than they pay out for salaries, programming, satellite time, and the other costs of doing business.

In recent years, the ownership of many broadcasting organizations has changed hands. In some cases unprofitable companies have been bought by profitable ones. In other cases one company has been able to invest enough money in another company to gain unwelcome financial control—a situation referred to as a hostile takeover. In 1985, ABC, which had been an independent company, was bought by Capital Cities. A year later NBC, which since its founding in 1926 had been owned by RCA, was purchased by General Electric (GE). Although neither of these was referred to as a hostile takeover, the culture clash between the old employees and the new owners often reached "less than friendly" proportions. U.S. entertainment companies have also increasingly been bought by companies from other countries, primarily Japan, England, and France.

Some large companies own a variety of media-oriented entities. For example, Time Warner, Inc., owns many cable TV systems throughout the country, and it also owns the cable network Home Box Office. In addition, it produces and distributes movies that are rented in video stores. The Gannett Company runs sixteen radio stations and ten TV stations, as well as a large number of newspapers. ABC has a large financial stake in two cable networks, the all-sports ESPN and the cultural Arts and Entertainment. Westwood One, which at one time was a very small radio network, bought the NBC radio networks from GE and became a much more important media player.

At the other extreme are very small companies that operate only one radio station or one TV station or one cable system. An example is Bay Radio, Inc., which owns one AM radio station in the small town of Coos Bay, Oregon. Often these small companies are family-owned, with the only investors being a husband and wife. Perhaps the wife is responsible for station management chores, the husband sells ads, and the couple hires several college students part-time to act as disc jockeys.

The profit motive is predominant in all forms of radio and TV except for public broadcasting. Public broadcasting is, by law, nonprofit. The organizations that own public radio and TV entities can bring in and pay out money, but any excess that they generate must be plowed back into the station. They do not have individual investors who are expecting a return on their investment. Some public broadcasting stations are owned by colleges or school systems that obtain money primarily from the government. Other stations are controlled by nonprofit community organizations that oversee finances and general operations but do not earn money.

Specifics regarding the organization of the various forms of electronic media vary widely, but the overall need for financial stability is universal.

Most of the money that supports radio and television comes from advertising. Private companies trying to sell products buy time on radio or TV networks or stations in order to run commercials.

Many companies do not actually buy the time themselves. They hire an advertising agency (another privately owned company) to make decisions concerning how best to advertise a product. General Motors (GM), for example, hires an agency named Lintas to make advertising recommendations concerning its Chevrolet automobile. The executives at Lintas may decide that GM should spend 10 percent of its advertising budget on roadside billboards, 20 percent on radio stations that appeal to 20- to 25-year-olds, 20 percent on cable networks, 40 percent on network TV, and 10 percent on flyers that are mailed to people's homes. The agency then buys the specific radio and TV time.

Stations, too, deal with intermediate companies called station representatives. Inefficiencies would abound if every radio and TV station in the country sent a salesperson to Lintas' New York headquarters to try to line up Chevrolet ads. So instead, one company represents about forty stations and tries to convince the Lintas executives to buy time on all the stations.

Sometimes, however, commercial buying is very direct. The owner-salesperson of a small radio station walks down the street and tries to convince the owner of a local hardware store to advertise on the station.

The cost of advertising time is directly related to the number of people who see or hear the commercial. Small radio station commercials can be as low as $10, while TV network time can run into hundreds of thousands of dollars for 30 seconds. Of course, the more money a broadcaster or cablecaster charges for commercials, the greater the likelihood of making a substantial profit.

Advertising is just about the only source of income for commercial networks and stations. Occasionally broadcasters make small amounts of money from selling their programming to one another or to other countries. But most of the money from these sales goes to the production companies (Universal, Paramount, Columbia) that produce the programs, not to the broadcasters.

Cable TV networks and systems also depend greatly on advertisements for their income, but they have another important income source—fees from subscribers. Commercial TV is free to everyone in the country, but only those who pay a monthly fee to their local cable company can receive the multitude of cable TV channels. The basic services (ESPN, CNN, MTV, etc.) are usually offered as a group to consumers for about $12 a month. The pay services (HBO, Showtime, etc.) are sold individually and are likely to cost $15 each per month. Pay-per-view charges vary from $3 for a movie to $50 for a major sports event. The money collected from the subscribers is divided about 50-50 between the cable systems and the cable networks.

Public broadcasting receives a little less than half its money from the government, some of it in the form of a yearly allotment from Congress and some of it from government-run educational institutions. The rest of the revenue comes from a variety of sources. Public radio and TV stations ask their listeners to contribute money. Such contributions are purely voluntary. Anyone can receive public radio or TV without paying a cent, but people who feel the service is worth something to them send money to the local stations they watch or hear. Public broadcasting also receives money from charitable foundations, often earmarked for the production of a particular program that covers a subject the foundation finds worthwhile. Although there is no advertising per se, private companies do give money to public broadcasting in return for on-air statements mentioning their contributions. As the years have passed, these on-air statements have become more elaborate. Once simple slides that merely listed the company name, these announcements now feature logos, slogans, and descriptions of products and services.

Americans are bombarded by commercials. During each hour of commercial TV viewing, they are subjected to somewhere between 7 and 17 minutes of commercials. Radio statistics are similar. An hour's programming is interrupted six or more times so that these commercials can be heard. Most of them last 30 seconds, but some are as short as 10 seconds. The ads are slick, employing fast cuts, special effects, and convincing acting.

Controversy surrounds commercials, not only because they are so numerous and frequent but also because of what they supposedly do to society. Critics feel the constant message of "Buy, buy, buy" has turned U.S. citizens into materialists who are up to their ears in debt. Aiming advertising at children who then badger their parents for products, some of which are sugary and unhealthful, has been decried by various parents' groups. As a result, the government occasionally places restrictions on the type of advertising that can appear in children's programs. For example, the hosts of children's programs cannot endorse a commercial product within the confines of the show because children develop faith in the hosts and willingly do whatever they say.

On the plus side, buying is what drives the U.S. capitalistic economy—one of the strongest in the world. Ads, even though they mostly use superlatives such as "best" and "most sensational," do inform people about products that are available and that may be genuinely useful. Advertisements pay the bills for radio and television programs, making them free or inexpensive to the consumer. People in the United States do not pay government-mandated TV set license fees as people in many other countries do. However, those who wish to subscribe to cable TV have to pay a monthly fee. One of the original ideas of cable was that it would sport fewer commercials than broadcast TV and so would be worth paying for. Most of the expensive channels are commercial-free, but the rest run the same commercials as broadcast TV and show them just as frequently and with just as many interruptions. So the consumer is faced with both commercials and fees but gains a larger variety of programming. Despite its downside, advertising will no doubt remain the main source of income for a radio and television system that is closely tied to the U.S. capitalistic economic system.

PROGRAMMING

Both radio and TV programming in the United States are overwhelmingly entertainment-oriented. Programs exist that are intended to inform, but most of them are presented in as entertaining a manner as the producers can devise.

Music Popular music dominates radio. Classical music (of the Bach and Beethoven variety) is rarely heard except on public radio. In large cities, classical music may be heard on one or two commercial stations, but for many radio programmers, the word "classic" is often used to refer to music that is over 10 years old. The record industry produces a vast number of hits and potential hits each year, and the success of this material is often determined by the amount of radio play it receives; the record industry and the radio industry have a symbiotic relationship. Music recorded in England (and to some extent, Western Europe) is also quite popular on U.S. radio.

The main purveyor of music on television is the cable channel MTV. This upstart company developed a whole new concept that altered music marketing. When the idea was first bandied about in 1980, skeptics felt no one would sit in front of a TV set watching disconnected visuals accompanying hit music. How wrong they were. Although other cable channels have been formed to play music videos 24 hours a day, none have been as successful as the original MTV.

But aside from music videos, TV does not highlight music. Public TV tapes classical concerts and sometimes features works of well-known composers and artists. Commercial networks hardly ever program strictly musical material. Someone simply sitting and playing a guitar does not have enough visual interest to attract a large U.S. audience.

Some of the explicitly sexual or violent lyrics of modern music have been highly criticized. In a similar vein, MTV has been verbally chastised for all its scantily clad women in fishnet stockings and high-heeled shoes. But in the United States, individual freedom is valued (and protected by the First Amendment of the Constitution—see the section on laws and regulations), and so ultimately individuals involved in the media business make most decisions regarding taste, ethics, and morals.

Drama and Situation Comedy The most common entertainment form on TV is fiction—both drama and situation comedy. These shows come in the form of series, soap operas, miniseries, and movies.

On commercial, public, and cable networks, series are usually shown at the same time each week. When these series are rerun on local TV stations, they usually air every day at the same time. For example, a station in San Francisco might run *I Love Lucy* every morning at 11:00 and *Star Trek* every afternoon at 4:00.

Soap operas, primarily a commercial TV network product, are aired at the same time each weekday, usually during the late morning or early afternoon. These continuing dramas with plot lines that stretch out over years are called soap operas because when they were on radio in the 1930s and 1940s, most of the advertisers were companies that sold soap. Soaps have occasionally been featured on a weekly basis during evening hours; *Dallas*, *Dynasty*, and similar shows were popular in the 1980s.

Miniseries became popular in the mid-1970s, spurred mostly by the success of *Roots*, Alex Haley's story of his black slave ancestors. This show aired eight nights in a row on ABC to the largest TV audience up to that time. Since then many other short series with definite beginnings and ends have been aired.

Movies are seen on all forms of TV—commercial networks, local stations, cable networks, public broadcasting. Most of these movies have already been shown in motion picture theaters, but some are made specially for TV.

The main criticism registered against dramas and sitcoms is their emphasis on sex and violence. Groups of citizens occasionally band together to try to reason with TV executives that the amount of sex and violence they show is harmful to society. If reason doesn't work, they threaten not to watch the programs or to convince companies not to advertise on the network or station by boycotting their products. Several times over the past decades various government bodies have investigated the subject of violence on TV, but little specific action has been taken. Sex and violence sell. People watch these types of programs. If they didn't—if they really did turn off their TV sets when two people climbed into bed or when the detective pulled out a gun—the networks and stations would not program sexual or violent material. Again, the dilemma rests in part with the democratic philosophy of giving the people what they want, not necessarily what is good for them.

Game Shows Another category of entertainment programs is game shows. Seen most often during the daytime, these shows feature ordinary citizens trying to win prizes through such feats as guessing how much certain products cost, filling in crossword puzzles, or trying to answer personal questions the same way that their spouse would answer them.

These shows are often criticized for being inane and encouraging avarice, but they provide a vicarious thrill for many people. The shows are easy and cheap to produce—most of the talent is free and the prizes are usually donated by companies that want the publicity. Probably no other country in the world would bother to dispute a U.S. claim that it was first to air a game show. Fortunately, or unfortunately, this genre is now being imitated in many other countries.

Talk Shows Both radio and TV produce talk shows with hosts and guests. Some of these feature interviews with celebrities, and others deal with problems or events in the lives of ordinary people. A number of talk programs deal with important current or sociological issues and so can be quite informative, but they are organized with entertainment in mind. Serious topics such as economic indicators and environmental problems are not dealt with at great length (except on public broadcasting, some specialized cable channels, and a few commercial network programs aired on Sundays). Topics are more likely to be of a sensational or titillating nature such as interpersonal problems faced by children of movie stars or the life of a prostitute.

Children's Programs The "entertainizing" of information is very common in the United States. Very few programs are dull. They move quickly and contain gripping sequences. This applies to programming aimed at children, as well as that produced for adults. Some children's programs, such as cartoons, are purely entertaining. But even programs designed to inform children feature actors rather than teachers and tend to cover material in short bursts.

The most successful children's program, public broadcasting's *Sesame Street*, assumes a very short attention span. Some say, only partly in jest, that American children, because they have been exposed to so many commercials, have developed attention spans that last only 30 seconds. At any rate, *Sesame Street*'s short segments, some of which mimic commercials in that they are "brought to you by the letter M," have been very effective in teaching concepts to children. Overall, the fast-paced visual entertainment that Americans are exposed to from childhood on has greatly influenced the kind of programming that is available to U.S. adults—and hence the rest of the world.

Sports Sports events are not just presented; they are hyped with emphasis on "the thrill of victory and the agony of defeat." If the action stops, pretaped interviews with team players can be shown. Most sports programming occurs on the weekend, but Monday night football has also been a popular staple in the United States. The 24-hour-a-day sports cable network, ESPN, is available for sports addicts—of which there are many in the United States.

TV networks and stations pay athletic teams rights fees in order to broadcast or cablecast their games. Sports have been such a drawing card for radio and television that bidding wars among the various networks seeking exclusive rights to show certain games have sent rights fees sky high. Teams have made enormous amounts of money from TV, a fact that has not escaped the notice of players, who demand increasingly higher salaries. As commercial networks have come upon hard economic times, they can no longer afford the escalating rights fees. The TV-sports relationship is in a period of shakeout.

Documentaries and Reality Programs Long documentaries that deal in depth with one issue have become rare on both commercial radio and TV. Public broadcasting airs several documentary series, and a number of cable networks feature documentaries, but this type of programming does not attract a large audience and so is generally avoided by the whole commercial sector. The documentaries produced tend to be tight and fast-paced, like the rest of U.S. programming.

The documentary form that Americans are most likely to watch is what has become known as the magazine minidoc. These are short issue-oriented stories placed one after the other within a single program. The most renowned is CBS's *60 Minutes*, which has been one of the most watched TV programs for most of its 20-plus years.

One of the newer forms of programming on U.S. TV is reality programming—semidocumentary, semidramatic material that is based on real events, often of a somewhat sensational nature. Commercial networks, in particular, have taken to this type of programming in part because it is much cheaper to produce than dramas.

News News is abundant in the United States. Anyone who wants to can be brought up to date on what is happening in the world at any hour of the day or night. CNN and some radio stations air news 24 hours a day. Commercial TV networks have regularly scheduled news each evening, and most local stations have their own news programs. Because the organizations gathering and presenting the news are privately owned, the government has little or no say about what is broadcast. Criticism of the government and investigations into the conduct of public officials are common.

Many different sources are used in the gathering of news. Newsrooms subscribe to wire services and buy special radios that can receive police communications. Reporters fan out from the local city hall to Bosnia. At some point someone at a network or station decides which stories should be broadcast to the public. These radio and TV employees are the gatekeepers who decide what is and what isn't news. There are many of them, however, and often they do not agree as to what is important. While station A may lead off with a story about a bank robbery, station B may emphasize an upturn in economic figures.

Elements of show business are present in

news programs. The stories are presented by attractive, personable, glib men and women who often become more famous than the people they report about. Stories are capsulized, again taking into account the fact that viewers might switch to something else if the material becomes boring.

Electronic media news organizations are criticized for presenting news in an overly sensationalized manner just to attract viewers or listeners. U.S. reporters are aggressive and may shove a microphone in front of grieving relatives just to obtain gripping footage. Reporters are also competitive, with each network or station trying to scoop the others. Sometimes in their hurry to be first with a story, they do not gather all the facts correctly. But U.S. news, on the whole, is current, thorough, informative—and often entertaining.

Religious Programs Religion plays only a minor role in radio and TV, but radio and TV play a major role in some religions. The United States prides itself on freedom of religion, and hundreds of different religions coexist peacefully. Most make little or no use of the electronic media. Numerous churches exist in each community that have services on Sunday (or Saturday) and other on-site activities for church members during the week.

Some TV stations air church services or other religious programs on Sundays, but the main religious programming is on radio or TV stations or cable TV networks devoted entirely to religion. Generally the stations or networks are owned by one particular religion that uses the electronic media as its main method of communicating with the people it serves. In the late 1980s, these "electronic churches" were involved in a scandal when it was discovered that some of the TV ministers had engaged in unbecoming sexual behavior and had also used money sent in by viewers to buy themselves expensive homes and cars. For a while the credibility of religious TV was shaky, but in the long run most of the organizations that had been using TV have continued to do so successfully.

Educational Programming Of all forms of programming, the United States does this the least well. Commercial radio and TV rarely broadcast anything that would be considered purely educational. Some public broadcasting stations and a few cable networks show programs designed to be utilized in school classrooms or as college courses, but such use is not widespread throughout the country. Teachers, on their own, might suggest that students watch certain commercial, public, or cable programs that relate to lessons being taught, but a well-structured, organized relationship between education and the media does not exist.

Other Programming Because Americans have so many channels to fill with radio and TV programs, just about everything imaginable has been programmed at some time or another. There are programs on fly-fishing and gardening. Cable channels, called home shopping channels, exist that do nothing but demonstrate products that people can buy by calling a particular phone number. One cable network shows the proceedings of the House of Representatives; another discusses the weather all day long.

Most programming is in English, the most widely spoken language in the United States. But the country has many immigrants who speak other languages. Some radio and TV stations and cable channels program entirely in a foreign language such as Spanish, Japanese, or Korean. These organizations, some of which have been quite successful, create their own programming and import material from other countries that speak the appropriate language.

LAWS AND REGULATIONS

The U.S. government is divided into three branches—executive, legislative, and judicial.

The head of the executive branch is the president, who is elected by the people every 4 years. Associated with the executive branch, but separate from it, are independent agencies that regulate various forms of business, including electronic media. The legislative branch, known as Congress, consists of two bodies, the Senate and the House of Representatives. The Senate numbers 100 people, 2 from each of the 50 states. The House has 435 representatives elected based on population. A city with a large population, such as New York, has more representatives than an entire state with a small population, such as Alaska. The judicial branch consists of many courts presided over by judges. The highest court is the Supreme Court.

One of the overriding principles of the U.S. government is separation of powers. In order to prevent any one person (or one branch of government) from wielding too much influence, each branch of government has checks and balances on the others. Congress passes laws, the president enforces them, and the courts interpret them when questions arise. Also, the president can veto bills, and the Supreme Court can declare that laws are in opposition to the U.S. Constitution and therefore must be rescinded.

Another aspect of government is that not all the power is held by the national government in Washington. States and local areas, such as cities and counties, also have governments. Many of the laws that affect the citizens of the country, including some related to radio and television, apply only in particular states or local areas.

The Federal Communications Commission
The main government body that broadcasters must interact with is an independent agency, the Federal Communications Commission, which was set up by the Communications Act of 1934. The FCC is headed by five commissioners who are appointed by the president but must be approved by the Senate (an example of checks and balances). This body, taking the Communications Act of 1934 as its framework, makes decisions and establishes regulations that affect the day-to-day operation of commercial and public radio and TV stations, as well as telephones and other forms of telecommunication. (Unlike the broadcast regulatory body in many countries, however, it does not oversee the post office.) If broadcasters do not like what the FCC devises, they can appeal to the courts. Cable TV must live by some of the regulations of the FCC, especially those that affect the interrelationships between cable and broadcasters, but many cable rules come from local city governments—an example of local regulation.

One of the primary duties of the FCC is overseeing the technical quality of radio and TV. It makes sure that stations broadcast on the right frequencies and with the right amount of power so that their signals do not interfere with one another.

It also grants, renews, and revokes station licenses. In order to operate, radio and TV stations must obtain a license from the FCC. Periodically (every 7 years for radio, every 5 years for TV) stations must apply for renewal of their license. As long as they have been abiding by FCC regulations, they can be fairly sure of obtaining renewal. If, however, a station consistently broadcasts with too much power, the people who own it will lose control and a new group of people will be given the license. Sometimes a station can lose its license because of its programming practices, especially if citizens complain. In the 1960s a large portion of the black populace in Jackson, Mississippi, complained that TV station WLBT was not presenting racial issues fairly. After a lengthy, involved hearing that eventually wound up in the courts, WLBT was stripped of its license and a nonprofit group was given the station. But, overall, the FCC rarely revokes a license. Usually the FCC warns a miscreant station by sending it a written complaint or by fining it several thousand dollars. This is usually enough to whip a station into shape so that revocation is not called for.

The First Amendment Another element of government that strongly affects the nature of electronic media is the U.S. Constitution—a document drawn up in 1787 that established the basic form of the U.S. government. The First Amendment to the Constitution reads "Congress shall make no law . . . abridging the freedom of speech, or of the press." Freedom of the press is taken very seriously by those in the radio and TV business, especially journalists. They feel they have an obligation to report everything to the people, even if it exposes inadequacies of the government. Sometimes the government tries to withhold or censor information, especially if releasing it might endanger the security of the nation. Exactly what constitutes "endangerment" is debated by members of the press and government officials. The First Amendment is also used in debates involving sexual explicitness, such as the lyrics of some modern music and the bedroom scenes of dramas and comedies. Literalists feel the First Amendment allows anyone to say, print, or broadcast anything. But indecency and obscenity are outlawed by the U.S. Criminal Code.

The problem comes in defining content that is protected by the First Amendment versus content that is indecent or obscene. Generally indecency involves broadcasting something offensive in relation to the standards of a particular community. Because the United States is such a vast country, what might be considered indecent in the middle of the country might be quite acceptable on the West Coast. How is a national network to decide when it has exceeded the bounds of decency? Obscenity was defined by a 1973 court case to include anything that appeals to the prurient interests of the average person and lacks serious artistic, literary, political, or scientific value. Needless to say, debate abounds as to what qualifies as obscene. The FCC can fine stations for broadcasting what it considered to be obscene or indecent material, but in most of these instances stations can appeal to the courts, which may or may not agree with the FCC.

Equal Time Another highly controversial regulatory subject involves Section 315 of the Communications Act of 1934. It states that if a licensee allows any person who is a legally qualified candidate for any public office to use a broadcasting station, it must afford equal opportunity to all other candidates for that office. This statement, which has become known as the equal-time provision, seems straightforward. If a station allows Senate candidate X to talk on the station for 5 minutes at 6 P.M., it must also allow candidate Y 5 minutes at approximately the same time.

But what happens if the president is a candidate for reelection and wants to use the airwaves to address the people about an urgent crisis? Should all the other candidates get equal time? (The FCC decided that crisis-oriented speeches are exempt from Section 315.) Or what happens if a presidential candidate is an ex–movie actor; if a station airs one of his old movies, does it have to give equal time to opposing candidates? This of course occurred when Ronald Reagan was running. The issue never came to a head because stations voluntarily refrained from showing old Reagan movies. Also, his opponent, Jimmy Carter, made light of the situation by joking that the showing of those old movies might cause Reagan to lose votes.

Many other laws, regulations, and court cases affect the electronic media. Copyright laws keep networks from using material without paying the creator. A variety of state laws prevent journalists from unduly invading the privacy of individuals. Court cases have decided when a broadcaster is or is not libeling a person. But overall, the hand of government brushes only lightly on the activities of the radio and TV industry, especially as compared to the situation in other countries.

THE AUDIENCE

In line with its democratic principles, the United States values the opinions of audience members. Citizens are encouraged to write to the FCC or station and network management if they have complaints—or if they have compliments. During the 1960s and 1970s, citizen groups were very much involved in the license renewal process. Some of their complaints led to license revocation, but mostly these groups succeeded in convincing stations to accede to their demands or face the threat of complaints at license renewal time. This degree of citizen involvement has waned in recent years, but the public is still very much involved in the electronic media.

Access Channels Cable TV systems have channels, referred to as public access, that are set aside for use by members of the community. Individuals or groups produce programs of their own choosing using their own equipment or equipment supplied by the cable company. The cable system has no say over the content of these programs. It simply distributes them to the community over the cable system's public access channel. When cable was growing rapidly in the early 1980s, these public access channels were used extensively. Enthusiasm has decreased, however, as amateurs have found what professionals have known all along—producing TV programs is hard work. In all other aspects of the electronic media, employees of stations or networks determine what will or will not be aired.

Ratings The major input from the audience comes in the form of ratings indicating how many and what type of people are watching or listening to a particular program. These ratings can mean life or death for much commercial station and network programming. Because the amount that can be charged for an advertisement is dependent on the size of the audience, shows with poor ratings are taken off the air quickly.

Several private companies supply ratings data, most notably A. C. Nielsen and Arbitron. Nielsen concentrates on television, while Arbitron measures radio. Both companies select sample households and ask family members to keep track of their viewing or listening. The number of people selected to participate is small, but Nielsen and Arbitron go to great pains to try to make their samples representative of the entire U.S. population.

In some cases the audience members selected fill out diaries listing what they heard or saw. In other instances a meter is installed on the TV set to record when the set is on and what channel it is tuned to. The most modern of these meters are Nielsen's "people meters." Each person in the household has a button to push when he or she is watching TV. In this way Nielsen knows which member of the family is watching the program—the 12-year-old son or the 48-year-old mother.

Nielsen and Arbitron gather the information, process it through a computer, and publish reports indicating how many people watch or listen to what. They also break the audience members down by demographics such as age, race, and sex. All the people meters are connected by phone lines to a central computer, and so the data gathered from them can be analyzed overnight. Diaries take longer and are considered less accurate because people can forget to fill them out. However, the accuracy of people meters is also questioned because people watching TV must remember to push their buttons regularly.

In fact, there are many in the United States who are opposed to the use of ratings. Newscasters, disc jockeys, and producers who have lost their jobs because of low ratings decry the system and point out all the possibilities for inaccuracy within the data that are collected. But unless someone devises a better system for determining how much advertisers should pay

CHICAGO, IL

WK1 4/23-4/29 WK2 4/30-5/06 WK3 5/07-5/13 WK4 5/14-5/20

MONDAY-FRIDAY 3:30PM - 6:00PM

TIME PERIOD

METRO HH RTG	METRO HH SHR	STATION	PROGRAM	DMA HOUSEHOLD RATINGS WEEKS 1	2	3	4	MULTI-WEEK AVG RTG	MULTI-WEEK AVG SHR	SHARE TREND FEB '92	NOV '91	MAY '91	DMA RATINGS PERSONS 2+	18+	12-24	12-34	18-34	18-49	21-49	25-54	35+	35-64	50+	WOMEN 18+	12-24	18-34	18-49	25-49	25-54	WKG	MEN 18+	18-34	18-49	21-49	25-49	25-54	TNS 12-17	CHILD 2-11	6-11
1	2			3	4	5	6	7	8	11	12	13	15	16	17	18	19	20	21	22	23	24	25	26	27	28	29	31	32	34	35	36	37	38	39	40	41	42	43
LT LT			R.S.E. THRESHOLDS 25+% (1 S.E.) 4 WK AVG 50+%	1 LT	1 LT	1 LT	1 LT	LT LT					LT LT	LT LT	1 LT	1 LT	1 LT	LT LT	LT LT	LT LT	LT LT	1 LT	1 LT	LT LT	2 LT	1 LT	1 LT	1 LT	1 LT	1 LT	LT LT	1 LT	1 LT	1 LT	1 LT	1 LT	2 1	2 LT	2 1
		3:30PM																																					
4	10	WBBM	LOVE CONNECTN	3	4	4	3	4	10	12X	12	13	2	2	1	1	1	1	1	2	2	2	3	2	2	1	2	2	2	2	1	1	1	1	1	1	2	1	1
<<		WCIU	HOLA AMERICA	<<	<<	<<	<<	<<		X																													
3	10	WFLD	DENNIS-ANIMATD	4	3	3	3	3	10	10X	11	7	2		2	1	1							1	2	1	1	1									4	7	8
1	4	WGBO	JUDGE	1	1	2	1	1	4	4X	5	5	1	1						1	1	1	2	1						1	1					1	1		
4	11	WGN	AVG. ALL WKS	5	4	4	2	4	11	10	9	10	2	1	1	1	1	1	1	1	1	1	2	1	1	1	1	1	1		1	1	1	1	1	1	2	6	4
5	13		#CHIP&DALE-RNGR	5	4			4	12				2	1	2	1	1	1	1	1	1	1	2	1	1	1	1	1	1		1	1	1	1	1	1	3	7	5
2	7		CHIP&DALE-RNGR				2	2	7				1		1					1	1	1		1			1	1	1								1	7	
9	26	WLS	JEOPARDY	9	9	9	10	9	26	27X	27	28	4	5	2	2	2	3	3	3	7	5	10	7	2	3	4	4	4	3	3	1	2	2	1	2	2	1	1
8	23	WMAQ	DONAHUE	9	7	7	7	8	22	21X	16	14	3	4	2	2	3	3	2	3	5	4	8	6	3	4	4	4	4	3	2	1	1	1	1	1	1	1	1
2	7	WPWR	MERRIE MELODES	3	2	2	2	2	6	6	7	9	2		2	1									1	1	1										3	7	6
1	2	WTTW	AVG. ALL WKS	1	1	1	1	1	2	3	2	2									1		1															1	
1	2		#BEST-NTL GRPHC	1	1			1	2												1		1															1	1
<<		WYCC	VARIOUS	<<	<<	<<	<<	<<																															
34			HUT/PUT/TOTALS*	38	35	34	32	34		38	39	35	18	16	14	12	10	10	10	11	20	14	29	21	16	14	14	14	15	11	11	6	6	6	6	7	19	27	24
		4:00PM																																					
7	20	WBBM	PEOPLE'S COURT	7	7	8	8	7	20	20X	19	20	4	5	2	2	2	2	2	3	6	4	9	6	2	3	3	3	3	3	3	1	2	2	2	2	2	1	1
<<		WCIU	HOLA AMERICA	<<	<<	<<	<<	<<		X																													
4	12	WFLD	TINY TOON ADV	5	5	4	4	4	12	11X	13	13	3	1	3	2	1	1	1	1	1	1		1	3	1	1	1	1	1	1	1	1	1	1	1	7	10	13
1	3	WGBO	HIGHWAY-HEAVEN	1	1	1	1	1	3	3	2	3									1		1	1													1		
4	10	WGN	AVG. ALL WKS	5	4	4	2	4	10	10	9	7	2	1	1	1	1	1	1	1	1	1	2	1	1	1	1	1	1		1	1	1	1	1	1	2	7	5
4	11		#TALE SPIN	5	4			4	11				2	1	2	1	1	1	1	1	1	1	2	1	1	1	1	1	1		1	1	1	1	1	1	3	9	6
2	6		TALE SPIN				2	2	6				1		1	1	1			1			1						1			1					2	5	
8	22	WLS	4.00 EYEWT NWS	8	8	8	8	8	22	23X	23	24	4	5	1	2	2	3	3	3	7	5	9	6	1	3	4	4	4	3	4	1	2	2	2	2	1	1	1
7	19	WMAQ	HARD COPY	8	6	7	7	7	19	20X	16	10	3	4	2	2	2	2	2	3	5	4	7	5	2	2	3	3	4	3	3	2	2	2	2	2	2	1	1
2	6	WPWR	B BUNNY&FRNDS	2	2	2	2	2	6	5	6	7	1		1	1									1												2	7	7
1	2	WTTW	AVG. ALL WKS	1	<<	1	1	1	2	2		2											1																
1	1		#WILD AMERICA	1	<<			1	1														1																
1	2		WILD AMERICA			1	1	1	2														1														1		
<<		WYCC	AVG. ALL WKS	<<	<<	<<	<<	<<																															
<<			#SESAME STREET		<<	<<	<<	<<																															
37			HUT/PUT/TOTALS*	40	37	37	35	37		42	42	37	21	18	15	13	10	11	11	13	23	17	32	22	15	13	14	15	16	12	14	7	8	8	9	9	22	32	34
		4:30PM																																					
9	22	WBBM	CH 2 NWS-4.30	9	8	9	8	8	21	21X	19	17	4	5	1	2	2	2	2	3	7	4	11	6	1	2	3	3	3	2	4	2	2	2	2	2	1	1	1
<<		WCIU	NOTICIAS&MAS	<<	<<	<<	<<	<<		X																													
4	9	WFLD	BEETLEJUCE-FOX	4	4	3	3	4	9	8X	10	11	2		3	2	1	1	1					1	3	1	1	1				1	1	1	1	1	6	7	9
1	3	WGBO	HIGHWAY-HEAVEN	1	1	1	1	1	3	3	3	4		1							1		1	1													1		
3	8	WGN	AVG. ALL WKS	4	3	3	2	3	8	10	9	7	2	1	2	1	1	1	1	1	1	1	1	1	1	1	1	1	1	1	1	1					3	7	6
4	9		#DARKWING DUCK	4		3		4	9				2	1	2	1	1	1	1	1	1	1	2	1	1	1	1	1	1	1	1	1	1	1	1	1	3	6	5
3	7		DARKWING DUCK	3	3		2	3	7				2		2	1	1							1	1	1	1	1	1	1		1					3	7	6
9	22	WLS	4.00 EYEWT NWS	9	9	8	9	9	22	22X	23	25	4	5	1	2	2	3	3	4	7	5	10	6	1	3	4	4	5	3	4	1	2	2	2	3	1	1	1
8	19	WMAQ	CH5 NWS-4.30	8	7	7	7	8	19	18X	15	10	4	5	1	2	2	3	3	3	6	5	9	6	2	2	3	3	4	3	3	2	2	2	2	2	2	1	1
2	5	WPWR	TEEN-NNJA TRTL	2	2	2	2	2	5	5	7	10	1		1	1									1							1					2	6	6
1	1	WTTW	AVG. ALL WKS	1	1	<<	1	1	2	3	2	1											1															1	
1	2		#WORLD-SURVIVAL	1				1	2												1		1	1														1	
1	1		#TRAVELS-EUROPE		1			1	1				1				1						1			1	1	1	1									2	
<<			TRAVELS-EUROPE			<<	1	<<																															
<<		WYCC	AVG. ALL WKS	<<	<<	<<	<<	<<																															
<<			#SQUARE ONE TV	<<				<<																															
<<			#SESAME STREET		<<	<<	<<	<<																															
40			HUT/PUT/TOTALS*	43	40	39	38	40		45	46	39	22	20	15	14	11	13	13	14	26	19	36	24	16	14	16	16	18	13	16	9	10	10	10	11	23	29	32
		5:00PM																																					
9	20	WBBM	CH 2 NWS-4.30	8	8	8	8	8	19	19X	17	15	4	5	1	1	2	2	3	3	7	5	11	6		2	3	3	3	3	4	2	2	2	3	3	1		1
1	2	WCIU	NOTICIAS&MAS	1	1	1	1	1	2	1X					1	1									1	1	1	1									1	1	1
4	10	WFLD	COSBY SHOW	5	4	4	4	4	9	10X	11	13	3	2	4	4	3	2	2	2	1	1	1	3	5	4	3	4	3	2	1	1	1	1	1	1	6	4	5
1	3	WGBO	HAWAII 5-0	1	1	1	1	1	3	3	3	3	1	1							1	1	2	1							1								
4	10	WGN	AVG. ALL WKS	5	4	4	4	4	10	11	11	8	3	2	5	4	4	3	2	2	1	1	1	3	7	5	4	3	3	2	1	2	1	1	1	1	4	6	5
4	10		DIFFERENT WRLD	5	4		4	4	9				3	2	5	4	4	3	2	2	1	1	1	3	7	6	4	3	3	2	1	2	1	1	1	1	5	6	6
5	10		#DIFFERENT WRLD			4		4	10				2	2	3	4	4	2	2	2	2	1	2	3	4	5	3	3	2	2	2	2	2	2	2	2	3	3	
10	22	WLS	5.00 EYEWT NWS	10	10	10	9	10	22	22X	24	25	5	6	2	2	2	4	4	4	8	7	11	7	2	2	4	5	5	4	5	2	3	3	3	4	1	1	1
8	19	WMAQ	CH5 NWS-5.00	9	8	8	7	8	19	17X	15	12	4	5	2	2	2	3	3	4	7	5	9	6	2	2	3	3	4	3	4	3	3	3	3	3	2	1	1
3	6	WPWR	GROWING PAINS	3	2	3	2	3	6	6X	6	9	1	1	2	2	1	1	1	1	1	1	1	1	1	1	1	1	1	1	1	1	1	1	1	1	3	3	4
<<		WTTW	AVG. ALL WKS	1	1	1	1	1	1	2	3	2																										2	2
1	1		#CARMN SANDIEGO	1				1	2				1																									3	
<<			CARMN SANDIEGO		1	1	1	1	1																												1	2	2
<<		WYCC	AVG. ALL WKS	<<	<<	<<	<<	<<																															
<<			#HERITAGE	<<		<<		<<																															
<<			HERITAGE		<<			<<																															
44			HUT/PUT/TOTALS*	47	44	45	41	44		49	51	41	25	26	20	19	18	19	19	20	30	24	40	30	22	21	22	22	23	20	21	14	16	16	17	17	24	26	30
		5:30PM																																					
7	16	WBBM	CBS EVE NWS	7	7	7	7	7	15	15X	12	13	4	5	1	1	2	2	2	3	6	4	9	5	1	2	2	3	3	3	4	2	2	2	3	3	1		
1	1	WCIU	NOTICRO UNIVSN	1	<<	1	1	1	1	X																													
4	9	WFLD	FAMILY TIES	5	4	4	4	4	9	10X	12	12	2	2	3	3	3	2	2	2	1	1		3	4	5	4	4	3	3	1	1	1	1	1	1	4	4	5
2	4	WGBO	HAWAII 5-0	2	2	1	2	2	4	3	3	2	1	1							1	1	2	1							1			1	1	1			
6	13	WGN	AVG. ALL WKS	7	5	6	5	6	12	15	13	11	4	3	4	4	4	3	3	3	3	2	4	4	4	4	3	3	3	3	3	4	3	3	2	2	5	5	5
6	13		PERFCT STRNGRS	7	5		5	6	13				4	3	5	4	4	3	3	3	3	2	3	4	5	4	4	3	3	4	3	4	3	3	3	2	5	5	6
6	12		#PERFCT STRNGRS			6		6	12				3	3	2	3	3	2	2	2	3	2	4	3	2	4	3	3	3	2	2	2	2	2	2	2	4	4	
11	23	WLS	ABC-WORLD NWS	10	12	11	10	11	23	23X	25	26	5	7	2	2	2	4	4	5	9	7	12	8	2	3	5	5	5	5	6	2	3	4	4	4	1	1	1
8	18	WMAQ	NBC NITELY NWS	8	9	8	8	8	18	15X	14	14	4	5	2	2	2	3	3	4	7	5	9	5	1	2	3	3	4	4	5	3	3	3	3	4	2	1	1
3	7	WPWR	GIMME A BREAK	3	3	4	3	3	7	6X	6	8	2	1	3	2	2	1	1	1	1	1	1	2	4	3	2	2	2	1	1	1	1	1	1	1	5	4	5
1	1	WTTW	NITE BSNSS RPT	1	1	1	<<	1	1	1X	2	1									1		1								1								
<<		WYCC	AVG. ALL WKS	<<	<<	<<	<<	<<																															
<<			#JOBMAN CARAVAN	<<	<<	<<		<<																															
47			HUT/PUT/TOTALS*	49	48	47	44	47		52	55	45	27	28	19	20	20	21	21	23	33	27	43	31	20	22	23	24	26	23	25	18	19	20	19	20	21	23	26
1	2	MONDAY-FRIDAY 3:30PM - 6:00PM		3	4	5	6	7	8	11	12	13	15	16	17	18	19	20	21	22	23	24	25	26	27	28	29	31	32	34	35	36	37	38	39	40	41	42	43

FIGURE 2–2

A sample page from a Nielsen ratings report. (*Nielsen Media Research*) to air commercials, the use of ratings is bound to continue.

TECHNOLOGY

Because the United States is a rich country, it is able to keep up with most technological advancements in the fields of radio and TV. Stations, networks, and production companies have the money to buy or rent the latest in cameras, videotape recorders, microphones, editing systems, satellite dishes, and other production and distribution equipment. Well-trained technicians keep the equipment running.

The distribution system has evolved through several layers of complexity. Radio and TV stations have always sent their signals out through antennas into the airwaves. These signals travel as far as they can, usually about 30 miles from the antenna. The exact distance depends on the power of the station, the shape of the terrain, and where the transmitter is located. Some radio stations are AM (amplitude-modulated signals on frequencies ranging from 535 to 1705 kilohertz) and some are FM (frequency-modulated signals from 88 to 108 megahertz). Almost all U.S. radios are capable of receiving both. A new form of radio broadcasting called digital audio broadcasting (DAB) has been proposed, and its fate and placement will probably be decided fairly soon.

Some TV stations are in the very high frequency (VHF) range (54 to 216 megahertz), and some are in the ultrahigh frequency (UHF) range (470 to 890 megahertz). VHF stations have much better transmission characteristics than UHF stations and so tend to be the most popular ones.

As mentioned previously, radio networks used to transmit their programming to stations through wires, and TV networks used to transmit through microwave dishes spaced out across the country. But now almost all programming, including that of cable TV, is sent by way of a satellite.

The other major way that program material is distributed in the United States involves a very simple pickup and carry. This is used for the distribution of videocassettes that people buy or rent to play on their home VCRs. Distribution companies truck or fly copies of tapes to video stores located throughout the country. Individual consumers visit these local stores and select what they want.

As discussed in Chapter 1, one of the big technological question marks for the United States involves high-definition TV (HDTV). The present NTSC system yields a picture quality far below what is possible technically, but the exact direction that the United States will take to replace its NTSC system with some form of higher definition has yet to be decided.

EXTERNAL SERVICES

Traditionally the United States has been one of the leading countries in external broadcasting. Most of this international broadcasting is prepared by Voice of America (VOA), a radio service that is under the auspices of the government-controlled United States Information Agency (USIA). Started during World War II, VOA occupies thirty-three Washington, D.C.–based studios where it produces programs in about fifty different languages.

The centerpiece of the programming is carefully prepared newscasts, but talk shows and U.S. music also attract listeners. VOA cannot tell how many people actually listen, but it receives over half a million letters a year from overseas. VOA is aimed at audiences throughout the world and is intended to supplement the national radio services.

In 1983 the USIA set up Worldnet, a television service designed to explain U.S. government policies to viewers overseas and to strengthen worldwide understanding of American society. Worldnet consists of specially prepared programs such as *Dialogue*, a live hour-long forum in which journalists, politicians, and people from around the world debate U.S. experts on various topics. It also includes programs supplied by the commercial, cable, and public networks—PBS's *MacNeil/Lehrer Newshour*, ABC's *This Week with David Brinkley*. This service is available to TV stations, cable systems, cultural centers, and any other entities around the world that wish to use it.

Several other U.S. government–run services are intended to replace radio services in other countries. These are Radio Liberty, aimed at the former Soviet Union; Radio Free Europe, aimed toward Eastern European countries; and Radio Martí, beamed to Cuba. The United States hopes that citizens in these countries will listen to the American version of information rather than that of their own countries. These services were set up primarily to combat communism, but now that many ex-Communist countries have changed their form of government and are more open to outside information, the services are in a state of flux.

A wide variety of distribution systems are used for external services. Signals are sent by satellite, microwave, shortwave, telephone lines, and regular broadcast transmitters, some of which are rented in such countries as Germany and Israel.

Very few people in the United States hear the external broadcasts of their own country (or any other country, for that matter). They are not aired on the regular AM or FM bands, and shortwave radios (which can pick up signals from around the world) are few and far between.

Although CNN is not formally an external service, in some ways it acts like one. As mentioned in Chapter 1, it is privately owned by cable TV magnate Ted Turner and several cable TV companies and has no connection with the government. But it is distributed to countries throughout the world and gives the U.S. point of view on national and international events.

IMPORTANCE IN THE WORLD COMMUNITY

Programming has been the United States' most important area in terms of world influence. Music is America's ubiquitous contribution to the world; the latest U.S. hits can be heard coming from radios all over the world. U.S. TV programming sells better in foreign countries than programming from any other country, even though it is frequently criticized for its emphasis on sex, materialism, and violence.

For several decades the advertising-based structure of U.S. broadcasting was frowned upon throughout the world. Other countries did not want commercials cluttering up their airwaves. Governments could afford to pay for radio and early TV with money collected through general taxes or through license fees charged to people who owned radios and TV sets. They did not see the need to make advertising revenue a major source of income. But as TV expenses have grown and media systems have been privatized around the world, more and more countries are looking to the U.S. structure as a model—rightly or wrongly.

At one time the United States was important in terms of equipment and distribution techniques. Companies such as Ampex, Motorola, RCA, and Westinghouse developed and manufactured equipment. To some extent they still do, but most of the equipment leadership has been ceded (not necessarily intentionally) to the Japanese.

The United States is a primary player in world media and no doubt will continue to be as the worldwide telecommunications industry continues to expand.

MAJOR ISSUES

The 1990s will prove very important to the fate of the overall structure of electronic media in the United States. The three networks, once so dominant, are losing their power base. No longer do they call the shots in terms of what people will see and hear. Once they earned almost embarrassing profits; now some are in the red. The audience is abandoning the networks, and advertisers are reluctant to pay the high prices that networks have been in the habit of charging. Television is fragmenting, just as radio did in the 1950s.

Radio is in less of a state of flux than television, but it too must adjust to the economic reality of advertising dollars being spread thinner and thinner among the various media. Predictions are that some of the 10,700 radio stations now in operation will go out of business in the next decade.

Cable TV companies have enjoyed economic prosperity, but are under threat. The FCC has ordered them to reduce the basic rates they charge subscribers because, in the FCC's opinion, they have been overcharging. In addition, U.S. telephone companies are starting to enter the video business in a way that may cut down cable's profitability. Phone companies envision themselves as the one wire into the home. They will deliver not only voice and data but also video information and entertainment. Telephone, computer, TV set, radio, fax—all may be tied into one interoperable system.

Thorough development of direct broadcast satellite could also further endanger the economic health of both commercial TV and cable TV. If consumers, by placing small receivers on the sides of their houses, can receive as many channels of information as they presently do but receive them directly from a satellite, they may abandon both their local stations and their local cable TV companies.

Of course, changes in the electronic media structure are not new to the United States. Television caused radio to alter its focus; cable TV brought changes to commercial TV. Americans absorb (and even relish) change. Privately owned companies switch gears and begin supplying the new products that seem most in demand by consumers. U.S. electronic media, aided by the democratic and capitalistic systems, have a history of adapting.

However, the most important issue of all facing U.S. radio and television will probably relate to the fate of the electronic media in the rest of the world. U.S. media cannot isolate themselves. They must keep their eyes firmly fixed on the future directions taken by the rest of the world.

SELECTED BIBLIOGRAPHY

Auletta, Ken. *Three Blind Mice: How the TV Networks Lost Their Way.* New York: Random House, 1991.

Barnouw, Eric. *A Tower in Babel: A History of Broadcasting in the United States to 1933.* New York: Oxford University Press, 1966.

Block, Alex Ben. *Outfoxed: Marvin Davis, Barry Diller, Rupert Murdoch, Joan Rivers, and the Inside Story of America's Fourth Television Network.* New York: St. Martin's Press, 1990.

Blum, Richard A., and Richard D. Lindheim. *Primetime Network Television Programming.* Boston: Focal Press, 1987.

Buzzard, Karen. *Electronic Media Ratings.* Boston: Focal Press, 1992.

"Cable: The First Forty Years," *Broadcasting*, 21 November 1988, pp. 35–49.

Dominick, Joseph R., Barry L. Sherman, and Gary A. Copeland. *Broadcasting/Cable and Beyond*, 2d ed. New York: McGraw-Hill, 1993.

"The First 60 Years of NBC," *Broadcasting*, 9 June 1986, pp. 49–64.

Gross, Lynne S. *Telecommunications: An Introduction to Electronic Media*, 5th ed. Dubuque, IA: Wm. C. Brown, 1995.

Head, Sydney W., and Christopher H. Sterling. *Broadcasting in America*, 6th ed. Boston: Houghton Mifflin, 1990.

McNeil, Alex. *Total Television.* New York: Penguin Books, 1991.

Sarnoff, David. *Looking Ahead: The Papers of David Sarnoff.* New York: McGraw-Hill, 1968.

Sherman, Barry L. *Telecommunications Management.* New York: McGraw-Hill, 1987.

Witherspoon, John, and Roselle Kovitz. *The History of Public Broadcasting.* Washington, DC: Current, 1990.

PART TWO

SOUTH AMERICA

Overview of South America

Many of the countries of Central and South America started both radio and television earlier than Third World countries in other parts of the world. By 1925 Argentina, Cuba, Brazil, Chile, Costa Rica, and Peru all had radio stations. Cuba and Brazil started television in 1950, and Argentina followed in 1951, with Venezuela, Chile, Nicaragua, Uruguay, and Peru all establishing systems in the mid-1950s.

Part of the reason for this early start was that electronic media businesses in the United States (and to some extent, Canada), feeling they could earn money, invested in the development of Latin American media. For example, NBC assisted Argentina, Peru, Uruguay, and Venezuela; Canada gave advice to Jamaica; ABC was active in Venezuela and Central America; CBS invested in Uruguay; and, as we shall see in Chapter 3, TV Globo in Brazil had alliances with Time-Life.

In other ways, however, the media structure is much like that of many other Third World countries. The rich have considerably more media access than the poor, especially the rural poor. Almost everyone on the continent can receive radio coverage, but TV is more accessible in urban areas than in rural ones.

Latin American countries have undergone enormous political turmoil resulting in numerous civilian and military government turnovers and coups. The political parties and their leaders have usually understood and utilized the power of the media.

All of these factors—U.S. involvement, Third World social structure, and political instability—have influenced the ownership and programming of the Latin American electronic media.

[*Note*: The term "Latin America" is used to refer to Mexico and all the countries south of it to the tip of South America—basically the countries whose language, religion, arts, and customs came largely from Spain, Portugal, and France and are based on those of ancient Roman (Latin) culture. Included in this are a number of Caribbean islands—Cuba, Haiti, the Dominican Republic, etc. Excluded are the English-speaking Caribbean islands—Jamaica, Trinidad, and some other smaller islands. "Central America" refers to the corridor of countries between Mexico and the continent of South America—Guatemala to Panama. "South America" is used to refer to the continent itself. This overview considers all of Latin America except Mexico, which was discussed with North America. The emphasis is on Central and South America with some mention of the islands in the Caribbean.]

OWNERSHIP AND CONTROL

The countries of Central and South America, like their northern neighbors, have emphasized private ownership of media and its accompanying advertising. One of the reasons a private rather than a government-owned structure arose was because of the influence of North America. However, ownership has been more family- and individual-oriented than in Canada or the United States; it more resembles that of Mexico, with its strong media families.

Expulsion of North American Interests The direct U.S.–South America electronic media relationships of the past are no longer operating. After the 1930s in radio and the 1960s in TV, Latin American countries decided they could operate the media on their own and were fearful of foreign investment in an area as sensitive as broadcasting.

For example, after the 1968 revolution, Peru's military government forbade foreign media interests from operating in that country. At present not only must owners and employees be Peruvian citizens, but they must also be native-born Peruvians. In 1974 the government of Venezuela tightened ownership rules and gave foreign networks only a month to sell their interests. However, by then U.S. companies (NBC in this case) had already concluded that the expected profits from South American TV would not materialize and had somewhat lost interest in the area. Foreign ownership lingered somewhat longer in Central America.

Foreign involvement in new media, particularly satellite television, seems likely to increase. There are partnerships between HBO and Latin American channels, and there are local MTV franchises.

Family Group Ownership The private ownership pattern of Central and South America, like that of Mexico, is heavy on family group ownership (the Genero Delgado Parker family in Peru, the Roberto Marinho family in Brazil). Many of these families also own newspapers because unlike the situation in the United States, electronic media–newspaper cross-ownership is generally accepted and even encouraged in South America. On occasion one of these countries has second thoughts about the fact that most news and information are coming from one source, but these concerns are usually short-lived. For example, in 1980 Argentina passed a law ruling out as broadcast owners anyone with a press connection. However, when the government sought bidders to buy new TV stations, the first auction did not attract any offers.

In most South and Central American countries (e.g., Brazil, Costa Rica, the Dominican Republic, Ecuador, Guatemala, Honduras, Nicaragua, Panama), governments have a limited role in media ownership. Private stations are the ones most watched and listened to, but government stations do exist. Even in countries controlled by military governments that exert a great deal of influence over media, ownership has still been largely private. Family owners support the government and, as we shall see in Brazil, are often quick to switch loyalties when new governments take over.

Government Operations However, there are exceptions to the media mogul model in that there are countries where the government owns and operates radio and television—Cuba, for example. The first fully commercial TV network in Cuba was formed by a media mogul, Goar Mestre, but when Fidel Castro took over in 1959, he nationalized the media, which then worked under a system similar to that of the former Soviet Union. Of course, there are those who feel Castro is his own special brand of media mogul.

In some countries, such as Peru and Argentina, ownership of radio and TV has passed briefly from industry to government depending on the ideas of the regime currently in control. Government takeovers of private media have been short-lived, however.

Chile presents a good example of the intertwining of private and government influences. The radio stations in Chile, some 160 of them needed to cover Chile's length, are primarily privately owned, although the government does own some. TV was started as an educational innovation at the Catholic University of Chile in 1958. Several years later the station was infiltrated by Communists, and so the Christian Democratic party then in power established another station that was government-owned. During the 1960s, a bitter political battle was waged between the Christian Democratic party, supported by the Catholic church, and the Socialist party, whose leader was Salvador Allende.

Allende was elected president in 1970, but both before and after the election the two political parties, knowing how important broadcasting was, did everything within their power to gain control of the media. Party loyalists infiltrated staffs, founded new stations, canceled frequencies, and purchased existing stations. One of Allende's methods between 1970 and 1973 was to take advantage of the president's legal right to require private radio stations to make time available for the president to address the nation. He kept the stations tied up with programming from the presidential palace, effectively excluding the opposition from the airwaves.

Allende was overthrown and killed by a military junta in 1973. The new government continued to own the TV network but canceled government grants and told the network administrators to make the operation self-supporting. Network programming changed from political pronouncements to the entertainment programming that would attract the most advertising. New private stations have since been started.

PROGRAMMING

Because of their commercial nature, electronic media in Central and South America are devoted more to entertainment than to education. Advertisers (including many foreign ones) who support the programming want material that will attract middle-class consumers. They are less interested in programs that will help, or even appeal to, the lower classes who do not have disposable income. However, there are entertainment-oriented channels in several countries that target lower-middle- and working-class viewers: the number two channel in Brazil has been commercially successful with this approach.

The commercialism of South American programming draws many of the same criticisms that it does in North America. It is accused of making people materialistic and conformist and of promoting the values of industrialized nations to the detriment of indigenous values.

For example, one of the first major pieces of critical media study in Latin America was *How to Read Donald Duck* or *Imperialist Ideology in the Disney Comic*. It was written in Chile in the early 1970s and pointed out that Disney comics and cartoons are materialistic, individualistic, capitalist, conformist, and condescending to Latin cultures. About the same time, other critics pointed out many of the same things about *The Flintstones* and other cartoons shown in Latin America.

Violence in U.S. programs so concerned the Brazilian military regime in 1970 that it pushed the television networks very hard to reduce the use of U.S. programs. The Brazilian government considered its culture much less violent than that of the United States and did not want to see television increase violence in Brazil.

Imported Programming Most of these criticisms are expressed toward programming imported from non-Latin countries such as the United States. Countries in Central and South America depend on these programming sources less and less as they develop their own program material. During the formative years, particularly the 1960s, U.S. programming was quite common. In 1968 ABC organized the Latin American Television International Network Organization (LATINO) to sell programs to most South and Central American countries. Now most of these countries go to sales meetings in the United States and Europe and select which U.S. programming they want. When enough countries express an interest in a program, it is sent to Mexico City or Brazil for dubbing into Spanish or Portuguese.

More and more Latin American countries are producing their own programming and importing material from other Latin countries, especially Brazil and Mexico. They are also exporting programs to other parts of the world, especially Spanish services in the United States. Italy imports quite a bit from Brazil and Mexico, and Poland has honored a Brazilian program as best program of the year.

Latin American countries give careful consideration to much of what they import. For example, when *Sesame Street* was brought into Latin America, it was adapted very carefully, using Mexican-American and Brazilian-American translating teams, so that the basic educational concepts were transposed into a locally produced version of the show. Despite this, the series was eventually abandoned because of criticism from educators who said it had the wrong cultural values for their nations such as consumerism, resolution of problems by outside intervention rather than individual initiative, and a general "middle-class" emphasis.

External broadcasting, such as Voice of America and the British Broadcasting Corporation's World Service, are not as popular in this part of the world as elsewhere. Foreign radio is usually listened to by less than 1 to 2 percent of the population. However, it is listened to from time to time both by the people and by media organizations. For example, during the 1980 Falklands War, South American broadcasters relied heavily on the BBC for war news. Even stations in Argentina, which was fighting Great Britain, carried interviews with BBC staff members until stopped by the government. Uruguay and Chile carried the World Service throughout the hostilities. Although the South American countries disagreed with the British, they trusted the BBC.

Foreign news programming is more common now on satellite television. CNN has a regional service directed to Latin America that is carried on many new cable systems.

Program Forms The most popular form of programming throughout most of Latin America is the telenovela. A cross between a soap opera and a miniseries, a telenovela runs for many episodes (up to a year) but does not go on indefinitely. The form came from radio where the plots originally involved romantic themes and family intrigues, such as a man searching for his parents. Later, upward mobility became a theme—a poor peasant girl moves to the city where she becomes a maid and then a seamstress. A number of the plots are based on national or regional history and literary classics.

Another popular form is the hosted variety show, which often runs on for hours, particularly on Saturdays and Sundays. The style of the host is distinctive in each country or region. The shows include amateur performers, professional musicians, comedy acts, games, political debates, giveaways, and even matchmaking.

Comedy programs are also popular. Sometimes they feature stand-up comedians, and sometimes they are short comedy sketches on the order of the U.S. program *Laugh-In*. Spanish-speaking countries that import comedy shows tend to purchase them from Mexico more often than from Portuguese-speaking Brazil because comedy (especially puns) does not travel well in translation.

Other entertainment genres include drama, miniseries, game shows, movies, music (especially on radio), and sports.

Informational programming exists in the form of news and interview shows. Some of the interviews focus on problems such as poverty, malnutrition, and crime, but it is usually middle-class people who are interviewed.

In the past much of the news in South American countries was influenced by their governments, often in an informal manner. For example, in the 1970s Argentina's military government adopted a method of encouraging dependence on the official news agency, Telam, without forbidding the use of foreign sources. Telam bought out a small advertising agency that handled government advertising, an important income source for the private stations. Telam then linked the government news handouts with advertising contracts; the more the news editor chose Telam stories, the more government advertising the station received. New government intervention in the reporting of news is less frequent (or as least less blatant), but it still occurs.

Most governments still require the media, particularly radio, to give the government a certain amount of time each day to broadcast what it wishes. These programs are not widely listened to or watched, however, and are often jokingly referred to as "the silence hours."

Cuba is an exception to the entertainment-based media emphasis. Here radio and television are used for education and political socialization. Fidel Castro's political speech marathons that often last up to 4 hours are an interesting genre in and of themselves. Cuba also broadcasts sports, music, and Eastern European programs. Before Castro, Cuba had a unique form of broadcasting that included thousands of commercials a day—repetitious, noisy, and often in bad taste. They were often incorporated into miniprograms that consisted of 30 seconds of news, 25 seconds of commercials, and a time check for 5 seconds.

Programming and the Newer Media Latin American countries were slow to develop their own cable TV and satellite TV. However, in recent years some of them have moved rather rapidly. Argentina, for example, now has 3 million homes cabled. A number of countries are developing pay-satellite services. Some are also using microwave and ultrahigh frequencies for pay-TV.

Most of the countries in Central America and at the top of South America are within the footprint of U.S. satellites and have helped themselves to U.S. cable network services, often illegally. For example, two entrepreneurs in Guyana bought satellite dishes, captured U.S. signals, and relayed them over the air to paying customers in their country without bothering to pay the U.S. copyright holders. Because each entrepreneur had only one broadcast channel on which to send the numerous cable services, the programming was a potpourri that often resembled someone flipping through channels with a remote control—part of a basketball game followed by the end of a movie followed by the middle of an evangelist's sermon.

So popular were U.S. services in Guatemala that the satellite dish became known as the "national dish of Guatemala." Rich people who could afford dishes watched CNN and HBO, while the poor watched Mexican telenovelas on government TV.

Illegal video piracy was also rampant in South and Central America for a while, but now the business has become more legitimized. Pressure from Hollywood on national governments has forced them to enforce copyright laws.

Brazil Brazil has been selected as the country to represent Central and South America. Although its language is Portuguese and most of the inhabitants of other countries in the area speak Spanish, it has become the leader in program production.

It is typical of many of the countries of the region because it has had both military and civilian governments, it was originally allied with a U.S. company and then forced that company to leave, and it has a rural and an urban society of both rich and poor.

Like many other countries, it originally imported a great deal of programming from the United States, but now it produces much of its own material and is the leading exporter of program material in South America.

(*Editor's Note*: I wish to thank Joe Straubhaar, professor of telecommunications at Michigan State University, for his input to this overview.)

CHAPTER 3

Brazil

Joseph Straubhaar

Joseph Straubhaar is a professor at Michigan State University, where he specializes in international and comparative telecommunications. He lived in Brazil for 3 years as a U.S. foreign service officer and then worked at the foreign service office in Washington for another 4 years, during which time he visited Brazil often. His doctoral dissertation dealt with the influence of the United States on Brazilian television, and he has published a number of articles related to Brazilian media. Each year he conducts the Brazil Overseas Study Program, taking Michigan State University students to Brazil.

Joseph Straubhaar.

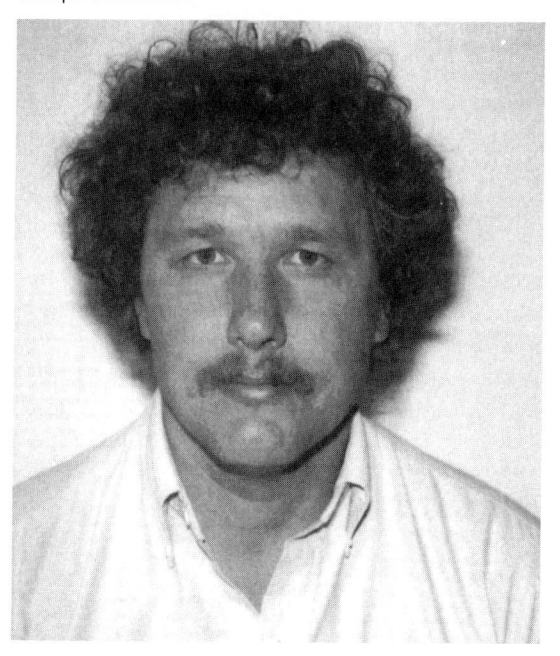

STATISTICS

Geographic Area: 3,286,470 square miles
Capital: Brasília
Population: 148,000,000
Religion: Roman Catholic
Language: Portuguese
Type of Government: Federal republic headed by a president
Gross Domestic Product: $388 billion
Literacy: 81 percent

GENERAL CHARACTERISTICS

The United States of Brazil occupies most of the eastern coast of South America and contains over one-third of the total population of Latin America. The majority of the population resides along the Atlantic coast and in the southern part of Brazil.

Geographical barriers to broadcasting have been overcome for most regions in Brazil. The proliferation of small commercial radio stations covers most towns, and the extension of television via microwave and satellite systems has brought almost all of the population within the reach of television signals.

However, a significant minority of Brazil's population is still involved in subsistence or small-scale agriculture. Particularly in the western and northern Amazon regions, the extensive distances to be covered and the limited attractiveness of the population as an advertising market have restricted extension of the commercial broadcasting system. In these areas, the government radio system is considerably more important than elsewhere in Brazil.

Even more significantly, the economy has been industrialized, and the population has been rapidly shifting to the major cities. Since 1940 the population has shifted from being 70 percent rural to being 75 percent urban. This is important for electronic media since almost all urban Brazilian households have radio and around 80 percent are estimated to have television. In contrast, probably only one-third of rural residents have television, although most now see it on a fairly regular basis in public places. Most rural people have radios.

New video technologies have been limited in Brazil to date because of high costs and the highly stratified distribution of income in Brazil. Cable TV and Satellite Master Antenna TV (SMATV) are available in only a few cities. Direct Broadcast Satellite (DBS) antennas are beginning to appear in small towns and on some farms. Cable TV, SMATV, and DBS are all limited to the upper middle class and upper class because of their cost. VCRs were limited in the same way in the 1980s but are beginning to diffuse more widely into the middle class as prices decrease.

Income in Brazil is highly stratified. Brazil has among the world's highest concentration of income in the upper classes. While the Brazilian economy as a whole grew 385 percent between 1940 and 1987, the actual value of a minimum salary declined by 64 percent. Regional differences are strong in income distribution as well: the average salary in the industrialized Southeast is over twice that in the more rural, less industrialized Northeast.

Both high rates of illiteracy and poverty exclude many Brazilians from access to print media, which cost more as a proportion of the average salary than in most developed countries. Poverty excludes fewer from access to broadcast media because there is extensive group viewing and listening in many rural communities and villages and because the purchase of radio and television receivers is an extremely high consumer priority.

Brazil is primarily a one-language country. Aside from a small indigenous population in the Amazon and western regions, virtually all Brazilians speak Portuguese. This means Brazilian media do not have to cope with the communication problems common in many countries where people do not speak the same language.

Brazil, perhaps simply because of its size, has more regional and ethnic diversity than most Latin American countries. The major stock comes from Portuguese colonists and the descendants of their black and Indian slaves, frequently mixed together since Portuguese settlers tended to intermingle more with both indigenous and slave populations than many Spanish colonists. Since the 1800s, these populations have been supplemented by other Europeans, particularly Germans and Italians, and more recently by Japanese and other Asians. In broad terms, however, Brazil is a remarkably homogeneous culture, at least by Third World standards. These diverse groups share a language and, particularly since the increasing unification of the country by broadcasting, a common notion of Brazilian culture.

While television production in Brazil incorporates some aspects of various regional cultures, most television content reflects the dominant cultures of São Paulo and especially Rio de Janeiro, production base of TV Globo, the main national commercial network.

THE DEVELOPMENT OF ELECTRONIC MEDIA IN BRAZIL

A main thread in the history of both radio and television in Brazil is that the stations and networks were developed in association with newspaper chains owned by a few families, commonly called *Grupos*. This cross-media ownership has made many of the media barons of Brazil rich and influential.

Radio Brazilian radio began with amateur experimental clubs in the early 1920s. Commercial stations began in the late 1920s to promote the purchase of radio receivers and increased in number as advertising revenue began to flow to the new medium. Most programming was live, emphasizing news, variety programs, and comedy. The number of both broadcasters and receivers grew dramatically in the 1930s and 1940s, with recorded music and *rádionovelas* (radio serials or soap operas) becoming popular genres.

Commercial radio networks were also developed in the 1940s and 1950s, primarily by newspaper chains. Networks developed as the commercial advantages of sharing program and news material among stations in different cities became clearer. Network growth also had a strong political motivation. Favors and patronage came more often to media owners who could provide geographically extensive multimedia coverage to politicians.

The major radio network was Diários e Emissoras Associadas: by 1938 it consisted of five radio stations grouped with twelve newspapers and one magazine in a chain, led by Assis Chateaubriand. Also notable were Rádio Bandeirantes (Grupo Carvalho) and Rádio Globo (linked with the newspaper *O Globo* and its owner, Roberto Marinho).

National and provincial governments also established networks and stations, but their main purpose was (and is) to serve areas that are not economically viable for commercial interests.

Hundreds of local commercial stations also emerged, however. The number of AM stations increased from 440 in 1956 to 1557 in 1990, while the number of FM stations went from zero to 1215. Furthermore, the largest numbers of stations have developed in states with many small and medium-sized towns not within broadcast reach of the capital cities. Most of these stations are independent. However, market research has shown that in major cities the network-affiliated stations, such as Rádio Globo and Rádio Bandeirantes, tend to be the most popular.

Television Television historian Ségio Mattos described four phases in the development of Brazilian television. There was the elitist phase (1950–1964) when television was limited to the upper and upper middle classes in cities. Then came the populist phase (1964–1975) when the audience expanded rapidly and programming became more popularly oriented. In the technological development phase (1975–1985) broadcasting expanded via microwave and satellite, and the number of networks increased. In the transition and international expansion phase (1985–1990), civilian government returned, and TV Globo and others began to export programs widely to the world. Since 1990 a fifth phase has been characterized by the advent of cable, DBS, and SMATV, and further segmentation of the audience.

The First Phase Television broadcasting began in Brazil on September 18, 1950, Assis Chateaubriand, of the radio network Diários e Emissoras Associados, opened a commercial station in São Paulo that was the beginning of the TV Tupi network. He started the station almost on a dare, after he was told by a U.S.

engineer that television was economically unfeasible in Latin America.

Other entrepreneurs, usually those who already owned radio stations and newspapers, started rival television stations. TV Tupi started early and was the largest network for some time, covering twenty-three cities in 1976, but TV Excelsior, TV Rio, and TV Globo were more innovative in programming and network organization. However, TV Excelsior's parent group was crippled by economic regulations established by the post-1964 revolutionary governments, causing the network to go bankrupt, and TV Rio prospered for a while before TV Globo raided most of its staff. TV Globo became the dominant network, expanding to cover virtually all urban areas of Brazil. TV Tupi, meanwhile, lost organizational coherence after its founder, Assis Chateaubriand, died in 1966, and the network went bankrupt in 1980.

Although TV Globo is still the main network, three other commercial national networks are currently in operation: TV Manchete, Bandeirantes, and SBT. There are also two regional networks. Rede Brasil Sul in the South carries TV Globo programming but supplies local news and other shows to people in a wealthy region that represents 12 percent of the actual consumption in Brazil. TV Record consists of loosely affiliated independent stations in Rio and São Paulo and a few other cities in the heavily populated Southeast.

Some educational television stations have developed. The most productive is TV Cultura, which is financially supported by the state of São Paulo. The state of Rio de Janeiro also operates TV Educativa, and other states have put together educational stations. The federal government also owns stations in Brasília and other cities. These have developed into a loosely organized public and educational network, TV Educativa, operating in many of Brazil's larger cities.

The Second Phase Between 1968 and 1985 TV Globo dominated both the audience and the development of television programming. It tended to have a 60 to 70 percent share of the viewers in the major cities at any given time, and at times had over 90 percent. During this period TV Globo was accused of representing the view of the government, of being its mouthpiece. TV Globo still often has a majority share of the audience but has encountered steadily increasing competition throughout the 1980s and 1990s.

Other networks have had difficulty in competing with TV Globo. Efforts by several networks, first TV Tupi and then TV Baneirantes and TV Manchete, to compete with TV Globo for a broad general audience have failed. So the oligopolistic, imitative competition among commercial networks for the general audience typical of the United States never took place. Instead, other broadcast television networks found themselves pursuing smaller, more specific audience segments largely defined by social class. For example, SBT (owned by Sílvio Santos) targeted lower-middle-class, working-class, and poor audiences. That strategy gained it a consistent second place in ratings in most of the 1980s and early 1990s, but advertisers were not always attracted to that particular audience segment.

TV Manchete targeted a more elite audience initially but found that this segment was not large enough to gain adequate advertiser support. TV Bandeirantes wavered on program lines but tended to emphasize news, public affairs, and sports, which proved economically viable. Ultimately, SBT, TV Manchete, and Bendeirantes wished to pursue a general audience with general-appeal programming, such as evening serials (telenovelas), but tended to find that such efforts still did not gain enough of the audience to pay for the increased programming costs.

The Third Phase From 1975 until at least 1985, Brazilian television was marked by an expansion phase. Coverage of the population by television greatly expanded with microwave and

TABLE 3-1
PATTERNS OF BRAZILIAN MEDIA USE BY SOCIAL CLASS

Social class	TV networks	Radio	Print media
Elite (5–10%)	Manchete, Globo	FM music	Elite papers, newsmagazines
Middle (15–20%)	Globo	FM music, talk	Elite papers, newsmagazines
Working (10–15%)	Globo, SBT	FM music, AM music, talk	Popular newspapers
Poor (50–60%)	Globo, SBT	AM music, talk	
Marginal (10%)		AM music, talk	

Source: L. G. Duarte, J. Straubhaar, and J. Stephens. *Audiences, Policy and "Cable" Technology.* International Communication Association, Miami, 1992.

satellite distribution systems. The number of television networks also increased from two to four. In fact, this expansion phase still continues but at a slightly slower pace. Efforts are still being made to start new television networks and to extend the coverage of new and existing networks to all parts of the population.

In the 1970s government telecommunications systems extended microwave systems to most parts of Brazil, carrying both telephone and television. This made it easier to conduct simulcast network broadcasting and sell national advertising.

The new technology with the greatest effect on Brazilian electronic media is the satellite distribution of television to small repeaters throughout the country. Brazilian television stations first used Intelsat and then BrasilSat (the government-owned satellite) to extend the reach of television into the rural areas and small towns of the Brazilian interior and Amazonian North. In the 1980s thousands of small towns in rural Brazil purchased satellite dishes and low-power repeaters to bring in television. Many times the systems were purchased by local mayors or political candidates as public works. In one month (April 15 to May 15) during the local and state political campaign season of 1990, in just one state (Bahia) 600 such systems were installed, all purchased by local politicians.

The Fourth Phase From 1985 to 1990 Brazilian television went through a fourth phase, marked by its role in the transition to a new civilian republic. In 1984 TV Globo initially supported the military government in opposing a campaign for direct election of a civilian government, while other media, including other television networks, many radio stations, and most of the major newspapers supported the campaign. Perceiving that it might literally lose its audience to the competition, Globo then switched sides and supported the transition to a civilian regime, which, in a compromise, was indirectly elected. The civilian government immediately reduced political censorship and pressure on broadcasters, although some censorship on moral issues remained.

The role of television, particularly TV Globo, as the regime's banner carrier was also diluted by the creation and effective growth of new networks. Growing television competition was marked by market segmentation, where most newer networks positioned themselves around the programming strengths of the dominant network, in essence counterprogramming one another.

Another main aspect of the fourth phase of Brazilian television was its internationalization. Imported television programs (feature films, adventure series, and cartoons and children's

TABLE 3-2

PERCENTAGE OF NATIONAL, U.S., AND REGIONAL PROGRAMMING IN PRIME TIME AND TOTAL BROADCAST DAY IN SÃO PAULO

Program source	1963 Prime	1963 Total	1972 Prime	1972 Total	1982 Prime	1982 Total	1991 Prime	1991 Total
Brazilian	70	69	86	55	64	63	75	64
U.S.	30	31	14	44	36	37	19	30
Regional	0	0	0	0	0	0	6	4

Source: Joseph Straubhaar, "Beyond Media Imperialism: Asymmetrical Interdependence and Cultural Proximity," *Critical Studies in Mass Communication*, Vol. 8, 1991.

programs) flooded Brazil in the 1960s. They were cheap, slickly produced, and popular. However, during the 1970s and 1980s the importation of television programs into Brazil actually declined, and imports were gradually replaced by domestic productions. By 1982 only 22 percent of Brazilian audience time was spent watching imported programs, down from about 48 percent in 1965.

In addition to reducing imports, exportation of Brazilian programming (particularly telenovelas) to the rest of the world became a significant phenomenon. It was during this period that Brazil began to be noticed as one of the world's major exporters; its programs, dubbed into various languages, were in demand not only in Latin America but also in North America, Europe, Africa, and Asia.

The Fifth Phase The recent fifth phase of Brazilian television has been marked by the appearance of some new video distribution systems. The first new technology to be widely diffused in Brazil was the home videocassette recorder. The proportion of homes with a VCR increased from less than 1 percent in 1980 to about 8 percent in 1989. This growth was slower than that in many other Latin American countries but seemed to accelerate in the late 1980s, with an estimated 250 percent growth in 1989 to a total of 5.3 million VCRs. However, many Brazilian viewers remained loyal to television and did not use VCRs extensively. Data from the Brazilian Video Association showed that roughly 40 percent were not actively used. The number of video rental outlets increased from 200 in 1982 to 4669 in 1989. Nearly all of the videos available in various rental catalogs surveyed by the author were from the United States.

New video technologies entered the Brazilian television market in the 1990s, offering focused or segmented programming through additional advertising-supported UHF (ultrahigh-frequency) channels or through pay-TV systems such as cable TV systems, multichannel multipoint distribution systems (MMDS), and Direct Broadcast Satellite (DBS). These main systems compete with conventional VHF television and with one another in terms of both programming and technological platforms.

A number of UHF licenses have been issued, and several UHF TV operations have entered the market. The main one is a licensed Brazilian adaptation of MTV (Music TV) owned by the Editora Abril publishing group and supported by commercials. It uses a great deal of programming from the U.S. MTV, with local announcers, local ads, and some Brazilian music videos. There is also an all-news channel in São Paulo operated by Rádio Jovem Pan, which had been successful with a radio news channel.

There is one major scrambled operation, TVA, that uses MMDS technology. In 1992, it offered five channels (films, CNN news, ESPN sports, a superstation-type channel, and TNT). Its technological approach and marketing are targeted at individual upper-middle-class households in major cities.

In contrast, GloboSat (owned by TV Globo) is a DBS and SMATV satellite channel aimed at some rural viewers and condominium owners in major cities. It has a programming lineup similar to TVA's, with four channels (films, news, sports, shows). Both TVA and GloboSat are very expensive, about $30 monthly plus installation costs that averaged $200 in 1993. This limits their potential market considerably.

A limited amount of cable TV exists but, as will be discussed later, its organizational structure has not yet solidified.

ORGANIZATION AND FINANCING

Broadcasting was begun by private initiative and took on a strong commercial orientation in its early development, following the model of U.S. broadcasting. There had been a tradition in the Brazilian press for both commercial and political party–owned newspapers, but party newspapers had been suppressed by several governments, both the Vargas government (1937–1945) and the military governments (1964–1978). Commercial newspapers gradually gained complete ascendancy, and even after 1978, when the military government removed the ban on party-related newspapers, the only significant one was that of the Communist party of Brazil. There was thus little tradition of party- or government-owned media for radio to follow.

Private Ownership Most broadcast media in Brazil are privately owned and operated. The federal government owns an extensive shortwave broadcasting system in the Amazon region and also some other radio and television sta-

TABLE 3-3
TOTAL BROADCASTING HOURS ADDED BY NEW CHANNELS IN BRAZIL

Company and channel	Daily hours	Program source
Pay-TV		
TVA		
Filmes	24	U.S. (99%), European (1%)
Notícias (CNN)	24	U.S.
Esportes (ESPN)	24	U.S.
Supercanal	18	U.S. (99%), Italian (1%)
Clássico (TNT)	24	U.S.
Total 114		
GloboSat		
Filmes (Telecine)	24	U.S. (99%), European (1%)
Notícias (GNT)	16	U.S. and European (99%), Brazilian
Esportes (Top Sports)	16	U.S. and European (99%), Brazilian
Shows (Multishow)	18	German, Japanese, French
Total 74		
PluralSat	12	German, French
Open channels		
MTV-Abril	24	U.S. (50%), Brazilian (50%)
Jovem Pan	16	Mainly foreign
Grand total	240	

Source: Abril, GloboSat, and Jovem Pan, January 1992, compiled by L. G. Duarte in *Television Segmentation: Will Brazil Follow the American Model?* M. A. thesis, Michigan State University, 1992.

tions, as do some state governments. However, these government-owned media have much smaller audiences and less impact than private media.

A 1990 survey showed that of the then total 2888 radio stations licensed, a number were owned by local businesspeople, business groups, or, increasingly in the late 1980s, local politicians. A number of these independent stations had large audiences, but the most popular (and profitable) ones were affiliated with five major networks operating AM and FM stations. Of these, Globo, RBS, Jornal do Brasil, and Manchete are major media conglomerates. Competition for the audience among all stations, large and small, is intense.

Until the mid-1960s advertising revenues were not sufficient to support all the private television operations that were initiated. Throughout the 1950s, the television audience was limited to an economic elite in a few cities, and so advertiser interest grew slowly. However, in many cases, television stations were seen as desirable for the prestige they added to media empires, even if advertising income could not support them.

Since the mid-1960s, however, television has become very profitable. The share of advertising it receives went from 25 percent in 1962 to 59 percent in 1981 to 49 percent in 1991, largely at the expense of radio and non-mass-media advertising. Furthermore, until recently these revenues were highly concentrated in the Globo network, which usually drew at least 60 percent of the nationwide television audience.

TV Globo was started in 1964 by Roberto Marinho, owner of the Globo group, using capital and technical expertise from Time, Inc. Although Time-Life was forced out in 1968–1971 by Brazilian government intervention, its association with TV Globo did reinforce the commercial pattern of television use that had developed in Brazil. To a much greater degree than any of its predecessors, TV Globo (with Time-Life's help) introduced sophisticated network operation on the U.S. pattern, which

TABLE 3-4
ADVERTISING INVESTMENT SHARES IN BRAZIL

Year	TV, %	Newspaper, %	Magazine, %	Radio, %
1991	49.0	35.0	10.0	5.0
1989	55.4	26.6	12.8	2.7
1987	60.8	13.2	16.3	6.2
1985	59.0	15.0	17.0	6.0
1983	60.6	13.3	12.2	10.5
1981	59.3	17.4	11.6	8.6
1980	57.8	16.2	14.0	8.1
1978	56.2	20.2	12.4	8.0
1976	51.9	21.1	13.7	9.8
1974	51.1	18.5	16.0	9.4
1972	46.1	21.8	16.3	9.4
1970	39.6	21.0	21.9	13.2
1968	44.5	15.8	20.2	14.6
1966	39.5	15.7	23.3	17.5
1964	36.0	16.4	19.5	23.4
1962	24.7	18.1	27.1	23.6

Source: Leda-Nielsen Serviços de Mídia, and McCann-Erickson Brasil, cited by L. G. Duarte in *Television Segmentation: Will Brazil Follow the American Model?* M.A. thesis, Michigan State University, 1992.

led in large part to TV Globo's subsequent success.

TV Globo has been extraordinarily successful. Roberto Marinho is now considered the second richest man in Brazil. He has branched out both vertically into all aspects of television (research, production, marketing, and syndication) and horizontally (magazines, books, video distribution, recording, cellular telephony, and other telecommunications) and beyond media into agriculture and other businesses. The group is also diversifying internationally, having acquired one of the new private channels in Portugal.

The other main television networks are also owned by family groups. Nine family media groups own most of the main Brazilian media, particularly the networks and main stations in the major cities.

TV Manchete is owned by Adolfo Bloch, a prominent publisher, but in 1992 was put up for sale because it was operating at a loss. TV Bandeirantes is owned by the Saad family, who are also landowners and industrialists. SBT is owned by Sílvio Santos, who started as a salesman, became a variety show host, and still hosts his own program.

The opening up of new licenses has admitted some new companies into "broadcasting," but a number of the companies involved are familiar, such as TV Globo. The major new entrant with UHF is the dominant publishing house, Editora Abril, owned by Victor Civita, which now has two UHF stations, one dedicated to MTV and one as yet unutilized. Editora Abril also now has a major interest in the TVA multichannel pay-TV operation.

Finance The Brazilian government historically has not invested directly in the ownership of media. Since private capital took the initiative to create and build up media companies in most parts of Brazil, the government tended to reserve its capital for other sectors in which private investment was judged inadequate.

However, government leaders developed an interest in using electronic media in the late 1930s. Early governments had been somewhat ambivalent about the commercial development of radio, but President Getúlio Vargas found it a very useful tool for mobilizing popular support for his "populist" regime. Vargas encouraged the development of commercial radio and used it extensively to promote his government from 1937 to 1945. After Vargas, from the 1940s to the late 1950s, commercialism in broadcasting continued to be accepted, even fostered, as the Brazilian government development plans increasingly stressed the development of a consumer economy.

Commercial radio was successful because it fit well into the developing Brazilian market economy. As the principal mode of advertising, it became a principal stimulus for economic growth. Radio stations were relatively cheap to start and operate, and given the advertising market, profitable. As elsewhere in Latin America, small private radio stations proliferated rapidly throughout Brazil from the 1920s on in every town large enough to support one.

Some research indicates that U.S. corporations who wished to advertise in the Brazilian market played a direct role in promoting the commercial approach to radio broadcasting. It is clear that Brazil's extensive trade and investment ties with the United States encouraged adoption of the U.S. advertising–based approach to broadcasting in a more general way, as an aspect of the overall consumer market system.

As of 1990, of the 2888 radio stations in Brazil 90 percent were commercial and wholly financed by advertising revenue. The other 10 percent were owned and supported by the Catholic church (110 stations), state and national governments, universities, and educational or cultural foundations. Although the number of stations has increased steadily, the percentage of all advertising expenditures devoted to radio has declined, going from 24 percent in 1962 to 10 percent in 1976 and 5 percent in 1991. Radio declined in importance as a medium for advertisers as television grew.

The military governments were far more active and interventionist in media, including the financial aspects. They financed microwave, satellite, and other aspects of the television network infrastructure. The government favored certain networks, particularly TV Globo, with government advertising, which was considerable since federal and state corporations, banks, trading companies, steel mills, and so on, contributed nearly half the GNP for several decades.

The military governments initially tolerated and then intervened in 1968 to end a joint venture agreement between TV Globo and Time-Life involving financial and technical assistance. This enforced specific provisions of the Brazilian constitution and the 1962 and 1967 communication laws that prohibited foreign ownership or decision-making input by foreign citizens in mass media. The fact that enforcement was delayed for 4 crucial years in TV Globo's early establishment and consolidation of its basic network was seen as a military government financial favor to TV Globo. Government loans were then used to repay Time-Life.

Television also received a strong financial base from advertising. The share of advertising investment drawn by television increased dramatically in the 1960s and 1970s and only really declined again slightly in the 1990s.

TV Globo augmented its advertising in the 1980s by creating a new form of product exposure called merchandising, especially in telenovelas. Specific products are either shown or mentioned in dialog within programs in return for a negotiated fee. For example, from 1983 on, a number of telenovelas on TV Globo have carried in-program propaganda for a major bank, Banco Itaú. In the telenovela *Tieta*, in 1989–1990, a modern, colorful branch of the bank was frequently shown in the middle of a small, traditional northeastern Brazilian town. The bank branch opening was shown, characters later did business there, used its credit cards, and so on. In another example, a 1990 TV Globo telenovela called *Top Model* presented a fashion show featuring the real-life fashion lines of a company partly owned by the daughter-in-law of Roberto Marinho, owner of TV Globo.

In a related phenomenon, TV Globo uses its various media branches to promote one another's products, thus enhancing overall revenue. Telenovela soundtracks are released as records, and key songs are promoted on radio, so that all three media reinforce one another.

In the late 1980s, despite increasing competition, TV Globo still dominated television in terms of revenue. Its revenues of $596 million were twice those of SBT, Bandeirantes, and Manchete combined.

The financing of new video technologies is a bit uncertain. In May 1992 the companies then operating pay services estimated that they would need at least 70,000 subscribers paying a monthly fee of $20 to $40 to break even. By 1992 neither of the two main operations (TVA and GloboSat) had reached that, but market potential seems to be there. Given that TVA is backed by the major Brazilian publisher, Editora Abril, and that GloboSat is backed by the major television broadcaster, TV Globo, both seem to have deep pockets and the staying power to develop an audience and market. It will be hard for other companies to break the financial barrier to entry at this point, however.

PROGRAMMING

Radio set a pattern for broadcasting in Brazil that television was to follow: a predominance of entertainment over educational or cultural programs, a clear dominance of advertiser-supported stations, a tendency in the early years to import a good deal of material as well as program ideas, and a countervailing tendency in later years to use a great deal of Brazilian material.

Radio Although an emphasis on entertainment emerged fairly early in the history of Brazilian radio, the question of what entertainment reflects which regional, national, or foreign cultures is still open and varies tremendously among stations and areas. A study of the cultural changes wrought by the mass media in the rural São Paulo town of Ibitinga, Milanesi, noted that radio started out being popular because of its rapid delivery of news and then gradually became an entertainment medium. While broadcasting was still completely live, local "hillbilly" (*caipira*) music and classical music groups dominated. Later they were replaced by recorded music: samba from Rio, other Brazilian popular and classical recordings, and popular music from abroad. Sports and talk shows also became popular on radio as stations began to specialize in order to capture particular audiences.

Other entertainment forms also emerged, some indigenous and some based on ideas borrowed from the United States or Europe. Notable among these were radio dramas, rádionovelas (serials or soap operas), and variety shows.

Rádionovelas developed from several sources. One was the serialized French novels that were popular in Brazil in translation. Rádionovelas were also imported from other Latin American countries, such as Cuba, Mexico, and Argentina, in the 1940s and translated from Spanish into Portuguese. Particularly important were the scripts imported from Cuba, where rádionovelas were first developed as a Latin American form of the U.S. soap opera. They were sponsored by Colgate, a U.S. corporation that wanted to sell soap in Latin America with the same advertising vehicle that had proved successful in the United States.

Many aspects of the U.S. radio variety show were probably also copied by Brazilian programs. They used live interviews, singers, games, show hosts, audience participation, amateur performances, and so on, but tended to insert distinctly Brazilian cultural elements: characteristic personality types, situations, and references to history, popular music, literature, and folklore.

As in other Latin American countries, these variety shows evolved into a rather distinctive format, the show de auditório, which featured a charismatic host combining many elements live in front of a studio audience. These shows were often very long and went from games to music to interviews to news. Some writers on Brazilian mass culture think this is one of the few formats in which traditional Brazilian oral folk culture, storytelling, song challenges, circus-type patter, and folk music (albeit commercialized into mass-culture forms) are brought into mass communication media.

Radio remains diverse in its content in Brazil. In fact, market segmentation and competition are making it more diverse, at least in major cities. On many stations much time is given to sports, particularly soccer, both in live coverage and in discussion on talk shows. Depending on the political climate, a good deal of political discussion also takes place on radio talk and variety shows. Local talk shows are in many cases the format that best reflects local culture and issues.

Radio is an important medium for news. Audience surveys tend to rate radio the most popular as a source of musical entertainment and less preferred than television or newspapers as a source of news. Still, studies of the 1989 presidential elections showed that radio programs, particularly radio talk shows, were an important source of information for people, par-

TABLE 3-5

1989 BRAZILIAN PRESIDENTIAL ELECTION SOURCES OF INFORMATION BY RESPONDENTS' LEVEL OF EDUCATION*

Source of information	Primary %	Middle %	Secondary %	University %
Talking with friends or family	41	43	40	34
Political advertising on radio or TV	30	25	39	42
Talking to colleagues	23	29	33	30
Television news	21	20	19	23
TV debates between candidates	13	28	41	55
News in newspapers	8	17	22	42
Seeing candidates at rallies	12	18	18	14
Radio news	12	11	6	6
Radio commentators	4	6	6	4
Information from the Catholic church	6	5	4	0
Information from labor leaders	3	6	9	3
Neighborhood associations	4	10	7	3
Poll results	4	6	7	6

*Note: Multiple responses were possible.

Source: Joseph Straubhaar, "The Role of Television in the 1989 Brazilian Presidential Election," in T. Skidmore, ed. *Mass Media and Democratization in Latin America*. Washington, DC: Woodrow Wilson Center, 1993.

ticularly those who are poorer or live in more rural areas.

As in the United States, radio in Brazil moved toward fairly extensive segmentation of both formats and audiences in the 1980s and 1990s. AM and FM have developed differently. AM radio is still somewhat more widely available, in terms of both transmitters and receivers, particularly in rural areas, smaller towns, and lower-class suburbs of cities.

Even within cities, AM remains focused on musical formats that appeal primarily to lower-class audiences, which include a large number of recent immigrants from rural areas. These genres include Brazilian country music, Brazilian popular music, sports, and talk. AM talk shows and a slowly increasing number of all-news stations do cross class boundaries, particularly during commuting hours.

FM has tended to be a primarily urban phenomenon, although it is expanding into smaller towns as well. The number of FM stations has grown rapidly in the 1980s and 1990s and, as in the United States, FM stations have tended to become ever more segmented, primarily in terms of musical format. While FM stations play more imported music, particularly pop, rock, jazz, and classical, Brazilian popular music is apparently more popular, even on FM, than imported music. A survey of the playlists for São Paulo FM stations in 1989 showed that seven of the ten most widely played songs in 1989 were Brazilian.

One result of radio competition with considerable implications for programming as well as economics has been the increasing segmentation of the radio audience. Particularly in the larger cities, twenty to thirty radio stations often serve specialized audiences: all-news, talk and sports, classical music, light rock, heavy rock, Brazilian rock, Brazilian pop, and Brazilian samba and jazz. Aside from the continuing popularity of Brazilian rock, pop, and samba, the evolution of formats resembles that of U.S. radio markets.

Television As in many other Latin American countries, television stations in Brazil have often been started or bought out by radio station owners, particularly those with national or regional networks. Because of this association and because of the lack of a Hollywood-type film industry, television tended to draw on radio for mass-culture formats, personnel, and traditions.

Like radio, the first decade of television in Brazil was essentially produced live. Most of the program genres and even a number of specific programs were brought over from radio. Television took most of radio's best talent: the best writers, actors, and directors for telenovelas, as well as comedians, musicians, and dramatic script writers.

While the television audience remained limited to the wealthier upper and middle classes in a few major Brazilian cities in the 1950s, programming had an elitist orientation. Favored were theater, ballet, classical music, and *teatro de revista* (music and comedy revues).

By the mid-1960s, the industrial situation had changed for commercial television in Brazil. The economy had been growing rapidly as the government invested in infrastructure and basic industries and as multinational and local manufacturing firms grew in capacity. This led to accelerated growth of the consumer economy within Brazil. With this, the television audience grew to include the middle class and lower middle class in an increasing number of cities. The number of television sets in Brazil went from 760,000 in 1960 to 6,746,000 in 1970 to 19,602,000 in 1977 to 33,000,000 in 1990. This growth of a mass audience for marketing mass-consumption products began to attract more advertising revenues. As in other countries, television was favored by the new multinational and domestic advertisers over other media as a means to reach the mass of consumers.

Several television organizations, particularly TV Rio, TV Excelsior, and TV Globo, responded to this commercial opportunity by changing their programming to appeal to a broader mass audience. They began to create or import programs that would sell products like soap, tobacco products, foodstuffs, and fairly simple appliances. Advertising for limited elitist consumption products gradually began to shift to magazines and a few television stations which continued to target an upper-class audience.

In the 1980s and 1990s, advertising investment began to shift visibly away from television toward newspapers and magazines, as the decade-long recession of the 1980s eroded consumption among the working class and the poor. Television still retained considerable advertising investment, though, for items that were still consumed by the lower classes: soap, soft drinks, beer, small radios, and clothes.

Development of the mass market and television mass audience led to a major shift in domestic programming. The demand for mass-audience television material also coincided with and stimulated the beginning of imported programming on a massive scale in the 1960s. Within Brazilian-produced programming on television, the focus shifted toward mass-audience genres like telenovelas, shows de auditório, game shows, popular music, and comedy. All of these had been present during the 1950s, but the shift in relative emphasis was clear.

Throughout most of this period, TV Globo and the other television networks and major independent stations produced virtually all their own programming (except for what was imported from abroad). For example, TV Globo produced 12 to 14 hours of programming a day. There were no independent production companies like those that supply programs for television broadcasters in the United States and some other countries.

Telenovelas Telenovelas were introduced in Brazil in 1952 and were popular throughout the decade. Unlike U.S. soap operas, they did not go on for years. Most of them lasted several months and so were more like extended mini-series. Also, although they were aired on a daily basis, most of them were shown during prime viewing time rather than in the afternoon, as in the United States. In the 1960s, the plots of telenovelas became increasingly nationalized, and sophistication was added by bringing in writers, actors, and directors from the theater and cinema.

By the 1970s, telenovelas were the most popular programs and dominated prime time on the major networks. TV Globo, in particular, began to hire major writers and actors from films, the theater, and telenovelas at other stations to dominate the competition.

Telenovelas increasingly drew on popular novels. The dominant themes were upward mobility, consumption goals, and lifestyles—messages that appealed broadly to the mass audience in a growing consumer society. At TV Globo at least, the production values of telenovelas became high enough to rival those of programs imported from the United States or Europe. Brazilian telenovelas are good enough, as commercial television entertainment, to be exported throughout Latin America and to Europe, Africa, and parts of Asia.

In the 1980s, other networks attempted to break into telenovela production to compete with TV Globo for a broader general audience. Neither SBT nor Bandeirantes had commercial success in producing telenovelas, but TV Manchete achieved fairly high ratings for an ecology-oriented serial, *Pantanal,* set in Brazil's western subtropical region. Since 1990 SBT has imported dubbed Mexican telenovelas.

Building upon the telenovela industry, TV Globo also successfully created a few series—self-contained 1-hour episodes with a continuing cast and theme patterned on the series that the United States and the United Kingdom export. The contents are well adapted to Brazil, though. A crime reporter focuses on abuses of *favela* or slum dwellers, truck drivers traverse Brazilian roads and encounter Brazilian character types and situations, and a newly separated woman tries to be independent in Rio. TV Globo has also successfully exported these series, particularly the one about the "unmarried" woman, which was shown on Spanish International Television in the United States as *Malu Mujer*.

Shows de Auditório, Music, and Comedy Another major genre of the 1960s was the show de auditório, also adapted to television from radio. Shows de auditório were extremely popular with the lower middle and lower classes and played an extremely important role in drawing them into television viewing. Shows de auditório tended to feature entertainment that was *popularesco* (vulgarized or extreme versions of popular culture). Some topics were scandalous by the previous middle-class standards of television taste and, for a combination of moral and political reasons, the military government of the early 1970s forced many of these programs off the air. After the relaxation of censorship in the late 1970s, the genre expanded again.

Some variety shows became much more polished during the 1970s. TV Globo, in particular, developed the program *Fantástico—o show da vida* (*The Show of Life*), which included music, dance, comedy, news, documentary films, and interviews. More specialized variety programs developed around different kinds of popular music and comedy. Music programs were either general or centered around a type of music like current Brazilian pop or more traditional bossa nova. Comedy programs were sometimes dominated by a single ensemble, and nearly all of TV Globo's major music and comedy programs are quite popular in prime time.

News and Information Programs Brazilian television is clearly entertainment-oriented. However, certain kinds of news and information programs have been very popular, and so they have prospered on television. The evening news program on TV Globo, *Jornal Nacional* (*National News*), is always popular, even among working-class viewers. News interview programs have been very well accepted, particularly among the upper middle class. Relaxed censorship beginning in 1978 permitted more open discussion of public issues on television, but self-censorship persisted until the civilian regime of 1985, and even in the 1990s the understood rules of the game at some stations are still quite limited.

For years, sports coverage was more limited on television than might be expected, because of past contractual conflicts between the television networks and the soccer leagues. Sports are popular and draw relatively large audiences but are not in the same league as a popular telenovela. Sports programming has increased, however, in the 1990s.

Educational programs have been the major fare of state and federally owned television stations. However, the most widely seen educational programs have been produced, at least in part, by TV Globo.

VCR and Pay-TV Programming The most widespread new video technology in Brazil is the VCR. It is also in some ways one of the more creatively used. Along with Venezuela, Chile, and some other countries, Brazil has produced a fairly widespread alternative video production movement. This has been made possible by the rapidly falling prices and portability of video production equipment. A number of groups related to labor unions, the Catholic church, neighborhood associations, environmental groups, feminist groups, Indian and indigenous rights groups, and so on, have started to use portable video equipment to produce a variety of materials. Some are documenting their history and encounters with others, such as the Amazonian Indians who use video recorders both to preserve their heritage and to document promises made by government officials. Other groups create "how-to" material, and others produce alternative news and documentaries since they feel that their views are not included in the mainstream media. Various groups have joined together to form a Brazilian Association of Alternative Video Producers.

One of the major questions about the new pay-TV (MMDS and satellite-delivered) technologies in Brazil, as in Europe, Asia, and the Middle East, is whether they will bring in a renewed wave of imported programs.

The new channels vary considerably in how much foreign, particularly U.S., programming they will bring in. While TVA and GloboSat have similar lineups, TVA's material is imported almost entirely in the original languages. That may well limit its appeal over time. In contrast, GloboSat draws on TV Globo's resources to fill much of its time. It has its own correspondents, resources in journalism, and a film library of 10,000 dubbed titles.

LAWS AND REGULATIONS

Broadcasting media have been largely privately owned, and government involvement, while often considerable, has historically tended toward prohibiting or censoring certain subjects rather than proactively directing the media to create programming and news consistent with government ideology.

For many years, the main thrust of the goals and de facto policy followed by broadcasting in Brazil were very similar to those of the United States, which had served as a model in many particulars. While broadcasting was frequently described as having education, information, and culture as priorities, in fact, it primarily served as a source of entertainment. In terms of broadcasting's owners and financiers, its main function was to generate advertising revenue by delivering an audience to those who wished to promote their products in the Brazilian consumer market.

More recently, the Brazilian government has begun to assert its own priorities through broadcast media. Radio stations have long been required to carry a 1-hour evening news program, produced by the government, called *Hora do Brazil* (*Hour of Brazil*). Ratings data show that it has not been widely listened to; in fact, jokes abound to the effect that the click of radio receivers being turned off at that moment can be heard throughout Brazil. To achieve more effective communication of their point of view, recent governments have concentrated more emphasis on television.

Government Policies before 1964 Initially, the Brazilian government followed much the same approach to the regulation of broadcasting taken by the U.S. government: minimum regulation of frequency usage and transmitter power to ensure that broadcasters did not interfere with one another. In 1917 the first regulatory law stated the government's intention to control and run radio, telegraph, and radiotelephone services, but the typical broadcast operation has been private enterprises operating under government concessions or licenses for 15 years which can, however, be quickly canceled. Subsequent regulations have focused on governing the behavior of private operations.

Government involvement in radio grew from 1937 to 1945. President Getúlio Vargas, in particular, spurred the growth of Rádio Nacional in Rio de Janeiro, which was the most influential station in Brazil for two decades. Vargas kept very tight control on the political content of radio news through an extensive news and censorship operation, the Departamento de Imprensa e Propaganda, which set a pattern for the authoritarian use of radio.

Post-Vargas civilian regimes between 1945 and the late 1950s paid relatively little attention to radio and television broadcasting. Broadcasters attempted to create self-regulation codes to avoid further interference. A slightly stronger government role was asserted and a communication law was issued in 1962.

Government Policies under Military Control Brazil's rule under military governments between 1964 and 1985 strongly affected the development of electronic media. The military governments tended to intervene more strongly in broadcasting than preceding or succeeding civilian governments in that they often exercised considerable control over broadcasting, both in direct censorship and through investments in infrastructure and advertising.

For example, after the 1964 revolution, the government initiated a low-interest loan program for the purchase of television sets, built a microwave network which enabled television networks to reach the more remote parts of the country, and contributed a good deal of revenue through advertising by government-owned corporations and banks. Development of the telecommunications system—telephones, telegraph, telex, radio, and television—was a high priority directly related to the military regimes' perception of national security needs. The military governments saw telecommunications as a vital economic infrastructure and perceived broadcasting, in particular, to be a means of reinforcing a sense of national identity (particularly in the more remote regions of the country), communicating government development plans and messages to the people, and ensuring a supportive political climate.

Television networks formed since 1964 have tended to have a fairly close working relationship with government officials, communicating government messages in frequently informal and sometimes subtle ways. In particular, TV Globo has been singled out as being particularly responsive to the government. In the early 1980s, it broadcast a Sunday evening prime-time program featuring speeches and questions answered by the president, and TV Globo's news coverage was often assumed to reflect, or at least not contradict, government viewpoints. That function of TV Globo has probably continued, in the view of most scholars and press critics.

The military governments also encouraged national television program production. In the early 1970s, several government ministers pushed commercial networks hard to develop more Brazilian programming and reduce their reliance on imported shows, particularly those that contained violence. TV Globo, in particular, increased national production considerably since it had discovered that audiences, and consequently advertisers as well, preferred nationally produced musicals, comedies, and telenovelas to all but a few imported programs. Government also intervened to cancel programs that it considered immoral or in bad taste. In some cases, it censored a theme from a telenovela but did not cancel the entire program. In a few cases it canceled entire episodes and even one or two complete series.

Government censorship of news was also extensive under the military governments between 1966 and 1978. Broadcasters were often notified by any of several federal- or state-level military, police, or judicial entities that certain topics, incidents, or people were not to be covered. While such formal censorship is now infrequent, broadcasters tend to display a finely ingrained knowledge of the current rules concerning what is permissible, so that a state of self-censorship exists to varying degrees on different stations.

After the 1964 revolution and continuing under the subsequent civilian regimes, the process for granting and maintaining broadcasting licenses became a source of political control and political patronage. Until the 1988 constitution, the president could and usually did essentially grant licenses to those applicants he chose. The Ministry of Communications, while responsible since the 1962 Telecommunications Law for standards and allocation of frequencies, did not make the actual decisions.

The political nature of license allocation in Brazil had not been too much of an issue before 1964, but the military governments created controversy and opposition by using the licensing process in two ways. The threat of license cancellation, which could also be ordered by the president, effective instantly and without appeal, was used to control the behavior of broadcasters, along with ongoing day-to-day censorship as noted above. The license-granting power, particularly in the newly profitable medium of television, was also used to reward allies or at least those thought to be politically safe. In the 1981 redistribution of licenses belonging to the former TV Tupi network, for example, licenses were given to Adolfo Bloch, publisher of *Manchete* (*Headline*) magazine, who supported the military governments, and to Sílvio Santos, a popular game show host. No licenses were given at that time to the publishing group Editora Abril, whose journalistic credentials were excellent but whose weekly newsmagazine, *Veja* (*Look*), was often openly critical of the government.

Recent Government Approaches One recent example of this tendency to use broadcast licenses as a means of political patronage is the increasing ownership of electronic media by politicians. In December 1991, a press magazine found 29 television stations and 91 radio stations owned or controlled by federal deputies and senators. President José Sarney gave 1028 radio and television station licenses out between 1986 and 1988, when the new constitution required review of licenses by the federal congress. The journalism magazine *Imprensa* observed that almost all of the licenses were given to politicians (either national or local) and noted, as had many newspaper articles, that many of the licenses were given to federal congressmen in explicit trade for their votes conferring a fifth year of presidential mandate on President Sarney.

The licensing process for new terrestrial and satellite broadcast services has also been controversial in Brazil. The presidential decrees that created the services specified that they were special concessions for pay television, apart from regular broadcast licensing rules, including the need to obtain congressional approval of broadcast licenses. However, one of the decrees also allows the Brazilian president to give away UHF concessions without congressional approval. MMDS has not been formally regulated yet and is still in the formal testing stage, but it is being used in São Paulo and other cities on a commercial basis already, which government regulators have chosen to ignore. Despite opposition, the government decided in 1991 that the use of rented satellite transponders for DBS was not broadcasting but ordinary retransmission of television signals and did not require any special license or regulation. This cleared the way for GloboSat to begin operation unregulated.

Another controversy surrounds the granting of access to the rental of transponders on the government-owned BrasilSat satellites. In 1970 TV Globo was granted five transponders even before their use for the GloboSat DBS/SMATV operation was confirmed. TV Cultura, the educational service run by the state of São Paulo, had requested a transponder to transmit its cultural and informational programming to other potential users and retransmitters throughout Brazil but was denied in 1976, despite vacant transponders, and again in 1990, just before their allocation to TV Globo. The reasons were apparently both political (TV Cultura had been critical of the minister of communications when he was governor of the state of Bahia) and commercial (as a noncommercial entity, TV Cultura was eligible for a 50 percent government subsidy of the transponder's cost).

Development of cable television was controversial as well. In the late 1970s a number of critics of commercial television in Brazil pressed to see cable television reserved for university or other educational users. Controversy was sufficient to delay attempts in 1975 and 1980 by the minister of communications to regulate and allow cable television. Discussions resumed again around the convention in 1986–1988 to draft a new constitution. A potential threat from the political left to redistribute or change existing broadcast licenses left an uneasy compromise. Broadcasting stayed private, and wired telecommunication stayed in the hands of the state.

However, a 1988 decree by the Ministry of Communications permitted cable TV for simple retransmission of broadcast signals. Some system construction began immediately, and thirty-six companies started the Brazilian Association of Community Antennas. In 1991 granting of franchises was suspended pending further debate on proposed legislation, which is still pending. By 1992 ninety-five franchises had been given out. Many of these were speculative, intended for resale, but several were being actively developed into multichannel systems with retransmission of national broadcast signals, national pay signals, some foreign channels, and in some cases local channels.

THE AUDIENCE

Brazil has been characterized in its own media as the "country of television" because the television audience is so large. Critics note that while a large majority of Brazilians either can afford a television set or have communal access to one, many if not most are too poor to have other leisure options, and so that is why they watch so much television. In a survey by a São Paulo newspaper in 1983, 24 percent said they watched TV because it was "the cheapest form of entertainment," and 17 percent because they "lacked other leisure options."

A 1992 study by the market research firm Marplan noted that in breaking down the Brazilian national audience, 77 percent "habitually" or regularly watch television, 62 percent listen to the radio, and 51 percent each read newspapers and magazines.

Both radio and television transmitters and receivers are concentrated in the more affluent South and Southeast of Brazil. The Southeast has 40 percent of the radio transmitters, and 81 percent of households there have radios, as of 1990–1991. Radio penetration is even higher in the South (84 percent), which is overall somewhat more affluent.

Brazilians watch a lot of television. Average household daily viewing is generally over 5 hours. The viewing is tracked by an audience measurement company, IBOPE, which uses

TABLE 3-6
PENETRATION OF MASS MEDIA IN HOUSEHOLDS IN BRAZIL

City of state	Magazines (%)	Television (%)	Newspapers (%)	Radio (%)
Brazil	51	77	51	62
Metro São Paulo	47	74	42	59
State of São Paulo	65	83	63	68

Source: Blecher, cited in L. G. Duarte, *Television Segmentation: Will Brazil Follow the American Model?* M.A. thesis, Michigan State University, 1992.

people meters and conducts ratings research in a manner similar to that in the United States.

A number of independent and academic studies have also addressed the nature of Brazilian audiences and, to a limited extent, the effects of media on them. For example, a study on young people in São Paulo found that sixth graders tended to watch 5 hours a day, and tenth graders 3 hours. Sixth graders also listened to 2.1 hours of radio, and tenth graders 2.4 hours, indicating that radio is relatively more important for adolescents than for younger children. On television, young people preferred comedies, movies, rock music, telenovelas, and action or adventure programs. On radio, they preferred rock and international music, although girls also preferred more Brazilian pop.

TV Globo has dominated television audiences. This is especially true on weekdays; a May 1990 São Paulo survey showed that TV Globo had 70 percent, TV Manchete 12 percent, SBT 7 percent, and others 5 percent. The weekend percentages were slightly different. TV Globo had 53 percent on Saturdays, while SBT (emphasizing variety shows) and TV Bandeirantes (emphasizing sports and talk) each had 9 percent, and Manchete 8 percent.

TV Globo's hold is being challenged, however. It is interesting to notice that in the same 1990 survey, two non-Globo programs achieved a higher spontaneous recall than any Globo program.

TV Globo has dominated television news audiences. In 1988 TV Globo news was preferred by 84 percent of the national audience, in part because it is considered easy to understand.

Both television and radio are thought to have considerable impact on their audiences in Brazil. In a survey in 1987 in São Paulo, television was rated both "more powerful" and "more prestigious" than any other institution. Radio was rated second most prestigious and seventh most powerful (behind multinational companies, banks, the president and ministers, the print press, and the armed forces).

Relatively little behavioral science research has been done on the effects of television on the Brazilian audience, but a 1992 study by Bradley Greenberg et al. found that television seems to affect certain kinds of perceptions in young people. Sixth graders tended to see characters, behaviors, and locales portrayed on television as more realistic than do older tenth graders. Young people also seemed to be influenced by advertising, which most considered to be relatively truthful, informative, and appealing. Most agreed that they were frustrated when they couldn't buy what was advertised, a major problem in a poor nation like Brazil.

Also, three major anthropological studies have found evidence of the impact of long-term viewing on issues such as male and female roles, social mobility goals, social permissiveness, what it means to be Brazilian, and social class identity. Consumption and mobility goals seem to be among the most affected. A 1990 study by anthropologist Conrad Kottak concluded, "In addition to spurring savings accounts and installment purchases, Brazilian TV has honed viewers' wishes to own a home and to be upwardly mobile. We have seen that *subir na vida*, 'to rise in life' is one of the main telenovela themes, and home ownership is a constantly expressed goal of lower-middle-class novela characters. . . . With its fashionable society women and powdered milk ads, Brazilian TV promotes early weaning and bottle feeding. Both our main TV variables correlated negatively with breastfeeding . . . the public health effect is likely to be negative. . . ."

Although the importation of programming into Brazil has led some to fear cross-cultural impacts of U.S. and other programs, two anthropological studies found that the greatest impact seems to come from domestic programming, particularly telenovelas. It also seems clear from these studies and a survey by the author that social class is the factor that most determines what programs people chose to watch. Furthermore, ethnographics indicate that class is the most crucial variable in how viewers interpret what they see, but that even lower-class viewers are fairly independent in their interpretations.

New video technologies are arriving in Brazil, but real questions exist as to who their audience will be. One respected audience analyst, Homero Icaza Sanchez, former research director for TV Globo, estimates that the new channels on the new technologies will succeed in segmenting the audience, as U.S. channels

TABLE 3-7
SÃO PAULO AUDIENCE PREFERENCE FOR TELEVISION GENRES, BY EDUCATION

Genres	No schooling (%) ($n = 9$)	Primary (%) ($n = 37$)	Secondary (%) ($n = 35$)	University (%) ($n = 27$)
U.S. programs				
Miniseries	22	40	46	41
Series	22	37	43	48
Rock music	20*	32*	49*	58*
International programs				
Movies	30*	68*	60*	84*
Mexican comedies	22*	18*	17*	4*
Cartoons	56	54	62	39
Japanese heroes	22*	22*	14*	4*
Brazilian programs				
Telenovela	80	66	63	56
Miniseries	44	38	60	59
Comedies	78	66	66	48
Variety	44***	66***	34***	27***
Pop music	80*	78*	91*	77*
Rock music	40*	30*	46*	62*
News	20***	84***	89***	93***
Debates	40*	54*	69*	85*
Films	56**	50**	71**	73**
Political ads	33**	40**	71**	73**
Sports	11**	57**	83*	60**

Statistical significance: *$P < .05$, **$P < .01$, ***$P < .001$

Source: Joseph Straubhaar, "Beyond Media Imperialism: Asymmetrical Interdependence and Cultural Proximity." *Critical Studies in Mass Communication*, 1991.

did. He expects the segmented channels to draw one-third of the audience away from conventional broadcast television within 10 years. This raises the prospect that access to new technologies will serve to isolate the Brazilian upper middle class and elite from the rest of the country in terms of access to information, whereas as of the 1990s, mass media, particularly television, have been a common source of information for all and a force for strengthening national identity.

Income and social class stratification place significant limits on the penetration of new technologies. As of 1992, even broadcast television (UHF or VHF) programming or format segmentation was limited because only 45 percent of Brazilian television households had a second television set. With only one television set, viewers tend to stay tuned to general-audience channels, not channels segmented by age or interests. This is widely seen in Brazil as a limit on the MTV audience, for instance. Even though younger people may wish to watch MTV, they may not control family viewing decisions.

Beyond the economic aspects of access to new technologies, however, there is the question of what people choose to watch. A sample week in São Paulo in 1991 showed that of the 45 percent who had more than one set, the main set accounted for an average of 78 percent of household viewing hours. Furthermore, on the average, two or more sets were turned on simultaneously only 13 percent of the total time and only to different programs 5 percent of the time. This indicates that even households that could choose to watch different, potentially segmented channels on different sets seldom do so.

TECHNOLOGY

In the early days of radio, equipment tended to come from the United States, supplanting British and French technical equipment that had been used for telegraph and other earlier technologies. By the 1950s U.S. equipment was dominant. In recent years, however, sources of equipment have become diversified as European and Japanese equipment makers have become very competitive with U.S. suppliers.

Relying on a commercial system that encourages small local stations anywhere a remotely profitable advertising market can be found, Brazil has developed an extraordinary number of radio stations.

Similarly, radio receivers are widely available. As of 1987, radio manufacturers' figures indicated that there were about 57 million radios in Brazil, about 2.3 per household, but that at least 50 percent were concentrated in the most affluent southeastern region.

Although television reaches a considerable proportion of the Brazilian population, its coverage is somewhat smaller than that of radio. As

TABLE 3-8

RADIO STATIONS LICENSED AND OPERATING IN BRAZIL (AS OF JULY 31, 1991)

Frequency	Total	Operating	Being installed	Commercial	Educational
AM	1557	1398	159	1544	13
Tropical band	87	79	4	82	1
Shortwave	33	30	3	24	9
FM	1215	912	303	1166	49
Total	2888	2419	469	2816	72

Source: J. Borin. "Rádios e TVs Crescem eom o Festival de Concessões." *Comunicaço e Sociedade,* 1991.

of 1991, television sets were found in a total of 65 percent of Brazilian households: 78 percent in urban areas, but only 28 percent in rural areas. Estimates of the total TV coverage of the population range from 75 percent to 85 percent, given that a great deal of viewing takes place in bars and public places. In many small towns, one set is available to the public in the town square or at a meeting house.

In the 1960s and 1970s television networks were extended throughout the country to repeater stations by microwave and by rented transponders on an Intelsat satellite. The government extended television coverage further with more earth stations in the Amazon and western regions which received signals from a Brazilian satellite (BrasilSat) launched in 1984.

VHF television has become extensively diffused throughout Brazil. UHF stations have also spread out in many areas, but most Brazilian sets still do not have a UHF capability. In the 1990s both open broadcasting and scrambled pay-TV were introduced on UHF. However, limits imposed by the slow diffusion of UHF receivers seem likely to keep the UHF audience small in the foreseeable future. In 1991 the IBOPE ratings company estimated that only 37 percent of households in its São Paulo people meter sample could receive UHF signals.

The main pay systems compete both with conventional VHF television and with one another in terms of both programming and technological platforms. So far, program channels in the two main pay operations, TVA (using MMDS) and GloboSat (using DBS and SMATV), have competing and incompatible technological platforms. Both could be carried by cable TV systems or by broadcast repeaters but are not being marketed that way yet.

In 1988 channel concessions for scrambled pay-TV in the UHF band were given in São Paulo and other state capitals. By 1990 fourteen UHF licenses had been distributed, not to exceed four in each city. Both open UHF and scrambled pay-TV UHF channels were in operation in São Paulo and Rio de Janeiro by 1991. The same pattern seemed likely to spread to other cities.

Direct Broadcast Satellite (DBS) service also began in 1991–1992 on GloboSat. BrasilSat II, which relays GloboSat's channels, delivers a relatively weak signal focused on the equator. So in northern Brazil, closer to the equator, the dishes may be 2 meters in diameter, while in São Paulo they must be at last 3 meters across.

Researcher L. G. Duarte notes that the DBS services of GloboSat are gaining subscribers. "Today, the industry estimates that 160,000 dishes are installed in Brazilian backyards, including those that serve more than one household. In this case, the earth stations can be more appropriately called SMATVs (Satellite Master Antenna Television). Even though American cable operators are strong enemies of SMATVs, in Brazil these systems may very well be the embryo of future cable plants, as one operator may be tempted to cross its fence to serve more houses."

EXTERNAL SERVICES

Brazil has one government external service, the Voice of Brazil, that broadcasts programs intended for reception in other countries. More importantly, as noted below, Brazil exports quite a bit of its programming.

Shortwave external services from other countries are available in Brazil, although the overall potential impact is rather insignificant because Brazilians prefer to listen to their own stations. Voice of America surveys in the early 1980s found an audience of under 1 percent, slightly larger in rural areas.

IMPORTANCE IN THE WORLD COMMUNITY

Brazil has interacted with the world telecommunication structure in a number of different ways. It has been influenced by other countries and has been an influencer. Some of the major international relationships have included program importation and exportation, foreign investment in stations and production, advertising, the adoption of foreign programming models, and the commercial mode of operation and organization.

Imported music has been popular on Brazilian radio since recordings have been available. However, Brazilian music has also demonstrated remarkable resilience and popularity. Although this music has absorbed a great deal of foreign influence, it has also exported some models, songs, and artists to jazz and pop in the United States, Europe, and other Latin American countries. Especially in jazz, a number of Brazilian artists have recorded for the North American market, both in Portuguese and in English and both on their own and with U.S. artists.

Imported television programs were abundant during the 1960s, but once the Brazilians mastered domestic production, the audience definitely preferred homegrown programs to the available alternatives. In the 1980s and 1990s, Brazilian television networks, particularly TV Globo, emerged as major exporters of programming to the rest of Latin America and the world, supplying particularly telenovelas, but also music videos, variety shows, comedies, and miniseries. TV Globo started in 1975, exporting the telenovela *Gabriela* to Portugal, followed by telenovelas dubbed into Spanish for the Latin American market. Despite dubbing costs, about $150,000 per series, TV Globo earned over $1 million in 1977 from exports and currently earns about $20 million per year from exports.

TV Globo had exported programming to 130 countries as of 1991. Its programming was sufficiently successful in Italy, Portugal, and France that European scholars Armand and Michelle Mattelart considered its productions, particularly telenovelas, potential models for European production. In 1992 a Brazilian children's variety program, *Xuxa's Show*, which originated on TV Globo and which had been produced for syndication in Spanish for Latin America, was successfully syndicated in English in the U.S. market by MTM.

In the early 1990s, in the face of increasing competition in Brazil, TV Globo began coproductions aimed at the European market with Spanish, Swiss, and Portuguese television companies. At the same time, TV Manchete and TV Bandeirantes also began to export programs, mostly telenovelas and miniseries, to the rest of Latin America.

Research has shown that foreign investment has pulled back from its position of ownership in Latin American broadcasting and program production companies. It has, however, left behind continuing influences. In Brazil the only significant foreign investment was by Time-Life in TV Globo for the period 1962–1971. Time-Life was forced out by the government intervention, but at least one major Time-Life advisor became a Brazilian citizen in order to stay with TV Globo in its own management group.

TV Globo also more generally borrowed organizational prototypes and successful program formats from several U.S. networks. An interesting point is the degree to which these borrowings have been adapted to the peculiar logic of the Brazilian system and market, where TV Globo is now considered a serious international competitor, in fact the fourth largest commercial network in the world after the North American networks NBC, CBS, and ABC.

It is difficult for countries involved in the international market economy to be independent of multinational advertisers, even in a fairly prosperous system such as Brazil's. Foreign advertisers are among the major sources of advertising revenue, and foreign advertising agencies handle a large proportion of the total billings. Even beyond their immediate influence, U.S. advertising agencies have served as models for Brazilian agencies in developing their own methods and approaches. In recent years, however, local corporations and governments themselves have become relatively more powerful as competing sources of advertising revenue in some countries.

Some of the major variety, soap opera, news, and comedy programs seem to owe quite a bit to borrowed U.S. formats. Questions of originality in formats are difficult, however. The soap opera is such a basic notion that the effects of copying seem minimal. Brazil has developed the telenovela genre to such a high degree that it influences how other countries produce their soaps.

MAJOR ISSUES

Although the question of Brazilian cultural dependence on the United States has been extensively debated in Brazil and in the United States, Brazilian radio and television seem to be well established as major cultural industry successes in economic terms. Extensive quantities of mass-culture programming are produced by Brazilian television, and Brazilian music continues to be fairly prominent on radio.

This programming, though popular, is clearly commercial, and all the criticisms of commercial, industrialized culture can be addressed to it. Some critics feel that by adopting a commercial model, Brazilian television has veered away from focusing on Brazilian reality and has become too dependent on the wishes of advertisers.

Since a thriving industry with a largely nationalized content exists, the critical question about Brazilian radio and television as a mass culture now relates to the character of "national" programs. Within that concern, the major issues are the lingering effect of formats and techniques borrowed from abroad, the continuing influence of multinational advertisers and, until recently, the control of content by the Brazilian government. In their close cooperation with the government up through the mid-1980s, the electronic cultural industries tended to produce programs that conveyed a vision of Brazil that was picturesque, dynamic, and developing.

The chief vehicles for this were the telenovelas, described in 1984 as "shot through with materialism, empty of political content, and laced unfailingly with forward-looking optimism." Much more criticism of Brazilian problems appears on television and radio now, even in telenovelas, but television and radio can still be powerful collaborators in image making for governments or candidates.

Renewed concern is also raised about program flow into Brazil via the new technologies: VCRs, cable, and DBS. Increased importation of music, films, and programs is apparent from these channels, but so far, the audience seems limited to the upper middle and upper classes. That in itself raises a new concern. Will the new technologies further stratify in television a population that has been stratified in almost everything but television already?

In radio, program and music importation, models, and advertising are issues. However, radio is a more localized, hard-to-characterize medium. It conveys a great deal of foreign cultures through pop music, but it also preserves and diffuses a good deal of Brazilian culture via pop music as well.

SELECTED BIBLIOGRAPHY

Durand, José Carlos. "The Field of Advertising in Brazil, 1930–1991." In José Marques de Melo, ed. *Communication for a New World: Brazilian Perspectives*. São Paulo: Escola de Comunicaçõ e Artes, University of São Paulo, 1993.

Fadul, Anamaria, ed. *Serial Fiction in TV: The Latin American Telenovelas*. São Paulo: Escola de Comunicaçõ e Artes, University of São Paulo, 1993.

Kottak, C. P. *Prime Time Society—An Anthropological Analysis of Television and Culture*. Belmont, CA: Wadsworth, 1990.

Mattelart, Michelle, and Armand Mattelart. *The Carnival of Images: Brazilian Television Fiction*. New York: Bergin and Garvey, 1990.

Mattos, Sergio. "A Profile of Brazilian Television." In Josée Marques de Melo, ed. *Communication for a New World: Brazilian Perspectives*. São Paulo:

Escola de Comunicaçõ e Artes, University of São Paulo, 1993.

Michaels, Julia. "Globo Goes for Europe," *Electronic Media*, April 1986, p. G-3.

Morreira, Sonia. "Radio in Brazil." In José Marques de Melo, ed. *Communication for a New World: Brazilian Perspectives*. São Paulo: Escola de Comunicaçõ e Artes, University of São Paulo, 1993.

Oliveira, Omar Souki de. "Mass Media, Culture and Communication in Brazil: The Heritage of Dependency." In G. Sussman and J. A. Lent, eds. *Transnational Communications—Wiring the Third World*. Newbury Park, CA: Sage, 1991.

Richeri, Giusseppe, and Cristina Lasagni. "Precocious Broadcasting," *Intermedia*, May 1987, pp. 22–33.

Rogers, Everett M., and Livia Antola. "Telenovelas: A Latin American Success Story," *Journal of Communication*, Autumn 1985, pp. 25–36.

Straubhaar, Joseph. "The Decline of American Influence on Brazilian Television," *Communication Research*, No. 2, 1984, pp. 221–240.

Straubhaar, Joseph. "Beyond Media Imperialism: Asymmetrical Interdependence and Cultural Proximity," *Critical Studies in Mass Communication*, Vol. 8, 1991, pp. 1–11.

Straubhaar, Joseph. "The Role of Television in the 1989 Brazilian Presidential Election." In T. Skidmore, ed. *Mass Media and Democratization in Latin America*. Washington, DC: Woodrow Wilson Center, 1993.

Vink, Nico. *The Telenovela and Emancipation—A Study on TV and Social Change in Brazil*. Amsterdam: Royal Tropical Institute, 1988.

"The World According to Globo," *The Economist*, 4 July 1987, p. 44.

PART THREE

WESTERN EUROPE

Overview of Western Europe

The term "Western Europe" is used to designate those capitalistic countries on the European continent that were never under Communist control. Most of them (Britain, Spain, France, Norway, Belgium, etc.) are truly in the western part of Europe, but some, such as Finland and Greece, are actually quite far east. However, they are usually grouped with Western Europe because they were not behind what used to be referred to as the Communist iron curtain.

Most of these countries are also part of what was known as the First World in that they are industrialized and prosperous and their media systems are well developed. Radio and, to some extent, television were started early in this part of the world. In fact, many of these countries claim contradictory "firsts" in radio broadcasting.

SIMILARITIES

Although each country of Western Europe developed its electronic media system in its own way, there are many similarities throughout the region. These similarities involve the basic structure, the methods of financing, the types of programming, the transmission systems, and the trend toward European integration.

Basic Structure At present the countries of Europe have a structure that includes both public and private electronic media systems. However, the private ones are relatively new—having grown up during the 1980s. The public systems are the original ones, and they existed as monopolies for many years.

These public systems are tied to the governments but not overtly controlled by them. In most countries the government has given a charter, a franchise, or some other authorization for operation to a nonprofit organization that then operates radio and television broadcasting. In Great Britain this is the BBC; in Finland it is the YLE; Norway has the NRK; and Portugal has the RTP.

The closest thing to this in the United States is the public broadcasting structure which consists of the Corporation for Public Broadcasting (CPB), the Public Broadcasting Service (PBS), and National Public Radio (NPR). However, there are really more differences than similarities between the U.S. and European systems. While the U.S. system is noncommercial, many of the European public systems broadcast ads; the U.S. system was not formed until the late 1960s, whereas the European ones date back to the 1920s; U.S. public broadcasting has never attracted large audiences, while the European systems, which were the only systems in existence for many years, were all that people had to listen to or watch.

Most of the European public systems are overseen by a board of political appointees, some from government and some from social organizations. This board appoints and oversees a director general who runs the day-to-day operation of the broadcasting entity. The employees are akin to civil servants, and over the years their numbers have ballooned.

Organizationally, most of the original public radio systems were put under the government body that also controlled the post office and the phone system, usually called the PTT (post, telegraph, and telephone). Most of these bodies have changed their names to something more modern (Ministry of Communications, Department of Telecommunications), but Europeans still sometimes refer to them as PTTs.

Because European countries are rather small, one national broadcasting system usually sufficed for the entire country. The national system had several different radio and TV services, which were often referred to as "programmes." This is not an individual program in the U.S. sense. It is more like what Americans know as a network or a channel. For example, in Britain the old Third Programme was one of the three national radio services all run by the British Broadcasting Corporation. Each one was on a separate frequency, and listeners could tune into whichever one they wanted.

Although there were cracks in the monopolistic public systems before the 1980s, that was the decade when the dam broke. Privately owned radio and TV stations and networks, along the lines of those in the United States, were established. As might be expected, established government organizations fought the introduction of these new services. In many countries the original private stations were illegal local radio stations that operated without any kind of license. They became so popular that eventually they were legalized. In Ireland these stations existed for most of the decade and were finally licensed in 1989. In other countries, the government monopolies disappeared earlier. Both Norway and Switzerland authorized local private stations in 1982, and Finland did likewise in 1985. In most countries, once private radio was authorized, private TV was not far behind. Both local and national private services sprang up. In addition, internationally oriented satellite-delivered channels started and were readily accepted by many European viewers.

The face of Western European electronic media changed greatly during the 1980s. Some homes that could receive only two or three television channels at the beginning of the decade had a choice of about forty offerings by the end of the 1980s.

In most countries, the public systems are suffering because of the addition of private systems. Burdened with huge staffs and methods of operation grounded in years of monopoly and political influence, they cannot respond as quickly to changing tastes and methodology as the new organizations can. However, they realize that in order to survive they must be responsive to the desires of the people, and so some have changed their structure, primarily by creating more services, many of them of a local or regional nature.

Greece provides an example of a typical modern public broadcasting structure. Its government company, Greek Radio and Television (ERT), has two national television services (ET-1 and ET-2) based in Athens and a third (ET-3) based in Salonica that has a limited range. It has four national radio channels (ERA-1, ERA-2, ERA-3, and ERA-4) and twenty-one regional stations, whose programming partly coincides with that of the national services.

The public systems, however, are losing listeners and viewers and public support as people tune into the flashier offerings of private enterprise. Their financial viability, stable for many years, is being threatened.

Financing The most common form of financing during the years of the public broadcasting monopolies was a license fee. Each household that owned a radio and/or TV set was charged a yearly fee. The government collected this money and turned it over to the public broadcasting organization which then used it for programming and other operations.

Some of the public systems also made money by airing commercials. However, the inclusion of advertisements within programs has been politically controversial in most European countries because they fear the social consequences of turning their populace into U.S.-style materialistic consumers. Also, the governments did not want to degrade their programming by inserting commercials into it. Parliaments have undergone vigorous debates concerning whether or not advertising should be allowed and, if so, under what circumstances. In 1965 the cabinet in the Netherlands fell because of a controversy over advertising.

License fees brought in enough money to support public radio, but television was more expensive, and the extra income possible from advertising became tempting. When ads were first introduced on public channels, they were soft-sell, decorous, and grouped in a block that did not interrupt programming. Most countries placed strict regulations on advertising. For example, in Denmark, no more than 10 percent of TV time can be devoted to ads, and no more than 6 minutes of commercials can be played during any one hour.

By the time private companies established electronic media operations, advertising had been accepted as a concept by most countries, and the private services, from their beginning, were commercially based. Some of these private stations or networks program as many (or more) commercials as U.S. networks. In general, Europeans have accepted ads as part of their new television services.

But private corporation advertising did not come easily in a number of countries. In Belgium, for example, cable TV operators who imported program services with commercials in them from other countries were required to delete the ads, but most did not do so. The Belgian government finally capitulated in 1987 and passed a law allowing commercials. The government of the Netherlands banned satellite advertising in the Dutch language, but a European court said this ban was discriminatory and made the Dutch rescind it.

The arrival of private services has undermined the financing of public systems that programmed ads because these systems are now losing advertising revenue to the newer services. In addition, citizens are questioning their license fees and are wondering if it is worth paying a fee for public programs when they prefer the "free" private programming. Some Europeans have always found ways to "cheat" on license fees and view TV without paying them, but of late the opposition to these charges has become more general. A number of countries are considering eliminating these fees, which would of course further undermine the viability of the public systems.

Through the years other methods for raising revenue have been utilized in Europe, generally in addition to license fees and/or advertising. Countries try to sell their programming internationally, and some, such as Britain, have been quite successful. In some countries, such as Greece and Spain, part of the money comes from the general state budget. Greece also has a special fee attached to electricity bills that goes toward the support of broadcasting. In Denmark small local radio stations run by volunteers obtain money from the profits of large stations. In the Netherlands, part of the media's money comes from subscriptions paid for various broadcasting magazines. Norway has a special tax on radio and TV equipment. Sweden has an interesting financial arrangement through which another medium profits from video. Videocassette recorders are rented, not purchased, and a special tax on the rented VCRs is used to support the Swedish film industry.

Programming The overriding concept of public broadcasting was originally based on public service. Programming was paternalistic—intended to give the people what they needed, not necessarily what they wanted. For example, Luxembourg's government charge says it should broadcast "programmes of a high intellectual level." The objectives of Danmarks Radio (Denmark) are "quality, diversity, plurality, fairness, and impartiality." Switzerland's programs are to "define and develop the cultural values of the country, contribute to the intellectual, moral, religious, civic and artistic education of the public, contribute to the free formation of opinions and satisfy the needs for entertainment."

Because European public programming was rather stodgy, a certain amount of discontentment arose that led to a restructuring of the systems. The first rebellion against the programming came from "pirate" radio stations that sprang up illegally in the 1960s to play rock music, which the public systems had chosen to ignore. For example, in the early 1960s, ships anchored off the Swedish coast and broadcast rock music that could be heard within the country. Swedish government radio responded by changing its classically oriented music services and playing some of the hit music.

In the 1980s a similar phenomenon occurred

involving "pirate" private TV stations that programmed illegally until they were recognized and licensed by the various countries. Private programming is quite different from that of the older public systems. Most of the private systems are geared toward entertainment rather than enlightenment. A number of countries have regulations regarding violence on TV, but nudity on Western European television is more common than on U.S. TV. The number of TV channels of programming in Western Europe has grown from 39 to 120 in the last 10 years. This includes new private terrestrial stations, cable TV channels, and direct broadcast TV. Europeans have access to, among other things, pay-TV, music videos, news channels, a variety of movies, and almost unlimited sports.

At first all the new private services provided a huge new market for programming—a boon to the United States, the country that had the most programming to sell. However, the trend has been for each European country to produce more and more of its own programming. Countries also join together to coproduce programming that is European-financed. Most Western European countries have now entered the marketplace as sellers attempting to distribute their programs internationally. This does not mean that U.S. programming will disappear from Europe. It is still among the most popular fare, but when the General Agreement on Tariffs and Trade (GATT) treaty was negotiated in 1993, the Europeans were successful in keeping U.S. entertainment programming out of it, thus paving the way for setting up rules to minimize U.S. program imports.

Public broadcasting systems have responded to the popularity of private systems by altering their programming lineups to include more popular fare. They, too, produce game shows and air locally produced and U.S. sitcoms. Radio services, both public and private, are format-based and include a wide variety of music and talk formats. Typical of public offerings, Austria's ORF has three channels, one for classical music and high-quality informational programs, one for Austrian pop music, and one for light entertainment and popular music of interest to young people.

Throughout the years, freedom of information has not really been a problem for either the public or the private systems. Although the public systems have government ties and are often required to program material about the government, such as sessions of Parliament, governments are not known for restricting what can and cannot be reported. European countries, although they do not have an equivalent of the U.S. First Amendment, have a relatively high degree of freedom of the press.

Distribution Systems In Western Europe, as in the rest of the developed world, the original broadcast systems were over-the-air (terrestrial) AM radio systems. (In Europe AM radio is often referred to as "medium-wave" or "medium-frequency" broadcasting because of the location of the amplitude-modulated radio frequencies on the electromagnetic spectrum.) If medium-wave frequencies could not be received throughout the country, repeater antennas were used to bring the signal to those parts of the country that could not receive it from the main antenna. Eventually most of the countries developed FM as well as medium-wave radio.

TV was originally terrestrial also, but the need for repeaters was greater because of the nature of the TV signals. Some countries were relatively late in establishing TV systems. Norway, for example, did not have one until 1960, and Sweden not until 1956. Belgium's TV was delayed until 1953 because its receivers had to be very complicated. Many people in Belgium speak French and wanted to be able to watch French TV. However, the French, unlike the rest of Western Europe, which had adopted PAL, used an 819-line SECAM TV system. Therefore, the TV sets in Belgium had to be able to receive both the French SECAM and the PAL signals. The French still operate with SECAM, but they use the 625-line version utilized in many other countries.

Cable TV has had varying degrees of success in Western Europe. In Belgium, 91 percent of the people subscribe to cable, making it the country with the highest cable penetration in the world. Switzerland, because its hilly terrain makes broadcast signal transmission difficult, is also heavily cabled. However, cable has not been very successful in Britain, and Portugal has cable TV only in tourist areas where it is subscribed to mainly by hotels.

The newest transmission technology in Europe is satellites. Satellite distribution has provided more international political intrigue than other distribution systems because programming placed on a bird by one European country can easily be received in other countries. The exceptions are Spain and Portugal which, because of their location, have more difficulty picking up signals from satellites aimed toward the more northerly areas of Western Europe. European countries value their cultural identity and originally were less than happy about cultural infringement from neighboring countries. However, most countries have gradually accepted the idea of satellites and have even embraced the programming they bring. For example, at one time the Greek government said it would shoot down any satellite that flew over Greek airspace, but by 1988 the Greek government broadcasting system was itself airing foreign programs brought in by satellite. In most countries satellite programming is more likely to be shown on cable TV systems than on over-the-air broadcasting.

Text services are also prevalent in Europe. These consist of words rather than moving pictures displayed on the TV screen. Information includes traffic conditions, the weather, news, stock market quotes, sports scores, want ads, and recipes. Sometimes this information travels along with the television signal, in which case it is called teletext. People who own TV sets that have a special built-in decoder can view the teletext, either instead of a picture or on top of a picture. Many public TV systems developed teletext in the 1970s and still program it. In other instances, text information comes over a separate wire under the aegis of the post office or phone company and is usually referred to as videotext. Some videotext systems require a separate receiver, and some can utilize the TV set. In some countries cable TV companies provide text material on one or more channels. These systems have varying degrees of interactivity, but at minimum a customer can use a remote control to call up certain pages of information, such as the weather report.

As with cable, text services are more successful in some countries than others. Denmark's teletext service, Tekst TV, is used in 45 percent of homes, and 40 percent of Dutch homes use their system, Teletekst, an average of 10 minutes a day. However, in neighboring Finland and Luxembourg, text services, although available, are not widely used, and in Norway they are used more by commercial companies than by home consumers.

Videocassette recorder penetration is also high (about 50 percent) in Europe. Unlike the situation in many other parts of the world, most of the cassettes viewed in Europe are legal copies for which copyright fees have been paid.

European Integration Because Europe consists of a number of fairly small countries in a rather confined space, many Europeans have been able to see and hear one another's signals for years. Because most of the countries use PAL, technical incompatibility is not a problem. Terrestrial radio and television signals do not stop at country boundaries, and so people living near the border of one country can receive the signals of a neighboring country. Most Danes, for example, have been able to receive signals from Germany and Sweden. The Swiss near the German border have always had access to German programming. Parts of Austria are within reach of German, Swiss, and Italian signals. In fact, since the disintegration of communism, people have set up stations in Hungary and in the Czech and Slovak Republics that are intended to be listened to or viewed primarily by Austrians.

Governments are not happy when their constituents watch programming from other countries because, as mentioned previously, most European governments want their countries to keep their cultural identity. At one time the Netherlands government prohibited subtitling of foreign programming in the Dutch language, but production companies objected and the government was forced to renege. The Irish have always had trouble with too much British programming coming across the Irish Sea.

With satellites and cable TV, the cultural problem has been accentuated, but most European countries have adjusted, knowing that their citizens like diversity. One of the reasons Belgium is so highly cabled is so that people can receive satellite-delivered programming from a variety of countries. Advertisers also like the concept of integrated media in Europe because they can reach the entire continent easily.

A number of Western European countries are now trying to one-up one another in serving the entire European continent so that they can cash in on the financial rewards of a mass market. The country that has most aggressively taken advantage of European integration is tiny Luxembourg. It programs very little that is intended for local distribution in its own country; rather, it sets its sights on providing programming for the rest of Europe. To this end, it has become involved in both the programming and ownership of services in other countries, primarily France and Germany. It is also the force behind the Astra satellite, a successful programming project discussed in detail in Chapter 4.

DIVERSITY

Each nation within Western Europe has its own electronic media characteristics, many of which have been mentioned above. Chapter 4 on the United Kingdom and Chapter 5 on Germany will show the individual traits of these countries as well as amplify the similar characteristics discussed above. Great Britain was chosen because of its leadership role in establishing the modus operandi of broadcasting in Europe. Most of the countries, in one way or another, looked to the British model. The British were also very influential in establishing their brand of broadcasting in other parts of the world where they had colonies. Germany is a major world power with a broadcasting system influenced by the Hitler regime and the aftermath of World War II. It provides an excellent example of what is happening in Western Europe today.

Several other distinctive aspects of Western European radio and television deserve special note. In Greece, the army has operated broadcasting stations aimed at the general public. During the reign of Francisco Franco (1936–1975), the media in Spain were more tightly controlled by the government than in other countries in Western Europe. Beginning in the 1960s, Franco released his grip on the media slightly because he wanted his country to be accepted by the other countries so that it could profit from the economic gains of a European market.

The Netherlands had an organizational methodology known as pillarization. Broadcasting time was divided among organizations with strong ties to "streams of society." Thus the radio service VARA was programmed by the Socialists, KRO by the Catholics, NCRV and VPRO by the Protestants, and AVRO by a liberal faction. The amount of broadcast time allotted to each group was determined by the number of members the group had. This was often based on the number of people who subscribed to broadcasting magazines produced by the organizations. During the 1960s, the broadcasting structure was "depillarized," but vestiges of the streams of society allocations still survive.

Switzerland has different services for each of its three linguistic groups—Italian, French, and

German. Although over 70 percent of the license fees come from the German-speaking part of Switzerland, the German service receives only about 40 percent of the money. If the output of money were divided according to the income, the Italian and French services would not be viable.

The diversity within Europe can also be seen by briefly examining some of the main characteristics of the electronic media systems of two uniquely intriguing countries, France and Italy.

France France has gone through many of the same phases as other European countries, but it has done it with more flair and turmoil, mainly because the media are highly politicized. When a right-wing party comes into power, it changes many of the media policies and overseeing bodies established by the previous left-wing party, and vice versa.

France's state monopoly is Radiodiffusion-Télévision de France (RTF), formed in 1945 to oversee radio. (At that point it was called Radiodiffusion de France.) The present public radio service, Radio France, has three national programs: France-Inter, which broadcasts a variety of programs including current events, music, and discussion; France-Culture, which features art, literature, and music; and France-Musique, which presents mainly classical music and jazz. In addition, Radio France operates about fifty local stations.

The present public TV structure consists of the over-the-air national service, Antenne 2, launched in 1964, and France Régions (FR3), a national and regional service begun in 1972. In 1989 a public service satellite channel emphasizing European culture was launched. Called Société d'Éditions de Programmes de Télévision (SEPT), it can be received only by homes with satellite dishes or homes connected to cable TV systems. The original French public television station, Télévision Française 1 (TF1), was started in 1935 but in 1987 was privatized.

During its existence RTF has been under a wide variety of government departments. Almost every new government has abolished the ministries of the old government and created new ones, altering the broadcasting structure along the way. Similarly, new regimes have instituted new laws governing broadcasting.

As a reaction to staid public service radio programming, pirate radio stations sprang up in France much as they had in other countries, but the government succeeded in suppressing most of them. Then in 1981 the Socialist candidate, François Mitterrand, came out in favor of them, and when he won, he saw that a law was passed allowing local private radio. In 1986 these local private stations were permitted to form networks and operate on a national scale. At first private radio networking was bit haphazard, with many people involved and many ideas being tried, but it has now settled down and a few major players have emerged.

In the television arena, Canal Plus, an over-the-air pay service launched in 1984, was the first private service. It had a difficult beginning because it did not attract many subscribers, and to stay alive it had to diversify with a host of subsidiary functions such as audiovisual production, newspapers, and TV reception equipment. Now it is profitable.

Two other private channels, La Cinq and M-6, were awarded in 1985. However, when a new government was elected in 1987, it rescinded the licenses and gave the services to different groups of people. La Cinq operated for a while but after several bouts of internal turmoil went bankrupt. M-6 is struggling. The most controversial of all privatization actions occurred when the French government decided in 1987 to turn the leading public TV service, TF1, over to private interests. The channel is quite healthy in private hands, but it has changed from somewhat lofty programming to more entertainment-oriented fare, including U.S. soap operas.

There are also three local over-the-air private TV channels, all losing money, and there are local origination channels on fifteen cable TV systems.

The French government had grand plans for cable TV, but they never materialized. In 1982 the government announced a large-scale systematic plan to cable the entire country. It took almost 2 years to come up with the specifics of the plan, which met with a great deal of opposition from people who thought the idea was too expensive in relation to its value. Also companies that manufactured cable did not like the idea of a government cable monopoly because they could not profitably supply cable for the price the government was willing to pay. In 1986 the government abandoned the cable plan, and, as a result, what little cabling there is has been undertaken in a piecemeal fashion by various private companies. Only about 15 percent of French households subscribe to cable.

French government TV services developed a high-quality teletext service called Antiope that was extensively used for a while but now is not particularly popular. The most widely used text service in France is Minitel, a videotext service that operates from a terminal supplied free by the French PTT. Almost 5 million terminals have been distributed to businesses and homes that pay phone charges for the information they retrieve.

The present French electronic media landscape is quite complicated because of the variety of media forms—private, public, terrestrial, cable, satellite, local, regional, national, European. No doubt new changes will occur as the political and media forces converge both within France and within Western Europe as a whole.

Italy Italian broadcasting began with the same sort of state monopoly public service radio as in other countries. Italy's government system is Radiotelevisione Italiana (RAI), which operates radio and television stations and networks using money from commercials and license fees. Over the years it has evolved into a very large organization that employs about 13,500 workers, many of them at one of its four production centers. RAI has also accumulated a $1 billion debt, and in 1993 the government had to pass a stopgap emergency funding bill to prevent it from going bankrupt. Needless to say, cost cutting is now a top priority.

The first threat to RAI's monopoly status occurred in 1979 when an Italian court ruled that a private company had the right to construct a cable television system. In 1980 another court ruled that radio stations and UHF TV stations could also be held by private interests, but that only RAI could own a network that could distribute live material to all its stations. Entrepreneurs figured out that it was cheaper to put up a transmitter for a UHF station than to wire an area for cable, and so private radio and TV have proliferated in Italy, but cable has died.

The major entrepreneur of private media, Silvio Berlusconi, was a real estate builder who bought numerous private TV stations and established a popular "network," Canale 5. He circumvented the RAI network exclusivity rule by distributing videotapes to each of his stations by airplane and motorcycle couriers and having the stations broadcast the tapes simultaneously throughout the country. Eventually he did this with two other networks. He lured top RAI entertainment talent to work for him by giving them large salaries, and he programmed a great deal of U.S. material.

In 1983 Berlusconi's illegal networks were ordered off the air by the courts but were ordered back on after a few days when the prime minister, a close personal friend of Berlusconi's, petitioned Parliament to reinstate them because of public clamor that shutting down the networks was interrupting episodes of *Dallas*. A compromise was arranged to permit the Berlusconi stations to carry the tapes but stagger them by a minute or two at various stations in order to avoid "simultaneous" live broadcasting. The solution did not last long and ultimately microwave relays and repeater transmitters linked the Berlusconi networks and Parliament ignored them.

Soon Berlusconi's stations were garnering

about 45 percent of the total television audience and beating RAI's programs on a regular basis. RAI responded by importing U.S. movies and TV shows, going from programming 90 percent of its own material to programming under 70 percent.

Meanwhile, Berlusconi expanded, to the extent that his company attracted more than 60 percent of the television advertising market through his media conglomerate Fininvest, which controlled three commercial networks, newspapers, magazines, an advertising agency, production companies, a motion picture theater chain, and interests in other media properties in Italy and elsewhere.

Until 1990 the only laws regulating radio and television were directed at RAI. After private radio and television stations went on the air and Silvio Berlusconi acquired such media power, Parliament, broadcasters, publishers, advertising companies, and the public began to ask for television regulation.

The new law, passed in 1990, had some antitrust regulations aimed at Berlusconi. For example, it stipulated that no one could own more than three TV networks, and anyone who owned three could not own a daily newspaper. This forced Berlusconi to divest himself of *Il Giornale*, an important newspaper in Milan, which he transferred to his brother. He also had to sell his majority interest in a pay-TV system and drop his interest in an all-sports network originating from Yugoslavia, an outlet that permitted him to skirt the network law and carry live soccer games and other sports events.

Another provision permitted only three commercial breaks in films, dramas, or concerts that lasted longer than 90 minutes. For RAI this was helpful because it interrupted films only once, in the middle. But it curtailed the Berlusconi networks because they had many commercial breaks during a film.

Private networks could now go live whenever they wanted, giving Berlusconi a competitive edge because he could compete against RAI with live soccer games on his own networks since he also owned the championship soccer team.

The law also placed some restrictions on program content. For example, films that cannot be seen in theaters by people under 18 cannot be broadcast on television.

Another law was passed in 1993 requiring that in 1 year pay-TV will be permitted only via cable and satellite, but there are virtually no cable systems or DBS systems in operation at this time. There are an estimated 30,000 homes with satellite dishes receiving non-Italian programming from other parts of Europe.

The Italian media scene is in a dynamic state. RAI needs to change because of budget problems. The new laws are sure to affect the private sector and create greater competition between RAI and the private networks. Add to this the fact that in 1994 Silvio Berlusconi threw his hat into the political ring and gained such popularity (in part because his media empire unabashedly promoted him) that he became prime minister of Italy. Obviously, Italy does not have the strict conflict-of-interest rules the United States has, and it has yet to be determined exactly what the new prime minister will do with his media conglomerate.

(*Editor's Note*: The section on Italy was written by George Mastroianni, Professor of Communications at California State University, Fullerton, who recently spent 7 months in Italy studying its electronic media systems and following the television bill as it was being debated in Parliament.)

CHAPTER 4

United Kingdom

Brian T. Evans

Brian Evans runs a United Kingdom–based consultancy that encourages the development of digital television and digital radio broadcasting. He holds an undergraduate degree in electrical engineering and a doctorate in medical electronics and is a senior member of the IEEE. During passage of the 1990 Broadcasting Bill, he was the technical advisor and wrote speeches and amendments for the opposition front bench. He has presented papers on digital television at international conferences and has recently published a nontechnical guide to this new technology

Brian Evans.

STATISTICS

Geographic Area: 94,226 square miles
Capital: London
Population: 55,486,000
Religions: Church of England, Roman Catholic
Language: English
Type of Government: Constitutional monarchy headed by a prime minister
Gross Domestic Product: $858 billion
Literacy: 99 percent

GENERAL CHARACTERISTICS

The term "United Kingdom of Great Britain" is a rather confusing one. The country is really four countries (England, Scotland, Wales, and Northern Ireland) united under one government. The southern part of Ireland is an independent country. Sometimes the four countries are referred to as the "United Kingdom of Great Britain and Northern Ireland." A short version of that lengthy name is either "United Kingdom" or "Great Britain." Even shorter designations are "Britain" and "U.K." In this chapter the terms will be used interchangeably.

By whatever name, the United Kingdom has had an esteemed broadcasting history. The United Kingdom has been a major world power since the 1700s and oversaw many colonies during the era when radio was being established. As a result many countries throughout the world have a broadcasting system that was originally modeled after the British Broadcasting Corporation (BBC). This model had a high regard for the public service nature of broadcasting. It emphasized enlightenment and the philosophy of raising public taste to a high level. The government oversaw broadcasting and set some of the standards, but the BBC, which operated under a government charter, was also given autonomy and independence.

Known throughout the world for its high broadcasting standards, the BBC executed its charter well. For 70 years the brilliant partnership that existed between the creative talents of program makers and the husbandry of the technical and administrative staff created something of esteemed value. The BBC's creativity remains unchallenged for it has never lost that magic touch that inspires audiences around the country and around the world.

However, times are changing. Throughout the world governments are yielding to privatization. Staid government-run broadcasting organizations, modeled after the BBC, are finding they must change if they are to compete with the systems that are set up by private corporations. The BBC itself is under attack in that its broadcasting charter is now being subjected to intense political scrutiny. There are many who envy its successes and, out of self-interest, seek to privatize them. Can the BBC retain its popular appeal or is this magic partnership to be broken up? Will the BBC be stripped of its profitable ventures and thereafter be consigned to a ghetto of unwatched public service broadcasting?

Since the beginning of 1993 U.K. commercial television has been regulated by a new broadcasting authority, the Independent Television Commission (ITC). Its mandate is to exercise a "lighter touch" than before. Many fear that this signals the end of quality peak-time programming on non-BBC channels and may thereby force the BBC into presenting more popular fare in order to compete.

Then there are other forces such as cable TV and satellite. To date, cable TV has not been particularly successful. The United Kingdom is a little smaller than the state of Michigan, and terrestrial over-the-air television is available to more than 99.4 percent of the 23 million homes. There has been little need for cable, and where it has been tried it has not been financially successful. In the last 10 years U.K. investors have been grateful to sell out to U.S. interests who now own about 90 percent of British cable. Will the U.S. companies regret their investment or will the recent change in laws that allows cable companies to offer telephone services provide a much needed change in their fortunes?

Satellite television has won a niche market. During the last 5 years over 10 percent of homes have installed their own 2-foot satellite dishes. Monthly installation figures are now declining. Many of the 70 percent of homes that have videocassette recorders (VCRs) turn to local video rental stores for more up-to-date movies than are seen on satellite TV channels. Is the satellite TV market reaching a plateau?

The following discussion will cover themes that may appear common to both the U.K. and the U.S. experience. Dare we assume that this commonality will lead to similar market developments in both countries? Perhaps the historical differences in the political and regulatory regimes will lead the United Kingdom instead into a quite different media environment. At present no one knows. We can conjecture and we can certainly lobby for our own point of view. A look back over 70 years of broadcasting may just yield some clues to where we are heading.

THE DEVELOPMENT OF ELECTRONIC MEDIA IN GREAT BRITAIN

Both radio and television started out as BBC-only services. However, over the years independent commercially supported services were begun, and more recently satellite has been added.

The Early Days of U.K. Radio Broadcasting

There have been two BBCs. The original British Broadcasting Company was formed on October 18, 1922, and started daily broadcasting from London a few weeks later on November 14.

It did not take politicians long to realize that broadcasting was a medium of great power and intimacy. The Crawford Committee was set up to investigate the new services, and in 1926 committee members presented their report to Parliament.

They said firmly that broadcasting is a national asset to be used for the national good and that there must be an overall adherence to the idea of public service broadcasting. They recommended that a broadcasting authority be established as trustee of the national interest and that it should be free of government interference. They expressed and endorsed the idea of universality; viewers in all parts of the country who pay the same license fee should be able to receive all public service channels.

As a result of the Crawford Committee's work, the first BBC was dissolved and was replaced on January 1, 1927, by the British Broadcasting Corporation, the BBC as we now know it. Its royal charter guaranteed its independence from the government. Sir John Reith, later Lord Reith, was appointed to the top management position of director general. Three years later in 1930 a second Regional Programme was added to the existing National Programme.

At the start of World War II in 1939 the Regional Programmes were merged into one Home Service, and the high-power regional transmitters were replaced by many low-power stations, all radiating the same program and all on the same frequency. If this technical measure was not in itself sufficient to deny radio location assistance to incoming German bombers, then the radio transmitters near a threatened city or town were turned off completely for the duration of the raid. Many years later these low-power transmitters were to form the basis of local radio.

At the end of the war regional services were resumed. The Third Programme, which was entirely devoted to classical music and literature, began its broadcasts on September 29, 1946.

FM broadcasting lagged U.S. developments by many years. From a slow start in 1955 the simulcast FM service was to remain a poor relation of AM until the introduction of stereo in the early 1970s. Even today barely more than 50 percent of the U.K. radio audience listens to BBC radio on FM.

For a teenager growing up in the mid-1950s BBC music radio was extremely dull. In 1955 the popular music Light Programme offered a mere 30 minutes of rock and roll on its regular *Skiffle Club* Saturday morning show. The rest of the schedule was mostly filled by dance music from BBC resident light orchestras. The distant 200-kilowatt Radio Luxembourg transmitter at 1440 kilohertz AM did provide an alternative, but listening to its service was sheer frustration. The nighttime broadcasts regularly faded away into the background static.

But then "radio pirates" came to the rescue. They dropped anchor just outside the U.K. territorial waters 12-mile limit and broadcast modern pop music. Best known were the two Radio Caroline pirate stations which played everything, including demo discs from budding musicians.

Caroline's main competitor was another pirate, Radio London, which had anchored a mile away from the Radio Caroline vessel. Unlike Radio Caroline, Radio London kept to a strict format top-40 playlist.

It was all too good to last, and in 1967 the good times came to an end. The government could not directly outlaw broadcasting from international waters, and so it did the next best thing. The Marine Broadcasting Offences Act prevented any U.K. company from doing business with the radio pirates who were to be both physically and financially starved off the airwaves.

But it was not all bad news; there was a quite unexpected surprise. Good old "Auntie BBC," or "Auntie" for short, woke up and responded to the competition. The BBC hired the best of the pirate disc jockeys and started its own new pop program, Radio 1, on AM. The Light Programme "oldies" channel became today's Radio 2, the classical music Third Programme became Radio 3, and the talk-based Home Service became Radio 4.

The fifth national BBC radio network, Radio 5, was added in 1990 on AM. It was aimed at the youth and sports markets. However, it was chopped before it could either find its feet or gain a cult following for its informative and entertaining style. In early 1994 its name and format were changed. Radio 5 became "Radio 5 Live"—a rolling news and sports service that no longer encourages teenagers to listen to talk radio. We shall discover the reason for this change further on.

Local broadcasting has been even less successful. Starved of money, BBC local broadcasters have struggled to fill their airtime. Independent commercial radio has also found the going tough. Many of its early promises to provide local flavor with local news and current affairs have been relinquished to the BBC. A recent trend of automating commercial stations and linking some of them together may improve their financial condition.

Grassroots community radio has enjoyed more success. These low-power stations are staffed primarily by volunteer enthusiasts who gain valuable experience for a possible future career in electronic media.

The Early Days of U.K. Television In the early 1920s John Logie Baird captured the public imagination with his early demonstrations of television. In 1926 he "borrowed" a BBC transmitter for experimental 30-line TV broadcasts and 2 years later transmitted TV pictures across the Atlantic. Despite his pioneering work, his mechanical "televisor" proved too clumsy for domestic use. If television was to succeed, much sharper pictures would be needed.

In 1935 the United Kingdom held perhaps the first competition in the world to select a "high-definition" television system for public broadcasting. Baird's new 240-line mechanical TV system lost out to the all-electronic 405-line TV system from a consortium formed by Marconi and the phonograph company EMI.

EMI's electronic television system was based on research first undertaken in the United States by Vladimir Zworykin, a Russian émigré, and by his countryman and protégé Isaac Shoenberg. Shoenberg left Zworykin to lead the EMI research team in the United Kingdom and obtained many thousands of research dollars for this speculative venture. In the United States Zworykin was given even larger funds by David Sarnoff at RCA.

Shoenberg's team included Alan Blumlein who was probably the greatest British electronics engineer of the twentieth century. His ideas and innovations allowed such rapid progress to be made that the BBC first started a regular 2-hour-a-day public television service on November 2, 1936. Zworykin's equivalent 525-line system was not to be demonstrated for another 3 years.

In those days there were lots of "firsts." On May 12, 1937, the first televised outside broadcast was of the coronation procession of King George VI, who had come to power following the surprise abdication of his elder brother, Edward VIII.

At the outbreak of World War II, the TV service was shut down, and much of the television transmission equipment was cannibalized for use in early radar sets. Although the TV service resumed in 1947, it was not until the next big royal occasion, the live telecast of the coronation of the young Queen Elizabeth II in June 1953, that television really caught the popular imagination.

TV sets were expensive and money was tight, so very few people were able to afford an outright purchase. Consumer demand was met instead by the emergence of a new industry, rival chains of television rental stores. Since those early days the British public has often chosen to rent new technology rather than risk an outright purchase. Ten years ago videocassette recorders were first rented rather than bought. At present there is a brisk business in renting out 34-inch wide-screen sets.

The Start of Independent Television On July 30, 1954, after a series of heated debates in Parliament about the effects of commercial TV on the public service orientation of broadcasting, the British government permitted the setting up of a second TV channel in direct competition with the BBC. The new service was called Independent Television (ITV). It was regulated by a new body—the Independent Television Authority (ITA). When independent radio was permitted nearly 20 years later in 1973, the ITA changed its name to the Independent Broadcasting Authority (IBA).

Unlike the BBC, which was funded by a compulsory license on every household that had a radio or television set, the new service was expected to raise revenue from televised advertisements. The United Kingdom was divided into a number of regional markets, and the major three markets were further subdivided into weekday and weekend franchises. Various companies bid to obtain franchises that would put them in charge of programming in the various markets.

The first U.K. commercial television service based in London therefore opened twice, on September 22 and September 24 of 1955. Associated Rediffusion won the weekday franchise and ATV the weekend franchise.

Services in other areas started gradually, and by 1962 the ITV network was complete. The major market contractors produced nearly all the programs, which were then redistributed or networked throughout the United Kingdom. To this day the antitrust implications of these cozy network agreements continue to haunt the industry.

ITV was an overwhelming success. U.K. viewers were fed a diet of variety shows, big-money game shows, pop music programs, and soaps. BBC ratings plunged. All the fears that had been expressed in Parliament now seemed to be coming true.

BBC2 How was the BBC to meet this challenge? Matching game show with game show might court popularity in the battle for ratings but would violate its public service obligations. The answer was a second BBC television channel—BBC2. BBC1 was now free to broadcast more popular programs while the BBC could salve its conscience with a better-quality diet on BBC2.

In practice the formula has worked very well. BBC2 was given the mandate to provide choice and to experiment with program formats that were less overtly popular. Many of the programming innovations have been transferred successfully to BBC1 and have subsequently enjoyed worldwide sales.

Following the introduction of BBC2 on April 20, 1964, the BBC was able to cut back some of the lead that ITV had gained. It could now play tag by scheduling two programs against ITV's one. The BBC could intertwine and cross-promote two separate themes during peak time, which allowed two or three "natural" change-over points at 7 P.M., 9 P.M., and 10:30 P.M.—just when ITV was showing advertisements.

The strategy paid off. BBC1 offered more popular programs, and the channel ratings rose. The BBC was not only meeting its obligations to public service broadcasting, it was also competing head to head with popular ITV programming. Public opinion shifted. If the BBC could put up such a good performance on a fixed license fee income, then surely the richer ITV companies should do even better?

The shoe was now on the other foot. Under intense political pressure the ITV regulator, the ITA, was forced to insist that its contractors meet their obligations for quality programming and localism.

Who were to be the fall guys? In the 1968 round of license renewals the main casualty was the Wales and West of England contractor, TWW. Because its program quality was not considered to be high enough, it was replaced by Harlech Television, later to become HTV. In the following round in 1981 the English south coast contractor, Southern TV, was replaced. No longer was an ITV franchise a license to print money; program quality had to equal if not exceed that of the BBC.

Channel Four During the late 1960s and 1970s ITV program contractors were busy reequipping their studios for color. Color television broadcasting was a great success, and ITV advertising revenues rose. By the late 1970s ITV was once again turning its thoughts toward expansion. Were the 1980s to see the dawning of the much hyped second ITV channel?

The politicians thought not. They did not want a clone of ITV. Instead a new independent channel should follow the BBC2 example and offer viewers a choice of good-quality programs. Thus the 1981 Broadcasting Act that created the new Channel Four specifically charged the new channel to create a distinctive character of its own. Under the stewardship of two charismatic leaders Channel Four has done just that. It does not produce its own programs. Rather, it commissions them from independent TV production companies who have come up with some excellent fare.

Satellite Television In the past 4 years about 2.5 million of the 22 million U.K. homes have installed Astra satellite dishes in order to receive a variety of English-language services through direct broadcast satellite (DBS). The Astra satellite system is owned and operated by the Société Européenne de Satellites (SES), a private company based in the Grand Duchy of Luxembourg. Snuggled between the borders of France, Belgium, and Germany, the Grand Duchy continues to retain its historic independence from its bigger neighbors even though it is only half the size of the state of Delaware.

Luxembourg likes maverick broadcasting deals. In the early 1930s it supported Radio Luxembourg, which was then the only commercial radio broadcaster in Western Europe. The Astra satellite venture offered local investors another bet on the media. It is therefore no surprise that 20 percent of SES was taken up by the Luxembourg government. The remainder of the equity has been acquired by European financial institutions and banks with a branch office in the Grand Duchy's tax haven. The British ITV company, Thames TV, also retains a small stake.

Astra's success in Britain has an interesting political history. In 1982 the U.K. government decided that the BBC should broadcast on two of the five DBS satellite channels allocated to the United Kingdom. By 1985, however, the cost of the venture was proving too high and it was abandoned.

Also in 1985 ministers from various European countries agreed on a directive—a set of Europe-wide regulations—that was intended to control direct broadcasting by satellite across Europe. These involved some technical parameters that will be discussed later in this chapter.

The British, despite the cost problems, were still intent on having a DBS system and decided it should be a private venture as opposed to a BBC one. In 1986 the IBA readvertised three of the five DBS channels, and the franchise was won by the British Satellite Broadcasting consortium (BSB). It was to spearhead the new age of multichannel satellite broadcasting. It spent enormous sums of money on new London studios and a head office that lay empty until the QVC Shopping Channel took over the building in 1993.

Meanwhile, the people involved in Astra discovered some technical loopholes in the Europe-wide technical standards that enabled them to broadcast more channels more cheaply than BSB engineers were able to. In addition, the vice-president of marketing for Astra had learned his craft as a record promoter and knew that time was never on his side. Just like any new recording artist, Astra either had to sell today or be consigned to the trash can. Astra moved while the BSB executives were still bogged down with technical and managerial details.

Another important ingredient for Astra was provided by entrepreneur Rupert Murdoch. His News International Corporation signed long leases for four of the sixteen transponders on the first Astra satellite. Not for him the lavish central London studios of his rival, BSB. He assembled the best international broadcasting talent and then launched his four-channel free-to-air Sky TV service in February 1989 from a business park near Heathrow Airport—months ahead of BSB's three-channel subscription service.

In 1991 BSB, which had been struggling to play catch-up, finally admitted defeat. It merged with Sky to form British Sky Broadcasting (BSkyB), leaving the original BSB investors nursing a US$1 billion loss.

But Astra is not without other competition, most notably the European Telecommunications Satellite organization (Eutelsat). This organization is an intergovernmental cooperative, ultimately owned by thirty-nine European countries. It was formed in 1983 to provide telephone links across Europe, but these never proved popular. Instead Eutelsat has seen a big expansion in its market for television distribution and audio services. It operates four satellites that are placed in adjacent orbital slots and carry Italian, Greek, Turkish, Serbian, Spanish, English, German, Dutch, Arabic, Hungarian, and Croatian television. It is a sign of the times that the Croatian TV service from Zagreb and the Serbian TV service from Belgrade are on identical frequencies but on neighboring satellites.

One of the satellites carries three international radio services previously obtainable only through the static of a shortwave radio. The BBC offers its World Service in both English and European languages. Deutsche Welle offers its equivalent international service from Germany. Perhaps most impressive of all is the U.S. Voice of America radio service which is broadcast in stereo.

During the late 1980s and early 1990s, Astra and Eutelsat expanded their services so that the European viewer is now being offered seventy channels of satellite TV. Both companies have plans for further expansion.

ORGANIZATION AND FINANCING

The BBC and ITV are poles apart in their organization and financing. The BBC enjoys a guaranteed income and is centralist in its approach, whereas ITV is a regional structure whose income depends on the buoyancy of the economy. Although popular programming is often boringly similar, both organizations offer a wide variety of distinctive programs for discerning audiences.

The BBC The BBC is a public corporation which raises US$2 billion a year by the levy of a US$125 license fee on every U.K. household with a color TV or VCR. This money is used to run two television channels, five national radio services, and many local radio services. Although the issue of allowing commercials on

BBC Television Centre. (Barbara Huemer)

the BBC, mainly as a way of increasing its funding, has been hotly debated in Parliament several times, at present neither BBC radio nor BBC television accepts advertisements.

The BBC is overseen by a Board of Governors consisting of twelve people appointed by the monarch on government advice for 5-year terms; however, its day-to-day operations are carried out by a director general and a management team. Its royal charter, last renewed by Parliament in 1981, provides independence from the government of the day.

The charter defines the BBC's responsibilities in providing both domestic radio and television services and overseas broadcasting. The BBC, through its board and various advisory councils, must seek public views and opinions of its programs and consider the criticisms and suggestions so obtained. (The various Broadcasting Acts stipulate that independent television must do the same.)

Independent Broadcasting The organization of independent radio stations is fairly straightforward. The stations are local in nature, and they receive their funding through advertising.

The 1990 Broadcasting Act allowed for the creation of three independent national radio networks, INR1, INR2, and INR3. Two are now in place: Classic FM and Virgin Radio on AM. The third independent network, INR3, which has yet to be established, is to be a news and talk station. Many bidders for this franchise are dismayed that the BBC has transformed its own Radio 5 AM service into a news and sports "Radio 5 Live" format in order to foil the success of a rival commercial talk network. These days Auntie BBC has very sharp teeth indeed!

Independent television, however, is more complex. The central organization (at various times called the ITA, IBA, or ITC) is actually a regionally based network. It does not produce any programs itself; they are all now produced or acquired by the companies (ITVs) that have won the local franchises awarded by the central organization. These ITVs produce programs for their local areas and also contribute to the national feed. Although all sixteen ITVs are eligible to produce national programs, in reality most of them come from the large population centers such as Birmingham, London, and Manchester. This independent television structure is somewhat akin to the American Public Broadcasting System structure wherein local stations produce programs aired on the PBS network.

The sixteen U.K. ITV companies are all public limited companies and are therefore all quoted on the London stock exchange. Cross-ownership restrictions are strictly enforced in that newspaper groups may not hold more than a 30 percent share of any TV company. The combined advertising income of the sixteen ITV companies is similar to the BBC's income of US$2 billion a year.

Channel Four Channel Four is unique. It earns revenue from advertising yet offers high-quality programming to minority audiences. How is it done? The answer is in the provisions of the 1981 Broadcasting Act. Under this act, ITV was made to guarantee the fledgling Channel Four a 14 percent share of its own advertising income. In other words, Channel Four, in the beginning, derived its income from its direct competitor, ITV. In return the ITV sales departments could sell airtime across both ITV and Channel Four networks, giving them the potential to increase their overall sales.

When Channel Four first started out, no one wanted to buy airtime on it, but as the channel gradually picked up audience share, advertisers were attracted to its audience profile. Although the 1990 Act now allows Channel Four to sell its own airtime, the 14 percent guarantee from the ITV companies still remains in place, but ITV must supply only the amount Channel Four does not earn itself that would add up to 14 percent of ITV's income. In practice Channel Four's own airtime sales have now risen to this level, and the guarantees are no longer such a burden on ITV profitability.

Like BBC2, Channel Four is intended to serve tastes and audiences not catered to on the popular ITV channel. Unlike the other three channels, however, Channel Four produces virtually no programs of its own. It is required instead to obtain a substantial proportion of its programs from sources other than ITV companies and has thus fostered an independent TV production sector which provides much of its output.

The Welsh Fourth Channel Following a period of intense political lobbying, the 1981 Broadcasting Act, primarily intended to set up Channel Four, was also used to establish a distinctive fourth TV channel for Wales. It is commonly known as S4C, which is an abbreviation of three Welsh words: sianel (channel), pedwar (four), eck (C, the first letter of "Cymru"—the Welsh word for Wales).

S4C broadcasts about 27 hours per week of original Welsh-language programming and about 80 hours of English-language programming rebroadcast from Channel Four. The Welsh-language program production is provided by three sources, BBC Wales, HTV (the ITC franchisee for Wales), and a number of independent producers. Like Channel Four, S4C is guaranteed a steady income. This is set at 3.2 percent of ITV revenue but is paid from government funds.

In the last 10 years there has been a change in Welsh middle-class opinion. The availability of peak-time Welsh television programming on S4C and the introduction of a Welsh-language radio service, BBC Cymru, from the BBC alongside its national English-language services have made people reexamine their cultural identity.

Many English-speaking parents have come to regret their lack of ability in their national language and want to put this right. By popular demand Welsh-speaking grade schools have sprung up in what were very "English" areas of south Wales. These initiatives are wide-ranging; parents and children now elect to be taught Spanish and French, for example, without the use of English as the intermediary means of understanding.

But Welsh viewers have paid a price for

S4C's popularity. Because of a lack of frequency spectrum, S4C programs are broadcast instead of rather than as well as Channel Four. It is a source of much frustration that many Channel Four programs, such as the 7 P.M. 50-minute flagship *Channel Four News*, are completely lost to viewers in Wales.

PROGRAMMING

Programming can be discussed by looking at a typical London evening TV schedule (Monday, April 18, 1993).

BBC1

				Audience
5:35*	(NI)	Neighbours	Australian soap	9.84 million
6:00*		National News		
6:30	(All)	Regional News		
7:00*		Eldorado	Unsuccessful soap set in Spain; discontinued in summer 1993	
7:30*		The Doctor	Documentary on primary care physician	
8:00*		Bruce's Guest Night	Light entertainment	5.5 million
8:30*	(S)	Waiting for God	Comedy	
9:00*		National News		
9:25	(All)	Regional News		
9:30		Panorama	Current affairs: What to do with the over 85s	
10:10	(NI)	Film 93	Movie reviews	
10:40*		Cagney & Lacey	USA	
11:25	(NI)	Germany Means Business	Düsseldorf boat show	
11:55		Weather		
12:00		Close		

BBC2

6:00*	The Addams Family	USA
6:25	Def 11—The Fresh Prince of Bel Air	USA
6:50	Standing Room Only	Soccer review
7:20*	The Great Picture Trail	Titian painting
7:30	Soundbites	Modern classical trombone
8:00*	Horizon	Documentary on carbon molecules
8:50*	Lucinda Lambton's Alphabet of Britain	A portrait of an old-fashioned Leeds jeweler
9:00	World Snooker	Competition
10:00*	Open Space	Personal view of female rape
10:30	Newsnight	Weeknight current affairs —tougher than Larry King
11:15	World Snooker	
11:55	Weather	
12:00	Writers in the 30s	Left-wing views
12:25	Close	

ITV: Weekday franchise, London Carlton

5:40*		ITN News		
6:00	(All)	London Tonight	Regional newsmagazine	
7:00*		Busman's Holiday	Team game show	9.52 million
7:30*		Coronation Street	Famous north of England soap	17.86 million
8:00		Cluedo	Whodunit game show	9.22 million
8:30		World in Action	Current affairs—Virgin v. British Airways	7.59 million
9:00*		Medics	Hospital drama	9.37 million
10:00*		News at Ten	From ITN	9.25 million
10:30*	(All)	Local News		
10:40	(All)	The Next Man	Movie	
12:35		ITN News Headlines		
12:40		Night Time Sequence		

Channel Four

5:00	The Late Late Show	Talk show from Dublin
6:00	Children's Ward	Hospital drama
6:30*	The Cosby Show	USA
7:00*	Channel Four News	From ITN
7:50	Comment	Personal view of U.K. life
8:00*	Brookside	Another north of England soap
8:30*	Surgical Spirit	Medical comedy
9:00*	Naked Sport	Documentary on basketball
10:00	Northern Exposure; My Sister, My Mother	USA drama
10:55	Channels of Resistance	Documentary on African rejection of U.S. TV
12:00	States of America	President Clinton v. gays
1:00	Close	

Key: *, closed captioned; NI, Northern Ireland breakaway; S, Scotland breakaway; All, seven BBC or fifteen ITV regional breakaways. Audience percentage share, January 4–April 25, 1993: BBC1, 32.8; BBC2, 9.8; ITV, 40.4; ChFour, 11.4; satellite and cable, 5.5. (Ratings courtesy of BARB, William Philips, and *Broadcast Magazine*.)

Both BBC1 and ITV slot a current affairs program in between peak-time light entertainment shows. *The Doctor* (BBC1, 7:30) discusses his professional dilemma in visiting and treating Bill, an 85-year-old gentleman with pneumonia who does not want to die in the hospital. (In the United Kingdom domiciliary visits and hospital treatment are free.) Later that evening *Panorama* (BBC1, 9:30) picks up the same theme.

Coronation Street (ITV, 7:30) is a 30-year-old success story. Note how its loyal 17 million viewers drop to 9 million for the following game show of average popularity.

In mid-1993 the BBC killed off the lavish but unsuccessful Spanish soap, *Eldorado*. In early 1994 it extended its more successful twice-weekly *East-Enders* soap to a third episode at 8:00 P.M. on Mondays. It attracts a regular audience of 11 to 13 million, coming second in popularity only to ITV's *Coronation Street*. Under such intense mid-evening competition from the BBC, ITV companies lobbied the regulator to move the 8:30 P.M. *World in Action* investigative journalism program to another slot outside peak time. At first the ITC refused to relax its rules on the amount of serious programming that must be broadcast in peak time. It cited the pro-

Coronation Street. (Granada Television)

gram's good ratings and pointed out that skillful scheduling and serious programming need not devastate peak-time audience shares. In the past more popular *World in Action* topics had occasionally attracted audiences of over 11 million. All to no avail. Despite promises from ITV, *World in Action* has disappeared from the screens.

Note also the inclusion of fill-in 5- and 10-minute programs; they are a delight.

Advertisements ITV and Channel Four are restricted to a maximum of 144 minutes of advertisements per day. In peak time, which extends from 6 P.M. to 11 P.M., the limit is 37.5 minutes. There are no more than three or four breaks per hour which always occur on the hour and often on the half-hour.

News at Ten (ITV, 10:00) attracts premium rates for its central break at 10:15. On the other hand, many 30-minute documentary programs run without a central break, even at peak time.

Once or twice a day independent broadcasters check that there is no correlation between program and advertising content. When Princess Diana addressed a convention on eating disorders in April 1993, the ITV network decided to broadcast her speech live. At the early morning meeting they checked carefully to see that any advertisements for dietary products had been reassigned slots elsewhere in the day. This procedure is strictly adhered to. If a movie actress or television personality makes a guest appearance on a show, then any advertisements in which they appear, either in person or just as a voice-over, are rescheduled.

Rival independent broadcasters watch one another's miniutage like hawks. ITV companies, for example, spotted that Channel Four was showing programs that allowed a central program break of not 1 but 2 minutes. This contravened the 37.5-minute peak-time ITC rule and had to be corrected. Over the next few months Channel Four had to "lose" 50 minutes of revenue.

Localism The London evening schedules show a number of breakaways from the network programs. These are times when the local area programs its own material rather than that being offered by the network.

BBC2 and Channel Four are the closest to being a national network, though there are some programs, such as BBC2's weekly 30 minutes of parliamentary regional reports, that take on a local flavor. As mentioned previously, the Channel Four service in Wales is quite different.

BBC1 usually provides the same light entertainment programs throughout the United Kingdom, though it offers many breakaways during the day for its seven separate regions. It can therefore come as a surprise to a Londoner that his favorite program is not being broadcast as close as 150 miles away from his house.

BBC Northern Ireland breaks away from the main network more often than Scotland or Wales and produces a lot of its own programming. By a quirk of popularity, these programs are watched in southern Ireland as well. Away from the misdeeds of the politically disaffected on both sides of the border, the Irish enjoy access to a wider choice of television than those living elsewhere in the United Kingdom.

Thanks to the efforts of many licensed (and unlicensed) cable television operators, the Eire State broadcaster RTE is widely available in British Northern Ireland. By the same token, BBC1 and BBC2 are available throughout politically independent southern Ireland. Market forces have determined that BBC Northern Ireland and RTE both produce local programs for Irish people on whichever side of the border they live.

There is, of course, a downside. Few local Northern Ireland programs ever get U.K. national airtime, for the programs are considered to be too Irish for English tastes. Some Irish shows do make the reverse trip, however. *The Late Late Show* (ChFour, 5:00) is an abridged repeat of the weekend talk show anchored by Gay Byrne from the studios of RTE Dublin.

Teletext Teletext is a 20-year-old technology that allows extra data signals to be transmitted in the black edges at the top of a normal TV picture. With a suitably equipped TV set these signals can be decoded to provide hundreds of pages of textual information on the screen. These pages can be shown on the TV set either in place of or overlaid on the normal TV picture.

The selected page of information can take many seconds before it is displayed, and the graphics are crude. Teletext in the United States has been a resounding failure. Yet 40 percent of all homes in northern Europe have paid a premium of US$100 or more to acquire a TV set with teletext.

The plain truth is that Europeans are addicted to teletext. Why? U.K. teletext provides a breaking news service that is often faster than CNN. Saturday football results are updated goal by goal for fifty or more professional games around the country. The secret is simple. There are direct links from the wires of the press agencies to the teletext computer and hence on to the screen at home. News flashes are just that—often way ahead of the next scheduled BBC or ITV news bulletin at the top of the hour.

The direct computer link brings other benefits. Arrival and departure information for every major airport in the United Kingdom is available at the touch of a button. Is the information up to date? It should be; it is the same information that is displayed on the monitor screens at the airports. Meeting a friend at Heathrow is that much easier as it no longer requires a phone call to the airline to check whether the plane is on time.

Financial data, such as currency exchange rates and stock options, are updated every 3 minutes. It is nearly as good as a place on the trading floor. Nearly, but not quite. The big rollers need split-second updates, and for that they need to pay. A fee of US$20,000 a year buys a special (custom) decoder and, with it, access to the private encrypted teletext pages which offer real-time access to stock market computers. It also buys access to the computer networks of the big retail corporations which use private teletext to update the price of every grocery item in every cash register in their chains of stores across the country.

Teletext is big business for television program makers and advertisers. It is also good business for the winner of the separate ITC teletext service franchise for ITV and Channel Four.

Did you miss the special offer from the local car dealer? No matter, full details of the offer are available on a teletext page. Do you need a discount flight, or would a romantic cruise suit you better? Look at teletext. Did you miss that French recipe on the cookery show? It's there on teletext. No need to scribble down the instructions. From within the show the French chef will remind you that it is all there on page 123. Keen on a job in the U.K. media? Check BBC teletext page 696 for the latest BBC jobs and then ring BBC corporate recruitment at 081 749 7000 for an application form. Teletext is just like air conditioning in your car. How can you admit to your friends that you don't have it?

The most popular teletext service is closed captioning. Many programs already carry closed captioning for the deaf and hard of hearing, and broadcasters are committed to increasing this service year by year. The BBC currently subtitles more than 25 percent of its programs.

BBC teletext.

Check the London TV schedule on pp. 108–109 where every captioned program is marked with an asterisk. The inherently high teletext data capacity allows a number of captions to be carried simultaneously. This feature is used by Filmnet, a European commercial satellite broadcaster, to subtitle movies in four languages (English, German, Swedish, and Danish) simultaneously. Just select your own language from the TV remote control.

The latest VCR innovation is Startext. Call up the television schedule on the appropriate teletext page and highlight the programs you want to record. Then, the VCR does the rest. If the program makes a late start or overruns, then the Startext data stream reprograms the VCR so that nothing is lost from the recording. It can even pause the VCR during advertising breaks. Surely this is interactive television at its best.

LAWS AND REGULATIONS

All of the British electronic media come under some degree of government control. BBC radio, which started in 1927, was authorized by Parliament, and many of the changes within the BBC have been spearheaded or approved by Parliament. Independent broadcasting could not be launched until it received a stamp of approval from Parliament. Once it received that stamp, through the 1954 Broadcasting Act, independent TV became a very good business. The industry made such high profits that the government introduced a special tax, an ITV levy, to cream off any excess. However, there was public and government dissatisfaction with the independent structure, mainly in terms of the quality of the programming, much of which was imported from the United States.

1981 Broadcasting Act The renewal of the BBC's charter in 1981 provided an opportunity to take a fresh look at ITV. The 1981 Broadcasting Act reiterated independent television's public service obligations, in effect matching the charter obligations placed upon the BBC.

- Programs should offer a wide and balanced range of subject matter. High standards should be maintained.
- A proper proportion should be of British or European origin.
- The service should inform as well as entertain.
- News must be presented with due accuracy and impartiality.
- Programs must not offend against good taste or decency.
- Violent scenes must be avoided before 9 P.M. when large numbers of children are likely to be watching.
- A suitable proportion of programs should specially appeal to the tastes and outlook of the audience served by the station whether in English or another language.

The 1981 Act also established Channel Four and the Welsh Fourth Channel, S4C. It also gave the IBA permission to advertise a U.K.-wide breakfast television franchise. (Early morning was to be given a franchise separate from the rest of the day—similar to the separate weekend franchises discussed earlier.) The winner, TV-AM, was soon to offer programs that plumbed the depths of public discontent and thus lost its franchise in 1992.

The Peacock Report In 1986 Alan Peacock was asked by the Thatcher government to inquire into the financing of the BBC. His committee reported that required changes would need to be introduced in three stages.

Stage 1 would retain the existing license arrangements. Any requests for increases in funding should be linked to the cost-of-living index. Stage 1 would continue until advances in technology overcame frequency spectrum scarcity.

The second stage would involve funding the BBC by subscription and allowing other broadcast services to proliferate.

Stage 3 would allow an indefinite number of subscription and pay-per-view services to flourish. These might be supplied through a nationwide grid of fiber-optic cables.

Peacock also floated the idea of a public service broadcasting council that would oversee the "quality" programming of both the BBC and ITV. His committee also suggested the formation of a broadcasting transmission authority which would take over the separate BBC and ITV engineering and transmission functions.

The government was displeased with his conclusions and commissioned independent research to check out the likely uptake of subscription television. The research report concluded that there should be a viable market for some high-value subscription or pay-per-view programs. However, for widespread use, the mandatory license fee was less expensive to collect than subscriptions. The report also expressed concern that a large number of people, once offered the choice, would choose not to subscribe, thereby invalidating the prevailing public service concept of universality.

ITV Back in the Spotlight In 1988 the government asked its Home Affairs Select Committee to examine the future of broadcasting in the United Kingdom. They held public hearings and called many witnesses including people from the BBC and IBA.

At its third sitting on February 3, 1988, the committee gave the IBA a rough ride. One Labor member asked the director general of the IBA, "[Do I understand that] you are satisfied with the legal framework within which you operate as far as the ownership and control of program companies is concerned?"

"Yes, Chairman," came the reply. This astonished the committee because the IBA head was indicating that he felt no improvements needed to be made, even though numerous criticisms had been leveled at the IBA by the press and by many diverse broadcasting interests. It was at that point that a number of senior members of the Thatcher administration were persuaded that the IBA must be disbanded.

The 1990 Broadcasting Act Following the recommendations made by the Home Affairs Select Committee, the 1990 Broadcasting Bill set out to replace the Independent Broadcasting Authority with a light-touch regulator, the Independent Television Commission (ITC).

Previous Broadcasting Acts (1954 and 1981) had entrusted the IBA with responsibility for everything broadcast by its sixteen television program contractors. In the government's eyes the IBA was "the broadcaster" who was there to be rapped for any shortcomings of its program contractors. This responsibility was not extended to the new ITC. Its mandate was to act as a regulator who was there to merely smack the hands of the sixteen regional franchised broadcasters if they were seen to breach program codes.

There had been strong criticism of how the IBA had dealt with program contractors in the earlier 1981 relicensing round. The possibility that cozy deals had been struck in smoke-filled rooms was no longer acceptable, and a more open selection process was to be followed. Although rough and ready, the most straightforward method appeared to be a sealed tender competition in which the highest sealed cash bids would determine the winners.

The independent television industry was stunned; their licenses to print money hung in the balance. Crocodile tears fell like rain. Had they not provided the British public with hours of "quality" programs at great expense to themselves? Surely the quality of their programs should be weighed in the balance along with their sealed cash bids.

The broadcasting minister, David Mellor, was torn between the industry's cogent lobbying for quality television and his leader's wishes. Prime Minister Thatcher sought to create a streamlined broadcasting industry set free from restrictive labor practices. Could David Mellor steer a middle course?

He won permission to add amendments to the Broadcasting Bill which, he said, would "make it clear that there are indeed requirements for certain high quality programs. That may not amount . . . to public service broadcasting but is not much of a notch below it."

"One notch below," rang out the cry of derision from the opposition benches. The minister had been forced to admit it: going for the highest bids meant that the winners could not afford to keep up the same program quality as before. For the Thatcher administration the once clear aim of an open-bid process was beginning to cloud over. How does one judge a bid that mixes quality with cash? Who can judge the quality of programs before they are made?

As the bill passed through both Houses of Parliament it grew in size. Every week saw the addition of new clauses and new schedules. In the space of 10 months the bill grew in length from less than 160 pages to 289 pages.

An individual franchise application would not be considered unless it could clear two hurdles:

Quality: the proposed service must comply with the code of practice, and

Security: the bidder must be able to maintain the service throughout the 10-year period of the license.

This second clause was soon to eliminate a few applicants who were not thought to be financially sound.

In order to determine the quality threshold, the ITC was to seek examples of the kinds of programs that would be broadcast by the franchisee. They must include the following:

- High-quality programs that include regional programs mainly produced within the region (90 minutes per week of current affairs).
- The offices and studios should be situated within the area. (This was to prevent a recurrence of an earlier abuse in which the Midlands contractor's studios were situated near London—100 miles outside the franchise area!)
- A proper proportion of European origin (65 percent must be originally commissioned for ITV).
- Not less than 25 percent of programs must be created by independent producers.
- Peak-time news (plus lunchtime and early evening bulletins).
- Specific religious (2 hours) and children's (10 hours) programs.
- Programs suitable for the blind and deaf (closed-captioning requirements.)

The bill passed into law, and regional broadcast franchises were advertised. The result was a farce. The ITC turned down some really high bids because it appeared that the high bidders might go broke trying to recover their costs. Subsequent litigation centered on the different predictions of different economic computer models. It emerged that one overbidder had assumed that his advertising sales would increase by 5.5 percent per year over the 10 years, whereas the ITC's own (secret) economic model had assumed a more modest 4 percent.

Four existing program contractors were unsuccessful in their bids. Most successful bidders paid between US$10 million and US$50 million for their 10-year franchises.

However, it was Central Television, the Midlands contractor, that stole the limelight. Its managers played a brilliant hand of poker. They first provided their senior staff with generous financial handcuffs in order to prevent their defection to rival counterbidders. With this security in place they then gambled that no one could then oppose their bid. No one did. They gambled high—and they were right. The ITC could not deny them a further 10-year franchise on the strength of a nominal US$3000 bid. In early 1994 Central Television sold out to Carlton (the London franchisee) at a handsome profit.

The multimillion-dollar bidders are now in trouble. Their advertisers know that finding the bid money has left them strapped for cash. The advertisers are calling the shots and are striking tougher deals for airtime.

THE AUDIENCE

The Broadcasters Audience Research Board (BARB) undertakes joint television audience measurement studies for the BBC and ITV companies. Under a 7-year contract that started in August 1991 two firms, AGB Research and RSMB Television Research, provide data on domestic TV viewing across the United Kingdom.

The system uses a panel of about 4500 private households whose TV sets are provided with special metering. Minute by minute the meter records when the set is switched on and to which channel it is tuned. Individuals use a handset to record when they are viewing the set. Overnight a central computer facility calls up both sets of data over the telephone lines.

Complementary to the quantity measurement is the BARB Television Opinion Panel (TOP). A self-completion booklet is sent to a 3000-viewer national panel from which a weekly Appreciation Index (AI) is determined for all programs with an audience of above 1 million. More detailed questions about viewers' responses to individual, regional, ethnic, and children's programs are also asked.

Until very recently BBC radio and independent radio used different forms of audience measurement. From 1939 until late 1992 the BBC used a very thorough system in which 1000 listeners a day were interviewed in their homes about their previous day's listening. These figures were aggregated to produce monthly statistics.

Since September 1992 there has been a new joint industry nonprofit measurement called the Radio Joint Audience Research (RAJAR). The basis of measurement is a 7-day self-completion diary. A 1000-person sample is generated each week for the national radio audience. These data relate to the five national BBC radio channels and the two national independent radio channels. The national data are supplemented by a sample of 500 diarists twice a year from each BBC and independent local radio station. A sample size of 3000 listeners per week reports on program appreciation on BBC national radio programs.

Aside from audience measurement, there are two statuary bodies that deal with adverse public reaction to broadcast programs.

One is the Broadcasting Complaints Commission (BCC) which was set up by the 1981 Act. Its task is to adjudicate upon two sorts of complaints.

1. Unjust or unfair treatment in sound or television programs that are actually broadcast
2. Unwanted infringements of privacy associated with the obtaining of material that is included in an actual broadcast

Complaints are entertained only from those who are directly affected or from someone considered sufficiently close to the complainant. Frivolous complaints are discounted.

The second is the Broadcasting Standards Council (BSC), which was set up by the 1990 Act. Its task is to monitor the portrayal of sex and violence. It receives complaints from the public and takes surveys of public opinion as to the limits of acceptability. Some share the view that these two bodies should be merged; one complaints body is probably more than sufficient.

TECHNOLOGY

Early TV sets were capable of receiving only BBC1. When independent TV started, some viewers were able to afford a new television set that could receive the new second channel, but most chose to have their old set modified. I remember that, as a schoolboy, I thoroughly enjoyed two summer vacations spent in the workshop behind the local TV store. My task was to convert used television sets to the new channel. Much of the fun came later in climbing across roofs to erect antennas for the new service.

Terrestrial Television In the hilly country of the United Kingdom good ghost-free TV reception was often difficult to achieve. As a matter of broadcast policy, and probably with an eye on the high cost of electricity, transmitter powers have never been as high as in the United States. "Rabbit ears" that came free with the TV set were quickly discarded. Everyone knew that good TV reception needed a big US$35 antenna on the roof. By the late 1950s this started to present a problem. BBC and ITV needed different antennas, each pointing in a slightly different direction toward different transmitting towers.

This issue was solved in the early 1960s by the government's acceptance of a recommendation to switch U.K. television from black and white to color. It was agreed that the United Kingdom would come into line with other European countries and adopt the higher-definition 625-line TV system. To do this all television broadcasting was to be switched from VHF to the previously unused UHF band.

British broadcasting was starting afresh. For the broadcaster the new 625-line picture standard was a bigger challenge than the proposed later switch to color. The new 625-line television system needed its own brand-new 625-line studio equipment, as interworking with the old 405-line standard was too difficult.

Television set manufacturers faced a bigger challenge—625-line television would not arrive overnight; there would be a period of perhaps 10 years in which viewers would require a TV set that could switch between the old and new standards. Dual standard 405/625-line sets were introduced and were a great success, in part because they were no more expensive than before.

In order to pull off this change in technology, in 1964 the BBC introduced a new upscale TV channel—BBC2. At first it was pitched at high-income early adopters who could wallow in the highbrow programming. To watch BBC2 you needed a new 625-line TV set; old-fashioned 405-line sets just would not do. Although BBC2 switched to color in 1967, very few color television sets were sold at first. Widespread consumer interest in color TV remained low until 1969 when BBC1 and ITV joined BBC2 on UHF. All programs were now in 625-line color, and so everyone could buy or rent a new color set with confidence.

However, the change from 405 lines to 625 lines took a long time to complete. It was not until 1984, 20 years after the introduction of 625-line television, that the 405-line service was finally discontinued.

Both the BBC and the ITC are obliged to provide a nationwide system of TV broadcasting in order to meet the requirement of universal access first set out by the Crawford Committee in 1926. A large number of repeater transmitters are needed to reach the last few percent of the population. Repeater stations have been provided for groups of as few as 200 people who live in small, isolated villages. In the face of this virtually universal high-quality coverage, it is hardly surprising that cable television has experienced an uphill struggle in its efforts to establish itself in the United Kingdom.

Satellite Television Although international agreement has allowed satellites to be positioned every 3 degrees or so across the heavens, the regular U.K. home viewer knows of only one—Astra. In addition to the political and marketing factors discussed earlier, which established Luxembourg-based Astra's dominance over its British rival, BSB, it engineered a number of unique technological coups.

In 1985 when the various European ministers agreed on DBS parameters for the entire continent, they bowed to intense lobbying from equipment companies Philips and Thomson and agreed that TV broadcasts must be produced according to an enhanced television technical standard called MAC. MAC had been developed in Europe and was now to be hailed as the savior of the European consumer electronics industry. On no account was MAC technology to be licensed to the Japanese.

Astra engineers knew that MAC pictures were generally sharper than conventional European PAL or American NTSC color pictures, but they knew, too, that most viewers were unlikely to notice much difference. What they did not know was that the new-technology MAC satellite receivers, forced on them by the European directive, had yet to settle down.

Astra's attorneys spotted a loophole in the regulations that enabled Astra to sidestep the MAC specifications. The restriction of five channels per country and the need to use MAC instead of PAL applied only to the 12-gigahertz frequency band that had been specially set aside for DBS. No such restrictions were placed on the adjacent 11-GHz band used every day for "internal" satellite hookups between broadcasters or for special telecasts to cable head ends.

Astra engineers knew full well that technology had moved on since 1979. Satellite receivers were now twice as sensitive as was thought possible 10 years earlier, and so satellites could operate at lower power. This was important because less power per channel could translate directly into revenue dollars. The engineers also knew that it was just as easy to design a satellite with lots of medium-power transponders as one with a few high-power transponders.

While Astra was working on its lower-power transponder concept, BSB, which had applied initially for only three DBS channels, applied for and won the franchise for two additional channels. But the IBA insisted that BSB provide a second "backup" spare five-channel satellite in orbit alongside the first—just in case. What an expense!

Back on earth these technicalities were of little interest to the owners of local TV stores. Their concerns were much more straightforward. They wanted to know whether satellite TV was an easy sell and whether the customer could then carry away the satellite dish in the trunk of a car.

The critical success factor was the size of the receiving dish. In the United Kingdom local environmental planning restrictions require each householder to seek written permission for the installation of a dish larger than 35 inches in diameter. The trade knew that unless dish size could be held to below this critical 35-inch size, bureaucracy would kill satellite television.

The BSB consortium was not at all worried. Its high-power satellite allowed the use of 18-inch dishes that were way below the critical limit. But Astra engineers were also able to show that, even at medium power, their dishes would be no more than 27 inches across.

Astra had another technical trick up its sleeve. The marketeers invented the concept of the "hot" bird, the stacking of two or more satellites next to one another in the same orbital slot so as to make them appear as one. International regulations did not specifically prohibit more than one satellite in the same frequency band in one spot—for every sane engineer knew that this was an impossibility.

But Astra engineers pinned their long-term business case on it. They argued that, unlike the 30-foot-diameter dishes of earlier times that needed to track the satellite with precision, 27-inch satellite dishes would be much more accommodating. Such a small dish would not notice any change in signal strength if the satellite, which was 23,000 miles away in space, was to move over 50 miles or so from its true position in order to make room for another. They were right. With their lower power, small receiving dishes, and hot birds, Astra became the leading satellite programming supplier.

Astra's current competitor, Eutelsat, knows it cannot beat Astra as the hottest bird in the sky and so has adopted a different technical game plan. If it can't beat Astra, it plans to join it. It suggests that viewers fit their Astra satellite dishes with two heads, or LNBs (low noise blocks), rather than one. The technology is simple. Unscrew the old LNB at the end of the supporting arm and fit two LNBs in its place. With a bit of juggling the left-hand LNB still picks up Astra and the right-hand LNB receives an equally good signal from Eutelsat's own bird a few degrees away. No need to motorize the dish. The viewer gets two satellites for just a little more than the price of one.

Satellite technology is moving rapidly, and it is likely that engineering one-upmanship will continue to play a major role in determining who wins the programming race.

EXTERNAL SERVICES

External BBC radio broadcasts are known and listened to throughout the world. When Mikhail Gorbachev was held captive during the failed Soviet coup in 1991, his radio remained tuned to the BBC Russian Service as the most likely source of independent news. Of late, the BBC has tried an external television service, but it has not yet met with as much success.

BBC WORLD SERVICE RADIO

In the early part of this century Britain's colonial empire still spanned the world. Although

Chinese students with a "Thank you BBC" banner in Tiananmen Square, April 1989. (*BBC World Service*)

Marconi had established point-to-point links across the Atlantic in the 1900s, some radio pioneers held a wider dream. Could radio signals be trained on faraway colonial audiences in Australia, Hong Kong, and India?

Shortwave radio was found to be the answer. Unlike medium-wave AM, these signals have a range of not hundreds but thousands of miles. After 5 years of intensive experimentation the BBC started its Empire Service that first reached faraway colonial audiences in December 19, 1932. It was such a success that the BBC formed an independent empire news desk 2 years later.

In 1937 Benito Mussolini's fascist Italian army invaded Ethiopia and set up a shortwave station to broadcast anti-British propaganda in Arabic to the Arab world. No longer could the Empire Service be just a private BBC trial of long-range broadcasting; the U.K. Foreign Office was suddenly eager to pay for counter-propaganda transmissions.

The BBC was in a fix. It badly needed the extra money but was not prepared to sacrifice its charter's guarantee of independence from the government. After much heart searching Lord Reith took the money on the proviso that BBC editorial independence was to be preserved, even to the point of broadcasting news that the Foreign Office thought was not in the U.K. interest.

Since that day the Empire Service, now the BBC World Service, is entirely funded by a grant-in-aid from the U.K. government. The current forty-one-language service is provided at a cost of US$250 million per year. Apart from its flagship 24-hour English service, the most extensive foreign-language service is in Arabic. Regarded by its audience as an Arab network in its own right, it is probably the single most influential broadcasting voice in the Arab world.

The BBC World Service is a good example of British understatement. It is on the air for fewer hours, broadcasts in fewer languages, and has fewer transmitters than its main competitors, yet its audience reach is astonishing. Its regular listenership, excluding China where no reliable figures are available, exceeds 120 million.

BBC World Service Television In the last 10 years both the BBC and the IBA have found out the hard way that English-language satellite broadcasting is a tough market. When the BBC pulled out of its two-channel DBS experiment in 1985, the frequencies were picked up by the IBA. Within a few years their chosen franchisee, BSB, had gone broke as well. Even Rupert Murdoch's Sky channels on the Astra satellite have yet to show a profit.

By 1988 the BBC wanted to try again with a scheme to broadcast its domestic television service into Europe. The BBC external broadcasting service already received a government grant to support shortwave radio broadcasts, and so it asked the U.K. treasury to help underwrite its new satellite television venture. The answer was a very definite NO. Any further satellite broadcasting experiments were to be met from the BBC's own funds—no government money would be forthcoming.

In 1988 the BBC leased a transponder on a low-power Intelsat satellite. The new BBC Europe TV service proved popular, especially for expatriate British who were working or had retired abroad. It was also picked up by cable head ends and widely distributed throughout many Western European countries.

In order to exact payment for the service it was necessary to encrypt the picture. Individual decoders were needed in order to restore the distorted picture to normal. Apart from the US$400 purchase price of the decoder there was a further charge of US$100 a year, payable via the manufacturer to the BBC, for a descrambling "dongle" that plugged into the back of the set-top decoder. The running cost was about the same as for a U.K. TV license.

Then disaster struck. A rival electronics company designed a pirate decoder that did not need to use a dongle and whose lower selling price did not include a contribution to BBC funds. The BBC took the company to court but lost because it was judged that the rival's electronic decoder circuits used a totally different method of descrambling than that used in the approved decoder.

It was only at a later hearing that the U.K. Court of Appeal decided that the supplying of decoders that had not been authorized by the broadcaster or sender of encrypted transmissions was contrary to Section 298 of the recent U.K. Copyright Designs and Patents Act 1988. During this process of litigation very few approved decoders were sold, production came to a halt, and the approved manufacturer eventually went broke.

The growing popularity of the rival Astra service brought another problem. The BBC was no longer able to simulcast its BBC1 service across Europe because program producers had become increasingly aware of their additional satellite "rights." Movies and sports gradually disappeared from the schedule and were replaced with reruns of stale documentaries. Many expat Brits complained bitterly that BBC TV Europe had changed out of all recognition from the simulcast BBC1 domestic service to which they had subscribed a few years before.

In 1991 the BBC changed tack. From the ashes of BBC TV Europe it formed BBC World Service Television (WSTV). Programming was no longer aimed at Brits working and living abroad but was directed at the indigenous populations of Asia, Europe, and Africa. Even this has been hard going. Although World Service Television was conceived as one brand, it has had to develop a three-channel service with three completely separate transmission controls.

In East Asia viewers receive BBC WSTV as part of a five-channel package from STAR, the satellite TV free-to-air commercial service uplinked from Hong Kong. The WSTV Asian service includes slots for advertisements which are inserted by STAR TV. At first many viewers found the TV programs too Anglocentric, and so the WSTV Asian service was refocused more closely on Asian news and Asian viewpoints. In April 1994, following the takeover of STAR television by Rupert Murdoch's News International Corporation, WSTV lost access to the STAR satellite's China beam. A month later WSTV announced a deal with the Pearson media group to recommence transmissions on an adjacent satellite. The European WSTV service is scrambled and carries no advertising. Each European subscriber must purchase an annual US$120 smart card which plugs into the set-top MAC decoder. The May 1994 WSTV-Pearson deal includes a second news channel alongside the more general entertainment carried on the current WSTV European service. WSTV is also available over Africa but requires a much larger dish to receive the signals.

IMPORTANCE TO THE WORLD COMMUNITY

"Our policy is so ill defined, the disorganization so great, there are so many changes of plan. The organization is so overstaffed that numbers of people have almost literally nothing to do." So runs the June 21, 1942, diary entry of the head of the Indian section of the BBC Empire Service. He was later to become better known as George Orwell, the author of *Animal Farm* and *Nineteen Eighty Four*.

Despite its many failings, the BBC has shown how broadcast programs can transcend the chaos that bedevils any large organization. The secret is simple—it has achieved a critical creative mass that acts as a magnet to all those with creative talent. It is this inflow of new blood that keeps the organization young and the programs so refreshingly different.

With a little legislative encouragement this approach has also blossomed in the independent sector. Independent Television News (ITN), which is owned by a number of ITV companies, produces news programming that is every bit as good as that of the BBC.

BBC set the standard and organizational pattern for broadcasting in many parts of the world. When radio was reaching its ascendancy and TV was being started, "the sun never set on the British Empire." Its colonies were everywhere, and its BBC advisors went to these colonies to help them establish broadcasting services. The British influence can still be seen and heard in the underlying public service philosophy that permeates many of these systems.

MAJOR ISSUES

The major issues concerning British electronic media are bound, in some way, to revolve around the BBC, the independent structure, and/or satellite broadcasting. For the moment, the independent scene has gone quiet. New franchises have been awarded; people are licking their wounds and getting down to work. However, satellite broadcasting regulation and the new BBC charter are hot topics.

Satellite Broadcasting For sheer legislative nonsense it is difficult to beat the 1990 Act's attempt to regulate satellite broadcasting. The Act created three categories:

Domestic: The domestic satellite broadcaster who is allocated channels in the 12-gigahertz DBS band must obey the same codes of practice as a terrestrial broadcaster. In the United Kingdom this species is now extinct; BSB went bust and its two satellites were sold off.

Nondomestic: The nondomestic satellite broadcaster who uses the adjacent 11-gigahertz band need only meet the much lighter regime that applies to minor market cable channels. Rupert Murdoch's Sky channels have few conditions imposed upon them.

Foreign: A foreign satellite service is defined as one uplinked from outside the United Kingdom. It may be proscribed if it repeatedly offends against good taste or decency or incites to crime or disorder or offends public feeling.

The ITV companies have taken issue with the U.K. government over the definition of "nondomestic." They claim it is unfair for the 1990 Act to require them to include high-quality programs and to commission 65 percent of their output, whereas their competitor, Murdoch's BSkyB nondomestic satellite service, has no such restrictions placed upon it.

Renewing the BBC Charter At first sight the regulation of U.K. broadcasting must look like a parliamentary game of leapfrog. First, the independent sector regulations are updated with a new Broadcasting Act, and then the BBC is brought up to date by changes in its Royal Charter.

This time around it has been different. As the BBC watched the damage inflicted on independent television by the 1990 Act, it realized that it had better put its own house in order—for the changes that Parliament may impose on its Charter in 1996 could easily kill not cure.

The opening shots of the renewal debate have already been fired. In November 1992 the government issued a formal consultative document, called a Green Paper, which sets out options for the future of the BBC. Although the Green Paper lists many questions, most of them are no more than rhetorical. The fundamental issue is accountability. What does and should the public get for its US$125 license fee a year? If the license fee is to be frozen, should some BBC services be sold off to the private sector so as to contain the running costs?

In reply the BBC has issued its own glossy document entitled "Extending Choice." It is a disappointing read, full of committee-generated corporate-speak that leads to few conclusions. However, it does confirm senior management's growing awareness that misspending its income will draw heavy flak from politicians.

As part of the drive for greater efficiency, the BBC has recently introduced a new and controversial accountancy system called Producer Choice. The theory is simple. Each program maker must choose between the BBC's internal production resources or those of independent companies. It is claimed that Producer Choice will reduce tiers of administration, cut overhead, utilize capacity more fully, increase investment in programs, and demonstrate value for license payers' money. In the process many staff have been switched from permanent staff posts to short-term contracts and there is much uncertainty in the air.

Is the BBC in crisis? A student of Chinese would probably agree. The Chinese translate the English meaning of "crisis" into two words "danger" and "opportunity." The BBC will need to draw on all its creative skills if it is to avoid the first and take advantage of the second.

SELECTED BIBLIOGRAPHY

Amdur, Meridith. "Astra Out Front in Europe's Satellite Race," *Broadcasting*, 7 June 1993, p. 22.

Cain, J. *The BBC: 70 Years of Broadcasting*. London: BBC Information, 1992.

Chapman, R. *Selling the Sixties, the Pirates, and Pop Music Radio*. London: Routledge, 1992.

Chippindale, P., and S. Franks. *Dished! The Rise and Fall of British Satellite Broadcasting*. New York: Simon and Schuster, 1991.

Dawtrey, Adam. "Auction Action Shakes Up U.K. TV," *Variety*, 17 October 1991, p. 1.

Evans, Brian. *Understanding Digital Television, the Route to HDTV*. Piscataway, NJ: IEEE Press, 1994.

Groves, Don. "Sky's the Limit for BSKYB," *Variety*, 20 October 1992, p. 18.

Hayward, A. *Street Cred: A Spotlight on Coronation Street's Rising Stars*. London: Boxtree, 1992.

Independent Television Commission. *The ITC Programme Code*. London: ITC, 1991.

Lewis, P. *A Right Royal Do: The Making of an Outside Broadcast*. London: BBC Television Training, 1991.

Lynch, T. *The Bill: The Inside Story of British Television's Most Successful Police Series*. London: Boxtree, 1991.

MacDonald, Barrie. *Broadcasting in the United Kingdom*. Dorset, England: Mansell, 1993.

McCalle, D. L. *Monty Python: A Chronological Listing of the Troupe's Creative Output*. London: McFarland, 1991.

Rolson, B., ed. *The Media and Northern Ireland: Covering the Troubles*. London: Macmillan, 1991.

Seymour-Ure, C. *The British Press and Broadcasting since 1945*. London: Blackwell, 1991.

Walker, A. *A Skyful of Freedom: 60 Years of the BBC World Service*. London: Broadside, 1992.

Wyver, John. "The English Channel 4," *American Film*, July–August 1986, pp. 46–49.

CHAPTER 5

Germany

Wolfgang Hastert

Wolfgang Hastert has recently finished shooting a feature-length docudrama on the U.S. painter Edward Hopper—a coproduction of German television's ZDF and ARTE (European Culture Channel). He has worked as camera assistant for many German TV programs and as art director and director of commercials. He was educated at the University of Darmstadt where he received an M.A. in photography and communications. In 1985, as a Fulbright scholar, he studied fine arts—photography, film, and television—at California State University, Fullerton.

Wolfgang Hastert.

STATISTICS

Geographic Area: 137,838 square miles
Capital: Berlin
Population: 79,548,000
Religions: Protestant, Roman Catholic
Language: German
Type of Government: Federal Republic headed by a chancellor
Gross Domestic Product: $1157 billion
Literacy: 99 percent

GENERAL CHARACTERISTICS

Germany has not exactly made a name for itself with its entertainment culture. Rather it is looked at as a country of great philosophers and literary people. This fact explains why the country has been somewhat reluctant to support the growth of electronic media.

At the outset of the twentieth century, a highly regarded cinema culture existed in Germany that could have led to a blossoming in entertainment, but many Jewish artists were killed in the 1930s and 1940s by Adolf Hitler's terror regime or fled the country when the dictatorship was about to be established. This resulted in an exodus of German talent. Both German cinema and radio served as propaganda tools for the Third Reich. After the war, the country was split into two separate entities: in West Germany electronic media and cinema tried to find an identification, and in East Germany they were used as a propaganda tool by the socialist dictatorship in the former German Democratic Republic (GDR).

The now reunited Germany has witnessed two separate histories—even in the area of electronic media. Currently, the electronic media in Germany are characterized by a competition between the public broadcasting structure and privately owned electronic media. The strong influence exercised by other media systems—above all that of the United States—also plays an important role.

Germany's position in the world economy is behind only those of the United States and Japan. Even though the costs imposed on Germany by the reunification of West and East Germany create a difficult situation for the national economy, there is no doubt about the importance of the German economy on a global level. The overall wealth in Germany and its political system of democracy, as well as its economic system of capitalism, create conditions similar to those in the United States for development of the electronic media. The major differences are accounted for by Germany's geographic situation. Germany is not isolated; it is situated in the center of European politics and economics.

Overall Wealth Like most people in the United States, many Germans are well off. Before the fall of the Berlin Wall and the reunification of the two German nations in 1989, West Germany's economic status was excellent. The situation has changed considerably since reunification because the costs involved in reconstruction of the former GDR have imposed an as yet undetermined burden on the German taxpayer. Mass unemployment, the collapse of industries in the east, and the loss of Eastern European markets have caused economic chaos. Many citizens in the west and a large majority of the people in the east are dissatisfied with their social situation.

Leisure Time Despite the recession and economic slump at the beginning of the 1990s, German employees are still comparatively well off: they enjoy a 37.5-hour workweek; their per hour wage ranks among the highest worldwide; and no other country offers more holidays.

Thus the German nation has a lot of leisure time to fill. And whenever the typical German citizen does not spend vacation time on some remote continent but instead stays at home, watching television is his or her favorite leisure-time activity. Almost every household has at least one TV set, and almost 60 percent own two. The percentage of households subscribing to cable is rapidly increasing. In addition, almost half the households own a VCR. As a result, Germany has been inundated by video rental outlets. Many small villages that do not even have a gas station have several video rental establishments. The rental rate is between DM 2 and DM 5 (about $1 to $3) per video per day, which is about 20 to 30 percent of the price of a cinema ticket.

Telephones are installed in almost every West German household. In the east the telephone supply is still catching up. It is this lack of voice communication that aggravates reconstruction of the East German economy, and this is why East Germany is awash in cellular telephones—a new technology that is not tied to the outdated, ineffectual phone system of the former GDR.

Ever since privately owned television stations were allowed to go into service, Germany has been witnessing yet another revolution. Formerly the TV audience could receive only two to four German channels, but for 3 years now people have been able to tune in to as many as thirty channels. This has caused a dramatic change in the behavior of the German television audience. Germans, who previously watched very little TV, now watch on the average about 4 hours a day.

Every German who owns a television set also has at least two radios and one stereo system. People listen to the radio in just about any situation. Depending on geographic location, dozens of radio stations can be tuned in.

The transmission technology for radio and television is provided by the Deutsche Bundespost/Telecom (Ministry of Posts and Telecommunications, often referred to as the German Post). It has, however, no influence on the actual programming of radio and television broadcasting.

In addition to over-the-air radio and TV, Germans can choose between cable and satellite TV. For example, in places such as the Alpine areas, where it is impossible to set up cable, people increase their programming options by installing satellite dishes.

With more programs to tune in to, the German people have obtained more electronic gadgets for their households. They are equipped with the latest in remote controls, VCRs, and stereo systems. Other hardware components such as camcorders and an ever-increasing number of personal computers inevitably complete the picture.

Germany and Europe Germany is located in the center of western Europe. Almost 80 million people live in an area encompassing half the size of California, a fact that makes Germany the European state with the highest population density. It is surrounded by many different nations. France and the Benelux states, Denmark, Poland, the Czech Republic, Austria, and Switzerland are Germany's neighbors. The capitals of these countries can be reached within a few hours. This creates an active exchange as far as economics and culture are concerned. The geographic proximity of these European neighbors also causes radio and television programs to mix. People who live close to the borders have always been able to tune in to the TV and radio programs of neighboring countries.

This proximity created a unique situation when Germany was still divided into two separate states. Many people in East Germany who lived close to the west were able to tune in to West German programs. Thus they were furnished with information about the "golden west," and West German television developed into a propaganda tool for the democratic world. Unfortunately, a distorted picture about the west was conveyed to East German citizens. This fact manifests itself in the integration difficulties now experienced by the former East Germans.

Democracy's Influence The electronic media have been highly influenced by Germany's political anchorage in democracy. For fear of a second Reichsrundfunk—the propaganda station of the Nazis—the Deutsche Rundfunkgesellschaft (German Broadcasting Society) was founded after World War II. It emphasized regional radio areas rather than a centralized one. (Later these regional areas were also used for broadcast television.) This decentralized organization was in line with what the Allied forces had done with Germany itself by dividing the country into so-called *Länder* (states). It is this political division that has imprinted the German electronic media with a particular national-local character.

The democratic element is evident in the programming content as well. The electronic media in Germany have a very distinct function in that they are asked to supply the population with information, participate in the formation of political opinion, and exercise control and criticism. In accordance with the *Rundfunkgesetz* (broadcast law), wireless broadcasting is to be controlled neither by the state nor by any particular interest group or economic society; instead, it is expected to function as a public institution providing for the welfare of the people. Unfortunately, this contradicts the audience's desire for pure entertainment and also clashes with the profit-oriented operation of privately owned stations.

Influence of Capitalism German broadcasting is more strictly regulated than, for example, broadcasting in the United States. Even though all the principles of a free-market economy are applied, financing of the radio and television stations under German public law is accomplished by a combination of selling commercials and collecting fees from people with sets. These public stations compete with privately owned stations operated totally on the principles of a free-market economy in that they sell advertising but do not receive government money collected from fees. Private stations are, however, required to offer information programming.

The two systems—public and private—are in competition with each other. Recently there has been an exodus of advertising money from public stations to privately owned stations. Thus, to a greater and greater extent, there is only one decisive element for both systems: audience size.

HISTORY

"Hello! Hello! This is radio Berlin speaking to you from the VOX studio on 400-meter airwaves. Ladies and gentlemen, we are proud to inform you that German entertainment radio starts its wireless telephone-based service today. . . ."

This was the first announcement of the first program on German radio. It occurred on October 29, 1923. However, wireless systems had already been in existence for many years. During World War I (1914–1918), armies used this technology, and soon after the war a radio station near Berlin broadcast the opera *Madame Butterfly*. Amateurs over 1000 miles away were able to receive this program.

Nobody knew exactly what to do with this toy called "radio," let alone how to organize it. This changed when Hans Bredow, the founding father of German radio, suggested using "airwaves to provide mass entertainment and education." Bredow, an engineer who at the time was director of the German Post, was to put his ideas into practice.

Thus in 1923 the first radio announcement was aired. It was broadcast from an office in the VOX House in Berlin and was transmitted via a 250-watt transmitter. The organizational structure of the radio system had previously been devised by the Ministry of Posts and the Ministry of the Interior. The system was not based on laws that had been enacted by Parliament but on guidelines drawn up by the government.

In 1923 German inflation had just about reached its peak. The price for a receiver was DM 3 billion. Nevertheless, within a few weeks of their availability, receivers were registered by 467 listeners, and 1 year later there were 100,000 registered listeners, each of whom paid a monthly fee of DM 2.

At that time, the government would have preferred to cover all of Germany with just one central radio station. This plan failed because in the 1920s it was technically impractical to transmit one signal to all the little towns and valleys. As a consequence, Germany was divided into nine broadcast regions. To a large extent, these nine regions still exist today, although the reason has more to do with preventing political centralization than with technical difficulties.

As early as 1926 there were 1 million registered listeners. To tune into the various stations or to "speed through the ether" developed into a fascinating evening pastime. Program designers looked at radio as a mediator and also as an initiator in the arts, science, education, and the good and beautiful things in life. It was even regarded as an official assistant of the state.

State Control It was the government, however, that created the guidelines to an ever-increasing extent. It held the majority interest in broadcast stations and exercised control, primarily through committees. As a result, individual stations were forced to air central news programs prepared by the Drahtloser Dienst AG (a wireless service agency). This organization included the government, the political parties in power, and newspaper publishers.

In the late 1920s Germany experienced the last critical days of the Weimar Republic (the government structure between World War I and the rise of Hitler's Nazi party). The leaders of the republic warned about the dangers from the political left. The economic situation was poor. Radio was not an information carrier during the beginning of the crisis of parliamentary democracy. Information and propaganda were conveyed to the people through newspapers. This, however, changed abruptly with the boom in radio sales. The government realized the possibility of using radio as a means of influencing the masses and made extensive use of it by either arranging or preventing certain programming. In effect, programming was subject to censorship.

During the Weimar Republic, the government was able to control what was on radio because the German Post, as a state-operated body, assumed responsibility for the technical infrastructure, and as a result all stations grew dependent on this executive power for technical knowledge. In addition, the German Post set up control councils to supervise each station, one responsible for political programming and the other for cultural programming.

Radio as Hitler's Propaganda Weapon
When Adolf Hitler and his National Socialist (Nazi) party began to create a dictatorship in the early 1930s, radio reported the events as rapidly as newspapers—and Hitler was quick to use the powers of radio. The 4.4 million radio owners in 1933 meant more potential listeners were available than readers of the Hugenberg Press—the most powerful publisher in Germany at the time.

Things moved quickly. On March 11, 1933, the cabinet, controlled by the National Socialists, decided to establish a Ministry for Public Information and Propaganda and place radio under its control. Joseph Goebbels was appointed the minister of this new authority and immediately commissioned the state police (SS) to arrest and deport the members of the radio management to concentration camps. A large majority of the employees, mainly editors, Social Democrats, Communists, and Jews were suspended from their jobs. All stations were "made even" and put under the control of the Ministry of Propaganda. Within a few weeks German radio was turned into an organization of the National Socialist party. "The German radio belongs to us and nobody else! . . . It has to submit itself to the goals of the government of the national revolution!" declared Joseph Goebbels in March 1933 in front of the radio superintendents.

From that moment on all information programming was subject to restrictions and directives. Entertainment, however, still played an important role, provided it was not "destructive." Jewish composers and their compositions were immediately forbidden. Jazz also disappeared from the airwaves. What was aired eventually had to comply with the Nazi "view of man and society." National Socialist rituals such as rallies and parades were aired. The statements and reports aired on radio were not supposed to inform but to extol. This applied, above all, to Hitler's speeches. To make sure that everybody could receive the programming, a simple radio receiver called a *Volksempfänger* was introduced. The goal was to enable every citizen to listen to the *Reichssender* (official radio station). One of the jokes of the year was

"What's the difference between a *Volksempfänger* and a good radio?: All you will hear on the *Volksempfänger* is Germany above everything but on the radio you will hear everything about Germany."

According to the *Reichssender*, "The German nation is not only the topic and goal but also the sole breeding ground of the programming design." Within a very short period, radio developed into a propaganda tool of the government through which, via short- or long-range waves, every German, even those abroad, could be reached. Thus the regime started to fear foreign stations capable of entering the German realm. Tuning into foreign stations was forbidden and could be punished by death. During the war, radio programming was basically national, with a standardized program. Regional stations were not allowed to contribute anything more than a few household tips and information pertaining to regional agriculture.

As Hitler's power began to crumble, he intensified his control over radio. After Germany's defeat in Russia, popular music was entirely banned from the radio. Eventually, by the end of the war, air combat information and warnings of upcoming air raids became the most important news apart from "stick-it-out" slogans. The end of the Third Reich came fast. The last broadcasting station to survive, which was located on the coast in northern Germany, announced the capitulation on May 7, 1945.

After the War The Germans who set out to reconstruct their country after the war thought radio should be the responsibility of the state, despite their unfortunate experience under the Nazi dictatorship. However, the victorious powers of the West (England, France, and the United States) had a different idea in mind. They withdrew control over broadcasting from the German Post. In 1947 General Lucius Clay, in charge of the U.S. military government, gave the order "that the influence exerted by such media as press and radio—which contribute to the formation of the public opinion—should be evenly distributed and be defunct of any government interference."

The Allied powers established three independent entities to supervise radio: the Broadcasting Council, the Administrative Council, and the Director General. They also helped set up the Arbeitsgemeinschaft der Rundfunkanstalten Deutschlands (ARD, which means roughly Association of Public Broadcasting Corporations in West Germany) that was to serve as an umbrella organization for all broadcasting. The ARD was very decentralized in that the radio stations operated within regions of the country but did not broadcast nationally.

After the Allies left in 1955, the German government and political parties started to regain influence in broadcasting. The regional aspects of the government and the sovereignty of the *Länder* were able to create a natural balance between national and regional control. In the zone occupied by the Soviet forces a totalitarian system was established in place of the old one, and radio was put under state administration, just as it was in the Soviet Union.

The Advent of Television Even before the war, attempts at transmitting pictures had been tried. In 1934 the first test program was put together. One year later Germany was the first country in the world to broadcast a television program on a regular basis. The citizens of Berlin could watch television three evenings a week in public TV rooms. The Olympic games of 1936 were also broadcast on TV. Although the new technology seemed very promising, it was not something the National Socialists were particularly interested in, and television was not given much attention until after the war.

The development of television after the war continued under ARD, the regional organization that was formed under Allied control. On Christmas 1950 the television service of the Federal Republic of Germany officially went into operation. It took TV much longer than radio to develop. It was not until 1955 that the 100,000th television viewer was registered. A real boom did not take place until 1967 when color TV was introduced.

Centralism within the organization of ARD had been carefully avoided. But, for pure financial reasons, not every institution of the *Länder* could produce its own TV programs. Thus a contract was hammered out according to which each area of the country was to contribute a fixed percentage of television programming which would then be shared with the other *Länder*. In essence, ARD became a network controlled and contributed to by the states.

In 1959 Chancellor Konrad Adenauer played a lone hand, something that was not to be without consequences. Adenauer founded the Deutschland Fernseh GmbH (German Television, Inc.), a private company dependent on the federal government. Other private companies immediately appeared on the scene, indicating that the central government was trying to become stronger. At the beginning of 1961 the Federal Constitutional Court, however, decided that these companies were unconstitutional. It was reiterated that radio broadcasting was to be related to the *Länder*. A strict division of responsibilities was set up in which the Bund (the German national legislative body) was responsible for broadcasting technology as part of public telecommunications and the *Länder* were endowed with programming power.

In a reaction to this decision by the Federal Constitutional Court, the minister presidents of the *Länder* turned "Adenauer TV" into the Zweite Deutsche Fernsehen (ZDF), a second network, which is organized as an institution under public law. Contrary to ARD, ZDF is managed centrally. ZDF started its broadcasting service in April 1963. In an attempt to counter this competition, the institutions of the *Länder* of ARD introduced their regional channels, the so-called 3rd Programs.

Ever since that time both programming institutions have been politically biased. The institutions of ARD vacillate between Social Democratic and Conservative tendencies depending on the setup of the parliaments in the *Länder*. ZDF, however, which started as a Christian Democratic Union party broadcasting station in the Adenauer era, still has a conservative political character.

Developments in East Germany Broadcasting in the German Democratic Republic was centralized when the Official Radio Broadcasting Committee was founded in 1952. At this time, radio and television were separated into two different government institutions. Radio broadcasting consisted of five program services that could be received anywhere in the country and twelve regional program services that could be received in the various districts. As television developed, it consisted of two national TV program services that did not include any regional programming. Radio and television programs produced in East Berlin, which were characterized by only a small amount of regionalism, were to present propaganda for the "socialism" of the GDR and serve as showcases for it.

The competition between the governments of East and West Germany carried over into radio and television. Time and again the media officials of East Germany tried to win this competition by means of ideological education and powerful arguments. The entire audience, however, judged this rivalry by a different criterion: Which of the two systems offers better entertainment? In almost all cases viewers preferred West German broadcasting.

Revolution and Media Switch In October 1989 the political situation in the former GDR came to a head. As in other Eastern European states, a large part of the population started to protest against the state. On October 9, 1989, for the first time in the history of East Germany, an invitation by the government of the GDR to open up a dialogue with the people was aired. This was followed by many programming changes. Protest actions by the population, which had been recorded using camcorders, were broadcast by radio and TV. The government lost control over its electronic media.

Events followed in quick succession. When the Berlin Wall was torn down, the political leaders of the GDR gave in to the pressures exerted from within. Erich Honecker, head of state of the GDR, who only a few weeks earlier had celebrated the fortieth anniversary of the GDR with an unparalleled media spectacle, gave up and took refuge in the USSR. After that, the East German state dissolved. On March 18, 1990, the first free elections of the *Volkskammer* (people's chamber) were held in which, for the first time, the German political parties participated. On October 3, 1990, the GDR was officially reunited with the Federal Republic of Germany.

After reunification, the broadcasting stations of the former GDR were integrated into the ARD system. Following the West German example, *Landesrundfunkanstalten* (broadcasting stations of the *Länder*) were created. ZDF started to establish regional studios. The process of integrating the East German broadcasting stations into the West German stations turned out to be a tedious one. Poor technical conditions, financial difficulties, reductions in personnel, and problems with the espionage department of the former GDR (Stasi) made reorganization difficult.

Commercial Broadcasting Television in Germany It all started with cable television. In May 1978 the heads of the states of West Germany agreed to launch four cable TV pilot projects. Everybody knew that cable television could improve the quality of television reception, and initiation of the pilot projects seemed to open up the opportunity for program experimentation. For example, privately operated programming suppliers were asked to supply material for the cable projects.

The starting point for the cable systems was large communal antennas from which signals were distributed directly to households. However, these cable projects, which initially were started as experiments, soon failed. The problem seemed to be a combination of cost and a lack of clear guidelines. The German Post was to collect fees from people who wanted to subscribe to cable TV. However, what it did was charter independent companies across Germany to install cable in private homes and collect the monthly fees. Consumers did not like the tactics of some of these companies. For example, one company charged a monthly fee of about $15 and forced customers to sign a 12-year contract. Viewers were already paying $10 a month for public services (ARD, ZDF, and the regional programs) and were confused and upset about the added fees. As a result, very few of them subscribed.

The states, in an attempt to solve the cable problems, amended their broadcasting laws in such a way that private programming suppliers, who were supposed to deal with the experimental cable pilots, were able to begin operating in other ways. For example, they started commercial television stations that mainly adopted the U.S. private enterprise system. Depending on revenues from advertising, these commercial TV stations offer mostly inexpensive American movies or copy the format of U.S. game shows and soaps.

Today these suppliers transmit their programs conventionally by station antennas; they distribute them via satellites to homes with satellite receiving dishes or route them to cable systems (which by now have recovered from their shaky beginnings and have been enhanced considerably).

During the period when commercial TV was floundering and fluctuating, commercial radio also started. However, it was not subject to as many problems. Commercial radio stations, like public stations, are local in nature. The addition of commercial stations gave people more

CHAPTER 5: GERMANY   **131**

BOX 5-1

Why *Sportschau (Sports News)* Had to Go

The manner in which ARD was forced to give up *Sportschau* is an example of how public television often loses in the battle between public and commercial broadcasting. It demonstrates how cruel the evolution of TV can be.

For decades, every Saturday evening at 6 P.M., Germans switched on TV to watch the most famous German sports broadcast dedicated almost exclusively to one thing: soccer, the number one national sport. It was always a very popular program on ARD, and apart from having high audience numbers, it also guaranteed a large income from commercials shown before and after the program.

However, this model program fell victim to the trend toward increased commercialization. While in the beginning it was mainly soccer clubs which, by raising rights fees, forced television stations to pay more and more, this competition for transmission rights increased even more sharply when private interests saw in the soccer program an ideal environment for their audience members.

After a pitched battle for the TV rights, the program was finally sold to Sat.1, a relatively new satellite service. According to the contract, public broadcasting corporations can supply only short reports about soccer in accordance with their duty to supply information. And they cannot air even this material at the 6 P.M. time when Sat.1 broadcasts its soccer sports program, now called *RAN*. The overall result is that public television has lost access to one of its best programs.

Sportschau is not the only casualty of the public-private battle. TV hosts switch to better-paying jobs with private stations; entire programs switch to different stations with commercial clients in tow. But *Sportschau*, because of its popularity, is the most glaring example of German TV on the move.

---

options but did not drastically change the operating structure.

Germany fulfills all the prerequisites needed to grow rapidly into a country with many television program options. Currently, a German household can, if it wishes, receive about twenty services. These include public stations, private commercial stations, and satellite programming, some of which come from other countries.

Thus the increase in programming delivery systems not only opened up a wide field in the area of commercial television but also created an arena in which public broadcasting corporations from the past and newer privately owned services compete for income from commercials.

ORGANIZATION AND FINANCING

The overall organization of the public broadcasting system is based almost entirely on decisions made by the Allied forces in the zones of occupation immediately after World War II.

As previously stated, any influence by the central government on radio broadcasting was to be prevented. This was the primary goal of the victorious powers as they oversaw the establishment of ARD. This principle of organization was also enforced through laws and government contracts when more broadcasting entities (ZDF, 3rd Programs, commercial stations) were established at a later time. Thus all the broadcasting stations in the Federal Republic are legally and economically independent and have sovereignty over their programming content.

There are, however, slight differences in organization among the three public broadcasting systems—ARD, ZDF, and 3rd Programs—and there are some rather extreme differences among the commercial systems.

ARD Altogether, fourteen broadcasting corporations are joined together in ARD. Three of these are new corporations from East Germany that are still in the process of being incorporated

FIGURE 5–1
ARD's nine regions in what used be West Germany. (1) Bayerischer Rundfunk; (2) Hessischer Rundfunk; (3) Norddeutscher Rundfunk; (4) Radio Bremen; (5) Saarländischer Rundfunk; (6) Sender Freies Berlin; (7) Süddeutscher Rundfunk; (8) Südwestfunk; and (9) Westdeutscher Rundfunk.

into the system. Two are not really part of the main national broadcasting service. They are Deutsche Welle and Deutschlandfund, Germany's external services. The remaining nine corporations are regional broadcasting organizations whose service areas for both radio and TV roughly correspond to the individual federal states of West Germany. Some of the smaller states have combined to form joint broadcasting corporations.

For television, each regional station contributes a percentage of programming based on the number of license holders in its state. Therefore, Westdeutscher Rundfunk contributes about 25 percent of the programming, whereas Saarländischer Rundfunk contributes only about 3 percent. The programs contributed by each state are broadcast throughout the nation. Radio stations are purely local; ARD does not operate a national radio network.

ARD consists of three independent entities: the broadcasting council, the administrative council, and the director general. The broadcasting council represents the public in broadcasting. It is composed of a representative of the state government and five members of the regional parliament elected by proportional representation. The other members are chosen by specific groups and organizations (churches, schools, universities, cultural communities). Every other year one-third of the council members are replaced by drawing lots. The members of the council are not representatives of any political party, and they may not be employed by the broadcast station. The council adopts a constitution, advises the director general on fundamental editorial questions, ensures adherence to editorial principles, has the final say about complaints, and approves the budget, annual account, and annual report.

The administrative council consists of six members, each appointed for 4 years. Four of the members are chosen by the broadcasting council, and two by the station's staff. Members must not be employed by the station and cannot be members of the broadcasting council. Their decisions are made at their own discretion, and they are not subject to instructions from any other group. Members audit the budget estimate, the annual account, and the annual report. The council draws up the director general's employment contract and controls the corporation's conduct of business.

The director general is the chief executive and administrative officer of the corporation and is in charge of its program. He or she is appointed by the broadcasting council for a term of between 5 and 9 years. The director general cannot appoint or dismiss any of the top managers of the station without the administrative council's approval. Such approval is also needed for legal acts of major financial scope.

ZDF ZDF (Second German Television) is also regionally organized in that it was established by a treaty signed by the minister presidents of the federal states. However, it is more centrally organized in that most of the programming emanates from its headquarters in Mainz, and, unlike ARD, it programs only television, not radio.

ZDF is organized around three bodies—the television council, the administrative council, and the director general. The members of the councils are selected in a slightly different way than ARD council members, but the three groups have roughly the same duties as the three ARD entities.

ZDF was set up so that Germans could choose between two distinctly different television programs. For this reason ZDF and ARD have ongoing coordination agreements concerning their program schedules. They must program in such a way that their offerings complement each other. In other words, if ARD is programming sports on Saturday afternoon, ZDF cannot air a sports program; it must show drama, a children's program, or some other genre.

3rd Programs The 3rd Programs function under ARD. They are, in essence, regional radio and television services whose programs can be heard only in a particular region. They were set up by ARD after ZDF was established as a means of competing with ZDF programming. In reality, they have become a third choice for the German people. ARD tends to program them with the less attractive educational and public service information so that it can use its national programming service for more popular programming and still fulfill its obligations in regard to service to the public.

Commercial Programming Services Commercial stations, cable systems, and satellites are all relatively new in Germany and have not settled down into any uniform organizational pattern. The following descriptions of some of the main commercial players give some idea of how much the German electronic media have changed in the past few years.

Sat.1 and RTL Plus are two of the most successful German satellite companies. Both compete directly with the public broadcasting stations. RTL's main shareholders are Radio Luxembourg and the Bertelsmann publishing house (one of the largest mass media trusts in the world). Sat.1 is owned mainly by the Axel Springer publishing house (its range of tabloids includes the popular *Bild Zeitung*) and the PKS-Programmgesellschaft. PKS belongs to the Kirch group which owns the majority of German feature film rights.

Less than a year after the Persian Gulf conflict and the outstanding performance of CNN, N-TV was set up to act as a German version of CNN. It started with an initial capital stock of DM 100 million, 25 percent of which belonged to the U.S.-based Time Warner group. Shortly after its formation, CNN announced that it would buy 49 percent of N-TV.

Smaller stations can also be successful. The station Fernsehen aus Berlin (FAB) is run by a collective. Five film directors from Berlin seized the opportunity when Deutscher Fernsehfunk (DFF), a former East German station, discontinued its service. FAB bought its transmission frequencies and set up the new station, which is governed by forty-one shareholders. The station is commercial and includes 6 minutes of ads in each hour of programming.

In addition, there are several pay-TV program suppliers. Some of them specialize in sophisticated movies available shortly after they arrive at the cinemas. But there are also specialized programs on the brink of legality. For example, one service offers pornographic programs which are transmitted via satellite from neighboring European countries to Germany. The legal position in this case is very interesting: in accordance with German law, it is legal to sell the decoders for these programs but not to operate them.

Finance Broadcasting in Germany is financed primarily through license fees and by revenue from advertising on radio and television. License fees have to be paid by every viewer and listener except low-income families and recipients of national assistance. The money collected from the license fees goes only to the public stations, not to the newly formed commercial ones. Both public and private programmers sell advertising.

License fees are fixed by the minister presidents of the federal states. The monthly fee for a television or radio license is now DM 23 ($15). People are required to pay DM 23 for each television set and radio they own—even car radios and portable radios. Inspectors visit homes to check on the number of radios and television sets, but many people do not allow these inspectors inside. In reality, many Germans are not paying license fees for all their radios and TVs. A comparison with the cost of a monthly newspaper subscription ($0.90 a day) and the price of a movie ticket (between $7 and $8) indicates that the services offered by broadcasting corporations are anything but expensive.

Advertising on the public and private systems is quite different because there are regulations that the public, but not the private, systems must adhere to. Advertisements on public radio can be broadcast any time of day but cannot be broadcast at all on Sundays or holidays. The rules for public television are more stringent. All public TV advertising must be broadcast between 6 P.M. and 8 P.M. as a block, that is, in several individual spots. The idea behind this is that the ads are not supposed to interrupt program content. Often these commercial blocks also contain short cartoons. In addition, there is also a legal provision limiting television advertising to 25 minutes a day. As in the radio system, there is no advertising on Sunday and holidays. Advertising in the private broadcasting realm can occur in any quantity and at any time. Usually there are commercial breaks every 20 to 30 minutes—similar to U.S. television.

A comparison of the amount of money collected by the satellite services (RTL and Sat.1) and by the public services (ARD and ZDF) in 1992 shows the difference in the financial structure between public and private services.

RTL: Return from commercials, DM 1.9 billion

Sat.1: Return from commercials, DM 1.2 billion

These figures make both corporations the largest advertising accounts in Germany. Their annual profit is said to be DM 50 million each.

ARD: Return from commercials, DM 940 million (TV), DM 735 million (radio); return from TV and radio license fees, DM 4.5 billion

ZDF: Return from commercials, DM 700 million (TV); return from TV and radio license fees, DM 1.05 billion

It should be noted that the private stations are much more tightly organized than the public stations and that they produce programs more inexpensively. Therefore their costs are not as high as those of the public stations.

PROGRAMMING

The airwaves of modern Germany are filled with a large variety of program types that differ in context, expression, and structure. However, not all possibilities have been exhausted.

German broadcasting corporations with their various radio and television programs are legally committed to offer a well-balanced variety of programs. In almost all public laws governing electronic media the mandate is identical to the one established many years ago for radio: "The duty of the radio is to broadcast news and performances from the field of education and entertainment."

Legalities aside, it is important to understand that the German electronic media philosophy places restrictions on programmers, and this is where the idiosyncrasies of German radio and television programs have their origin. Quite the opposite is true for other countries where entertainment plays the leading role. In Germany, information and education are the supporting columns of radio and television. The audience's desire for entertainment is nevertheless fulfilled. During peak airtimes, radio as well as TV presents almost exclusively entertainment shows.

During the first decades of the history of radio the government felt it was doing people a favor by giving them radio programs to listen to. Today, radio stations recognize that they must operate in such a way that they provide a service to their listeners. They offer information on the traffic situation, special news shows, pop music, and, of course, advertising.

Early Television Programming In December 1992, German TV celebrated its fortieth anniversary. Bazon Brock, one of the most distinguished art critics in Germany, considers this an anniversary that should not be celebrated in a positive way. He believes that television has changed our lives but not improved them. For example, for only a few hours, Shakespeare involved the audience in the "life, lust, and vices" of a royal family, while today the staging of even the most boring and trivial events is spread out over what seems to be a never-ending series of TV programs.

Formerly, that is, before private stations existed, everything was a bit different as far as programming philosophy was concerned. Public broadcasting stations offered a notable variety of programs in which even small interest groups got their money's worth and still do so today. A look at the *Program Chronology* of ZDF or the *Almanac of the ARD* shows a rather comprehensive palette of programs divided into the following areas.

- Culture (fine arts and literature)
- Children (adolescents and family)
- Feature films and movies
- Variety shows
- Talk shows
- Sequences and series (late-afternoon programs)
- Theater and classical music
- Current events
- Political magazines
- Domestic policy
- Foreign policy
- Economics, society, and environment
- Social and educational politics
- Reports
- Sports
- Live folk music shows

This structure has grown over a period of 40 years and closely follows the editorial division of newspapers and magazines. German television has a strong journalistic heritage. It took several years before elements from show business started to play a more important role. This explains why some of the early programs of German TV strike us as being a little bizarre, at least by today's standards.

One of the most popular early shows on German TV was *Ein Platz für Tiere (A Place for the Animals)* which was hosted by Professor Bernard Grzimek, director of the famous Frankfurt Zoo. On every show Professor Grzimek brought along a "guest animal" which would sit next to him during the program.

As the years went by, the shows—especially those that were part of the evening entertainment—became increasingly complex. There were sophisticated shows with audience participation, and quizzes, which were hosted by famous show masters. Most of the time these programs were live performances and could be received in many European countries simultaneously. To this end the organization Eurovision was founded. When the Eurovision logo came up on the television screen, Germans knew the program was being viewed by others in Europe,

Professor Grzimek and one of his "guest animals"—an ape. (*Hessischer Rundfunk, Frankfurt*)

Eurovision logo. (*Courtesy of the European Broadcasting Union*)

most likely Swiss and Austrians who shared the same language and the costs of production.

For many years the programs of the two public broadcasting corporations remained stable. Series were started, and ambitious political program features, as well as documentaries, were established. Special programs for children and citizens from other countries were included. But even at that time, a large number of programs—mainly feature films—were imported from other countries. Above all, American productions—*Sesame Street, Dallas*, and many others—became part of German TV programming.

In addition, Germans copied the program formats of other countries when they developed their own programs. An example of this was *Lindenstrasse* (*Linden Street*), the first German soap opera, which by now has aired at least 300 episodes.

Programming Today A look at today's television magazines shows an almost unlimited offering. And with some luck the former program structures of the public broadcasting corporations can still be recognized. Even at the private stations, there are program formats established by ZDF and ARD that have found a regular audience.

The main types of programs include the following.

1. *Drama and situation comedy*: This category is made up of films written for TV and feature films that are often continued in the

Members of the cast of *Lindenstrasse*. (*Westdeutscher Rundfunk*)

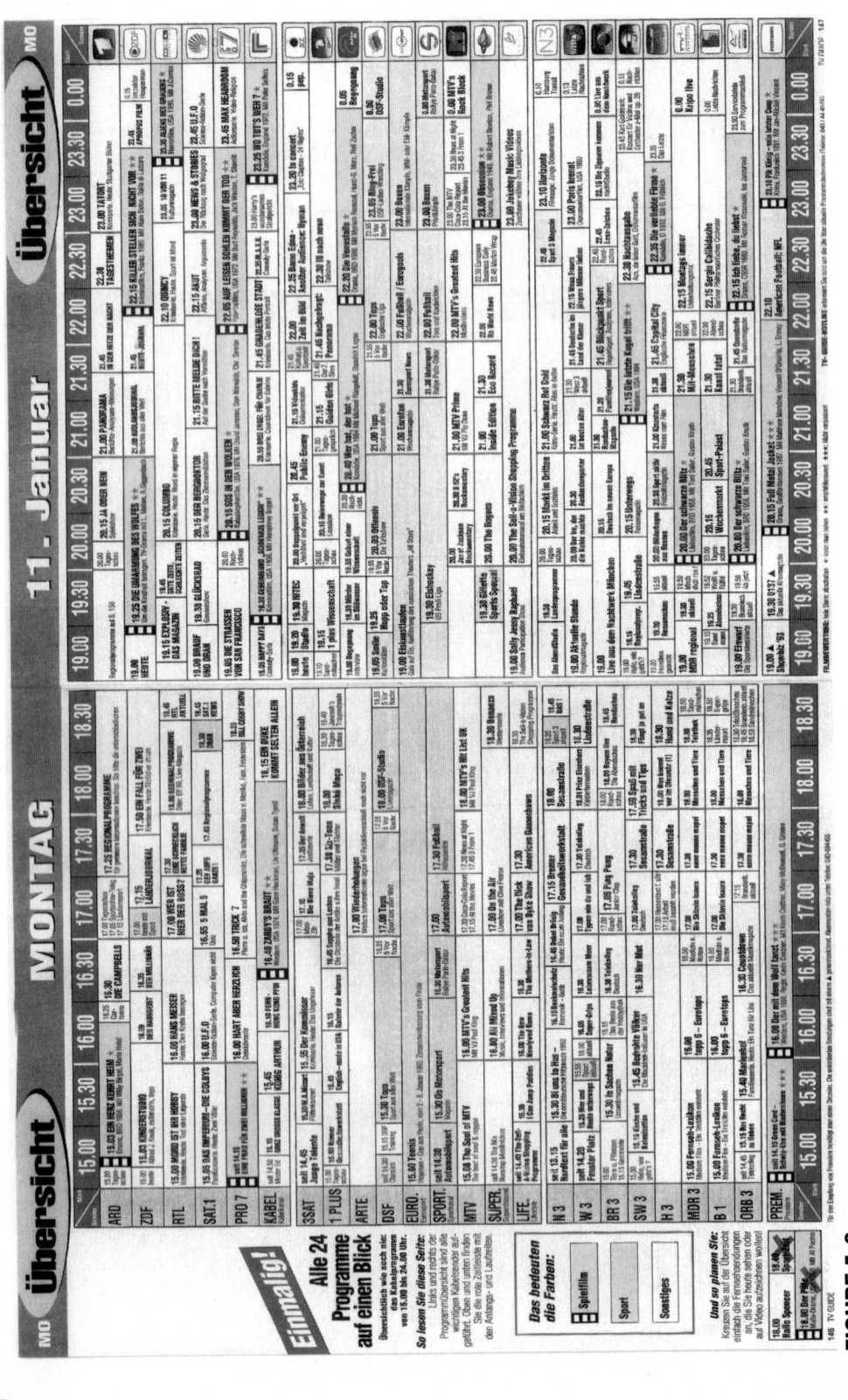

FIGURE 5–2
An evening schedule from the German *TV Guide*.

form of series. One example is *Heimat*, a film divided into twelve parts which runs on the European cultural channel ARTE (a joint venture of ARD, ZDF, and TV1 of France). This category also includes many U.S. series, as can be seen in the schedule from *TV Guide*.
2. *Game shows*: This type of show came into existence when the private stations started their services. The game shows have the same design and to some extent the same producers as their American counterparts. These shows are quite popular, but they are also subject to harsh criticism. The East German audience especially enjoys this type of program, which may be related, in part, to their backlog demand for consumer goods. Following the U.S. example, a kind of game show tourism has developed—busloads of game show visitors travel across the country to wherever the recording studios are.
3. *Talk shows*: This is the type of program Germany could have invented. Whenever one switches to a channel on German television "talking heads"—the German form of entertainment—can be seen. However, most of the time, serious topics prevail over sensationalism.
4. *Sports*: A large part of German television is occupied by sports programs. As in many other countries, in Germany, too, sports is important to millions of citizens. This is why negotiations for transmission rights have become so dramatic [see Box 5-1, "Why *Sportschau (Sports News)* Had to Go"].
5. *Documentaries*: Early documentaries often lasted up to 45 minutes. Today they are mostly limited to a maximum of 30 minutes. In this genre, too, the minidocumentary (6 to 8 minutes) is becoming increasingly popular. Generally speaking, the trend among program designers is to reduce the number of documentaries because they are unlikely to produce high ratings.
6. *News shows*: Public broadcasting corporations have at their disposal a large network of reporters and bureaus in foreign countries. This explains the high quality of their news broadcasting and the topicality of news programs on German television. There have been many changes during the past few years in the way these programs are presented. Newscasters are livelier, and newscasts are more fast-paced than they used to be. News shows also have to be sold in a very competitive market. This is why the structure of the newscast has become increasingly important. Still we have not yet come to the point where presentation of the news is more important than the news itself.
7. *Religious programs*: These programs are occasionally found on ARD and ZDF. One example is *Wort zum Sonntag (Sunday Word)* and the broadcasting of Sunday church services. Religious programs play only a minor role on television and are transmitted mainly on radio. There is no station in Germany engaged in purely religious programming.
8. *Educational programming*: This is the domain of the 3rd Programs. This type of programming includes language classes and early-morning school television with an emphasis on science. There are also programs for foreign citizens in their respective native tongues.
9. *Other programming*: There are of course special programs that address the do-it-yourselfer and hobby gardener, but there is also stock exchange information which is aired live from the Frankfurt stock market. This field of programming, in particular, still seems to hold a lot of potential for the future.

The Issue of Sex and Violence Compared to the United States, there are considerable differences regarding sex and violence on TV. The representation of violence is severely restricted and subject to constant supervision. Foreign series, which very often include violent scenes, are therefore subject to a lot of criticism. In contrast, nudity and erotic scenes are handled much more liberally. While a program may include nudity, actual pornographic scenes are not allowed.

Sources of German Programming According to statistical data collected by ZDF, the sources of German programming are as follows. For editorial material, which covers all political and journalistic programs, 90 percent are German productions and 10 percent are purchased productions. In the area of entertainment there is a considerable shift—25 percent are home productions, while about 30 percent are accounted for by commissioned works or coproductions usually prepared in conjunction with a television entity from some other country, and 39 percent are purchased abroad. These figures seem to point to an ever-increasing dependency on foreign productions.

LAWS AND REGULATIONS

After World War II, when freedom of radio broadcasting was established as a counterpart to freedom of the press, the founding fathers of the Basic (constitutional) Law of the Federal Republic of Germany anticipated the important role radio and television broadcasting was to play in the formation of public opinion. "Every citizen has the right to express and to stand by his or her opinion in speaking, writing, or in pictures and turn for information to a public source. There is no censorship." (Article 5, Basic Law.)

Functions of the Regional Broadcasting Corporations The democratic social system of the Federal Republic of Germany with its parliamentary democratic government system gives every citizen the chance to participate directly in shaping social interest. As a result of this, regional broadcasting corporations have three political functions.

1. *Providing information to citizens*: It is the duty of broadcasting corporations to report objectively, comprehensively, and popularly in such a way that citizens can have a clear idea of the political, social, and economic relations in which they are involved as members of society. This makes it possible to participate in the process of political codetermination.
2. *Participation in the formation of political opinion*: In a democratic system, political decisions are legitimized by the fact that they are first subject to free and open discussions. It is the task of the electronic media to inform citizens about this exchange of opinion and become involved in this process independently through its commentaries. It is the task of the electronic media to bring into focus the opinions and requests of the public, discuss them in public, and inform the instruments of state about them.
3. *Supervision and criticism*: From what has been said above, it is the duty of both the press and radio broadcasting to prevent certain individual groups and those with a distinct economic interest from influencing the decisions of the government to an undue extent.

Other Regulations Many of the rules governing both private and public radio and television stations stem from the laws of the states in which they are located. Others are in accordance with the act on the freedom of press and radio. According to this act, everyone has the right to send out programs. This right is restricted, however, by the allocation of frequencies. Frequencies and other technical matters are overseen by the Ministry of Posts and Telecommunications. The act also stipulates that the supplier of radio and television programs must establish a legal business. What is more, every broadcasting corporation (public or private) has the duty to supply information.

In addition, as mentioned earlier, public TV stations can air commercials only at certain times and for a limited number of minutes per day. This puts a lot of pressure on the competitive situation between public and private broadcasting corporations. ARD tries to compete by placing most of its allotted commercials on its national service where it programs its entertainment programming, while leaving the regional stations (3rd Programs) to carry commercial-free informational programming.

THE AUDIENCE

German television is dependent on market research to obtain a representative picture of its audience. While cinema can draw clear evidence of a movie's success from the number of tickets sold at the box office, with TV the situation is different. Although TV does have direct feedback in the form of letters from the audience, incoming telephone calls, and press reviews, it must resort to other means such as indirect surveys or opinion polls to come up with figures about audience quantity and quality.

Ever since the public broadcasting stations stopped competing against each other and instead began to assert themselves against private stations, statistical data on audience numbers have become the basis for programming decisions.

Audience Research Producer to talent: "In the beginning we had a 2 percent rating, but when your part came on 0.3 percent switched the channel. Try to be a little bit more commercial and entertaining, and less ambitious." Everything is judged by the ratings.

In order to find out how many viewers switch on and off, and how many switch channels between commercials, the four biggest corporations, ARD, ZDF, SAT.1, and RTL, have commissioned the Gesellschaft für Kommunikations/Marktforschung (GfK). For this purpose, GfK set up a representative audience panel. In 2900 households in West Germany, which contain some 6600 people, television viewing is recorded.

In each of the selected television families the GfK meter—a small microcomputer—is installed. The tune-in hours of every family member are recorded with a simple keystroke. At night these data are collected via modem, evaluated down to the second, and statistically projected.

Broadcasting corporations use these data to find out how their programs performed statistically. They also use the results in making programming decisions. Often they are particularly interested in the behavior of certain target groups. They convey this information to their advertising partners who, after all, are interested in precisely predictable audience groups.

Audience Research in East Germany In East Germany, it is quite difficult to collect ratings because so far there is no complete telephone network that would allow for the collection of data. Thus audience behavior has to be examined the conventional way, by means of opinion polls. This of course means that the results are never up to date.

Evaluating audience behavior has traditionally been difficult in East Germany. During the cold war, the west made attempts to collect data on the listening and viewing practices of radio and TV audiences in the east. In 1960, the West German government commissioned a market research group to conduct an opinion poll on the radio and TV habits of their East German neighbors. One of the goals was to find out what opportunities existed for receiving West German programs. The data collected at that time were based on opinion polls carried out among refugees who had just left the GDR. Several areas could be distinguished in which it was not

> **BOX 5-2**
>
> ## The Valley of the Unsuspecting
>
> What follows are comments from a short interview with a citizen from Leipzig, East Germany, which was conducted in December 1992.
>
> On the "Mittelwelle" (intermediate range) we were able to receive a lot of West German radio programs. I mostly listened to them under my blanket. Not because of my parents, but because it was generally badly looked at.
>
> With the exception of Dresden, western television could be received just about anywhere. The people in Dresden really did not have any firsthand information; as a result of this we referred to this area as the "valley of the unsuspecting."
>
> This is why shortly after the destruction of the Wall many people, especially from that area, emigrated to the west. They knew the "golden west" only from hearsay and immediately wanted to cross over to paradise.
>
> East German television did not start until the evening and stopped shortly before midnight. However, even during that period of time, most people watched western programs. At the beginning of the isolation, that is, shortly after the construction of the Berlin Wall, only very few people dared to direct their antennas toward the West. Later, this changed altogether and everybody had his or her own west antenna.
>
> The people in East Germany mostly enjoyed watching the West German entertainment shows. After all, it was mainly in these shows that the problem of the divided nation was always made a topic. And those viewers who wanted to be informed about the political situation of course watched the political programs on West German TV, especially the famous *ZDF-Magazin*, which tried to come to terms with the separation of the two German states.
>
> Western television and radio were tolerated. However, the program designers in the east tried to manipulate the material through commentaries or by just presenting a few individual sections of a program. A very good example of this is *Der Schwarze Kanal (The Black Channel)* by Eduard Schnitzler, which acted as a smear campaign against western imperialism for almost thirty years. This was ideological warfare.
>
> As students, we were not allowed to quote information from western media. The hard-liners of the party tried to cut access to these media, even at home in their own families.
>
> Of the East German programs produced, the children's programs were remarkable. Even though they, too, were used as propaganda tools, their cinematography enchanted the viewer. Similar to other eastern countries this was a stronghold of the TV and film producers.
>
> There were also advertising films, some of which were quite ingenious. Of course, these were used only for products from state-owned companies. And there were educational films which explained how to wash your car, plant flowers. . . .
>
> During the revolution, in September 1989, there was no information available at first. This is when everybody turned to western television for information. The information on East German TV started to change very quickly, however, and in addition we were capable of reading between the lines and the pictures. It went so far that we started to watch the *Aktuelle Kamera* (news program in East Germany) again because it was more up to date with the events and included more current information than the programs on West German television.
>
> The new broadcasting corporations of the former GDR now offer a program similar to the 3rd Programs in the west. They offer a complete daytime and evening schedule and a much larger choice of information than there used to be. Naturally, for the most part, they use journalists and film craftspersons who worked for public television before the new era started in 1989.

even technically possible to receive any programs. Mainly, these included the sections around Rostock and Dresden.

The survey also tried to find out what East Germans wanted from West German television. Almost 60 percent requested information, but a large percentage also wished to be better educated about the west, the Soviet-occupied zone, and general political events. Other important objectives dealt with the special situation of the divided Germany. There was a desire to "stress the bond (between the two German states) and to inspire hope and resistance." The people in the east wanted to join in the events in the west and felt locked out by the Berlin Wall:

"It's like living on an island. They should provide guidelines to the man in the street, instruct him on how to behave because many mainly join the party because they want to protect their families." (Statement by a worker, 48 years old.)

"More programs must be available to show the East German population that they are not left in the lurch." (Statement by a pensioner, 67 years old.)

In its investigation the market research institution came to the following conclusion: "The reasons for turning to western television did not involve a pro-western attitude but rather an emotional antipathy to television in the east. The tasks of western television were to act as a balancing counterpart and, in the long run, enable a conscious identification with the values and standards of the west."

A sociologist maintains that the reunification of the two German states was accomplished much earlier in the living rooms of the two nations. But despite many similarities, there are still big differences in the television behavior of the people in the west and those in the east. As a result of the difficult social situation in the east, many unemployed people consume more television. Private stations, in particular, have witnessed an increase in audience numbers. This trend is further enhanced by the fact that there are fewer possibilities for filling leisure time and there is still an overall backlog demand for video programs.

TECHNOLOGIES

"It's a Sony" is one of the principal statements that can be made about German media technology today. There are still some areas of technology in which Germany assumes a leading role, but most of today's major developments are dependent on Japan. Germany's electronics industry which, until a few years ago, ranked among the first in the world, now uses components from the Far East.

Throughout various stages and generations, the distribution and transmission systems have been adjusted to the latest technological standard. The system of the future for all areas will be satellite transmission; before long it will replace the transmission of information via UHF and VHF. Radio stations broadcast via either AM or FM frequencies, which in the near future will be replaced by digital audio broadcasting (DAB).

In Germany, high-definition television (HDTV) is also a popular topic. The current PAL system, which is the most advanced system with a resolution quality of 625 lines, is to be enhanced to 1250 lines with a 16:9 aspect ratio. This will mainly cause problems for program developers, as current programs probably will not be compatible. The hardware industry hopes to sell new devices. No matter what the decision is, companies from the Far East will probably supply the required technology to everyone.

One of the technical areas where Germany excels is in the dubbing of films from one language to another. The majority of German programming is of U.S. origin. Although many Germans speak English, dubbing material into German makes it more understandable. Thus, in Germany, a renowned dubbing industry has developed.

EXTERNAL SERVICES

There are two public broadcasting corporations in Germany that are responsible for radio services abroad. They are both members of ARD. One of them is Deutschlandfunk, which offers radio programs for Germany and other European countries. The other is Deutsche Welle, which is a shortwave service for listeners abroad.

While Deutschlandfunk plays a somewhat minor role and has limited its range of service to the local European market, Deutsche Welle plays an important role and ranks fifth among external radio services worldwide. It can be compared with ZDF and ARD in that it is not a government station, yet it has a programming mandate according to which it must supply information on German events and developments. In addition, it is required to present opinions on events that happen on the international scene.

There are three target groups: the most important consists of listeners all over the world with German roots; second are German employees abroad; third are foreigners who either speak German or want to learn to speak it. The programs of Deutsche Welle are aired in 35 languages, with more than 100 news programs a day being beamed to all corners of the world. In 1992 a total of 43 transmitting installations with a transmission capacity of 11,550 kilowatts was available to ensure this service.

Despite the fact that the audience for whom these programs are designed is distributed all over the globe, there is comparatively strong feedback. In 1992 alone some 400,000 letters from listeners were received, two-thirds of which came from countries of the Third World. This same audience will soon be able to watch the television programs of Deutsche Welle. A satellite television service started in 1992 and is expanding continually.

For many Germans in the remotest parts of the world Deutsche Welle very likely is the only direct link to their homeland. But the political importance of this station will decline as news networks such as CNN and N-TV transmit globally and exercise a news monopoly (which happened, for example, during the Persian Gulf war). When this happens, foreign radio services will be reduced to simply supplying commentaries, a kind of secondhand news.

IMPORTANCE IN THE WORLD COMMUNITY

As already pointed out, Germany is a less important production center than the United States. Only a few movies make it over the Atlantic into American movie theaters or into movie theaters anywhere in the world for that matter. This has something to do with the highly intellectual composition of German movies, but it also has to do with the distribution policy. This policy makes it difficult for a German product to access a market controlled by a few U.S. distributor groups. The same applies to television productions. Another obstacle is the German language, which does not exactly enjoy an important position in the world.

On an international level, Germany is one of the most important buyers of foreign programs. Hardly a day goes by without a dozen feature films—mainly of U.S. origin—being played on the various German channels. In addition, German television corporations, as coproducers, participate not only in European but also in other international projects. ZDF, the largest broadcasting corporation in Europe, regularly coproduces television and feature film projects.

Formerly, Germany was a major producer of radio and TV sets. Companies such as Bosch, Siemens, and Telefunken enjoyed a worldwide reputation, especially where reliability and workmanship were concerned. But, as mentioned earlier, this market position was lost to manufacturers in the Far East. Germany is a primary *follower* in world media and no doubt will continue to be as the worldwide telecommunications industry continues to expand.

MAJOR ISSUES

The ramifications of commercialization will be a major issue in Germany's near future. The privately owned television stations that were allowed to go into business in the middle of the 1980s changed not only the history of TV but also the programs to a large extent. The conflict between commercial radio and TV stations and public ones will cause a great deal of tension in the future. One other related question is whether the programming choice will be enriched or whether too much second-class mass material offered by all the television stations will result in a loss of profile.

What strategies will private stations come up with in order to further increase their audience size? When will public broadcasting corporations have to become even more commercialized in order not to miss the boat? It will take some time for this conflict to be settled. The more the old broadcasting stations have to abide by the rules of the marketplace and the more they have to fight for audience share, the more the public broadcasting stations will have to give way to public taste. One could argue that this is consumer-friendly in the sense of consumer sovereignty. This, however, is not entirely true because TV programming financed through advertising is characterized by many taboos determined by the advertising environment: no television commercial is allowed to conflict with a program message—this would mean disaster for the effectiveness of the commercial. Does this not also spell disaster for the program variety that has characterized German TV so far? Are we facing a future in which TV will be mainly made up of inferior series and programs taken over from foreign stations?

However, commercialization can no longer be stopped. Thus an ever-increasing number of broadcast stations are offering more and more programs. This development also causes changes in the advertising business. Printed advertisements are becoming less important as the trend favors radio and mainly television commercials.

German citizens, in both the east and the west, are exposed to an increasing number of commercials. Within a short period Germany has adopted the television habits of other countries to an alarming extent. The German programs of the early 1990s are very internationalized and tend to favor easy entertainment. Public broadcasting institutions appear to have little to offer in opposing this trend, but they also have to adjust.

Yet the two German television systems themselves are involved in the biggest conflict. The near future will tell how long the public broadcasting system will survive in its current form. Very likely, these two institutions will be allowed to program more commercials, while reducing their license fees at the same time; maybe the latter source of income will be done away with altogether. Some sources even say that one of the public services (ZDF) might have to go commercial soon.

Radio does not seem to be endangered by such drastic changes. Commercialization has already progressed much further. The problem of the future will be how to divide the (advertising) cake. Everybody will have to be prepared for a small slice.

We do not know as yet how the increase in programs and the change in programming content will affect the population. Some tendencies seem to be obvious from what has been observed in the United States. American programs and productions, as well as copied program formats, will characterize and manipulate German television—but maybe also inspire it.

In the course of this development we will lose some of that cranky charm that had become so typical of Germany's semiprofessional television. A current symbol of this trend: at the end of 1992 many programs stopped using the beloved television announcers the Germans were so fond of. These people were replaced by flashy trailers with a highly commercial image—in the true sense of the word "a loss of character" for German television.

SELECTED BIBLIOGRAPHY

ARD Jahrbuch. Frankfurt: ARD (yearly).

Browne, Donald R. "Germany: State's Rights, National Ambitions, and International Communism." In *Comparing Broadcast Systems: The Experiences of Six Industrialized Nations.* Ames, IA: Iowa State University Press, 1989, pp. 175–246.

Dill, Richard. "Broadcasting in the Federal Republic of Germany." In William E. McCavitt, *Broadcasting around the World*. Blue Ridge Summit, PA: TAB Books, 1981.

Door, Renate. "ADF Prepares for a Reunified Nation," *Almanac: The Annual of the International Council of NATAS*, 1990, p. 97.

Fernsehempfang in der SBZ. München: INFRATEST, 1961.

"Germans Get New Private Web," *Variety*, 25 August 1992, p. 18.

Guild, Hazel. "German Cable Cost Controversy Keeps Viewers from Signing Up," *Variety*, 3 February 1988, p. 68.

Phänomen Fernsehen. Düsseldorf: Econ Verlag, 1978.

Radio and Television in the Federal Republic of Germany. Frankfurt: Hessischer Rundfunk, 1980.

Schwarzkopf, Dietrich. "A New Germany Brings New Opportunities for ARD," *Almanac: The Annual of the International Council of NATAS*, 1990, p. 94.

ZDF Jahrbuch. Mainz: ZDF (yearly).

PART FOUR
EASTERN EUROPE

Overview of Eastern Europe

The term "Eastern Europe" used to refer to all the countries that were behind the "Iron Curtain"—countries that were Communist and had little communication either in or out with Western Europe and the rest of the Western world. It was often referred to as the "Second World" to distinguish it from the industrialized capitalistic nations of the "First World" and the poorer developing nations of the "Third World." The leader of the Second World was the Union of Soviet Socialist Republics (USSR), and the other countries (often called "satellites" or "puppets") were Poland, Czechoslovakia, Hungary, Albania, Romania, Bulgaria, and East Germany (which was geographically in western Europe but politically in what was referred to as Eastern Europe). Yugoslavia, although Communist, was independent of the USSR.

However, all that started to change in the late 1980s when communism toppled. Old leaders were ousted, new ones were voted in, and the countries wended their way toward a market economy. Old religious and cultural hatreds that had been stifled under authoritarian rule surfaced. The most violent conflicts were in Yugoslavia where pent-up bitterness exploded, neighbors killed neighbors, and the country was split into several warring factions. Czechoslovakia also split, but much more peacefully because its fractionalization had been a historical one between the Czechs and Slovaks, as will be outlined in Chapter 6. The USSR disintegrated, with Russia being the largest surviving country of what had been fifteen republics during the days of the Soviet Union.

Through all of this the media transformed and were transformed. Radio and television were given credit for much of the downfall of communism. Media practitioners (and ordinary citizens armed with camcorders) got word to the outside world about what was happening, thus solidifying the cause and soliciting help. Once the old guard had been overthrown, the media had to reinvent themselves. This has not been an easy process, as is thoroughly discussed in Chapters 6 and 7 which deal with the two countries chosen to represent Eastern Europe.

Russia, as the leader of communism, is the most obvious choice for showing the media characteristics both before and after the downfall of communism. The discussion of Russia naturally includes a description of the Soviet media system that endured for many years. The other part of Eastern Europe discussed in detail is the former Czechoslovakia. Now separated into two countries, this area was considered one of the more advanced economically of the Communist satellite countries. Its emerging model will no doubt influence its neighbors. Also, the reunification of a country (Germany) was shown in Chapter 5. Examining the Czech and Slovak Republics shows the effects of taking apart as compared with those of putting together.

The general characteristics of the old system and the evolving new systems of Eastern Europe deserve some attention. This is an area where very recent electronic media history (from the early 1980s to the mid-1980s) must be comprehended in order to even begin to understand what is happening in the area in the 1990s.

THE COMMUNIST MODEL

The Soviet Union was more stringent in its enforcement of authoritarian principles than were its satellite countries. It had adopted communism after a 1917 revolution, but the rest of the countries did not come under the Communist yoke until after World War II. There were more people in the satellite countries who remembered pre-Communist ways and tried to incorporate them, clandestinely or subtly, within the authoritarian structure. The media were given freer reign in these countries in terms of local autonomy, importation of programming, and journalistic initiative.

Power of the National Government In most Eastern European countries, the central government owned and operated the media for the whole country. Policies were set by the Communist party leaders, and most of the programming emanated from the city where the government was located. The government imposed strict censorship over programming, and financial support came from the state. (In these countries and others, the word "state" is used differently than it is in the United States. It refers to the central government, not to an individual state such as Utah or Minnesota.)

The government was actually subservient to the party. Often media organizations had two chief executives: one was a member of the Communist party who often did not know much about broadcasting but made sure that party dictums and decrees from the country's leader were followed. The other (who may or may not have been a party member) handled the day-to-day operation.

The purpose of media was to validate the party. As a 1987 booklet put out by the Hungarian television service, Magyar Television (MTV), stated, "The task of MTV is to promote and promulgate the policies of the Hungarian Socialist Workers' party and the Hungarian People's Republic via the special means of television broadcasting."

People who worked in the television industry had secure jobs—as long as they were obedient to the party. They, like other workers in Communist societies, were guaranteed work. The bureaucrats who had to generate statistics regarding audience size or radio penetration did so in a manner that would please their bosses. For this reason, many of the statistics that came from the Communist era cannot be trusted to be accurate.

The pattern of central control was not as heavy-handed in the satellite countries as it was in the Soviet Union. For example, Hungary had local cable TV. Unlike the United States, where cable TV became popular because of the national pay channels and basic network services, Hungarian cable was born because the people saw it as a way of showing locally produced programming. The areas that were wired produced their own programs and cabled them into local dwellings.

The country with the most local autonomy was Yugoslavia, where six states and two provinces created their own programming. These areas had diverse ethnic, language, and religious differences and were jealous of one another (factors that led to bloodshed in the 1990s). There was a central broadcasting agency that supervised overall operations, but the eight centers had their own facilities and a great deal of independence. Programming choices were made by local stations, but purchase of equipment and international programs was handled by the state agency in order to obtain the best prices.

Electronic Media Programming Programming had to please the party leaders, not the audience. As a result, it was very didactic, educational—and dull. Radio programming consisted of classical music, theatrical presentations, literature, news, children's programs, and educational programs, some of which were broadcast for children in schools and some of which were various forms of adult education dealing with history, social science, natural science, literature, biology, and foreign languages.

Some typical programs shown on Hungarian TV included *Growth Rings*, a 30-minute weekly information program for pensioners; *Hello Mum*, a series that gave practical advice to would-be parents and young families with small children; and *Us, You, Them*, a series for secondary school students that featured different youth groups.

A common form of television programs was documentaries, but not in the sense of modern U.S. documentaries that look at controversial or sensational subjects. Nothing as hard-hitting as *60 Minutes* was shown on Eastern European broadcasting. What was shown were documentaries about how well the workers were growing wheat or weaving cloth, how national artifacts were being preserved, or how wildlife lived. Also, a large number of documentaries dealt with the virtues of the Communist party.

News programs, too, sang the praises of Communist rule. Much of the newscast time was devoted to the activities of Communist leaders. Reporters would ask questions of the politicians and then listen obediently as the politicians talked on and on, using radio and television as a platform for whatever ideas they wished to deliver. In some countries adventuresome news readers would exhibit certain mannerisms that viewers learned to decode; these mannerisms indicated to viewers that what was being said should be dismissed as propaganda.

Sports programming was popular in all the countries and was the most entertaining fare available. It was used to glorify the winning records of Eastern European athletes.

Artistic programs such as serious drama, ballet, opera, and films were also shown. Artists had a particular status in this part of the world that they do not have in the United States. They were highly revered and were actually paid more than many of the other workers. They constituted most of what there was of a middle class in these countries. Artists were paid weekly salaries by the state to write scripts or direct films; they were not paid for particular projects as they often are in the United States. As a result, they had little pressure on them to finish projects. The hard part was getting an idea accepted; it had to be politically correct. Once through the labyrinth of the party approval process, an artist had almost unlimited money and time to complete a project.

The content of films and other artistic programs was quite different from that which people in the United States are used to. It was much more along the line of art for art's sake. The creations were as much for the creator as for the audience and often dealt with the inner mind of the artist. Abstract, lofty human dilemma themes were common. Chase scenes and fast-paced cuts were not part of Eastern European dramatic programs. The area held many festivals to show its films and TV programs. Sometimes these works were awarded prizes, but often the festivals were noncompetitive; they were simply places where media artists could display their works.

The restrictions on programming, as in other facets of the electronic media, were stricter in the USSR than in other countries. One place where this manifested itself was in imported programming. The Soviet Union imported very little from other countries. When it bought the 90-minute special *Glenn Miller—Moonlight Serenade* from British Thames Television in 1987, it was the first program it had purchased from the British since 1983 when it bought a special on Charlie Chaplin. It secured even less programming from the United States.

In contrast, Poland imported as much as 80 percent of its programming, and Hungarian TV bought 40 percent of its programming from overseas, half of it from Western Europe. Yugoslavia bought more programming from the United States than it did from any other country, and it bought more from Great Britain, France, and Italy than it did from the USSR. For the most part these countries bought cultural material that they used in their own ways. For example, Bulgarian broadcasters bought episodes of *English House* and *English Garden* from Britain and used them for a series they created on European architecture. However, these countries also bought telenovelas from Brazil and a few U.S. crime series such as *The Streets of San Francisco*, *Columbo*, and *Kojak*. Poland and Yugoslavia broadcast *Sesame Street*, but the USSR condemned it as capitalistic propaganda.

Generally no religious broadcasting was allowed in Communist countries. However, Poland relaxed the ban in 1979 when Polish-born Pope John Paul II visited Poland. It was the first time Mass had ever been seen on TV in that country, which was overwhelmingly Catholic. There were government orders, however, not to show on TV the huge throngs that greeted the Pope everywhere he went.

Advertising Advertising was banned in the USSR from 1935 to 1947 but gradually was accepted there and in other Eastern European Communist countries, with Albania holding out the longest. The Yugoslavian broadcasting system pursued advertising revenues the most vigorously of any of the Communist countries and allowed up to 5 percent of airtime for ads.

However, throughout Eastern Europe, the purpose of ads was more to inform consumers than to persuade them to buy or to build brand loyalty. The state owned the businesses, so there was only one brand of most products, and there was obviously no competition. About as "commercial" as ads got was when they were used to try to move surplus consumer goods that had built up in state warehouses.

Outside Sources of Information Communist governments worked very hard to keep their citizens from obtaining information from outside the Iron Curtain, as well as from any dissidents who might be within the country. They jammed signals from European and U.S. external services, and some of them had wired radio that carried only government stations.

Nevertheless, information did seep in, in part because Western countries were occasionally able to circumvent the jamming. Some of the countries near Western Europe could receive broadcast signals. This was easiest in Yugoslavia because, unlike other Soviet satellite countries, it used PAL rather than SECAM and therefore did not have to put TV signals through a technical system to convert them from one format to another. Signals from Italy were shown underground in Yugoslavia, and vice versa—to the chagrin of both governments.

Some of Hungary's cable TV systems managed to show satellite signals from the outside. In some instances individuals constructed homemade satellite dishes. Estimates were that Czechoslovakia had 30,000 illegal satellite dishes and that 10 percent of Hungarians received satellite signals through either cable TV or their own dishes.

Videotapes were another avenue of outside information. People traveling overseas could buy both recorders and tapes and smuggle them through customs—usually by paying off customs officers with hard currency or giving them a videocassette recorder (VCR). Anyone who could bring in a number of VCRs could sell them on the thriving black market. The same was true of videotapes, which could also be duplicated once they were in the country. Videotape piracy became quite commonplace.

From time to time there were clandestine radio services within a country. Poland's dissident labor union, Solidarity, was granted access to television for a short period of time, but then the government reasserted its exclusive right and banned Solidarity from further use. But Solidarity was able to establish an underground radio service.

Most of the citizens within Communist countries knew they were not getting completely unbiased information from their government broadcasting systems. The desire for more communication with the outside world was part of what led to the uprisings that undermined communism.

THE EVOLUTION TOWARD A NEW ORDER

Beginning in the 1980s, Eastern European media systems began to establish a whole new set of rules. Times have been chaotic because political stability has not been the order of the day. The Communist party is not top dog anymore, but it is often hard to tell who is. New laws and methods of operation need to be devised not only for electronic media but also for all other aspects of society. The job is enormous, and the needs of the media are not high priorities when compared with providing food, establishing a stable economy, and setting up election procedures. In Hungary the new leaders of state-owned radio and television weren't named until about 4 months after a new government was elected. There and elsewhere parliamentary bills affecting electronic media are slow in coming and greatly debated before being enacted. Sometimes things just happen, and no one knows for sure if they are legal or illegal.

Another problem is that although the structure of the media is supposed to change, many of the same people who were part of the old structure are now in charge of the new structure. Their old jobs were low-paying but relatively easy. There was a saying in the Soviet Union, "I'll pretend to work and the state will pretend to pay me." Many people supplemented their state jobs by working in the underground economy. State taxi drivers sold vodka; waiters sold pirated videotapes. Human nature being what it is, many people do not want to change their lifestyle. It is difficult in countries that disdain the rich to use profit and individual financial gain as incentives. Many people do not want to use their initiative to try new media ideas; they liked being told what to do because it was easy. They admire the idea of freedom, but they still look upon it as something bestowed by the state. In the past they were assured jobs for life; with the changes they are not sure from day to day whom they will be working for or even if they will be working.

To make matters worse, the people who oppose change (primarily the hard-core Communists) sometimes appear to be gaining back their power, as evidenced in Russia by the coup attempts against Yeltsin. People know that if they are among those who have advocated change and the old guard comes back into power, they will be severely punished. Best to straddle the fence. Most of Eastern Europe represents the epitome of the old Chinese curse, "May you live in interesting times."

Although the structure of the media changes from day to day, certain trends do seem to be evolving, especially in relation to economic and programming changes.

Economic Changes The new directions for Eastern European media involve having competition and efficiency, gaining an audience, cutting costs, and serving viewers and listeners—all of which are in line with a market economy.

One result is that the search for advertising dollars is becoming more important. But people who were raised in societies where minimal needs were provided by the state and frills were frowned upon are not skilled in sales or commercial production. In addition, inflation within the countries has eaten away money people once had to buy things. A lack of supply of goods also works against advertising. Why pay for advertising when you are selling all you make and can't keep up with demand?

Governments appear to be in favor of coexisting public and private systems. However, they don't have enough money to give adequate support to public systems, and they generally don't provide training for private endeavors. Many of the people who were running state operations in Eastern Europe have little or no knowledge of economics or accounting; they may not even know how to prepare budgets.

Joint ventures with Western companies have been eagerly sought. Chase Enterprises of Hartford, Connecticut, is undertaking a joint venture in Poland establishing cable TV with Polska Telewizja Kablowa. Chase, whose chief executive officer is a native of Poland, is providing financial support, know-how, and a willingness to gamble. International media moguls such as Rupert Murdoch and Ted Turner are checking out possibilities in Eastern Europe. HBO is considering setting up channels in Hungary and the Czech and Slovak Republics.

But joint ventures have a downside. Eastern European countries, because of their unstable economic conditions and their lack of knowledge of the intricacies of free-market enterprise, are somewhat at the mercy of their benefactors. All the cultural imperialism factors that have plagued Third World countries come into play. Countries searching for a new identity do not want a Western mentality thrust upon them.

Western countries, on the other hand, find dealing with Eastern European countries to be frustrating. Because of all the changes that are going on, it often takes forever to accomplish something—to push it through the old and the new red tape. Added to that are cultural misunderstandings and language problems. Companies see that the hurdles they face are going to irrevocably damage profits. They fear the financial impact and back out.

In addition, the rules change as companies begin to undertake joint ventures. In Hungary, for example, radio and TV were taken over by the new government after the revolution. Many of the same people who had been in the Communist Magyar Television and Magyar Radio were still employed in the non-Communist Magyar broadcasting organizations. Although the government leaders wanted to pass a full-scale broadcasting law encouraging privatization, MTV leaders opposed this because it would dilute their control over electronic media.

Organizations interested in joint ventures watched from the sidelines as the new law jockeyed and stalled. In July 1993 Hungary lifted the ban on *local* licensing of new radio and TV stations saying it did not, as Magyar broadcasting claimed, violate the country's constitution. The ban was kept on new *national* media services, however. But even the lifting of the local ban is being fought and may not be enforced. To complicate matters, media organizations may have up to 49 percent foreign ownership and sometimes up to 100 percent with special government approval.

What does a company wishing to invest in Hungarian electronic media do—wait to make sure the local situation is secure, start investing in a local station and hope for the best, wait and hope for a lifting of the national ban in order to undertake a more potentially lucrative venture, invest in a Hungarian company, or try to determine the methods for obtaining special government approval for 100 percent foreign ownership?

The economic situation in this part of the world will, in all probability, improve. With all that has happened there is no turning back to the communism of the past. Once time has passed, people have adjusted, and the political climate has settled down, interesting patterns could develop. In many ways Eastern Europe is not hampered by its past. The infrastructure of equipment and facilities is broken down and must be replaced. The area has the option of jumping to new technologies and new methods without going through many of the intermediary ones.

Programming News is a programming form that has undergone great change. Although non-Soviet countries had more freedom of expression than the USSR itself, all of them had state-controlled news services. Journalists are now free to criticize government (at least in theory), but many of them need training in this type of reportorial style. The Poles, for example, asked Israel for guidelines on how to create objective news. Politicians, used to giving long-winded answers to friendly questions, don't know how to handle hard questions.

Sometimes politicians still crack down on news media. For example, in Hungary in the fall of 1993, Magyar Television canceled *Evening Balance*, the most objective current affairs program, and fired its editor in chief. The program had frequently criticized Hungary's coalition government, and some felt that the leading political party in the coalition, Magyar Democratic Forum, didn't want the show on during an upcoming election campaign. The stated reason for canceling the program was that it had broadcast falsified and erroneous coverage of a political event in which President Arpad Goncz was making a speech that was disrupted by hecklers. The program did show the hecklers. Politicians are keenly aware of the power of the press and that, historically in Eastern Europe, those who rule the media can rule in politics.

Entertainment is a concept that is now being seriously considered in Eastern Europe. With the dictum to gain and serve viewers and listeners, Eastern European media must take into account the needs of the people rather than the needs of the party. This has meant that more foreign programming and foreign popular music are being imported. The U.S. miniseries *Winds of War* and *North and South* were on the air at the same time in Poland as early as 1990.

The role of artists is slowly evolving. Whereas previously they had difficulty getting ideas accepted, but once accepted could be assured of money, now they can write scripts on just about any subject they wish, but they have great difficulty finding someone or some organization to fund production. In order to sell their ideas, artists need to change their mind-set from serving the party to serving an audience. This switch in thinking is not particularly easy.

Eastern Europe has many skilled practitioners of media arts. Once the countries have settled down, they could contribute greatly to the artistic and commercial stockpile of programming. For the innovative, Eastern Europe is a clean sheet of paper.

CHAPTER 6

The Slovak Republic and the Czech Republic (Formerly Czechoslovakia)

Ivan Stadtrucker

Ivan Stadtrucker.

Ivan Stadtrucker is a professor of film and television theory at the University of the Arts (VSMU) in the city of Bratislava in the Slovak Republic. He is the author of numerous books on film and television, including *Beauty of Darkness, Time of Projective Culture*, and *Theory of Film Dramaturgy*, and has also written screenplays for more than twenty television dramas and feature films, some of which have won major prizes. He was a member of the international jury for the television festival "Golden Prague" and has read papers and conducted workshops at universities abroad, including Harvard University and the University of Missouri in Kansas City.

(*Editor's Note*: When this chapter was commissioned, Czechoslovakia was a single country. In 1993 it split into two countries, the Czech Republic and the Slovak Republic. This chapter has been updated to reflect the change, but in reality little has happened to media in either country to give them a distinctive identity. Because the split between the two countries was peaceful, the media forms, although they are slowly developing their own structures, continue to coexist without pressure for rapid changes. The roots of the electronic media in the Czech and Slovak Republics are closely tied to Czechoslovakian media history and structure, and so the background originally written for this chapter is valid for an understanding of the media of the new nations.)

STATISTICS

Geographic Area: 49,365 square miles
Capitals: Prague (Czech); Bratislava (Slovak)
Population: 15,724,000
Religions: Roman Catholic, Protestant
Languages: Czech, Slovak
Type of Government: Federal republic headed by a prime minister
Gross Domestic Product: $120 billion
Literacy: 99 percent

GENERAL CHARACTERISTICS

The development and function of electronic media in the Slovak Republic and the Czech Republic cannot be comprehended without a knowledge of the social, cultural, and geographic factors that have determined the development of the Czech and Slovak societies. Without taking these determinants into consideration, radio and television development in both the Slovak Republic and the Czech Republic as well as in other Eastern bloc countries, particularly the former Soviet Union, cannot be understood.

Social and Cultural Factors Throughout most of its existence, the territory known in recent years as Czechoslovakia was not a unified nation. Therefore it was not really surprising that it split again in 1993. The northwestern section, peopled by Czechs, was at one time part of Austria. The southeastern section, populated by Slovaks, was formerly part of Hungary. The two were joined together for a short duration (A.D. 833 to 906) as the Great Moravian Empire, but the union did not last.

The Czech area consisted of the territories of Bohemia, Moravia, and Silesia, and the Slovak area was called Slovakia. Bohemia was influenced by the German language and culture and the Protestantism espoused by Martin Luther. Slovakia was largely Catholic, and its social development was often negatively influenced by wars and invasions of nomadic tribes and outlaw Hussites from Bohemia. Prague was the largest city in the Czech region, and Bratislava was the main Slovakian city. Each area had its own language (Czech and Slovak), but the languages were so similar that the people could understand each other.

When the Austro-Hungarian Empire disintegrated after World War I, the language similarity and cultural connections between Czechs and Slovaks became a good basis for the establishment of a common state, and Czechoslovakia was established in 1918. However, the more highly developed industry, greater work productivity, and lower unemployment in the Czech part of the country, as well as its larger population, resulted in social differences and social tensions between Czechs and Slovaks.

The political system in Czechoslovakia between World War I and World War II was based on democratic principles. The function of the press and radio was similar to that of media in other democratic countries. Before World War II even began, Czechoslovakia was truncated by the direct military impact of Hitler's Germany, and two separate states were formed: the Protectorate of Bohemia and Moravia, and the Slovak State. Bohemia and Moravia were occupied by the Nazis until May 1945. Czech newspapers and radio broadcasts were censored, and listening to foreign broadcasts was forbidden and punishable. The Slovak State was proclaimed autonomous and was not occupied, but the threat of occupation hung over its head. For instance, the frequencies of foreign Slovak-language broadcasts from London and Moscow were locked out of radio sets.

An attempt to establish a common state of Czechs and Slovaks based on democratic principles was not successful after World War II. The Democratic party won the elections only in Slovakia; the Communist party was the winner in Bohemia, and the result was the installation of a totalitarian regime which persisted for 40 years.

In 1989 the citizens of Czechoslovakia overthrew the Communist government and returned to democracy. The social differences between Czechs and Slovaks were still evident, and on January 1, 1993, the nation was split in two—the Slovak Republic (Slovensko) and the Czech Republic (Česko).

Geographic Factors Both the Slovak Republic and the Czech Republic are situated in the central part of Europe and, from time immemorial, have been a crossroads of trade routes from the north to the south and from the east to the west. Apart from this central position, the overall communications situation has been influenced by another factor—the rugged relief of the terrain.

Both factors are important for the reception of radio broadcasting, but they are crucial for the reception of television broadcasting. Mountain chains are barriers to the propagation of electromagnetic waves, and this is why some villages in deep valleys still are not covered by terrestrial broadcasting in the Slovak Republic. Transmission of television broadcasts from neighboring democratic countries (Germany and Austria) to the inhabitants of Prague and most of the Czech Republic is impossible.

Reception of neighboring broadcasts is better in the Slovak Republic; since the late 1950s, Austrian television channels, ORF1 and ORF2, have been received in Bratislava. These telecasts exerted an important influence on Slovak viewers, and the political machinery had to take this fact into account. Because they have had an opportunity to watch Austrian TV programming, basic ideas of humanism, principles of democracy, and the Western way of life have long been on the minds of Slovak citizens. New types and methods of programming, including the visualization of news, have inspired and influenced the work of the television center in Bratislava. That is why many programming innovations of the past did not come from the broadcasting center in Prague but from Bratislava.

Apart from the two Austrian channels mentioned above, two Hungarian TV channels can also be seen because of the geographic features of the Slovak Republic. Hungarian broadcasting extends into the rural, most fertile parts of the Slovak Republic where agriculture is highly developed. The area is inhabited mostly by a Hungarian minority that has become a target of intentional propaganda and a source of permanent tensions in recent years. The administrators of the newly formed Slovak electronic media structure have placed restrictions on use of the Hungarian language on radio and TV, and this has raised the concerns of the Hungarian minority.

A third channel from outside the country must be mentioned. This channel was used to receive Moscow television broadcasting aimed especially at soldiers of the Soviet occupation dislocated in Czechoslovakia. After communism was overthrown in 1989, the channel was no longer needed for that purpose.

The Growth of Electronic Media The trends regarding electronic media are generally the same in both the Slovak and Czech Republics as in the rest of the world. In comparison with Western countries, there has been a delay in development of several years, but these two countries are ahead of the other former Communist countries. The reasons are a well-developed domestic electronics industry and the availability on the market of foreign equipment such as color TV sets, VCRs, and satellite dishes.

For political reasons (especially the possibility of recording political events by private persons), the importing of VCRs was blocked for a number of years. Only in the 1980s did the firm AVEX, established in Bratislava, start licensed production of Philips VHS VCRs in cooperation with the electronics producer TESLA.

The liberation of foreign trade in 1990 brought a dramatic change to the market. While the price of an imported VCR had been about half the price of an automobile before 1990, it was only about one-fifth that cost in 1992. The price relationship for satellite TV reception equipment has been similar. In 1992, the price of a VCR or a satellite dish was about twice an average month's pay.

THE DEVELOPMENT OF ELECTRONIC MEDIA IN THE CZECH REPUBLIC AND THE SLOVAK REPUBLIC

Articles on the history of electronic media in Czechoslovakia usually start with the invention of wireless radio and then introduce the name of Josef Murgaš, a Slovak living in Wilkes-Barre/Scranton, Pennsylvania, who made radio broadcasting experiments parallel to those of the Italian Guglielmo Marconi. Even before 1910, he was a holder of nine U.S. patents.

Early Radio Regular Czechoslovakian radio broadcasting started on May 18, 1923, in Prague. Later on, radio stations in Brno, Bratislava, Košice, Ostrava, and Banská Bystrica started their broadcasting with news, music, educational programs, and the reading of fiction. All broadcasts were live until 1937 when the first experiments with recorded broadcasts were made. The company Rádiožurnál was a programming producer that monopolized the whole territory until the disintegration of Czechoslovakia in 1939.

During World War II, radio in Bohemia and radio in Slovakia were completely separate institutions. For the most part these media were stifled by the Germans, but radio did play a role in an armed uprising that broke out in Slovakia in August 1944. The aim was to attack the German army in the rear, create a new front, and accelerate the advance of the Allied armies. This uprising picked up strength the day the rebels seized the radio station at Banská Bystrica, and it fell apart 2 months later on the very day the station ceased broadcasting.

Radio after World War II After the war, radio became a subject of intense political fighting between the Democratic and Communist parties. With the support of the Soviet Union, a political revolution took place in February 1948, and in April 1948 Czechoslovakia Radio began broadcasting as the proclaimed tool of the Communist party's propaganda. Media were quickly nationalized and were fully controlled and censored by the state until 1989.

Until 1952 there was only one common radio network, with all stations contributing to filling the airtime. In 1952, the Slovak National Network and a common network called Czechoslovakia were organized. Another radio network, Czechoslovakia II, was established in 1962.

In 1971, a diversification took place. Five radio networks were established: one federal whole-state network, Hviezda (Star); two regional networks broadcasting general entertainment programming and news, the Slovak network Bratislava and the Czech network Prague; and two regional networks with music and educational programming, the Slovak network called Devin and the Czech network called Vltava.

Radio broadcasting was not continuous until 1952. Before 1952 there were breaks between the morning and afternoon and afternoon and evening programs. After 1952, the only break was at night, from midnight until 4:30 A.M. When the Hviezda network started operation in 1971, there was continuous 24-hour broadcasting in Czechoslovakia.

During the cold war years, the state spent a great deal of money and technology building a special system, cable-radio. Uniform programming (with the exception of local news) was transmitted to the whole republic through a network connecting central amplifiers with radio sets placed everywhere—in homes, schools, offices, and public institutions. Cable-radio served not only as a means of suppressing information and creating uniformity in the news but also as a system of preparation in case of war.

The change in the political system in 1989 was reflected in the organizational structure of radio broadcasting. Now, private persons are

Equipment used in Slovak television in Bratislava in 1961. Ivan Stadtrucker is the man in white. (*Photo by Eduard Holly*)

able to obtain licenses for radio broadcasting. By the end of 1992, there were about fifteen private radio stations in Prague, broadcasting in the FM range. They supply prevailingly popular music but also classical music, talk shows, and cultural and religious programs. Apart from that, another twenty-one radio stations operated in the Czech territory. In Slovakia, seven stations had been licensed in the FM range, four of them in Bratislava.

Since the creation of the Slovak and Czech republics, the main problems facing radio have been financial. They have been more severe in the Slovak Republic. It found itself unable to support foreign radio news correspondents and so joined with the Czechs in an arrangement to have joint correspondents provide news for both republics.

Television during the Communist Era The first reference to television in a Czechoslovak official document occurs in a 1934 communication. It can be found in the official correspondence of the Ministry of Posts and Telegraphs, where the term "television" is defined as "picture-radio broadcasting."

In 1953 the Communist party initiated broadcasting from a television station in Prague, at first only two times a week. The party applied Lenin's thesis, "As for us, film is the most important of all arts," to television and made of it a most effective medium for mass distribution of information and propaganda.

In 1956 TV stations in Ostrava and Bratislava started broadcasting, and within the next 2 years the stations in Prague, Bratislava, and Ostrava were interconnected to form a network. Throughout the years, the number of stations entering the network increased, as did the number of broadcast hours. In 1970 color broadcasting began and a second channel was started. By 1980 Channel 1 covered 98.5 percent of the country and Channel 2 covered 72.5 percent. About 73 percent of programming was in color.

The number of homes with TV sets also increased from 75,800 in 1956 to 3,091,000 in 1970 to 5,824,000 in 1990. In general, a little over one-third of the sets were in the Slovak part of the country and two-thirds were in the Czech part.

Through the years the Slovaks pushed for their own television station, and this was the subject of many negotiations. In 1968 the Slovak Parliament established Slovak Television as an institution operating in the territory of Slovakia. However, its independence from television in Prague was only relative. The director of Slovak TV had to be nominated by the Central Committee of the Slovak Communist party, and his or her activity was controlled by the Central Committee of the Czechoslovak Communist party in Prague. Often there were different official standpoints emanating from Prague and Bratislava concerning the operation of Slovak TV.

The situation changed in 1989 when Communist party control ceased. Between 1989 and 1993, Czechoslovak TV, the national network, was responsible to the federal government in Prague for its operation. Czech Television was established as a counterpart to the already existing Slovak Television. Both of these broadcast independently of each other on different channels and only in their respective territories.

When the split came in 1993, the two systems were already fairly separate, and the two countries began to operate their television broadcasting independently. As with radio, financial problems ensued, and both countries were forced to reduce the number of broadcast staff employees. The Czech Republic has started the process of introducing private television. In early 1994 its first nationwide private TV service, Nova, went on the air, offering a mix of Czech public affairs shows and Western entertainment. Nova's parent company, CET-21, obtained U.S. financial backing for this TV venture.

Major Broadcasting Events There are two events in the history of Czechoslovakia that were greatly influenced by television and radio.

The first occurred after censorship was abolished by the Slovak political leader Alexander Dubček in 1968. This is frequently referred to as Prague Spring. Both radio and television played a major role in broadcasting information about these reforms. However, in August 1968, troops from the Soviet Union and other Eastern bloc countries entered Prague to put down the reforms. The occupation armies soon paralyzed the television operation. Then radio became the basic information channel for the whole country and in this way prevented the collapse of the social structure and reported on the disintegration and chaos that followed.

The second important influence of broadcasting manifested itself in the spring of 1988 from abroad. Because of strong Christian traditions in Slovakia, the suppression of religious freedom by the totalitarian regime was felt there intensely. The fighters for religious freedom received much help and support from Anton Hlinka, a reporter for Radio Free Europe in Munich. A peaceful protest demonstration against the suppression of religious freedom, though forbidden by the authorities, took place on the night before Good Friday (March 25, 1988) in Bratislava. Radio Free Europe then broadcast direct reports by participants calling in from street telephone booths. The high point of this program was a radio communication about the interfering police units that one radio hobbyist managed to send to Munich. The broadcast of this intervention against praying people was considered a moral fiasco of the Communist regime by listeners abroad.

The same principle of public confrontation was used several months later by students in Prague. Their politically successful provocation in front of cameras on the main street of Prague on November 17, 1989, was shown by television staffers who disobeyed their bosses in order to present the protests on screen. This led to the final downfall of the Communist government, followed by the coming of democratic forces.

Commercial Television When the Communist government fell and the Soviet occupation troops left Czechoslovakia, the channel that had been coming into the country from the Soviet Union was no longer needed. The idea of using this channel for civilian purposes was initiated in Czechoslovakia. As a result, a commercial network was set up in May 1990, operated by Intendancy OK 3 and subordinate to the director of Czechoslovak Television in Prague.

This OK 3 network could air advertisements and obtain foreign programming by bartering commercial time in exchange for programs. Material from France (La Sept, MCM, Euromusic, Canal France International), Germany (RTL Plus, Deutsche Welle), England (Screensport), and the United States (CNN, Worldnet) was broadcast.

Because Intendancy was part of the federal network Czechoslovak TV, the profit from commercials stayed in the Czech purse. This was the main reason the management of Slovak Television decided to set up Intendancy TA 3. In June 1991 this independent group started to operate Channel 3 in Slovakia, broadcasting foreign and regional programs.

Some programming from sources that had cooperated with OK 3 became inaccessible to TA 3, but TA 3 succeeded in obtaining programs from other programming sources such as Britain's Sky News and Granada TV. TA 3 broadcasts 24 hours a day and airs news obtained from four different foreign agencies in English, Russian, French, and German, as well as Sky News in Slovak translation. During its existence, TA 3 has aired 450 hours of programming in Slovak. Original foreign programs have been translated into Slovak by the use of subtitles, dubbing, or voice-overs.

Satellite Television Because Czechoslovakia is geographically in the center of Europe, a broad spectrum of programs transmitted through satellite television can be received. Satellite broadcasting is received either individually through private dishes or jointly; that is, the received signal is transferred to a wire which is then run into each of the neighborhood homes as cable television.

Some of the satellite signals that are available include: RTL Plus, SAT.1, Super Channel, Sky Movies, Music TV, Premiere, Lifestyle, Eurosport, Sportkanal, and Filmnet. The schedule for these satellite signals is published weekly in newspapers.

None of the programs delivered by satellite is translated into Czech or Slovak. As a result, their capacity to communicate to viewers within these countries is reduced because of the language barrier.

VCRs In the 1980s VCRs became available in Czechoslovakia. If a Slovak or Czech citizen had to choose between a VCR and a dish, the VCR would be preferred. Videocassette recorders utilizing the VHS system and the European PAL standard dominate the market. Mainly, the citizens are interested in feature films (dramas, comedies, science fiction adventures, thrillers, pornos, cartoons). Videocassettes with such programs are available in specialized shops either in the original version or in Slovak or Czech translation.

It is a well-known fact that regulation of the videocassette market is unclear and that illegal activities abound. Legislative regulations regarding import have not been stabilized; thus not all imported videocassettes are legal productions respecting copyright laws. Piracy and illegal copying, as well as clandestine production of Slovak and Czech versions, are not unusual. Such video programs are usually distributed and sold outside legal stores and distribution networks. Videocassettes with all types of programs are available on the black market.

In stores that rent videocassettes legally, the choice is not as rich, but the cassettes are of higher technical quality. Video stores are mostly privately owned, and renting cassettes from video stores is not as common as in the United States; exchange and lending on a home-to-home basis prevails. Thanks to favorable prices, videocassette recorders are abundant in schools, offices, firms, and institutions, as well as in homes. They are used in promotion and information dispersal, and for educational uses such as language courses.

Simultaneously with the advent of videocassettes, many private video production centers have sprung up in Czechoslovakia. They produce Czech and Slovak translations of foreign video programs as well as their own commercials, popular shows, educational programs, documentaries, and dramatic programs of a high professional level. They create television programs for Czech and Slovak television and for foreign TV companies.

ORGANIZATION AND FINANCING

Until 1990 radio and television were owned exclusively by the state. Since that time, numerous changes have occurred to convert the system structure from a totalitarian one to one that is more democratic.

Structure during the Communist Era During the early 1950s, both radio and television were run by one administrative unit, the Czechoslovak Committee for Radio and Television, operating out of Prague. Starting in 1958, the two media were operated separately. In 1964 the Czechoslovak Parliament passed a television act stating that the head of television would be a director, nominated by the government, who would have overall responsibility for programming and economic decisions. Ideological control of television by the Central Committee of the Communist party in Prague was also embodied in that act.

The director had deputies responsible for different areas: programming and political issues, production and technology, and finance and administration. The programming deputy was the head of the editorial offices, each of which produced a certain type of program: entertainment, dramas and fiction, news, music, sports, children's programming, and so forth.

Each editorial office had to submit projects for programming, and programs could not be produced until they had been approved and included in the ideological and thematic plan (ITP) by the station management. Programs were produced in television studios or made to order in film studios. The main editorial office decided when individual programs would be broadcast. Broadcasting times of programs distributed by the federal network had to be approved by the main editorial office in Prague.

The director of the TV station in Prague was the central director of Czechoslovak TV as a whole and decided on the allocation of federal government grants and made final decisions as to whether or not a program could be broadcast.

The structure of broadcasting as a whole, as well as details regarding individual types of programming in the schedule, was decided by the Central Committee of the Communist party in Prague. For instance, its directives determined the percentage of feature films, documentaries, and dramas that were to be produced. It also prescribed how many of them could be classical, how many could be based on works by Western authors, and how many had to be by Communist authors. For new, original productions that were made to order, the theme, genre, and often even director and actors were prescribed.

All these directives were usually decided 2 to 5 years in advance of when they would be put into effect. Then the editorial offices presented elaborate plans for programs, and the Central Committee of the Communist party decided which projects would be actually realized. Once approved, the thematic plans and ideology became binding. The same was true for radio. It was practically impossible to produce a program not included in the plan.

Before 1968 the question of language was a sensitive one. The management in Prague determined the percentage of programs that Slovak viewers could watch in their own language, and this did not always sit well with the Slovaks. Then, in 1968, television was set up in Slovakia and its director was chosen by the Central Committee of the Slovak Communist party. Radio went through a similar development pattern, including the establishment of Slovak Radio and Czech Radio. Channel 1 was the federal channel, and its programming went to both Czechs and Slovaks. Channel 2 was controlled from Prague for broadcasting in the Czech part of the country, and from Bratislava for Slovak broadcasting.

The influence of the central director in Prague on Slovak Channel 2 programming underwent several changes that resulted in Slovak Communist party leaders taking more control over Slovak broadcasting. The ideas of freedom, democracy, and equality of nations proclaimed by Dubček and his Prague Spring brought about a gradual diminishing of influence from Prague over the next decade; yet radio and television broadcasting in Slovakia was obviously controlled and censored by its Communist party. Financially, the operation of Czech and Slovak broadcasting was supported by the respective budgets of those regions. Federal television was financed by both.

Structure after the Fall of Totalitarianism
After the fall of the totalitarian regime in 1989, a process of transforming state institutions into public institutions started, and technical equipment and communication lines were partly privatized.

The activities of both public radio and public television were overseen by the Council for Radio and Television Broadcasting, consisting of nine members. The council was the highest authority and was the group that licensed broadcasters. Based on the respective councils' suggestions, the national parliaments of both republics nominated general managers of Czech Radio, Czech Television, Slovak Radio, and Slovak Television. Federal television, broadcasting on Channel 1, was still under the patronage of the federal government in Prague.

Each general manager had his or her own editorial board consisting of nine members representing various fields of culture. Their membership in a political party was not of primary importance. The editorial board members gave their views on overall programming, broadcasting schedules, economic and budget issues, and equipment and technology.

Managers of production departments such as news, children's programming, sports, arts, and exchange programs were subordinate to the general manager and had their own budgets. Each prepared program had an editor, and the production center manager decided whether the program would be produced in-house or ordered from an outside organization.

The financing for public broadcasting came from subscribers' fees, money from the state, and profits from advertising. Each household with at least one TV set paid a monthly fee that was approximately equivalent to the price of two theater tickets or five cinema tickets. Each household with at least one radio also paid a fee that was about half the TV fee.

Besides the stations and networks that came under the Council for Radio and Television Broadcasting, there were commercial radio and television stations that operated exclusively off the profits of advertising. Most of them had both foreign and domestic investment capital.

When the two countries separated in 1993, their broadcasting organizations separated, too. However, because they were already divided into Slovak Television, Slovak Radio, Czech Television, and Czech Radio, only minor adjustments needed to be made. For example, there are a number of relay antennas on the border between the two countries, and eventually a decision must be made as to whom they belong to. But, at present, the two countries are operating them jointly—and peacefully.

PROGRAMMING

Though the Communist party and its representatives proclaimed that radio and television were cultural institutions providing for the intellectual development of Czechoslovakia's population, in fact, they were always considered tools of political propaganda. Continuous and intense manipulation of minds, as well as a unification of public opinion, was exerted directly through news and public affairs programs and, in a concealed form, even through artistic and entertainment programs.

Because of their obviously tendentious character, radio and television programs were excluded from the sphere of culture and the arts. To mask the essentially propagandistic character of mass media, the Communist party gave some support to works that actually fulfilled artistic criteria. This marginal sphere—from the material and financial point of view—became an oasis that saved the Czech and Slovak nations from cultural degeneration and moral decline. In this way, talented artists had an opportunity for relatively autonomous creation, and critics were challenged to raise their standards.

Thus a possibility for manifestation of the Czech and Slovak nations' creative potential was found. The continuity of intellectual development was secured, and under favorable circumstances even outstanding works were created. These persist as works of great value, but what is more important, they were recognized and prized abroad when they were created.

The international successes of radio, and especially television, were claimed by the Communist party and used as a "proof of its correct cultural policy." But in fact the successes were something else; they were a form of ideological support and cultural diversion from Western countries against what the Communist administration could not defend. Works that became famous abroad could hardly be questioned, and their authors could not be persecuted.

Television and Radio Journalism In the early period of TV broadcasting in Czechoslovakia, the major task of television journalism consisted of direct transmission of the most important political events. Domestic and foreign news was taken from radio and read over TV by radio newscasters. The news was supplemented by a newsreel, *Týždeň vo filme (Week in Film)*, which was projected in cinemas as well.

Starting in 1958, a major program, *Televízne noviny (TV News)* was broadcast. It was prepared by teams of journalists, and film shots from all the important events in Czechoslovakia were shown on the screen. The central editorial office in Prague was in charge of reporting news from abroad. Its reporters were stationed in many countries, and news was also obtained from the UPI and VISNEWS agencies.

In the following years, news was always presented in prime time and in two editions. The first, broadcast sometime between 7 and 8 P.M., lasted 30 minutes on television and 15 minutes on radio and mainly involved serious topics dealing with domestic and foreign policy. There were also a few brief reports on culture and sports. TV news and radio news were presented at different times so that they did not overlap.

The second edition was broadcast between 9:30 and 10:30 P.M., and more time was devoted to political and economic reports. There were always special supplements for sports, *Góly—body—sekundy (Goals—Points—Seconds)*, and for culture, *Okienko do kultúry (Glances into Culture)*. This final edition was always prepared by the editorial office in Prague. Although reports on Slovak topics were prepared in Bratislava, they could be broadcast only after they were approved by Prague, where all decisions were made concerning which stories might be broadcast to the whole territory, which would be shown in Slovakia, and which would not be broadcast at all.

The news was read by speakers in an impersonal, official manner. These speakers evoked an impression of official representatives of television, and they were not allowed to act in other TV programs as entertainers.

This situation changed after 1989, and announcers have now started to behave in a more relaxed manner, addressing each other by their first names just as U.S. newscasters do. Their mannerisms also imitate those of American newscasters—taking papers from the table or putting a pen into a pocket at the end of the newscast. But from the viewpoint of their role as communicators, they have remained impartial, passive interpreters allowed at most to conduct short interviews. The role of anchorperson, as performed by people like Walter Cronkite and Dan Rather in the United States, is unknown in the Czech and Slovak republics.

Recently, the relationship of the broadcasters to the audience has become less formal. For example, one moderator started a radio psychological advising program for lonely people. Gradually this program changed its format to one that involved authorities and then ordinary listeners calling in by phone. The program has become one of the most popular on Slovak Radio.

Shortly before the Czechoslovakian nation split, anti-Czech and anti-Slovak feelings started to appear in the mass media. Anti-Slovak attitudes manifested themselves mainly in federal radio and television broadcasting controlled by Prague. In reaction, Slovak Radio and Slovak Television started broadcasting their own news programs on their own channels. These programs were independent of Prague, and their time slots were shifted in an attempt to paralyze the effect of news from Prague. The federal news broadcast on Channel 1 from Prague was a major factor in swaying public opinion and contributing to the disintegration of the common state. Once separated, the Slovak news took on primary importance in the Slovak Republic.

Documentaries After the end of World War II, a strong tradition of documentary production existed in both Czech and Slovak film studios. Up until 1970 the studio in Brastislava alone produced about 300 documentaries a year, and Czech production exceeded 500 titles a year. These documentaries were shown in cinemas or were produced for schools and other institutions.

After 1970 the demand for documentaries for cinemas decreased, and most of the documentaries made in the studios of Prague and Bratislava were designed for television broadcast. In practice, three types of documentaries were produced: current affairs journalism (reports, interviews, inquiries); TV documentaries (wildlife programs, films of expeditions, films about the arts); and educational films (language courses, teaching and training programs). Documentaries created for television were a hybrid genre with elements of reality, as well as fiction subordinate to the ideological design.

From 1958 to 1968 the program *L'udia, roky, udalosti (People, Years, Events)* provided a mixture of current and historical events. Similarly, individual parts of the series *Toto je moje město (This Is My Town)* introduced historical facts about various towns and chronicled their current social, ecological, and cultural problems. Most importantly, the prospects for a favorable future were described using bright colors.

In spite of censorship, some unexpected documentaries appeared on the screen that produced a significant reaction from the government. This was especially true for the documentary *Kysuca, Kysuca*, directed by Ivan Rumanovský, which was inserted in the series *Namiesto výrobkov l'udia (People Instead of Products)*. In this film, the poor social situation of people living in northern Slovakia was described by the secretary of the district committee of the Communist party. After the program was broadcast, the secretary-general of the Czechoslovak Communist party and the president of the republic, Antonín Novotný, protested. This brought Novotný into conflict with the leader of the Slovak Communist party, Alexander Dubček. The conflict eventually led to the recall of Novotný, the ascent of Alexander Dubček, and eventually the onset of Prague Spring!

In 1968, during Prague Spring, programming

was marked by thematic and genre heterogeneity but especially by freedom of speech. Parts of a television series featuring the Czech actor and writer Jan Werich were outstanding because of their intellectual riches, wisdom, and wit. They have remained popular up to the present day.

The 1970s was a time of strict totalitarian control. It was a period of censorship and self-censorship. The two main documentary-type series were talk shows, *Na aktuálnu tému (On Topical Themes)* and *Kreslo pre host'a (Chair for Our Guests)*, where celebrities and people from political life explained their opinions. During this period, programming was characterized by conformity, ideological sterility, and uniformity. Programs were broadcast simultaneously in both republics, and those produced in Prague and Bratislava were identical.

In the late 1970s, viewers were attracted by the series *Kto je vinný (Who Is Guilty?)*. Each part of this series consisted of two installments: the first one was a reconstruction of a trial, and the second was a talk show where lawyers and journalists answered questions from viewers.

Documentary production reached its peak with documentaries dealing with artistic works, cultural memorials, and well-known personalities. The value of these films has persisted, and they have become part of the national culture. There has always been a demand for such documentaries in the international television programming exchange.

Since the beginning of the 1990s, political change has brought about changes in the role and forms of documentaries. Because of a shortage of money needed to produce works of artistic ambition and some of the technical limitations of video, documentaries lack sophisticated composition, well-ordered scenes, and other aesthetic qualities. They concentrate on information that is topical and reveals viewpoints through interviews.

During 1992 the most remarkable program was the documentary series *OKO* by Fero Fenič, a Slovak director living in Prague. It was devoted to topics and celebrities, and it usually conveyed a definite point of view. However, one aspect of its originality that disturbed some of its viewers was the appearance of the film director who often made a point of showing himself in the film. At the beginning or end of the program he was seen standing at some unusual place such as the platform on which politicians deliver their speeches or at the state border.

Documentaries on expeditions and sociological documentaries have remained very popular with TV viewers, but wildlife series are the most popular of all.

Sports Sports events televised to Czechoslovakia from abroad, and vice versa, have a tradition and are of great importance. In the years of the totalitarian regime, transmissions from the Olympics and from world championships were the only window to the outside world. International sports events transmissions from Czechoslovakia have helped to improve the technological aspects of television broadcasting as well as the professionalism of TV staff members.

Direct transmissions of top competitions, such as the world and European championships in skating, ice hockey, volleyball, wrestling, handball, and so forth, have always tested the quality of television technology and staff. They have provided opportunities for confrontation with developments elsewhere.

Among numerous sports events transmissions, a special place belongs to the transmission of the world championship in classic skiing held in High Tatras, Slovakia, in 1970 where, for the first time in the history of not only Slovak but also Czech television, direct transmissions were made in color. Those transmissions were received in more than thirty countries, and were such a success that the president of the United States sent Czechoslovak Television a congratulatory telegram.

Children's Programs Children's television programs in the Czech and Slovak republics cover all age groups from very small children to teenagers. Many genres are present on the screen—cartoons, fairy tales, educational programs, talk shows, game shows, pop music concerts, and teleplays.

Even in times of the greatest centralism in Prague, Bratislava's broadcasting for children and youth retained a remarkable sovereignty. This was due to cultivation of the Slovak mother tongue in children. All children's programs, Czech and foreign alike, were dubbed into Slovak.

As a consequence, no tradition of cartoon animation in Slovakia, except for the works of V. Kubal, existed. This differed from the situation in the Czech part of the country where cartoon production was undertaken by well-known animators. However, in the late 1980s Slovak children's program editor H. Minichová succeeded in organizing a group of talented people, and in cooperation with Film Studios Koliba, created a new phenomenon—the Slovak animated film. Their international success has been comparable to the success of Czech animators. This development was influenced by the fact that short cartoons (lasting about 10 minutes) broadcast at children's bedtimes (after 6:30 P.M.) have been very popular with children, as well as adults, for decades in both Bohemia and Slovakia.

Music Music, both classical and popular, is the mainstay of radio programming. Disc jockeys introduce the music, which consists of popular instrumentals and vocals from tapes, records, and CDs. Public radio music is intended for the general audience and often consists of dance music and symphonies. Commercial stations tend to be more youth-oriented and broadcast the top hits. Public station announcers are fairly formal, but commercial disc jockeys imitate their U.S. counterparts by joking, talking to listeners on the phone, and presenting advertisements.

There are all genres and forms of music in the archives of Czech and Slovak television: folk songs, video clips, variety shows, pop music, jazz, musicals, operettas, and operas sung by famous soloists, some composed and first performed as special TV operas.

Classical concerts, interpreted by the Czech Philharmonic, Slovak Philharmonic, and Slovak Chamber Orchestra, are of high and persistent quality. Classical music has been one of the most successful Czechoslovak exports. Each year there are two international classical music festivals: Prague Spring in the spring, and Bratislava Music Festival in the autumn. Videotape recordings of all concerts given by well-known soloists and orchestras and transmitted abroad are kept on file.

Drama When television broadcasting started in Czechoslovakia, there were theaters in all the larger towns. Those theaters had permanent companies playing all season on the home stage and occasionally in other towns. Their performances were often presented on TV by use of a stationary camera showing the action from in front of the stage. In both republics, such companies became a broad platform for teleplay casts and directors.

At first, film directors did not cooperate with television. They were not interested in a live broadcasting technology that necessitated the use of shots from four or five on-air cameras without any possibility of repetition.

However, political support for television was manifested in material support. There was money enough to buy raw materials, and there was more opportunity for various proposals than in state cinematography. Professionally well-prepared graduates from the Prague Film University (FAMU), not influenced by tradition, saw an opportunity in television and took their chances. When first starting out, they were inspired by Western TV authors, especially Paddy Chayefsky, who wrote the U.S. teleplay *Marty* about a growing love between a homely schoolteacher and a butcher. They concentrated on common people's problems in situations of everyday life.

Giving up theatrical methods (one camera showing the proscenium arch) and employing film production techniques have produced television of fine quality; since 1979 all internationally important and successful productions have used film technology.

Before the short period of Prague Spring concluded and Communist reality returned, three trends evolved in dramatic television programming: the transmission of theater productions performed on home stages or in TV studios, the production of original Czech and Slovak screenplays, and the adaptation of literary and dramatic works by foreign authors. Czech TV was successful in the production of original screenplays, while television adaptations of foreign works became the domain of Slovak TV.

The arrival of Soviet occupation troops brought the short period of free artistic creation and freedom of speech, Prague Spring, to an end. The Thirteenth Congress of the Communist party criticized television mercilessly for "taking over modern influences from abroad and meeting the lifestyle and philosophy of the western world." Many editors and staff members were dismissed, and others were no longer allowed to work in television.

The range of themes narrowed, and the ratio of domestic to foreign authors changed from 2:3 to 3:2. Only screenplays describing life in a glib, optimistic way were allowed to be produced. Gradually, the situation started to improve. Works by Plautus, Machiavelli, de Vega, Balzac, Dostoyevski, Kaufman, and others were eventually put on the screen.

During the period after the suppression of Prague Spring, Communist ideologists preferred nonfiction programs. They supported reconstructions of historical events such as the Yalta and Potsdam conferences, as well as docudramas from milieus and times distant from Czech and Slovak viewers.

The 1989 "velvet revolution" that led Czechoslovakia from communism toward free enterprise brought about many basic changes in the social structure of Czechoslovakia. In the field of TV dramatic production, this revolution changed values as well as criteria. Programs on subjects that used to be forbidden can now be produced. However, conditions for creative work have deteriorated as economic depression has advanced. Now a market economy, based on business profits, demands productions that meet a standard mass culture.

LAWS AND REGULATIONS

Before 1990, when radio and television were exclusively in the hands of the state, the process of approval that all programs went through before their broadcast was an elaborate system of censorship and control applied by the ideologists of the Communist party. The approval process made it practically impossible to broadcast anything that would not be in accord with the policy of the Communist party.

Censorship was exerted by specialized censors or ideological experts, but editors, deputies, and directors of the respective television stations were responsible for the content of programs. If a program was broadcast that resulted in an unfavorable political effect, in spite of censorship, repressive measures were taken to punish the responsible persons. Usually the editor of such a program was dismissed.

In 1990 basic changes were undertaken in mass media. First, Slovak Radio and Slovak Television were proclaimed independent entities, and then Czech Radio and Czech Television were similarly organized. All four have been transformed from state enterprises (corporations owned by the state) into public corporations (supported, at least in part, by the state). Now that the countries have split, Slovak Radio and Slovak Television are funded by the Slovak Republic government budget, and Czech Radio

Headquarters of Slovak Television in Bratislava.

and Czech Television are likewise funded by the budget of the Czech Republic. The fact that each of these institutions is supported, at least in part, with money from the respective republics raises the question of whether such institutions can be really independent and how loyal they must be to the current government.

The primary law governing radio and television broadcasting in both the Slovak and Czech Republics stems from a 1991 act passed when Czechoslovakia was still one country. It states that broadcast programs are not allowed to promote war or describe or show violent acts in an exciting or approving way. Programs that might jeopardize the psychological or moral development of children and youth may not be shown between 6 A.M. and 10 P.M. No commercials may be broadcast that encourage behavior jeopardizing morality, consumer interests, health, security, or the environment, as well as commercials designed for children or featuring children that threaten their health or psychological and moral development. Advertisements for tobacco products must include data on the actual nicotine content and a warning that smoking is hazardous to one's health. Commercials must not be inserted into broadcasting immediately before or after a religious service.

Original enforcement of the law was assigned to the Federal Council for Radio and Television Broadcasting for the whole territory of Czechoslovakia. Although this council disappeared on January 1, 1993, when Czechoslovakia was divided into two autonomous states, the two countries kept the basic provisions of the act until their respective parliaments could pass new laws.

THE AUDIENCE

Under totalitarianism the government decided what the audience should see and hear. The desires of the people did not really come into play, so there was no need for anything resembling the ratings methodology used in the United States. Whether or not audience numbers will become important will depend on the direction radio and television take in the future.

A few facts are known about the audience. The accompanying table shows the percentage of people who view television at various times of the day on various days of the week.

Time	Mon.	Tue.	Wed.	Thu.	Fri.	Sat.	Sun
7 A.M.–1 P.M.	8	10	10	9	10	28	45
1 P.M.–5 P.M.	10	11	11	10	14	35	46
5 P.M.–7 P.M.	43	44	41	43	50	61	68
7 P.M.–10 P.M.	78	80	82	81	83	85	83
10 P.M.–1 A.M.	20	20	21	21	50	63	36

TECHNOLOGY

The SECAM standard for broadcasting, rather than the PAL system, was adopted by Czechoslovakia and other Eastern bloc countries mainly to make the reception of Western television stations impossible. Although this did not totally preclude people from finding ways to receive programming from Western nations, it definitely made it difficult.

During the Communist years, vast sums of money were spent on the development of technical equipment—from vacuum tubes to transistors to cameras and transmitters—not because of a lack of foreign currency needed to import the equipment from abroad but because of the Stalinist doctrine of technological independence from the West.

TV cameras, microphones, recorders, and other instruments were produced in Czechoslovakia in small numbers on a semiprofessional level. Hence there was a high failure rate. However, the products could not be replaced with standard foreign-made products. Now, foreign-made equipment can be imported and is gradually replacing Czechoslovakian-made equipment. The new production studios are equipped with up-to-date technology, usually Sony cameras and recorders and highly computerized editing and graphics systems.

EXTERNAL SERVICES

Before 1989 Czechoslovakia broadcast intensive propaganda programs in several languages through Radio Prague. Since the disintegration of Czechoslovakia, Czech Radio broadcasts for listeners abroad in English, French, Russian, German, and Spanish. It also broadcasts programs in the Slovak language aimed at Slovakia. Slovak Radio broadcasts for listeners abroad in Slovak, German, English, French, and Russian but does not produce programs in the Czech language to be broadcast to the Czech Republic. Letters from listeners in North and South America, Australia, and other remote territories prove that this broadcasting can be heard all over the planet.

The Czechs and the Slovaks listen to external services from other countries, particularly Radio Free Europe, Voice of America, the BBC, and Radio Vatican.

In addition, during the cold war period, Prague served as the seat for the Intervision Consortium, an association of the Soviet Union,

Hungary, Bulgaria, Mongolia, Finland, and Czechoslovakia. Through Intervision these countries exchanged programming with one another and also with the Eurovision countries.

IMPORTANCE IN THE WORLD COMMUNITY

Of all the Eastern bloc countries, Czechoslovakia had the highest standard of living. That characteristic makes it something of a bellwether as Eastern Europe makes the transformation from totalitarianism to democracy. The direction that Czechoslovakian electronic media take may well influence the direction taken by neighboring countries. In addition, the two countries into which Czechoslovakia has been divided may become buyers of programming if their economies improve and if commercial television and satellite television progress and the videocassette market becomes more legitimate. These countries will need to establish laws and regulations because the old ones have lost their validity and do not take into account any of the newer media structures.

Most importantly, Czechoslovakia has the innate ability to produce programming for the world market. In the past, Czechoslovakian television generated an impressive list of international successes, in spite of the fact that the country is relatively small, with only about 15 million inhabitants. Even though Czechoslovakia produced only five films in 1956 when television broadcasting first started, it has been able to make such an impressive step forward that now its TV production can be internationally appreciated.

Slovakian television, in particular, has made enormous strides. One of the reasons has been its cultural traditions, but there have also been some special conditions and influences. On the broadcast program schedule, Bratislava obtained a rather undesirable time slot—Monday evening—for presentation of its dramatic programs, but this time has remained the same for 30 years. Thus viewers have developed an expectation of seeing high-quality works of art on Monday nights. In this way television cultivated the perceptiveness of viewers so that their desire for high-quality productions increased.

Slovak actors have had more opportunities to work in television because their numbers have been smaller than those of Czech actors. Besides acting in front of the camera, they have dubbed foreign films, and in so doing they have been able to analyze artistic performances by the best actors and film stars in the world. That has been good professional training for them and at the same time has increased their self-confidence.

Thanks to videocassette recorders, actors have been able to watch themselves as though looking in a mirror. They have learned to respect the position of the camera and the microphone. They have been cast in movies and teleplays of Slovak, Czech, and even foreign productions. For instance, the Slovak actor Jozef Króner played the main character in the movie *Obshod na korze (Store on the Promenade)* which was awarded an Oscar by the American Academy of Motion Picture Arts and Sciences.

Professionally, very well-prepared camerapeople, graduates of the Film University (FAMU) in Prague, have had many artistic opportunities in Slovakia. They have applied film techniques in their television works and have undertaken very careful editing. Though past self-regulations allowed no more than sixty cuts in a 75-minute teleplay, some plays now have as many as 400 cuts.

About 100 teleplays a year are produced in Slovakia, and another 100 in the Czech territory. Their quality is equal to, or even higher than, the usual European standard. The programs deal with human fate and fortune from ancient times to the present. They feature the dreams, luck, and sorrow of individuals. They are artistic works with themes that should have consistent appeal to viewers everywhere.

MAJOR ISSUES

The main issues of electronic media in both the Slovak and Czech Republics revolve around the changing political situation. The disintegration of Czechoslovakia and the rise of the Czech and Slovak Republics took place in an atmosphere of high political drama. Both republics must create their own new internal political, legal, and economic structures and define the relations between themselves and also with other countries. It is a manifestation of the mutual regard and tolerance between the two republics that some TV programs are prepared jointly and transmitted live to both countries. Every day Slovak viewers can see news from Czech TV that is broadcast on Slovak TV. Czech TV also broadcasts Slovak TV news.

As the two broadcast systems develop their new structures, they will probably be affected by their cultural background. Historical factors left over from totalitarianism will no doubt play a role as the media continue to develop. Both parts of Czechoslovakia must free themselves of the mindset engendered by generations of Communist control over the electronic media and must establish an electronic media system that can survive in a democratic society and a market-driven economy.

The economy will have a great effect on radio and television because production and transmission of programming are very expensive. Both Czech and Slovak radio and television are accustomed to receiving funds from general budgets. Now that capitalism is taking hold and more and more of the money will need to be raised in other ways, the media structures must readjust. This may lead to at least a temporary period of economic hardship.

The countries' geographic position at the crossroads of Europe will also affect their media structure. Satellite reception is plentiful, and if the technology develops so that more people can understand the language of the satellite feeds from neighboring countries, the traditional Czech and Slovak radio and television networks may be threatened by an outside invasion of programming.

Overall, however, Czech and Slovak radio and television have already produced immense cultural wealth, which has been and will long remain a contribution to human progress and people's understanding—mediated by the global electronic village.

SELECTED BIBLIOGRAPHY

Abercrombie, Thomas J. "The Velvet Divorce: CzechoSlovakia," *National Geographic*, September 1993, pp. 2–37.

"Broadcasting in Czechoslovakia," *Communication's Update Service*, June/September 1979, p. 24.

"Czechoslovakia: Redrawing Media Boundaries," *Broadcasting*, 16 July 1990, pp. 90–92.

"Czechs to Get Commercial TV," *Journal of Commerce*, 17 September 1993, p. A-4.

Draxler, V. *Solovenské rozhlasové dramatické vysielanie (Slovak Radio Broadcasting of Drama)*. Bratislava: Čs. rozhlas, 1985.

"From Bratislava with Love," *Cleveland Plain Dealer*, 17 September 1993, p. B-4.

"Ownership of Private Czech TV Agreed," *Screen Digest*, June 1993, p. 23.

Palkovič, P. *Cestami rozhlasovej tvorby (The Ways of Creativity in Radio)*. Bratislava: Čs. rozhlas, 1986.

Perkner, S., G. Kopaněvová, and K. Bílková-Belnayová. *Řeč dramatu—Film a televize (Language of Drama—Film and TV)*. Prague: Horizont, 1988.

Stadtrucker, Ivan. *Čas projektívney kultúry (Time of Projective Culture)*. Bratislava: Tatran, 1983.

Stadtrucker, Ivan. *Who Is that Man on the Screen?* in *Cultural Content of TV Programmes*. Prague: UNESCO, 1982.

CHAPTER 7

Russia

Sergei V. Erofeev

Sergei Erofeev.

Sergei Erofeev is the current director of the International Department of the Russian State Television and Radio Broadcasting Company in Moscow. Before that he was deputy editor in chief for Soviet Central Television. He has been a producer and/or reporter for many international programs shown on Intervision and Eurovision and for the Emmy Award–winning series *Capital to Capital*, coproduced with ABC News. He has written many articles and a book, *Space-Bridges*, and he currently serves as director of foreign affairs for the International Radio and TV Association.

STATISTICS

Geographic Area: 6,592,800 square miles
Capital: Moscow
Population: 148,542,000
Religions: Nonreligious, Russian Orthodox
Languages: Russian (official) and many regional ones
Type of Government: Republic headed by a president and a prime minister
Gross Domestic Product: $2.5 trillion
Literacy: 99 percent

GENERAL CHARACTERISTICS

Until relatively recently, the market in Russia for entertainment and information was strictly ordered. The broadcasting industry was heavily regulated and dominated by the state and the Communist party. The late 1980s saw a change in this relationship, but it would be hard to understand the present without looking at the past.

It would be simple just to say that the state monopoly of television and radio in the former Soviet Union was absolute. However, it was more than that. The former chairman of the USSR State Committee for Television and Radio (also known as Gostelradio or Gostel), Sergei Lapin, wrote in his 1973 article in the *Great Soviet Encyclopedia*: "In the U.S.S.R. and other socialist countries, television . . . demonstrates individual features of the socialist way of life, molds public opinion, and helps provide the ideological, moral, and aesthetic education of the masses."

Audience members were presented with the Communist party point of view; they did not see or hear any other opinions. They regarded the USSR State Committee for Television and Radio as the state committee on the *security* of television and radio.

For several decades, it was Gostelradio that decided everything concerning broadcasting in the former Soviet Union. By the late 1980s its total staff exceeded 82,000 workers of all ranks; in number of employees it was second only to the USSR Defense Ministry.

To say that the mass media were a state monopoly is not quite right because they were really a *party* monopoly, and the state was an obedient servant. In the everyday life of television and radio, all major decisions were made by party committees, and station management had to follow these decisions.

This situation prevailed until the Soviet Union started to disintegrate. Then all the Soviet republics claimed that they would control broadcasting in their own territories. Soviet authorities discouraged this tendency and in January 1991 ordered a military seizure of the Vilnius television center in Lithuania and then attacked the Latvian television center. Leaders of the rebel Baltic republics tried to organize underground television and radio stations but were too weak to compete with the media giant Gostelradio.

A crucial point for the media was reached in the summer of 1991 during the attempted coup against then President Mikhail Gorbachev. For broadcasters in Moscow and the republics, its failure meant that the days of party monopoly were over. But the situation was not so simple. Most of the key positions in television and radio were held by professionals who were voluntarily or involuntarily members of the party, and for many of them it was (and is) not easy to change from the mentality of a slave to "Big Brother." After a short period of time, USSR Gostelradio disintegrated.

At the same time, an entirely new phenomenon—independent broadcasting—appeared in almost every former Soviet republic. It started with very small cable television stations that provided pirated programs for several blocks of apartments in big cities. These were followed by on-air television and radio stations created when central and local authorities removed frequencies from the control of the KGB and the military and made them available for public use. There are roughly between 100 and 200 medium and large independent television and radio stations in the former Soviet Union.

Within a short period of time during the early 1990s, the situation in television and radio changed dramatically. From a state and party monopoly, it was transformed into a symbiosis between state and independent broadcasters. How this happened will be described in the following.

THE DEVELOPMENT OF ELECTRONIC MEDIA IN THE SOVIET UNION

Both radio and television were created and operated by the state for many years, and their development was fairly orderly and unchallenged.

National Communist Radio From the beginning, broadcasting in Russia was a state and party monopoly. The Communists, who seized power in October 1917, soon realized the importance of mass media in holding together a country as vast as Russia. Within 6 months the Council of Ministers, headed by Vladimir Lenin, issued a decree that centralized radio broadcasting in the Russian federation.

In December 1918 a radio laboratory in Nizhniy Novgorod was set up to develop radio. Less than a year later, it started regular test broadcasts, but because of civil war in the country, they were stopped. In 1924 broadcasting was resumed, and an organization called Radio for All Society was founded. Within 2 years the society had set up radio stations in major cities. They broadcast mostly so-called radio newspapers—news that was controlled by the Communist party. *Pravda*, the main daily newspaper, reported in 1927 that the total number of listeners in Russia exceeded 2 million that year.

To control the contents of the broadcasts, a special Commission on Radio (Radiokommissia) was set up within the Central Committee of the Bolshevik party (the original name for Lenin's followers, later to be called the Communist party). A little later, a state body in charge of radio broadcasting was established. It was called the Radio Council (Radiosovet), and it became the nucleus of the future Gostelradio.

Unlike many other countries, the Soviet Union relied heavily on state-subsidized radio by means of wired (or cable) radio, which enabled party and government authorities to enlarge the regular radio audience considerably. It was a system for receiving state broadcasts at local redistribution centers and forwarding them by wire to speaker boxes in homes (the most favored place was, and still is, the kitchen), offices, factories, and public places.

Wired radio is very popular even in the 1990s. The monthly license fee is very modest, and the technical quality is good. Listeners can receive up to two national radio programs and one local program via a speaker box, which usually has three program buttons. In some large cities, they can even receive stereo programs.

Radio broadcasting in the Soviet Union was developed so that listeners would be limited in their program choices. Wired radio was under control, and the majority of radio sets were manufactured so that their tuners had certain limitations, especially in receiving the shortwave bands. Until recently, listening to foreign external services stations was officially prohibited, and the government jammed the signals as best it could.

In general, Soviet radio had a distinctly authoritarian outlook with little regard for popular tastes. Most programs had a propaganda or, at best, educational goal, and light entertainment programs were scarce. Marketing and advertising were not developed because all radio stations throughout the country were financed by the state.

In 1985 the total number of radio sets in the Soviet Union was estimated at 81 million, including 6 million stereo radios. The potential audience was said to be about 250 million. It is hard to say how accurate these figures are because Soviet statistics reflected false figures given to please the authorities. Nevertheless, Gostelradio relied on these figures and produced programs accordingly.

By the end of the 1980s and the beginning of the 1990s, USSR Gostelradio was producing four radio channels that were distributed throughout the country via satellites and land lines. First Program was considered the major service. It emphasized news, political commentary, and classical and folk music. It was said to cover 97 percent of the general audience in the Soviet Union. Second Program, better known as Radio Station Mayak (the Lighthouse), was the first to start 24-hour broadcasting of news and music. It was estimated to cover 85 percent of the Soviet audience. Third Program and Fourth

Program reached, respectively, 40 percent and 7 percent of the audience and were devoted mostly to serious music and radio plays.

The Advent of Television The first patent for electronic television was given to B. Rosing of Russia as early as 1911. (In 1922 Soviet authorities confirmed this patent for a radiotelescope.) But the development of electronic television at that time was premature, and there was no technology to make it a reality. Instead, Soviet scientists experimented with a less sophisticated low-definition television system that used German Paul Nipkow's mechanical disk to produce pictures.

In 1930 scientists at the television laboratory at the Electro-Technical Institute in Moscow produced the first black-and-white picture of a dancing couple. She was in white, and he was in black. The picture was received about 1000 kilometers (600 miles) from the transmitting point. The screen had a definition of 1200 elements in thirty lines. A year later, the television laboratory started to broadcast regular test programs for thirty television sets in Moscow.

After 1934 these low-definition television programs became regular broadcasts, and they attracted the interest of the general audience. The programs consisted mostly of documentaries and theatrical plays shot on film and broadcast twelve times a month to about 2000 television sets. Although these television sets had small screens (less than 3×4 inches), the programs were usually watched by neighboring families together.

At this time, electronic television was developed as well. Instead of 30 lines, it used 441 lines and was more attractive to consumers. By 1938 special television centers for electronic television had been built in Moscow and Leningrad, and low-definition television had been abandoned. Moscow television began regular transmission on March 10, 1939. Every night it showed a movie or theatrical play produced exclusively for television.

During the Great Patriotic War (1941–1945), television broadcasting was stopped and not resumed until 1945 after the victory over the Nazis.

The Culmination of USSR Broadcasting In the 1980s Gostelradio reached the summit of its development and became the ideal model of authoritarian broadcasting. The USSR State Committee for Television and Radio was headed by a chairperson appointed by the Communist party's Central Committee. The chairperson held a ministerial post and was a member of the Council of Ministers of the Soviet Union. By tradition, the chair was also a full member (i.e., a member with the right to vote) of the Central Committee. The position provided a unique combination of influence on government and the party. For example, Sergei Lapin, who chaired Gostelradio for more than a decade (longer than any other chairperson), was one of the most influential figures in the Soviet hierarchy. It was not a coincidence that he became a close friend of Leonid Brezhnev, the Soviet Union's Communist party leader during the 1960s and 1970s. All other key positions, from those of deputies to those of commentators, were filled with the approval of the Central Committee.

Unlike any other broadcasting organization in the world, Gostelradio created within itself a new designation of so-called political observers. They were talented journalists picked by the Central Committee who were in charge of explaining party policy at home and abroad to listeners and viewers. In the hierarchy of the organization, they were on the level of deputies to the chairperson but, unlike other journalists, they had to report only to the chairman of the Central Committee.

USSR Gostelradio was subdivided into Soviet Central Television, Soviet Central Radio, and Radio Broadcasting for Foreign Countries. These divisions were headed by deputies to the chair. The divisions were further subdivided into editorial departments. For example, Central Television had departments for news, propaganda, drama, children, youth, sports, music, movies, and foreign programs.

The main body of Gostelradio was made up of editors and senior editors who were in charge of the production of programs. In truth, they were producers (although this word was banned from the vocabulary of Gostelradio as being too "Western") who combined the skills of director, film and text editor, production group manager, and accountant.

Independent of Central Television but within the framework of Gostelradio was a film production studio, Ekran (Screen), that produced movies, documentaries, and animation films for television. Central Television, based in the Ostankino television center in Moscow, produced programs for several channels, which were distributed nationwide by land lines and satellites.

By official Soviet statistics, in 1988 television was available to 95.6 percent of the country's population. Statistics also show that about 12 million people were not technically able to receive television at all and that an equal number could not receive good-quality television signals. Only 20 million people had color television, which accounted for 24 percent of the country's TV sets.

Television Channels For several decades, First Channel was the main source of television programs for the bulk of the Soviet people. When Brezhnev was in power, there was a joke that television could be described as the Brezhnev show with a little information about the weather. Its main news program, *Vremya (Time)*, which was shown at 9 o'clock each evening, carried mostly political and industrial news and major official announcements. Gostelradio claimed that *Vremya* was watched by more than 80 percent of viewers. This was close to the truth because *Vremya* was shown at the same time on all channels. To this day, many people call the 9 P.M. news *Vremya*.

First Channel also carried a daily Soviet movie (or, on rare occasions, a foreign film), children's programs, sports, and other fare. In the 1980s it was on the air from 7 A.M. until 1 A.M. Because the Communist ideology considered television a tool for "mass political education," there was even a notorious program, *Lenin University of Millions*, which educated Soviet people about socialism.

Second Channel was considered a wastebasket by both Gostelradio officials and viewers. It was launched in the early 1970s as an experimental color television channel but in two decades failed to find its own image. Mostly it showed reruns of First Channel programs, failed programs that were not suitable for First Channel, and some educational programs. Gostelradio executives tried to create a new image for Second Channel several times, but these attempts were in vain. It was clear that there was to be no competition for First Channel.

The Third (or Moscow) Channel was on the air from 5 or 6 P.M. until midnight. It was seen only in the Moscow area and was watched the least of all the channels. It carried mostly city and regional news and some rather unsophisticated entertainment.

The Fourth (or Educational) Channel was the kind of channel Soviet leaders could brag about. It was a Soviet model of the BBC's Open University. It carried programs on biology, history, foreign languages, mathematics, and other subjects that could be used in classrooms. The channel was distributed by land lines to ten large cities throughout the country.

Leningrad's television station was also included in the Central Television system. In the 1980s Gostelradio made the decision (approved by the Central Committee) to distribute Leningrad television beyond its local reach. It was carried by land lines to major cities in the European part of the Russian federation, and like the other channels, it had to give its 9 P.M. time slot to *Vremya*.

Nationally, television broadcasts from the Ostankino center in Moscow were picked up from satellites or land lines by local television stations that distributed them locally to individual or collective antennas. Almost every republic (except Russia) had its own national television station in the USSR Gostelradio system. They had programs in native languages that were usually modeled after those on Central Television.

In Russia, Gostelradio allowed local stations to carry their local news and public affairs programs up to 2 to 4 hours a day on the Second Channel frequency. According to Gostelradio statistics, in 1990 there were 120 television programming centers in the Soviet Union.

Glasnost Broadcasting In 1986 the former Soviet leader Mikhail Gorbachev announced a new policy of glasnost (openness) that encouraged Gostelradio to change. For the first time in history, Soviet broadcasting was allowed to cover such topics as domestic disasters (though the Chernobyl nuclear disaster story has still not been well reported), the war in Afghanistan, corruption in the government, and the crime situation throughout the country. Of course, glasnost had its limits. There was still a tight system of censorship in television and radio: military censors, literary censors with lists of taboo names and topics, and most importantly, political censors from party committees and the administration.

Television news and other public affairs programs began to brighten their image by using more open reporting. Both television and radio stations scheduled live shows and spontaneous interviews (before glasnost almost 100 percent of programs were taped so that their content could be reviewed and controlled) and telephone call-in shows. The hours of broadcast were extended to early morning and late night.

A new television phenomenon was started with U.S.-USSR "space bridges," a series of talk shows that included exchanges between U.S. and Soviet citizens. The first programs were hosted by Phil Donahue of the United States and Vladimir Posner of the USSR. They were tremendously successful with the Soviet audience and were the programs that were watched the most. Many people still remember the dialogue between an American woman and her Russian counterpart. Answering the question whether or not there was sex in the Soviet Union, the latter answered, "No, but we have sports clubs."

But even with glasnost, the situation in broadcasting was very much controlled and the contents of programs were strongly guarded by party watchdogs. The Marxist approach to broadcasting was officially abandoned only after the failure of the coup against Gorbachev in August 1991. However, it would be naive and unrealistic to expect that a huge broadcasting monster could be transformed by magic into a more effective institution in just a few years.

Radio and Television in Russia Though Russia introduced television and radio to the Soviet Union, the republic itself had no national broadcasting authorities until 1990. It was understood that Soviet Central Television and Radio represented Russia. (The same thing happened with the Communists: in the late 1980s they suddenly realized that there was no Communist party of Russia.)

The real cause of the establishment of Russian television and radio was the political situation in the Soviet Union in 1990. By then democratic forces in Russia clearly realized that without mass media they could not overthrow the Communist regime. The democratic press, which was mostly concentrated in Moscow and Leningrad, was financially weak and could not reach remote areas. Television and radio were under the control of Soviet authorities, and so the Russian Parliament, which was in opposition to the central Soviet government, could not introduce any new laws to the population through Soviet mass media. New Russian legislation contradicted Soviet law in many ways, and party officials made many efforts to block the release of information.

The Russian Parliament had no other way to cope with the situation than to establish a Russian national broadcasting authority, and it did so in August 1990. By the fall of that year, about thirty journalists had left Gostelradio to organize the Russian State Television and Radio Company (RTR). They started from scratch in an old building erected in 1938 for the construction department of GULAG (the main management of concentration camps).

By December 10, 1990, they managed to launch Radio Russia. It broadcast for 6 hours a day on Soviet Central Radio and instantly became popular. Soviet authorities had to allow Radio Russia to occupy that particular time slot because (so it was said) Boris Yeltsin, who headed the Russian government, said that if they did not, he would order Moscow authorities to switch off the power and water supply to the Ostankino broadcasting center. In January 1991, when Soviet military forces seized the television center in Lithuania, Radio Russia backed the rebels. Central authorities were furious, and Mikhail Gorbachev described Radio Russia as a "foreign radio like the Voice of America."

Meanwhile, television programs were being prepared for the coming establishment of Russian Television. Yeltsin and Gorbachev decided that Russian Television would have 6 hours a day on Second Channel starting in January 1991, but its initiation was delayed several times for many reasons. At last, on May 13, 1991, Russian Television was inaugurated. From the very start it was sabotaged by Soviet Central Television officials. That was easy because Russian Television had no technical base at the time. Most of the needed equipment was leased from Gostelradio, and this equipment could conveniently "break down." Central Television officials succeeded in reducing Russian Television's airtime to 5 hours a day.

It is difficult to predict how Russian Television and Radio would have evolved if it had not been for the attempted coup against Gorbachev in August 1991. As the result of a decree issued by the hard-core Communist rebels, the activity of the Russian State Television and Radio Company was banned and it was switched off the air. The chairman of the company, Oleg Poptsov, who was also a deputy of the Russian Parliament, was put on a priority execution list and labeled a most dangerous person.

Meanwhile, the company had evacuated all available equipment to homes in order to start underground broadcasting. In the White House, which was the location of the Russian Parliament, Radio Russia organized, with the help of amateurs, a shortwave radio station. Television reporters from Russian Television made live reports for CNN via its Moscow bureau. On the second day of the coup, Russian Television technicians made it possible to broadcast "illegally" via satellite a 20-minute report on the situation in Moscow directed to the Ural Mountains and west Siberia. It was reported later by the press that within an hour of that broadcast, a crowd of 1 million had gathered in the central square of Yeltsin's home city of Sverdlovsk in the Urals as a show of support in opposition to the Communist rebels.

After the coup collapsed, the broadcasting situation changed dramatically. In September, Yeltsin and Gorbachev reached an agreement on the division of Gostelradio between the USSR and Russia. According to the agreement, Gostelradio kept First Channel and Russian Television received control over Second Channel. Third Channel still broadcast from Moscow, although eventually it experienced a strange transformation involving the merging of a Russian state television company, Moskva, with commercial Channel 2 × 2. The latter leases time from Moskva for 12 hours a day to show foreign movies, news (BBC, ITN, CNN), entertainment programs, and reruns from other channels. Moskva, itself, produces a daily evening 2-hour show consisting of local news and features under the name *Good Night, Moscow*. The airtime on Fourth Channel was divided between Gostelradio and RTR. RTR's Radio Russia was given the so-called first button in wired radio and a frequency for 24-hour broadcasting.

RTR was also given an old television center in downtown Moscow which had been used by Gostelradio for many years for the production of educational and children's programs and which was sarcastically nicknamed "the museum of television."

In general, by the end of 1990 the whole television and radio system in Russia became obsolete and could have been described as the museum of Soviet mass media. New political powers came in to play the mass-media game by the same rules as their predecessors. In the first part of the game (from August 1990 until the presidential elections in June 1991), there were two major players—democrats, under the leadership of Boris Yeltsin, and old party members, who still were influential even though the Communist party had been officially banned by a decree issued by Yeltsin.

In the spring of 1991, the first elections for president of Russia were announced, and for the first time both Gostelradio and RTR carried live television debates featuring the candidates. Gostelradio played mostly on the side of the old guard, and RTR was on the side of Yeltsin and the democrats. Yeltsin won, and the balance of power changed.

After the presidential elections, democrats took control of executive and legislative power in the country, but at the same time they separated into many factions. Since then, there have been three major players in the mass-media game—President Yeltsin and his team, the Russian Parliament and the conservatives who dominate Parliament, and many new political parties.

The Plight of Russian Television and Radio

After the attempted coup against Gorbachev in August 1991, Boris Yeltsin was sharply criticized by the Russian media for attempting to close down major Communist newspapers, including *Pravda*. But this was just the first skirmish in the war over control of the mass media.

Television and radio, traditionally monopolized by the central government, were taken over by the Russian government, and thus far, the government and Parliament have shown no signs of loosening their hold.

By decrees from Yeltsin, Gostelradio was divided into several state broadcasting companies. In 1991 it was transformed into the Russian State Television and Radio Company Ostankino (RTO) and at that time was still the strongest broadcasting company. It controlled First Channel and the best airtime on Fourth Channel, and it still had its radio services, the names of which it changed in 1991. The former First Program became Radio-1, Third Program was changed to Radio-2, and Fourth Program was renamed Ortheus. Radio Station Mayak retained its name.

The leadership of RTO was worried about competition from the young RTR, which had the clear distinction of being a "Russian" medium from its origin. The main worry was the budget, which was provided by the Russian government to RTO and RTR. The scarcity of money resulted in a transformation of RTO into the broadcasting company of the Commonwealth of Independent States (C.I.S.)—nine of the former republics of the Soviet Union. In January 1993 an agreement was signed by C.I.S. leaders stating that a new television company, although it would not replace RTO, would use a part of the RTO facilities and broadcast its programs on First Channel.

The disintegration of RTO (formerly Gostelradio) was furthered by a decree from President Yeltsin on January 19, 1993, declaring that RTO did not control the Fourth Channel airtime. This channel, the old Educational Channel, was transformed into the Russian Universities Channel. Its philosophy has not yet been developed, though it is clear that it will broadcast educational material.

As a result of all these developments, the former Gostelradio, now RTO, was demoted to a secondary position.

Nevertheless, First Channel (which RTO controls) is still the most watched television channel in the former Soviet Union. It is transmitted by satellite and land lines to more than 90 percent of the potential audience in the former Soviet Union. Between 30 and 50 percent of the audience regularly watch First Channel.

President Yeltsin's decree of January 19, 1993, had another purpose—to transform the Russian State Television and Radio Company into a major state national company. In other words, the decree clearly stated that RTR was the main broadcasting entity in the country. Many observers think that this was done by the president in the hope that RTR, which always helped him fight political opponents, would back him again in the turmoil of political chaos, especially on the eve of a national referendum. Another reason was Yeltsin's concern that Parliament, which opposed him, would take control of Russian television and radio. Furthermore, Yeltsin no longer believed he had the support of RTO.

Yeltsin's support of RTR helped him during the unsuccessful coup against him by staunch Communists in the fall of 1993, Anti-Yeltsin rebels attacked the Ostankino facility, shared by RTO and RTR, and succeeded in taking almost all programming off the air. However, RTR was able to continue broadcasting because its facilities were not in the Ostankino building but rather in the old facilities in downtown Moscow referred to as "the museum." RTR had installed a fiber-optic link from these studios to the Ostankino tower, and this kept its pro-Yeltsin service operational. In fact, for a period of time RTR's programming was seen on all Russian television channels.

Broadcasting in St. Petersburg and Other Parts of Russia The third major broadcaster in Russia is former Leningrad Television (Leningrad's name has been changed back to St. Petersburg), which experienced several structural transformations within just a year. The first occurred in 1992 when journalists attempted to privatize the station. On January 19, 1992, Yeltsin signed a decree creating St. Petersburg Russian State Television and Radio Company to replace the Leningrad Committee on Television and Radio. This ended a long-standing dispute between St. Petersburg journalists, who wanted the city's television and radio to be independent, and city authorities, who insisted on complete control over broadcasting in St. Petersburg.

St. Petersburg Television is seen in major cities in the European part of Russia. That has made it a target of Ruslan Khazbulatov, the chairman of the Russian Parliament. It was said that because he had failed to gain control of RTO and RTR, he attempted to change the status of St. Petersburg Television into an Inter-Parliamentary Television of the C.I.S. (In the fall of 1992, St. Petersburg was chosen as the capital of the C.I.S.) When Yeltsin learned about this attempt, he signed a decree that changed the St. Petersburg Russian State Television and Radio Company into the Federal Radio and Television Service Russia within a few days. Bella Kurkova, a longtime supporter of Yeltsin, became chair of the new service, and it, like the Moscow-based RTR, supported Yeltsin.

There are also 100 state television programming stations throughout Russia operating in local areas. Before 1992 they were an integral part of RTR as its affiliates. Then it was decided that they should be given independent status and would receive money from the state budget through the special department of the Ministry of Press and Information. Following a tradition that goes back to the period of the Soviet Union, they mainly receive and redistribute national television programs (i.e., RTR programs). But many of them produce local programs that are broadcast between 2 and 4 hours a day. Some local stations have their own frequencies, independent of the frequencies of the RTR programs, and therefore can broadcast more than 4 hours a day. All of the local stations lack proper financing, modern equipment, and qualified staff.

Independent Radio and Television In June 1990 the former Soviet Parliament adopted a law regarding the press and other mass media that acknowledged the decay of central control over the airwaves and the disintegration of the Communist party's monopoly of radio and television. On paper, the law gave people's deputies, social organizations, political parties, and even individuals the right to operate television and radio stations. In practice, this form of ownership was not made clear because of the lack of detailed legal regulations and the opposition of Communist party authorities. Almost simultaneously, Gorbachev signed a decree covering the democratization and development of broadcasting in the USSR. These two documents were the first to legalize the establishment of new mass media which would be independent of the state.

Within a few months, many applications for new radio and television stations were made to the Moscow City Council and the Ministry of Press and Information. Many of the applications were simply filed away because only a few frequencies were available and they were strongly guarded by Gostelradio, the Ministry of Communications, the KGB, and the Defense Ministry.

The first rift in the state broadcasting establishment occurred in August 1990 when a group of young radio journalists convinced the Moscow City Council, the journalism faculty of Moscow University, Novosti News Agency, and the USSR Ministry of Communication that they should become founders of a new radio station, Echo Moskvy (Moscow's Echo). Five journalists started with 3 hours a day of news, music, and talk on medium waves for the radio audience in the Moscow area. Within a year, the station was broadcasting 8 hours a day. When the coup broke on August 19, 1991, Echo Moskvy was immediately closed by the KGB. The next day, with the help of deputies of Russia and Moscow, journalists resumed broadcasting for 20 hours a day only to be shut down again—but only for a few hours because the coup was over.

Now Echo Moskvy is just one of several FM stations in Moscow. Between 1990 and 1992 several others started: Radio M, formed by journalists who were expelled from Gostelradio; two Russian-French joint-venture stations, Europe Plus (which now has affiliates in St. Petersburg, Nizhniy Novgorod, and Volgograd) and Radio Russia-Nostalgie; two joint ventures with Americans, Radio Rocks and Maximum; and Svobodnoye Radio (Free Radio), which rebroadcasts the programs of external services of other countries such as Voice of America, BBC, and Deutsche Welle.

The process of privatization (as opposed to state ownership) in television is more complicated for two major reasons: lack of available frequencies and lack of financing. The main developments in television have involved the rapid establishment of a large number of small cable television networks in big cities.

Cable TV development was made somewhat easy by the already available system of so-called collective antennas in block apartment buildings. Such antennas installed on the roof of a building to receive over-the-air television had cable outlets in every flat of that and neighboring buildings. Thus it was easy to connect a videocassette player to the system and play back available programs. In Moscow there are about 1500 such collective antennas.

The first cable network was founded in

Moscow in October 1990 by a private citizen, Nikolai Loutsenko. He registered his independent broadcasting corporation, NIKA TV, with the Ministry of Press and Information in hopes of producing programs for Gostelradio. But Soviet Central Television was not willing to share its airtime. So Loutsenko launched the first private cable television system in Moscow, and in the following years the concept of cable spread to other cities, reaching many locations in Russia where collective antenna systems were available.

New, independent on-air stations have also been started. For example, Marathon TV received a license in January 1993 to program to businesspeople in the Moscow area. Marathon TV was founded by several companies with an interest in communications and the home video industry. Founders hope that the station will become commercially viable, with revenues from advertising covering operational costs.

Another commercial station was launched in Moscow simultaneously with Marathon TV. It was the long-awaited Channel 6, a joint venture with Ted Turner's TBS. It started with 4 hours a day of programming via a low-powered transmitter on January 1, 1993, that reached only a small number of households near the Ostankino television tower. However, it increased its transmitter power and expanded its hours of transmission and can now be received in approximately 70 percent of Moscow. Programming on Channel 6 consists of news from CNN with Russian voice-overs, old movies from Turner's library, and Soviet- and Russian-made movies.

Independent radio and television in Russia are in the early stages of development. It seems clear that within several years they will equal state broadcasting.

Video Distribution In the late 1970s and early 1980s, foreign-made videocassette recorders (VCRs) and videocassettes of foreign programming appeared in the apartments of families who traveled abroad and managed to circumvent customs. Until the mid-1980s it was dangerous to have a VCR at home because the militia might come to see what you were watching. There were several trials at the time at which people were convicted because they were watching movies featuring nude actors. According to the statistics of the Procurator's Office of the USSR, in 1987 and 1988 more than 200 people were imprisoned for watching pornography.

In the middle of the 1980s, Soviet industry introduced homemade VCRs and videocassettes. Although the quality of the recorders and the cassettes was low, people lined up to buy them. However, the bulk of the recorders still came from abroad. By 1989 the Soviet industry had manufactured only 73,000 videocassette recorders, but by 1992 it was estimated that Russians had between 3 and 6 million.

With growing numbers of home video recorders, the state decided to go into the business of producing software and in 1985 set up Videofilm, a studio that was part of the USSR State Committee on Cinematography. The studio was in charge of the production and distribution of programs for home video. However, its cassettes were outnumbered by those available from the black market industry that delivered to its customers fresh, new movies pirated from the West. As a result, *Terminator 2* was "released" in the Russian market several months earlier than in the United States. It was estimated that the video black market in Moscow alone collected revenues of 6.5 million rubles a month in 1990.

The much publicized early 1990s campaign of U.S. moviemakers to boycott the Russian market because they did not receive royalties on these black market tapes did not influence the revenues of black marketeers. But it did one good thing—it attracted public attention to the problems of copyright and piracy. Even President Yeltsin expressed personal involvement in this hot issue. In 1992 he signed two decrees—

one to establish a Russian Copyright Agency and another to establish a commission in charge of formulating a state policy on piracy of intellectual property. In 1993 the Russian Parliament enacted comprehensive copyright legislation that should provide a great deal more protection for films and television programs.

ORGANIZATION AND FINANCING

During the Communist era, both the organization and financing of broadcasting were very straightforward. The state owned and operated all radio and television, and all the money came from state coffers.

However, beginning in about 1990, the structure started to change. Now there are two main categories of media ownership in Russia—state and independent. State ownership has undergone many changes because of power struggles involving the old guard and the new. "Independent" can mean anything—from a joint venture with foreign broadcasters to private ownership. There are still no laws governing different forms of broadcasting in Russia and, more importantly, there are no standards of practice—legal or otherwise. An independent station can be "public" or "commercial" or a combination of both. The ownership of media is pragmatic—consisting of whatever sources are available in the changing political and economic climate of Russia.

In the times before perestroika (restructuring), radio and television were strictly censored and the people involved were limited as to what they could program. However, money was not a problem. The projects that were approved by the state were amply funded. Now the media have freedom of speech, but they also have huge financial worries. The key question for most of the independent stations is whether they can find enough advertisers and sponsors to survive. They have no financial support from the state and must rely only on themselves.

The problem of finding advertisers does not concern state-budgeted stations in such a dramatic way. In the case of RTO and RTR, the revenues from advertising make up no more than 5 to 7 percent of their budgets. Still, the future of all state broadcasting companies depends largely on whether the Russian government will find finances (both in rubles and hard currency) to maintain state television and radio. In rubles, the costs will be tens of billions per year.

Both RTO and RTR are looking for ways to change the ownership of the companies to avoid dependence on the state. There are projects for transforming them into shareholder companies with the participation of the state, but it is unlikely that this will happen for at least a few more years.

In a climate of political and economic instability, state-owned and independent companies are trying to find ways to increase their revenues. An obvious answer is advertising. At present the advertising industry in Russia is like the Wild West in that there are no real laws regarding advertising, such as those restricting the volume of advertisements during and between programs or limiting subjects for commercials. As a result, every station establishes its own advertising rules. It is quite usual to see and hear advertising for hard liquor and tobacco.

In 1992 it became quite clear that big foreign advertisers were looking at the Russian market. Johnson and Johnson, Pepsi, Unicap, Upjohn, Kodak, and other large companies ran advertising campaigns on Russian television. Several audience surveys found that the Russian audience found Western advertising quite convincing.

Laws have been drafted regulating both advertising and ownership, and it is expected that at some point advertising will be limited to occupying no more than 10 percent of broadcasting time. Also, foreign investments in broadcasting may be limited to up to 25 percent of ownership.

PROGRAMMING

Information and culture dominated radio and television programming in the former Soviet Union. Each program was in some way planned to mold harmonious people, oppose hostile ideologies, and display the benefits of the Soviet way of life. Politicians talked for long periods of time. Occasionally they were interviewed by journalists, but the questions were benign, and the answers were *long*—and uninterrupted.

Documentaries about work in the factories and on the farms abounded. Ballet and opera were shown, but entertainment programming, as it was known in the West, was virtually nonexistent. People rarely had reason to laugh while watching Soviet television. The most entertainment-oriented form of programming was sports, which usually emphasized the superiority of Soviet athletes. News was frequent and of course *Vremya* permeated the nation each night at 9 P.M. Programming for children was propaganda-oriented, and educational programs designed to increase the intellectual knowledge of Soviets were abundant.

Now both radio and television are changing rather dramatically. The major radio and television stations in Russia are on the way to adopting Western-style programming that is oriented toward consumers.

Many radio stations are now broadcasting 24 hours a day. State-owned stations specialize in news, public affairs, talk shows, and light and classical music. The programs are aimed toward the general audience. New FM stations (mostly independent and commercially oriented) are geared toward the younger generation and broadcast mostly Western music and news.

Television has introduced such formats as talk shows, game shows, soap operas, miniseries, morning programs, and late-night shows. There is a good deal of foreign programming, mainly from the United States, on all television channels. The most popular program in terms of ratings is *The Magic World of Disney* on RTR on Sundays.

The daily television menu for the Russian viewer has at least ten news bulletins, several movies in prime time, light entertainment at late

RTR's news presenter, Vladislav Vlyarkovski. (*Photo by Pavel Klimov*)

hours, educational programs, programs for children, sports, and a selection of documentaries. Game shows and religious programs are delivered on selected days. Viewers can watch state-owned television from early morning until late night.

The following schedule shows the prime-time programs on RTO and RTR for Tuesday, January 26, 1993.

RTO

6:00 P.M.	News
6:15	Travelogue (C.I.S. Television)
6:50	Documentary
7:05	*Return to Eden* (Australian Series, Seventeenth Episode)
7:55	Talk Show
8:40	Program for Children
9:00	News
9:40	Movie (Russian-made, 1991)
10:50	Animation Film (Russian-made)
11:00	Music (Part 1)
12:00 A.M.	News
12:25	Music (Part 2)
1:25	Movie for Television (Russian-made)

RTR

6:00 P.M.	Program about Russian History
6:30	Religious Program
7:00	Parliament Messenger
7:15	Documentary about Russian Scientist
7:45	Program for Children
8:00	News
8:25	*Santa Barbara* (U.S. Series, Episode 123)
9:15	Program about Russian Theater
10:00	*Letters from Provincia* (Feature)
11:00	News
11:20	Astrology Forecast
11:25	Sports Magazine
11:30	Game Show
11:45	Report on the Session of Russian Parliament
12:15 A.M.	Entertainment Program

LAWS AND REGULATIONS

Like other aspects of broadcasting (and almost everything else in Russia), present laws and regulations are quite different than they were during the many years of communism when the state was omnipotent.

RTR's program *Face to Face*, a regular live program where leading journalists interview well-known politicians and public figures. (*Photo by Pavel Klimov*)

Before February 6, 1992, when the Russian law on mass media took effect, television and radio had been regulated by the All-Union Law on Press. The draft of the new Russian law was heavily debated in Parliament. A total of twenty-six amendments were introduced during the debates, most of them by the conservatives who were trying to limit the freedom of the media.

After the law was debated and amended in Parliament, the authors of the draft signed an open letter in which they asked President Yeltsin not to sign the revised version because the law, as amended, was a step backward from the All-Union Law. This criticism was backed by Russian mass media and the public, and under the pressure of public opinion and journalists, Yeltsin refused to approve the amended text. When the law was finally signed, it was in its original form.

Under the law, a citizen, an association of citizens, an organization, or a state entity may establish a media concern. Its activities may be halted or suspended only by the founder's consent or through a court order.

During 1992 there were debates in Parliament and in the press about the introduction of a separate law governing radio and television that would not involve the print media. Many leading foreign consultants were summoned to Moscow to help draft the law, but it has not yet been passed because other issues have prevailed. The most advanced draft foresees the establishment of a Federal Broadcasting Commission (FBC) and Regional Broadcasting Commissions (RBCs). The FBC would be made up of eight members and would report annually to the president of the Russian federation. The RBCs would be made up of three members and would report annually to regional authorities. Federal and regional commissions would have the responsibility of publishing a list of available frequencies which would be approved by the FBC, announcing the rules for license applicants, and selecting applicants and giving out licenses.

THE AUDIENCE

Until recently, the major information about television and radio audiences in Russia came from letters viewers and listeners sent to stations. Unlike their counterparts in other countries, the managers of state-owned stations were not interested in unbiased audience feedback. Their boss was the party, not the audience.

Now the situation has changed as competition and advertising have been introduced into the Russian broadcasting industry. Managers need accurate reports from the broadcasting battlefront telling which program, station, or network claims to be ahead in the struggle for survival and supremacy.

For many years, audience research in Russia was conducted only by the sociological department of Gostelradio and from time to time by the Institute of Sociology of the Academy of Sciences. But many Western researchers did not believe the figures obtained by these two organizations because the methods of audience research were inadequate and many figures were biased to please broadcasting authorities.

In the last 2 or 3 years, many independent audience research groups have been founded in Russia, but none of them can be compared to Arbitron or Nielsen in the United States. They mostly use the less expensive methods of coincidental telephone calls and telephone recall to gather audience size information. From time to time, they employ personal interviews and diaries, but there are no meters.

The most serious market measurements are being made by the Russian Media Monitor, a joint venture formed by Gallup, BBDO Marketing, and Invizible Arts, with the assistance of RTR. The Russian Media Monitor conducts 1000 personal interviews each month and collects diaries from respondents every 2 weeks. The group publishes quarterly reports on the Russian media, including television, radio, and print. These reports include month-by-month analyses of viewing and listening patterns with weekly average audience figures per quarter-hour for both television and radio.

The groups that have been conducting surveys since 1992 have found that three out of four Russians watch television every day. On a typical day viewing time is between 2 hours, 50 minutes and 3 hours, 30 minutes. Approximately 50 percent of the audience members prefer to watch First Channel, and 30 percent prefer Second Channel. The audience likes to watch movies on First Channel and news on Second Channel.

The surveys also discovered that about 60 percent of Russians listen to the radio every day. An average Russian listens 6 days a week for a little less than 2 hours a day. The percentage of people who listen to the various major radio services is as follows: Radio Russia, 70 percent; Mayak, 60 percent; Radio 1, 20 percent; Radio 2, 15 percent; Europa Plus, 10 percent.

TECHNOLOGY

Most of the television and radio equipment used in Russia is imported from Japan, Germany, France, or the United States. The Russian electronics industry manufactures mainly radio and television transmitters, switches, satellite ground stations, relay equipment, and communication satellites. Russian-made videocassette recorders and cameras have proved to be unreliable, and television professionals prefer to use Western-made equipment.

Because Russia is a huge country, it pioneered the use of communication satellites as early as 1965. Now it has a developed system that utilizes satellites, terrestrial and microwave relays, and cable (including fiber optics) for the distribution of television and radio programs throughout the country.

Television uses a 625-line SECAM system for broadcasting. RTR is the only television company in Russia that uses the PAL system for editing its programs. Before these programs go on the air, they are converted into SECAM.

EXTERNAL SERVICES

From the very beginning Communist leaders realized that radio was a good propaganda tool, not only for Soviet citizens but also for foreigners. Thus an elaborate jamming system was established to block out Voice of America and other Western external services.

The Soviet government developed the largest external service in operation in the world. November 7, 1925, might be considered a launch date for this Soviet foreign broadcasting service, which would later be known as Radio Moscow. On that day the first live report about a military parade and a civilian demonstration in Red Square was broadcast for foreign listeners in three languages—English, German, and French. Within a few years the foreign broadcasting service became a stronghold of Soviet radio. By the late 1980s, it was broadcasting 2257 hours a week in 80 languages.

During the course of its Communist existence, Radio Moscow often changed the languages it broadcast in and the number of hours devoted to each. Whenever the government faced problems, as it often did along the Chinese border, it would expand its hours of broadcast to that area. Likewise, when it gained a foothold, as it did in Cuba, it expanded hours. It also programmed in many neglected languages that other external services never even considered—mainly African and South American dialects.

Gostelradio also operated what was referred to as the Fifth Program. It was launched in 1963 as a 24-hour radio service in Russian for Soviet people who worked abroad (diplomats, military personnel, sailors). Later, a television channel, Moskva Globalnaya (Moscow Global), was established for the same audience. It offered a 2-hour selection of the best programs from Central Television.

The international services are presently under RTO, but their status is uncertain in a changing world.

IMPORTANCE IN THE WORLD COMMUNITY

As the leader of the former Eastern bloc, the Soviet Union's electronic media structure was very influential. The iron curtain countries operated radio and television systems that were similar in design and philosophy to those of the Soviet Union. For many years, the Soviet system was the primary model of authoritarian broadcasting. Its state-owned structure and censorship patterns were emulated throughout most Communist societies.

Although communism seems to have collapsed, Russia is still a dominant world power. The future direction of its media (along with the future direction of many other facets of its society) will be closely watched by the rest of the world.

Russia's media play an important role in world politics. What these media say about events and ideas of the outside world greatly affects how the citizens of Russia and the C.I.S. think and act. The government fully understands the importance of the media, and friends and foes of democracy and the free market try to control the press. Meanwhile the people within radio and television are trying to assert their own independence. The last few years have seen a tug-of-war among the various factions that are asserting themselves throughout the entire former Soviet Union. Control of the media is very definitely tied to political power.

Because Russia is a world power, the direction taken by its media organizations and programming greatly affects other nations. If democracy is to be successful in Russia, the media must assume a dominant role.

MAJOR ISSUES

The year 1991 may be considered a turning point in the development of electronic media in Russia. After the coup against Gorbachev failed that year, television and radio took a step toward more freedom of speech and press.

The state-owned networks and stations play a major role on the broadcasting scene, although they are losing their audience. At the same time, it is quite clear that a new phenomenon—independent broadcasting—is acquiring more influence and in the coming years could take a leading role. The interrelationship between the state system and the new independents will no doubt create many major issues in the coming years.

State-owned television and radio are still under pressure from the government and politicians who tend to interfere in broadcasting matters. If a new broadcasting law is passed by Parliament, this interference could diminish. The whole area of freedom of speech within Russia bears close watching.

For the first time in broadcasting history, television and radio stations in Russia have to work in an environment of competition. They also have to rely more and more on advertising revenues. How well they succeed in both these areas will determine how important their role in society will be.

As in many other countries, both state-owned and independent broadcasters are threatened by home video and by satellite broadcasts from abroad. The old Soviet structure has suffered political and economic upheavals that have created a situation suitable for new technological forces such as VCRs and direct broadcast satellite (DBS) to gain a strong foothold.

In summary, one may say that electronic media in Russia are awakening from many years of lethargy and are finding new ways into the future.

SELECTED BIBLIOGRAPHY

Browne, Donald R. "The Soviet Union: Of, By, or For the People?" In *Comparing Broadcast Systems: The Experience of Six Industrialized*

Nations. Ames, IA: Iowa State University Press, 1989, pp. 247–301.

Dawtrey, Adam. "Yank Distrib: To Russia with Commercial TV," *Variety*, 18 February 1992, p. 1.

Fraser, Hugh. "Turner Cohort Wins Moscow TV License," *Variety*, 23 November 1992, p. 1.

Gillette, Robert. "Soviets Hungry for News from the Outside World," *Los Angeles Times*, 21 August 1984, p. 1.

Harasymiw, Bohdan, ed. *Education and the Mass Media in the Soviet Union and Eastern Europe.* New York: Praeger, 1976.

Hickey, Neil. "Good Morning, USSR!" *TV Guide*, 3 September 1988, pp. 3–9.

Hopkins, Mark. *Mass Media in the Soviet Union.* New York: Pegasus, 1970.

Ignatius, Adi. "Life-Style Pitch Works in Russia Despite Poverty," *Wall Street Journal*, 21 August 1992, p. B-1.

Lieb, Rebecca. "Gostelradio Faces Competition from New National Soviet Web," *Variety*, 12 December 1991, p. 2.

Lisann, Maury. *Broadcasting in the Soviet Union: International Politics and Radio.* New York: Praeger, 1975.

Redmont, Bernard. "Soviet TV: Ballet and Brezhnev, Serials and Symphony," *Television Quarterly*, Spring 1981, pp. 27–35.

"Russian Hard-Liners Target Moscow TV, Radio Facilities," *NAB World*, November 1993, pp. 1–3.

Smith, Hedrick. "Part Two: The Awakening." In *The New Russians.* New York: Random House, 1990.

Tinsley, Elisa. "Soviets Open Video Shops," *Electronic Media*, 21 April 1986, p. G-12.

Vachnadze, Georgi. *Secrets of the Press in the Times of Gorbachev and Yeltsin.* Moscow: Books and Business, 1992.

Wharton, Dennis. "Russia Passes C'right Reform," *Variety*, 4 May 1993, p. 1.

Yaroshenko, Vladimir. "Broadcasting in Russia." In William E. McCavitt, ed. *Broadcasting Around the World.* Blue Ridge Summit, PA: TAB Books, 1981.

PART FIVE

THE MIDDLE EAST

Overview of the Middle East

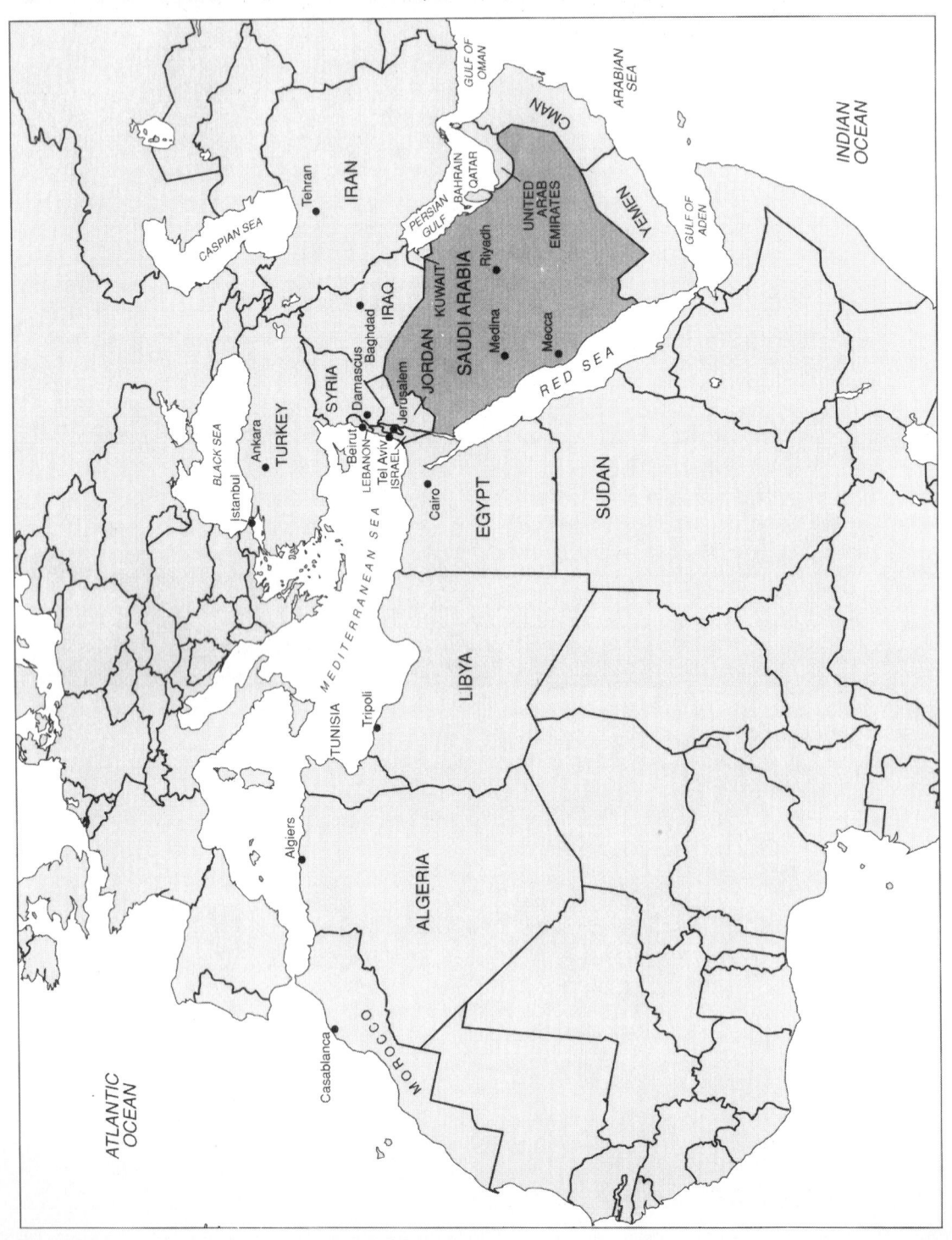

The "Middle East" is hard to define. Geographically, it is an area in the vicinity of the Persian Gulf, the Arabian Sea, the Red Sea, and the southern Mediterranean Sea, but it is not a discrete continent as are many of the regions dealt with in the other sections of this book. It is rather an area devised largely by the media whose practitioners often refer to "trouble in the Middle East."

Sometimes Turkey is part of the Middle East, and sometimes it isn't, depending on the nature of the problem being reported. Sudan is often included in the Middle East, although the southern part of it has much more in common with the rest of Africa. Similarly, Morocco, Algeria, Tunisia, and Libya are all African and Middle Eastern. Egypt, which is actually on the African continent, considers itself a leader in Middle Eastern media and politics.

One element that unifies the area is the Arabic language and culture. But Israel, a key player in Middle East politics, uses the Hebrew language and considers itself in conflict with Arab politics. Also, the official language of Iran, another major Middle East player, is Farsi, and the Turks speak Turkish.

The Islamic religion is another unifying factor, but again, Israel is an exception, and many Muslim countries, such as Indonesia and Malaysia, are definitely not considered part of the Middle East.

Yet the Middle East is a part of the world that needs to be considered by itself because of its unique characteristics, its often explosive political nature, its economic importance, and its promise for the future.

Saudi Arabia was selected as the country to illustrate the Middle East in part because there is no doubt that it is located there: it is Muslim and Arab, and it is bounded by the Persian Gulf, the Arabian Sea, and the Red Sea. Because of its size and wealth, it is one of the most important countries in the area. It is the region's largest oil exporter, a fact that makes it important to the United States and many other countries. Although it has its own distinctive characteristics, it illustrates most of the electronic media characteristics that are common throughout the Middle East: the influence of the Western world on broadcasting systems, the interrelationship of the countries' media systems to one another, the government-run aspects of the electronic media structure, the sway religion has over broadcasting practices, the impact of the culture on radio and TV, the ramifications of internal strife on the broadcasting structure, the effects of fluctuations of wealth, the dominance of equipment over programming, and the changes brought about by newer media such as satellites and the VCR.

WESTERN INFLUENCES

Most of the countries of the Middle East were European colonies during the era when radio was developed. As a result, their broadcasting systems were established to resemble the systems of the colonial powers—British in the case of such countries as Jordan, Kuwait, Oman, and Qatar; French for Lebanon, Algeria, Morocco, and Tunisia; and Italian for Libya. When the countries gained their independence in the 1950s and 1960s, some of them retained the basics of the broadcasting systems that had been developed for them.

In most instances settlers from the colonial powers aided in the establishment of native broadcasting systems and trained at least some local people to operate them, but in some cases they were much more heavy-handed. In Algeria, for example, the French totally dominated the broadcast structure, even airing only programs that were produced in France. When the French left (or were forced to leave) very quickly in 1962, the Algerians had no one capable of maintaining or operating the broadcasting structure. Almost all the technicians had been French, and when they left, the entire broadcasting system came to a temporary standstill. The Algerians still resent the French; they do not import any French programming—but import mostly U.S. programming dubbed into French, a language that many of them speak.

Even countries that were never colonized (Saudi Arabia and the former North Yemen) had strong ties with the West. For example, the U.S. Army Corps of Engineers was responsible for building most of Saudi Arabia's early television system, with RCA receiving the contracts to supply most of the transmission and production equipment.

In many Middle East countries, the selection of a television color system was strongly tied to political relationships with Western countries. The French lobbied strongly for adoption of their SECAM system, while the rest of Europe pushed for PAL. The selection (as will be seen in the chapter on Saudi Arabia) often had nothing to do with technical superiority but was politically motivated. As might be expected, Algeria opted for the PAL system so that it would not be feathering the French nest.

Today the West has less influence over Middle East broadcasting systems, each of which has developed its own unique characteristics over the years. However, many of the Western external services (BBC World Service, Voice of America, Radio Monte Carlo Middle East, etc.) are beamed into the area because of its political importance. These programs have large listenerships because the people in the area know that their own broadcasting services carry only the views of their leaders and they are eager to hear other points of view.

Quite a few of the countries also have national broadcast services aimed at Westerners who live within their boundaries. For example, both Jordan and the United Arab Emirates have channels with all-English programming to appeal to the many English-speaking people still working in these countries.

MIDDLE EAST COUNTRY INTERRELATIONSHIPS

Most of the countries of the Middle East broadcast (unintentionally or purposefully) to one another. Part of the reason for this deals with geography. Broadcast signals travel very well over warm salt water, especially during the hot, humid summer months. In addition, most of the countries have opted for high-power transmission systems because they want their ideas to be heard in other countries. As a result, it is difficult to distinguish between internal and external broadcasting in the Middle East.

Antagonistic Interrelationships This fluency of transmission is a double-edged sword. On the one hand, countries are able to get their points of view across to residents of other countries. For example, South Yemen broadcast derogatory material about the leaders of Oman when it wanted Oman's people to overthrow their government. Iraq's leader, Saddam Hussein, believes all Arab countries should unite (with himself as head, of course), and Iraq's broadcasts regularly espouse this theme. On the other hand, leaders of different countries listen to one anothers' broadcasts to ascertain changes in political philosophy that might affect them. For example, Jordan's leaders regularly listen to Syrian broadcasts to learn if Syria is considering any change in policy that might result in an attack on Jordan.

Israel and Jordan engage in an ongoing propaganda war—even when they are actually at war. Jordan attracts Israeli audiences by programming Western programs interspersed with Jordan's version of the news presented in Hebrew. Israel's radio and television services program in Arabic several hours a day with programs of general interest and programs designed to show Israel in a positive light. These programs are intended for Jordanians as well as well as other Arabs within or near Israel.

In some instances, one of the main motivations for the leaders of a country to establish a broadcasting system was to counter the negative information about them coming into the country from other Middle East countries. As will be seen in the chapter on Saudi Arabia, broadcasts from Radio Cairo were instrumental in the Saudi decision to increase radio services and introduce television. The same was true of Iraq.

Egypt Egypt's broadcasting system deserves special mention because it is so influential in the Middle East. Early Egyptian radio was influenced by the British. In fact, the British Marconi Company managed Egypt's radio system in the 1930s. The quality was rather high because Egypt, unlike other Middle East countries, had thriving film and theater industries and therefore had people available who could perform and operate equipment.

Egypt's early radio had little influence on the rest of the Middle East. That phenomenon awaited the arrival of Gamel Abdel Nasser who came to power as a result of a revolution in the early 1950s. Nasser, who was a skilled orator and an ambitious politician, used radio to build support for his policies. Radio Cairo, the main radio service, could be heard throughout much of the Middle East, but Nasser's real jewel was Voice of the Arabs, which he established in 1953. It was totally in Arabic and consisted of Nasser giving his points of view interspersed between Egyptian singers, drama, and news. Most of the other Arab countries did not have well-developed national radio services as yet, and so their citizens were easy prey for both Radio Cairo and Voice of the Arabs. Nasser's persuasive personality and his attacks on various Arab leaders led a number of countries to establish or improve their radio systems.

Nasser also supported television with more money than it received in many other countries. Egypt had three TV services—the Main Program, which was news, drama, and other information and entertainment aimed at general viewers; the Second Program, which was more sophisticated fare; and the Third Program, which was aimed at the foreigners in the country and programmed mostly in English and French. (Radio had several services that somewhat paralleled the TV channels.) TV did not reach the rest of the Arab world to the extent that radio did, but Nasser's version of TV did put other countries on the defensive.

In 1967 Egypt was defeated in a war with Israel. Anyone following the reports on Egyptian media would have thought Egypt was winning easily. When even Nasser had to admit that Egypt had lost, he pulled back and stopped courting the international audience as much as before. He abolished the Third Program and, for a period, developed stronger ties with the Soviet Union.

In 1970 Nasser died and was succeeded by Anwar Sadat, who was not a fiery orator and not as media-oriented as Nasser. As a result, Egyptian radio and TV became rather bland. In 1973 Egypt and Israel again fought a war, and this time the Egyptian media were more honest in their coverage. The outcome of the war itself was rather nebulous, with neither side emerging as a clear victor.

In 1979 Sadat signed a peace treaty with Israel. This made him unpopular with most of the other Middle East leaders who were more militant in their relations with the Israelis. Some of the Arab leaders boycotted, as best they could, Egyptian movies and radio and TV programs. Today many Arab countries air Egyptian television programs, and Egypt is the most important television producer in the Arab world.

Friendly Interrelationships Not all is antagonistic and propagandistic among the Middle East countries. Frequently they cooperate and help each other. The larger, richer, and more populous countries often send people to operate equipment in the smaller, poorer, less populated countries. Lebanon, Jordan, and Egypt have trained technicians and run equipment in Kuwait, Oman, and the United Arab Emirates. Sudan's commercials are produced in Egypt and Lebanon. The Middle East countries also join together to produce certain programs, such as an Arab version of *Sesame Street*.

GOVERNMENT POWER

In general, Middle East electronic media systems in Arab countries are under tight government control. News is scrutinized almost as carefully as it was in Eastern Europe during Communist days. Political leaders appear on radio and TV with great frequency, and their every move is followed—in a positive manner of course. A number of the area's leaders, including Iraq's Saddam Hussein, have used media to bypass the upper classes who regularly read newspapers, in order to establish their personalities with the common citizens of their countries.

The government is in charge of the financing of media. Most systems have commercials, and some also have license fees. A unique form of financing was developed by Egypt and copied by other countries. Originally, Egyptians who owned radios had to pay a license fee—in the British mode. However, the Egyptian government had trouble collecting these license fees and so instead added a fee to everyone's electricity bill on the theory that the people who had and used electricity were probably frequent radio listeners. Jordan, Tunisia, and Morocco now also have broadcasting fees added to electric bills.

Some governments have tried to use the electronic media to improve the health and literacy of their citizens, but these campaigns have not been very successful. Responsibility for electronic media is often transferred from one ministry to another to another, making for general instability. Governments feel no need to conduct research about the effectiveness or effects of the media; they just give the people what the leaders want them to have.

In a few countries underground radio stations have existed for periods of time with alternate points of view, but these have not made much impact. Except in Israel and Lebanon, privatization has not reached the Middle East, although Algeria is flirting with the idea. The main non-government viewpoint comes from illegal videocassettes.

RELIGION

The Muslim religion (Islam) that permeates most of the Middle East has a strong influence on the electronic media. Programs are very heavily censored for sex, violence, and "improper" religious references. Strict codes exist throughout the region, several of which will be discussed in the chapter on Saudi Arabia.

Because the conservative Islamic religion has tenets against reproduction of the human form, the area does not have a history that includes any of the visual arts—painting, sculpture, photography, and so on. Its outstanding area in the arts is music. The lack of personnel with a visual arts background has hindered development of the electronic media. On the other hand, radio and TV are quite popular in the Middle East because not much else exists in the field of visual arts or culture.

Religious programming appears on both radio and TV regularly. Readings of the Koran and discussions of religion are numerous. Of course, the situation is different in Israel where the Jewish religion predominates. Because religion is such an important part of the media structure, a few words should be said about Israeli broadcasting, especially in terms of its differences from Muslim-based systems.

Israel Israel was not a country when radio began. From 1917 to 1948, the territory it now occupies was overseen by the British under a

League of Nations mandate, and they established a Palestine Broadcasting Service along the lines of the BBC. In 1948 the United Nations decided that Israel should become the homeland for the Jews; however, the Arabs were vociferously opposed to the idea. British control ended on May 14, 1948, and the next day Israel was attacked by five Arab nations. After defeating the Arabs and establishing what has become a long, uneasy truce, the Jews started to build their nation, including their broadcasting system. It was formed from what was left by the British and from clandestine services run by Jewish groups during their fight for independence.

What eventually emerged were six government-run radio services, five operated by civilians and one by the military. Two of the civilian services were commercial, and one noncommercial one broadcast totally in Arabic—mainly to promulgate the Israeli version of events to nearby Arab listeners. The overall radio programming is lighter in nature than that of surrounding Arab radio. It features popular and classical music in addition to news and information, and some of the disc jockeys have become well-known personalities.

Television was slow in coming. As in some of the conservative Arab countries, it was opposed by religious leaders, in this case the extreme orthodox Jews. But it was also considered by many to be a frivolous waste. The 1967 war with Egypt, however, demonstrated that indigenous TV was needed to counter the spillover from Arab countries. Israeli TV was started in 1968 with one rather dull government-run channel well known for its many talk shows featuring long-winded politicians. This channel was slow to change to color; it did so mainly because people in Israel were buying color TV sets to watch the programming coming from Jordan.

The channel broadcasts $1\frac{1}{2}$ hours a day in Arabic, again to promulgate positive information about Israel. This includes a regular newscast and programs featuring information about Israeli achievements in science, literature, and education. Some of the programming is of a nonpropagandistic nature (jazz concerts, stories about the circus), and one comedy series dealt with Arab-Jewish prejudices in a humorous way.

Both government-run radio and TV are overseen by the British-modeled Israel Broadcasting Authority and are supported by license fees. The Israeli government wields significantly less power over its media than do the rest of the governments in the Middle East, but it has prevented the airing of programs that depict Israel treating Arabs cruelly, and in the past it has banned interviews with Palestine Liberation Organization (PLO) leaders.

Unlike most of the rest of the Middle East, Israel has established cable TV and embraced a limited amount of privatization.

Cable TV began in 1990, giving Israelis about twenty channels' worth of programming including music videos, CNN, the British Sky services, and entertainment from many countries including France, Germany, Turkey, and Russia. This is the first time that Israel has had this much exposure to outside programming. Israelis have taken to cable TV, with over 70 percent of them subscribing.

The second TV channel was born in 1993 and is operated by three different private companies, each of which program 2 days a week. Saturday programming is rotated among the three organizations, and plans are under way for private radio stations.

The effects of cable TV and the commercial channel are not clear, but the government-run TV channel is quickly sprucing up its image by building a more attractive set for its nightly news bulletin (generally viewed by 90 percent of the population), making sure its programs start precisely on the hour and half-hour, and reducing the number of talk shows featuring politicians. Also, now that the Israelis have a choice within their country, they do not watch Jordanian TV as much as they used to.

In general, Israeli electronic media are more Westernized than the media of Arab countries. They do not have as many censorship restrictions, and productions from the United States and other Western countries receive more acceptance.

IMPACT OF ARABIC CULTURE

For most of the Middle East outside Israel, the Arab culture has an impact on electronic media. This culture is oral in nature, making it more adaptable to the aural nature of radio and TV than to the written form of newspapers and magazines. As a result, most countries in the Middle East had an electronic revolution before they had a print one.

INTERNAL STRIFE

The Middle East is far from a peaceful area. The Arabs have a common enemy in Israel, but they also do not get along well with one another. The wars, alliances, and falling-outs have affected and been reflected by the media. For a number of years Egypt and Syria had an alliance, the United Arab Republic. During that time Syria was able to start to develop TV because Egypt helped it. When the two countries split, Syria's TV system met with hard times.

Wars sap money, leaving little for less important matters such as the development of radio and TV and the repair of equipment. In Syria (which, in addition to its on-and-off relationship with Egypt, has been involved in internal military coups and disagreements with its neighbors), the shortwave transmitter deteriorated completely, and service was shut down before anyone made plans for a new transmitter.

When Iraq retreated from Kuwait after the 1991 Gulf conflict, the Iraqi army took all of Kuwait's television equipment along—as well as sets, costumes, and even the puppets for a children's show. It also took 50,000 satellite dishes, causing some to postulate that the Iraqis weren't really after Kuwait's oil—what they wanted was uncensored TV. Kuwait has now rebuilt its entire television system.

In Lebanon, which is approximately half Muslim and half Christian, the constant conflict leads to a multiplicity of partisan and clandestine media without one official point of view. In the 1970s the stations reported very little about a raging Muslim-Christian war, but an army officer forced his way into one of the studios and demanded airtime.

In other countries, such as Iran and Iraq, when wars are under way, each country uses the media as a propaganda tool. Each country broadcasts to the other that it is winning the war—even if it isn't—in an attempt to demoralize the enemy.

Overall, the turmoil in the area keeps the electronic media from reaching their full potential and increases the need for the countries' leaders to maintain tight control of radio and TV. One result is that the people in the Middle East are the largest consumers of international radio broadcasting in the world.

FLUCTUATIONS OF WEALTH

For centuries much of the Middle East was considered by Westerners to be rather useless hot, dry land. The stereotypical picture was one of nomads on camels roaming the desert. Then in the 1930s, oil was discovered. Now some of these countries had a resource that was much in demand, and they became very wealthy selling it. In 1973 alone, oil prices quadrupled. But by the 1980s, oil prices had fallen, and the countries found that they were overextended.

All of these phases affected broadcasting. Very little radio and TV existed in the pre-oil years; broadcasting developed and expanded (especially in terms of equipment) during the oil boom years of the 1970s; now the media are more sanguine.

Disparities have also occurred between countries that have oil and those that don't. Oil-rich countries like Saudi Arabia, Iraq, and Kuwait have more developed media systems than nonoil countries such a Sudan and Tunisia. Poor countries have trouble supporting electronic media; there are not many takers for advertising in such countries.

EQUIPMENT AND PROGRAMMING

Lack of training has hindered both the operation of equipment and the development of programming in the Middle East. Some colleges, including the American University in Cairo and King Saud University in Saudi Arabia, have radio and television courses, but educational possibilities in this field are few and far between.

When some of the countries were rolling in oil money, they could buy whatever equipment they wanted, and even make mistakes and buy it all over again. They could also buy maintenance in the form of foreigners who would operate their systems for them. Although natives were trained, not enough of them were available to keep radio and television operating. Most Middle East countries have small populations, and all aspects of life, not just broadcasting, burgeoned during the 1970s. The population was stretched too thin. As a result, the technical quality of radio and TV sometimes suffers. Still, the equipment used in most Middle East countries is top rate.

Hardware is much easier to handle than software, however. Developing local programming without an arts background was difficult. Foreigners could not be trusted to abide by the strict religious regulations.

The main Middle East country to produce "acceptable" programming has been Egypt, but some countries do not like what they perceive to be the pro-Israel, pro-West political stance of Egypt and, as a result, boycott its programming.

Programs from the West are definitely shown in the Middle East, but sometimes they are edited to such a degree that they are almost unrecognizable. Sex and violence aside, the conspicuous consumption seen in many foreign imports (especially American) creates false hopes and demands from the youth.

The homegrown programming of the Middle East is gradually improving. It contains numerous political pontifications by leaders and "politically correct" news, but a number of the children's programs produced are of good quality and some of the local dramas even deal with sensitive subjects such as the generation gap.

NEWER MEDIA

The "official" electronic media structure in most of the Middle East is government-operated over-the-air broadcasting, with Israel of course being an exception. Several pay-TV multichannel multipoint distribution services (MMDSs) are in operation and more are planned, but their programming content is supervised by the government. In a number of countries home satellite dishes are illegal, although royalty and the rich have them.

The Arabs know the value of satellites, however, and in the mid-1980s launched their own satellite system, Arabsat. These satellites were to make the Arab countries self-sufficient in terms of satellite transmission and reception. No longer would they need to depend on what they perceived as a Western-dominated system, Intelsat. However, it didn't work out that way. Many of the countries that were supposed to use Arabsat did not have the money to buy downlinks, and in general, not enough money was available for it to operate effectively. Partly because of this, Intelsat's rates are cheaper, and so when countries do want satellite feeds, they often choose Intelsat over Arabsat. Arabsat still exists, but it is on shaky grounds financially.

The nonbroadcast media form that has taken over in the Middle East is the videocassette recorder. Most of the cassettes are illegal duplicates. As mentioned in the chapter on Saudi Arabia, the first imported cassettes were legal

Arabia, the first imported cassettes were legal copies brought past censors who didn't know what they were. Once they found out what could be seen from those little black cases, they stopped them at the border. So the whole operation went underground. It is estimated that there are more VCRs and videocassettes per person in the Middle East than in any other part of the world.

The electronic media of the Middle East have undergone a rapid evolution in a very short period of time. Their significance in this politically unstable area will no doubt continue.

(*Editor's Note*: Much of the material for this overview is from Douglas Boyd's book *Broadcasting in the Arab World: A Survey of Electronic Media in the Middle East*, published by Iowa State University Press in 1993.)

CHAPTER 8

Saudi Arabia

Douglas A. Boyd

Douglas Boyd.

Douglas Boyd is currently dean of the College of Communications and Information Studies at the University of Kentucky. He has made many trips to the Middle East as a scholar and media practitioner, spending a year as a Fulbright professor in Cairo and serving a stint as an announcer for a Saudi Arabian radio service. He has published numerous research articles about the Middle East and is the author of *Broadcasting in the Arab World: A Survey of Electronic Media in the Middle East*, published in 1993 by Iowa State University Press. This chapter is an edited version of a chapter from the second edition of that book and is used with the permission of the publisher. Boyd, who received his Ph.D from the University of Minnesota, is the recipient of many internationally oriented research grants, including ones from Japan's Hoso-Bunka Foundation, UNESCO, and the government of Quebec.

STATISTICS

Geographic Area: 839,996 square miles
Capital: Riyadh
Population: 17,869,000
Religion: Muslim
Language: Arabic
Type of Government: Monarchy with a council of ministers and a sixty-member Consultative Council appointed by the King
Gross Domestic Product: $79 billion
Literacy: 62 percent

GENERAL CHARACTERISTICS

The two factors that have most influenced Saudi Arabian society (including its electronic media) are religion and oil. The kingdom is very conservative, adhering to the basic beliefs of the Islamic religion. The consumption of alcoholic drinks is illegal, and public cinemas are not allowed; the country's legal system follows closely the teachings of the Koran.

In the 1930s, oil was discovered in the Eastern Province, but almost no revenue was realized by the government until after World War II. Income then increased steadily, during the 1950s and 1960s, but not until the rapid increases in oil prices after the 1973 Middle East War did the country accumulate enormous wealth and put into effect its remarkably energetic development plan. An important supplier of oil to the United States, Europe, and Japan, Saudi Arabia is the largest oil exporter of the Arab countries.

It was the Iraqi invasion of Kuwait on August 2, 1990, that placed the Saudi desert kingdom firmly in the minds of those in the West and much of the rest of the world. With the possibility of Iraq's invasion of the Saudi Eastern Province, the U.S. government proposed a multinational force composed primarily of United States, British, French, and Egyptian troops. Subsequent Operations Desert Shield and Desert Storm gave the world a comprehensive view of the religion, culture, and character of Saudi citizens. Those paying attention also were witness to some of the activities of the government-run broadcasting services.

THE DEVELOPMENT OF ELECTRONIC MEDIA IN SAUDI ARABIA

Saudi Arabia is one of the few Middle Eastern countries that was never colonized or otherwise dominated by a foreign power. The area's modern history began when Abdul Aziz ibn Saud captured the old walled city of Riyadh in 1902; over the next 30 years, his sons and followers conquered various sections of the country, which occupies most of the Arabian peninsula. In 1932 that land was proclaimed Saudi Arabia.

When ibn Saud and his followers captured the Western Province, which contains the holy cities of Mecca and Medina, they found wireless stations and a telephone line that had been left behind by the Turks, who before World War I had nominal control over the area. The king realized that he would need the help of wire and wireless communication facilities in order to rule effectively over such a vast, sparsely populated country, and so he purchased and installed a network of transmitters in various cities in the kingdom and also acquired portable transmitters to accompany him when he traveled.

But he realized at the same time that he and those who followed him would need to strike a delicate balance between modernization and Islam because the *ulema*, the religious leaders, were grimly opposed to the Western gadgetry that would almost surely change the traditional ways of the area. Unable to see the manner of its working, they had to suspect that wireless was literally the work of the devil.

Ibn Saud's way of proving that it was not was characteristic of him: he devised an "experiment" to satisfy them. He asked a group of *ulema* to travel to Mecca, where they were to await a wireless transmission from his headquarters in Riyadh. At the appointed time he had passages from the Koran read to them over the system. He then reportedly observed that, as the devil could not pronounce the word of the Koran, the "miracle" they had just witnessed had to be the work of man and nature rather than the devil. Opposition to wireless communication ceased. Television, however, was to be another matter.

Radio Broadcasting before 1960 There was no early need for a radio broadcasting service in Saudi Arabia. No foreign power was influencing government decisions, and ibn Saud ruled the country with an ongoing system of interpersonal communication, traveling to visit the various tribes on a regular basis. But by the end of World War II, when he was showing signs of aging, ibn Saud may have reasoned that when he became older and found it difficult to travel extensively, radio could be a substitute for his visits. Also, Saudi citizens started acquiring radios after World War II, and they listened to Arabic programs on foreign stations in order to hear news and other programming. Therefore, the minister of finance arranged in May 1949 for International Telegraph and Telephone, Inc., to build a transmitter and studio in Jidda, and ibn Saud put his son Faisal in charge of the station. Neither women's voices nor music (military marches excepted) was allowed on the air, and most of the broadcasting time was devoted to religious programming.

Faisal was influential in 1953 in establishing the first identifiable office within the government to handle broadcasting and information activities, which later became the Ministry of Information. But no other major broadcasting developments took place in Saudi Arabia in the 1950s, though the number of radio receivers increased because of growing affluence and the new availability of electricity. Smaller, more reliable battery-operated transistor sets also appeared on the market and, as was the case in many other Arab countries, coffeehouse owners acquired radios to attract customers.

As the decade ended, radio service was still restricted to the Western Province and operated for only a limited number of hours per day. Listeners interested in news events tuned to the BBC; those more interested in entertainment, especially popular Arab music, tuned to one of the Egyptian radio services. And when, in the late 1950s, the Egyptian services (most notably Voice of the Arabs) started attacking the Saudi royal family and suggesting revolution, the government was initially powerless to counter them. The popular Egyptian radio services, which were only to grow more hostile during the 1960s, were therefore probably the single factor most responsible for the expansion that took place in Saudi Arabian radio in that decade. The kingdom could not defend itself against radio attacks without adequate transmitting facilities.

Radio Broadcasting in the 1960s Primarily because of increased listening to foreign broadcasts, the government announced in 1957 that it would build a station in Riyadh. The first Saudi radio station outside the Western Province, the Riyadh Domestic Service, was on the air about 16 hours per day. Then in the early 1960s construction started on a new broadcasting studio complex in Jidda: its service was to be known as Radio Mecca even though it did not originate from there, and it operated for about 17 hours per day. In 1965 these two domestic radio services were operating quite separately, 500 miles apart, with no means existing to connect them. They reached only their respective cities and the surrounding towns: national coverage was not yet a reality.

Indeed, the only radio broadcasting in the large oil-rich Eastern Province was done by Arabian American Oil Company (ARAMCO), the U.S. company later acquired by the Saudi government. Not until the late 1960s did the Ministry of Information inaugurate service in the eastern portion of the country. But it had been announced in 1964 that a series of transmitters would be built in major Saudi Arabian cities to broadcast a Voice of Islam program to compete with the Egyptian anti-Saudi radio services. The plan was frustrated by failure of the French-built transmitter to operate as designed until it was refitted in the early 1970s, by which time Egypt's Gamal Abdel Nasser and Saudi Arabia's King Faisal had reached agreement over the chief source of friction during the 1960s, the civil war in Yemen, and the need to counter Egyptian broadcasts had diminished.

As the 1960s ended, the fact that the kingdom was no longer under constant radio attack by other countries gave planners an opportunity to review the future of radio broadcasting in Saudi Arabia. During this period, a plan was conceived to provide a strong signal to the sparsely populated northern portion of the country and to reach other countries such as Egypt, Lebanon, Iraq, and Jordan. The Ministry of Information was relocated to the capital city, Riyadh, in 1967, and plans were consolidated to centralize radio administration and most production and transmission there as well. The U.S. Army Corps of Engineers (COE), which had built the initial television facilities in the kingdom, was asked to supervise the design and construction of the new central radio studio and administration building.

The chief problem of the period was that the Ministry of Information had grown dramatically and it was hard to find enough qualified Saudis to fill the major management positions in expanding radio and television services. In Saudi Arabia those positions were reserved for natives of the country, and all too often, those who assumed administrative responsibilities had no previous media experience.

Radio Broadcasting after the 1960s The October 1973 Middle East War had a great effect on Saudi Arabia and consequently on its radio system. Though not directly involved in the armed conflict among Egypt, Syria, and Israel, the kingdom for a time joined other Arab countries in stopping shipments of oil to the West, quadrupling the price on resumption of shipping. Saudi Arabia found itself with more oil income than it could absorb—and a new international role.

The increased income was earmarked for an energetic development plan that included additional high-powered radio transmitters able to reach other countries. In the mid-1970s the completion of a Saudi national telecommunications system made reliable radio networking possible, both throughout the country and to other countries.

Television before 1970 Plans for Saudi television were not announced until 1963, and by that time the Saudi government had several reasons for building a national television system. First, it needed to provide the population with an innovation that was at least symbolically modern. Despite the fact that some religious leaders had interpreted sections of the Koran to mean that any kind of cinematic art was a form of idolatry, wealthier Saudis had by that time traveled to other countries and had become enamored of television. National television, it was reasoned, would at least give the government some control over the kind of news, developmental, and entertainment programming that was provided to Saudis at home.

The second reason for the introduction of television was the preoccupation of the Ministry of Information with hostile broadcasts from Egypt's radio stations: a television service operating during evening hours would provide an attractive alternative to Radio Cairo and Voice of the Arabs. Third, the government counted on using television for educational purposes—to help with basic health and literacy training as well as to support classroom teaching. Finally, television would help provide a sense of national unity not before possible. No longer would the Eastern Province be isolated from the capital and the cities near the Red Sea.

The U.S. Army Corps of Engineers hired American firms to develop the television facilities that operated from both Riyadh and Jidda. Contracts were awarded to Radio Corporation of America (RCA) to supply the equipment, and another contract went to the National Broadcasting Company International (NBCI) for the operation and maintenance of the stations. On July 17, 1965, both stations officially went on the air.

OPPOSITION TO TELEVISION

It is unlikely that the full story of the opposition to television from conservative religious ele-

Early TV facilities at Riyadh.

ments in Riyadh will ever be known. What is certain is the profound and far-reaching effect that one incident had on the country many years later.

Essentially the same religious leaders who had opposed radio broadcasting opposed television, but television was a more serious problem because of its visual element that Muslim religious leaders saw as counter to the prohibition against graven images.

In the summer of 1965, during the test transmission period in Riyadh, a conservative royal family member named Khalid ibn Musad gathered supporters for a march on the television station, intending to destroy its tower and transmitting equipment. What happened next is still a matter of speculation. Several sources reported that the transmitter had been destroyed, but this was not true. When police dispersed the crowd, Khalid returned to his house, where he was shot and killed by a policeman during a struggle with an official of the Ministry of the Interior. Though Khalid's immediate family appealed to King Faisal to punish the person who shot him, Faisal ruled that the policeman, whose identity was never officially disclosed, had acted appropriately.

But the incident was not really over. Almost 10 years later, Faisal ibn Musad, Khalid's younger brother, shot and killed King Faisal while he was receiving guests in Riyadh. *Newsweek* reported that after the shooting Faisal ibn Musad shouted, "Now my brother is avenged." King Faisal's death came when his leadership was badly needed in the kingdom. He was a moderate who had attempted to balance social progress with the constraints imposed by conservative Islamic beliefs, and it is one of history's ironies that he was thus killed over an incident involving television—a medium he had supported and helped to develop.

Television Expansion In 1967, two years after the opening of the Jidda and Riyadh stations, a second television project was completed by the Corps of Engineers: a series of microwave relays was built to send the Jidda station signal to transmitters in Mecca and Taif. In that same year an operation called the Training Transmitter Project was also completed—one

King Faisal. (*Marc and Evelyn Bernheim/Woodfin Camp and Associates*)

that the COE and RCA undertook only reluctantly. The innocuous name of the project notwithstanding, its four transmitters in a building near the Jidda television station were in fact intended to jam Egyptian television signals. The importance of this project to the government can be understood only within the context of the Egyptian anti-Saudi radio propaganda that was so virulent before the 1967 Middle East War; and indeed by the time the transmitters were operational, improved relations between Saudi Arabia and Egypt had made them, like the Riyadh Voice of Islam radio transmitter, unnecessary.

In early 1968 two more television stations, in Medina and Qassim, came on the air. These were smaller than the Jidda and Riyadh facilities—though they contained living quarters for the foreign engineers who were needed to operate them. RCA and National Broadcasting Company International built and operated the new stations.

The final Saudi television project involving the COE was the construction of a powerful television station in Dammam in the Eastern Province. The good working relationship that the COE had with the Ministry of Information soured when the station became operational. The Saudi government had placed a high priority on completion of the Dammam station because neighboring countries were building stations that might reach the Eastern Province. A Kuwaiti station was already available there, and Saudi Arabia, which had traditionally had a friendly rivalry with Kuwait, wanted especially to make a similar showing in that neighboring oil-rich state. With uncharacteristic speed, plans for the station proceeded. RCA was asked to supply two transmitters, but apparently it misinformed the COE, or the COE misunderstood some of the technical advice provided by RCA, and the transmissions did not reach Kuwait. The government was furious, and with the cooling of relations between the COE and the Ministry of Information, the COE stopped contract work on broadcasting in the kingdom.

Television in the 1970s Considerable changes had taken place in Saudi Arabian television by the mid-1970s. After a decade of experience with television, the Ministry of Information felt more comfortable with the medium. Under the supervision of the Corps of Engineers, a small number of Saudi television employees had been sent to the United States for training in all facets of television: production courses, English-language training, graduate work in broadcasting, and electrical engineering. By 1974 the entire television system was Saudi-managed. A local Saudi company, BETA, had taken over the contract for operation and maintenance of the kingdom's television stations, although the technicians and engineers who worked for the company were virtually all non–Saudi Arabs. European personnel generally supervised the work done by Jordanian, Egyptian, and Lebanese engineers.

In August 1977 a new television facility was opened in Abha in the southwestern part of Saudi Arabia. The station is used to broadcast the national television service and has the capability of producing local programming. Very little has been done with station building since then. The growth in Saudi Arabian television has been in the increase in coverage provided by transmitters that broadcast the Riyadh signal via a leased Intelsat system satellite transponder. Thus, although behind other Gulf states such as Kuwait in the construction of production facilities, Saudi Arabia has expanded its television coverage to include the entire country; and, moreover, two ground stations linked to the Intelsat system are used to receive and transmit television signals internationally.

Television in the 1980s Three developments most affected the visual medium during the 1980s: (1) the decrease in worldwide oil prices that dramatically slowed the booming Saudi economy, (2) the addition of a second channel, and (3) the decision to permit advertising on television.

Between early 1974 and 1980, the high price of oil supplied by the Organization of Petroleum Exporting Countries (OPEC) fueled a financially healthy Saudi economy, resulting in an immense transfer of wealth from the West to Gulf states. Large sums of money were spent by the government on development projects, with the electronic media receiving large sums of this money. Old television equipment in the stations built by the COE in the 1960s was replaced, and some new buildings were built. However, the most impressive project was the new state-of-the-art studio and administrative complex for Saudi television in Riyadh.

The additional studio space and associated equipment made possible the addition of a second national channel. From its beginnings in August 1983 the second channel has evolved into a genuine alternative source of broadcast television for viewers who know English. The entire channel consists of locally produced or imported programs that are dubbed into, or subtitled in, English.

Advertising was not considered necessary to help finance the system until the kingdom started experiencing financial difficulties in the early 1980s because of the drop in oil prices. At first, advertising was permitted only on the English-language Second Channel. But after its January 1, 1986, start, wide acceptance on the part of the public allowed the Ministry of Information to permit advertising on the Arabic-language First Channel.

Videocassettes In the early 1980s the business of providing videocassette recorders in the Gulf states, particularly in Saudi Arabia, was a major industry. By the mid-1980s, Gulf state businesses became more active in videocassette software—in both the production and distribution of tapes for rent. The Gulf area is probably the largest home videocassette market in the world; it is surely one of the world's largest outlets for pirated tapes of first-run American and British films and television programming, as well as Egyptian video and film material.

Part of the explanation for this situation can be found in the cultural and economic conditions that exist in the kingdom. Only a few private cinema enterprises have been allowed to operate—small businesses that rent 16-millimeter projectors and older Egyptian and Western films for home showing—and no public cinemas exist. In most areas of the country, the only television programming available is on the two national Saudi Arabian television channels. Yet, from their travels upper- and middle-income Saudis have become accustomed to a diverse film and television diet. That Saudi Arabia is a culture that is fascinated by modern gadgetry also boosts business, as does the fact that import duties on home entertainment equipment are low to nonexistent.

ORGANIZATION AND FINANCING

Television and radio are organized in an almost identical manner. They are operated by the Ministry of Information, and funding is provided by the government and commercial advertising; there is no license fee.

Riyadh is the center of program transmission, providing the bulk of programs for all stations and relay transmitters in the kingdom. Jidda and Mecca also provide radio programming, and for television, the cities with studios large enough to tape programs—Jidda, Riyadh, Dammam—are assigned the task of specializing in the production of certain kinds of programs that are then placed on the national network. Both Riyadh and Jidda tape some programming for children; quiz programs are taped in Dammam, as is a program about Saudi Arabia that is produced as part of a Gulf states cooperative programming arrangement.

Advertising The Saudi government has never really objected to advertising per se. In a consumption-oriented, market-driven economy, advertising appears in Saudi newspapers and magazines, on billboards, and in stores. However, during the period when the government could afford it, the Ministry of Information felt that it did not have sufficient numbers of trained personnel to operate the stations and that the organization of advertising would only make matters worse. All this changed when the Second Channel began and the Ministry of Information was forced to find an alternative source of funding to that provided by the government.

Not only did Saudi television wish to gain income from television advertising, but also the government had grown resentful of Western and Asian manufacturers of consumer goods who were selling millions of dollars worth of products in the kingdom by advertising on the commercial radio and television stations in other Gulf states and via international radio operations. The economic impact of Saudi Arabian television advertising on outside media is obvious from what happened to advertising revenue on the most popular Western radio station heard in the Arab world: after the introduction of advertising on both Saudi television channels, gross advertising revenue for Radio Monte Carlo Middle East (RMCME) fell 50 percent.

Corps of Engineers Involvement For the first 8 years of television's existence, the United States was deeply involved in television planning and operation in the kingdom. The U.S. connection started when then–Crown Prince Faisal, who later became king, made a visit to the U.S. ambassador asking for help in solving the problem of contracting for a reliable television system, believing that the United States could build stations for him quickly, bypassing the Saudi Arabian commercial firms that could be expected to slow the introduction of television and increase the cost of the project.

The ambassador passed the request along, and eventually the implementation became the responsibility of the U.S. Army Corps of Engineers, whose efficiency in constructing he Dhahran airport facility and several small projects involving the Saudi Arabian military had impressed the Saudi government.

ARAMCO Radio and Television Broadcasting A discussion of the organization of broadcast media in Saudi Arabia would not be complete without further examination of the broadcasting activities of the Arabian American Oil Company. This firm was originally owned by major U.S. oil companies that participated in Middle East petroleum exploration in the 1930s. Company headquarters are in Dhahran, in the Eastern Province, where almost all oil activity is centered. During the 1970s the kingdom purchased the company, but it continues to contract with a consortium of U.S. oil firms to manage and market the country's entire output. Americans have always played an important part in Saudi Arabia's oil industry: by January 1980, 3000 Americans were directly employed there by ARAMCO, and 3600 more were employed by various company subcontractors. The compound in Dhahran, then, could function as a model American community, complete with cinemas, a bowling alley, supermarkets, beauty shops, and a school system with an American curriculum; women, not allowed to drive in the rest of Saudi Arabia, were permitted to do so there. Naturally, in such a setting, a broadcasting system similar to that in the United States could operate.

ARAMCO started television transmissions in Dhahran in 1957 and soon was providing entertainment not only for its American employees but for Saudis in the surrounding area who could receive the signal, broadcasting its soundtracks in two languages, English and Arabic. In 1964 the company moved its studios from their previous location above a snack bar to a larger building, specifically to accommodate an increased local production schedule including religious programs, drama, and a children's series—mostly in Arabic.

When the government built a station in Dammam in 1970, the ARAMCO station ceased all Arabic-language transmissions but still continued to provide English-language—mostly U.S.—programming. The station operates daily from midafternoon to approximately 10:00 P.M., featuring those U.S. and British programs that the company believes conform to local Saudi cultural standards. Indeed, all programs are censored by the ARAMCO public relations department in spite of the fact that most offerings purchased for the station are intended primarily for a Western audience. The station is presented by ARAMCO as Channel 3 and is never identified as being operated by ARAMCO.

When U.S. and other "coalition" armed forces arrived in the Eastern Province of the kingdom to participate in Operation Desert Storm in 1991, Channel 3 was important because it was an immediate source of American television programming for U.S. and other English-speaking troops. In fact, the Saudi Arabian military asked ARAMCO television to increase transmission hours slightly to meet what was believed to be a need for "home-style" entertainment for the mostly American military contingent.

Like its television services, ARAMCO's radio broadcasting dates from the 1950s: not until the mid-1960s to late 1960s did records and tapes become generally available for sale in the kingdom, and ARAMCO reasoned that FM radio music would fill a real void. So too would a 15-minute newscast of international news from United Press International (UPI) read by an employee of the ARAMCO public relations department. But the original small radio operation of the 1950s has, like the company itself, greatly expanded. By 1963 popular and easy-listening music services were available. After 1970 the company decided that more variety was important and designed a new system to broadcast four separate 24-hour FM stereo music services: the operation, assembled wholly from components, resembles a U.S. automated radio station.

PROGRAMMING

Although ARAMCO provides Western-style programming, most of what is seen and heard by the Saudi Arabian people is Middle Eastern in style and content.

Radio Services Dependent on announcers and producers from other Arab countries, Saudi Arabia can claim relatively little that is uniquely Saudi about its programming: Egyptian, Jordanian, and Lebanese personnel particularly have had a major influence on programming style and format, and some of the recorded music and drama broadcast in Saudi Arabia was taped in other Arab countries before the kingdom had built adequate studios for its own productions.

By the early 1960s the initial restrictions on music had gradually changed, one reason being that popular songs could easily be heard on the Egyptian radio services. Religious leaders did object to the introduction of female announcers on the Jidda-based radio service in 1963, but King Faisal reportedly told the protesting *ulema*, "You'd better get used to women's voices on the radio, because you'll be seeing their faces on television soon."

As of 1990 the two services in operation were the General Program and the Holy Koran Broadcasts. The General Program is transmitted for 20 hours per day and originates from the studios in Riyadh and Jidda with a certain number of hours going out from each location each day. Intended to be the country's main domestic and international Arabic radio voice, the General Program is structured so that special programs appropriate for military personnel, children, women, students, and housewives are aired at appropriate times. Much of the religious programming offered on the General Program is supplied by another radio service that originates from the holy city of Mecca and is heard on the General Program at the times of the daily prayers. Besides the calls for prayer from the Mecca Mosque, this service, called Voice of Islam, broadcasts news and features about Islam.

The Holy Koran service traces its origins back to 1972 and is actually two separate services, one from Riyadh and the other from Mecca. Designed for listeners in Arab, Asian, and African Islamic countries, the Riyadh service lasts for 18 hours per day and the Mecca service 14 hours a day. The Holy Koran Broadcast appears to differ from Voice of Islam in that the latter is more oriented toward news and information about the Islamic world, while the former is designed to broadcast serious religious discussion and lectures, as well as readings from the Koran.

Television Programming It is easier, given sufficient funds, to acquire hardware than to produce software, and generally speaking the Saudi Arabian television administration has been more successful in managing the equipment-related aspects of television than the programming side. The Corps of Engineers and National Broadcasting Company International (NBCI) were ready to provide production advice when asked by the government, but programming decisions have been the responsibility of the Ministry of Information—and, when television was first introduced, very little thought had been given to the kind of daily schedule that the ministry would provide. It was after the 1965 incident in Riyadh, which showed how militant the opposition to the medium could be, that officials became concerned about the possible consequences of the start of actual programming.

Early Programming In July and August 1965 the test pattern was telecast in the morning; in the early evening about an hour's worth of programming was provided, including Koran readings, background music, and scenic slides of various sections of the kingdom. Mighty Mouse cartoons were shown, and off-camera announcers read the news while still news pictures appeared on the screen.

By almost any measure, these first television signals were received with tremendous excitement by the citizens of Riyadh and Jidda, the majority of whom had never seen a motion picture. I remember the scene in downtown Jidda during the brief evening transmissions in August 1965; people stood five and six deep on the sidewalks to catch a glimpse of the television sets in shop windows. Every morning when the test pattern transmission stopped, the station's switchboard was flooded with calls wanting to know where the "programs" were. The minister of information would drop by the station at night to see how the programming was progressing. On one occasion he came to the station with a press delegation and decided on the spot that the visit should be televised.

Early planning by the Ministry of Information and NBCI projected that nightly programming was to be limited to about 2 hours. But receiver sales soared. Those who could not afford to buy, such as lower-income families and expatriate workers, watched television in the coffeehouses and restaurants at night. By the end of the first year of operation, each station was operating between 5 and 6 hours daily.

The Jidda and Riyadh stations had only one studio each; and although the studios were large, only limited amounts of local programming could be produced in a single studio that could be used only when the station was off the air. Programs were, moreover, limited by the lack of production, engineering, and artistic personnel. Some dramas were taped, but most locally produced programs consisted of interviews with officials and religious leaders. Children's programs and dramas were written and produced by Arabs from other countries, most of them from Syria. The only live programming consisted of the news and press reviews, reviews of the evening's schedule (which was not yet published in Saudi newspapers), and station identification.

Religious Programming Religious programming, important in all Arab countries, has special importance in the country in which the most holy cities of Islam are located. Each telecasting day begins with a Koran reading. Evening prayer calls are heard over a slide or short film of the famous mosque in Mecca. King Faisal reportedly promised religious leaders, when he was trying to secure approval for the construction of the system, that television would be used as an important means of disseminating religious doctrine; and one of the first programs to be videotaped at the Jidda station, a popular religious series that continued into the 1970s, therefore deserves special mention. Former U.S. Ambassador Hermann Eilts described it and its creator:

> At least one distinguished *alim*, Shaykh Ali Tantawi, is demonstrating the value of television in the cause of religion. Possessed of an engaging television personality, this savant conducts a regular question and answer program on religious subjects. He invites written questions, reads them before the television camera, and with homely anecdotes about and relevant allusion to contemporary everyday life instructs his viewers. Lacking his imagination, some of his colleagues shortsightedly criticize him. He deserves more credit.

When the Jidda station acquired a mobile broadcasting unit, it began originating both live and taped broadcasts from Mecca during the important religious days of Ramadan and Hajj. By 1980 about 25 percent of programming was devoted to religious subjects.

Other Programming Sources The increase in programming hours during the first year of operation required buying material from other countries. Egypt, as previously noted, was not considered an acceptable supplier: relations between the two countries were at an all-time low between 1965 and 1970. Some programming, generally of low quality, was purchased from the two privately owned Lebanese stations, but little else of Arab origin was available.

The only answer to the immediate need for even more programming, then, was to purchase packages of old movies from the United States and Great Britain. Some of these films were shown, but many proved to be unacceptable because of content offensive to Saudi religious sensibilities. During the first 5 years of television in the kingdom, imported made-for-television programs were limited to those that had been sold to other Arab countries and therefore were already dubbed or subtitled in Arabic and were suitable for Islamic viewers. These programs proved to be so popular that the Ministry of Information was willing to purchase additional such programs to help fill the expanded television schedule. Until about 1972 the percentage of imported Western programming on the Saudi Arabian television system ranged from 25 percent to 33 percent.

After 1972 the kingdom started purchasing large amounts of Egyptian programming while continuing to buy from Lebanon; and by the late 1970s, it was also buying programs from Jordan, Bahrain, and Dubai. While the percentage of imported, mostly entertainment, programming has not decreased, the percentage of imported Western programming has. This is due not only to increased program production in the Middle East but also to the new permissiveness in television programming in the West: the earlier programs had been more acceptable and had required little editing.

Educational Programming The government has commissioned several studies on how the television medium can be used for educational purposes, but relatively little educational programming is shown except for a few programs on health, safety, and literacy. The main reason for this dearth is that the Ministries of Information and of Education have never been able to agree on which has primary responsibility over such programming.

Commercials As is occasionally the situation on commercial television, some of the commercials on Saudi television are more interesting than the regular programming. Many of the commercials, featuring automobiles, cooking oil, watches, processed food, soap, bug sprays, and cosmetics, are produced in the West or in Egypt.

However, some of the commercials do rankle Muslim sensibilities. For example, in early January 1991, just before the Gulf conflict, some influential conservative religious elements in the kingdom are said to have officially protested to the Ministry of Information about females being used in some commercials.

As noted previously, from the very beginning of Saudi television in 1965, the appearance of females—especially Arab females—on television has been a very sensitive matter. There has been a general understanding that females will not be shown in commercials, especially those that do not directly advertise female-oriented products. But the television administration has become rather lax about this, particularly when commercial producers become very clever. For example, males and females are never seen dancing on Saudi television. However, in a bath soap ad shown in 1990, bars of soap—rather obviously sex-typed as male and female—did dance! This was reportedly one of the commercials to which the religious authorities objected. The Ministry of Information decreed that females would appear only in commercials where their presence was appropriate, for example, in commercials for disposable diapers.

Generally speaking, however, female roles in commercials are very carefully presented. For example, in a 1991 commercial for a brand of cooking oil, viewers see only the hands of the woman using the product. Another commercial shows an obviously satisfied husband and children eating food prepared by the wife and mother. The woman is not shown; she assumes the position of the camera viewing the happy family.

Programming Events Some of the government's programming choices have unquestionably helped unify the country. National leaders, most of whom are members of the royal family, have been given the kind of national visibility not possible before the introduction of television.

The medium has been used with some degree of effectiveness during periods of crisis, the first instance being in 1967 when a series of bombings occurred in Riyadh. Yemenis, allegedly supporting Egypt's role in the Yemen Civil War, were arrested and executed; but first they were shown on television in an interview during which they admitted their role in the bombings. These telecasts were apparently well received by citizens. Seeing the people responsible for the acts somehow added credibility to the government's statements about the nationality of the bombers and their motive and stopped rumors and speculation about the causes of the explosions.

During the November 1979 Mecca Mosque incident, television helped again in a national crisis—though it began the exercise less than smoothly. The takeover of the large mosque on the day corresponding to the end of the Islamic fourteenth century caught Saudi Arabian authorities by surprise: for several days, Ministry of Information officials withheld information about the "incident" and Saudi citizens listening to foreign radio reports began to suspect that the government was minimizing the seriousness of the situation at the mosque. When the government decided to release specific information about the extent of the fighting, television was unable to react promptly: pictures of what was actually happening were difficult to obtain because no trained Saudi national was available to take the necessary news footage, and Arab expatriate employees of the film department hesitated to undertake the assignment until their security in Mecca could be guaranteed. But as soon as film of the fighting became available, it was included in newscasts. Following his capture, the leader of the takeover was interviewed on television. The ministry used this and other footage to produce a 90-minute documentary that was shown on what was then the national channel. As the interviews with the Yemeni bombers had done 13 years earlier, this program defused rumors—and it apparently helped satisfy Saudi concern about the extent of damage to a holy Islamic structure.

LAWS AND REGULATIONS

The Ministry of Information controls all radio and television content, which generally reflects what the ministry believes to be the mood of the country. When conservative religious elements become more forceful, programming, too, becomes more conservative. Even in the most liberal of times (by Saudi standards), censorship is abundant.

Program Censorship One of the advantages of television over public cinemas was that television could more easily be controlled by the government. This was especially true before Egyptian television could be seen in Saudi Arabia and before the proliferation of videocassette recorders in the kingdom. News and other information about the royal family and the country itself could be—and was; and is—placed first on the news: the royal family and ranking government dignitaries have thus always been ensured a great deal of exposure on the medium.

The government believes, moreover, that it must regulate cultural trends toward modernization, and controlled television is one means of expressing and affecting, often indirectly, the prevailing mood. The use of the medium itself of course reflects a government orientation on the question of how quickly society should move away from traditional Islamic practices. The alternations of cultural liberalism and conservatism in Saudi Arabian society since the introduction of television have been clearly seen on the TV screen: for example, women were only gradually allowed to be seen on television, and there remains a kind of double standard on the two national channels. Western women are considered to be properly attired when their arms are covered and their skirts are not above the knees. On the other hand, Arab women are usually more conservatively dressed, with at least a scarf covering the hair. With the conservative crackdowns that came following the 1979 Mecca Mosque incident, Saudi women were banned from television altogether for a short time.

Every program purchased for Saudi television, whether bought from an Arab or a Western country, is reviewed by a special department within the Ministry of Information that must screen both its visual and its audio portions. For example, some words on the English sound track of an American-made program may be deleted even in a subtitled program because the original sound track can be heard. The basic guidelines established in the late 1960s for censoring imported programs still apply and prohibit:

1. Scenes that arouse sexual excitement
2. Women who appear indecently dressed, in dance scenes, or in scenes that show overt acts of love
3. Women who appear in athletic games or sports
4. Alcoholic drinks or anything connected with drinking
5. Derogatory references to any of the "heavenly religions"
6. Treatment of other countries with praise, satire, or contempt
7. References to Zionism
8. Material meant to expose the monarchy
9. All immoral scenes
10. References to betting or gambling
11. Excessive violence

Of course, Saudi Arabia is not the only Arab country to screen programs before showing them on television, and these criteria are generally used by all the Gulf states; but they are more strictly applied in Saudi Arabia. An example of what can happen to a program when the guidelines are applied to an ordinary U.S. western was related to me by an employee of the film department:

> The town sheriff walks into a bar—censored because alcohol is forbidden. Sheriff talks to woman who is unveiled—censored because woman's face is shown. Sheriff pets dog as he walks down the street—censored because the dog is considered an unclean animal. Finally all scenes involving the sheriff are omitted because it is discovered that the sheriff's badge closely resembles the Star of David and is unacceptable because of the association with Israel.

Except for some residents of the Eastern Province (who can see ARAMCO programming) and those in the Jidda area with equipment for receiving Egyptian television, viewers have little opportunity to compare the Saudi television service with that of other Arab countries and are therefore unaware of the extent of program censorship. Because the kingdom is such an important market for Arab television programs, particularly dramatic programs dealing with Islamic history and culture, many programs are conceived and produced with the requirements of the Saudi system in mind.

The censorship requirements of Saudi Arabian television depend on the prevailing political, economic, and social climate in the kingdom. The 1992 *Index on Censorship* published a list of what is not permitted in Egyptian-made programs shown on Saudi television:

1. Unmarried couples acting the part of a married couple are not allowed to sit on the same bed together.
2. Unmarried actors are not allowed to be shown sitting in the same room together with the door closed.
3. A father cannot be shown kissing his daughter, nor a mother her son, unless the actors themselves are so related.
4. Certain names cannot be used as they are theologically suspect.
5. Women are not allowed to be shown singing or dancing.
6. No women may appear on Saudi television during the month of the religious observance of Ramadan.
7. It is forbidden for any character to use the expressions "by my life" or "by your life."
8. The name of the Lord may not be taken in vain.

9. No statues of figures may be shown that represent the human or animal form as these are graven images and hence forbidden by Islam.

Videocassettes and Censorship Once videocassette recorders became popular, the immediate problem was to provide enough programs on cassettes to meet the demand. At first, cassettes were openly imported into the kingdom. Before the arrival of high-speed duplicating equipment, a company would acquire the rights to programs and then have the duplicates shipped to Saudi Arabia. Customs inspectors and the Ministry of Information, which is responsible for censoring such material, were initially accommodating; they did not understand what the cassettes were and had no means of previewing the programming. When they awoke to the realities and required that all material be censored, importers simply circumvented the system by smuggling.

Several businesses in Saudi Arabia sell selected television programming taped in various U.S. and British cities; so little attention is paid to the editing of their tapes that in many instances identifications from stations in New Orleans and San Francisco may be seen and heard. Even the commercials are often left in the programs. And after the advent of copying machines, pirated U.S. and British first-run films were regularly shipped to Saudi Arabia for duplication and local sale or short-term rental. Eventually, the pirating importers almost wholly prevailed over those who were purchasing the rights to programming. Foreign business firms in the kingdom became their willing customers because their wares cost so much less than legal equivalents.

The videocassette business has, then, circumvented the government's policy of controlling the kind of visual material shown in the kingdom. One need no longer rely wholly on Saudi Arabian television for entertainment. Indeed, in some instances the censored Western programming shown on the national television channel is locally available in full on videocassettes.

The efficiency of the cassette pirates is evident from the speed with which the controversial British program of April 1980, *Death of a Princess*, reached the kingdom. Purporting to detail the death of a Saudi Arabian princess and her lover for adultery, the film was flown to the Eastern Province the morning after its showing on British TV; copies were duplicated and made available in Dammam for sale the same day. Though luggage is thoroughly searched by Saudi customs authorities, a compact VHS or Beta tape may be carried through customs in a coat pocket. So, doubtless, came the *Princess* to Arabia.

The videocassette business is still growing rapidly throughout the Middle East. Though Saudi Arabia is the liveliest market, because of its prevailing cultural conditions and the economic position of its citizens who want video programming, the kind of activity described above occurs in many other Gulf states.

THE AUDIENCE

Relatively little audience research has been done by commercial firms in Saudi Arabia. First, the government has been hesitant to allow foreign companies to come to the kingdom and ask questions that might, by local standards, be sensitive. Second, when permission has been granted for survey work, it has been given with the stipulation that women not be interviewed, even by trained female interviewers. Whatever reliable data are available, then, regarding radio and television audiences in Saudi Arabia apply only to the male half of the population.

Although in 1991 the British Broadcasting Corporation estimated there were 4.5 million radio receivers and 3 million television sets in Saudi Arabia, it is impossible to know the exact number of receivers there. Customs figures on the importation of sets are not helpful because many of the imported receivers are purchased by Arab expatriate workers, mostly Egyptians and Jordanians, and taken home to their families or sold to friends. Even a low-paid laborer from another Arab country can afford to buy an imported radio in Saudi Arabia; and the same statement may apply to television sets, as many workers come to the kingdom without their families, and several men, often renting a small apartment or room, pool their financial resources to purchase a stove, refrigerator, television set, and VCR.

In 1987 Morad Asi and I undertook a kingdomwide study of the international radio–listening habits of 2000 Saudi university students. Students were most likely to listen to Radio Monte Carlo Middle East and the BBC, preferring the BBC for news and public affairs programming, and RMCME primarily for entertainment as well as news. This finding is generally consistent with the results of studies done by the leading foreign international radio broadcasters. The BBC's long tradition of credible service to the Arab world as well as its signal strength advantage make it an important information source, particularly during times of crisis.

There was no more appropriate crisis during which to examine radio listening than during the time that Iraq occupied Kuwait. A U.S. Information Agency (USIA) study in Saudi Arabian urban areas between December 5 and December 25, 1990, highlights Gulf crisis radio-listening levels in the kingdom. All respondents in the USIA national Saudi survey used radio as a daily information source. To illustrate the impact of radio listening before and after the invasion, Saudi nationals were asked about regular listening before the August 2 invasion, during August and September, and finally in December. Results indicated that before the invasion, 1 percent listened regularly to the BBC; in August and September, 35 percent were regular listeners; in December, the percentage had increased to 40 percent. All radio services, but especially those from the West, had increased listenership.

TECHNOLOGY

Saudi Arabia has been strong on technology. With the help of the U.S. Army Corps of Engineers, it has succeeded in building some excellent production and distribution facilities. Along the way it has encountered some interesting technological dilemmas and situations.

The Color Choice Determining the color system for the national TV service to use was a complicated process, rife with politics. The feeling in Saudi Arabia and many other Gulf states was that the German PAL system ought to be the common Gulf states color standard. In 1971 the Ministry of Information hired a San Francisco broadcast engineering consulting firm to study the SECAM and PAL systems to determine which would be better for the kingdom: they too concluded that PAL should be the choice.

Despite this, the country decided on the SECAM system, invented and promoted by the French, who have been successful in some countries in tying SECAM standard acceptance to various economic, military, or cultural agreements. The SECAM decision was thus political rather than technical and was made by the Saudi Arabian cabinet, possibly at the request of King Faisal.

In any case, whatever lengths the French went to in order to secure acceptance of the SECAM color system in the kingdom, it was worth it to them: the majority of the color equipment bought by the Saudis since, whether for new stations or for upgrading older ones, has been purchased from French manufacturers.

Inconveniently for the Saudis of course, most of the other Gulf states use PAL. In order to compete in international television in the Gulf states region, Saudi Arabia had to convert its powerful twin RCA transmitters in Dammam to PAL so that those outside the kingdom could see the Saudi signal in color.

Technical Aspects of ARAMCO ARAMCO's early broadcasts were from its 525-line monochrome transmitter. Once the Saudi broadcast system started with 625 lines, local Saudi nationals received the ARAMCO programming by purchasing multistandard sets that were able to receive not only both the ARAMCO and the government stations but the services of other Gulf states as well. In November 1976 ARAMCO modified its transmitter to broadcast NTSC color. In March 1979 a new 625-line PAL color transmitter became operational, thus making ARAMCO TV's signal compatible with those of neighboring Gulf states.

When the ARAMCO station was broadcasting in both English and Arabic in its early days, all English programs were dubbed into Arabic. The Arabic sound was transmitted with the picture, and the English sound was provided by FM radio. ARAMCO's American employees, for whom the service was originally started, used a standard U.S. television set with an FM radio tuned to an ARAMCO FM radio frequency.

Satellites Saudi Arabia is an active participant in the Arabsat project headquartered in Riyadh, in which members of the Arab League participated in the launching of two satellites in order to improve all forms of communication, including the distribution of broadcast signals among Arab countries.

It also uses an Intelsat satellite to distribute its programming around Saudi Arabia. The country has a system of twenty ground stations throughout the kingdom that pick up the TV network signals from transponders leased on the Intelsat satellite. Radio also uses the Intelsat satellite for standby purposes for linking the Jidda and Riyadh stations, In December 1979, when the national telecommunications network malfunctioned, the satellite circuit was activated so that the distribution of radio signals would not be interrupted.

At one time Saudi Arabia had plans to design, build, and launch a satellite for its own exclusive use. The government apparently believed that having such a satellite would lessen its dependence on Intelsat for circuits, and the $500 million voted for the project by the Council of Ministers in December 1979 was thought to be a good investment of excess funds gained from oil exports. However, the Arabsat satellite project was more expensive than anticipated, and as the mid-1980s approached, it became clear that the kingdom would not have the funds for its own satellite because of declining oil prices.

At present, home satellite receiving dishes are not legal in Saudi Arabia, and there is no indication that there is widespread use of illegal dishes to view satellite-delivered programming.

EXTERNAL SERVICES

Saudi Arabia's external language services are beamed primarily to other Arab and non-Arab Islamic countries. The Indonesian- and Urdu (Pakistan)- language services were started as early as 1949 and were transmitted for only a short time each day. The original enthusiasm for this kind of broadcasting did not continue because of limited facilities and the higher priority given to the establishment of a domestic service in the 1950s and 1960s. Essentially a product of the 1970s, then, the language services feature religious subjects and some information about Saudi Arabia as an international economic entity.

European Service Saudi Arabia also has an external-type service intended for people who live within the country, namely, English-speaking and French-speaking foreigners residing there. In January 1965 the Ministry of Information began an English service in Jidda in the hope both of reaching the large foreign community there and of communicating Saudi news, views, and other information to diplomatic missions that might not (it thought) have personnel to translate the daily Saudi newspapers from the Arabic.

For the full two years of the service, the staff consisted of two full-time British ex–BBC announcers and one full-time American announcer (myself). Special programs were taped on a weekly basis by native English speakers who were employed part-time. The hours of service fluctuated, depending on availability of transmission time and programming personnel. During the first 5 years, there were two 1-hour transmissions, one in the early morning and one in the early afternoon; the evening program lasted for $3\frac{1}{2}$ hours. On Friday, the afternoon transmission was lengthened to include a program of popular Western music for people at the Red Sea beach, introduced with patter by a popular Saudi Arabian disc jockey. Between 1966 and 1968 the Jidda service was broadcast simultaneously from Riyadh, using the radio link supplied by the telephone authority; the link was of poor quality, a fact that discouraged listening in Riyadh, and the rebroadcast was discontinued when a separate Riyadh-based English service was started.

The Jidda French service, which began in 1965, has not received much attention because French is not an important language in Saudi Arabia. The kingdom has good relations with France, however, and appears interested in continuing the service for public relations purposes.

Although intended mainly for listeners within the kingdom, at specific times the English and French services are broadcast on shortwave for listeners in the rest of the Middle East and in Europe.

Services Coming into Saudi Arabia As already mentioned, Saudis listen to quite a few external services from other countries—Radio Monte Carlo Middle East, BBC World Service, Radio Cairo, Radio Kuwait, Voice of America.

In addition, as part of the infusion of military personnel into Saudi Arabia after the Iraqi invasion of Kuwait in August 1990, the British and U.S. military secured permission to operate FM radio stations to entertain and inform troops in central and eastern Saudi Arabia. Both the British and Americans have had a policy since World War II of providing troops with entertainment and news from "back home." For U.S. troops, the Armed Forces Radio and Television Service (AFRTS) operated several stations under the generic name Desert Shield Radio. Beginning in late October 1990 one station came on the air in Riyadh and several in the Eastern Province. I monitored several of these stations for a week in late December 1990 and early January 1991.

In Dhahran, for example, a station operated at 99.9 megahertz with the on-air call: "This is your oasis station, FM 99.9 on the Desert Shield Network." In Riyadh the FM station could be heard on 107 megahertz. Much of the programming came via satellite from the Los Angeles studios of AFRTS. Music-oriented, with public service announcements for military personnel in Saudi Arabia, Associated Press radio news, sports, and some local disc jockey–type programs, the stations seem to have been popular with some Saudis. Although no audience figures are available, from discussions with a number of Saudis and from listening to the Western music coming from car radios and shops, it seems that the popular music stereo service was a change from either the conservative-oriented government radio or the numerous medium-wave and shortwave radio services available from neighboring or Western states.

In the Eastern Province, the British operated an FM station at 103.5 megahertz. Known as British Forces Broadcasting Service (BFBS)—and similar to the service provided to British troops stationed in Germany—it was a satellite relay of BBC World Service news and information from BFBS London.

IMPORTANCE IN THE WORLD COMMUNITY

Because Saudi Arabia is the Arab world's largest oil producer, the country is very important to the international community. What is broadcast over radio and television is very significant, in part because it influences Saudis, but even more because it is very indicative of what the government thinks. What is said about other countries over Saudi media can indicate how the kingdom feels about its relationship with those countries.

MAJOR ISSUES

In the 1990s the kingdom faces the difficult problem of coping with an escalating demand for appropriate programming. But the future of radio and television broadcasting in Saudi Arabia depends on many factors, including the stability of the present government, the future level of oil incomes, and the kingdom's position internationally and within the Arab world.

The kingdom has completed installation of the most extensive system of radio and television transmitters in the Arab world; added studio space allows the production of as much locally produced radio and television programming as the government deems appropriate. The second television channel that started in August 1983 provides a choice of programming for viewers who do not have access to alternatives from other countries; that additional service, when the English channel is not operating, could also be an opportunity for the Ministries of Information and Education to cooperate on educational and/or instructional broadcasting, particularly instructional programming designed to help alleviate the kingdom's lack of qualified native teachers.

But the country's development has been so rapid since 1965 that the government has still not been able to install within the Ministry of Information a cadre of skilled administrators able to establish, and then effect, a consistent broadcasting policy. Most particularly, the government has not agreed on the manner in which it will present itself to its own citizens, to the Arab world, or to the rest of the world. The government's practice (as it was during the 1979 Mecca Mosque incident) has customarily been to react to events, usually after a period of silence during which rumors abound. The information apparatus of the kingdom must then act to attenuate the rumors and minimize the incident or situation that started them. This procedure may be culturally Arab in nature, but the government appears to be interested in making changes in it, especially in light of its position in the international political and economic community.

The Council of Ministers has created a commission to study and deal with information problems. Known as the Higher Media Council, the organization is headed by the minister of the interior, rather than the minister of information, in part because of the widespread belief that it was the information ministry that was the gatekeeper causing past information flow problems. The government realizes that it must be more aggressive and prompt in providing information about internal matters. An example of such a possible change in the previous policy is the manner in which the media handled the 1990 death of 1400 pilgrims in a Mecca tunnel accident. The information given to both the domestic and international press was straightforward.

The acquisition of the broadcasting infrastructure has been the easy, albeit expensive, part of the establishment of a comprehensive Saudi Arabian radio and television system. More difficult to achieve is a lasting practical consensus on the way in which that nation's broadcasting facilities are to be used. The videotape revolution in the kingdom presented television programmers with a considerable challenge. With VCRs in almost all Saudi television homes, the two national channels are no longer a monopoly. Owners of videotape recorders are, in fact, their own television station program directors.

However, the ultimate test of the system will take place when direct satellite broadcasts become more practical financially for viewers and when and if home satellite receivers are officially permitted by the Saudi government. Direct satellite television programming is already available in the Gulf region. Egyptian television offers programming via SpaceNet, although for the most part this is a satellite-to-television station service whereby the Egyptian Ministry of Information distributes material to stations in the Arab world. The satellite service with the most potential to have a major impact is in fact Saudi-backed. London-based Middle East Broadcasting Centre (MBC) is owned by a group of wealthy investors headed by Saudi King Fahd's brother-in-law. MBC started operating in September 1991; in late June 1992 it purchased the U.S. wire service United Press International that had been in financial trouble for a number of years. The kingdom is not only moving to take advantage of new communication technology but is also expanding its decade-long policy of starting Arabic-language media outlets in and outside the Arab world with the apparent goal of favorably influencing public opinion both inside and outside the kingdom.

When satellite services become possible, those in the affluent state will be able to do with television what they now do with shortwave and mediumwave radio broadcasts—tune to the outside world.

SELECTED BIBLIOGRAPHY

"Aramco TV on the Air," *Aramco World Magazine*, May 1963, pp. 3–7.

"Battling Radios Vie for Arabs' Ears," *Business Week*, 16 March 1957, p. 48.

Benoist-Mechin, J. *Arabian Destiny*, translated by D. Weaver. Fairlawn, NJ: Essential Books, 1958.

Boyd, D. A. "Saudi Arabian Television," *Journal of Broadcasting*, Vol. 15, No. 1, 1971, pp. 73–78.

Boyd, D. A., and M. Asi. "Transnational Radio Listening among Saudi Arabian University Students," *Journalism Quarterly*, Vol. 68, 1991, pp. 211–15.

Boyd, D. A., and A. M. Najai. "Adolescent Television Viewing in Saudi Arabia," *Journalism Quarterly*, Vol. 61, No. 2, 1984, pp. 295–301, 351.

Crane, R. J. *The Politics of International Standards: France and the Color TV War*. Norwood, NJ: Ablex Publishing Corporation, 1979.

Eggerman, M. "BBC Doubles Daily Audience in Saudi Arabia," *ARC News*, December 1992, p. 1.

"Faisal the Fabian," *The Economist*, 13 November 1965, p. 742.

Goldman, K. "Saudi-Controlled Firm Wins Bidding for Troubled United Press International," *Wall Street Journal*, 24 June 1992, p. B-10.

Holden, D. *Farewell to Arabia*. London: Faber and Faber, 1966.

Ibrahim, Y. M. "Saudis Pursue Media Acquisitions, Gaining Influence in the Arab World," *New York Times*, 29 June 1992, p. D-8.

"The Murder of King Faisal," *Newsweek*, 7 April 1975, pp. 21–23.

"Saudi Arabia: No Singing or Dancing," *Index on Censorship*, February 1992, p. 22.

United States Department of State. *Saudi Arabia, Establishment of Television System in Saudi Arabia*. Washington, DC: U.S. Government Printing Office, 1964.

United States Information Agency. *Media Habits of Priority Groups in Saudi Arabia. Part II: Appendix*. Washington, DC: USIA Office of Research, 30 August 1973.

United States Information Agency. *Foreign Radio Listening Rates High in Four Arab Gulf Nations: VOA Increases Audience during Crisis*. Washington, DC: USIA Office of Research, 14 February 1991.

PART SIX

AFRICA

Overview of Africa

In most of Africa, radio was established between 1920 and the mid-1950s by the European powers who governed these nations as their colonies. In all but a few African nations, television systems were initiated after independence, during the 1960s and 1970s, usually with outside direction from the former colonial powers. Colonial rule is now a 30-year-old memory for most African nations, but a new cultural imperialism, spawned largely by the media, is in force. Other factors affecting most African radio and television operations are the low standard of living and the political fragility of most of the nations.

Nigeria has been selected to represent African electronic media. It was once a British colony and, with its more than 150 ethnic groups, can be considered in many ways a microcosm of Africa. Within its borders are vast cities, both ancient and modern, together with wide stretches of rural lands where peasant farmers eke out an existence using the traditional farming methods of their ancestors. Nigeria is blessed with substantial oil resources and for this reason is wealthier than most other African countries. But Nigeria's wealth has not made the nation immune to the political turmoil that has rocked the continent over the years.

Before the discussion of the electronic media in Nigeria, however, the major factors affecting African media (especially sub-Saharan African media) will be considered. This will be followed by a discussion of media in South Africa, a country that for many reasons does not share the characteristics of its northern neighbors.

COLONIALISM

France and Great Britain were the dominant imperialistic powers in Africa, though Belgium, Spain, Portugal, Italy, and Germany were also involved in the colonial scramble for Africa in the late nineteenth and early twentieth centuries. French colonial policy, known as "assimilationist," involved radio broadcasting systems that were intended to tie the peoples of the colonies firmly to the motherland. Thus most of the programs were broadcast from colonial capital cities, in French, by Frenchmen.

The British had a different approach. They were somewhat more inclined to encourage their subjects to use radio to preserve the local culture. This attitude grew out of the British colonial policy of "indirect rule," which favored the retention of local rulers provided their loyalty to the British crown was secure. The British trained indigenous broadcasters, and by the 1940s stations in several of the British-run colonies offered vernacular-language services in the major languages of the people, along with English.

Despite differences in colonial approaches to broadcasting, the programming in both French- and British-controlled colonies aimed to foster the interests of the colonial metropoles, each albeit influenced by its own national model. The French model was one considerably more controlled and more closely allied to French government policies. The model Great Britain supplied to her colonies was that of a public corporation along the lines of the British Broadcasting Corporation (BBC)—one designed to guarantee some measure of autonomy from government.

After independence, it was the British-inspired systems in Africa that were altered the most. By the 1970s most broadcasting systems in the former British colonies had lost in name or in fact their semiautonomous status, as insecure governments reined in the media firmly under their control. The French systems, which had enjoyed little autonomy, continued their central position in government, albeit under new masters.

NEW CULTURAL IMPERIALISM

Today the influence of the West is still very strong in Africa. It is the area of the world where external services from other countries are most used. The majority of persons having shortwave radios in Africa listen to the BBC World Service, Voice of America, Radio France Internationale, and other services, in large measure because they feel these services provide more accurate and more complete news services than their own national services do.

While most African countries produce most of their radio programming and much of their television news, few have the resources to develop significant quantities of entertainment programming for TV. Only Zimbabwe, Nigeria, and South Africa produce dramatic fare. Most countries rely heavily on imported entertainment programming, especially that which they can obtain cheaply or free. Many European national cultural organizations offer either free of charge, or highly subsidized, cultural and educational television programming, as do the United States and Canada. Such free programming is supplemented with inexpensive reruns of commercially syndicated material chiefly from the United States. U.S. evangelical broadcasters have been known to pay African broadcasting organizations for the use of airtime on their national systems. For example, in the mid-1980s, Jimmy Swaggert visited Swaziland and attracted a following. When he returned to the United States, he bought airtime in Swaziland for his evangelical television programs. Eventually he stopped paying for the airings when he learned that not many people in Swaziland had TV sets.

Satellite services are also starting to penetrate Africa. Rich, influential Africans have satellite reception dishes on which they receive CNN, Sky services from Britain, and other channels. Nigeria is currently in the throes of a debate over whether, and to what extent, CNN-supplied news and other feeds should be rebroadcast over national broadcasting services.

Beginning in the late 1970s, videocassettes, most of which were illegal, took Africa's urban areas by storm. The central African nation of Cameroon, for example, which had delayed the establishment of television, finally set up a television broadcasting system in 1986, in part as an effort to lure wealthy viewers away from home viewing of imported programming on videocassette recorders.

Another new phenomenon that will no doubt increase Western influence on African airwaves is privatization. At present, most of the African electronic media systems are still run by governments, but many countries are at least studying the question of adding privately owned stations to the mix. Some entrenched political interests understandably prefer the status quo in broadcasting, for government ownership of media clearly makes it easier to control broadcast output. Nevertheless, "privatization fever" has reached Africa, and in the wake of political shifts occurring on the continent, many would-be broadcasters have seized the opportunity, found foreign investment money, and begun broadcasting even before legal and regulatory mechanisms governing these new structures are firmly in place.

The West African nation of Burkina Faso, for example, began flirting with non-government-owned radio as early as 1987. When the Burkinabe government changed after a coup that year, private broadcasting temporarily ceased. But the initial service had given the people of Burkina Faso a taste for private radio. A number of entrepreneurs found foreign partners and began tentative efforts at radio broadcasting. Though most of these early pioneers floundered for a combination of technical, financial, and legal reasons, the new government was gradually forced to accept a new era in privatization. In 1990 the government of Burkina Faso authorized the creation of Horizon FM. This popular youth-oriented radio service broadcasts from the nation's capital and a few provincial capitals. Private Canadian interests backing the enterprise hope to expand into private television as well.

Meanwhile, the Burkinabe government has opened up the FM band to other broadcasters.

The services of Radio France Internationale are now available in Burkina Faso, and the BBC has requested FM transmission rights in the country. While not all African governments are moving as quickly to open up their airwaves, the events taking place in Burkina Faso in the 1990s are rather typical of shifts occurring throughout much of the continent.

POOR ECONOMIC CONDITIONS

The media of Africa, as a whole, are the least developed of any continent. This is due largely to the fact that, overall, the average standard of living in much of Africa is very low. For example, Ethiopia's per capita annual income is only $130, Zaire's is $183, Uganda's is $290, and Angola's is $620. In contrast, the per capita annual income in the United States is $21,800. With food and shelter being the most pressing needs, there is not much money left for radio and television. The only access that some people have to television is community viewing areas set up in towns or villages. The advertising market is in its infancy. Most of the people are information-poor as well as economically poor.

Despite this poverty, most nations developed television as a matter of pride and as a signal that their nation had entered into the modern world. For example, in 1963, Haile Selassie of Ethiopia persuaded the newly formed Organization of African Unity to hold its first meeting in his capital, Addis Ababa. A European manufacturer supplied closed-circuit TV for the historic event. Visitors and the press could watch proceedings in an adjoining hall. Selassie was impressed and ordered installation of a regular television station in Addis Ababa to open in time for the imperial birthday—always a big event during his reign. Thomson Television, a British firm, built the station in 6 months—just in time for the emperor's birthday. Thus it was in 1964 that Ethiopia, a country with one of the world's lowest per capita incomes, had a national television service but hardly any sets on which to view its programs. At present, Ethiopia has only one set for every 500 people.

Many African countries received their radio and TV equipment from grants-in-aid from industrialized countries. While equipment grants may have been well meaning, they have often come with strings attached, strings that typically mandate that supplies be purchased from the donor country. This dependence on outside sources of funding has often resulted in the proliferation of incompatible technologies. The problem is compounded by the fact that electronic equipment suffers badly in the humid tropical climates characteristic of many of the equatorial African countries and in the dusty atmospheres of the desert-fringe countries. Furthermore, the national electricity supplies in many African countries are often erratic, making climate control within the stations and transmitting sites a daunting prospect.

Training media personnel and retaining those who have been trained is also a problem. Donor countries and multilateral agencies of the United Nations, such as the International Telecommunications Union (ITU), are active in training technical personnel. In fact, the ITU sends more technical experts to Africa than any other part of the world. However, once trained, technicians sometimes leave the services of government broadcasting organizations for work in the private multinational sector where their skills are at a premium.

The inadequacy of technical infrastructures and the shortage of technical personnel in government broadcasting operations means that broadcasting equipment in Africa often works badly or not at all. The Swaziland Broadcasting System, which once had eight radio studios equipped with gear given to it by Britain and the United States, gradually cannibalized these radio studios in order to keep the main control room operational and eventually was left with only one workable studio.

The combination of low literacy rates and

widespread poverty in the region has meant that radio has become the medium of the masses. Other factors supporting this trend relate to the availability of TV signals and electricity supplies. For example, TV signals reach only 30 percent of the landmass below the Sahara Desert, and many rural villages do not have the electricity needed to operate television sets even if a signal were available. In contrast, radio signals are more widespread throughout the continent, covering a median of 60 percent of the landmass, and radio receivers can operate effectively with batteries. In addition, radios are much less expensive than TV sets, which often cost a year's wages for a peasant or semiskilled worker. TV then, to the extent that it exists in Africa, is primarily an urban medium. Newspapers seldom circulate in rural areas because distribution is patchy, costs are high, and reading ability is generally low among rural peoples.

Most governments have made some effort, at least intermittently, to produce radio programs for developmental purposes. Such programs attempt to provide important health, educational, and agricultural messages for their listeners. Usually a great deal of thought and creativity are put into the programs so that instruction and entertainment are combined. In Gambia musicians on the radio sing songs telling people to wash their hands with soap and water. A lesson for rural mothers on how to prepare a diarrhea remedy for children masquerades as a soap opera. Such programs are appreciated by rural populations whose traditions have long incorporated song, dance, and stories into lessons about daily living.

Overall, however, African production values are not high, especially on television. The news is merely presented—often by one person who sits facing the camera reading bulletins. On-the-scene reports are included only when the remote equipment is working and tend to concentrate on the speeches and public pronouncements of government officials, particularly the head of the state.

Radio is often used as a personal message board. People report their major life events—births, marriages, deaths of next of kin—to radio stations that then broadcast the information nationwide. Most radio stations charge people to air this material, and these announcements become an additional source of funds for cash-strapped radio services. Although it is the governments that operate most radio stations, they typically do not spend a great deal of money on broadcast operations. The result is that well over half of the continent's government radio stations air commercials. This airtime is largely filled by local subsidiaries of multinational corporations interested in selling locally made soap, pharmaceuticals, manufactured food products, and soft drinks.

What little money there is in Africa is sometimes subject to corruption. One result of this is that there are pockets of wealth within the continent, and people who have money are likely to spend it on media. The rich were the first to obtain TV sets and then the first to own VCRs. Now they are first in line for satellite dishes.

POLITICAL TURMOIL

Political insecurity, that is, the precarious position of many African governments that rarely enjoy a true democratic mandate from their people, has also contributed to the inadequacies of the media. Governments have been reluctant to allow broadcasting that might lead to the empowerment of their people. Political leaders have opted instead for broadcasting services targeted to the few who are in power rather than to the many who are powerless.

When governments are fighting for their lives, they do not discipline themselves to develop goals and objectives for broadcasting. Leaders have made many promises regarding radio and television that they have not kept. Radio and television facilities are generally run with insufficient coordination of national goals and a lack of long-range planning. Some of these problems derive from Africa's dependence on the whims of outside sources of financing; some come from internal deficiencies in broadcast management and policy planning.

At present, many of the top people in government-run radio and TV had little broadcast training or experience in the day-to-day activities of the profession. Senior managers are very often political appointees. Such persons have approached broadcasting very cautiously, eschewing the watchdog role of the media expected in more libertarian systems. Self-censorship of news personnel is the order of the day. It has not been uncommon for African media personnel to broadcast one evening in the pay of one government and wake up the next morning with that government overthrown and a new one in place. The broadcaster who has been cautious with news bulletins is able to remain employed.

Two relatively new African political phenomena affect media. One is the birth of multiparty democracy, and the other is decentralization. Many countries in Africa, even those that claimed to be democracies, were ruled by one party. The authoritarian regimes were propped up by Western capitalistic countries or Eastern bloc Communist countries. Because the East and West were competitive, they courted African leaders, mainly with financial support, to win their loyalty—or at least to ensure they didn't go firmly into the other camp. The disintegration of Communist countries had profound effects within Africa. Eastern Europe and the Soviet Union have ceased to be players in African affairs, and the Western powers have no need to give the support they once did in order to gain African leaders' lip-service praise of capitalism.

As a result, African leaders of the 1970s and 1980s have found their support, and their power, undermined. In the wake of these power vacuums, African middle classes and even some rural peasant groups have called for a restructuring of government and for the holding of multiparty elections. Since 1990 a number of countries have held elections, and many have voted out the old rulers. Many others are in the throes of election planning, activities that often include the resurrection of long-dormant local citizens' groups and inactive political parties.

Government broadcast organizations are being enjoined to participate evenhandedly in these processes, airing campaign speeches, political platforms, and political ads of all contenders. This is often easier said than done, for the ingrained habits of the one-party state rule often weigh heavily on broadcast organizations and personnel whose stakes in the outcomes of these elections are often considerable. Nevertheless, many African broadcast organizations are experimenting with schemes designed to make them less partisan, at least during the election periods. Their efforts at democratizing broadcasting are refreshing if not always tidy. But it must be recalled that the transition to democracy anywhere in the world has seldom been smooth and has rarely occurred without upheaval.

A corollary to multiparty democracy is broadcast decentralization. Until the 1990s most broadcasting systems were controlled by central governments. Repeater stations were generally used to distribute program material to the different regions of each nation. But democratic restructuring in politics has given fresh impetus for media more responsive to local needs. One reason many people feel decentralization is needed is that Africa has so many different languages. For instance, in Ghana no indigenous language is shared by as many as half the people. The Ghanaian radio service uses six different local vernaculars in addition to English. Each language runs for about 15 minutes before another takes over.

The political situations in Africa are far from stable. Their future will determine what happens to the media. By the same token, what happens to the media will undoubtedly help shape the future of African political life.

SOUTH AFRICA

Media in South Africa developed quite differently than in other countries on the continent, mainly because of the policy of apartheid. South Africa's colonial history was filled with wars between the Boers (Dutch, German, and French Huguenot settlers who had arrived in the seventeenth century) and the British who had arrived about 150 to 200 years later. The British won decisively in 1902, but many Boers continued to live in the country as they had long since severed their ties with their European fatherlands.

The Union of South Africa was formed in 1910 as a dominion of the British Empire. The Union attempted to form a single united white people, one which would incorporate the best of British and Afrikaner (Boer) cultures. The Union also sealed the secondary-class fate of other members of the population—the black Africans, the coloreds (people of mixed racial origin), and people from India who had been brought to South Africa as indentured servants by the British.

In 1934 South Africa became a fully independent state, and the Boers living there took political control. In 1948 they developed the program of apartheid designed to keep racial groups separate and to maintain power in the hands of the white minority.

The radio that started in the 1920s was based on the British system. When the Boers took over the country politically, they continued the radio service set up by the British as the South African Broadcasting Corporation (SABC), but it was an AM service, and there weren't enough AM (medium-wave) frequencies available to develop a truly national service. During the 1960s the Boers developed an extensive FM radio system that was national but segregated. The whites had services in the Afrikaner language and in English, and the other racial groups had services that included seven native African languages. Although the nonwhites understood and used English, they were supposed to listen only to the stations in African languages; the Boers were trying to use language as a method of ensuring apartheid.

The Boers set up, within South Africa, homelands for the native Africans (similar to U.S. Indian reservations). They hoped this would be where all these people would live, and they arranged for four of these homelands to have their own FM radio stations, which again were to program in local languages.

Television was even more affected by apartheid. It did not start until 1976, making South Africa the last industrialized country to establish TV. It started out as a color system, however; South Africa never had black-and-white TV. Its introduction was late because the ruling Boers saw many evils in it. They did not want to disturb the "South African way of life." They feared programming from outside the country because of the effect it might have on the white culture and because they thought it would create dissatisfaction among the nonwhites who might see how people of their races lived in other countries.

When it was finally introduced, television, too, was supposedly segregated. TV1 was started first and was in Afrikaans and English, alternating nights in each language. It was rather staid programming, but it had high production values and much of it was produced within the country. The news, for example, sported state-of-the-art sets and special effects, but the news items themselves were primarily government pronouncements. Rarely was any racial turbulence mentioned—unless it was in some far-off country such as New Caledonia or Ireland.

What was imported was "safe" programming that was highly censored. It was not censored so much for sex and violence as for themes that might undermine the concept known as "Christian nationalism." This concept was basically apartheid—it stated that each ethnic group had a right to its own cultural identity and separate nationhood. Therefore, violent programs such as *The A-Team* and sex-oriented series such as

Dallas had full runs on TV1, but *Roots*, the saga of Alex Haley's search for his African ancestors, did not air.

Often the South Africans had program-importing difficulty because of sanctions against the government of the country. For many years the British refused to sell any programs to South Africa. Many U.S. production companies did likewise, while some individual casts, such as that of *Cagney & Lacey*, donated the royalties from South African airings to the black African National Congress.

In 1982 SABC established two networks for nonwhites. These were less extensive services than TV1 and were programmed in native African languages.

In addition, the homelands had their own TV stations just as they had their own FM stations. One of these, the station from the homeland Bophuthatswana (nicknamed Bop TV), caused quite a stir in the mid-1980s. Although it was overseen and largely financed by the South African white government, it had a certain amount of independence because it was operated from a homeland. It exercised this independence by programming in English, by airing *Roots*, and by including in newscasts members of the black underground who could not be quoted in South Africa under penalty of law, as well as blacks who had been involved in racial unrest.

In addition to serving its homeland, Bop TV was beamed by directional antenna into the black ghetto of Soweto in south Johannesburg but not into the nearby white area. However, the antenna system was not perfect, and the signal spilled over into some of Johannesburg. White viewers watched and liked it; it was more lively than TV1. Home sellers in Johannesburg advertised that they could receive Bop TV, and it was generally agreed that good Bop TV reception could add $1000 in value to a house.

The government went to great lengths to try to keep whites from watching the station, saying it was a breach of apartheid, but whites continued to watch. The government did have the signal narrowed down, but Bop TV continued to be popular with whites—and with people in other African countries. In 1988 Bop TV leased a transponder on an Intelsat satellite to distribute its programming to parts of its homeland that could not receive the signal. However, what this really did was to expand Bop TV's reach to both black and white audiences in various parts of Africa, including Nigeria.

Now that South Africa has abandoned its apartheid policy, production companies and broadcasters in other countries are willing to sell the government programs. Plans are being made to desegregate the media so that services, including a new pay channel, M-Net, are for both blacks and whites. Bop TV, however, does not want to lose its identity. The media are now more open, and criticism of government is allowed, but a great deal still needs to be worked out regarding how radio and television will operate in a postapartheid era.

(*Editor's Note*: I wish to thank Dr. Louise Bourgault, professor of mass communication, Northern Michigan University, for providing much of the information and editorial assistance for this overview. It is difficult to find facts, figures, and other current information regarding African media, and so I appreciate her sharing with me some of the research she has gathered for her book *Mass Media in Sub-Saharan Africa*, published by Indiana University Press.)

CHAPTER 9

NIGERIA

Louise M. Bourgault

Louise Bourgault.

Louise M. Bourgault is a professor of mass communication in the Department of Communication and Performance Studies at Northern Michigan University in Marquette. She lived in Nigeria from 1980 to 1984 where she taught mass communication at Bayero University, Kano, and was a founding partner of Media Development Consultants, Ltd., of Kano. In 1992 she returned to Nigeria to deliver lectures for the U.S. Information Agency (USIA) and to conduct research on the broadcast media. Overall, she has worked with the broadcast media or related areas in fourteen African countries. In her most recent assignment in 1993, she served as an international election monitor in the Republic of the Congo. She has written a book, *Mass Media in Sub-Saharan Africa*, published by Indiana University Press.

STATISTICS

Geographic Area: 356,667 square miles
Capital: Abuja
Population: 88,500,000
Religions: Muslim, Christian
Languages: English, Hausa, Yoruba, Igbo
Type of Government: Military headed by a president
Gross Domestic Product: $28 billion
Literacy: 51 percent

GENERAL CHARACTERISTICS

Nigeria is Africa's giant, having more people than any country in Europe or Africa. One in five Africans is a Nigerian. The West African nation is about the size of California, Arizona, and New Mexico combined. Nigeria's landmass includes five major geographical zones: lowland coastal areas along the Gulf of Guinea; hills and plateaus to the north of the coast; the fertile Niger-Benue River valley; a broad plateau of 1200 meters high in the central northeast; and a higher mountainous zone along the eastern border with Cameroon.

Nigeria is the home of over 250 ethnic groups and nearly 400 mutually unintelligible languages. Of these, three major vernaculars dominate: Yoruba in the southwest, Igbo in the southeast, and Hausa in the north. English is the national language and is widely spoken throughout the country, particularly in the southern half. At the last officially recognized census, 47 percent of the population were Muslims, 35 percent were Christians, and 18 percent were followers of indigenous animistic religions.

Since obtaining its independence from Great Britain in 1960, Nigeria has enjoyed two periods of civilian rule, 1960–1966 and 1979–1983. These two eras represent Nigeria's First and Second Republics. In between, the country was been led by a series of military rulers. The current ruler, General Ibrahim Babangida, who came to power in 1985, has promised to cede power to an elected civilian government in the mid-1990s.

The Economy By African standards, even by world standards, Nigeria is a wealthy country. Oil was discovered in the Niger River delta in the 1950s. During the 1970s Nigeria experienced an unprecedented period of economic growth known as the "oil boom." Nigeria's income soared as the Organization of Petroleum Exporting Countries (OPEC) twice dramatically increased the price of oil. But overspending, rampant corruption, and poor management, combined with the collapse of OPEC control, left Nigeria with a massive national debt by the mid-1980s.

A series of budget-cutting exercises, Nigeria's own version of a structural adjustment program, led to massive reductions in the standard of living of the people. By 1989 the per capita gross national product (GNP) had fallen to $250 per annum from a high of $830 in the early 1980s. The present low per annum GNP figure is, however, deceptive, as the gap between rich and poor is extremely wide. One percent of the nation's population controls 75 percent of its wealth, and Nigeria is home to more millionaires than any other African country.

Today the nation's economy is still enormous. Nigeria is the world's ninth largest oil producer and has the world's fourth largest reserves of natural gas. And Nigeria is Africa's largest market for manufactured goods.

The Mass Media The mass media in Nigeria reflect the enormity and diversity of the country. Nigeria has over 80 magazines and newspapers and over 100 radio and television stations.

Electronic media outlets have proliferated with changing political structures and shifts in governments and the creation of new states. By any yardstick, the electronic media in Nigeria represent a huge, complex, frequently changing system.

Nigeria is said to possess a three-tiered structure of broadcasting. At the top level is a network service offered for all radio and television stations by the two federal broadcast authorities, the Federal Radio Corporation of Nigeria (FRCN) and the Nigerian Television Authority (NTA). The second tier consists of regional divisions of the federal broadcasting services. There are four zones for radio and six for television. The third tier incorporates radio and television stations operated by the individual states. This organization can be diagrammed as follows:

Federal Radio Corporation of Nigeria (FRNC)
|
Four radio regional zones
|
Individual state radio stations

Nigerian Television Authority
|
Six television regional zones
|
Individual state television stations

Plans are currently under way to create what some might call a fourth tier: privately owned stations. Much of the interest in private broadcasting has come in the wake of a boom in so-called new communication technologies. In 1992, even before private broadcasting guidelines had been officially considered, new retransmission services were available. Using multichannel multipoint distribution service (MMDS) technology, these systems were collecting satellite signals, mainly from Europe but also from India, Saudi Arabia, South Africa, and the United States, and rebroadcasting them to subscribers. In Nigeria, this service is referred to as "cable television," although it does not represent a wired service. It is, as all MMDS systems are, a through-the-air transmission service that broadcasts signals at higher frequencies than conventional broadcasting. MMDS signals cannot be received on a regular TV set unless a converter is attached to the set to change the high frequencies to lower ones that the TV set can recognize.

Meanwhile, satellite-to-home reception has mushroomed in Nigeria since the late 1980s, with satellite reception dishes dotting the landscape in wealthy neighborhoods of Nigeria's major cities. In 1992 there were an estimated 700 to 1000 privately owned satellite dishes in the city of Kano, Nigeria's second-largest city with an estimated population of over 1 million people. Lagos, the largest city, with its soaring population of over 8 million, supports easily ten times as many reception dishes. Satellite-to-home reception represents the latest media craze in Nigeria. Among those wealthy enough to own a satellite dish (the installation cost was estimated at $10,000 in 1992), it has certainly supplanted rented or purchased videocassette use.

Statistics are extremely difficult to obtain in Nigeria, and they are notoriously unreliable. Since independence, the extent to which Nigeria has become a "mediated society" is quite remarkable. In 1960, according to the Marcomer Research Firm, there were 143,000 radio receivers in Nigeria. In 1981 there were 12 million. A more recent estimate, from 1991, sets the Nigerian radio distribution figure at 10 million. This decline may be indicative of decreasing disposable income in Nigeria or it may simply reflect estimate discrepancies. UNESCO estimated in 1960 that there were 4 radio sets per 1000 persons in the population. By 1986 that figure had risen to 162 per 1000, just below Africa's average of 164 per 1000.

UNESCO places the number of television receivers in Nigeria at 5.6 per 1000 inhabitants. This figure falls considerably below the continent's average of 25 per 1000. It is worthwhile to note that UNESCO's figures are drawn from official Nigerian figures and are therefore based on numbers of television and radio sets legally imported or assembled in the country. The vast quantity of electronic goods smuggled into Nigeria to avoid costly customs charges are therefore underrepresented in the UNESCO statistics. Other enterprises tend to include illegal receivers in their estimates and thus are undoubtedly more accurate. In 1987 *Screen Digest* estimated that there were 2 million television sets in Nigeria, while the BBC set the figure at 6.5 million. Both of these were much higher than UNESCO's 550,000 figure for 1986. And in 1990 the *World Radio Television Handbook* listed 5.6 million as the number of television receivers in the country.

In the late 1970s the videocassette recorder boom began with the importation of ¾-inch U-matic machines for home use. Wealthy Nigerians purchased the first ones abroad, and soon local electronics merchants began making them available for sale. By 1980, ½-inch VCRs, in Beta and VHS formats, made their way onto the Nigerian market. Many of the VCRs were also purchased outside the country. Though the early 1980s to mid-1980s marked the end of the oil boom, heavy borrowing and an overvalued currency still provided a sense of enormous prosperity. Nigerians traveled widely to Europe and the United States on business or for studies, and many Muslims traveled to Saudi Arabia for the Hajj pilgrimage.

Video viewing was extensive in the early 1980s. Electronics shops did a brisk business selling and renting bootlegged movies and television series from the United States, Europe, India, and the Far East (karate films from Hong Kong). Feature-length movies rented at the time for about $4.00 a tape. By 1992 the video rental business was floundering. Proprietors of electronics shops were charging as little as about $0.25 for a tape rental and still failing to attract customers, so severe has been the economic downturn.

The use of video rental tapes was so significant in the early 1980s that many of the cinemas catering to the civil servant and/or big business class closed for lack of patronage. And today, with ever-increasing competition from satellite viewing, they are not likely to reopen.

Screen Digest provides some tracking of the growth of videocassette recorders in Nigeria. In 1982 there were an estimated 15,000 VCRs in the country. Two years later (when the country was still basking in the afterglow of the oil boom), there were five times as many. By 1989,

A customer selecting videos in an electronics shop in Kano, Nigeria.

the figure reported was 277,000. Again, the BBC's estimates of VCR ownership are much higher at 1.5 million.

The mass media are extremely important and firmly established in Nigeria. Radio has long been a medium for the masses, and television is becoming increasingly so. Those at the top of the social pyramid have already shifted their attention to VCRs, and now, increasingly, they tend to watch satellite broadcasting.

The entire surface area of the country has been within the reach of at least one Nigerian radio signal since the mid-1970s. And television signals (at least one) have covered at least 70 percent of the land surface since the early 1980s to mid-1980s. Because not all rural areas have been electrified, radio, which can easily be battery-operated, is still the dominant medium in rural areas. In villages served by electricity, there are likely to be several television sets and, as in the rest of Africa, group viewing is common in both rural and urban areas. Except among the "bourgeois classes," African life is still very communal and people tend to share resources.

At varying times, both the states and the federal government have established community TV reception sites. And urban shopkeepers often keep a TV set flickering in their shops. It lures a steady stream of customers to their businesses, provides companionship, and promotes discussion among passersby.

While Nigerian radio serves rural and urban dwellers alike, Nigeria's television services tend to serve somewhat more urban audiences. This includes a vast swath of middle-income individuals: lower-level civil servants, shop owners, craftspeople, artisans, small-scale entrepreneurs, and students. This is a group likely to own TV receivers but have no access to VCRs or satellite broadcasts. Meanwhile, unskilled workers and the unemployed must make do with someone else's set.

THE DEVELOPMENT OF ELECTRONIC MEDIA IN NIGERIA

The development of Nigerian electronic media was influenced by the country's British colonial heritage, but modern-day media are most heavily influenced by the political structure that the country adopted after independence.

The Colonial Period The first radio service was a wired repeater signal provided by the British Empire Service. It was established in Lagos in 1932. The Empire Service was designed to serve the British colonies and dominions of Canada, Australia, India, and Anglophone Africa. By 1950 the service had been extended to many other areas of Nigeria.

The radio service was initially run by the Post and Telegraph Office, but in 1951 the colonial government inaugurated the Nigerian Broadcasting Service (NBS) as a separate entity. That year it also set up studios in Kaduna, Lagos, and Enugu. Local production had begun in 1949, and by 1953 the NBS was offering 58 hours a week of local production transmitted in English and some local languages. By the mid-1950s, a wireless service had been established. Indigenization of the staff came early in the NBS. By 1952 there were 186 Nigerians employed by the NBS as opposed to 22 British.

In 1957 the Nigerian Broadcasting Service was transformed to the Nigerian Broadcasting Corporation (NBC). Modeled after the BBC, the NBC was structured to provide a good deal of public service coupled with considerable autonomy from the government.

Shops such as this one may bring out TV sets in the evenings so that passersby can join in the viewing.

The three major geographic regions of Nigeria had enjoyed considerable political autonomy since 1945. In 1959 the western region of Nigeria established the first television station on the African continent. And in May 1960 it opened a radio station of its own at Ibadan. The eastern region quickly followed suit and began radio and television broadcasting from Enugu in October 1960. The northern region began broadcasting from Kaduna in 1962. Thus, even before independence, Nigeria had developed a two-tiered system of broadcasting—national and regional.

Radio after Independence At independence in 1960, the federal minister of information declared his intention to maintain the independence of radio. But in 1961 the statutes on the NBC were amended so as to provide greater federal government control and to decrease the power of regional governments over existing NBC stations.

Military rule came to Nigeria in 1966, and soon afterward the three regions were divided into twelve states. Efforts were made to provide radio stations for all twelve states. Meanwhile, the federal military government went about the task of centralizing Nigerian broadcasting. It took over the ownership and management of all existing state stations. In 1976 seven new states were added, and a further expansion of radio was planned. By 1978 each of the nineteen states had a radio station. It was then that a major reorganization took place, one which was mandated by the Federal Radio Corporation Decree of 1978.

The stations were handed back to the states and were to broadcast on medium wave only, with limited power. The Federal Military Government created the Federal Radio Corporation of Nigeria which was divided into four large zones. FRCN's headquarters was to be in Lagos, and together with the three former regional capitals, it would broadcast on shortwave. This restructuring of broadcasting was designed to balance the competing needs of the regions with those of the federal government.

In 1979 a civilian government, headed by President Shehu Shagari, ushered in Nigeria's Second Republic. State radio had considerable power at this time, particularly in states where parties rivaling Shagari's party (the National party of Nigeria, NPN) were dominant. The NPN was eager to provide a counterforce to its political rivals in broadcasting.

An amendment to the FRCN decree was created to allow the creation of more FRCN stations in each of the nineteen states, and construction of several new medium-wave radio stations soon proceeded. All of this resulted in considerable confusion and a good deal of overlapping of services within the industry.

The competition among stations allied with one of five political parties became even more keen before the 1983 elections. Some stations began violating the spirit of the FRCN decree by increasing their transmission power. Other states established multiple stations, particularly FM stations, all in an effort to provide political propaganda in connection with the upcoming elections.

Though Shagari was returned to power by the electorate in the summer of 1983, the military again took over by the end of that year. The new military government undertook an overhaul of the system, combining some state and federal stations and once again returning radio broadcasting to the states, by then under military governors. The FRCN was once again restricted to the shortwave operation beamed from major cities.

Television Television broadcasting originally started on a regional basis with WNTV in Ibadan in 1959. Within a few years, both the northern and the eastern regions had established their own television services. And a limited television service was established in Lagos in 1962.

In the late 1960s the three regions were divided into twelve states, and the process of creating new state television stations began. A 1977 military decree created the Nigerian Television Authority (NTA) as the only body authorized to broadcast television signals. By then there were ten TV stations in Nigeria, and all of them were taken over by the federal government.

By the early 1980s, state governors, particularly those not aligned with the civilian party in power, began to clamor for permission to operate their own television services. Thus began a spiral of television station development similar to that for radio. Twelve new state stations were created during this period. All of them were assigned the use of ultrahigh-frequency (UHF) signals rather than the very-high-frequency (VHF) signals reserved for the NTA.

When the military returned to power at the end of 1983, the new state television stations were allowed to remain in the control of state governors, subject to certain administrative directives of the NTA. In 1988 there were thirty-four television stations in Nigeria, twenty-two owned and operated by the NTA and twelve controlled by individual states.

Recent Trends Throughout the history of Nigeria, there has been constant pressure to increase the number of states, as state status is a means by which groups can more easily access federal resources and revenues. By 1990 there were thirty states in Nigeria, plus the new federal territory at Abuja. By this time there were over 100 radio and television stations.

A new Nigerian constitution, prepared in 1989 in anticipation of the return to civilian rule, allows for the eventual establishment of private broadcasting. It is likely that future private broadcasting will provide some mixture of local origination plus redistribution of international satellite feeds. As previously noted, several feisty entrepreneurs are already providing (through MMDS) the redistribution of a panoply of signals—CNN, British Sky Movies, MTV Europe, Eurosport, and South Africa's Bop TV.

Quite apart from the very latest developments brought about through foreign satellite services, the Nigerian television system is a vast one. Because of the presence of the state and the federal system, viewers in Nigeria, particularly in the south, enjoy multiple television services. Some areas can pick up four different channels. Parts of the north are less well served.

ORGANIZATION AND FINANCING

The Federal Radio Corporation of Nigeria is administered by the government through a board of directors. The board, representing a variety of interests including youth, women's affairs, and culture, advises the FRCN director general on matters of policy. Both the board and the director general are appointed by the minister of information in consultation with the head of state.

A parallel structure exists for the regulation and administration of television within the Nigerian Television Authority.

These structures guarantee considerable control from the top. Nigeria is nevertheless one of the few countries in Africa to regularly appoint chief executives (director generals) with backgrounds in broadcasting rather than in politics or nonbroadcast branches of the civil service. The appointment of "media men" to top positions helps to ensure a degree of professionalism in broadcasting and somewhat curbs the tendency, seen in so many other African states, to use the media chiefly to create and foster a personality cult around the president.

State broadcasting organizations are run by general managers and advised by boards similar to those operating at the federal level. The state minister of information appoints general managers for radio and television and selects members for their respective boards. All this is done with the advice and consent of the state governor. State stations vary in their degree of autonomy, depending upon personalities and politics within the state government.

Budgets Budget figures for broadcasting are difficult to obtain. In 1982 the budget for the NTA was about 100 million naira (about $130 million) or about one-third of the budget of the BBC. Ninety-eight percent of the NTA's budget went for salaries and administration.

Since the mid-1980s life has been economically difficult for Nigeria. President Ibrahim Babangida has introduced a series of contractionary fiscal policies designed to help ease the serious debt burden inherited from the economic mismanagement of the Second Republic. Belt tightening has meant an overall decrease in social spending. Between 1981 and 1988, for example, 3.7 percent of the government's budget was destined for the federal communications sector. But in effect only 2.6 percent was allocated to the federal media. These percentages, moreover, included subsidies to the government-owned newspaper, *New Nigerian,* and the partially government-owned *Daily Times.* By the late 1980s the NTA's budget had been halved, and NTA personnel had been reduced from 9719 in the early 1980s to 5200 by 1985.

Commercialization and Government Subsidies In 1988 the federal government established, through Military Decree No. 25, a Technical Committee on Privatization and Commercialization (TCPC). The body was charged with devising plans for partial commercialization of the FRCN, the NTA, and the News Agency of Nigeria (NAN). In July 1992 the TCPC signed an agreement with the NTA, the FRCN, and the NAN to allow government media organizations to operate as purely commercial enterprises.

Even before the agreement, the NTA had been putting increasing pressure on stations to generate their own funds. Each station is given a target based on the potential to generate advertising revenues within its coverage area. The 1992 advertising budget of the NTA regional service located in Kano (NTA Kano), for example, was set at about 40 percent of the station's entire budget.

The NTA is attempting to decrease station dependency on the networks for revenue and is working toward a system where the NTA will provide funds only for capital investment. As one general manager explained, "When you make your [advertising] target, they increase it the next year." At present, it seems that only NTA-Lagos 2 is consistently able to meet all of its running costs through self-generated funds. It is having difficulty maintaining service levels with the reduced number of personnel.

Perhaps more onerous is the practice of commercializing television news that was introduced by the Babangida administration in 1989. Anyone outside the government who wants an event covered must pay for the coverage. NTA network news coverage now costs about $4000 for an event in Lagos, and about $5000 in some of the other areas. Presidential hopefuls running in Nigeria's primaries in the summer of 1992 were not spared these charges. The NTA demanded about $500 each for recording and broadcasting interviews with the candidates.

The FRCN, which began accepting commercial announcements in 1987, has operated a similar scheme for news coverage since that year. Only renowned individuals outside government circles can expect to be exempt from news coverage fees.

State television and radio stations, long dependent on advertising, receive proportionally smaller subventions from their state governments. The proportion they receive depends on the degree of importance their states attach to broadcasting combined with the potential of the marketplace in their coverage area to generate revenues. Today most state stations are trying to make their product more attractive to advertisers so as to compensate for shortfalls in state budget allocations.

Advertising has been well established in Nigeria since 1928. Major advertising agencies such as Lintas Worldwide, McCann-Erikson, and Ogilvy-Benson all operate agencies in Nigeria. The greatest proportion of advertising is sponsored by multinational corporations, some having local subsidiaries in Nigeria. Soap, toothpaste, laundry detergents, beverages, packaged food items, and nonprescription drugs are the products most commonly advertised on Nigerian radio and television. In television many programs are sponsored by one company. In 1980 Nigeria's United Bank of Africa sponsored the well-known series *Cock Crow at Dawn*. The series was designed to encourage urban dwellers to return to rural areas and take up modern agricultural methods.

Other Forms of Income Other than advertising, news coverage fees, and government subventions, Nigerian media occasionally avail themselves of a few other opportunities for generating funds.

Most notably, they receive payment for participating in coproductions. The NTA has worked on coproductions with the BBC and the U.S. Corporation for Public Broadcasting (CPB). Basil Davidson's series, *Africa*, contained segments shot in cooperation with the NTA, as did the BBC documentary *The Squandering of the Riches*. And segments from CPB's major series on Africa, *The Africans*, narrated by Kenyan scholar Ali Mazrui, also benefited from NTA assistance.

There are no license fees collected for broadcasting in Nigeria. The size of the country and the complexity of the broadcasting system would undoubtedly render such an undertaking unwieldy, while opening up a plethora of opportunities for graft.

PROGRAMMING

NTA stations begin transmission at 3:00 P.M. on weekdays and earlier on weekends. Sign-off is usually around midnight. The timetables of the state television stations are more varied, depending on their budgets and the importance attached to the service by state authorities.

The NTA mandates that no more than 30 percent of the programs on all Nigerian television can be imports. The stations tend to fall just shy of this goal. Sixty-nine percent of Nigerian television is locally produced; 31 percent originates outside the country.

Programming in Nigeria falls into three broad categories: news and current affairs, public enlightenment, and entertainment. A typical breakdown for an NTA station reveals that 48 percent of the programming is entertainment, 36 percent is news and current affairs, and 16 percent is public enlightenment.

With the advent of the UHF state stations created during the Second Republic, there was a marked overall increase in entertainment on Nigerian television. This occurred initially because the new state stations found themselves with a great deal of airtime and satisfied this demand with inexpensive imported fare.

News and Current Affairs News and current affairs encompasses national and international news, sports, and documentaries. National news is broadcast on the NTA three times in the evening, at 7:00 P.M. (for 30 minutes), at 9:00 P.M. (for 45 minutes), and at 11:00 P.M. (for 15 minutes). State stations are required to hook up for the 9:00 P.M. broadcast. These stations provide their own locally produced news, as do the NTA affiliates. These are typically 30-minute English broadcasts repeated in different time slots in one or more local languages.

The news sometimes includes CNN feeds. The NTA has a contract with CNN which permits the network to redistribute within its broadcasts a specified proportion of material supplied by the Atlanta service. Many state-owned stations also have similar contracts. CNN has become a ubiquitous feature at many of the state stations. In the summer of 1992, CNN international feeds blared out through the day and evening in the producers' room at the state-operated station in Kano (CTV Kano), providing a backdrop for the work of the producers. Some newspeople indicated the feeds were giving them new ideas on news production. For example, inspired by CNN business news, the news department of at least one state station is now trying to provide more news on the private sector. Impressed by live, on-the-scene reporting, this station sometimes asks reporters who have covered a particular item to appear on a newscast to discuss the event with the anchorperson. Some Nigerian producers and camerapeople scrutinize the technical aspects of particular CNN scenes and try to incorporate them into their own work.

The use of CNN feeds has raised concern in some circles, and cries of "cultural imperialism" have been heard in conjunction with its use. To quell the criticism, the NTA has mandated that "local contexting" of CNN stories be provided before the CNN feeds are used. More regulation of these services may be in the offing for the future.

National news from the NTA is delivered in flawless English. National news broadcasters vie with one another to be the most flamboyant in dress. Lavish headties crown the heads of female newscasters; newsmen dress in national costumes or Western business suits.

News and information has long tended to be top-heavy, concentrating excessively on the speeches, pronouncements, discussions, debates, and activities of state and federal officials. NTA policies charging for coverage of those outside the government have exacerbated these propensities.

Network sports is offered to affiliates every Sunday evening from 10:00 P.M. to 11:00 P.M. The network also devotes Saturday afternoons to sports. Soccer and wrestling are the most popular sports shown.

Public Enlightenment The public enlightenment program category includes women's, children's, religious, public service, and educational programs. Some of these programs are considered to be "development programs" because their aim is to help the country develop improved social conditions such as better sanitation and more efficient agricultural practices. For example, a number of years ago, the NTA created a program in cooperation with the Family Planning Council of Nigeria. A drama entitled *My Brother's Children* was designed to illustrate the problems of large families and to discourage polygamy. Research conducted on the program's effects show that the intended message overall was not grasped. The program was nevertheless very popular and was appreciated by audiences for its dramatic qualities.

A more recent public enlightenment program aimed at women was the *Better Life* series produced by state broadcasters. The overall project was chaired by President Babangida's wife and involved the wives of governors. It provided home study courses on child rearing, cooking, and crafts. One program showed women how to prepare guinea corn the "old-fashioned way" using traditional clay pots.

Children's broadcasts include games, storytelling, dramatized fables, traditional children's dances, craft shows, health and safety exposés, and magazine programs especially designed to attract young audiences. Imported cartoons are shown, as is *Sesame Street*. The NTA holds an annual festival of children's programs. Such festivals are designed to promote program and idea exchange among TV stations throughout the country.

Public enlightenment programs also include the category of religious programs. Religious programs tend to feature coverage of religious services, particularly on or around religious feasts. In Muslim areas, religious broadcasts often begin with readings from the Holy Koran. CTV Kano, located in the Muslim heart of Nigeria, begins each daily transmission with a prayer.

Public enlightenment programs include agricultural programs. For example, Oyo state TV carries agricultural programs which are viewed by farmers at community viewing centers. It also carries an original program on health called *Ilera*. A traditional healer, a herbalist, and a modern doctor hold weekly on-air discussions regarding the treatment of common ailments.

They compare and contrast approaches to the cure of headaches, burns, and diarrhea.

CTV Kano uses public enlightenment program slots to alert viewers to possible dangers or scams facing them in their environment. In 1992 thieves posing as representatives of the Nigeria Electrical Power Administration (NEPA) were marauding Kano's neighborhoods, levying a variety of fees and collecting unpaid charges from customers. CTV Kano alerted viewers to these practices through the use of dramatized sketches and announcements urging caution in the face of urban tricksters.

Educational broadcasting intended for schools has not fared very well in Nigeria. Nigeria's first TV service, WNTV in Ibadan, introduced educational television in the very early days of its service, but its efforts were short-lived. The United States Agency for International Development (USAID) launched an educational project, but conflicts soon developed between U.S. project personnel and the British television staffers who operated WNTV along commercial lines, not to mention British teachers who still occupied teaching positions in some Nigerian schools. In 1978, 16 percent of the TV broadcasts were educational, but educational television has suffered from a lack of coordination between television staffs and the various ministries of education.

Entertainment Entertainment categories include imported programs of all types and locally produced variety programs and dramas. Imports in Nigeria come largely from the United States, which supplies, on average, 54 percent of foreign programming in the country. British shows represent 27 percent of the fare. Nigerian TV has aired at one time or another most of the major United States TV series: *Dallas, Roots, Charlie's Angels,* and *Twin Peaks.* Black American sitcoms have been especially favored—*The Jeffersons, Sanford and Son,* and *Different Strokes.* Also popular was the comedy variety program *The Flip Wilson Show.* British series have included *The Saint, The Avengers, Mind Your Language, Are You Being Served?,* and numerous detective series.

Nigeria is Africa's biggest importer of television fare, but it is also Africa's biggest producer of TV programs. Figures for 1991 showed that Nigerian television produced 906 hours per week. This accounts for nearly one-half of all local television production on the continent.

One form of local production is the variety program which may include traditional and modern musical groups, storytellers, and traditional and modern dance skits. There are also game or quiz programs. Some of Nigeria's well-known musicians made their debuts on popular music TV programs.

Other than Zimbabwe and South Africa, Nigeria is the only sub-Saharan country to devote a large share of its resources to the production of local drama. Some of these are melodramatic soap operas and some are serious dramas, but most of the local productions are comedies heavily laden with visual humor and wordplay.

The NTA produced *Village Headmaster,* which was designed to promote education. The program began in the 1970s and was still going strong in the late 1980s. Other popular programs produced in Nigeria include the comedy *Alawada,* produced in Yoruba, *Case File,* a police drama produced in Kaduna, the drama *Kuliya,* produced by CTV Kano, and *Jos Play of the Week,* from NTA Jos.

CTV Kano, which airs only 10 percent imported fare, had five weekly drama programs in production in the summer of 1992. Of these, three were comedies depicting rural life in Nigeria's north. The other two were melodramatic soap opera–style productions. NTA Kano also had five drama series in production in 1992. The city of Kano enjoys the talents of numerous drama groups and individual actors who appear in these programs.

The NTA sponsors an annual television drama competition which all of Nigeria's TV

A scene from the drama *Kuliya* produced by CTV Kano.

stations are free to enter. This incentive helps keep producers and actors enthusiastic in these times of budgetary austerity.

Locally made programs produced on state stations are for the most part in local languages, as the state stations have a special mandate to serve their local constituencies. Such local programming tends to be done in one of the "big three" Nigerian languages: Hausa, Yoruba, or Igbo. Alternately, stations in the southern part of the country may also use English in entertainment productions. In keeping with the "federal character" of the network, the NTA network service produces programs only in English, though local NTA affiliates, like the state stations, often also produce programs in Nigerian languages.

By and large, dramas tend to depict the difficulties of modern urban life: troublesome landlords, dishonest tradespeople, corrupt civil servants, intransigent bureaucrats, love-marriages, divorce, and polygamy. One important aspect of these local productions, says one Nigerian author, is their classless quality. Typically, they poke fun at Nigeria's "big men," permitting Nigerians to laugh at the rich and powerful while secretly identifying with them. Nigerian audiences enjoy the local feel of these programs and delight in the typical Nigerian types presented. These are characters who speak the Nigerian way, that is, in a delightfully dramatic mixture of pure bombast colored with fractured British expressions and Nigerian phrases, all seasoned with indigenous language terms. These plays seem to provide a genuinely unifying popular cultural force for Nigerians.

Nigerian local productions are not without their critics, however. Nigerian newspaper columnists regularly denounce the poor lighting, bad recording, poor acting, and poor technical coordination which mar many of these productions. Others have complained that the dramas contain too much slapstick humor, too much shouting, and too many visual gags.

Radio Programming Medium-wave radio stations in Nigeria practice what is known as "conventional broadcasting." That is, they feature news and information, public enlightenment, and entertainment. News is supplied in English through the News Agency of Nigeria, rewritten, and sometimes translated according to the needs of a given station and its audience. President Babangida has suppressed the reception of all other wire services, mandating that all news must pass through the filter of the NAN. In earlier times, when international wire services were not available (often because of lack of funds), newsrooms would monitor international shortwave radio and incorporate this information into their news bulletins. Since the military took over in 1983, all radio stations hook up to the national service several times a day for national news bulletins.

As noted in the case of television, public enlightenment includes development programs. State radio in Kaduna produced a program targeted at rural development entitled *Don Manua*. The program, broadcast in Hausa, featured a series of sketches about a rural village. It was designed to encourage mechanized farming and the use of higher-yield seeds. Radio Enugu produced a weekly program, *Ekene Umunwany (Thank You to Women)*, in 1981. The broadcast discussed marriage, family planning, and questions of interest to the audience submitted by listeners.

One type of broadcast which is popular throughout Africa is the private message board. These programs are used by listeners to carry announcements to family members scattered throughout the listening area. News about important family events—births, deaths, naming ceremonies, marriages—are circulated through this form of broadcasting. Message board programs may also be used to send missives of love and greetings. People in countries poorly served by telephones very much appreciate this particular type of broadcasting service.

Educational radio has not been particularly successful on Nigerian radio. In 1964, during the First Republic, some "schools broadcasting" was undertaken. The Federal Ministry of Education cooperated with regional ministries in the three major regions. Other efforts in schools broadcasting were undertaken in cooperation with the USAID between 1963 and 1968. As is the case with television, there has been an absence of clear strategy as regards radio programming.

Nigeria's FM radio stations, whose installations began during the Second Republic, tend to provide a heavy diet of entertainment, mainly music. A content analysis performed in 1983 on one such station showed that 69.5 percent of the music played was of non-African origin; 26 percent was Nigerian; and the remaining 4.5 percent was from other African countries. An earlier study conducted before the proliferation of FM stations found that 54 percent of the music played on Nigerian radio was of Nigerian origin and 46 percent was foreign. These figures seem to suggest that the proliferation of FM stations has resulted in the airing of more Western music, a trend which has also been found in Ghana. Surprisingly, U.S. country and western music is extremely popular in Nigeria. And American country singer Don Williams is a major favorite within the genre.

The FRCN broadcasts from 4:30 A.M. to midnight and transmits in twelve Nigerian languages. This linguistic mix ensures that 85 percent of the population will be reached in a language it can understand.

LAWS AND REGULATIONS

The Federal Ministry of Communications issues all licenses for broadcast stations in the country. The Ministry of Information supervises the two broadcast authorities governing broadcasting, the FRCN and the NTA. As indicated above, the directors general and both boards are appointed by the minister of information with the approval and consent of the head of state.

Broadcasting Guidelines Broadcasting in Nigeria is provided with a set of general guidelines which allow a certain degree of flexibility in their application. The guidelines are the following:

1. Providing an efficient broadcasting service to audiences based on national and local objectives, and to external audiences according to Nigeria's foreign policy
2. Providing full quality coverage and promoting the growth of culture
3. Promoting the development of Nigerian society and fostering national unity by representing views from all parts of the country
4. Delivery of information promptly to the people
5. Providing a forum for free and responsible discussion of issues so as to foster two-way communication between the authorities and the people
6. Providing special broadcasting in education or other areas as requested by national policy
7. Fostering orderly technical development of broadcasting so as to better serve the nation and providing staff training and staff exchanges with other nations
8. Encouraging research on the effects of mass media on Nigerian society
9. Fostering pride in being Nigerian

During civilian periods in Nigerian history, legislation of radio broadcasting has come through parliamentary procedure. During military regimes, it has come through decrees of the Armed Forces Ruling Council.

Government policy stipulates that the aim of television is to promote the political, economic, cultural, social, and technological uplift of the Nigerian people. There is considerable latitude in how these guidelines are interpreted, particularly at the state level.

In both radio and television, the major differences in policy are over the question of emphasis. Federal stations are expected to express the national character in programming and in hiring practices. State stations are destined to appeal to a more limited local audience. In practice this tends to mean that at the state level there will be a preference for hiring "native sons," if for no other reason than a requirement for proficiency in certain local languages.

Broadcast Codes Television and radio at all levels are expected to adhere to a broadcast code. The code stresses impartiality, objectivity, and balance in programming. It also stresses the importance of moral and social values together with high professional standards. The depiction of violence and cruelty is to be avoided on television, though some stations clearly violate this mandate by showing karate films. Other than this example, there is little violence on Nigerian television. Detective programs containing killing scenes tend to be shown in the late-evening hours. Stations broadcasting in the Islamic north tend to be very cautious with sexual content. So as not to cause offense, they show only women who are modestly dressed. Though kissing couples may occasionally be shown, steamy love scenes are always cut.

An advertising code proscribes the use of immoral, misleading, and superstitious advertisements. It is designed especially to protect children and the less educated from unfair influence by advertisers. An advertising council was set up in 1976 to develop code guidelines and monitor advertising practice.

Sedition and Defamation and Freedom of the Press The first law of sedition was enacted in Nigeria in 1909 by British colonial rulers and was intended to counteract the nascent preindependence movement. The Nigerian sedition law is still very much on the books and forbids the publication of any utterance or the broadcast or depiction of any act which has "seditious intention." Seditious intention is seen to include hatred or contempt for the government or government officials, laws, or the constitution. Seditious intention has also been interpreted at one time or another so as to protect foreign governments allied with Nigeria.

The law of defamation forbids the publishing

or broadcasting of any information likely to injure people in their trade or profession by damaging their reputation. This law, which was put in place by the Newspapers Act of 1964, made it a punishable offense to knowingly publish a rumor whose veracity is in question.

In 1984 the Mohammadu Buhari (military) regime issued Decree No. 4, also known as the Public Officials Protection against False Accusation Decree. The decree made illegal the publication or transmission without justification of any false statement or any rumor designed to subject public officers to ridicule or disrepute and clearly strengthened the existing sedition and libel laws. This law also empowered the government to prohibit the circulation of newspapers and revoke the license of any station or newspaper deemed detrimental to the interest of the whole or any part of the country.

On August 27, 1985, the ruling military council retired Buhari and replaced him with General Ibrahim Babangida. In his first broadcast to the nation, Babangida promised to restore basic human freedoms and to repeal the hated Decree No. 4. Babangida released journalists detained under the decree, claiming the media would now be allowed "to disseminate information . . . without undue hindrance."

Yet Babangida did not act entirely as he had promised. Parts of the constitution suspended since 1984 remained so. These included sections guaranteeing press freedom and legislative oversight power to the judiciary. And a State Security (Detention of Persons) Decree remained in place. This decree allowed the government to intern "persons having committed acts prejudicial to state security or economic prosperity."

Babangida enacted a new press law that became known as the "*Newswatch* decree of 1987." The ruling allowed the military junta to close the office of *Newswatch* magazine and to prohibit its publication for 6 months. *Newswatch* had published so-called classified information on the government's deliberations about the return to civilian rule (then scheduled for 1992).

The Buhari military regime arrested a large number of journalists, but under Babangida arrests have been less frequent. Nevertheless, harassment of journalists has continued. In 1986 Dele Giwa, the editor of *Newswatch*, was killed by a letter bomb. The perpetrators of the crime have never been identified, but there is widespread belief among journalists and among the public that the Babangida regime was behind the killing.

Babangida also uses another less coercive measure to keep journalists in line. They are picked up by security forces and invited to security offices for "chats" about their reporting, and the chats may include a few days of detention.

In 1988 the Babangida regime issued a decree that established a largely government-appointed council to police the registration of journalists. The council requires practicing journalists to hold a degree or a diploma from an approved school of journalism or to have 5 years of work experience before 1988. Apparently the decree has proved unenforceable because journalists and their organizations have refused to cooperate with it.

The lessons of the Dele Giwa letter bomb and other harassments have not been lost on the broadcast media. Because the broadcast media are government-owned, media personnel have routinely engaged in self-censorship, leaving the work of daring, courageous journalism to the private print media. About half of the newspapers and magazines published in the country are privately owned.

Still, within the African context, Nigerian media have been considered quite free. Media personnel, for example, are comfortable discussing the pros and cons of their organizations with outsiders. These professionals exhibit none of the paranoia and furtiveness displayed by their counterparts in some other parts of the continent.

Nigeria's media have a reputation for being

among the freest in Africa. This freedom has come no doubt from the plurality of ownership, especially under civilian regimes during which journalists have enjoyed a right to trial by independent judiciaries. As Graham Mytton noted in 1983 in *Mass Communication in Africa*, "What one newspaper will not print another paper may be very happy to publish; what one radio station may silence may well be carried by another."

Over the years, a number of journalism scholars, L. John Martin, Raymond Gastil, and Ralph Lowenstein, among them, have monitored the level of freedom of the media in various countries. Using a range of quantitative measures, they have rated Nigeria's media high on freedom of expression. But successive military regimes have put a damper on the formerly outspoken Nigerian media, and the country's once preeminent position in this domain in Africa has slipped. In the 1990s a number of countries in Africa have held multiparty elections and have loosened the reins on their press.

THE AUDIENCE

Audience research in Nigeria, as in much of Africa, tends to be piecemeal and haphazard. One general manager of NTA Ibadan admitted to Canadian scholar Iain McLellan that he had little idea whether his programs were pleasing or even reaching his audience. Audience research data tend to come from outside sources: BBC or USIA surveys or estimates, or marketing research conducted by multinational firms concerned with penetrating Nigeria's vast market for consumer goods.

Audience Research Some stations do conduct surveys in an effort to generate numbers useful to advertisers. Oyo State Television Service, which obtains 40 percent of its revenues from advertising, collects data for advertisers through its advertising traffic office. The comptroller of programmes at the station admits that the research information is rarely passed on to producers. Like programmers throughout the country, Oyo's comptroller relies on letters from viewers for feedback. She blames frequent staff changes, budget cuts, and confusion about the political direction of the station for its inattention to surveys.

There is a factiousness and a general lack of discipline which characterizes much of Nigerian life, and broadcasting is certainly not immune from it. The nonuse of sometimes available data is symptomatic of a larger lack of coordination and sense of purpose which is often characteristic of the media. McLellan quotes one general manager within the NTA system who admits that the objectives of Nigerian television have never been clearly articulated: "There has been no planned strategy and programming has been uncoordinated with any other developmental efforts. The various officials have to decide what they want to do with television, identify the problems and allow us to go ahead and deal with them," he noted.

Of the few studies that have been undertaken, one published in a 1981 NTA handbook showed that 50 percent of the television audience was middle class, 40 percent was lower class, and 10 percent represented the elite. With increasing use of VCRs and satellites, since that time, local television viewing is undoubtedly down among the elite.

In 1980 a nationwide study of radio usage showed that 90 percent of the population had heard radio at one time or another. In rural areas, this figure stood at 86 percent, and in urban areas at 93 percent.

Scholarly Research Media research of a more scholarly nature is produced by Nigerian academics who teach media-related subjects in departments of mass communication and/or journalism or in related areas within Nigeria's vast university and polytechnic system. At least sixteen institutions of higher learning offer advanced training in media subjects.

Research on mass media is published in the *UNILAG Media Review*, a joint publication of the Departments of Mass Communication at the University of Lagos and the University of Maiduguri and the Department of Communication and Language Arts at the University of Ibadan. Research, mainly on the Anglophone African countries, is regularly published in the *Africa Media Review* produced by the African Council of Communications Education based in Nairobi, Kenya.

Much of the research published in these documents treats issues related to media policy and press freedom. There is a dearth of studies on media content, functions, and effects.

A range of problems plagues would-be media researchers in Nigeria. These include insufficient databases, undersupplied libraries, poor transportation, and limited or nonexistent budgets, as well as alien research paradigms and models derived from Western training and overall Western hegemony in the field.

TECHNOLOGY

Nigeria has a complex broadcasting system and a dizzying array of stations. By the end of the 1980s, it had twenty-two VHF television stations and twelve UHF stations, all using the PAL standard. It also had sixty-five radio stations, more than a dozen of which were FM.

Nigeria's technical facilities have grown in response to no clear-cut telecommunications policy. In 1973, after Nigeria's oil revenue export value had shot up sevenfold, President Yakubu Gowon told the world that Nigeria's problem was no longer money but how to spend it. World businesspeople and bankers rushed to Nigeria to help Nigerians spend their oil wealth.

Most of the early broadcasting equipment in place during the 1960s had been supplied by British firms, particularly British Cable and Wireless for radio, and EMI for television. During the 1970s and 1980s, radio and television stations proliferated. International businesspeople ferried around the country trying to pick up installation contracts: General Electric (USA), Harris (USA), RCA (USA), Philips (the Netherlands), Nippon Electric (Japan), and Thomson CSF (France) were among them. By 1978 Japan had become Nigeria's most important supplier of television equipment. Sony provided much of the material for upgrading the NTA stations during the oil boom. It also got many of the contracts for the new state TV stations constructed during the Second Republic.

During the mid-1970s construction of the Domsat, the Domestic Satellite Communication System, designed to handle sound and television broadcasting for the country, was begun. Now, nineteen ground stations, along with coaxial cable and microwave, link all major urban areas. The Domsat installations were built un-der so-called turnkey arrangements, whereby equipment and maintenance technology would be transferred to Nigeria after installation by whichever multinational provided the loan. Swiss, Japanese, West German, Belgian, and U.S. funding was made available, and consequently a variety of systems and equipment was provided.

Today, problems of compatibility, maintenance, and lack of spare parts have plagued the Domsat, and portions of it are frequently inoperative. The same is true for the rest of the radio and television infrastructure. Some of this reflects a larger pattern of lack of discipline that characterizes the entire operation of Nigerian broadcasting.

Budget shortfalls and massive external debt incurred since the mid-1980s ($27.6 billion at the end of 1992) have precluded Nigeria from repairing or replacing much of the equipment purchased during the boom years.

EXTERNAL SERVICES

Nigeria's external service, Voice of Nigeria (VON), was inaugurated in 1962. At first it broadcast only in English and French for 2 hours per day. By 1963 it had increased its transmission to 6 hours daily and had added broadcasts in Arabic and Swahili.

When the FRCN was established by military decree in 1978, it took over Voice of Nigeria. The service currently broadcasts 67 hours per week in English, French, German, Arabic, and Hausa. VON beams to Europe, North America, the Middle East, and West Africa. The broadcasts are also heard and appreciated within the country. External services are seen as a way to reach Nigerians living outside their country. They are also a means through which the Nigerian government can diffuse its point of view to the world, particularly neighboring countries. The service carries mainly news and current affairs but also sometimes features documentaries, cultural programs, development broadcasts, and Nigerian music.

External broadcasts from other countries are also widely appreciated in Nigeria. A 1984 survey showed that the British Broadcasting Corporation (BBC) enjoyed the largest share (20.6 percent) of the international shortwave audience, and Voice of America came in second with 11.4 percent. The BBC broadcasts in Nigeria in Hausa and English. Research on international shortwave listenership in Africa has shown that the predominant audience for shortwave is adult males with at least a secondary school education. International shortwave radio has always functioned to provide African listeners with alternatives to locally available newscasts. Today, there is some evidence that listenership at the highest economic levels of society may be decreasing as a result of competition from satellite TV news services.

IMPORTANCE IN THE WORLD COMMUNITY

Nigeria has been called at varying times, "Africa's largest democracy," the "most African country," and "Africa's big black hope." Its size and wealth make it a key player in African and world affairs. Admired and despised by its continental neighbors, often for the same reasons, Nigeria cannot be ignored.

Nigeria is one of forty-four members of the Union of National Radios and Televisions of Africa (URTNA). The organization is based in Nairobi and is charged with the task of facilitating program exchanges between member states. However, because of financial, technical, and political difficulties, the organization does little more than maintain a catalog of programs available for exchange.

The NTA is a regular contributor to the CNN *World Report*. It has also made tentative steps at program distribution, and some of the more successful series have been made available through specialized distributors catering to academic audiences.

Nigeria has long been recognized for its preeminence in the arts: literature, music, theater, sculpture, and bronze casting, just to name a few. It has the artistic and dramatic talent to build a formidable television export industry. Coordinated efforts in the production of television drama combined with improved attention to technical details and production quality could make these products salable to African television services throughout the continent. A growing number of African countries now have private television and would especially welcome the opportunity to distribute programming from neighboring African countries.

Marketing opportunities for Nigerian fare are available through the huge South African market, which is just beginning to open and which offers the promise of satellite distribution. Canal Horizon, which provides subscriber-supported services in Senegal and Gabon, might also be interested in dubbed high-quality Nigerian programming. And the U.S. Black Entertainment Network may provide yet another market for Nigerian programs. Such participatory ventures could in the long run generate needed funds for Nigeria's coffers.

MAJOR ISSUES

The electronic media industry is about to be faced with a major change—the introduction of private stations. In September 1992 Babangida authorized the creation of private radio and television stations and announced that a national audiovisual board would be set up to examine applications and monitor the media. Two likely applicants for broadcast licenses are Kano businessman Bashir Tofa, present presidential hopeful of the New Republican Convention, and M. K. O. Abiola, the Social Democratic party's current presidential candidate.

At present, the regulation of these private services is being considered. It is unclear to what extent private broadcasters will be required to provide public service. There is a danger that private electronic media will serve the needs of the wealthy, possibly providing a large dose of imported entertainment fare, creaming advertising revenues away from government broadcasting, and further impoverishing the existing stations. These are the stations that serve viewers unable to afford alternatives: VCRs and satellite reception dishes.

Two other Nigerian issues related to the media are paramount and cry out for resolution. The first is the issue of democracy. Nigeria's military rulers, having once willingly ceded power, are precariously poised to do so again. However, Nigeria's progress toward democracy has been delayed by a series of maneuvers on the part of General Babangida and the ruling junta. The nation was to return to civilian rule in 1992, but the date was pushed back. In the fall of 1992, after presidential primaries were held, Babangida nullified the results because of widespread vote buying. The only two allowed political parties, the Social Democratic party and the New Republican Convention, were asked to agree on new candidates. Babangida then postponed the election scheduled for December 1992 until June 1993.

The nullification of the primary results was widely supported, and the subsequent election delay was largely understood. Still, some observers are disquieted by fears that the military may be trying to prolong its stay in office. The rest of Africa trembles as it looks to Nigeria because what happens in Nigeria's bid for civilian rule will surely have repercussions around the continent. If Nigeria's military rulers decide to hold fast to government power, Africa's military classes will be emboldened, and the pace of democratic reform elsewhere will slow and may even reverse itself. This could easily mean another decade of stultifying government control of free expression by the press and more abuse of human rights in Africa.

The other issue involves the domestic level, where a more concerted effort must be made to improve the social situation in rural areas and narrow the yawning chasm between the rich and the poor. The growing rift between the haves and have-nots in Nigeria does not bode well for a civil society. Babangida has attempted to redress some public dissatisfaction by funneling more government funds to rural areas and by strengthening the role of local governments. These are good first steps. More assistance to rural areas is needed if Nigeria is to decrease its dependence on foreign food imports. This will improve its balance-of-payments standing in the long run. Judiciously employed and systematically coordinated, Nigeria's vast reservoir of entertainment programming could be put to use in solving social problems. And some of these development-style programs could also be used by other African countries.

The task before Nigeria is a formidable one. Yet Nigeria has no choice but to get down to business and to solve its problems. As Blaine Harden of the *Washington Post* noted, "Nigeria is Black Africa's principal prospect for a future that is something other than despotic, desperate, and dependent. If the world's poorest continent is going anywhere, Nigeria is likely to get there first."

SELECTED BIBLIOGRAPHY

Domatob, Jerry, Abubakar Jika, and Ikechukwu Nwosu, eds. *Mass Media and African Society.* Nairobi: African Council on Communication Education, 1987.

Edeani, David O. "West African Mass Communication Research at Major Turning Point," *Gazette,* Vol. 41, No. 3, 1988, pp. 151–83.

Ibie, Nosa Owens, "The Commercialisation of the Mass Media in Nigeria: The Challenge of Social Responsibility," *Journal of Development Communication,* June 1993, pp. 60–68.

Kinner, Joseph. "Nigeria." In Phillip T. Rosen, ed. *International Handbook of Broadcasting Systems.* New York: Greenwood Press, 1988.

Maja-Pearce, Adewale. *Who's Afraid of Wole Soyinka?* London: Heinemann, 1991.

McLellan, Iain. *Television and Development: The African Experience.* Ottawa: International Development Research Center, 1986.

Mytton, Graham. *Mass Communication in Africa.* London: Edward Arnold, 1983.

Nwosu, Ikechukwu E. "Mass Media Discipline and Control in Contemporary Nigeria: A Contextual Critical Analysis," *Gazette,* Vol. 39, 1987, pp. 17–29.

Sonaike, S. Adefemi. "Telecommunications and Debt: The Nigerian Experience," *Media Development,* Vol. 34, No. 1, 1989, pp. 2–6.

Tudesq, André-Jean. *L'Afrique Noire et ses télévisions.* Paris: Anthropos, 1992.

Uche, Luke Uka, "The Politics of Nigeria's Radio Broadcast Industry: 1932–1983," *Gazette,* Vol. 35, No. 1, 1985, pp. 19–29.

Uche, Luke Uka, "Youth and Music Culture: A Nigerian Case Study," *Gazette,* Vol. 37, No. 1–2, 1986, pp. 63–78.

Ugboajah, Frank Ukwu, ed. *Mass Communication, Culture, and Society in West Africa.* Munich: Hans Zell, 1985.

PART SEVEN
ASIA

Overview of Asia

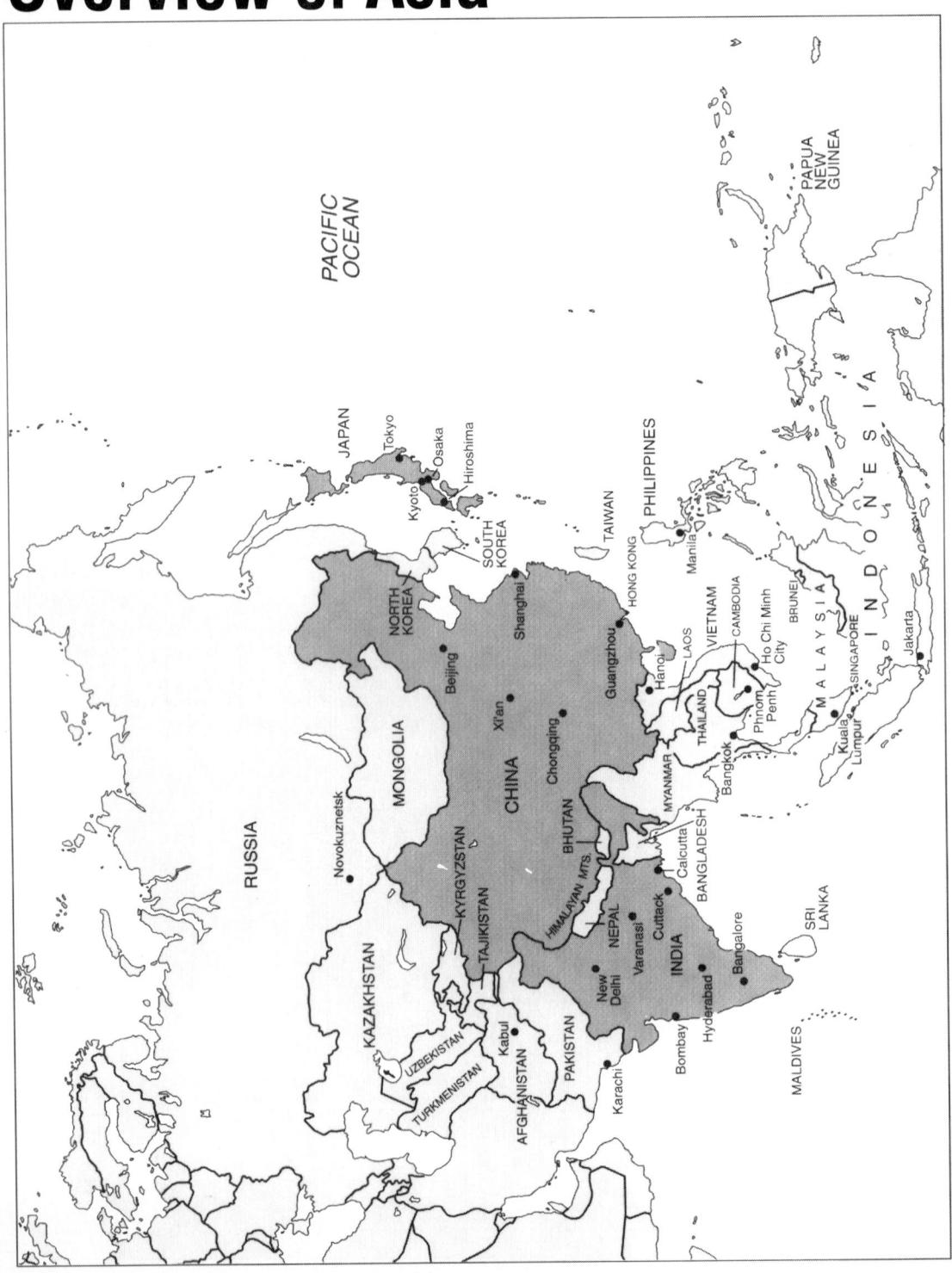

Asia represents both a unified and a diverse electronic media marketplace. It is considered *the* continent of the 1990s. Western Europe was the prime growth marketplace for programming and advertising during the 1980s because of the many private channels that were added during that decade. Now, the peoples of Asia, many of whom had had scant experience with electronic media before the 1990s, are embracing television with fervor. The media distribution form responsible for the surge is satellite. Because a satellite signal can reach many countries at once, Asia is now thought of as a unified marketplace.

And yet, Asia is a very diverse continent, harboring countries that are large and small, rich and poor, cold and warm, crowded and sparsely populated, democratic and Communist. Media systems have grown up in a variety of styles and exhibit their own national characteristics. The yin and yang of unity and diversity promise to be an outstanding feature of Asian media in the twenty-first century.

ASIA AS A UNIFIED WHOLE

One of the reasons Asia is considered *the* continent of the 1990s is that it is awakening economically. Although Japan has been an economic giant for many years, the rest of the Asian countries did not rank highly as either suppliers or buyers. Now areas that have been poverty-stricken for centuries are invigorating themselves. The gross domestic product growth rate for all of Asia is 8 percent per year. This means that at least some of the citizens are acquiring disposable incomes, and this of course makes advertising viable. The amount of money spent on advertising rose 15 percent between 1992 and 1993, with much of it going to the advertising means that have been successful in many countries—the electronic media. The increasingly affluent audience is starved for entertainment, and TV set penetration is growing faster in this part of the world than anywhere else. In fact, the sale of sets in China alone is growing twice as fast as in any other country in the world.

The unifying media force in Asia is satellite broadcasting direct to homes (DBS). Satellites are not entirely new to Asia. Indonesia, with thousands of islands across 3000 miles of ocean, had a need for some system of distribution other than terrestrial broadcasting many years ago. It was the first developing nation to have its own satellite when, in 1976, it launched Palapa. It then made its satellite available to its neighbors—Malaysia, Singapore, and Thailand.

But the real impetus for satellite-delivered programming for all of Asia has come from STAR.

STAR Satellite Television Asia Region (STAR) was founded in 1991 in Hong Kong by property developer Li Ka-shing and other members of his family. It is an advertising-based service that consists of five presently unscrambled channels—BBC World Service providing news, MTV with an Asian music video service, Mandarin-language entertainment from ATV in Hong Kong, English-language entertainment supplied by various Western companies, and sports, most of which comes from the Denver-based Prime Network. The satellite also carries Zee-TV, a Hindi-language service from India. The satellite's footprint covers thirty-eight countries from Japan to Egypt and from Upper Mongolia to Indonesia. STAR has created a huge appetite for its programming, as detailed extensively in the chapter on India. It has approximately 65 million viewers in 15 million homes and 116,000 hotel rooms.

In 1993 Rupert Murdoch's News Corporation purchased a 63.6 percent interest in STAR for $525 million. Li originally invested $250 million in the service, which is less than half of what Murdoch paid, and Li still owns one-third of the company. Murdoch also bought a 49.9 percent interest in Zee-TV. With this purchase, and with the other TV properties that News Corporation owns, Murdoch now has access to three-fourths of the world's population. He has plans to use STAR to distribute the British satellite service, BSkyB, of which he owns 50 percent, into Asia.

STAR's Competition Other companies are not standing by idly and letting Murdoch and Li monopolize the audience. Various forms of competition are in the works. Most notably, nine international broadcasters have joined together to form a consortium to operate a service out of Hong Kong with approximately sixteen channels of programming. The nine companies are Turner Broadcasting System, which could supply CNN; Time Warner, owner of HBO; Capital Cities/ABC, owner of ESPN; Discovery Communications with its Discovery Channel; Viacom, which owns MTV and will need to negotiate out of STAR; Dow Jones, provider of news; Paramount with its movies; the Australian Broadcasting Corporation; and Hong Kong–based Television Broadcasts, which owns many Chinese movies.

Also in the works is Asia Business News (ABN) produced in Singapore. It is advertiser-supported and will feature Asian anchors. Owners are Dow Jones, TCI (the largest U.S. cable system owner), and Television New Zealand.

Cable TV is also a potential competitor for the satellite services. The continent has historically had illegal cable systems and illegal copies of videotapes, some of which are programmed over cable. For example, Taiwan's cable pirates of the 1980s wired primarily apartment buildings and brought in Japanese programs that had been banned by the Taiwanese government because Japan recognized Taiwan's enemy, mainland China. The pirates also programmed material, some of it pornographic, for the late-night hours after regular stations had gone off the air.

Now cable is becoming legitimate in many countries. Wharf Cable in Hong Kong promises to be the world's largest single cable franchise, four times as large as that of New York City.

Singapore's government is starting to wire every home on the island because it doesn't want people watching satellite broadcasts and worries that dishes will be too small to detect. Phone companies are jumping into the fray to offer video on demand.

Success Potential The success of these new ventures is not ensured. Although STAR has captured an audience, it has not captured enough advertisers to make money. Many feel that in order for an Asian service to be economically viable, it must penetrate China, and China's present government is not obliging. In fact, it has ordered all those in China who have satellite dishes to haul them down.

Other countries are also suspicious of satellite services because of fears of what they will do to the national culture. The appearance of Rupert Murdoch, known for his sensational approach to media content, has not calmed their nerves. Malaysia recently outlawed satellite dishes for about 22,000 people who already owned them. The government dictum said the king, sultans, heads of the various states, and selected hotels could own the dishes, but not ordinary citizens. Whether or not the government will be able to make the people destroy their satellite dishes has yet to be seen.

Probably the most important stumbling block to media services that look at Asia as a unified entity is the diversity within the continent. Delivering one advertising message to all of Asia, with its multitudes of social and economic constituents, may not work.

ASIA AS A DIVERSE CONTINENT

Diversity abounds in Asia. Countries range in size from sprawling China with its 3.7 million square miles to tiny Taiwan with less than 14,000 square miles. Some countries, such as Sri Lanka and Taiwan, are single islands; Indonesia consists of thousands of islands;

Nepal and Mongolia are landlocked. China, with 1.5 billion people, is the most populous country in the world, holding one-fifth of the world's population, while Bhutan's population is only 1.6 million. Population densities also vary. In Bangladesh, on the average, over 2000 people inhabit each square mile, while Mongolia has 3 people per square mile.

Although Asia as a whole is increasing its economic viability, there are still many variances. Japan's $17,000 per capita gross domestic product (GDP) far exceeds that of any other country in Asia, but even beyond that there is great divergence. Taiwan's per capita GDP is over $7000, and Korea's is close behind at $5600, while Malaysia's is at $2500 and is climbing. But poor countries still abound: Nepal, $160; Bangladesh, $180; Bhutan, $200.

While many of the countries are democratic republics, the continent still hosts—in China, North Korea, Laos, and Vietnam—most of what is left of communism. Ethnic and religious differences abound. Some countries are Muslim, some are Christian, some espouse no religion, and some contain a number of religious groups that do not always coexist harmoniously. The number of languages spoken in Asia is essentially uncountable. For example, Pakistan alone broadcasts in Baluchi, Balti, Brahvi, Chitrali, English, Punjabi, Pashto, Shenna, Seraiki, Sindhi, and Urdu.

Media System Differences It is small wonder that differences also exist within the electronic media. Japan has one radio for every 1.3 people and one TV set for every 1.8 people; in Bangledesh there is one radio for every 24 people and one TV set for every 315.

A number of the countries, such as India, Pakistan, and Malaysia, were past British colonies and, as such, were influenced by the structure of the BBC, adding their own unique qualities along the way. In Malaysia, for example, state-operated radio was set up in 1946 while the country was still a colony. Although the country obtained its independence in 1957, the TV service Malaysia started in 1963 was modeled after the British example. Malaysia is a Muslim country, however, so more emphasis is placed on religious programs than in Britain. Also, Malaysia has three main ethnic groups—Malays who speak Bahasa Malaysia, Chinese who speak Mandarin, and Indians who speak Tamil. In addition, English is still used in some circles. As a result, the TV newsroom produces an average of seven newscasts a day—one each in English, Mandarin, and Tamil, and the remainder in Bahasa Malaysia. In 1984 Malaysia added a private TV network to its two government-run TV networks and four radio networks.

Indonesia was colonized by the Dutch who helped it establish a state-owned radio system. But the Indonesians, themselves, concurrently established a private radio station that promoted indigenous culture. When the country obtained its independence in 1949, its broadcasting system had a definite local flavor that both government and private radio and TV services have continued.

In Sri Lanka, privatization was an even more potent force in television. For many years the government resisted establishing TV, fearing it would destroy the indigenous culture. But in 1978 a private operator won permission to open a small TV station, and 45,000 sets were sold in the first year. Despite this success, the private owner ran out of money, and within a year the government took over the station to keep it on the air. By now, the government was espousing the idea that TV improved the quality of village life. However, for a short period of time, the state-run TV system did not broadcast from 9:00 P.M. until 9:30 P.M. so that people wouldn't be tempted to watch TV rather than listen to the main daily radio newscast. During the 1980s privatization returned to Sri Lanka, and the country now has both government-run and private TV services.

The United States introduced TV to South Vietnam during the Vietnamese war and did it in an unusual way—through airborne relay. In 1966 an airplane banked into an oval pattern above Saigon and broadcast a television signal. Inside the airplane were two transmitters, two videotape recorders, an audio panel, film projection equipment, and a small studio.

Some of the countries of Asia, like the countries in Europe, can receive one another's signals. The Thais in the southern part of the country could not receive their own country's radio signals during the 1970s, but they could pick up those of Malaysia. Even when the Thai government improved reception in the south, the Thais still preferred the Malaysian programming, which they considered less long-winded and boring than their own.

Programming Countries also use one another's programming to some extent. Hong Kong and Taiwan are the big producers of Chinese movies. These films are shown in countries with Chinese-speaking populations and are often subtitled in other countries. Asian countries also import U.S. and European programs and produce their own material. Bangladesh, for example, has within its radio organization a special unit to promote family planning. Among its productions has been a 20-minute early-evening serial called *Happy Family*. Bangladesh's latest media plans, however, involve exporting its programming. It is sending its best dramatic and musical TV programming to the United Kingdom where it is being delivered by cable and satellite to Bangladesh expatriates in England.

Although all countries in Asia have government and/or private radio, some of the least developed countries started TV late or have not started it at all. Nepal's first regular TV broadcasts began at the end of 1985, and Bhutan still does not have a national TV system. These countries and those like India, that have only sleepy, rather boring government services, have been prime targets for the programming of the newer satellite services.

SPECIFIC COUNTRIES

The three Asian countries covered in detail—India, China, and Japan—are all rather obvious choices. India is the leading country in southern Asia, generally acknowledged to be the most powerful of the nations that compose the South Asian Association for Regional Cooperation, a cooperative that includes Bhutan, Bangladesh, India, Maldives, Nepal, Pakistan, and Sri Lanka. China, as the most populous country in the world and the most powerful of the remaining Communist countries, is a sleeping giant ready for a media awakening. Japan, with its electronics industry and highly developed economy, is a media leader.

Before examining these countries, however, it may be wise to consider TV in Nepal, a small country tucked above India, that may in some ways predict the future of electronic media in Asia.

Nepal As already mentioned, TV did not start in Nepal until 1985. The delay was primarily due to economic and technological constraints. After decades of rule by hereditary prime ministers who stifled the education and the economic system of the country, Nepal's development has nearly all come since 1951. It was not until the mid-1980s that Nepal felt it had the technological and programming expertise to start a television station.

Even in the 1980s, television was not a given. Neer Bikram Shah, the founding general manager of Nepal Television (NTV) who had a background as an actor, lobbied furiously to convince those in power that the time for television had come. Eventually he had to stage a media event to get the country's attention. He jerry-rigged a transmitter, rented a camera, and went to Australia to cover the king's state visit there live. Soon after this public relations stunt, the king cleared the way for a television station.

Nepal Television has been on the air every evening since December 1985, but it still reaches only about 23 percent of the population. For awhile it carried both CNN and BBC World Service Television, but dropped CNN in 1992 because it could not afford the $3000-per-month license fee.

After being on the air less than 5 years, Nepal Television underwent a stern challenge in 1990 when political unrest forced the king to relinquish his absolute powers to an interim government. During this period, NTV was destabilized as politicians haggled over how the news media should be handled under a new form of government. After a democratic government came to power, there were massive staff reductions that robbed Nepal Television of some of its key senior staff.

Nepal Television's Neer Shah, who had close ties to the king, eventually decided to leave NTV under political pressure in mid-1992. Shah had been the motivating force behind Nepal Television, and his departure left NTV almost rudderless at a time when it was still trying to establish itself as a serious broadcaster.

While Neer Shah's departure was a blow to government terrestrial television, it opened the way for an era of new private forms of electronic media that could have a profound effect on the distribution and content of television throughout south Asia. Soon after leaving NTV, Neer Shah founded the Shangri-La Channel, a Nepali-language direct broadcast satellite channel that could eventually supplant terrestrial television transmission in Nepal and provide programming to an expatriate audience worldwide.

Neer Shah had been intrigued for some time with the possibility of developing a satellite channel for Nepal Television. When he left NTV, he retooled his plan for the private sector. Because Neer Shah was a former actor with close ties to the Nepali film industry, he had the best contacts to commission programming for a new channel.

Within 6 months of leaving NTV, Shah had the Shangri-La Channel operating, if only for 1 hour per week. To launch his service, Shah took advantage of the rising popularity of STAR and the introduction of the Hindi-language channel Zee-TV on the same satellite. Realizing that the Shangri-La Channel would be a perfect fit for Zee-TV, Shah signed a contract with Zee-TV to sublet 1 hour of satellite time per week beginning on a regular basis in January 1993. Shah's plans are to contract with film producers for product and sell advertising for his 1-hour-per-week slot on Zee-TV. He expects two sources of revenue: advertisers who want to reach Nepalis specifically and general advertisers who want to make a pan-Asian buy on STAR.

While the Zee-TV initiative has provided a glitzy premiere for Shangri-La, it is not to be the mainstay for Neer Shah's new programming service. Shah estimated that there were only 15,000 satellite dishes in Nepal in 1992 and realized that with such limited satellite dish penetration, cable was the only way he could successfully market the Shangri-La Channel in Nepal and achieve profitability with the service.

By the end of 1992 there were approximately fifty illegal cable systems in Nepal. Most of them are primitive, supplying only a handful of subscribers in a neighborhood. These bootlegged systems usually provide no switching mechanism to change channels. If a subscriber wants to watch one channel instead of another, he or she must contact the person in charge of the system's head end. Problems also abound regarding the replacement of defective or stolen equipment and the adding of new channels. Neer Shah is now supporting a government initiative to regulate cable so that larger, better-financed, and more professional cable systems can be established. He hopes to offer 3 hours per day of Nepali-language programming to these cable systems and enter the cable business himself, wiring many of the remote areas of the country.

Within a span of 10 years, Neer Shah has been active in terrestrial, satellite, and cable TV. He has not been overly successful with any of these media forms, but he remains a visionary and is perhaps someone who can lead the way for electronic media in Asia to reconcile their roles in relation to unity and diversity.

(*Editor's Note*: The information about Nepal was provided by Dr. Joe Foote, dean of the College of Mass Communication and Media Arts, Southern Illinois University at Carbondale, who has served as an academic specialist with Nepal Television.)

CHAPTER 10

India

Lalit Acharya and Surekha Acharya

Lalit and Surekha, husband and wife, are natives of India. Both have studied communications in India (at Osmania University in Hyderabad) and in the United States. Surekha has a master's degree from California State University, Fullerton, and Lalit has studied at the University of Southern California. Presently, Lalit teaches at California State Polytechnic University, Pomona, and Surekha is an English teacher at Riverside Community College.

Lalit and Surekha Acharya.

STATISTICS

Geographic Area: 1,266,595 square miles
Capital: New Delhi
Population: 866,000,000
Religions: Hindu, Muslim, and others
Languages: Sixteen languages including Hindi and English
Type of Government: Federal republic headed by a prime minister
Gross Domestic Product: $287 billion
Literacy: 48 percent

GENERAL CHARACTERISTICS

In November 1923 radio programs beamed by an amateur club invaded small pockets of British and Europeanized Indian homes in the city of Calcutta. Those signals heralded the entry of India, the world's largest democracy and second most populous nation, into the age of radio.

From those humble beginnings when India was still a colony of the British Empire, Indian radio, and now television, has grown into a monolithic communications network that informs and entertains about one out of every five human beings on earth.

The Land and Its People About one-third the size of the United States, this ancient land of 1.27 million square miles, known as the Bharat in the Hindi language, occupies most of the Indian subcontinent in south Asia and is home to some 866 million people, about one-fifth of the world's population.

It is bounded by the Himalayan mountain range on the north, the Indian Ocean on the south, the Arabian Sea on the west, and the Bay of Bengal on the east. Its neighbors to the northwest are Pakistan and Afghanistan. The countries of China, Bhutan, and Nepal lie along its northern borders, while Bangladesh and Myanmar (formerly Burma) line its northeastern borders.

India's population, soon expected to surpass China's, is distributed among four ethnic groups and about six religions. About seven in ten Indians are descendants of the Indo-Aryan tribes from Central Asia who settled India about 1500 B.C. About 25 percent of the Indian people are descended from the Dravidian people and now mostly live in the southern part of the country. The remainder of the population is divided between the aboriginal tribes that inhabit the forests and mountains in central India and the Mongoloid descendants of the Huns who settled northeastern parts of India around A.D. 450.

India is predominantly Hindu, with 83 percent of the population claiming Hinduism as their religion. The country is also home to many Muslims, who account for about 11 percent of the population. Christians, Sikhs, Buddhists, and Jains each account for 2 percent or less of the Indian population. There are also about 250 tribes in India, making up 7 percent of the population.

Fourteen major languages besides Hindi, the national language, and English, the business tongue, are spoken in India. Coexisting with the major languages are several thousand minor languages and dialects that are staking a claim for recognition.

According to the Indian government's Ministry of Planning, these diverse people have an average income of about $261 annually (compared to over $21,000 for the United States) from a variety of occupations. Farming claims about 75 percent of the Indian workforce. About 10 percent are employed by the nation's manufacturing industries, mines, quarries, and government. These, then, are the people who form the audience for Indian radio and television.

Media Sources Because less than half of the Indian population is literate, it is not surprising that Indians rely more on radio and television for news and entertainment than on newspapers and magazines.

In 1989 Indian audiences switched on an estimated 65 million radio receivers, according to figures released by India's Ministry of Information and Broadcasting. Included among these were radio receiver sets installed in community centers to maximize broadcasting coverage. Indian audiences have far more radio program choices now than they have ever had before. Listeners can tune into Radio Ceylon (Sri Lanka) for popular music and into the British Broadcasting Corporation's (BBC) external news service for both domestic and international news. Likewise, listeners in north Indian border towns and villages are often exposed to music, news, and propaganda aired by neighboring countries such as Pakistan and China.

This notwithstanding, the bulk of radio programs Indians listen to are broadcast by the state-owned All India Radio (AIR). In 1989 the Indian government's Ministry of Information and Broadcasting estimated that news and entertainment radio programs broadcast by AIR were heard by about 804 million people, or 95.3 percent of the Indian population, over an area of roughly 1 million square miles. That works out to about 84 percent of the total landmass of the country.

The television scene has changed greatly in the last few years. As recently as 3 years ago, the only force in television was the state-owned Doordarshan India, as it always had been since 1959. Programs were a dreary collection of instructive materials. But, thanks to satellite, videocassette recorder, and cable technology, much has changed since 1989, and an international alphabet of services (CNN, MTV, BBC, TV-5, WST, ATN, CFI, Zee-TV) is available. As M. Rahman comments in *India Today*:

> . . . ZAP . . . this is Ashis Ray of CNN reporting from Ayodhya in Uttar Pradesh . . . ZAP . . . *en se retrouvant, leur passion les submerge* . . . ZAP . . . De, de ek chumma de de . . . ZAP . . . and the L.A. Lakers once again demonstrated their . . . ZAP . . . Yo, so as I was saying . . . ZAP . . . The force is with us.
>
> The mundane television set has suddenly turned into an incredible technicolor dreamboat. The remote control has placed a glitzy new world at our fingertips. Enormous metallic objects, crammed with electronic gizmos circling the sky, are beaming down a bewildering collection of images. And, like a lost tribe discovering an oasis in the desert, lakhs [hundreds of thousands] of Indians are hotwired into this superbazaar of soaps, sports, news, music, sex and much more.

THE DEVELOPMENT OF ELECTRONIC MEDIA IN INDIA

It is difficult to understand what Indian electronic media are and do, or even make sense of the current explosion of international TV programming, without discussing the history of the state-owned radio and television systems.

Radio   The first shots in Indian broadcasting were fired by amateur radio clubs that sprang up in the nation's major cities in the early 1920s. In November 1923 the Radio Club of Calcutta was founded, followed in June 1924 by similar clubs in Bombay and Madras. These fledgling efforts, which beamed radio programs at small and often elite audiences for a few hours each day, languished for want of money and subscribers.

By the time they died in late 1927, these clubs, as well as the financial success of European broadcasting companies, had caught the imagination of a group of Indian entrepreneurs who founded the Indian Broadcasting Company on July 23, 1927. This two-station company, broadcasting out of Bombay and Calcutta to about 7000 listeners, lost money heavily over the next 3 years for the following reasons:

> Too little revenue from radio licenses. The licenses, which each cost 10 rupees (Rs 10), annually accounted for about 80 percent of the company's income and did not amount to enough to keep the company going.
>
> The unaffordable cost of radio sets, which then were priced at Rs 500.
>
> Limited audiences. The company made little effort to reach out to the Indian masses, preferring instead to cater to small pockets of Europeanized audiences.

By early 1930 it was clear that the Indian Broadcasting Company would not survive. Bending to political pressure to continue the broadcasting services provided by the company, the Indian government renamed it the Indian State Broadcasting Service (ISBS) and brought it under the control of the Department of Labor and Industries on April 1, 1930. By June of that year, the Indian Broadcasting Company filed for bankruptcy and went out of business.

Though it got off to a shaky start, ISBS survived and prospered. Two factors fueled the success of the state-run broadcasting service over the next decade.

First, there was a growing official interest in the propaganda potential of broadcasting, an interest that became more urgent as World War II loomed. The war threat presented colonial administrators with tremendous new public communication demands. In 1935 the viceroy (the colonial chief executive) asked for help, and the BBC sent Lionel Fielden, one of its senior producers, to India as the first director of government-sponsored broadcasting. Fielden, who believed that the name ISBS was unwieldy and tainted with officialdom, persuaded the viceroy to change the name of the organization to All India Radio (AIR) in June 1935.

Second, increased revenues resulted from the enactment of two laws. The Indian Tariff Amendment Act of 1932 doubled import duties on wireless receiving sets, while the 1933 Indian Wireless Telegraphy Act made possessing a radio set without a license a federal offense. These measures, together with government control and assistance, effectively protected ISBS from the vagaries of the marketplace that had felled its predecessors.

In its march to purveying news and entertainment to a fifth of the world's population, AIR has passed several milestones, among them the following:

In 1935 AIR began broadcasting rural programs to audiences in the Northwest Frontier Province (which includes northern parts of present-day Pakistan) and the United Provinces (the present-day Indian state of Uttar Pradesh along with parts of neighboring Madhya Pradesh).

In 1937 the network established the Central News Organization, precursor of its News Services Division. That year, control over the network passed from the Ministry of Labor and Industries to the Department of Communications. In 1941 AIR came under the control of the newly formed Department of Information and Broadcasting.

In 1939, reacting to World War II, AIR started broadcasting to foreign audiences. The first broadcast was in the Pushtu language and targeted at audiences in Afghanistan.

In 1947 India gained its independence from Britain, and AIR's parent authority, the Department of Information and Broadcasting, was upgraded to the level of a ministry. That year, AIR broadcast through eleven stations to about a quarter-million licensed radio sets around the country.

In 1957 AIR launched Vividh Bharati, a light entertainment and music service in the Hindi language. That year, AIR also began calling itself Akashvani for domestic audiences, which in Hindi means "voice from the sky" or "cosmic voice."

In 1967 AIR decided to accept advertisements on Vividh Bharati, and within 3 years commercially sponsored programs were airing on this service. By 1982 advertising had invaded the network's news programs.

In 1969 AIR launched its youth program, Yuv Vani (Voice of Youth).

Television By the time India became independent in 1947, British television was already more than a decade old and television in the United States was taking off in full force. Quite naturally, there was a clamor for this strange and exciting medium among newly independent India's industrialists, educators, and broadcasters.

Early Stations Despite such pressures, the Indian government resisted experimenting with television until September 15, 1959, when an experimental television broadcasting station was set up in New Delhi by AIR with help from the United Nations Educational, Scientific, and Cultural Organization (UNESCO); the U.S. government; and the electronics firms Philips India. Philips India and the U.S. government provided the transmitting equipment for the television station, while a $20,000 grant from UNESCO funded 180 community television sets for tele-clubs (public viewing centers) that were set up in and around New Delhi. This experimental station had a transmitting range of 40 kilometers.

The first telecasts, which were about 20 minutes long and beamed twice a week to the tele-clubs, were mostly cultural and educational and designed as much to discover how television could educate people as they were to train specialists to handle the new medium. By 1961 the Delhi television station was transmitting 20-minute lessons to high and middle schools in New Delhi. The lessons, which were telecast twice a day, covered a range of subjects from physics and chemistry to geography and current events. In 1965 AIR and the Indian government succumbed to public pressure and began producing entertainment programs at the Delhi station. In 1967 the Delhi station increased its transmitting range to 60 kilometers and started broadcasting weekly farm programs to villages around New Delhi and to the surrounding states of Haryana and Uttar Pradesh.

The 1970s set the stage for the expansion of television services to other parts of the country. In 1972 India's second television station was started in Bombay, and within 3 years six other cities got their own television stations.

By 1976 there were half a million television sets around the country, bringing the medium within reach of about 3 million people. About this time, the Indian government's Ministry of Information and Broadcasting decided that television could survive on its own, gave it the name Doordarshan (which means "seeing from afar" in Hindi), and separated it from AIR.

Satellite Instructional Television Experiment (SITE) For much of its history, Indian television programming has been consistent with the social, agricultural, economic, and political aims of the government. Taking their cues from Indian politicians, programming executives put aside the entertainment value to television in favor of its more instructive and educational usefulness.

This bias for wholesome, practical, and educational television became far more evident in 1975 when Doordarshan, still a part of AIR, launched the Satellite Instructional Television Experiment (SITE), one of the most ambitious experiments in television history.

SITE was the brainchild of Vikram Sarabhai, a brilliant physicist and chairman of the Indian Atomic Energy Commission. Sarabhai persuaded India's Department of Atomic Energy (DAE) and the U.S. National Aeronautics and Space Administration (NASA) to work with each other to bring satellite-based television to India. He also signed an agreement that provided India access to NASA's applications technology satellite (ATS-6) to conduct the 1-year experiment.

From August 1, 1975, through July of the following year, Doordarshan used the ATS-6 satellite to beam farm, health and hygiene, and family planning programs 4 hours each day to 2400 villages in rural India. SITE was also used to telecast entertainment programs, consisting chiefly of rural art, music, and dance. For the most part, since very few people had their own sets, they watched SITE programs in communal areas where TV sets were specifically set up for viewing purposes.

SITE's overarching agenda was not only to educate people about solutions to the country's problems, such as its wildly burgeoning population, but also to unify the diverse and multilingual audiences of India by exposing them to one another's cultures.

People watching a SITE program at a public viewing place. (*NASA*)

SITE programs were produced at production centers in New Delhi, Hyderabad, and Cuttack with the help of university teachers, social workers, and state and federal government experts. Some of the programs were also produced by the Indian Space and Research Organization (ISRO), a wing of the DAE. ISRO was also responsible for installing and servicing the television sets used for the experiment. These sets, for the most part, consisted of ordinary television sets that were each provided with a front-end converter and a chicken-mesh antenna for receiving satellite signals.

SITE's results were more modest than its designs. According to a 1980 report by Krishan Sondhi, the farm programs did not have the expected impact. Farmers in SITE viewing areas were not more innovative than farmers who weren't exposed to SITE programs, possibly because they had already learned about the innovations from AIR's farm bulletins and programs. Another weakness was that the farm programs were not adapted to the widely differing farming practices in the SITE viewing areas and consequently were not of much use to the farmers. The health and family planning programs did not result in significant improvements either.

Indian Television after SITE Whatever its shortcomings, SITE, for the first time, opened up the possibility of connecting people in far and unreachable corners of India through the magic of satellite communication.

NASA had loaned the ATS-6 satellite to the Indian government for only 1 year, and it would be 6 years before India would launch its own satellite. So there remained the question of what would replace SITE after July 1976. AIR wanted to extend its ground network of television stations and transmitters into cities and towns in the SITE viewing area so that urban as well as rural audiences could watch TV. ISRO, on the other hand, argued for low-power transmitters designed exclusively for telecasting to SITE's rural audiences. But none of these transmitters or SITE continuity centers was ready when NASA disconnected its satellite from Indian audiences in mid-1976. And so ended a chapter in India's television history.

Meanwhile, Doordarshan was passing other milestones. By 1977, a year after SITE ended, the newly independent network had increased its audience to 100 million people, and political parties were allowed to pitch for votes on television.

In 1982 India launched the Insat-IA satellite, enabling Doordarshan to televise programs in color to audiences across the land. That year, Doordarshan telecast the Ninth Asian Games live to national audiences and set the stage for live coverage of sports such as cricket, table tennis, and soccer. In August 1983, Insat-IB was launched from the space shuttle *Challenger* to replace the short-lived Insat-IA. Regional stations supplemented the programming from the national network by producing news and information programs of interest to, and in the language(s) of, their local audiences.

Videomania Even as Doordarshan was beginning to improve its technology and increase its audience, videocassette recorders (VCRs) and players (VCPs) were starting to alter the broadcasting landscape. In 1984 there were an estimated 300,000 VCRs and VCPs in India, with ownership of these machines growing at the rate of 20,000 sets a month. Today the number hovers around 3.5 million and is still growing.

India took to this new medium in a big way. Video clubs and parlors sprang up all around the country with the single-minded intent of showing English and Indian movies. It became the fashion to ride around in buses that showed videos. People could rent a VCR and could also eat at a restaurant that showed videos.

Even so, for every individual who obtained access to videos, there were several thousands who did not. To get around this limitation, ingenious entrepreneurs rigged up rudimentary cable systems, especially targeting large apartment buildings. For a fee, each apartment was wired to a VCR in the basement from which the entrepreneurs showed movies to willing audiences, sometimes all day long. Soon the cable operators (of which there are an estimated 10,000) discovered that satellite dishes could expand the range of their program offerings as well as their audiences.

The real proof of this came during the 1991 Persian Gulf conflict when the demand for news in India became insatiable, in part because India provides a large workforce to many countries in the Middle East, including Iraq. Cable operators bought satellite dishes capable of receiving CNN and hooked them up to their cable systems. Generally they charged customers about Rs 600 ($20) for installation and Rs 150 ($5) a month for the service.

The VCR and the satellite dish affected Indian television in three ways.

First, they cracked open Doordarshan's monopoly on television content.

Second, they exposed the flaws in the Indian network's slow and heavily bureaucratized approach to news programming. CNN beat Doordarshan by about 12 hours in reporting the 1991 assassination of Prime Minister Rajiv Gandhi.

Third, they paved the way for the globalization of Indian broadcasting space by opening it up to a number of international television networks.

Leading this invasion of Indian airwaves is Hong Kong's Satellite Television Asia Region (STAR) system. Founded by real estate mogul Li Ka-shing in January 1991 and later largely taken over by Rupert Murdoch, STAR uses the AsiaSat1 satellite to reach thirty-eight Asian nations from Israel in the west to Taiwan in the east with news from the BBC, sporting events from around the world, American daytime soap operas such as *The Bold and the Beautiful* and *Santa Barbara*, sitcoms such as *The Cosby Show* and *Murphy Brown*, and MTV. STAR's impact on Indian audiences has been phenomenal. Within 2 years, its viewership climbed to about 2 million households. Suddenly, life seemed incomplete without a remote control unit.

On October 2, 1992, in a move that further ate into Doordarshan's audience, STAR added Zee-TV, a Hindi-language channel that reaches audiences from the Middle East to the Far East with a daily fare of soaps, children's programs, and Hindi movies.

Meanwhile, waiting in the wings are other players with the promise of more and better television. For example, the Malayalam-language network, Asianet, will soon start using the Russian Ekran satellite to telecast programs to vast numbers of Malayali people in the south Indian state of Kerala (where they originally came from) and countries in the Middle East (where large numbers of them are employed).

ORGANIZATION AND FINANCING

The new services, because they are not legally sanctioned by the government and because the programming is primarily foreign, do not have an established form of organization within India. However, there is pressure on the government to regulate cable and to establish some sort of private broadcasting. Meanwhile, the state-owned radio and television systems, AIR and Doordarshan, continue with their fairly long-established organizational system.

Radio What began as a two-station radio venture in the 1920s is now a giant network that monopolizes India's radio broadcasting industry. Headquartered in the nation's capital, New Delhi, controlled by the Indian government's Ministry of Information and Broadcasting, and headed by a director general, AIR operates a network of 104 radio stations and 190 transmitters that reach over 95 percent of the country.

The radio stations of AIR are grouped into four zones. The eastern zone has twenty-six stations covering northeastern and eastern Indian states. The northern zone has twenty-five stations, while the southern zone has twenty-nine. Twenty-four stations service the western zone. The stations are generally located in major urban centers such as Calcutta, Varanasi (Benaras), Bangalore, Hyderabad, and Bombay.

The various departments of the Indian government are financed by a national fund called the Consolidated Fund of India. AIR is no exception. Its operating budget is presented as part of the overall budget of the Ministry of Information and Broadcasting for approval by vote in the Indian Parliament. AIR's budget is generally presented in two parts: one is for the annual operating expenses of the network, and the other is for development and expansion.

The Indian government outlines financial outlays for its various departments and projects in 5-year financial plans. In the seventh plan, covering 1985–1990, the government allotted Rs 70 billion (approximately US $2.3 billion) for operating and developing AIR, or Rs 14 billion (approximately US $0.5 billion) annually. This amount generally meets about 90 percent of the network's financial needs. The remainder comes from another Indian government fund called the Non-Lapsable Fund which contains all of the net advertising income earned by AIR and its television counterpart, Doordarshan India.

Television The New Delhi–based Doordarshan national programming service reaches an audience of about 700 million Indians through a network of 18 television stations and 522 transmitters scattered over an area of roughly 900,000 square miles. The 18 television stations are also under the supervision of Doordarshan and program material for their regions as well as retransmit national programming.

Doordarshan and AIR share many similarities. Though operationally independent of each other, they are both headed by the same director general and are controlled by the Indian government's Ministry of Information and Broadcasting. Like AIR, the two sources of funding for Doordarshan are the Consolidated Fund of

India and the advertising revenue–based Non-Lapsable Fund. Despite the far greater costs of producing and transmitting television programs, the Indian government gives Doordarshan about the same amount of operating money it gives AIR. Very few of its correspondents are allowed to travel by plane, and payments to performers have not kept pace with inflation. The sparse budgets of Doordarshan and AIR generally explain the poor quality of programming on these networks.

PROGRAMMING

By now it should be evident that the Indian government considers radio and television primarily a means of educating people and developing the nation. This is one reason why there is such a hunger for entertainment programming from the outside. However, AIR and Doordarshan continue a programming pattern that is largely paternalistic.

Radio News and music dominate radio as they do in many other countries. In addition, Indian radio provides some interesting services to unusual constituencies.

News Services Division The news and information arm of AIR is its News Services Division (NSD). One of the largest news organizations in the world, NSD broadcasts 208 daily news bulletins in 24 major and minor languages and 38 dialects. Eighty-one of these bulletins originate from NSD's home service headquarters in New Delhi and are relayed to remote corners of the country through regional broadcasting stations. The remaining 127 news bulletins originate from the regional broadcasting stations and are broadcast in 62 languages and dialects to local audiences.

As with other news agencies, AIR's bulletins cover a broad spectrum of developments in the fields of sports, medicine and science, international news, economics, and politics. Additionally, they pay special attention to rural and cultural topics, issues, and events. When the Indian Parliament is in session, AIR keeps the country informed by reviewing daily proceedings, providing commentary and analysis, interviewing key politicians from the ruling party and the opposition, and obtaining reactions from citizens to political and legislative events and issues.

News-gathering efforts at NSD are supported by the network's own full- and part-time correspondents. AIR also subscribes to international news agencies such as United Press International (UPI) and Reuters and domestic agencies such as the Press Trust of India (PTI), besides continuously monitoring the world's major radio networks such as Voice of America (VOA), Radio Moscow, and the British Broadcasting Corporation.

In the minds of many, however, there is a nagging suspicion that AIR is no more than a mouthpiece for the Indian government, capable of suppressing negative information or, at least, delaying such news. For example, Prime Minister Indira Gandhi was assassinated on October 31, 1984, at 9:30 A.M., but AIR did not report her death until 5:57 P.M., about 8 hours and 27 minutes after the assassination, and 4 hours and 27 minutes after the BBC reported it to Indian audiences on its 1:30 P.M. newscast. Much of this delay can be attributed to protocol—deaths of important personages cannot be broadcast without the permission of the home secretary—that gives the government a chance to hedge and wedge.

Vividh Bharati Perhaps nothing defines the Indian soul as well as music does. There is a constant sound of popular songs that are part of Indian movies, classical music, Indian rock music, bhajans (religious hymns), and folk music on the streets of India and in the homes of its people. There is not a store or restaurant that doesn't have a radio set blaring loud music. Even the buses and subway trains hum to the strains of music emanating from thousands of boom boxes. When people turn on television sets, it is often to listen to film and other kinds of music. Indian movies themselves, the most any country produces, are mainly musical extravaganzas. So, to understand India is to listen to its music.

Not surprisingly, the radio set is a prized and venerated object that is prominently displayed in Indian homes and businesses and often covered with an ornate embroidered cover to protect it from dust.

Ironically, for a long time, AIR dismissed music, especially film music, as vulgar entertainment and banished it from the airwaves. Network executives often screened records for good taste, which meant that only classical music and bhajans had any chance of being aired. While this worked for the cultural elite, it left masses of Indians unsatisfied and turned them away to Radio Ceylon, which, by the early 1950s, was using powerful shortwave transmitters to broadcast Indian movie songs to the subcontinent.

Faced with the prospect of losing a large part of its audience, AIR made music and light entertainment part of its service by establishing the All India Variety Program or Vividh Bharati on October 2, 1957. The enormously popular Vividh Bharati service is broadcast exclusively in the Hindi language. Most of its content is taken up by folk, classical, religious, and of course film songs. Movie stars host many of these programs, much to the delight of the Indian audiences. The remainder of the service is given over to skits, plays, documentaries, features and newsreels, movie trailers and excerpts, and quiz and game shows.

Vividh Bharati is unusual in that all programming is centralized at its headquarters in Bombay. AIR broadcasting stations around the country send musical selections on tape to Bombay. There, Vividh Bharati staff edit and package about 13 hours of content on tape and mail it back to the stations for broadcasting. Because Vividh Bharati borrows all of its material from the broadcasting stations, it is sometimes called a "library" service.

In 1967 AIR further commercialized Vividh Bharati by accepting advertisements on the service. Ads were first aired in Bombay, Pune (previously Poona), and Nagpur, but by 1970 radio advertising on Vividh Bharati had spread to the nation's other urban and trade centers such as New Delhi, Calcutta, and Madras.

Yuv Vani On July 20, 1969, AIR aired its first youth programming, Yuv Vani. The service, which literally means "voice of youth," consists of discussions, plays, features, musical selections, and sports commentary that are entirely planned, managed, and presented by high school and university students under the guidance of professional AIR staff. Yuv Vani thus not only provides a forum for India's youth to express itself but also creates rich and enjoyable broadcasting experiences for young people. Both authors of this chapter were briefly involved in Yuv Vani in the early 1970s when they were college students in India.

Programming for Other Special Audiences In addition to the services mentioned so far, AIR also broadcasts regularly to the country's farm and native tribe audiences. The daily agricultural and tribal broadcasts last a half-hour and focus on pertinent topics such as cultivation, crop rotation, animal care, folk music, and culture. Many stations broadcast news bulletins to these audiences as well.

Likewise, AIR has an armed forces channel which broadcasts news and entertainment to soldiers patrolling the country's borders. It also broadcasts programs to commemorate special occasions such as Wildlife Week and Arbor Day. Finally, AIR publishes the journal *Akashvani,* in Hindi and in English, to document events and issues in Indian broadcasting.

Television Doordarshan, through its national and regional services, telecasts 280 hours of programs daily. These programs, in large part, are designed to (1) speed social and economic change, especially among women, children, and economically disadvantaged people; (2) unify the multiethnic and multilingual peoples of the country; (3) spur scientific thought; (4) encourage responsible environmentalism; (5) promote interest in sports; and (6) expose audiences to the cultural and artistic heritage of the country.

News Programs News programs, which account for about 12 to 14 percent of Doordarshan's programming, generally consist of news bulletins, commentaries, and panel discussions (much like CNN's *Crossfire*). While the majority of news programs are telecast in the Hindi and English languages, regional broadcasting stations (or *kendras*) supplement these with news briefs and bulletins in languages such as Tamil, Telugu, and Kannada.

An important part of the news is the parliamentary report. When India's lower house of Parliament, Lok Sabha (House of Commons), and its upper house, Rajya Sabha (House of Lords), meet, Doordarshan, like AIR, provides daily coverage. Likewise, the regional broadcasting stations air proceedings of the state legislatures when they are in session.

Doordarshan does not have its own news service and depends on AIR for much of the news it disseminates. The rest is collected by Doordarshan's meager staff of full- and part-time news correspondents. The network has entered into news exchange agreements with international agencies such as the Asian Broadcasting Union (ABU). News feeds resulting from such agreements allow the network to broadcast international news at home and domestic news abroad. ABU's *The World This Week* is perhaps the most widely viewed of the news programs telecast by Doordarshan. A few privately owned production companies, such as New Delhi's TV News Features, provide the network with news features, documentaries, and science programs.

Educational Programs Educating school and university students has been a key priority for Doordarshan. Since 1961 the New Delhi station of Doordarshan has collaborated with the city's education department to supplement school curricula with 20-minute programs on, for example, physics and chemistry, and current events and geography. Three such programs are beamed twice a day, 5 days each week, to New Delhi's high and middle schools. In 1975 Doordarshan Delhi began transmitting 20-minute general education programs twice a week to primary schools in the city. Similar telecasts are in place in Bombay. Additionally, Doordarshan telecasts cartoons, puppet shows, and quiz shows aimed at children of various ages throughout the country.

When the Insat-IB satellite became operational in 1983, several government agencies bid for channel space. One agency that succeeded was the University Grants Commission (UGC), a government body that oversees and regulates the nation's colleges and universities. The UGC telecasts, most of which are on science and technology, are beamed nationwide in two 45-minute segments, one around noon, the other in the late afternoon. Much of the content of these programs is provided by Indian and British open universities. These are somewhat akin to university extension programs in the United States, but on the scale of a large, formal university.

Developmental Programs Consistent with its aims of speeding social and economic change, Doordarshan broadcasts weekly developmental programs to rural audiences about farming practices, and to both rural and urban audiences about health and hygiene. Because population control is a high priority for the Indian government, Doordarshan also addresses issues such as contraception and responsible parenthood in its features and documentaries. Many of these programs, such as the weekly *Amchi Mati, Amchi Manse* (meaning "our land, our people" in the Marathi language), use entertaining folk formats such as dance, music, and puppetry to get their messages across.

Sports Programs Much as American audiences are obsessed with football and baseball, Indian audiences are fanatical about sports such as soccer, badminton, cricket, hockey, and table tennis. When soccer or cricket matches are being played, life literally stops for the rest of India. Indians are glued to television sets in their homes and to radio sets at the office and on the road.

Doordarshan routinely telecasts important sporting events such as the Asian Games, Olympics, and cricket test matches between India and other countries belonging to the British Commonwealth. During the 1992 Olympics in Barcelona, Spain, Doordarshan carried live telecasts of events such as the opening and closing ceremonies, as well as sports such as field hockey that Indians either are interested in or have participated in.

Entertainment Programs About a third of Doordashan's programs can be classified as entertainment programs. Many more programs, be they educational or developmental, incorporate entertaining devices such as song, dance, and humor to get their messages across to audiences.

Entertainment programs on Doordarshan generally take four forms: music and dance recitals, movie-based programs, soap operas, and religious programs.

The first of these forms is self-explanatory. Recitals of prominent classical, popular, and folk musicians and dancers are routinely telecast to national and regional audiences.

Movies are a big draw in India. The country produces a larger quantity of theatrical movies than any other country in the world. Most of them are entertaining but not particularly high-quality musicals that are shown only in India. Television presents audiences with the opportunity to watch their favorite movie actors and actresses in the comfort of their living rooms. The typical programming is three movies per week, with Sundays reserved for Hindi movies. The other two showings are given over to English films or regional-language films.

In addition, Doordarshan telecasts interviews with famous movie stars and producers, as well as *Chitrahar.* This weekly show, whose title means "garland of pictures" in the Hindi language, consists of a 30-minute collection of song-and-dance sequences from popular Indian films. This genre is so popular that it forms a large part of Indian television shows such as *Namaste America* that are produced for Indians residing in the United States.

Soaps invaded Indian homes in 1984 when Doordashan began showing the Indian soap opera *Hum Log.* The program, whose title means "we people" in the Hindi language, documented the lives, loves, and struggles of a middle-class family in a social tapestry of political corruption and crime. One hundred and fifty-six episodes of this hugely popular soap, modeled after the telenovelas of Mexico and Brazil, were shown between July 7, 1984, and December 17, 1985.

Indian advertisers had traditionally been very skeptical about advertising on television, but *Hum Log* changed all that. By paying rich dividends to Food Specialties Limited, a subsidiary of Nestlé India and a maker of the now popular Maggi noodles, *Hum Log* proved the value of television advertising. Soon advertisers were lining up to advertise on Doordarshan, which began to produce soaps such as *Khandaan* (meaning "family" or "dynasty") and *Buniyad* (meaning "foundation") at a rapid pace; by 1987 Doordarshan was showing two serials every evening.

Matching India's obsession with movies and soaps is its preoccupation with religion. In 1989 Doordarshan staged a major religious revival by airing the two Hindu epics *Ramayana* and *Mahabharata.* For over a year, Indian audiences sat riveted as the stories about two mythical kingdoms unfolded across the screens of their television sets. During the hour-long episodes, of which there were more than 100 for the two epics, life came to a standstill as buses and trains lay empty while passengers and drivers alike watched the ancient drama on television sets in bus terminals and railway stations. For that hour, too, the television set became a shrine where devout Hindus took off their shoes, offered prayers, and sat reverently as they might in a temple. Quite suddenly, Indian audiences, which had long been fed a diet of well-meaning but dull programming, rediscovered the joys of television. The medium had finally come of age.

LAWS AND REGULATIONS

The only laws that regulate Indian broadcasting are two hopelessly outdated wireless and telegraph acts. The 1885 Indian Telegraph Act gives the Indian government exclusive rights to maintain and operate broadcasting and telecommunications systems in the country. The 1933 Indian Wireless Telegraphy Act gives the Indian government control over consumers by allowing it to collect license fees for radio and television sets.

The Indian Parliament passes laws that affect radio and television, but these have not been enacted in great abundance and have not significantly altered the original form of state-run broadcasting set up under the influence of the British. In 1990, responding to citizen pressure to make broadcasting more responsive to its audience, the Lok Sabha (House of Commons) passed the Prasar Bharati Corporation Bill granting more autonomy to AIR and Doordarshan. However, this bill has yet to be implemented by the government which wants more public debate on the subject.

Generally, what will and what will not be aired on All India Radio and on Doordarshan is dictated by a 1968 AIR code. While permitting the discussion of political and social policies followed by the government and various political parties, the code does not allow the broadcast of

Criticism of friendly countries

Attacks on religious or ethnic communities

Obscene, defamatory, inflammatory, and anarchic material

Content that undermines the integrity of the president of India, state governors, or the judiciary

Hostile criticisms of the state and center (federal government)

Content disrespectful of the Indian constitution

Content that advocates violence as a means for changing the Indian constitution

The code echoes many of the constitutional restrictions placed on the fundamental citizen rights of freedom of expression. Clause 2 of Article 19 of the Indian constitution gives the state the right to reasonably restrict such rights in the interests of the sovereignty and integrity of India, national security, public order, morality, decency, and the like. Many scholars argue that the code has often been so narrowly interpreted that it would make criticism and free discussion all but impossible.

Presently, the newer media (direct broadcast satellite and cable TV) are not regulated at all, in terms of either structure or content. The result is an entrepreneurial chaos of proliferation.

THE AUDIENCE

AIR and Doordarshan constantly monitor the impact of their programs and the attitudes of their listeners through their own audience research units. Field operatives of the units annually survey about 40,000 to 50,000 households and report their listening and viewing habits and preferences, as well as any attitude or behavior changes that have resulted from viewing AIR or Doordarshan programs, especially social programs. This information is sent back to program directors for use in modifying and adapting existing programs and in developing new programs.

However, a common complaint is that much of these data goes to waste since program directors have no control over program policy and are hampered by a slow-moving bureaucracy in their attempts to make any changes. As Mehra Masani says in *Broadcasting and the People*, AIR and Doordarshan are mired in bureaucratic red tape and suffer from "top-heavy officialdom, too much paper work, slowness of decision, unwillingness to admit shortcomings, a casual attitude to listeners, lack of flexibility in staffing and budgeting and therefore in planning programmes." In the words of Jeremy Tunstall, author of *The Media Are American*, "AIR is perhaps the least market-oriented national radio service ever operated in a sizable market."

In fairness, it must be noted that the Indian government in recent years has been trying to make broadcasting more responsive to its audience members. That was what stimulated the passage of the still-to-be-enacted Prasar Bharati Corporation Bill.

TECHNOLOGY

India is a land of paradox where it is not unusual to see a satellite dish pointing to the sky beside the spires of an ancient temple, and where Muslim clerics make the timeless call to prayer from the minarets of a mosque via microphone and loudspeaker. People not only travel vast distances by foot, rail, and airplane to visit holy shrines but also make electronic pilgrimages to their religious heritage through televised epics such as the *Ramayana* and the *Mahabharata*. And, as an *India Today* article puts it, "[Indian] housewives now discuss the latest episode of *The Bold and the Beautiful* and *Santa Barbara* with more animation than the vagaries of their cooks and dhobis [professionals who wash and iron clothes]."

What makes this physical and electronic movement across time and space possible is India's thoroughly modern communications and transportation technology. Crisscrossing India is the world's fourth-largest railway system. Its cities are connected by telex and interstate telephone systems which feed into about 5 million telephone receivers and rapidly growing numbers of computers and fax machines. The Indian Posts and Telegraphs Department provides microwave and telephone circuits for use by broadcasters, while the Overseas Communications Service connects India with the rest of the world by telegraph, telephone, and telex.

Satellite communication technology has vastly improved India's capacity to link remote and hitherto inaccessible parts of the nation. Since the early 1980s, Indian-designed, multipurpose communications satellites such as the Insat-IB, operating through 30 satellite earth receiving stations and about 400 relay centers, have boosted the reach of India's broadcasting, telecommunication, and meteorological services. Three more Insat satellites are scheduled to be launched in the 1990s. As previously mentioned, Hong Kong's AsiaSat1 satellite also covers India, greatly expanding television choices.

EXTERNAL SERVICES

In 1937 the newly formed Central News Organization, precursor of AIR's News Services Division, was preoccupied with composing news bulletins and commentaries for domestic consumption. But all that had changed by 1939. The imminent threat of war in Europe and the recognition that radio could be used as a potent propaganda weapon persuaded AIR to develop an external services wing.

In 1939 AIR reached its first international audience by broadcasting in the Pushtu language of Afghanistan. By September 1939 World War II had broken out in Europe, and AIR worked feverishly with the Far Eastern bureau of the British Ministry of Information to expand external broadcasts to counter the propaganda of Germany and its allies, notably Japan.

By 1945, when World War II ended, AIR was broadcasting seventy-four times each day in twenty-two languages to countries in the Middle East and south Asia.

The external services operations of AIR continued to grow after the war, informing international audiences about developments in India; promoting the Indian viewpoint on key national and international issues via commentaries, analyses, and interviews; and offering insights into Indian culture, traditions, arts, and music.

AIR separated External Services from News Services in 1949 and made it into an independent division. Today the External Services Division broadcasts sixty-eight daily bulletins in nineteen languages such as Arabic, Swahili, French, English, Indonesian, Chinese, and Russian. It also broadcasts international programs in Indian languages such as Bengali, Gujerati, Hindi, Punjabi, Sindhi, Tamil, and Urdu to countries such as Bangladesh and Sri Lanka as well as to Indians living abroad.

IMPORTANCE IN THE WORLD COMMUNITY

The size of India's population makes it an important player in any sort of world endeavor. It can provide more audience members than any other democratic country. However, it is a poor country and so does not attract those looking for quick economic gain.

It is the undisputed leader among the south Asian countries, seven of which have joined into a regional alliance known as the South Asian Association for Regional Corporation. The other six countries—Bangladesh, Bhutan, Maldives, Nepal, Pakistan, and Sri Lanka—look to India for leadership. However, some of the other countries have been quicker to incorporate the newer media into their electronic media structures. For example, Bangladesh has legalized satellite dishes and brought CNN free to every television household, and Nepal has a home-grown satellite service, Shangri-La. India will have to move forward in a formalized way if it is to remain a leader.

The film industry of India, the most prolific in the world, could become a program supplier if it concentrated on international distribution. The movies are criticized for their cookie cutter sameness, but they are extremely popular with the Indian people and would no doubt appeal to some of the services trying to fill the voracious appetite of international satellite delivery.

Likewise, television programs produced in India could be marketed to cable TV services located in areas with large Indian populations.

MAJOR ISSUES

All of the cable and satellite activity within India poses a problem for a government that never anticipated or addressed the issue of private broadcasting. Because its laws are so out of date, India is not equipped to deal with technology that rains pictures from around the world from space. Despite the experiences gained from SITE and from the Insat satellites, the Indian government has not attempted to incorporate this new and rapidly changing broadcasting technology into its laws.

The government also misjudged the Indian entrepreneurial spirit and the impact it would have on bringing cable and satellite-based television into India. The result has been that the government finds itself bereft of laws that can regulate cable operators and satellite dish owners. Unhappy with the flurry of unregulated cable activity that threatens to deprive AIR and Doordarshan of its listeners and viewers, the Indian government has promised to introduce laws regulating cable. When and in what shape remain to be seen.

The second issue the government faces that it never did when AIR and Doordarshan monopolized Indian broadcasting concerns changing its policies and programs to effectively counter the seductive programming of services such as STAR. Already in place are legislative bills such as the 1991 Prasar Bharati Corporation Bill granting more autonomy and programming flexibility to AIR and Doordarshan and allowing them to become more market- and listener-oriented. But long accustomed to having its own way and reluctant to relinquish control over radio and television, the Indian government has been slow to implement such measures.

Technology is the last major issue that the Indian government will have to grapple with. Competitors such as STAR and CNN are here to stay. The Indian government needs not only to figure out ways to allow these agencies to coexist with AIR and Doordarshan but also to put in place its own sophisticated satellite systems. It has acted to send into orbit its own satellites such as Insat-ID and Insat-2A. and three more satellites with C-band and Ku-band transponders are scheduled to go into orbit soon. These satellites will give Doordarshan enough transponders for itself as well as for leasing to private broadcasting companies.

Thus, the future of Indian broadcasting, as India prepares itself for the twenty-first century, appears to be chaotic but exciting and full of promise. Stay tuned.

SELECTED BIBLIOGRAPHY

Agarwal, Amit. "Fuzzy Picture," *India Today,* 15 November 1992, p. 31.

Bhatia, Jagdish. "An Epic Goes Electronic and India Gets Hooked," *Far Eastern Economic Review,* February 1988, pp. 70–73.

Chatterji, P. C. *Broadcasting in India.* New Delhi: Sage Publications, 1987.

Hanson, Jarice, and Uma Narula. "India: A Case Study." In *Communication Technologies in Developing Countries.* Hillsdale, NJ: Lawrence Erlbaum, 1990.

Ingelbrecht, Nick. "In India, a Market Slowly Develops," *Cableworld,* 30 November 1992, p. 120.

Krishnatray, Pradeep. "Radio and Television in India," *Combroad,* 1981, pp. 36–39.

Kumar, Keval J. *Mass Communication in India.* Bombay: Jaico, 1991.

Masani, Mehra. *Broadcasting and the People.* New Delhi: National Book Trust, 1976.

Nadkarni, Shirish. "Satellite Ends Doordarshan Party," *Asia-Pacific Broadcasting,* 30 November 1992, p. 14.

Palmer, Rhonda. "Stars in Their Eyes for Six New Channels," *Variety,* 5 April 1993, p. 59.

Panitt, Merrill. "In India, They'll Trash a Station . . . or Worship an Actor," *TV Guide,* June 4, 1988, pp. 44–45.

Rahman, M. "The New TV Superbazaar: Now at Your Fingertips," *India Today,* 15 November 1992, pp. 26–32.

Singhal, Arvind, and Everett Rogers. "Television Soap Operas for Development in India," *Gazette,* 41, 1988, pp. 109–26.

Sondhi, Krishan. *Problems of Communication in Developing Countries.* New Delhi: Vision, 1980.

Traub, James. "New Delhi Gold Rush," *Channels,* July–August 1986, pp. 34–35.

Tunstall, Jeremy. *The Media Are American.* New York: Columbia University Press, 1977.

Wallace, Charles P. "'Dish Wallahs' Plug India into the World," *Los Angeles Times,* 20 October 1992, p. H-8.

CHAPTER 11

China

Joseph S. Johnson

Joseph Johnson.

Joseph Johnson is professor and chairman of the Department of Telecommunications and Film in the School of Communication at San Diego State University, where he teaches courses in media management and performance. His Ph.D. is from Michigan State University. His other writings have been both for and about the media and include two books. A former broadcast executive, he regularly narrates educational and commercial films and television programs. He has traveled extensively in China and spent one year there as a foreign expert lecturing on American culture and mass media.

STATISTICS

Geographic Area: 3,696,100 square miles
Capital: Beijing
Population: 1,151,486,000
Religions: Officially atheist, but Confucianism, Buddhism, and Taoism are traditional
Languages: Mandarin (official); many local and regional dialects use the same nonalphabetic written language; the spoken language varies greatly.
Type of Government: Communist party–led state
Gross Domestic Product: $393 billion
Literacy: 70 percent

GENERAL CHARACTERISTICS

The modern People's Republic of China dates back to "Liberation," 1949, when the present government took over, instituting the existing pseudo-Marxist system of government and establishing present communication policies and infrastructure. China's sense of nation is far older, however, and its history is rich, filled with some of the world's greatest dynasties.

China has nearly one-fourth of the world's population, the world's largest standing army, and several of the world's largest cities, including Shanghai, Beijing, Chongquing, and Guangzhou, although three-fourths of the population lives in rural areas. (Chongquing is pronounced "chong ching," and Guangzhou, also known as Canton, is pronounced "gwong joe.")

Today China must be considered a developing nation. According to government figures, 1992 per capita income used as living expenses was $275 per year for urban residents and $125 for farmers.

Historical Facts China has undergone a great deal of adversity in the past century. A corrupt imperial dynasty rotted away, and warlords filled the void. Western powers bullied and exploited the nation, using opium as an instrument of foreign policy. There was a cruel invasion by Japan in the late 1930s. Extended civil wars finally ended when Mao Zedong's (pronounced "mow dzuh dong") ragtag army defied tremendous odds and won control of the country from the Kuomintang (Nationalist party) in 1949. The Nationalist party leaders fled to Taiwan where the Kuomintang remains the governing party.

Mao's army started out against tremendous odds and made one of the most amazing retreat maneuvers in military history, living off the land and making friends in the countryside. After holing up in caves in the cold north, they counterattacked until a combination of opposition corruption and Maoist tactical brilliance gave the present government power. "Liberation" began with the Maoists' consolidation of power and elimination of dissent.

Had Mao retired to let others run the new government, he would be universally considered one of history's great liberators. His later excesses have dimmed his luster, even in China, though he is credited with giving China back to the Chinese and restoring their sense of nationhood. The new government took power with widespread public support because it threw the foreigners out, it promised to correct the extremes of past exploitation by feudal lords of various stripe, and in a short time corrected a great number of wrongs.

Mao's reforms culminated in the Great Cultural Revolution between 1966 and 1976. An aging Mao, by then firmly in power, became increasingly corrupted by it, and paranoid. He encouraged the excesses of a new generation and institutionalized youthful rebellion. He encouraged the youthful Red Guards to throw away all vestiges of the past, including their rich cultural heritage, and to crush all opposition. Tests of ideological purity were everywhere. Enemies were sent away, jailed, or killed. Anything Western was considered bourgeois and unacceptable: in the West they grow flowers, so get rid of yours because they are a sign of bourgeois decadence; women in the West wear long hair and makeup, so cut your hair and lose the makeup; and get rid of all temples and monuments that remind of the past.

Mao's little red book became assigned reading for the nation, in some cases the only safe reading. Populations were forced to move to places their leaders assigned them to. Universities were shut down. The youth were sent to the country to "learn from the peasants." Cities like Shanghai were felt to be overpopulated, and so many of their youth were sent elsewhere and not allowed to return. People who were teens and young adults during this time call themselves "the lost generation." The Great Cultural Revolution was a cataclysmic occurrence.

Then, in 1976, Mao died.

A more pragmatic Deng Xiaoping (pronounced "dung show ping") was brought back from exile in the countryside far from Beijing, where he had been a waiter, and ascended to senior leader status. Deng had earlier been a major leader under Mao, was banished by him, brought back, and banished again. As Mao's successor, Deng played down ideological purity, saying that it was "not so important what color a cat is, so long as it catches mice." Relations with the Soviet Union, which Mao had cultured, soured. Tentative relations with the West resumed. Deng said to "let a thousand flowers bloom," meaning to let different viewpoints be heard. This new openness soon led to a testing of how far it could lead. In 1978 Deng felt that it had gone too far, and he ordered a crackdown on students.

Still, things became much looser than in Mao's time. Deng's own children studied at U.S. universities. Chinese were encouraged to study English because it was considered the language of science and technology. Russian professors at the universities were recycled and assigned to teach English. Cultural exchanges were resumed, including the importation of some Western films and television programs.

Deng, who is in his eighties, went into semiretirement gradually in the late 1980s but remained the senior leader, the one with the most influence. He gave up all his official posts, including party secretary and chairman of the military commission, yet he remained in power. He never built a cult of personality as Mao did. He shared credit, consulted more, and kept a lower profile.

By sheer force of will, even after becoming old and feeble, Deng consolidated his power and tried to make sure his reforms would be continued by gently moving old Bolshevik leaders aside, bringing in new people who endorsed his free-market reforms. The 1992 party congress, in a significant reinforcement of Deng's vision and a blow to conservative hard-liners, affirmed the reforms. One of his last major public appearances was a trip to the coastal special economic zones, areas of the country that have been given free rein to develop economically using capitalistic free market policies. Deng's trip gave him an opportunity to proclaim publicly that these zones were the model of future Chinese economic development.

China is presently in transition toward its third phase of Communist leadership. Deng is still the leader, and no one is sure what position the emerging leaders of the future will take.

This background is important in order to understand the workings of the media. However the organization charts read in China, the reality is that the senior leader sets the tone for the nation, especially for something as pervasive and obvious as the messages in the press and electronic media, and particularly when the leadership believes that all communications are ideological and political and that their purpose is to serve the needs of those in charge. People who create programs and write news stories perform those functions with that background firmly ingrained. They are accustomed to being told what to do.

The Land and Its People With a landmass roughly the same size as that of the United States, China has more than four times as many people. It has great natural resources, including a long seacoast and two of the world's major river systems long used for irrigation and transportation. Its various dynasties were among the world's richest and most accomplished, with a historic reverence for the scholar and for learning in general. It has long been a highly populated country where an agrarian population raised large families to help with the crops. In the mid–twentieth century the government encouraged large families as a matter of national policy in order to accomplish the work leaders felt needed to be done. In recent years, however, government policy has been to control population growth by allowing most couples to have only one child.

Beginning in 1949 China began looking toward the Soviet Union for trade, and the Soviets provided assistance in the training of leadership and the setting up of new institutions, including the media. Eventually relations with the Soviets deteriorated as a result of border disputes and hegemony, and the Chinese began to steer a more independent course. China has sought leadership among Third World nations, including Arab nations in the Middle East. Recently it has looked increasingly toward the more prosperous Western nations for economic linkups. Its relationship with the regional economic power Japan has been wary, as the Chinese have had a hard time forgiving the Japanese for invading their country in the period leading up to World War II.

Other nations look at China and see over a billion potential customers. China looks at itself and sees a large population capable of producing goods to sell to the richer nations. Presently, the U.S. balance-of-payments deficit with China is the second largest in the world, behind Japan's.

In this decade China has had the fastest-growing major economy in the world. This reflects several things. It reflects dramatic real growth. It reflects previous underdevelopment; such dramatic percentage increases are rare in already highly developed large economies. It reflects the success of special economic zones where previous restrictions have been lifted and Chinese ingenuity and free-market concepts have been allowed to operate. It reflects a skilled workforce and incredibly low wages, including the use of prison labor to produce cheap products. It reflects the results of simply being allowed to trade with the rest of the world.

The special economic zones have become very freewheeling for China in more ways than just economic. Shenzhen (pronounced "shun jun"), near Guangzhou (Canton), is practically a suburb of Hong Kong, a very Westernized country that is to return to full control of the Chinese government in Beijing in 1997. Wages in Shenzhen are at least double the national average, and people have been given fairly free access to move there to take these jobs. The result is that the area increasingly emulates Hong Kong, whose unbridled capitalism is close to being the antithesis of everything the mainland has stood for the last forty-plus years. Hong Kong manufacturing jobs have been moving inside China, while Hong Kong has provided the management expertise and the outside marketing contacts. In this area, the dominant media consumption is the more diverse and open Hong Kong electronic media, circumventing Beijing control.

In the Yellow Mountains a path leads hikers for several hours up steep hills through the kind of scenery celebrated in Chinese scroll paintings. Perhaps the most scenic vista of the hike is along a narrow mountaintop that is called the Carp's Backbone. Even people with little fear of heights can feel a bit of vertigo walking along the rocky mountaintop that falls away sharply on either side. The view out across the other mountains is exhilarating, but a misstep to right or left could result in falling into a canyon. In the latter part of the Deng era the Chinese government has been walking the Carp's Backbone, attempting to open the country to foreign trade and expand the economy while preserving its central control over the institutions of government, media, and public life.

The leaders have seen what has happened to the Soviet Union, the government after which China's was most closely modeled, and the countries of Eastern Europe. They have seen the results of the economic collapse of those centrally planned economies. They have also seen the role outside media played in the fall of the old governments in those other countries. They want to have it both ways in their country, communism with Chinese characteristics—free-market economic reforms without the loss of control, free market without free thought.

They haven't yet proven that it can be done over the long run. For now the party remains in control because it has the army behind it and because it has moved the economy along, relying less religiously on central planning and allowing for more flexibility in developing economic growth. At the same time, the government has severely limited mass distribution of outside messages into the country and has stifled dissent.

It is impossible to think of China without thinking of the Great Wall. China was and is a nation of walls, a Great Wall, smaller walls around cities, factories, and compounds, and cultural walls indicating mistrust of those outside and even inside the walls.

Media Traits Chinese media are a mix of Chinese, Soviet, and Western influences. The government retains direct media control to reinforce the rightness of government policies and the validity of government. Media are there to unify the country in thought and in language. Chinese leaderships look at all media messages as having cultural and political effects and are not so sure there is such a thing as pure entertainment. To be sure, there is entertainment in the electronic media, but that entertainment must be consistent with national goals.

The mass media in China are clearly supplemental to more direct personal communication. The country is tightly organized from the top down, and word is passed quickly through interpersonal channels, with follow-up through those same channels. China is not a society of memos. It is a very oral society, a nation of grapevines and gossip. Interpersonal communication is used to sort out information received from media and other official sources. In general, family and close friends' opinions and observations have the highest credibility, then foreign media, and then Chinese media.

Language unification is a major concern throughout the country, and the government has assigned the media a major role. China has made great strides toward universal literacy since 1949. Because the language is written in characters simplified from pictures without an alphabetic representation of sounds, pronunciation varies widely by region and there are numerous dialects. One of the stated aims of government is to have everyone speaking and understanding *putonghua*, the dialect of Beijing, and that dialect is heard nationally on radio and television. Without one common language it would be difficult to create the necessary harmony and unity to be one country.

Throughout the country there are many fewer electronic media channels than in the West. The number of television and radio signals available varies by size of city, but virtually every small and medium-sized city in the West has more TV stations than even Beijing or Shanghai. The largest cities have four or five TV channels. At least two of them are from the national TV service, China Central Television (CCTV). The rest are provincial or local stations. Cable television is just beginning, though it has long been common for factories and residential compounds to have closed-circuit master antenna–type systems.

Individual TV sets within the home are now common, particularly in the cities, but a dominant pattern is to share one set among extended family members or to watch on sets available for common viewing in lounges and public locations. Availability is much greater than simply counting the number of sets would indicate.

The use of videocassette recorders (VCRs) is still limited, but the VCR is often used to acquire programs that are not available through normal channels, including bootleg copies of films and sexually explicit materials.

Education and training for media positions are evolving. University courses in media are much less common in China than in the United States, and many fewer students study the subject. The Beijing Broadcasting Institute was founded in 1959 to offer courses in engineering and technical operations, announcing, reporting, and a full range of broadcasting-related instruction, though a heavy emphasis is on the technical side. In addition to a 4-year course of study, the institute offers a 3-year advanced program. The Beijing Broadcasting Institute is highly selective, perhaps more so than any U.S. university, stating that "Admission will not be given to any candidate who opposes either in words or action the socialist road, the people's democratic dictatorship, the leading role of the Communist party, and Marxism-Leninism and Mao Zedong thought." Those specific qualifications are universal for Chinese universities. Chinese universities have little general education, and therefore a greater concentration of courses in the major, and mandatory Marxism courses. Students in media also study Chinese history and culture.

Other leading university media programs in China are available at Fudan University in Shanghai and at Hinan in Guangzhou. About thirty other universities have courses of study. China's news agency, Xinhua (pronounced "sheen hwah"), operates its own journalism school, in part to train Chinese to be foreign correspondents. In the 1980s a number of Chinese began to come to the United States and Europe for media studies, and American professors were brought in to teach in China.

THE DEVELOPMENT OF ELECTRONIC MEDIA IN CHINA

Early China operated as a society and a large, powerful nation in good part because of its systems of roads, communications, and walls. Chinese contributions to the printing press are well known. Modern China has made mass media an important part of governmental control and national development.

Radio's Development The nation's first radio station began operation in January 1923 in Shanghai. Set up by an American, it operated with 50,000 watts of power with the call letters XRO. Other early radio stations were also established by foreigners, who had set up exclusive foreign settlements in Chinese cities and were practicing robber baron capitalism.

The first Chinese-run station began operation in Harbin in 1925. By 1928 the Nationalist party was running its own radio station, the Central Broadcasting Station. By the late 1920s regulations had been established governing radio, and several other privately run stations went on the air, though set penetration remained low. Shanghai was the center of broadcast activity. During the Japanese invasion and occupation, from 1937 until the end of World War II in 1945, development was curtailed.

During the 1940s the Communists set up their own primitive services, which grew as their power grew. Early on, Mao realized the importance of activities that would sell his ideas to the people. He made great use of guerrilla theater to dramatize the sins of the opposition Nationalist party and promote the values he espoused. Like all revolutionaries of our time, he and his fellow revolutionaries made attempts to capture and control existing radio stations. They set up their own stations and consider the present system of broadcasting to have begun with their first radio station in 1940, built with a Russian transmitter and scavenged parts. It operated out of caves and partially destroyed buildings under very difficult conditions.

With the war victory, the Communist party took over all broadcasting and established the Central China Broadcasting Station (CPBS) in Beijing. Eventually the CPBS signal was sent to the entire country. In addition, some regional and local stations were established to bring people information of local interest.

The Development of Television Experimentation with television began in 1956, and by 1960 stations in a dozen cities were transmitting programs. Few viewers had sets, and programming was sporadic. The first television station in 1958 was initially called Beijing Television and then took the name China Central Television and became the heart of what eventually became a national TV service. As in the case of radio, local and regional stations also grew throughout the country, particularly in the more populous areas.

Color TV began in 1973 and became widespread in the 1980s. Most of the sets sold are made domestically, about 26 million in 1991, of which just under half were color sets. In 1980 China began to distribute TV programs throughout its vast country by microwave, and now it relies heavily on satellites. Local stations have also regularly traded program tapes.

Newer Media Newer forms of media have been slow to come to China. VCR penetration is very low, but VCR units are highly desired, and their use is increasing. There are few video rental outlets, but there is active smuggling and sharing. Western nations have long been critical of China for being casual about paying copyright fees. There are privately operated small viewing lounges throughout the country, unofficial backroom places, some with racy videos. The government periodically announces a crackdown on such places.

The public is very much aware of Hong Kong–based TV, though most in the country do not have access to it. Officially, it is illegal to own home satellite dishes in China, but some people do and thus have access to STAR TV and other signals that can be received within the Chinese borders. For a time, authorities ignored this satellite reception, although they did make sure that Cable News Network and BBC news were blanked out except in tourist hotels and the like. Then in October 1993 (coinciding with media mogul Rupert Murdoch buying into STAR), the Chinese authorities announced a crackdown on unauthorized satellite dishes, along with a crackdown on other unauthorized communication devices such as wireless phones.

A trial broadcast of experimental TV at a facility that became a local TV station in the province of Shaanxi in 1960. (*Photo courtesy of Shaanxi Television Station.*)

This follows a familiar pattern—permitting events to continue until they appear to be too threatening and then issuing a warning and exercising more firm control. In loudly announcing the satellite receiver ban, the Central Ministry of Radio, Film, and Television cited a "nonstop effort" by foreigners to "undermine China's stability."

Perhaps the future of electronic media development in China can be seen in what has happened in Shanghai during the 1990s. In 1991 Shanghai had the national CCTV service and two local channels. Shanghai and four other local governments then received permission to import entertainment shows without prior review from Beijing. Two new channels were started, Shanghai TV and Oriental TV. Shows like *Falcon Crest* and *Dynasty*, as well as U.S. movies, are included in the 30 percent of programs coming from foreign sources. Shanghai TV uses extensive excerpts from BBC World Service news broadcasts. Oriental TV became the first broadcaster in China to use live feeds from a foreign broadcaster when it reached an agreement to carry the Academy Awards live. During that broadcast, actor Richard Gere criticized China for human rights abuses, and the screen went blank for a time. Also in Shanghai, a cable network of eleven channels was started, using fiber-optic cable, with 700,000 subscribers by the end of 1993. All these services mentioned are essentially advertiser-supported.

Tiananmen Square One of the most intriguing aspects of modern China's television history involves the Tiananmen Square demonstration of 1989, which became a major worldwide media event. International media had been allowed into the country in unprecedented numbers to cover the state visit of Mikhail Gorbachev, then head of the Soviet Union. China was attempting to demonstrate to the world its new openness by allowing these media in to cover the event live and in the process to send a message to the world of its importance on the world scene. It was planned to be a grand ceremonial media event.

But China's own citizens had learned quickly about using the media and turned this event into an opportunity to publicly embarrass the leadership by demonstrating for additional freedoms and government reforms, and an irony is that if the government had not loosened up from earlier times, such an event could not have happened. The media sources were seduced by this high drama, with its strong visual elements, staged in a world-famous public location with good media access. In fact, the main difference between this event and what happened in 1978 (when Deng cracked down on students) was that outside media were present this time. The demonstrators showed they knew how TV works and how the improved Beijing infrastructure, including fax machines and direct-dial long distance, could be used to help get their message out.

Pesky CNN was able to get live pictures out to the world even after the government began to restrict media access. Dan Rather's tireless CBS coverage included his on-air negotiations with local officials before being shut down during a broadcast. Many pictures, including the celebrated one of a young man facing down a tank, are burned into our memories.

The government finally succeeded in shutting down foreign coverage, brought in troops, and stopped the demonstrations, killing protesters in the process. They jammed outside signals coming into the country to keep citizens from knowing what was taking place. They are still denying to their own public that much of what took place at Tiananmen Square really happened.

Tourism, an important source of foreign exchange dollars, immediately shrank dramatically. Foreign companies rethought business ties. Government conservatives were quite vocal for a while and brought pressure to reconsider economic reforms and the nation's more open relations. But Deng persisted, saying that free-market reforms would stay and that outside contacts would continue. By the mid-1990s the nation was as open as it had been since "Liberation," and the economy was booming. China made a serious bid to host the Olympic Games in the year 2000, but the world nations that had witnessed what they called the Tiananmen Massacre voted instead to give the games to Sydney.

ORGANIZATION AND FINANCING

Chinese radio and television receive direct government funding and supervision. The national radio service is China Central Broadcasting, and the national television service is China Central Television, both from Beijing. There are also local and regional radio and TV stations. The Central Committee of the Communist party controls the national services directly, while the regional and local stations are responsible to local party officials.

The national CCTV service operates three TV channels, but many parts of the country can receive only two of them. Major cities have up to two additional channels of their own, but some areas of the country have no local channels. Many of the services do not operate full-time. Further, when the national CCTV news or other major programming is on, all channels carry it. At other times local stations carry programs they produce, programs they trade with other local stations, and some programs they acquire from other sources.

CPBS operates five radio services that cover most of the country. As in the case of TV, there are also regional and local radio stations.

Most of the funding comes from the government; Chinese citizens do not pay media license fees. Commercials are permitted, and, in the emerging economy, advertising revenues are welcome sources of support. Radio and TV are being encouraged to become totally self-supporting through advertising, but media services are considered to be so vital that their continued government funding is quite secure.

Advertising Advertising first appeared on television in the post-Mao reform period in 1979, though the government itself has always been a major practitioner of institutional advertising using wall posters, billboards, kiosks, and all of the mass media. Huge billboards promoting the one-child policy, or the four modernizations, or "If we all work together we can stamp out rats" are a way of life.

Product advertising is increasingly common, and local commercials that once were voice-over stock footage are becoming increasingly sophisticated. Foreign companies often advertise products before they become available in China as a way of getting entry into the market. The government encourages advertising competition among the various product providers as a method of raising quality and lowering prices. Institutional image commercials are also quite common. Commercials do not interrupt programs but appear between programs or during natural breaks. Some of these breaks have become quite long, however, reaching 5 minutes, and are longer on weekends.

By Western standards ad rates are very low, but rising—to reach the entire Chinese audience costs less than buying an ad on a local station in many U.S. cities. Foreigners have to pay about three times what domestic advertisers pay, just as foreigners do for everything else in China. The Japanese are the largest foreign advertisers.

Most products and most advertising are in a universal mode, touting the usefulness of a product, the benefits to the consumer, its advantages over other products, and of course image. But some ads are quite colorful and even outlandish. Cigarettes have claimed that they are health-promoting, even on the label—a government-owned business yet. Cigarettes are a major source of government profit, although in January 1992 the government announced some changes out of concern for health effects. The Marlboro man has been successfully introduced into China, and his rugged individualism has been a hit; the horse has mythic values in China.

A sports drink advertised "Jianlibao can make you strong." Health claims for an earthworm fluid tell of marvelous results for those who drink the substance (yes, it is extract of earthworm). A brand of dried cherries claimed to be high in protein (we should hope not). Some claims seem strange to us—a brand of citrus-based sports drink claimed it "promotes expectorate." (Most foreigners think there is too much spitting already.) A restaurant advertised "three-snake gallbladder," including takeout service.

PROGRAMMING

Television programming is much more limited than in the West, both in number of channels and hours of operation, but it is growing. Within the more limited options there is nonetheless considerable diversity. China Central Television carries a combination of types of programs that would be found on public and commercial networks in the United States—news, variety shows, educational and instructional programs, dramas, serials, sports coverage, and the like.

Ideas for programs and the productions themselves undergo an elaborate multilayered review process. This process becomes more or less stringent according to the times and current sensitivities. Recently some programs have been produced in record time.

Apart from news, very little of what is seen on CCTV is produced at its own facilities. Much of it is created in Chinese film studios. These studios are quite competent and have been for a long time, though they have had a reputation for turning out stodgy, ideologically laced formulaic productions. In the 1980s the Xian Film Studio gathered a group of talented young filmmakers who made visually stunning films on modern themes and broke new ground for Chinese film. These filmmakers influenced Chinese television to become more topical, more questioning, and more satiric.

Although most of the programming is of domestic origin, emanating either from Chinese TV studios or film studios, programs from other nations are also shown. CCTV and the local stations regularly carry programs obtained from the BBC, particularly classic dramas. A surprising amount of U.S. programming can be seen, given the national concern about "spiritual pollution." *Hunter* and *Falcon Crest* were both viewed by large numbers of Chinese. U.S. films are shown on a regular basis, many of them the kind that have long since run on all the U.S. independent stations. CCTV has carried the Iditarod dogsled races from Alaska, the Super Bowl, the NBA All-Star Game, and a fairly wide variety of other sports. Table 1 shows weekend programming highlights on CCTV and two local Beijing stations. Included at the bottom are the regular morning and afternoon programs.

News The government-approved evening news is carried everywhere on every channel without competition at the dinner hour. Official figures say that CCTV news is watched by 84 percent of viewers in China. The first 15 minutes of the program show pictures of progress—computers, bustling factories, happy workers, helpful soldiers, and many many pictures of party leaders sitting in meetings smoking and drinking tea or touring places of progress where everybody smiles and shakes hands. Following that is a generally evenhanded account of world events, including a number of Western news stories picked off satellites. It is not uncommon to see Peter Jennings or Diane Sawyer with the original audio turned down and a dubbed sound track.

Striking to someone raised on U.S. news is the absence of conflict. News in the United States is reported by people trained to believe that the essence of drama is conflict, and critical views are sought. A Chinese citizen, hearing what Democrats and Republicans have to say about each other, would hardly realize that the adversaries may very well go out together afterward for drinks. Such open public conflicts,

TABLE 1

TYPICAL CCTV PROGRAMMING

Saturday		Sunday	
Channel 2, CCTV		**Channel 2, CCTV**	
19:36	Across the Country: On China's Territory: Hebei Province	19:49	Observation and Reflection
19:49	World Today	20:45	41-part Series: I Love You Definitely (32)
20:05	41-part Series: I Love You Definitely (31)	21:43	14-part TV Special: A Trip to Guangdong (9)
21:03	Everyone's TV	22:29	US Feature Film: Lion (2 Parts)
21:24	14-part TV Documentary: A Trip to Guangdong (8)	**Channel 8, CCTV**	
23:51	Five-part Series: The Year of Dragon (5)	11:25	TV Play: Black Cat Shock Brigade
Channel 8, CCTV		14:15	Feature Film: Unvanished Electric Waves
18:14	Series: Auntie Kaili Tells Science Stories (93)	16:56	Children's Programmes
19:30	The CT Group Programmes (141): 1. The Wonderful World 2. Facing the World 3. Chiatai Stage	18:13	Series: Auntie Kaili Tells Science Stories (94)
		19:30	Live Telecast: '93 Beijing World Cup Swimming Contest
21:30	Economy 30 Minutes	21:30	Economy 30 Minutes
22:55	English Programmes for Foreigners	22:40	French Programmes
Channel 15, CCTV		**Channel 15, CCTV**	
19:30	26-part TV Series: Jasmine Flower in Blossom (19–22)	19:30	26-part Series: Jasmine Flowers in Blossom (23–26)
22:58	Opera Special	**Channel 6, BTV**	
Channel 6, BTV		08:30	Children's Programmes
19:36	Film News	09:25	TV Market
19:41	Beijing Today	12:00	News Roundup in the Past Week
20:07	On TV Next Week	13:44	Grand View of Science (171)
20:23	Economic Hotline	15:24	Economy and Society 18 Minutes
20:28	Sanyo TV Theatre: 34-part Japanese Series: Sweet and Sour Apples (15)	15:44	Grand View Garden
		17:41	Cartoon World
22:16	41-part Series: Emperor Qianlong (8–9)	18:11	News Roundup in the Past Week
		19:41	Beijing Today
23:56	Life Guide	19:57	On TV Next Week
Channel 21, BTV		20:29	American Series
17:36	Series "Stories of a Newsroom"	23:02	British Detective Series
		Channel 21, BTV	
19:30	Children's Programmes	17:37	Series "Stories of a Newsroom"
20:29	Tonight We Meet (59)	19:34	Children's Programmes
21:09	The Window of China (2)	20:38	Global Sports (83)
22:04	English Programmes: 1. Looking at China; 2. Capital Guide; 3. Entertainment Theatre	21:28	TV Market
		21:46	BTV Response (12)
		22:06	English Programme

Regular programmes

Channel 2		21:35	Economy 30 Minutes (Monday to Sunday)
09:00	News (Monday to Sunday)	22:00	News (Monday to Sunday)
12:00	News (Monday to Sunday)	22:30	News in English
12:15	Economy 30 Minutes (Monday to Saturday)	**Channel 6**	
13:10	Weather Report	18:11	Story-telling (Monday to Friday)
19:00	News (Monday to Sunday)	18:40	Beijing News and Weather Report (Monday to Sunday)
22:00	Night News (Monday to Sunday)		
22:10	Sports News (Monday to Saturday)	19:00	News (Monday to Sunday)
Channel 8		19:36	Across Beijing
10:00	News (Monday to Sunday)	21:50	News (Monday to Sunday)
13:00	News (Monday to Sunday)	**Channel 21**	
13:15	Economy 30 Minutes (Monday to Sunday Except Tuesday)	17:31	Series
		19:30	Children's Programmes

with sharp questioning of government decisions and opposing points of view, are simply nonexistent in Chinese media.

The news also does not make a point of covering disasters. A flood in Sichuan Province may not be reported until 3 days later, and the slant of the story would be how well authorities have worked to clean up. To be sure, the news media cannot totally ignore disasters, but the spin on stories is generally on the heroism of those who rescued or fixed or were saved.

In China newspaper reporters do most of the heavy news gathering and story origination, and television illustrates these stories, except for those major visual stories and scheduled events, particularly ceremonial ones, that television can cover so well. As in the West, the heaviest use of print media is by those with the most education and those in leadership positions.

While television news is widely accessible, there are categories of newspapers that the average person does not get to see, four levels of restricted publications representing in a sense four levels of power and access or four levels of trust. These are in addition to the general-circulation papers posted on bulletin boards all around the country. *Reference News* is relatively widespread though not available to all. It is a compilation of news stories from foreign sources, mostly wire services. Slightly more restricted is *Reference Material,* a more detailed account of these articles, and in large print for easy reading by elderly eyes. Next are the internal documents distributed only to deputy cabinet ministers, status reports on the various areas of responsibility, prepared by each ministry. At the top of the secrecy ladder is *Cable News,* available only to the Central Committee and top military commanders. *Cable News* is the most candid and accurate of the news sources. There really is no television equivalent of these restricted publications, though the top party leaders have access to foreign satellite coverage that the average person is not allowed to see.

The Central Committee of the Communist party controls the major media entities directly, including the newspaper, *People's Daily,* Xinhua news agency, and central broadcasting. Reporters quickly learn to self-censor, being conditioned to present what is acceptable.

Both print and electronic media are given the responsibility to serve a national watchdog function for the nation, to build it according to approved principles. They are specifically given the task of criticism, though this must be within certain bounds. Sincere efforts to improve the country are fair game. Criticism of the central leadership is not.

This concept deserves elaboration. Criticism is commonly used to bring all sectors of society into conformity. Party leaders can call into line reporters or producers or anybody in society who may not be doing his or her job to the satisfaction of the leaders. This may involve talking to individuals privately, and if they are contrite enough, they are asked to confess their sins publicly as part of their rehabilitation. This is sometimes done quite lovingly, with public acceptance for pleas of forgiveness. If the leaders feel the individual is not contrite enough, the criticism may not be as benevolent. It will also be public, but the person may be criticized or even vilified by others. Under Deng, this practice has been used more as a tool of rehabilitation. Under Mao, particularly during the Cultural Revolution, it was a way of publicly humiliating and banishing people who could not prove they were sufficiently orthodox. This concept of public criticism to improve the nation and enforce orthodox thought and behavior has become part of the responsibility of mass media.

Watching television news is encouraged, as it promotes conformity to national behavior and goals. The government prefers to accomplish this with a light touch, as a gentle breeze that leaves no traces. At the time of Tiananmen the touch was heavier, and the army occupied newspaper offices and TV studios to make sure that orders were being followed. As an editorial in *People's Daily* put it, "As soon as elements of turmoil appear, we will not hesitate to take any means whatsoever to eliminate them as quickly as possible."

One 1993 incident illustrates how harsh the authorities can be in dealing with a seemingly minor incident. A Chinese journalist provided an advance copy of a speech by party secretary Jiang Zemin to a Hong Kong journalist. The copy was given one day in advance and was accurate. No new policies or international incidents or state secrets were involved. The speech was given as planned. It was the kind of thing that happens all the time in open societies, without penalties, but this journalist was sentenced to life in prison for circulating the advance copy.

China has seen periods of public and media openness—in the early 1960s, late 1970s, and mid-1980s—followed by periods of restriction. The periods of change have often been quite rapid. Following the brief chill after Tiananmen, the society has been relatively open, particularly as the nation was trying to put its best foot forward in hopes of getting the Olympics. When that bid was unsuccessful, there was a brief period of lashing out at various enemies. The general trend has been toward a cautious opening up.

Other TV Programming Sports programming is very popular in China. The whole nation literally stops to gather around a TV set when events showing Chinese excelling in world competition are presented. The women's volleyball team and Olympic champions have become national heroes. A champion gymnast cut a best-selling album as a singer. Domestic sporting events showing teams from such sports as soccer, basketball, and team handball are popular. The government is making the development of world-class Olympic athletes a major priority and has imported East German coaches to help.

A live broadcast of the closing ceremonies of a young people's sports meet. (*Eastfoto*)

During the Deng years China seems to have gradually become comfortable celebrating its cultural heritage, and programs such as Chinese opera, classical drama, and traditional music are produced.

A number of different types of educational programs are scheduled on a regular basis. Nearly a million people are enrolled in televised courses. China started the Television University in 1960, a full 10 years before Britain's Open University. The most popular courses have been instruction in English, although a great deal of math and science is also taught. An estimated 200 million Chinese have studied some English.

General-appeal English-language programs are also aired nationally to help Chinese learn the "language of science and technology." One

A scene from a televised Chinese opera. (*New China Pictures/Eastfoto*)

of the best known English speakers in the country has been an "overseas Chinese" woman who has hosted a program called *One World*, a weekly program featuring soft travelogs of different places all over the world, all showing pretty pictures and nice people.

The Chinese operate an agricultural radio and television broadcast education network to spread education in rural areas and promote agricultural production. Many of the other programs are simply for the greater good of the society, and any caring society would want to spread that kind of knowledge.

Audio Programming Radio is reminiscent of the BBC. It is less popular, less youth-oriented than radio in the United States, though there are programs that feature light popular music. There are also serious music, news, talks, sports events, educational programs, and features. Entertainment and sports make up just over half of all programming, with news at about 14 percent. There are still places where television is scarce, and so radio is relatively important.

Some programming is in English, and there is foreign-language instruction in English, Japanese, French, and German. One curious thing to us is that Radio Beijing broadcasts in Esperanto four times a day (and there are Esperanto clubs all over the country). Music accounts for about one-third of programming on CPBS, which is heard throughout the country on several frequencies simultaneously, carrying five programs at a time. The program that claims the largest audience is a summary of reports from the nation's largest newspapers. Talk radio has recently come to Shanghai, and people have begun to speak fairly explicitly about sexual and other personal matters on the air—a dramatic change for China—but so far there has been no criticism of government.

There is an extensive popular music industry. The variety of cassette tapes is more diverse than what is heard on radio. Radio music is mostly sedate, often with melodic string arrangements of songs from the West. Surprisingly, there is a lot of music by Stephen Foster and Jerome Kern. Many of the most popular performers among the youth are from Hong Kong and Taiwan, with a lot of bouncy, sugary dance music and a much tamer music scene than in the West. There is an amazing array of pirated tapes of every sort, from a recent Michael Jackson tape to old Kenny Rogers and John Denver tapes. In the presence of dissonant jazz or hard rock most Chinese become uncomfortable, as if they were being corrupted. Much music from the West has replaced traditional Chinese forms, though there are still many who play erhu, flute, and Chinese percussion in order to perform traditional pieces.

Another form of audio programming involves an elaborate loudspeaker system throughout China. These speakers extend the reach of radio beyond just those who have their own sets. Many of these loudspeakers are located outside living and work units. They go on at 6 A.M. to wake people up and get them on their way with programming official announcements, bouncy wake-up music, and an exercise lady—*yi, er, san, si* (one, two, three, four). Official government figures list 83 million of these loudspeakers nationwide. They are found in surprising numbers in rural areas, where group housing allows a single speaker to reach many people. Most farms have land surrounding apartment buildings rather than having individual housing units scattered among the farmland.

LAWS AND REGULATIONS

National broadcasting headquarters are in close physical proximity to government headquarters and are very responsive to central leadership. The Ministry of Radio, Movies, and Television is China's highest administrative authority for the media. In 1991 alone it ratified 138 new regulations, including a facilities protection law, cable TV regulation, regulation of programs received by satellite, and review and approval of foreign TV plays. The 1991 regulations regarding journalism ethics covered the following.

1. Serving the people wholeheartedly
2. Taking social benefit as the highest norm
3. Observing laws and regulations
4. Safeguarding the truthfulness of news
5. Persisting in the principle of objectivity and justice
6. Maintaining honesty in performing duties
7. Adhering to the spirit of unity and cooperation
8. Promoting friendly international cooperation

A comprehensive review and revision of regulations is continuing as China continues to modernize and adapt.

Media practitioners sometimes must deny what their eyes and ears tell them if those things conflict with the ideologies and directions of their leaders. To be sure, throughout the world all people of power and influence try to present their best public face and try to manipulate media portrayals of them and their causes. But in China the influence is direct and firm. The 1993 Chinese Cannes Film Festival prize-winning film, *Farewell, My Concubine,* cannot be distributed in its country of origin because it portrays homosexuality and is politically incorrect. The role of the media is to reinforce, not fight, the system.

One interesting aspect of government influence concerns the Chinese news agency Xinhua. In Hong Kong, it operates as the Chinese shadow government. Ostensibly a Chinese version of the Associated Press, in reality the Hong Kong office has many more police, government policy makers, and government functionaries than journalists. Estimates are that reporters are less than 5 percent of the workers in the Hong Kong Xinhua office. Beijing has become increasingly assertive in the affairs of Hong Kong, resisting proposed British political reforms, but at the same time it is integrating Hong Kong into the mainland economy. It uses the Xinhua office to try to balance its diplomatic concerns.

THE AUDIENCE

There are no equivalents to Nielsen or Arbitron ratings in China, though the government makes surveys of various sorts to assist in decision making. Published statistics tend to be self-serving. By all measures and estimates, internal and external, Chinese television and radio are popular and widely used, and use is growing dramatically.

Enthusiasm for the medium is mindful of U.S. television in its early days, with the same sense of wonder at all the new things the expanding medium brings. In a nation that loves lanterns, television is clearly a magic lantern. In a nation where people travel very little, television brings the nation and the world home. Television set penetration has not nearly reached saturation, particularly in rural areas, and a high proportion of sets are still black and white, and so there is much room for growth.

A recent Beijing survey showed that 30 percent of people watched TV daily, 57 percent watched frequently, and the remainder watched occasionally, with the average time spent watching at about 3 hours a day. In rural areas availability is probably much less, for now. In another survey comparing media use, 64 percent of respondents said they learned of national and international events from radio, 25 percent from television, and 11 percent from newspapers.

In a 1988 nationwide survey, CPBS radio estimated that its first two national channels had 623 million listeners and that about 60 percent of the population listened regularly. Of listeners, 70 percent said they listened to news regularly.

Complaints about the media do abound, and some sound remarkably like those heard in the United States. A 1992 study criticized CCTV for the very small amount of programming for children (reasons given for the dearth could have come from U.S. broadcast executives). Parents worry about what their children watch, worry that it takes too much time away from homework, complain about the cartoons, and claim that programs teens watch are contributing to rudeness and lack of respect for everything. Political leaders worry about the corrupting effects on society.

One friend said he had saved for 3 years to buy a set, limiting consumption of meat, cutting back on movies, and delaying purchase of clothes to come up with the money. Then he got his new set and now says that too much of what is on is a waste of time and that his son sits and watches a cartoon show made in Japan. Another friend, age 40, watched as young people sat enamored of a Taiwanese musician performing a currently popular song and shook his head, saying, "Young people really like this music. I can't understand why."

TECHNOLOGY

China has always prided itself on that which is homegrown. It values self-sufficiency and has been primarily a rural nation. Its technologies are not well developed, and even today you can ride the train through sections of the countryside for hours without seeing motorized vehicles. The number of cars in the whole nation is fewer than in California. The number of computers per 1000 people is less than 10 percent of what Mexico has, one-sixtieth of what Taiwan has, and less than one-half of 1 percent of what the United States has. It is only beginning to build an efficient workable nationwide phone system. Business phones in metropolitan areas are common and work well, but try to find a phone book. Residential phones are still scarce. China has a shortage of electricity and other forms of energy, roads, and transportation infrastructure.

Very few Chinese-made goods have been competitive on the world market until very recently. The special economic zones and foreign management, particularly through Hong Kong, are making major changes, and the biggest workforce in the world works cheaply. The major problems have been that Chinese industrial workers have been among the world's least efficient and that the government structures have been awkward to work with, to say the least. Communications, energy, transportation, sanitation, and general industrial infrastructure weaknesses have made it a difficult place to produce goods.

In line with this, China has so far not been a major exporter of electronics, although it does manufacture TV sets used extensively within the country and, to some extent, in other Asian countries. One of the ironies of Chinese production is that the country now manufactures satellite reception dishes, which are illegal within China. The country hopes to sell these dishes abroad to help its foreign exchange situation.

The best broadcast equipment used within China is made abroad, and facilities are full of equipment manufactured by Sony, Ampex, Otari, Thomson, Panasonic, and Silicon Graphics. China Central broadcasting operations have world-class state-of-the-art gear, but at regional and local stations quality is uneven. The nation is very cautious about balance-of-payment problems and requires a bureaucratic process before currency can be spent on foreign goods.

Until January 1, 1994, Chinese currency, *renminbi*, could not be spent abroad. It was not traded on the world market. Only a special class of currency could be spent—foreign exchange currency (FEC). The ordinary Chinese could get FEC only on the black market, where *renminbi* sold for much less than their official value. So a broadcast organization, if it could afford new equipment, could buy that equipment only by some questionable procedure or by going directly to the government for permission to export Chinese money abroad for foreign goods. The central government maintains a list of "controlled goods," including several broadcast items such as recorders and cameras, that may not be bought, and in general requires the purchase of Chinese goods if they are available. To purchase foreign goods, the broadcaster must apply for an amount of foreign money to buy the goods and then invite a government-owned import corporation to conduct the negotiations and purchase, frequently through Hong Kong.

Some Chinese broadcasters have been able to obtain donations of equipment or money from sister city organizations or private individuals abroad. Others have been able to make "back door" arrangements to smuggle gear in. Sometimes they just conveniently lose the records documenting equipment they are not supposed to have, in the time-honored fashion of bureaucracy fighters everywhere.

China uses a 625-line, 50-hertz broadcasting system in the Russian mode. When color was introduced, the Chinese chose the West German PAL system over the SECAM system used by the Russians.

EXTERNAL SERVICES

The international shortwave service, which became Radio Beijing, began in 1947 with a daily 20-minute program in English. As the service grew, it became a way of presenting China's message both inside and outside its walled borders. Radio Beijing now offers service in over forty languages. Chinese are bombarded by shortwave signals from offshore, and they are trying to return the favor, particularly targeting Taiwan, Hong Kong, and nearby Asian nations with the China story the government would have told.

The many ethnic Chinese living in regions outside Chinese borders are a particular target. People inside China refer to their nation as the motherland and encourage all ethnic Chinese to consider it so. Chinese have a great sense of family and origin, and the mainland has a special appeal. Programs in their own language also have a special appeal. Ethnic Chinese from abroad are not considered foreigners, but "overseas Chinese." When they visit China they get better prices than other foreigners, are welcomed at special shops and hotels, and receive favored treatment in general.

China has ambitious plans for the production of television programs for exchange with networks abroad. One such project is *Let the World Know China*, which explores the changes in Chinese life since Mao and is an attempt to update China's image.

Chinese regularly use shortwave radio to keep up with the world. Since the early 1980s to mid-1980s, this has even been encouraged by the government because on shortwave radio people can hear native English speakers and better learn to speak the language of science and technology. Voice of America has been the preferred choice, though the BBC is widely listened to for news. Universities regularly record VOA Special English broadcasts (those with slower delivery and simpler words), as well as other programs, and play them in classrooms. It is common for them to play John F. Kennedy's speech in which he said, "Ask not what your country can do for you, ask what you can do for your country," and Martin Luther King's "I have a dream" speech. It is also very common to walk through a neighborhood at night and hear the news broadcast by VOA emanating from numerous housing units. VOA broadcasts in Chinese as well as English and often transmits news reports of events within China that Chinese media will try not to cover or will give a locally favorable slant.

Chinese can receive good shortwave signals from Australia, Japan, Russia, and North Korea, among others. Surveys show that the Chinese are more apt to believe Western radio broadcasts than any of the domestic services because the Western media are more objective and more thorough.

IMPORTANCE TO THE WORLD COMMUNITY

So much of China's importance is obvious. There is just so much of it—so much land, so many people, and so much culture to learn from. It has military importance, partly because it has the world's largest army. It is seen by other countries as a major market for programming and for consumer products that can be advertised on the electronic media.

China has been a major exporter of people, frequently the best and brightest. The United States and Canada have been greatly enriched by that. China's own people have been a major undeveloped resource, but the country is working hard to change that.

So far, China has not been an important exporter of either broadcast hardware or software. A few films are now being shown abroad, but some of the best filmmakers have already taken their work outside where they are allowed more freedom to work. In a few short years China's inexpensive hardware could potentially be flowing into world markets, as outside companies are quickly learning how to work within the country. China has the potential to become, and is showing signs of becoming, a major world economic force.

MAJOR ISSUES

The Chinese media are an arm of government, helping its leaders to get their messages to the people. At the same time, they are increasingly a window on the outside world, letting in foreign commercials, foreign lifestyles, and foreign ideas. The leadership knows it needs the outside world for economic growth, but the outside world threatens in so many ways. China's relations with foreign nations over the last century have been traumatic. It is hard for China to forget the Japanese invasion, the opium, the ways Western nations bullied China, and how their businesspeople exploited the country. They are still ambivalent about the Western missionaries who taught them Christianity and foreign languages but did not always practice their own doctrines very well. Chinese fought with North Koreans against Americans in the Korean War.

In their own civil war the Western powers backed the opposition. China's revolution was primarily nationalist in character; that it became Communist was due as much to Western hostility, misunderstandings between the West and China, and Russian support during difficult times as it was to deep-seated ideology. The revolution itself was a violation of Marxist doctrine in that it was led by farmers in an agrarian society rather than industrial workers in a developed one. The collapse of the Soviet and Eastern European economies and the fall of the governments of China's closest ideological allies have left it as the last major Communist state, leaving it to ponder the contradictions in its own precarious position. To be sure, in the recent past, outside nations have provided important aid, trade, and friendship but all the while have been pressing China about its human rights record. China is trying to manage its own evolution, to reform from within, and to maintain order amid change.

The media reflect all of this ambiguity. They are opening up, but they are far from open. The West is portrayed in so many positive ways, and yet television programs and films selected for showing in China are those that show capitalism in its most extreme and unfavorable light, reinforcing Marxist training of more than 40 years. Since 1949, Chinese have been told by their government that capitalists are evil, that capitalism will destroy harmony and equality. Now they are being told that the way for the country to progress is to learn from the West in science and technology but to let the government continue to order their lives. Chinese are told to emulate free markets but not to think in the process. The leaders must know deep inside that it is impossible to have it both ways, that you cannot get people to unleash all of their potential unless they are allowed to be innovative and solve problems, to use logic and reason. How can people do that in their work and not continue to do that elsewhere?

The Chinese have every reason to be wary of Western excesses and foibles. Their own citizens also have every reason to be wary of the top-down leadership that has required average people to let the government make so many of the decisions about their personal lives.

In the Mao era ideological purity was important. In the Deng era pragmatism and economic reform were stressed. We do not know how far reform will lead in the post-Deng era. There is not yet the kind of rule of law that ensures continuity of direction; it could be a volatile period. Recently the special economic zones have brought the nation new prosperity, but other areas have suffered. Factories in the inland north have experienced worker unrest, and farmers in Sichuan who were paid by IOUs rather than cash for their products have demonstrated their anger.

The media are more entertaining and open than at any time since 1949, but many Chinese object to the "cultural pollution" they see as part of this openness. Mao's picture still looks out over Tiananmen Square, his mausoleum dominates the center of that most famous public location in the nation, and residual Maoism permeates the countryside. The Big Dipper in the sky is still considered by many to be a symbol of Mao. While Deng has resisted his own deification, the government has felt it necessary to exalt his status to counter those who would turn back the clock. A best-selling biography of Deng and the third volume of his writings have been receiving a major media push as part of the effort to continue reforms. Deng's picture has begun to appear in prominent squares in parts of the country—Mao style. Anyone who works in an important media position must be at least part weathervane, ready to respond to the climate in Beijing.

China is a poor and struggling country with a great past and great promise. The people themselves have great strength and resilience, great resourcefulness, a sense of family, and a sense of their worth in the world community—qualities that allow them to overcome significant obstacles.

On the outskirts of Nanjing, where the Yangtze is very wide, the Chinese have built a long and impressive bridge high over the river. Outside nations brought in engineers and workers to build the bridge but struggled with it and never got the job done—it was a difficult engineering feat. The Chinese themselves persevered and completed the bridge on their own. To stand on the observation deck with a group of Chinese and look out over the river and the city is impressive both for the view and for seeing the pride it brings to those who see how their fellow citizens have succeeded in that work. The Chinese are known as the country that built the world's best walls. They would also like to be known as a country that can build great bridges.

Du Ruiqing.

Du Ruiqing also assisted in the preparation of this chapter, particularly in providing up-to-date statistics and charts and photos. Du teaches English at Xi'an Foreign Language University in China. He was born in China in 1944 and educated at Xi'an Foreign Language University, Sydney University in Australia, and Brigham Young University in the United States, where he received a Ph.D. He is the author of numerous articles in both Chinese and English and has written *Chinese Higher Education: A Decade of Reform and Development: 1978–1988*, published by St. Martin's Press. A few of his observations about Chinese electronic media follow.

Chinese radio and television are intended to be the voice of the Communist party of China and the people. As such, they have to toe the party line and operate in strict accordance with the four cardinal principles, which means adherence to the socialist road, the people's democratic dictatorship, the leadership of the Chinese Communist party, and Marxist-Leninist-Mao Zedong thought.

More specifically, this general guideline entails that radio and television have to reflect the latest achievements of the drive for socialist modernization so as to unite, inspire, and educate the people. In other words, radio and television are the most powerful modern tools for educating and inspiring the whole Communist party of China, the whole army, and the people of all nationalities across China in their endeavor to build a socialist material and spiritual civilization. They are also one of the most effective means for the Chinese Communist party and the Chinese government to maintain their close ties with the masses. What has been emphasized most recently is that radio and TV must be subordinate to and serve economic construction, which is the focus of the whole nation.

The political nature of China's radio and television determines that they are didactic in nature. But with the country's deepening reform and growing openness toward foreign countries, there has emerged a fairly drastic change in China's radio and television programs. Political indoctrination, which was prevalent over a decade ago, is gradually giving way to a media system that is entertainment- and service-oriented. The concentration on good news which is characteristic of Chinese media is beginning to be modified. The straight-faced lecturing type of information service is also being replaced by a more pleasant, relaxed, informal approach. In short, as the nation's political climate is becoming more congenial, the radio and television service is undergoing a corresponding change.

This change can be evidenced in many of the radio and TV programs that have been released recently. *I Love You for Sure*, a TV play in forty-one parts, tells of the love and hate of a group of ordinary young people in their ordinary daily existence. It is a play permeated with rank humor and witty, philosophical remarks devoid of political message. What is also noteworthy about the play is that it passed the official censor almost immediately after it was completed in December 1992. It was broadcast on a CCTV channel which reaches every household in China in late December 1992. This is considered extraordinarily fast by Chinese standards. Usually, the bureaucracy is such that an official examination would last several months, even 1 or 2 years. Some of the programs not palatable to official tastes may never even see the light of day.

The recent loosening up of government control of radio and TV can also be evidenced in the establishment of a local business news station in Xi'an. Going into operation on July 1, 1992, the station provides timely and varied economic information to local businesspeople as well as to the general residents. Some of the reports are on-the-spot and instantaneous. The reporters are mellow-voiced and spontaneous sounding and do not read from a script, which still remains the standard practice for news anchors on both radio and television.

In addition to having a freer hand in their operation, radio and TV stations in China are also exhorted to play an increasingly greater role in supervision. What this means is that as part of the mass media, radio and TV must also report the seamy side of life and expose the dishonesty of government workers and their evil practices. This is perhaps all the more necessary in view of the nation's growing market economy. It will hurt the interests of consumers and lead enterprises astray if fake and shoddy commodities and lawbreaking practices in market competition are not exposed and effectively checked.

The growing trend toward a more liberalized and relaxed radio and television service and its supervisory role are, however, a far cry from radio and television services in relatively free Western democracies. But given China's socialist system, the progress seems to be phenomenal. And many people are continuing to make efforts for more changes. A recent article by a responsible member of the China TV Play Production Center, for example, argued for TV productions which are more entertaining, relaxing, and gratifying to the audience. In emphasizing that TV stations must offer the viewers programs to their taste and liking, not didactic political indoctrination, the article compared the operation of a TV station to the management of a restaurant—what is ultimately essential is to provide palatable and nutritious meals to the customers, not to bore or displease them with straight faces and food forced upon them after a busy workday. The article also advocated more humor in TV productions and a wider variety of entertainment.

One of the problems that China must cope with in the near future revolves around regulating the media. Though China has drafted and put into operation many pieces of legislation as regards radio and TV production, two problems still remain outstanding. The first is that the laws and regulations are far from comprehensive for one of the world's biggest radio and TV industries. To ensure a sustained and balanced development of radio and television, Chinese authorities may have to work out strategies from a long-term point of view. The formulation and implementation of laws and regulations at present seem to be piecemeal and tinted with spontaneity and impulsiveness.

The second problem is strict implementation of the laws and regulations that are promulgated. It is common in China that laws and regulations drafted and enacted are not at all properly carried out.

Abuses and violations are frequent, and countermeasures are sometimes devised for local or departmental interests. Therefore, a better and more workable mechanism for law enforcement is also imperative for China's radio and TV industry.

As one of the few countries that is still Communist, China has a type of centralized government-controlled media structure that has disappeared in most of the rest of the world. Pressure will no doubt be placed upon this structure, but the basic Chinese makeup is strong and should be able to respond and adapt to whatever pressures it faces.

SELECTED BIBLIOGRAPHY

Bishop, Robert L. *Qi Lai! Mobilizing One Billion Chinese: The Chinese Communication System.* Ames, IA: Iowa State University Press, 1989.

Chang, Won Ho. *Mass Media in China.* Ames, IA: Iowa State University Press, 1989.

China Radio and TV Yearbook. Beijing: Beijing University College Press, 1986, 1987, 1988, 1989, 1990, 1991.

Liu, Zhiyun. *Dianzi Zinwen Meijie—Guanboyu Dianshi (Electronic News Media—Broadcast and Television).* Beijing: Chinese People's University Press, 1988.

Lull, James. *China Turned On.* New York: Routledge, 1991.

Rittenberg, Sidney. *The Man Who Stayed Behind.* New York: Houghton Mifflin, 1993.

Salisbury, Harrison. *Tiananmen Diary: Thirteen Days in June.* Boston: Little, Brown, 1989.

Schell, Orville. *Discos and Democracy, China in the Throes of Reform.* New York: Pantheon Books, 1988.

Thirty Years of Shaanxi Television (1960–1990). Beijing: Beijing Broadcasting College Press, 1990.

Wang, Feng. *Guanbo Dianyi Dianshi Zhuanyefa Pufa Duben (Professional Laws and Relative Laws of Radio, Film, and Television).* Beijing: Publishing House of Law, 1992.

Yan, Yu. *Zhongguo Guanbo Dianshizue (On Chinese Radio and Television).* Beijing: Radio and Television Publishing House, 1990.

CHAPTER 12

Japan

Nobuo Otsuka

Nobuo Otsuka is a news director for the Asahi Broadcasting Corporation (ABC), a major commercial broadcaster in Japan. He is currently in charge of a 30-minute TV documentary program called *Telementary*, which is aired nationwide every Sunday morning. He received the 1994 Superior Award for a TV documentary and news feature. He has had many overseas

Nobuo Otsuka.

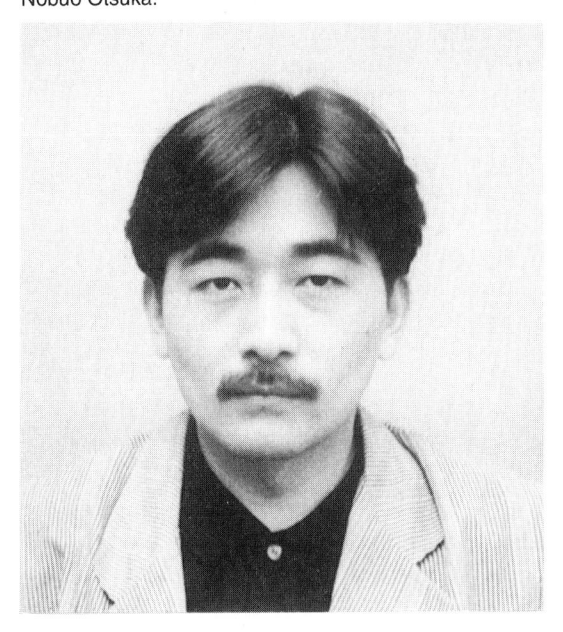

assignments, including covering the 1992 U.S. presidential primaries in New Hampshire, reporting on the confusion in Russia immediately after the breakup of the Soviet Union in 1992, and preparing a special program on the Silk Road in Syria. Early in his career he was a disc jockey for a popular late-night radio program for young people.

STATISTICS

Geographic Area: 145,856 square miles
Capital: Tokyo
Population: 124,017,000
Religions: Buddhism, Shintoism
Language: Japanese
Type of Government: Parliamentary democracy headed by a prime minister
Gross Domestic Product: $2.1 trillion
Literacy: 99 percent

GENERAL CHARACTERISTICS

If television sets disappeared from Japanese living rooms, the daily routine would definitely be upset. Just as with viewers in the United States, the daily lives of Japanese are too occupied by TV to do without it. In the 1950s television replaced movies as the top form of entertainment, and, ever since, TV and radio have been consistently more popular. Television news and weather broadcasts have been the main sources of information.

Generally, TV and radio are utilized to such a great extent because of the long working hours and lack of a leisure-time infrastructure in Japan. A short vacation for a Japanese family is very expensive. Even worse, Japanese businesspeople constantly work overtime and seldom take time off for a paid holiday. Consequently, families tend to spend their leisure in the easiest and least expensive manner: they stay at home and relax in front of a TV set.

Most of these homes are in cities; Japan has ten cities with populations of over a million. Only about 10 percent of the population lives in areas that can truly be considered rural. These rural dwellers also receive radio and TV, although, because Japan is mountainous, huge investments in relay stations have been required to bring over-the-air broadcast signals to everyone. One of the advantages of satellite broadcasting in Japan is that a satellite signal, beamed from the sky, can cover the entire country more easily than terrestrial broadcasting, which must cope with the mountains. Television and radio are predominantly attractive to the Japanese people as media that are available at any time, at any place, and at a relatively low cost.

Television's Present Status When you go into a Japanese house, you are likely to see a number of TV sets, not only in the living room but also in the children's room. A 1990 survey revealed that, on the average, each Japanese family has 2.4 television sets, and 18.5 percent of Japanese families have more than four TV sets. Furthermore, TV sets having screens larger than 22 inches are common, with approximately 70 percent of all families owning one. The reasons for the large number of sets are the following. First, since Japan's per capita income and gross domestic product are second only to those of the United States, people can afford the television sets; second, because of the scarce and expensive housing situation, the living style is such that two generations cohabit; and third, because each member of a family tends to have his or her own favorite programs, several television sets are necessary. The "my TV" trend is very evident in Japan.

Although television viewing time has gone down slightly over the last few years, the average viewing time is 3 hours, 21 minutes per day per person. According to 1990 research, TV occupies 40 percent of the free time of the Japanese people. For the elderly, television is literally the best form of entertainment. For the younger generation, the TV set has become a visual piece of furniture, especially in urban areas, not just by providing programs that are intentionally watched but by always being on. For children, TV is a tool for playing family computer games. For businesspeople, TV provides information, even when they are in a taxi or on a train. Thus television is the main provider of activities for people's free time, and TV is utilized in different ways by each generation.

Radio's Present Status Radio in Japan is not as popular a medium as television. However, nearly every home has at least one radio set, and the average home possesses about four. The average radio listening time is a half-hour a day, but that figure is somewhat misrepresentative because many people hardly listen to the radio at all, and those that do tend to listen about 2 hours a day.

Most people listen to the radio while they are doing something else, for example, when they are working outside the home, doing housekeeping, or commuting to and from the office. By and large, listening time has gone down year by year since 1980 because other media have attracted listeners. For example, TV has increased programming in the evening for the younger generation, and videocassette recorders (VCRs) and compact discs (CDs) have actively sought larger audiences. At present, the most common use of radio is not as a music medium but as an information medium for the aged.

However, in recent years radio stations have tried to attract younger listeners. Some AM stations have begun to broadcast music in stereo and have created new programs that encourage young people to send fax and modem messages to the radio station, such as pictures they draw or news about the students in their schools. Many FM stations have been started in the last several years, targeting the younger generation by playing different types of music. In addition, digital pulse code modulation (PCM) technology is being used for satellite-delivered music. This is significant because the PCM sound is of a higher quality than that of AM or FM stations.

Radio, which lost popularity to TV in the late 1950s, is obviously engaging in trial-and-error experimentation in terms of technology and function to regain the number of listeners it used to have and to close the popularity gap. In other words, it is trying to create a "radio renaissance" to help the medium survive into the next century.

THE DEVELOPMENT OF ELECTRONIC MEDIA IN JAPAN

An examination of the history of electronic media in Japan shows that they have been developed under strong governmental initiative. As a result, commercial stations and public stations coexist, and a special license system adopted by the government 40 years ago is still in operation. In addition, major newspapers have consistently regarded the electronic media as a most effective means of helping them improve their image and their profitability. So, major executive posts at commercial stations are often occupied by people from the newspapers that have invested money in the stations.

In the following sections, important phases in the history of Japanese electronic media will be discussed. Toward the end of the history section, the focus will be on the "new kids on the block" of Japanese electronic media—satellite broadcasting and cable television.

Before World War II With the success of radio stations in the United States and Europe in the 1920s, "radio fever" mounted among the people of Japan, and the government decided to establish a national policy on setting up new radio stations. However, because the government was financially squeezed by the recession that followed World War I, it developed the idea of a government-regulated broadcasting system that would be a nonprofit private enterprise but would be authorized to collect "receiver fees" to cover the cost of its operation. This licensing of radio reception, where a private company rather than the government collects the fees, is very rare outside Japan.

More than 100 applications from newspaper companies and influential businesspeople were submitted for the stations, and the Communications Ministry (then in charge of radio) examined their qualifications under a policy calling for the establishment of one station in each of Japan's three largest cities: Tokyo, Osaka, and Nagoya. The companies that applied were encouraged to combine their applications and own the stations jointly.

The first broadcasting station, the Tokyo Broadcasting Station, was established in 1924. The former minister of communications, Shimpei Goto, was elected to head the station. There were nineteen directors on the board, coming from different electrical appliance firms, newspapers, the stock exchange, and even a hat-making firm. The composition of the board reflected the unusual diversity of the original applicants and the difficulties faced in arranging a harmonious group.

For the first broadcasts in 1925, a school library was used as a temporary studio, where felt and woolen clothes covered the inside walls to reduce echoes. It had been decided that the license fees for the roughly 3500 homes that owned radios were to be limited to 1 yen

($0.50) a month. There were about 8000 listeners in all. They listened to news, weather, time signals, and stock and commodity reports that were aired 8 hours per day. Many phone calls and telegrams came in right after each broadcast from people who wanted to let the station know that they had been listening. The Osaka and Nagoya stations went on the air shortly after the Tokyo station.

The government, which was interested in propagating its policies through radio, decided to merge the three stations into a single network, although all of the stations and newspaper companies strongly opposed this plan. Nevertheless, Nippon Hoso Kyokai (NHK), the Japanese national public service network that still exists today, was organized in 1926. The Communications Ministry appointed several officials to major posts at NHK, and these government appointees began to control all of the programming. Since then, Japanese broadcasting has evolved in accordance with government policies.

Once the network was established, radio was able to broadcast sports programs, such as a national inter–middle school baseball tournament (1927), a sumo wrestling tournament (1928), and the Los Angeles Olympics (1932) nationwide. Radio attracted people into its audience through these sportscasts. As of 1944, approximately 50 percent of the population had radios. With the start of full-scale fighting in World War II, NHK was completely reorganized and radio programming was brought totally under state control. The maintaining of radio services was a high government priority during the war, with the number of stations growing from about eighty to ninety during this time period.

As for television research in this early period, Kenjiro Takayanagi of the Hamamatsu College of Engineering succeeded in reproducing the Japanese character "i" (ee) on a reception tube in 1927. This research continued at NHK with an eye on the 1940 Tokyo Olympics. Ultimately, the research was halted because the Olympic Games were canceled.

After World War II It was through the medium of radio that His Majesty, Emperor Hirohito, announced the end of the war. The occupation of Japan after the war was largely in the hands of U.S. forces headed by General Douglas MacArthur. Policies regarding radio came primarily from the General Headquarters of the Allied Powers (GHQ). It gave comprehensive instructions for radio programming and censored program content as well. Even music program scripts had to be cleared.

The Japanese government and the Western-run GHQ came up with an idea to reorganize broadcasting to include both NHK and new private commercial stations. To further this idea, three bills, the Broadcasting Law, Radio Law, and Radio Regulatory Commission Establishment Law, were approved in 1950. Based on these laws, the first two commercial radio stations, the Chubu Nippon Broadcasting Company (CBC) in Nagoya and the Shin Nippon Broadcasting Company (NJB) in Osaka, began operation, backed by newspaper companies. Thus in 1951 NHK's monopoly position ended, although it continued to operate much as it had before the war.

The new stations, unlike NHK which operated both a network and stations, were not allowed to form networks; they were intended to be local stations serving local or regional areas. However, large Japanese newspaper companies such as Asahi, Mainichi, and Yomiuri started a number of stations throughout the country and played the same taped programs on all of them, so they sounded very much like a network. This seminetwork status of commercial stations still exists today with both radio and TV.

NHK carried many popular programs such as the serial drama *What Is Your Name?* which almost vacated the public baths when it was on, and the music program *Red versus White Singing Competition,* which was a popular singers' contest held on New Year's Eve. (The latter program is still broadcast on TV every year with about 40 percent of the population tuning in.) These programs were very successful in bringing some relief to the people whose lives were still abysmal during the postwar period.

Japan's first advertisement on commercial radio was presented by the Seiko watch and clock firm. The commercial message was used to mark the broadcast time signals; however, the company's name was not mentioned in the jingle. This was mainly because of a lack of experience and understanding of broadcast commercials at that time. Later advertising became more sophisticated, and commercial stations saw a fairly fast rise in the amount of sponsored time sold.

The Television Age The first opportunity to introduce television into Japan was initiated by Matsutaro Shoriki, the former president of the *Yomiuri* newspaper. He obtained the idea for setting up a Japanese-run television service from U.S. Senator Carl Mundt, who was thinking of establishing international TV facilities around the world, including Japan, to fight communism. The company Shoriki led, Nippon Television (NTV), was not international, however; it was organized only to start a service in Japan. There has been an ongoing argument between Nippon Television and the NHK concerning which was the first television broadcaster. NTV got the preliminary license earlier than NHK, but NHK began TV broadcasting in 1953, before NTV. At that time, only about 16,000 receivers had been sold because the sets were extremely expensive for the average household. So, NTV set up large receivers in public areas to demonstrate TV to passersby.

The first program shown on NTV was a professional wrestling match between Japanese and American wrestlers. Viewers looking at sets out on the street became so excited about the match that they sometimes blocked traffic. Once NTV and NHK television caught on, other companies, many of which owned newspapers and radio stations, started local television stations. As in the case of radio, NHK had a true TV network, and the commercial stations shared programming.

One event that decisively accelerated the spread of TV sets into people's homes was the marriage of the crown prince in 1959. The bridal ceremony and parade were broadcast on television, and 15 million people watched. Typically, people watched 10 hours a day. This big event promoted the setup of nationwide news organizations with the Tokyo stations acting as a centerpiece. Because programming had become more complex and expensive, it was important to have local stations cover all the national news. Most national news happened in the capital, Tokyo, and so the Tokyo stations were dominant in the collection of news.

First, the Japan News Network (JNN) was formed. Following this, other news services were formed—NTV, NET (now TV Asahi), and Fuji TV. Later, in 1975, several major newspapers with national sales systems associated themselves with broadcasting organizations in Tokyo in order to establish national mass news distribution.

In the 1950s the advent of the transistor radio drastically changed the way people listened to radio. They began to listen while driving, eating, and studying. The AM stations purposely avoided competing with television. Instead, they tried to develop different types of programs, such as 5-hour shows that mixed news, music, talented disc jockeys, and phone calls from listeners. However, they lost much of their audience, particularly young people, as TV took over the front-runner position. AM stations (forty-seven in all as of 1992) are trying hard to regain their popularity in terms of number of listeners and advertising revenue.

Meanwhile, FM stations (thirty-nine in all as of 1992) are taking on all-music programming formats and, in pursuit of the younger genera-

This AM radio program, in which a host is talking to a comedian, is being broadcast from a public place in order to make potential audience members more aware of it.

tion, are inviting American and French disc jockeys to perform.

At present, traditional over-the-air television (119 stations, 5 commercial nationally linked organizations, and NHK) is being gradually replaced by satellite broadcasting, cable TV, and videocassettes in terms of ratings, viewing time, and revenues. However, the loss of viewership is not as severe as it has been for U.S. television networks and stations. Japanese TV entities broadcast news, dramas, talk shows, and music programs in various ways to attract continuous viewer attention. For example, they broadcast live reporting of the 1992 Los Angeles riots via satellite, a trendy serial drama located in New York, and all-night discussions on "taboo" issues by excellent panelists. Some of these late-night programs involve nudity and subject matter that is more risqué than material that can be shown on TV in the United States.

In both rural and urban areas, people in Japan can freely chose their favorite programs, depending on whether they wish entertainment, information, or culture, from an overflowing supply of programming 24 hours a day throughout the year.

Satellite Broadcasting Although other countries used satellites to transmit television signals to stations and cable TV systems, Japan was the first country that sent into orbit a satellite intended for broadcasting directly to home receivers (direct broadcast satellite, DBS). NHK started DBS in 1984.

One satellite, BS-3, is used for direct broadcasting. It carries three channels. Two are operated by NHK, and one is operated by Japan Satellite Broadcasting (JSB), an organization in which the main commercial television stations, newspaper companies, and trading companies have invested and for which a former high-ranking official of the Ministry of Posts and Telecommunications (the organization that now oversees broadcasting) was selected as the number one man. In addition to the three channels, high-definition television (HDTV) technology uses BS-3 experimentally by broadcasting programs in high definition 8 hours a day. NHK airs sports and news via the first channel, and through the second one international news (unedited news from ten foreign countries, almost in real time) and movies (an entire week might be dedicated to one director, for example,

Akira Kurosawa). More than half of all JSB broadcasting also consists of movies, with the rest being made up of news, sports, and music.

These services are facing financial problems because their revenue comes from people who pay for the service. NHK had 6.2 million subscribers as of July 1992, and JSB had 1 million subscribers as of August 1992. Neither of these figures reached the expectations people had for paid programming, and the systems are as yet unprofitable.

Anyone who wants to watch JSB broadcasting has to purchase a satellite dish and an exclusive decoder and become a member, which carries a fee of 27,000 yen (more than $200). In addition, they have to pay 2000 yen per month to subscribe to JSB. NHK's satellite services are similar in cost. People must pay additional fees of 1300 yen ($10) on top of the color TV viewing fees they already pay for regular broadcasting.

All of the television services in Japan are very much interested in the next broadcasting satellite (BS-4), which will be launched in 1997. This satellite will make the presently experimental HDTV broadcasting a reality, and the number of channels will increase from three to eight. This is based on the decision that broadcasts will be established as directed by the Ministry of Posts and Telecommunications, using the eight channels that are allocated to Japan for satellite broadcasting.

A crucial issue that must be decided very carefully concerns the way in which the channels should be allocated. The Ministry of Posts and Telecommunications wants to retain the 1957 governmental principle of discouraging the concentration of mass communications media; for example, no single station or network owner should have more than two BS-4 channels. NHK, JSB, and the commercial stations are all jockeying for positions and trying to keep newcomers out.

If satellite broadcasting is carried by people or companies other than established broadcasting organizations, an enormous amount of advertising revenue will be realized by the newcomers to the detriment of established busi-

Satellite dishes being sold in an electronics store.

nesses. This can happen with a system where expenses are considerably reduced by satellite broadcasts that send programs directly into people's homes, unlike terrestrial broadcasts that go through an indirect route, passing several ground relays on the way. It would be natural for national sponsors to air their commercial messages through satellite broadcasting which is relatively inexpensive. Therefore the established commercial television stations are likely to be ruined. Because of this fear, the key broadcasting stations have recently announced their fundamental concepts and specific plans for programming for the BS-4 in order to position themselves to acquire at least one channel.

However, during recessionary times, such as those presently faced by Japan, electronics companies refrain from participating in a project such as BS-4 because they are faced with the 60 to 80 billion yen ($500 to $600 million) investment required to launch it. Another factor that makes the prospects of the BS-4 more difficult in the near future is uncertainty about whether it will be profitable, a problem JSB is experiencing now in a very concrete way. Each channel of satellite broadcasting needs at least a few million subscribers to be profitable, but it is not certain how many families in Japan will spend money for paid satellite broadcasting. Viewers who acquire BS-4 channels will pay a high price for very little if the programming is the same as that of terrestrial broadcasting or if the satellite channel owners cannot produce software that utilizes the advanced features of HDTV.

A different kind of satellite started serving the public in 1992. Originally called a "communication satellite" (CS), to distinguish it from the BS-3 "broadcasting satellite" (BS), it operates at much lower power. There are two communication satellites in operation, JC SAT and SCC. Together they deliver six channels of specialized programming, for example, a sports channel, a music channel, and a channel that airs CNN in English 24 hours a day.

The difference between the broadcasting satellite and the communication satellite is the generating power and frequency. The current BS-3 generates 120 watts, while the two communication satellites produce 20 watts (JC SAT) and 22 watts (SCC). Because of the weakness of the communication satellite transmission, a BS antenna and tuner cannot be used to view it. Two antennas are needed for CS reception since the orbits of the satellites are different. Putting up the needed antennas is physically difficult because of Japan's tight housing situation. The antenna-tuner setup costs 130,000 yen ($1060), and the subscriber fee is usually between 800 and 900 yen ($6 to $7) per month for each channel.

The Ministry of Posts and Telecommunications, aiming at a multimedia system of communications, plans to increase the number of CS channels. The ultimate number will probably be at least fifteen. Therefore, each channel will survive in the near future by producing more special programs and focusing on program content. If the CS channels do not take an aggressive attitude in terms of software, their future will not be optimistic.

Cable Television "Excuse me, madame, I am a CATV salesman." "I am sorry, but we already have too many channels to watch." This is typical conversation heard in the suburbs of a big city in Japan today, and it shows how terrestrial television has dominated and how little the public knows about cable TV.

Cable television appeared in Japan to eliminate areas of poor TV reception, as happened in the United States in the 1950s. The complete name of the system is Community Antenna Television (CATV). It uses a high antenna that receives its signal through the air and transmits it by cable to nearby homes in areas of poor reception, for example, on islands and in mountainous areas. Eventually, the system developed from this complementary position to a modern

CATV system offering a multipurpose channel service.

To be more specific, there are two types of CATV in Japan. One is the urban type, and the other is the rural type. An urban CATV system, which is overseen by the Ministry of Posts and Telecommunications, is defined as a system with more than five channels that is able to function in two-way communication and has more than 10,000 terminals to transmit programs to homes. Rural CATV, which is overseen by the Ministry of Agriculture, Forestry and Fisheries and the Ministry of Home Affairs, is utilized to vitalize the agricultural district by presenting information about everyday life and about agriculture; this system is mainly run by local governments. Today, urban CATV is more popular and more generally used than rural CATV.

The first urban-type CATV, the Tama Cable Network, was set up in Oume City, Tokyo, in 1987. Shortly thereafter, 118 urban-type CATVs were established nationwide. This happened because the government agreed to promote cable TV in 1987 and eased the formalities of laying the cable. As a result, a private railroad company, a trading company, and a local government participated in the CATV industry. However, only about 550,000 households subscribe, according to 1992 research. This is equal to only 1.8 percent of all licenses for NHK terrestrial broadcasting.

The cable systems provide, in addition to news, movies, and music, special channels transmitting such programming as 24-hour weather forecasts, animated programs for children, programs produced by other Asian countries, narrowly focused spot reports on weather and traffic, and events involving the local government.

Most CATV channels are basic channels that people can watch by paying the basic fee, but there are also pay channels that have to be paid for separately. The average number of channels per system is about thirty; out of these, the number of local channels programmed by the local cable system can be as high as ten. The viewing fee, in most cases, is 3000 yen ($24) per month on average. So, it might be more reasonable to subscribe to CATV than to broadcasting and communication satellites separately, as long as the CATV can provide both BS and CS channels.

In Japan the first thing CATV has to resolve is the changing habits of viewers watching TV, and it has to make people recognize what CATV is so that the service can go forward by emphasizing more local information and providing channels that stress individual character. A single CATV system has certain limitations in terms of ability to finance and produce programming. Consequently, there have already been attempts by CATV systems to form networks for purposes such as cablecasting big events in the district to reach a larger number of people. Currently, CATV systems are strengthening the function of two-way communication. For example, people can order specific movies on a pay-per-view basis, and one system has begun experiments with a home security system in cooperation with a large security company.

In accordance with these trends, the urban-type CATV will in all probability not only provide multiple channels but also develop a compound communication medium.

ORGANIZATION AND FINANCING

The electronic media structure of Japan is organized in such a way that the government does not specifically own any radio or television services; all are privately owned. However, NHK has many government ties because high-ranking government or ex-government officials have been appointed to important positions within it. The commercial stations are truly privately owned, with newspapers as primary owners.

NHK is by far the largest media giant in Japan. It has two regular television channels, two satellite TV channels, two AM radio frequencies, one FM frequency, and seventy broadcasting stations. It has approximately 15,000 employees, which is about ten times as many as a key commercial station in Tokyo. NHK's revenue relies almost entirely on license fees—1 trillion 720 billion yen ($15 billion) in 1989. There are no commercials on NHK. License fees are $10 a month for each household with a color television set—that is, most Japanese households. The satellite broadcasting fee is an extra $10 a month. Of late, people have been rebelling against paying license fees, and they have become harder to collect.

NHK is a nonprofit organization and hence cannot show a profit. Recently, however, it has suffered losses, due in part to the fact that the number of subscriptions to receive satellite broadcasting has been below the original estimate. NHK was in the red by 27 billion yen ($225 million) in 1989. Reflecting on such an embarrassing situation, its executives have discussed certain issues over the last few years, such as turning NHK into a private profit-oriented company like commercial television companies and cutting down on the number of NHK employees. Resolving these tough issues is very difficult, partly because of strong resistance inside NHK and partly because of opposition from commercial stations which do not want NHK competing with them for advertising revenues.

By contrast, the commercial stations are financed by advertisement fees from sponsors. The gross advertising revenue of the Japanese commercial television and radio industry approached 2 trillion yen ($16 billion) in 1988. Most years, except during recessions, commercial TV stations have enjoyed nearly double-digit growth, which has been much higher than in other industries over the past two decades or so.

However, there are predictions that the commercial station revenue situation will not be as favorable in the future. According to a research-based forecast called "A Vision of Japan's Broadcasting in the Year 2000," published in 1991, terrestrial broadcasting earned 75 percent of all broadcasting industry revenue in 1990 but in 2000 this figure will be down to 54 percent. This means that the revenue for terrestrial broadcasting by both the commercial systems and NHK will be uncertain because of the multichannelization of satellites and cable TV.

PROGRAMMING

Since the electronic media, especially television, are the "department store of the mind," they provide news, dramas, sports, variety, and music in their showcases. The two systems, NHK and commercial, differ somewhat in what they present.

NHK has been featuring news and cultural programs since its inception, when it was set up by law to broadcast nationwide for the public welfare. It has two AM national services, one of which features news and discussion, while the other is geared toward educational programming for schools and people studying on their own. The one FM service features music—Western, traditional Japanese, and modern Japanese. Of the two television services, one is general, programming news, public affairs, drama, talk shows, and documentaries, and the other is educational, along the same lines as the second AM radio service.

Commercial stations have prospered mainly by emphasizing entertainment. Radio stations highlight music, news, and sports, and TV stations program general shows of various genres—game shows, sports, dramas, news, talk. Although theoretically the commercial structure does not have networks, most of the TV programs come from major stations in Tokyo and Osaka because local stations do not have budgets to produce expensive entertainment programming. There are five major commercial organizations that have what might be termed networks.

News Programs When television first started in Japan in 1953, news programs had no vitality because they had not found their style. One of the reasons for this was that the individuals responsible for the operation were not experienced in using electronics to broadcast TV programs. For instance, only a few people knew how to use a television camera. More importantly, however, the limited supply of TV journalists was quickly exhausted.

Nevertheless, these journalists handled TV news coverage faithfully in dealing with such topics as the incidents that led to bloodshed between the police and local citizens, and the opinions of labor union members on the matter of expanding an American army base in the suburbs of Tokyo in 1956. And the television camera of Radio Tokyo (now TBS) was able to record the flight of the first satellite launched by the USSR in 1957. The coverage of these events played a decisive role in opening people's eyes to television as a viable news medium that very quickly came of age.

Since then, TV news has been the cause of several social reactions and has developed at a rapid pace with up-to-date technology. As news programs were becoming established, ordinary people rearranged their days to accommodate the morning, afternoon, and evening time slots of the programs. Eventually, an individual who would just read the news into the camera was replaced by an experienced journalist. During a short span of 40 years, news programs have become a staple of TV programming and of people's daily activities.

Now that television has become so powerful, it seems to threaten the position of the older medium, the newspaper. According to research done by NHK in 1990, TV occupies the number one position (52.4 percent) as the medium helping people to understand political and social issues, while newspapers follow with 36.8 percent. Comparable research in 1985 gave newspapers 45.7 percent and television 43.4 percent.

A major change in TV news was started in 1985 by *News Station,* produced by commercial news service TV Asahi. Before that, TV news in Japan meant the NHK news, *NC 9,* which began at 9 P.M. But TV Asahi produced *News Station* starting at 10 P.M., Monday through Friday, for 1 hour, 18 minutes. This program started operating amid strong opposing comments: "too risqué," "reckless," from inside its organization, and "suicidal action" from rival services. The starting time seemed to be too late for a news program. However, it was very appropriate on two accounts: 10 P.M. is the time almost all Japanese businesspeople arrive home after "overworking" in the city, and the free time that people have after 10 P.M. has been increasing.

Before *News Station,* people had the impression that news was hard to understand. The main objective of *News Station's* policy is to provide programming that is understandable and interesting based on the concept that even junior high school students should be able to understand the news. The program features a main newscaster and a commentator to explain the news. *News Station* developed this style first, and currently there are nineteen news programs that have adopted the same format.

As for the content of *News Station,* it begins with news of the day, followed by sports, special reports, and live segments that have broken with accepted notions by offering such enjoyable visuals to viewers as cherry blossoms at night, waterfalls in Japan and abroad, and red leaves. These live segments have impressed the Japanese people, who appreciate nature in depth. And the news style, which adds explanatory comments to the newscaster's reports, grabbed the attention of viewers who had not watched much news before *News Station* appeared.

Moreover, live broadcasts of the revolution in the Philippines and a domestic volcano eruption boosted *News Station*'s popularity, and ratings went up to double digits. Noting its success, other newscasts used the same format for their programs, and even NHK challenged TV Asahi by extending its airtime. Ultimately, none of the others was successful. *News Station* constantly gets a 15 percent rating (1 percent equals 1 million households), which is considered a monster rating for a news program.

Sponsors are eager to advertise on *News Station* because of its high ratings. Often they pay twice what they pay on other programs because so many sponsors want to advertise on *News Station*. Advertising on such a news program contributes to a company's image more than advertising on an entertainment program.

"We think that there is definitely an amount of merit in sponsoring *News Station*, largely because the newscaster, Hiroshi Kume, appeals to the viewers by penetrating his sense of ordinary people into the whole news program," says one of the big sponsors.

The attitude of *News Station* received intense bashing from the government and the ruling party on the peacekeeping operation (PKO) issue that divided public opinion just before the election of the House of Councillors in July 1992. Hiroshi Kume kept making negative comments about the PKO bill because it would open the door to sending the Self-Defense Force abroad, and engaging in any sort of offensive military actions is against the post–World War II Japanese constitution.

At the time Hiroshi Kume was making his comments, the minister of health and welfare, Tokuo Yamashita, said, "If people continue watching his anti-PKO program, they will agree with his opinion and have a negative impression of the bill. The Liberal Democratic Party should organize a boycott against buying products of companies that sponsor *News Station*."

Before this the minister of home affairs, Masajuro Shiokawa, claimed that "The TV news about the PKO, which features a tank and a missile, makes the people misunderstand," and he asked the minister of posts and telecommunications to discuss it with the TV stations.

These remarks by ministers are considered by broadcasters to be an intervention by the government in the area of television news and a challenge to freedom of speech, which is protected by the constitution. The government has repeatedly put pressure on television news programs. However, broadcasters feel this criticism of *News Station* shows most symbolically the government's idea of what TV should be like, namely, obedient to authorities.

On this matter, TV Asahi has not made any specific protests to the government, partly because the commercial TV stations are licensed companies. Specifically, TV Asahi's silence is thought to be caused by a desire to avoid offending the government, especially the Ministry of Posts and Telecommunications, which will decide channel allocations when the BS-4 satellite is launched in 1997. TV Asahi is eager to acquire one of the channels through any means.

Information Programs Lately informational TV programs have been started, especially in the weekend time slots, that explain and look back on the week's events. These programs feature talented actors, experts, and interviews with politicians. For a long time, the morning time on the weekends was called the "sterile time" as far as ratings were concerned. But then, TBS's *Sunday Morning* started in 1987, and TV Asahi's *Sunday Project* became a pioneer in developing that time slot.

They succeeded because the 5-day workweek prevailed and people could afford to pay more attention to the news on the weekend. Financially, producing these programs is relatively inexpensive for the TV stations. At present, there are six such programs (almost all on commercial television stations) on Saturday and Sunday mornings.

One of the most popular features of these programs is interviews with important politicians. As the chaotic political situation involving ruling and opposition parties evolves, these interviews become all the more important. Producer Shoichi Wada of *Sunday Project* says,

Powerful Saturday, one of Japan's information programs.

"The Japanese political scene has been hidden, so far, behind the secret meetings in the Ryotei [a traditional highbrow restaurant]. But, through hard-hitting interviews the viewers can understand what the politicians are thinking, as if the real discussion in the Diet [Parliament] had been transferred to the studio."

NHK has been airing *Political Discussion* on Sunday mornings since 1953, giving equal time for each politician's speech. But *Sunday Project* emphasizes examining a politician's character by concentrating on an issue over a longer period—as long as 40 to 50 minutes. This gives people a different image of politicians than that previously given on daily news programs. "I realize that they actually have their own policies," says one of the viewers.

As a result, the ratings for these weekend shows are good—in the high single digits, which is excellent for a weekend morning program. In addition, the type of viewer is very favorable for sponsors because the major category of viewer is businesspeople in their thirties and forties. This program actually refuses to accept sponsors' offers because no time is available for more commercial messages.

Furthermore, there are many offers from politicians who wish to appear on these weekend programs because they realize the influence these shows have on the voters. However, the producers must take care to avoid politicians who intend to advertise their causes.

Entertainment Programming Entertainment is the dominant fare of electronic media in Japan. The entire range of entertainment programs is presented—drama, comedy, talk shows, music, variety, game shows. Most of the programs, whether on NHK or on commercial stations, are produced in Japan. Sometimes another country's idea, such as the idea for *Wheel of Fortune*, is used, but most of the programs feature Japanese and are taped in Japan.

Some of the program ideas from the past and present include an early-morning show featuring older people playing gateball, a game similar to croquet; a quiz show where people have to guess how much things cost in other countries; and wrestlers who are also rock stars—first they sing and then they wrestle with each other.

One of the game shows went on for many episodes. It started with over 1000 contestants, most of whom were eliminated through various levels of competition. When the number of contestants got down to about ten, they were taken to other countries where they competed in entertaining endurance feats such as running a relay race in Death Valley, California.

A noontime variety show features a lively host who will do just about anything. Included in his program are contests, pet tricks, interviews, and housewife wrestling.

The Japanese love sports, with televised baseball games being a big draw. Sometimes four baseball games can be seen at one time in Tokyo, which has six commercial and two NHK TV stations. Soccer, golf, judo, and sumo wrestling also attract large audiences.

Music shows are also popular and include concerts by symphony orchestras, traditional Kabuki opera/dramas in which women's parts are still often played by men, Japanese popular music groups, and awards shows similar to America's Grammy presentations.

Many of the dramas are based on elements of Japanese history. One, called *Oshin,* that went on for many episodes was about a poor girl who lived on a farm at the turn of the century. Over two-thirds of Japanese people watched at least part of it. A number of the drama programs, including shows featuring samurai warriors and police activity, are quite violent. Occasionally they are criticized for their violence, although violence on TV does not seem to have affected the Japanese society, which is generally nonviolent.

Children's cartoons, many of which are violent, proliferate. Other children's programming includes educational programs and studio shows where children are in the audience and interact with show hosts. One children's program that has been on for over 20 years is called *The Drifter.* It stars an acting company that performs skits for the children. These skits have been criticized for being violent and vulgar, but kids love them.

U.S. entertainment programming is sometimes shown, but it is not very popular. *Dallas* did very poorly when it was imported. American movies are usually relegated to the late-night hours.

LAWS AND REGULATIONS

The main government body concerned with broadcasting is the Ministry of Posts and Telecommunications (formerly the Communications Ministry). One of its main functions is awarding channels such as the BS-4 satellite channels that will begin operation in 1997.

The major laws governing the electronic media are those that were passed in 1950 to reorganize broadcasting after World War II. However, even before that, the government was involved in broadcasting. As already mentioned, NHK was established by a government initiative in 1926 and later reorganized as a public broadcasting enterprise based on the Broadcasting Law of 1950. Each year, NHK's annual account of revenues and expenditures has to be approved in the Japanese Diet (Parliament) at the same time as the following year's budgetary content.

The government cannot censor programs and does not have a formal role in creating radio or television programming. However, viewers doubt this since NHK sometimes ignores important news or gives low priority to items that are unfavorable to the government and the ruling party. This has increasingly strengthened the movement among viewers to refuse to pay license fees.

As far as commercial stations are concerned, the Ministry of Posts and Telecommunications grants licenses. If many groups submit petitions for one station, the ministry decides which one will get the license or, more likely, tries to convince the various companies to form an ownership group. Licenses must be renewed every 4 or 5 years, but this is essentially automatic unless there is some type of problem. If a problem has occurred, the ministry will tell the station to discontinue the practice or it might have its license taken away. So far no station has lost its license.

THE AUDIENCE

A saying in Japan goes, "Do you know of a job in which one can walk proudly in the middle of the corridor with a popularity of only 15 percent and not be obliged to walk on the edge?" "Sure, it is a TV producer!"

Though this seems to be exaggerated, it pointedly reflects the substance of Japanese television; the viewing rate is the absolute and sole measure for evaluating all the programs, as in the United States. This is because an alternative measure has not yet been devised. And sponsors are buying airtime and want to have their advertisements viewed by as many people as possible. In Japan, television viewing research is conducted by A. C. Nielsen and Video Research, and the people meter concept has been introduced. More than before, each station's financial situation is being affected by the viewing rate.

Thus the purpose of most producers is to aim more and more at exceeding the popularity of other programs shown at the same hour by even a slight degree in terms of viewing rate. This has sometimes made even the producers in charge of documentaries completely blind to the social mission of journalism, and they broadcast sensational episodes (so-called *yarase*) as if they were true.

The popular documentary *Sutekini Document,* produced by the Asahi Broadcasting Corporation, aired a misleading story in July 1992. The program gave the impression that, through hidden cameras, ABC was showing Japanese women seeking American gigolos by interviewing them. The program was very successful, with a rating of 18 percent, but the "interviewees" had been hired to appear, costumed, and coached by an outside production company. This incident brought about a great uproar throughout Japan. The Ministry of Posts and Telecommunications expressed great concern about this *yarase* because it damaged people's trust in television as a medium of journalism, and the ministry gave a severe warning to ABC. Ultimately, this program was halted, and some of the ABC executives and producers took a self-imposed salary cut for a few months to assume the responsibility.

Unfortunately, a producer is permitted to continue as long as he or she gets a high viewing rate regardless of who is viewing. Thus the demand to correct such evils and ask who is viewing the programs and why has often been heard, not only by the general public but also by sponsors.

TECHNOLOGY

Japan is a very high-tech country. Radio and television stations and networks have sophisticated production equipment that can create many special effects. Most of the equipment is Japanese-made because Japan is the leader in the production of electronic equipment.

The original technology of the Japanese electronics industry was developed by importing technological innovations from other countries and improving on them. In this way, Japanese companies, such as Sony and Matsushita, have become world leaders in the manufacture of cameras, VCRs, and other electronic gear.

HDTV However, some innovations, foremost among them high-definition television, had their beginnings in Japan. NHK initially started to develop and research HDTV in order to produce the "TV of the future." Japanese HDTV has 1125 scanning lines, more than twice as many as the NTSC system presently used in Japan, the United States, and many other countries. It also has a wider screen that has an 9:16 aspect ratio rather than the NTSC 3:4 aspect ratio. The HDTV system is not compatible with the NTSC system.

Since 1991 Hi-Vision Promotion Association, Inc., which consists of NHK and the commercial stations, has been tentatively airing sports, movies, dramas, and art programs for 8 hours a day on average, using the satellite BS-3. Full-scale broadcasting is scheduled to start in 1997 on BS-4. Little by little, HDTV programming material is being accumulated through these broadcasts, although some critics claim that both the quality and quantity do not do justice to the real characteristics of HDTV.

Japanese electronics companies are beginning to sell HDTV sets that cost less than 1 million yen (about $8300), as well as VCRs that can play both NTSC and HDTV. Companies are putting a great deal of emphasis on developing HDTV because it could have a 1 or 2 trillion yen ($8 to $16 billion) market in the twenty-first century. So far, approximately 100,000 HDTV sets have been brought into Japanese homes.

"Our HDTV is clearly advancing ahead of America and Europe in terms of practical applications," an HDTV researcher states proudly, "though great concerns are yet left about the technology for the near future." Japan's HDTV broadcasting adopts the Multiple Sub-Nyquist Encoding (MUSE) method, which relies on compressing the transmitting width of the HDTV signal. Specifically, 30 megahertz of the HDTV signal is transmitted by 8.1 megahertz when compressed. However, the compressed HDTV signal is not completely restored, and the amount of information is decreased. Thus the quality of the picture is sacrificed. Also, the Japanese MUSE technique is a hybrid method that combines digital and analog technology.

The digital transmitting method of HDTV developed in the United States is still under experimentation. However, the quality of the picture on the proposed American system is better, and there is still more room for improvement than in Japan's MUSE method.

EDTV II In the meantime, apart from HDTV broadcasting using a broadcasting satellite, so-called extended-definition TV (EDTV II), which will improve the current NTSC method for terrestrial broadcasting, is being considered by the Broadcasting Technology Association, which is supervised by the Ministry of Posts and Telecommunications.

This system improves the picture quality in that it diminishes flickering, improves vertical resolution, and widens the television screen from a 3:4 ratio to the same ratio as that of HDTV. Additionally, the sound will be digital. Although EDTV II broadcasting will be compatible with current TV sets, a special set will be needed in order to enjoy its full benefits. The Japanese viewpoint on picture quality is that HDTV is the "super express" and EDTV II is the "limited express."

However, to spend money, time, and labor on EDTV II research and then also to have to concentrate on preparing for HDTV broadcasting is a very heavy burden for commercial television stations. Even if EDTV II comes into common use, many people feel that it might possibly be replaced by HDTV, which is supposed to start in 1997. Thus one researcher has come to question what the Ministry of Posts and Telecommunications' real intention is in promoting both HDTV and EDTV II at the same time.

Nevertheless, viewers welcome this competition in pursuit of high picture quality. It is also welcomed by electronics companies that expect HDTV and/or EDTV II to be the main sales product of the near future.

However, the actions of the commercial television stations have been considerably overshadowed by political intentions regarding the favor or disfavor they might incur from the Ministry of Posts and Telecommunications. Their efforts in the research and development of the software and hardware for HDTV are obviously regarded as an appeal to the ministry, which is the real decision maker in allocating the eight channels of the next broadcasting satellite,

BS-4. And, as long as the Ministry of Posts and Telecommunications attempts to promote EDTV II, the commercial TV stations cannot discontinue research and development for fear that the ministry will award the satellite channels to individuals not presently in the broadcasting business. Thus research and development efforts have been undertaken by the commercial TV stations with a somewhat cynical attitude.

Sound Meanwhile, efforts to improve quality have moved forward at a rapid pace in Japan in the "sound" media (the new name that is becoming common for radio). In 1992 some AM stations adopted stereo broadcasting for sports and dramas using the Motorola method, and most listeners speak highly of the sound. Stereo has an important role in revitalizing AM stations, which have been overwhelmed by the recent surge of FM stations.

Broadcasting and communication satellites are very crucial, not only for television media but also for sound media. PCM (digital) stations have begun operating as paid stations by utilizing communication satellites, and the quality of the sound is superior to that of FM and CD sound. These sound-innovation stations are advancing their specialty in a way that distinguishes them from the traditional stations. For example, one station is airing an ecological sound that features sounds from nature.

If people want to listen to these stations, they need a special tuner and antenna that cost about $2000 to install. However, the reality is that not enough people have subscribed to these new sound stations, and so the stations have been forced to sell advertising. The importance of sound quality, made possible by technology, is not enough to attract listeners as long as it forces them to pay more money just to listen.

Thus radio and television technology in Japan consists of varied innovative hardware looking to a future that will make Japan the highest-ranking technological country in the world. However, as already pointed out, programming will not necessarily benefit from the hardware unless there is enough quality and quantity. In addition, new electronic media have to be affordable because they are not a necessity; they are used almost entirely for entertainment. Technology, which promises a bright future for people, cannot be truly meaningful until these difficulties are eliminated.

EXTERNAL SERVICES

In 1935 Japan started an international radio service with a 1-hour broadcast in English aimed at the western United States and Canada. During World War II, it was known for its Tokyo Rose broadcasts featuring dulcet-voiced women trying to talk Americans into deserting the military.

The present Japanese external radio service, Radio Japan, is run by NHK and broadcasts in 21 different languages. NHK devotes 200 of its staffers to the operation, and Radio Japan hires an additional 100 or so non-Japanese staff members as translators, writers, and announcers. The programming deals primarily with Japanese and international news, but feature material on Japanese life and popular culture is also included. Many of the people who listen to Radio Japan are Japanese who live overseas and individuals who are studying Japanese.

Japan does not partake of external services from other countries to any great degree. Formerly, people listened to Voice of America and to the BBC, but very few do anymore. The Japanese prefer their own media programming.

IMPORTANCE IN THE WORLD COMMUNITY

Japan's primary importance stems from the dominant position of its electronics industry. Almost every country in the world depends on Sony, Panasonic, JVC, and other Japanese companies for electronic equipment such as cameras and television sets. Purchases of this equipment have brought wealth into Japan and strengthened its economy.

Japan has led the way in research and development for some of the new technologies, such as HDTV and satellite-delivered programming. However, it has not always been successful in marketing its technological ideas to the world. For example, although it was first in the development of HDTV, it could not convince the rest of the world to adopt its technology.

Japan has much less influence in programming than in the realm of hardware. Very few programs are exported, in part because Japanese is not a universal language. The programs produced in Japan are meant mainly for the national audience.

However, the Japanese are trying to overcome this program inadequacy by buying production companies in other countries. Most notably in the United States, Sony has purchased Columbia Pictures, and Matsushita has purchased Universal Pictures.

MAJOR ISSUES

The future direction that radio and television structures will take is very uncertain. Radio is attempting a comeback, but no one knows for certain if it will succeed. AM, FM, and satellite sound are competing for whatever audience share the sound medium can generate.

The television landscape is even more unsettled. The terrestrial stations, both NHK and commercial, seem to be on the decline. But cable television and satellite-delivered services have not caught the people's fancy yet—at least not with the price tag now attached to them. Some observers point out other, structural, reasons why terrestrial stations have lost their superior position. These reasons include the increasing number of stations and the decreasing trust customers have in the electronic media. Also, videocassettes, personal computers, and TV games are competitors invading their market. Feeling the crisis, some commercial television stations have begun to build production companies to strengthen programming.

The new satellite channels that will be awarded for 1997 present opportunities, but for whom? The conflict between established broadcasters who want the channels and a government that wants to open them up to novices must be resolved. Even if it is settled in favor of the broadcasters, there are so many of them that competition for operation of the satellite channels will still be great.

The future direction of HDTV is important to Japan. If digital American HDTV is just around the corner, globally it may be the major method; at the same time, the Japanese MUSE method may be replaced by the U.S. method. If so, the $1.5 billion invested in the research and development of HDTV by Japanese electronics companies and broadcasting stations will have been for naught.

But most importantly, the Japanese electronic media, which have an overriding role in entertainment, should reconsider in depth their very significant role in journalism—in producing public opinion. They should resolve several of the evils that plague the industry. First of all, with the development of technology, information is received live from the other side of the earth as if it is coming from a neighboring village. However, this information is often not polished or immediately verified and can present facts or opinions that are not correct. Also, the commercial television stations and NHK must stop presenting misleading stories because they cause viewers to lose trust in television. Stations have also been accused of wasting public airwaves by airing very lowbrow programs that gain success by pandering to viewers.

In Japan, the electronic media can develop a bright future as they rapidly advance toward the twenty-first century if they change their course and get a new grip on their audience through well-organized, truthful programming that deals with the meaningful issues of the day.

SELECTED BIBLIOGRAPHY

Browne, Donald R. "Japan: From Kabuki to Crime Drama." In *Comparing Broadcast Systems: The Experiences of Six Industrialized Nations.* Ames, IA: Iowa State University Press, 1989, pp. 303–355.

Burton, Jack. "Japanese Say Cable TV Too Expensive," *Electronic Media,* 7 February 1985, p. 18.

50 Years of Japanese Broadcasting. Tokyo: NHK, 1977.

Japan Broadcasting Corporation. "Broadcasting in Japan." In William E. McCavitt, *Broadcasting around the World.* Blue Ridge Summit, PA: TAB Books, 1981.

Patterson, Richard, ed. *The International TV and Video Guide.* London: Tantivy Press, 1986.

Radio and Television Broadcasting Facilities. Tokyo: Tokyo Broadcasting System, 1985.

Rosen, Philip T. *International Handbook of Broadcasting.* Westport, CT: Greenwood Press, 1988.

Siegel, Mark. "Japan: The Ritual Roots of 'Ultraman,'" *Channels,* July–August 1985, pp. 48–49.

Yasuko, Muramatsu. "For Wives on Friday: Women's Roles in TV Dramas," *Japan Quarterly,* April–June 1986, pp. 159–63.

PART EIGHT

AUSTRALASIA

Overview of Australasia

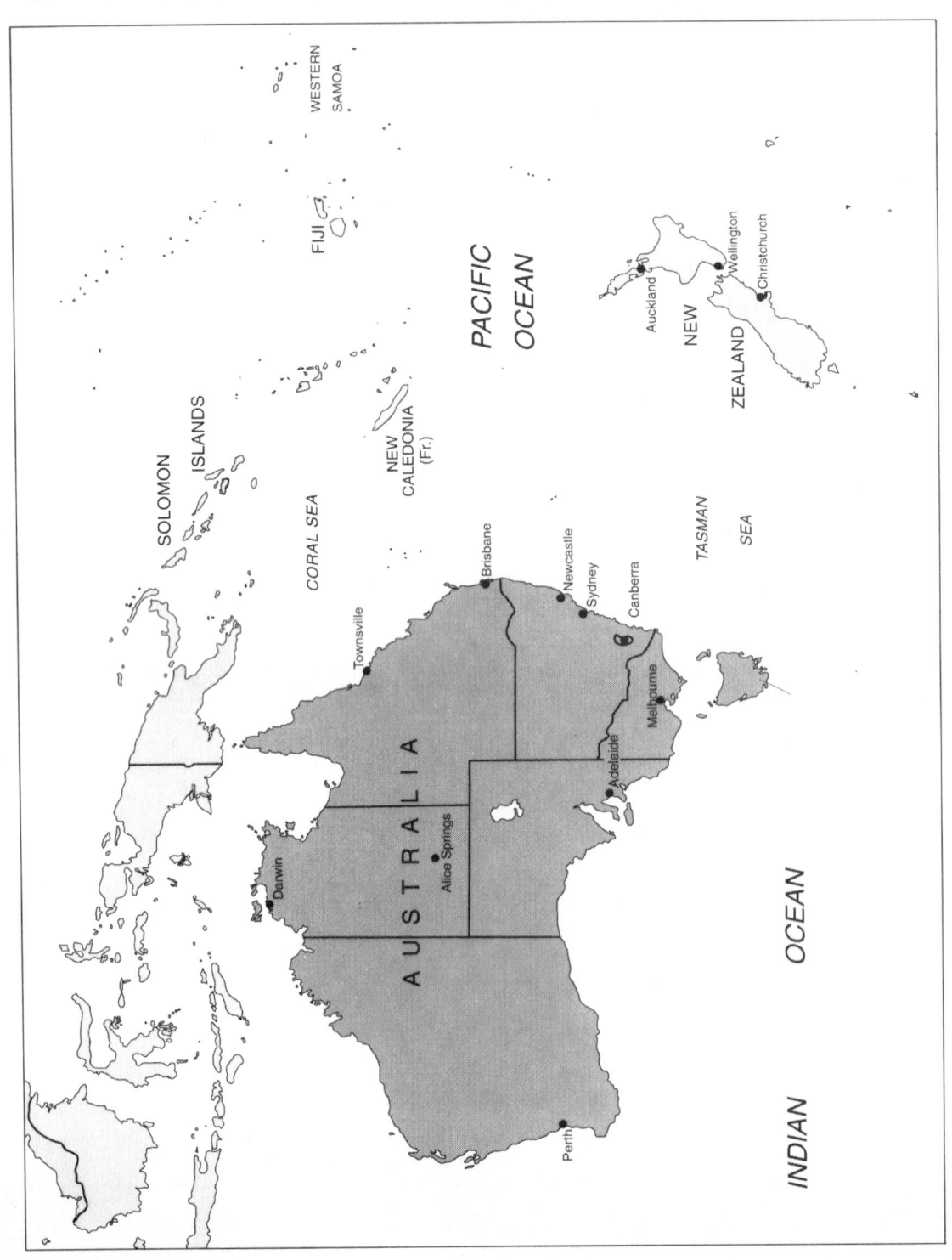

Australasia consists of Australia, New Zealand, and various South Pacific islands such as Samoa, Fiji, and the Cook Islands. While the term "Australasia" dates back to the last century, it has taken on a new dimension as the countries in the area reconsider their relationship with the rest of the world.

ELEMENTS OF CHANGE

Historically, because they were British colonies, Australia and New Zealand have considered themselves closely tied to the Western world. In fact, the truism "The sun never sets on the British Empire" was accurate because far-flung Australia and New Zealand were part of the British Empire. Australia (with New Zealand "tacked on") was a continent unto itself. Most people from the industrialized, more populous northern hemisphere thought of Australia and New Zealand as "down-under" remote areas. The countries were not important in the political interplay of the major powers—and the electronic media structure and programming of the continent were given little outside attention. Structurally, both media systems developed along the lines of the British Broadcasting Corporation (BBC), and the programming was produced to entertain and inform people with a British background. Very little attention was paid to the native people (the Aborigines in Australia and the Maoris in New Zealand), and even less note was taken of the continent's neighbors in Asia.

But all that is changing. Australia and New Zealand, both underpopulated countries, have always encouraged immigration. Among the first non-British to come were Europeans who did not speak English (Greeks, Italians, etc.) and the Chinese and Pacific Islanders who were brought in as laborers for the Australian gold mines. These people eventually wanted their cultures and languages reflected in media output.

During World War II, Japan threatened to invade Australia, and the Australians, with their limited population, looked to the United States for assistance in their defense. They were very appreciative of the aid they received and as a result began developing a relationship with the United States that included the acceptance of elements of American culture, involving, as time went by, U.S. television programs. New Zealanders, too, appreciate the United States and emulate its culture. This is not to say that either country wholeheartedly accepts American values. In fact, America bashing is common (small shop owners who are being put out of business because of the growth of shopping malls blame the United States for developing the mall concept). But both countries measure their accomplishments against an American yardstick. Having an Australian- or New Zealand–produced program shown in the United States (no matter how small the monetary payment or how insignificant the station or network) is considered a major accomplishment.

The British settlers who originally came to this part of the world (convicts in the case of much of Australia and gentry in the case of New Zealand) did not give consideration to the needs or rights of the indigenous people living on the continent. In a manner similar to what happened with the American Indians, they took their land and did their best to destroy native culture. In recent times these indigenous people have begun demanding rights, including access to the media. In both countries public broadcasting stations (somewhat akin to public access channels on U.S. cable) have been established to serve community groups, particularly Aborigines and Maoris. The national networks have also been encouraged, through regulatory actions, to direct some attention to indigenous needs in their mainstream programming.

As Asia has risen in political and economic stature, the Australians and New Zealanders have begun to pay more attention to their neighbors—and vice versa. Asians seeking a higher standard of living have begun emigrating to

Australia and, in lesser numbers, to New Zealand. Both countries are experiencing the "new Japanese invasion"—tourists. Japanese imports (long disdained because of the World War II experience) are now in great abundance. Perhaps even more importantly, Australia is intrigued with the possibility of becoming a leading country in Asian communication and a bridge between Eastern and Western trade and culture—hence the new importance of the term "Australasia." If it can position itself geographically within the Asian community, Australia stands to profit economically through trade and development. New Zealand, too, envisions itself taking a stronger role in the growth of the Asian market. Part of the influence Australia and New Zealand would like to exert on Asia involves the electronic media. Both countries have been involved in giving advice to evolving media structures in Asia. Hong Kong–based STAR TV's management at one point consisted of a number of New Zealanders—many of whom were "replaced" when ex-Australian Rupert Murdoch bought into STAR. Both countries consider the Asian region a prime target for the export of programming, and, indeed, many of these countries do purchase a fair amount of Australian (and some New Zealand) programming. On the other side of the coin, the new Asian immigrants want their needs taken into account within the media structure of Australia and New Zealand.

All of these factors—non-English-speaking immigrants, U.S. emulation, indigenous considerations, and a positioning within Asia—have given the media structures of Australia and New Zealand their own particular qualities. No longer are they clones of the British. They have their own distinctive, constantly evolving cultures.

IMPORTANCE OF AUSTRALIA

Australia was selected as the country to be highlighted in the Australasia portion of this text because it is the largest and most important country in the region. The South Pacific islands do not have well-developed media systems. Most of them have radio but no formalized television. Those that are engaged in television are doing so with the help of other countries, including neighboring Australia and New Zealand. For example, Fiji's government has begun a trial television network for which New Zealand is supplying the programming.

Australia has one other trait that is likely to make it a major player on the world media scene. It envisions itself as a major media production country. In the 1970s the Australian government poured economic resources into the Australian film industry with the intent of obtaining worldwide recognition for Australian films. It worked. Movies such as *Crocodile Dundee*, the *Mad Max* series, and *My Brilliant Career* were economic and critical successes worldwide. The government set up a highly endowed film school in Sydney, and many Australians became adept at moviemaking techniques. This interest and capability are now carrying over into television production as well as theatrical production. However, money does not flow as freely now as it has in the past, and this has affected the quality and quantity of the content, but many people within Australia have the mind-set and desire to make Australia a major television production producer and distributor.

New Zealand does not have this view of itself. Its film industry is very small. The government allocates about $9 million a year for filmmaking that it doles out in grants of $1 or $2 million to prospective filmmakers. With these small numbers, feature filmmaking is a passion, not an economically viable occupation. Nevertheless, New Zealand's radio and television structure is well regarded within its own country and by the countries it influences.

NEW ZEALAND BROADCASTING

Presently, New Zealand has one of the least regulated media systems in the world. A branch of the Ministry of Commerce auctions frequencies and makes sure stations stay on their frequencies, but there is no regulatory body equivalent to the Federal Communications Commission (FCC). There is a Broadcasting Standards Authority to which citizens can take complaints about broadcasting—but only after they have contacted the station or network involved and feel they have received an unsatisfactory resolution of the problem. However, prior to deregulation, which occurred in 1988, broadcasting was subject to a long period of political influence. Historically, the New Zealand legislature has passed more laws about broadcasting in the last 40 years than anywhere else in the world. The politicians could not keep their hands off broadcasting. Because of this, the deregulation of recent years is even more remarkable.

Because of the small size of New Zealand, most of the radio and TV is national—three radio networks and three TV networks. In addition, there are over forty independent local radio stations, twenty-three of which are operated by and programmed primarily for Maoris. Some of the local radio stations are also community access in that they are operated by volunteers from the community. Two regional TV networks already exist and there are plans for several more.

New Zealand originally had a radio structure modeled after the BBC except that commercials were accepted and the system was operated by a state-owned government department, not a chartered agency. However, in recent years the country has adopted more of an American model in that it has allowed privatization. The radio networks that were run by the government have been put under a form of commercial trust called a "state-owned enterprise." Many see this as a step toward selling them off to commercial interests. Two of the TV networks are still government-run, but the third one, TV-3, has been privately owned since its inception in 1989. New Zealand has no laws prohibiting foreigners from owning media, and TV-3 is presently owned primarily by a Canadian company that rescued it from bankruptcy encountered by its New Zealand owners.

New Zealand also has a pay-TV system called Sky TV. This is a multichannel multipoint distribution service that consists of three channels: news (largely CNN and BBC), sports (some ESPN and other international sports), and movies (with many U.S. films). Teletext is also fairly popular in New Zealand.

The government and private broadcasting systems are financed primarily by commercials. TV set owners do pay a license fee to a government agency that then distributes the money to fund public affairs and other programs that would not be produced on a commercial basis. This money also funds Maori and community access broadcasting.

New Zealand has no programming quotas, and so any amount of imported programming is allowed. As a result, the TV channels are heavily American, with some British and Australian input. Most New Zealand–produced programs are of a news and information nature. Some drama is produced in the country, including a highly successful early-evening soap that is partially funded from the license fee. It is argued that the soap reflects New Zealand culture, one of the objectives of the funding agency, which is appropriately titled "New Zealand on Air." The game shows that are aired use U.S. formats. Children's programs are produced internally, and these shows are the ones that New Zealand is mainly interested in exporting. There is a thriving industry producing, usually with international partners, what are termed "kidult" programs. Radio networks and stations program primarily music, news, and talk. The technical quality of the programs tends to be excellent, mainly because New Zealand broadcasters keep their equipment up to date and in good repair and respond very professionally in a very competitive market. There are over 70 radio stations for 3.4 million people.

New Zealand has an external service that sends radio programming to the islands in the South Pacific as a public service. It does not broadcast any propaganda material.

Because of the commercial nature of the

radio and TV media, ratings are very important. The people meter is used to record TV ratings. New Zealanders, on the average, watch about 23 hours of TV per week and are generally pleased with the service that the media provide.

HISTORY AND GEOGRAPHY

Both New Zealand and Australia are presently experiencing a history-versus-geography philosophical war. This is more intense in Australia where forces are trying to divorce the country from the queen of England, where a larger number of Asian immigrants reside, and where there is a stronger desire to become an economic leader in the Asian theater.

If Australia cuts its historical ties and becomes the economic leader among its geographic neighbors in Asia, it will truly be Australasian. But of course there are other powers in Asia, such as Japan and Hong Kong, that are not going to lie down and play dead while Australia takes over economic control. One thing is certain, however: Australia will never again be as British as it has been in the past. Despite its relatively remote location, it must interact with the world and especially with its nearby Asian neighbors.

After having felt the "tyranny of distance" for many years, it is eager to become a more active participant in world affairs, especially by contributing to the international media environment.

(*Editor's Note*: I would like to thank Brian Pauling, head of the New Zealand Broadcasting School at Christchurch Polytechnic, for providing the information about New Zealand broadcasting.)

CHAPTER 13

Australia

Bruce Molloy and Derek Wilding

Bruce Molloy and Derek Wilding.

Bruce Molloy retired as professor and head of the School of Media and Journalism at the Queensland University of Technology in Brisbane, Australia, in February 1994. A former president of the Australian Communication Association and a commissioner of the Pacific Film and Television Commission, he is the author of *Before the Interval: Australian Mythology and Feature Films 1930–1960* and coeditor of *Queensland Images in Film and Television*. Currently adjunct professor of media at Bond University on Queensland's Gold Coast, he is a consultant to the Australian film and television industry.

Derek Wilding holds a Bachelor of Arts–Bachelor of Law from the University of Queensland. Until early 1993 he was research officer in the Research Concentration in Media Policy and Practice at QUT. Now he is engaged in full-time doctoral research into media representation and policy as they relate to HIV/AIDS issues.

STATISTICS

Geographic Area: 2,966,200 square miles
Capital: Canberra
Population: 16,849,496
Religions: Anglican, other Protestant, Roman Catholic
Language: English, Aboriginal languages
Type of Government: Democratic federal state system headed by a prime minister
Gross Domestic Product: $311 billion
Literacy: 89 percent

GENERAL CHARACTERISTICS

Accidents of history and geography have significantly shaped the development of the electronic media in Australia and determined that they exert an important influence on Australian society. Australian history since European settlers arrived in 1788 has been dominated by social institutions largely based on British models. These institutions include systems of government and education, and so it is not surprising that the initial steps into radio and television followed patterns established in the United Kingdom. The development of national radio and television networks was similar to that of the British Broadcasting Corporation (BBC), funded, directly or indirectly, by the public.

History and Geography Internal geography has provided the Australian nation with sole occupancy of the smallest continent, although with a land area of 3 million square miles it is almost as large as the continental United States. The population, however, is still less than 20 million, and about half of it is located in the six state capitals, all positioned on or near the coast. This distribution of population in widely dispersed generally coastal locations reflects both the importance of sea travel during the nineteenth century and the generally arid nature of much of the interior of the continent.

Such a dispersed population depends largely on the electronic media for both information and entertainment. Consequently the media serve as a form of social cement that provides far-flung population centers with a sense of being a coherent community. Because of their important social and cultural roles, the Australian media are subject to a degree of government regulation unusual by U.S. standards.

This tradition of government intervention possibly results, at least in part, from the origins of European Australia as a repository for excess convicts from Britain. The harsh environment of the interior of much of Australia also contributed to a tendency for Australians to accept government assistance and consequent control of certain aspects of everyday life. For whatever reasons, the colonial heritage of Australia is still significant, despite its achievement of national status as a commonwealth in 1901. A major present controversy, almost entirely conducted in the media, concerns Prime Minister Paul Keating's campaign to sever monarchical ties with Britain's queen and have Australia declared a republic by 2001.

The ethnic composition of Australian society reflects a society composed largely of the descendants of immigrants. The indigenous people, the Australian Aborigines, constitute less than 1 percent of the nation. They have seen their tribal society disintegrate over the two centuries of European settlement, although in recent decades many Aboriginal groups have reasserted their cultural identity, often employing the media in the process.

Until the end of World War II in 1945, the predominant racial group in Australia was Anglo-Celtic, derived largely from initially involuntary, but later voluntary, migration from England, Ireland, Scotland, and Wales. The great population surge accompanying the gold discoveries of the second half of the nineteenth century involved a proportion of noncaucasians, mainly Chinese, but the Australian Immigration Act of 1901, which remained in force until about 1960, was designed to discriminate against nonwhites and was commonly referred to as "the white Australia policy."

After World War II, one of the world's great migration programs saw an influx of non-English-speaking European people, such as Greeks and Italians, into Australia. This changed the demography of Australia forever, with the proportion of British-derived Australians falling from about 95 percent in 1950 to less than 50 percent in 1990.

In recent years, in line with a government policy of establishing trade and cultural links with Asia and in recognition that its location makes Australia geographically, if not culturally, an Asian nation, an increasing proportion of Asians have been admitted to Australia. In recognition of this cultural diversity, and in line with the government policy of multiculturalism, special non-English-language radio and television networks, known as the Special Broadcasting Service (SBS), have been established with government funds. These will be discussed later in this chapter.

Although Australia has looked largely to Britain for social institutions, its location in the Pacific has provided a geographic insulation from British dominance, while its cultural traditions have separated it from the direct influence of its more populous Asian neighbors. Trade links with the United States, established in the nineteenth and early twentieth centuries, were reinforced by the popularity of U.S. media products and by a community of interest against Japan during the Pacific war between 1941 and 1945. In early 1942 Australia's wartime prime minister, John Curtin, foreshadowed a major shift in Australian relations when he stated that Australia had been forced "without inhibition of any kind, to look to America" for military support. The penetration of Australia by American cultural influences has produced commercial media systems that resemble those of the United States, while they operate in a largely British-derived regulatory environment.

Media Statistics The central role of the media in providing both information and entertainment is confirmed by statistical surveys. The average Australian watches in excess of 20 hours of television each week. Over 70 percent of Australians identify television as their principal source of information about news and current affairs, a fact which has not been lost on press proprietors as they redesign newspapers to be more competitive. While radio is more pervasive than television in terms of the number of sets in use, it tends to be a secondary activity with its audience listening as they perform some other task.

This dependence upon electronic media is reflected in the 98 percent of Australian homes that have one or more color television sets, have more than one radio, and are connected to a telephone service. The ratio of telephones to population, probably reflecting commercial usage, is more than one per person, with rapidly increasing numbers of mobile and cellular phones.

More than 78 percent of Australian homes have at least one videocassette recorder, and the practices of time shifting by recording programs for later viewing, zapping commercials on recorded programs, and zipping through available channels using remote controls are well established. Surveys indicate that a majority of Australians do not plan viewing but choose from available programs when they have free time.

Over 50 percent of Australian homes have some form of home computer facilities. Although domestic services are not yet fully integrated into information networks, the necessary fiber-optic cabling is already in place within and between major population centers. Australians have always enthusiastically welcomed new technology, and they are among the world's leading users of fax machines for business and domestic purposes.

Media and Society Because the electronic media are so widespread and influential, the provision, ownership, regulation, and control of broadcasting services have long been an important issue on the Australian political agenda. So, too, is the related question of cross-media ownership (one company owning numerous newspapers, radio stations, and TV services) since it involves the possibility of media monopolies with extensive information power concentrated in few hands. These issues became increasingly significant in the allocation of licenses to operate radio and television stations.

Another important issue in Australian media, itself a consequence of Australia's colonial past and of Australian resentment of cultural imperialism, is the regulation of content to ensure that a substantial proportion of Australian-produced material is shown across a range of program categories. These issues will be considered in more detail later in this chapter.

While the Australian people enjoy a relatively high quality of life because of the wealth of natural resources available to a small population, the Australian economy has experienced difficulties in recent years. These problems have resulted from an unfavorable balance of payments, with imports (including media hardware and software) significantly in excess of exports.

Since the economic turbulence of the late 1980s, unemployment levels have hovered above 10 percent, a figure five times that of a generation earlier and unseen in Australia since the Great Depression of the 1930s.

Paradoxically, tough economic times seem to increase domestic media consumption, perhaps because spending on entertainment outside the home diminishes. The video rental business has been a growth industry during the last decade, with most small retail shops offering videos for rent, while large specialist outlets have also developed.

With most working Australians spending fewer than 38 hours per week on the job, and with a mandatory 4 weeks' annual paid leave period, Australians rank close to the top of the developed world in terms of leisure time available for potential media usage.

THE DEVELOPMENT OF ELECTRONIC MEDIA IN AUSTRALIA

Experiments in the use of wireless (the original name for radio) began in the early 1900s based on a clause in the Australian constitution that gave the federal government control of postal, telegraphic, telephonic, "and other like services." Initially seen as a means of two-way communication, the first direct England-Australia transmissions occurred in 1918. Within a couple of years, public demonstrations of radio broadcasting were taking place in Sydney and Melbourne, and by 1921 experimental broadcasting of concerts was occurring every week.

Early Radio With the establishment of regular radio broadcasting services in London in 1922, impetus was added to move to establish regular broadcasting in Australia, with the structure of the BBC providing the model for development.

Following a conference organized by the postmaster general's department in 1923, public broadcasting was introduced using a system of sealed radio sets tuned to one station only. This system was designed to ensure that license fees were paid directly to the relevant station, but it was unwieldy and open to abuse through alteration of the frequency. Within a year it proved unworkable and was replaced in 1924 by a two-tier system which was to remain effectively in force for almost half a century.

Under this system, two groups of radio stations were established. One group, designated A-class stations, was maintained by license fees. These A-class stations eventually evolved into the government-funded national network called the Australian Broadcasting Corporation (ABC). The second group, B-class stations, commenced operations in 1925. These stations were to be supported entirely through revenues from advertising. These B-class stations became the nucleus of the commercial radio system. Under the two-tier approach, the number of license holders grew from 1400 in 1924, to 38,000 in 1925, to 310,000 by 1929.

The ABC In 1928 the Australian government decided to amalgamate all A-class stations into a national organization. This system would provide, under contract with the government, programs to all six states. Initially this organization was run by a private company, the Australian Broadcasting Company, which also had theatrical, music, and film interests. In 1932 the government decided to replace this private company as national provider, setting up a new government authority to take its place. The new authority was called the Australian Broadcasting Commission (ABC), along the lines of the British Broadcasting Corporation.

The establishing act for the ABC required it to provide "adequate and comprehensive" programming, thus creating continuing tension between the proportion of quality (i.e., "adequate") programs and the policy of broad or popular (i.e., "comprehensive") programs. The ABC encouraged Australian writers through its radio plays, established symphony orchestras for music lovers, and aired special agricultural programs for rural dwellers.

Two very important aspects of its programming were its educational programs for schools and its broadcasting of parliamentary proceedings from the Federal Parliament in Canberra. Naturally, such a diversity of programs meant that it had to develop more than one radio station in each state.

As the ABC expanded its activity, the revenue from license fees for radio and television sets paid by consumers fell short of the costs involved in offering comprehensive services. Consequently license fees came to be paid into the consolidated revenue of the government, with direct appropriations being allocated to the ABC in annual federal government budgets. In 1974 the government abolished broadcasting license fees for individual radio and television sets, and the cost of the ABC and other later national broadcasters like the Special Broadcasting Service (SBS) was met by taxation.

In 1982 the ABC was renamed the Australian Broadcasting Corporation and was restructured to broaden its accessibility to public opinion. In theory, the new structure provided an additional degree of autonomy, but in practice the ABC remained susceptible to government pressure through its dependence on government funding.

Commercial Radio Commercial radio broadcasters formed a representative body initially called the Federation of Australian Radio Broadcasters (FARB). This organization helped coordinate commercial networking arrangements and opened links with other countries in programming, particularly high-profile drama and serials. During the 1920s radio advertising became a significant industry, often involving multinational agencies.

Innovation was characteristic of both the ABC and commercial radio broadcasting. Along with parliamentary broadcasts and radio plays, Australian radio achievements included the first radio broadcast from an aircraft (1924), the introduction of religious broadcasts (1928), and the initiation of direct international sporting broadcasts with its coverage of a cricket series played in England in 1933.

World War II With the onset of the war in Europe in 1939, the state took a renewed interest in radio. Radio Australia was established under the auspices of the ABC to provide an international outlet for Australian views. The ABC national news took on a global complexion, though after the entry of Japan into the war in late 1941, the Pacific theater of war became its dominant interest.

In 1942 a full-scale government review of the broadcasting industry led to a single act of Parliament to regulate all sectors of the radio industry and to protect the ABC from political interference. This new act also addressed program content, requiring a set proportion of music being aired to be produced in Australia. This provision initiated a policy of regulating Australian content that continues to operate in radio and television to the present day and that has generated considerable controversy over the years. In 1949 the first statutory body to regulate broadcasting, the Australian Broadcasting Control Board (ABCB), was established.

One consequence of the war was an increase in the relative importance of radio, in terms of both news and especially advertising, as the shortage of newsprint drastically reduced the page length of newspapers. Another war-related shortage was created by a halt in the flow of American drama scripts and transcriptions to Australia, so that the demand for Australian-written scripts and Australian-produced radio drama increased sharply, laying the foundation for a solid export industry in the postwar years.

Postwar Media The decades following the end of the war saw a substantial growth in the Australian population. Between 1950 and 1970 the number of people in Australia doubled, in part because of the baby boom, in part because of migration. The number of radio stations did not increase, however, until the Whitlam Labor government was elected in 1972, ending 23 years of conservative rule. This new government was pledged to social reform. In the radio area it introduced frequency-modulated (FM) broadcasting; it also opened additional slots on the amplitude-modulated (AM) band; and it introduced another new element in Australian media—public access broadcasting (often called simply "public broadcasting") wherein community groups have primary input into station programming.

By 1978, 200 AM stations were in operation, along with 5 FM stations in metropolitan areas and about 50 public access stations. In 1976 the ABCB was replaced by the Australian Broadcasting Tribunal (ABT), which opened up the system of license allocation and license renewal to increased public scrutiny and participation. For the first time the question of cross-media ownership emerged as a serious issue, while the question of Australian-produced content received renewed attention, with the ABT setting the quota for Australian music on radio at 12.5 percent. Although the ABC did not fall under ABT purview, it usually complied with ABT directives to commercial stations.

Radio after the Introduction of TV The arrival of television in the late 1950s saw radio gradually abdicate such fields as quiz programs, family melodrama, and situation comedy, as the new medium appropriated them. Replacing these was an increased emphasis on popular music and sports. The development of talk radio provided a new low-cost program format, while the manufacture and sale of radios emphasized the shift away from standing models like consoles toward portables, a trend that accelerated rapidly as transistors replaced tubes.

Accompanying these changes was an increase in the youth market as the proportion of young people in the population grew and prosperity provided them with significant disposable income. As this demographic shift occurred, so also did the shift to such youth-oriented content as rock-and-roll music and programs devoted to listing music in terms of popularity. These radical changes, as always, caused no little perturbation to the guardians of cultural orthodoxy and moral standards, both self-appointed and statutory.

Commercial radio management became increasingly sophisticated in its approach to programming and marketing. Closer and closer attention was devoted to the details of market segmentation by age, gender, and ethnicity, while advertisers attempted to find the keys to unlock disposable income.

One initiative (opposed unsuccessfully by a rather conservative FARB) was the introduction of the Special Broadcasting Service to cater to the needs of ethnic communities within Australian society. This followed a 1972 determination that the ABC was not responsible for broadcasting to ethnic groups. SBS was a result of government recognition in the early 1970s that the desire of ethnic groups to maintain their language and culture was consistent both with the government's avowed policy of multiculturalism and with its goal of integration rather than assimilation of cultural and ethnic minorities. The basis of ethnic programming was to be language rather than national or cultural identification. Naturally this policy has involved SBS in a number of political issues where cultural animosity or rivalry has divided national groups. In recognition of these problematic areas, it has now been decided that public broadcasting should cater to ethnic groups (e.g., Aborigines, Chinese) as distinct from language groups (Greek, Polish) which remain the province of SBS.

Generally, the public broadcasting sector in Australia is distinguished from the commercial stations by its dedication to special-interest groups, community organizations, and educational needs. Some public stations are sponsored by and located within educational institutions, while others serve such interests as the visually disadvantaged or indigenous peoples. Most public broadcasters are heavily dependent on public donations, membership subscriptions, and volunteer workers for their activities.

One notable special-interest group is the Central Australian Aboriginal Media Association (CAAMA). This group caters to the scattered Aboriginal communities of central Australia, with English and Aboriginal language programming, and has been in operation since 1980.

Early Television Politics Despite experiments dating from the 1920s, Australian television broadcasting did not commence officially until 1956. By then television services had been available in Britain and the United States for almost a decade, but the delay in the Australian introduction was due to political factors.

Originally television broadcasting had been expected to commence in Australia by 1950. The Australian Broadcasting Control Board had been established, as noted above, to oversee the regulation of radio and television.

Foreshadowing a continuing theme in the development of Australian television broadcasting, political events overtook the development process. The Australian Labor party (ALP), which had been in power since 1940, was defeated in the 1949 elections by a conservative Liberal party and Country party (LCP) coalition, led by the staunchly pro-British Robert Menzies.

Prime Minister Menzies and his successors were to remain in power for an unprecedented 23 years, Menzies himself remaining as government head until 1966. This long term of LCP office was aided by the ALP's disunity and factional fighting, and the LCP coalition pursued policies based on selling raw materials (such as wool, wheat, and coal) rather than developing new secondary industries, and generally maintaining the status quo in terms of Australian society. What seemed at the time to be stable government is now viewed by many Australians as a period of social stagnation, and this stability or stagnation extended to the media.

The LCP attitude toward television was typical of this social conservatism. Soon after his election, Menzies announced that television broadcasting would follow the two-tier pattern of national (ABC) and commercial stations familiar to Australians from radio broadcasting. In 1952 he announced that the introduction of television had been "deferred temporarily" because of economic circumstances. Popular demand for the start of TV broadcasting led to the establishment of a commission of inquiry in 1953. This commission recommended a phased but simultaneous introduction of national and commercial services, with a licensing system for operation of stations similar to that for commercial radio.

The ALP suggested to the ABCB that metropolitan newspaper owners should not be eligible for television licenses in order to prevent the development of media monopolies potentially able to manipulate public opinion through the use of press and television. Despite this, applications from interests involved in the publication of newspapers and magazines dominated the license hearings. The ABCB granted the first two commercial licenses to companies with publishing interests, one in Sydney and one in Melbourne.

TV Up and Running   TCN Nine Sydney, the flagship of what was to become the Nine Network, a station owned by the Packer family which had extensive publishing interests, went on air for the first time in September 1956. These early decisions to allow cross-media ownership set the scene for continuing controversy about the control of press and television by the same companies.

By the time that the Melbourne Olympic Games started in late 1956, one national and one commercial station were operating in both Sydney and Melbourne. The well-known Australian obsession with sports made these and later Olympics powerful marketing tools for companies promoting sales of television sets.

By 1960 all state capitals had a national station (the ABC Channel 2), and two commercial stations (Channel 9 and Channel 7). Between 1960 and 1971, television coverage had been extended to most major cities, with about 98 percent of the Australian population having access to TV services.

While the ABC had established a national network, the ABCB refused to allow commercial proprietors to establish formal networks across the nation. Despite this decision, informal arrangements and affiliations developed, and regional stations benefited from the availability at reduced prices of programs already purchased by metropolitan channels. This ability to select from successful programs led the regional television broadcasters to become known as "the cherry pickers," a term which soon entered official terminology.

Rupert Murdoch and the Ten Network   One controversial ABCB decision was the introduction in the mid-1960s of a third commercial channel, now called the Ten Network, in five cities. Not surprisingly, the two existing channels, 7 and 9, opposed this development since it further fragmented an already small market. Eventually, however, this channel became profitable, though even today it is the least successful of the commercial channels.

Perhaps the most interesting aspect of Channel 10's history is its transformation from autonomous state-based stations to a national network, a move effected amid controversy by Rupert Murdoch in the early 1980s. Murdoch's interests in Australian television evolved from a position of relative obscurity in 1958 as owner of Channel 9 in Adelaide. It was not until 1979 that Murdoch's News Corporation, which had extensive newspaper holdings, entered the TV industry as a major player.

Fitting with his reputation as entrepreneur, Murdoch established his position in the industry through corporate takeovers. Having acquired Channel 10 in Sydney in this manner, he then embarked on a joint share raid on the Australian airline company Ansett, which owned Channel 10 in Melbourne and held a controlling interest in Channel 10 in Brisbane. Murdoch emerged not only with the stations but with half ownership of the Ansett airline in the process. Having acquired the stations, however, he still had to circumvent ABT restrictions on concentration of ownership.

Murdoch's first application to the ABT was for approval of his purchase of Channel 10 in Sydney. Although objections were raised even at this point in relation to concentration of ownership, the ABT announced that it had no jurisdiction to upset a completed commercial deal.

The tribunal made a similar ruling in relation to the Ansett deal when Murdoch applied for approval in 1980. On appeal to the High Court, however, the ABT was forced to reconsider the matter, having been found to have failed in its statutory duty to investigate the deal. The second time around, with a new chair of the ABT, the tribunal found there was a problem with concentration of ownership, but it was unsure whether it had the power to order a divestiture of shares by Murdoch. Furthermore, Murdoch took up his appeal rights to a government Appeals Tribunal with this tribunal ruling that concentration of ownership was not of itself against the public interest; it was a matter to be decided in each individual case.

In any event, Murdoch's interests were becoming more secure by the moment. While the Appeals Tribunal was considering his case, the government moved to introduce legislation abolishing the existing public interest standards and replacing them with the condition that the applicant for a license must be a "fit and proper person" who will serve the community and promote Australian programs (a condition that was to stick in the throat of another media entrepreneur, Alan Bond). From this point, Murdoch went on to rename the network Network Ten, before leaving the Australian network to pursue his current press and television interests in both the United Kingdom and the United States. News Corporation's current investment in Australian television is limited to a 15 percent share of the Seven Network.

The era that was characterized by what was to become known as the "Murdoch amendments" was therefore significant not only in terms of the developing network arrangements but also in its revelations of the play among commercial interests, government, and the seemingly independent broadcasting authority.

Special Broadcasting Service Another contentious issue was the introduction in 1980 of SBS television services providing foreign-language programs and more comprehensive international news coverage. By the mid-1980s SBS services were well established and strongly supported, so much so that a government proposal in 1986 to incorporate SBS within the ABC led to a public outcry that forced the planned merger to be abandoned. SBS remains a small but viable service, attracting a range of viewers from both ethnic and general audience segments, sometimes rating as high as 5 percent of the total audience compared with the ABC averaging between 10 and 15 percent and the strongest of the commercial stations, Channel 9, at about 25 to 30 percent. Since 1992 SBS has successfully supplemented its government grant and its corporately sponsored programs with paid commercials.

Color TV From the time of its introduction in 1975, color television, using the PAL system, has dominated Australian screens. Within 5 years color sets had almost totally replaced black-and-white receivers.

During the late 1970s the introduction of color transmission was accompanied by an increase in the quality and quantity of sports coverage, and this in turn helped promote the conversion to color sets. Even cricket, the most traditional of Australian sports, was revolutionized when Kerry Packer, proprietor of Channel 9, introduced 1-day international cricket (cricket games usually go on for *several* days) with specially modified rules and with the different national teams (England, New Zealand, the West Indies, and Australia) wearing colored uniforms instead of the traditional white gear, a change which caused its detractors to refer to it as "the pajama game." Inevitably, it was a huge success, and World Series Cricket, as Packer's cricketing circus was called, forced the world cricketing establishment to bring some overdue reforms to the game.

The introduction of color arrested a decline in television viewing during peak hours. The average number of households that viewed TV regularly had fallen from near 60 percent in 1965 to under 50 percent in 1974, but by 1977 the average number of viewing households had risen to 54 percent, while the penetration of households had also increased from 80 percent before color to 93 percent by 1977.

Growth in Program Production Contemporaneous with a revival of Australian-produced feature films in the late 1970s and early 1980s, an upsurge occurred in the production of Australian television drama. Partly this was a result of the "new nationalism" which followed the end of the long conservative hegemony in Australian politics in 1972; partly it was the result of the related change in the regulatory environment. These changes included the formulation of provisions to ensure that commercial channels showed a required proportion of Australian programs across a spectrum of program types, including drama and children's programs, during peak hours.

This period coincided with the development of high-quality Australian drama miniseries, often celebrating historical themes, which commenced in 1978 and reached its peak in the early 1980s. With titles such as *The Dismissal* (a dramatization of the real-life 1975 sacking of the elected Australian reformist prime minister, Gough Whitlam, by the governor general, John Kerr, the queen's appointed head of state) and *Bodyline* (recounting the violence and excitement of the England-Australia cricket matches of 1932–1933 which severely strained the relationship between the two countries), these series not only developed Australian nationalism but easily outrated imported British and American drama programs.

News programs had come to be dominated by the inclusion of satellite-delivered coverage of international events. This process had started with the American moon landing in 1969, and the increasing availability of satellite delivery systems enhanced the immediacy of images available to news and current affairs programs, reducing the tyranny of distance so long at the heart of a ubiquitous Australian sense of isolation from world affairs. No doubt this quality of placing the viewer close to the action in time as well as in space accounts in large part for the increasing audience reliance on television as the primary source of news. Direct news feeds are usually revoiced, with Australian newsreaders reading the same commentary to reduce the "foreignness" of the news and to increase the credibility of the constructed personae of the newsreaders. During satellite coverage of international sporting events held overseas, such as the Olympic Games and the Rugby World Cup, channels find that their ratings increase remarkably.

Social and Regulatory Changes In the late 1970s the process of commercial licensing underwent major change. In 1978 the ABCB was replaced by a new agency, the Australian Broadcasting Tribunal. This new body was more receptive to public input, with provisions for public participation in hearings to grant or review licenses. Although nominally independent of government pressure in its role of granting, renewing, and suspending licenses and determining standards in relation to commercial programming including advertising and levels of Australian content, the ABT was still susceptible to government influence. Nevertheless it developed a more accountable and coherent approach to regulation and established the principle that this regulation should take account of social and cultural factors as well as economic and commercial pressures.

During the early 1990s considerable opposition was mounted to some of the so-called "social engineering" practices of the ABT. This opposition focused upon the local content provisions and upon the amount of children's programming needed in order to meet licensing requirements. When a new act of Parliament, the Broadcasting Services Act, was legislated in 1992, the ABT was disbanded and replaced by a new regulatory agency, the Australian Broadcasting Authority (ABA).

While empowered to exercise the same responsibilities as its predecessor, the ABA has already indicated a preference for a less interventionist position on many of these issues. It encourages a greater degree of self-regulation by broadcasters, though it retains the right to intervene if necessary. A significant change from the ABT's role is that the ABA has some jurisdiction over the ABC and the SBS when complaints are lodged against them, as well as over the commercial channels. These changes in role are consistent with the increasingly deregulated policies of the ALP governments which have been in power in Canberra since 1983.

Recent Events Recent Australian television history has been marked by technological innovation, changes in ownership patterns, and economic turbulence. The first generation of domestic satellites, originally called Aussat but now privatized and renamed Optus after its owner, Optus Communication, was launched in 1985–1986. This development made possible networking of the total Australian continent with simultaneous programming as satellite delivery replaced the microwave links that comprised the informal existing affiliations and arrangements between metropolitan and regional stations.

Revised legislation allowed media proprietors to expand their interests from holding a maximum of two media outlets in any designated region to having access to a maximum of 75 percent of the Australian population. This meant that, for the first time, legislation recognized the possibility of national networking. At the same time, under the ABT policy of "equalization" or "aggregation," all programs offered by the three metropolitan commercial channels (9, 7, and 10) and the two national networks (ABC and SBS) were to be made available to regional viewers. The effect of this determination was to force the regional networks serving the four large designated regional markets into networking arrangements with the metropolitan stations. The consequences of this aggregation are that program costs have risen for the regional stations, no longer able to cherry-pick, and that centrally produced advertising, news, and current affairs are likely to replace those produced regionally. The full impact of networking has not yet been experienced.

Because of these technological and regulatory changes, ownership patterns in television (and also in radio) have changed significantly during the late 1980s and early 1990s. Almost all capital city radio and television stations changed ownership, ending two decades of relative stability. Often the new owners were entrepreneurs seeking profitable investments for funds generated in breweries or real estate developments. They accepted uncritically the folklore that television stations were licenses to print money, and their desire for the glamour and power associated with media, coupled with a lack of experience in the realities of media ownership, clouded their business judgment. Too often the prices paid were unrealistically high, and so the rising interest rates and economic downturn of the late 1980s drove these speculators into receivership. The control of two commercial networks was given to financial institutions for varying periods of time.

The third commercial network, Channel 9, was sold by Kerry Packer to Alan Bond and then several years later repurchased by Packer for a fraction of the price Bond had paid. In late 1992 the Ten Network was purchased from its mortgagee by a consortium comprising experienced Australian media and advertising interests and the Canadian network CanWest. Stability is slowly returning to the television industry, but the profits that funded the quality of Australian programs of the 1970s and 1980s have disappeared, at least temporarily.

During 1993 two major developments occurred in Australian television—the allocation of the first public access television licenses for the sixth channel in Australian capital cities and the call for bids for the first pay-TV licenses.

In March 1993 the ABA awarded the first public access television licenses to companies in Sydney and Melbourne, with other capitals expected to follow soon. As in the case of radio, these nonprofit companies comprise loose consortiums of educational, ethnic, and public interest groups that will prepare and provide programs for the sixth channel in each metropolitan region. Program categories will include news and current affairs, documentaries, educational programs, and drama. The programs are likely to be a mixture of orthodoxy and innovation and certain to be predominantly low-budget productions. It is anticipated that the sixth channel will provide an outlet for experimental and low-budget film and video which, apart from short segments on SBS, are rarely seen on Australian television.

Present plans call for allowing the sixth channel to broadcast commercials to establish viability. How successful these stations will be in attracting financial support remains to be seen. As with public access radio, these community access television stations will be heavily dependent on voluntary workers and on relationships with educational institutions. The provision of suitable training programs to ensure levels of competency will be among the conditions to be met for the award of licenses.

The most contentious issue in Australian television at present involves the establishment of pay-TV. In a familiar scenario, innovation has been delayed by political infighting. Following a range of sometimes contradictory statements by successive communication ministers (this ministerial turnover itself is indicative of a turbulent portfolio), the ALP government of Paul Keating announced the technological specification for pay-TV and called for bids. This specification called for a satellite-delivered service using a digitally compressed signal.

The provision for satellite delivery had been foreshadowed in the conditions of sale when the government-owned Aussat system was privatized and sold to Optus Communications. The decision on mode of delivery, however, did not end the confusion surrounding the introduction of pay-TV in Australia. Three licenses are to be issued, one reserving two stations to the ABC, and two more providing four channels each to two commercial licenses. All are to be delivered via the Optus satellite. The application process has seen three rounds of offers with both applicants in both the first and second rounds failing to acquire financing for the 5 percent deposit imposed by the federal government. While the third-round winners appear to have the required financial backing, they are nevertheless under investigation for cross-ownership.

One important condition imposed on licensees addressed the concern that pay-TV will provide only overseas drama by requiring that at least 10 percent of all budget for drama must be spent on first-release drama produced in Australia. This local content requirement is designed both to ensure continuity of employment in the film and television industry and to provide an adequate representation of Australian culture on pay-TV.

OWNERSHIP AND FINANCING

The current ownership structures of Australian electronic media are a direct result of federal government regulation in the 1950s. The decision to develop a dual system of television broadcasting in place of a wholly state-owned or wholly free enterprise system has led to the continued existence of the Australian Broadcasting Corporation in both radio and TV, as well as the introduction of the Special Broadcasting Service to operate alongside commercial stations.

Both services operate from government charters that reflect the commitment of the networks to fulfill certain public service roles. In the case of the ABC this is to provide innovative and comprehensive services which inform, entertain, and reflect the cultural diversity of Australia and contribute to a sense of national identity. Multilingual broadcasts are provided by the SBS, reflecting the cultural diversity of the Australian community. Both services stress their independence of the federal government, though both are funded through the Federal Parliament. Some discreet corporate sponsorship is permitted on the ABC, while a full commercial advertising structure was introduced by the SBS in 1992. Both are national broadcasters with established television networks and with SBS radio transmitting to five major cities and ABC radio providing five major radio services throughout Australia.

In addition to these government-funded national broadcasters, a public radio sector exists operated by nonprofit companies and funded by government grants, listener subscriptions, and limited commercial sponsorship. Public access television is just beginning.

The other aspect of Australian broadcasting involves the privately owned commercial stations. In June 1991 there were 43 commercial TV stations divided among 16 owners, and 149 commercial radio stations with 76 owners. As an indication of the concentration of ownership of Australian electronic media, 77 percent of shares in these TV stations and 45 percent of shares in radio stations were held by the four largest owners in each. Cross-media ownership concentration is recognized as a major problem in Australian broadcasting.

At present, the Nine Network metropolitan stations are controlled by Kerry Packer, while the Ten Network is owned by a consortium comprising the Canadian group CanWest Global Communications, the regional broadcaster Telecasters North Queensland Ltd., and some experienced media and advertising interests. The Seven Network is owned by a number of holding companies including banking interests currently expressing an intention to float the network on the stock exchange. Some metropolitan stations not owned by the major networks are nevertheless aligned with them. Since the aggregation scheme was introduced in 1986, four approved regional market designations have been created in which local stations are once again aligned with the networks. As of 1991 there were thirteen independent TV stations in Australia with a combined audience reach of 7 percent. This contrasts with audience reach levels of 81 percent for the Seven Network, 84 percent for the Ten Network, and 86 percent for the Nine Network.

The advancement of networking has been as significant for privately owned radio as it has for television, with the four major networkers forming powerful media groups: Hoyts Media (with 55 percent audience reach), Austereo (54 percent), Australian Broadcasting Company (50 percent), and Wesgo (37 percent). In contrast to television structures, however, a large number of radio stations are locally owned, with about 75 percent of proprietors owning no more than two stations.

A shift in the financing of the TV industry occurred in the 1990s, reflecting the departure of banking interests that had dominated commercial ownership for the previous 5 years. The profitability of the Australian electronic media has declined significantly since the boom era of the mid-1980s. In the 1990–1991 financial year, television and radio industries both recorded losses: A$225 million in the case of TV, and A$15 million in the case of radio.

While some losses incurred by the industry can be attributed to the recession, it is not just the commercial sector that has suffered from the economic downturn. The levels of government funding for the ABC and SBS are continually under threat from the economic rationalism that has dominated government thinking in recent years. Since July 1992 advertising has supplemented SBS resources. On the ABC, statements of corporate sponsorship are permitted, but commercials are not, though supplementary funding of about A$80 million is obtained through coproductions and merchandising.

The federal government derives revenue from fees imposed on broadcasters. In 1991–1992 it received A$114.5 million from TV and A$8.6 million from radio. In a bid to aid the struggling industry during 1992, the government cut radio fees by 50 percent.

PROGRAMMING

In 1991, 53.8 percent of television programs shown on Australian television were of Australian origin. This figure far exceeded the minimum level of 40 percent imposed by the government despite the much higher cost of local programs compared to imported products. Such commercial success for Australian production began in the 1960s, at about the same time that concern was growing about the possibility of U.S. programs swamping local products as broadcasters balanced reduced audiences against considerably reduced outlays.

The popularity of Australian drama, current affairs, talk, and music shows continued through the 1970s. During this period, it was evident that Australian content was not surviving solely by means of quotas. Australian products have continually been successful in ratings surveys.

This popularity of Australian productions was enhanced by the emergence of a new TV genre. The Australian miniseries appeared in the late 1970s with *Against the Wind* and gained momentum through the first half of the 1980s. Interest in Australian product was sustained during the 1980s by renewed nationalism associated with the 1988 Bicentennial, evident in such phenomenally successful Australian films as *Crocodile Dundee* and *Mad Max*.

In the early 1990s the most popular programs on Australian television were current affairs

A still from the ABC drama series *Brides of Christ*, a 6-hour series set in Australia during the radical upheaval of the Catholic church. The program premiered in 1991, won the Australian Film Institute award for best drama series, and has been successfully marketed on video and replayed several times on the ABC and commercial networks. (*Photo courtesy of the Australian Broadcasting Corporation*)

programs. Some of these, such as *Sixty Minutes*, are based on American program ideas that have been franchised to Australian broadcasters. Others, such as *Four Corners*, an ABC series that covers one subject in depth for a 45-minute period each week, are Australian productions.

In 1989–1990 expenditure on Australian programs was A$655.3 million, as opposed to A$284 million on foreign programs, while in 1990–1991 at least seven of the ten most popular programs in the five major metropolitan markets were Australian-made. Although SBS and the ABC are not subject to local content regulations, both national broadcasters have produced successful and critically acclaimed programs such as the ABC drama success of 1992, *Brides of Christ*, which dealt with Australian nuns trying to adjust to changes in the Catholic church. The ABC is widely acclaimed for both the quantity and the quality of its programs and for the innovation they display.

The success of soap operas, miniseries, and other drama programs is reflected in statistics showing that drama accounts for 26 percent of all programs. This is followed by light entertainment (14.8 percent), children's programs (14.3 percent), news, documentaries, and current affairs (13.4 percent), comedy (10.7 percent), sports (10.2 percent), education, arts, religion, and information (6.9 percent), and quiz, panel, and game shows (3.7 percent). It is interesting to note that the amount of children's and educational programming on the ABC is double that of the commercial sector.

LAWS AND REGULATIONS

Regulation of electronic media in Australia is a federal responsibility, established by the Australian constitution which refers to "postal, telegraphic, telephonic, and other like services." Three acts of the Federal Parliament have been generated by this provision, and three regulatory agencies have been established to oversee spectrum allocation and content requirements. The Australian Broadcasting Control Board (ABCB) operated from 1949 to 1976, the Australian Broadcasting Tribunal (ABT) from 1976 to 1992, and the Australian Broadcasting Authority (ABA) commenced operations in 1992.

TABLE 13-1

CATEGORIES OF TELEVISION PROGRAMS, 6:00 A.M.–12:00 MIDNIGHT: COMMERCIAL AND ABC STATIONS*

	Metropolitan Commercial %	Aggregated Commercial %	Solus Commercial %	Total Commercial %	ABC %
Drama, comedy	11.9	10.2	9.9	10.7	2.4
Drama, other	25.7	25.9	26.5	26.0	9.7
Children's	16.3	15.9	11.6	14.3	28.0
News, documentaries, and current affairs	13.1	14.0	12.7	13.4	21.8
Education, arts, religion, and information	5.5	6.2	9.3	6.9	17.8
Sports	9.8	9.7	10.7	10.2	12.3
Quiz, panel, and game programs	3.1	3.0	4.6	3.7	0.0
Light entertainment	14.7	15.3	14.7	14.8	8.0
	100.0	100.0	100.0	100.0	100.0

* Due to rounding, columns may not total exactly.
Source: Reproduced by permission of the Australian Broadcasting Authority.

The Australian constitution treats the airwaves as a natural resource of public interest. While the question of spectrum allocation has retained fundamental importance under the three successive regulatory bodies, the interpretations of licensing and ownership provisions have varied considerably. The initial stages of radio development in the 1920s and early 1930s saw little concern about multiple ownership of radio stations. By the 1940s, however, newspaper interests were influential in 44 percent of Australian radio stations, and fears of monopoly control and concentration of ownership led to the initiation of various parliamentary standing committees on broadcasting.

The need for a permanent regulatory body was finally recognized in a 1948 amendment to the Broadcasting Act which created the first of Australia's media regulators, the ABCB. The principal aim of the ABCB in the 1950s and 1960s was to prevent multiple ownership of radio and television channels, and the Broadcasting and Television Act of 1956 restricted media proprietors to one capital city TV station and no more than two stations nationwide. A secondary aim was prevention of excessive foreign ownership through an amendment to the act in 1965. These measures served to protect the interests of existing media players, while the ABCB concern for maintaining the commercial viability of these interests inhibited development of broader ownership patterns.

The 1970s and 1980s brought different conditions and new issues to Australian electronic media. Replacing the ABCB in 1977, the ABT was intended to be a more open, responsive body with the added function of allocation, renewal, suspension, and revocation of commercial licenses, operations previously performed directly by the relevant federal minister. The ABT was also charged with authorizing changes in ownership and inquiring into all broadcasting issues. It was given the power to create program and advertising standards. During 1986 the ABT played a central role in implementation of the most important policy change in broadcasting for decades, the networking and aggregation policy.

By the late 1980s the Australian Labor party was firmly entrenched in what was to become its longest consecutive period in federal government. In 1986 Prime Minister Bob Hawke announced a new communications policy which identified the avoidance of excessive cross-media ownership as the principal objective of spectrum allocation. Media magnates could no longer hold both television and press interests in the same service area, though service areas were redefined to allow for aggregation of rural markets. The ABT, through its public hearings, opened the licensing process to the public in an unprecedented way, most notably in its investigation of entrepreneur Alan Bond's suitability as a "fit and proper person" to hold a television license. Adding to the financial troubles the Bond Corporation has encountered since the high days of the mid-1980s, Alan Bond found himself under scrutiny from the ABT for a payout to the former Queensland premier in 1988. In June 1989 the ABT deemed Bond was not fit to hold a license, and he was ordered to reorganize the structure of the network so as to divest himself of control.

In this case and throughout the history of broadcasting in Australia, one fundamental principle dominated the operations of all three regulatory bodies. This was the belief that spectrum allocation involves the leasing of a public resource that has substantial power in representing and shaping Australian society. The issues in this process are consequently not merely economic. Rather there exists a cultural objective of nurturing a distinctively Australian media.

Yet there has always been an element of imposed cultural hegemony in any regulations aimed at establishing some single national identity. A similar attitude informs the imposition of notions of quality and concepts of good taste on broadcasters. Critics of these policies argue that commitment to the idea of a single Australian identity is untenable in a diverse and multicultural nation. Similar objections can be directed toward the requirements for media proprietors to prove themselves fit and proper persons to hold licenses, a situation that reflects the initial broadcasting philosophy devised for the BBC by Lord Reith who believed that entertainment in broadcasting should be balanced by education and moral improvement.

The ABT, as principal regulating agency, was responsible for developing programming restrictions. Specific restrictions were applied in the three areas of Australian content, children's TV, and advertising. Australian content provisions of the ABT required broadcasters to provide programs that were identifiably Australian, recognized the diversity of cultural backgrounds as represented in the Australian community, were intended for an Australian audience, and resulted from Australian creative control.

When it replaced the ABT in 1992, the ABA adopted a less interventionist stance, vacating previous areas of control and leaving regulation of many aspects of television content to the industry itself. A system of industry-developed codes has superseded the prescriptive regulatory schemes of previous decades. The ABA nevertheless reserved the right to reenter the field if necessary, while industry operators can renounce the scheme and opt for ABA-imposed standards if they decide self-regulation is unsatisfactory.

One program category remaining under direct ABA control is children's TV. Regulations governing C (for "children") classification programming times have existed since 1984. In 1990 these standards were expressed in terms of C-classification time bands when broadcasters were required to deliver a certain minimum amount of children's programming.

Concerns for the interests of children and for the propagation of Australian content are also found in the regulation of advertising. In 1987 the main commercial body, the Federation of Australian Commercial Television Stations (FACTS), applied to the ABT for a period of deregulation of advertising. A 2-year trial period followed in which advertisement length, placement, and number were deregulated. Though the overall number of advertisements during this period increased, by 1989 there was no increase in the rate of program interruptions. Despite deregulation, however, restrictions still exist during C periods. There is also an 80 percent overall quota for Australian-made advertisements, and all cigarette advertising is banned. This ban has attracted opposition from tobacco companies and from advertising agencies that fear its extension to alcohol products. The ban has led to creative attempts to circumvent its restrictions through sporting sponsorships by tobacco companies of events such as the Winfield Rugby League competition and the Benson and Hedges World Cup for cricket.

THE AUDIENCE

Electronic people meter ratings surveys were introduced in Australia in 1991. Previously, ratings had been measured using an often criticized diary system. Perhaps the most significant finding since the introduction of the new system is that viewers retain their viewing practices over the summer Christmas period, traditionally perceived as a ratings dead zone in TV and radio.

The implementation of this system has not been achieved without complications. A challenge to the integrity of measurement was revealed when a Melbourne afternoon talk show announced it would run a story on the households using people meters and managed to skew the ratings of an otherwise unremarkable ratings performer as the relevant households tuned in. The same network ran an "investigative" report on the people meter issue during another edition of the same program in a different state and during a prime-time current affairs program a half-hour later. A half-hour news bulletin was slotted between the talk show and the current affairs program, and the strategy succeeded in capturing an abnormally large audience for the news bulletin. Eventually an agreement was reached among the networks to invalidate the ratings period, and an order was given to refrain from targeting people meter households in the future.

Opportunities for audience feedback apart from ratings have changed considerably since the ABA came into operation. Previously, viewers could complain directly to the ABT, which would compile statistics on viewer complaints and investigate any potentially serious breaches of broadcasting policy. The last months of the ABT were marked by controversy about some of its rulings. These rulings involved decisions not to award a C classification to the program *Fat Cat and Friends* and to some episodes of *The New Adventures of Skippy*, as well as scrutiny of the adult educational program *Sex*.

The decision about *Fat Cat and Friends* was based on the ABT's view that the production values were low and that the central character, Fat Cat, lacked clear gender definition. While the criticism of low standards of production may well have been justified, the statements about lack of gender definition led to emotional editorials attacking the ABT for "social engineering."

When the ABT denied the Nine Network credit toward its required quota of children's program time for two episodes of *Skippy*, the network responded by following the screening of the program with a telephone poll which showed that three out of four respondents disagreed with the ABT decision. In the face of such criticism the ABT disbanded its Children's Program Committee, which had formerly classified each item of programming, and introduced a scheme of accrediting producers with a satisfactory track record so that their future programs automatically received classification. This incident severely diminished the credibility of the ABT.

The case of *Sex*, also on Channel 9, was quite different. *Sex* was a documentary program that addressed in relatively explicit terms issues such as sexuality, sexual mores, and particularly the incidence and causes of HIV/AIDS. *Sex* aired at 9:30 in the evening, and so it was clearly an adult program. Despite its educational objectives, it was heavily criticized by family lobby groups, some religious groups, and conservative viewers. Some sponsors dissociated themselves from the program. The ABT investigated the complaints and cleared the program of any breach of broadcasting standards. *Sex* was eventually awarded a commendation by the Australian Federation of AIDS Organizations for recognition of excellence in HIV/AIDS reporting. After some indecision, Channel 9 screened a second series of *Sex*, with Pamela Stephenson acting as host, replacing Sophie Lee, who was the focus of much of the media attention.

Sophie Lee, presenter of the first series of Channel 9's documentary *Sex*, receives a media award for the program. (*By permission of the Nine Network*)

With the demise of the ABT and the advent of the ABA, the procedures for viewers to register complaints have altered markedly. Viewers no longer complain directly to the regulatory agency but contact the television or radio station directly. This process removes the ABA from direct audience contact. Viewers and listeners approach the ABA only when no response from the broadcaster is received within 60 days or when the response is perceived as inadequate.

Racism and sexism in the media have been recognized as important social issues, and complaints about them are referred to the federal Human Rights and Equal Opportunities Commission or to state-based equal opportunity or antidiscrimination boards. It remains to be seen what complaint-handling procedures will be adopted by the commercial networks.

TECHNOLOGY

The relative affluence of Australia has enabled it to maintain a high standard of media technology, at least until comparatively recently. As in the United States, stations, networks, and production companies have access to high-technology video and radio equipment. Government support of national radio and television services has ensured that their technology is up to date and well maintained, and this in turn has motivated commercial stations to at least match this quality.

Also as in the United States, TV stations broadcast in both the very high frequency (VHF) and ultrahigh-frequency (UHF) ranges, the most notable UHF service being SBS-TV. SBS consequently has variable reception quality even in metropolitan areas. Radio stations broadcast using both AM and FM signals, though the shift to FM broadcasting is significant as new licenses are granted and as older broadcasters convert from AM to FM. Often, public broadcasters are able to buy superseded AM facilities as commercial stations move to FM.

Satellite TV transmission to remote areas has been in operation since the mid-1980s, supplementing the microwave links which initially linked capital cities. A wide range of microwave informational services also exists, on individual licenses, opening up the possibility for microwave delivery of pay-TV should legislation permit this. Special programs are available to clubs and pubs through these links.

The most notable recent innovation has been the move to digital technology in both radio and television. This is fast becoming the standard in radio and TV broadcasting by the national and commercial networks. The cost of new technology may cause its extension to public access areas to be slower. As already noted, government policy provides for pay-TV to be satellite-supplied using compressed digital video. Trials involving various forms of high-definition television have been under way for some years.

The downside of this technological innovation is that although much of the pioneering theoretical work and experimentation has taken place in Australia, it is highly likely that the actual manufacturing of this technology into commercial equipment will take place in Japan, Taiwan, and Korea, as well as in the United States, and its installation in Australia will add to the already great economic imbalance between imports and exports.

Video rental has long been an established practice in Australia, with its extremely high penetration of home VCRs now approaching 80 percent. No doubt this is due to the present unavailability of pay-TV services and perhaps to the disenchantment of audiences with a range of program choice perhaps best described as "more of the same" despite the availability of a range of channels. While recent releases rent for $A5 or $A6 a day, rentals as low as $A1 a week are not uncommon for older titles. Particularly among young teenagers, video is a popular form of entertainment, often allowing them to escape the age restriction placed on some restricted films in theaters, though legislators are threatening to close this loophole in some states.

EXTERNAL SERVICES

Australia has broadcast external radio programming for many years and has just recently begun external TV broadcasting. Radio Australia, since its inception in 1939 as an adjunct to the ABC, has broadcast information and entertainment programs to south and east Asia and to the Pacific basin.

Its policy is based upon the proposition that its effectiveness is proportional to its credibility, and even during the Pacific war it avoided distortion of news for propaganda purposes, though suppression of news items that might advantage the Japanese war effort was occasionally practiced. Radio Australia broadcasters have always been careful to avoid language or editorial tone that could be construed in any way as racist or prejudicial toward its Asian listeners, enhancing its acceptability within the region. Political interference has sometimes occurred, particularly as government departments such as Trade or Foreign Affairs have sought to influence Radio Australia broadcasters to reflect favorably upon their policies and achievements.

From its transmission facilities, Radio Australia provides 350 hours per week of specially produced news, current affairs, education, and entertainment programs in eight languages: standard Chinese (Mandarin), Cantonese, Thai, Indonesian, Tok Pisin (or Pidgin), Vietnamese, French, and English. Its policy of objectivity and its unwillingness to censor political material have caused tension with some of Australia's neighbors including Indonesia, Papua New Guinea, and Malaysia. The most serious incident followed the Indonesian appropriation of Timor in the mid-1970s, which led eventually to exclusion of the ABC and Radio Australia from operating a bureau in Indonesia for a 10-year period from 1980 to 1990. More usually, foreign displeasure leads to diplomatic notes or expulsion of particular journalists.

Surveys of Radio Australia listeners reveal that a surprisingly high proportion, about 30 percent, prefer the English-language broadcasts, while its reliability for news and current affairs is rated second after that of the BBC World Service but ahead of Voice of America. Estimates of the audience size for Radio Australia range up to 50 million daily, with the largest segments (each about 10 million) located in Indonesia and China.

Radio Australia does not interfere with or jam broadcasts from other services, nor is it subject to electronic interference in the southeast Asian and Pacific basin regions. Radio Australia operates in tandem with the ABC, and news is reported from the various ABC bureaus and correspondents in Asian capitals. It does not accept sponsorship or commercials.

In February 1993, as part of the Australian government strategy for establishing closer trade and cultural links with Asia, Australian Television International (ATVI) commenced transmission of programs to fifteen Asian countries. ATVI programs consist of domestic ABC offerings in drama, sports, variety, children's, and educational categories, and, most importantly, a 1-hour specially designed regional news service which is updated regularly each day.

This news service draws upon the network of the ABC news bureaus and correspondents throughout Asia and, like the other ATVI programs, is an English-language service. ATVI programs originate from the ABC facility in Darwin and are uplinked to the Indonesian-owned Palapa satellite using a PAL signal that is free to possessors of an appropriate receiver dish within the Palapa footprint. An estimated 1 million dishes with an average of four viewers per dish give ATVI a potential audience of 4 million.

The satellite that carries ATVI now also carries Radio Australia. The TV service, unlike its radio counterpart, is expecting to carry commercial sponsorship from companies endeavoring to tap the Asian market. In due course the Darwin facility may become an important hub, offering access to Asian audiences by other Australian and international broadcasters.

Radio Australia and ATVI are important players in the implementation of the Australian government policy of presenting Australia as an Asian nation rather than as an enclave of European culture in an Asian location.

IMPORTANCE IN THE WORLD COMMUNITY

As government policy statements and media developments have indicated, Australia seeks to play a major role in the Asia Pacific region. This is evident from attempts to dispel the perception that Australian culture is Eurocentric by increasing pressure to sever such traditional ties as the monarchical link with England. More significantly, perhaps, Australia provides a model for the operation of the electronic media in a democratic society that could be copied by emergent nations and by nations seeking to democratize governmental processes.

Within Australia there is a recognition that the media industries must adapt to a global media economy or succumb finally to the cultural domination which successive regulatory agencies have so strenuously resisted. The forms of integration of media and business interests that underpin the development of this global media economy have proved destabilizing if not disastrous for one short generation of Australian media entrepreneurs, suggesting that the economic base of the Australian media industries is too narrow to support such integration.

The introduction of pay-TV, with substantial involvement by international players like Rupert Murdoch and Time Warner, along with the expansionist domestic policies of Kerry Packer, will place further pressure on regulating agencies and government restrictions. This situation is complicated by the fact that satellite delivery systems do not recognize national boundaries or regulations.

At present, the regulations for the introduction of pay-TV ensure that the ABC will be a participant and that a significant proportion of Australian product will occur in the drama category. The international appeal of Australian miniseries and the success of such soaps as *Neighbours* and *A Country Practice* suggest that potential exists for export of this new drama product to offset the cost of foreign programs that will dominate the drama channels in quantity if not in quality. An indicator of one possible trend is the production of a number of U.S. television series at the Warner-Roadshow studio complex located on Queensland's Gold Coast. Coproductions and foreign-financed productions made in Australia may become a regular occurrence as part of this new global media.

As a small, predominantly English-speaking nation, Australia is vulnerable to various forms of media imperialism. American and British producers of television programs usually recover production costs and make profits from sales to their domestic markets. This means they can then sell these programs to overseas markets at prices well below their actual production cost. An hour of high-quality TV drama such as *LA Law*, *Minder*, or *Northern Exposure* can be bought by an Australian network for about 5 to 10 percent of the cost of producing an Australian program of similar quality. This makes the Australian product economically vulnerable, although it may be of substantial cultural value and provide continuity of employment for a range of Australian media workers.

Local content requirements provide some degree of protection for the Australian industry but are often criticized by overseas media interests. Big overseas producers advocate unrestricted two-way trade, a situation often referred to as a "level playing field" since it apparently allows all participants in the global media economy equal access to markets. In practice, however, it provides economic advantage to countries with large and relatively affluent domestic markets since production industries there can achieve economies of scale.

This vulnerability of Australian media producers will increase with the evolution of the global media economy and the proliferation of transnational delivery systems. The concept of a level playing field espoused by economic rationalists clearly favors the big, established players, many of whom do not enthusiastically practice what they loudly preach. The Australian model of self-regulation in most categories of media, coupled with direct intervention by the regulatory agency to control certain critical areas such as children's programming and minimum provisions for local content, may serve to keep the playing field tilted just enough to strike a healthy balance between the local team and the overseas heavyweights. If this allows the locals to maintain a degree of cultural integrity and national identity, the value of the Australian electronic media system as a model for other small and culturally vulnerable nations may be considerable.

MAJOR ISSUES

While many of the major issues facing the electronic media in Australia in terms of policy and regulation have been addressed above, some of the most interesting and important subjects currently being debated concern content. In particular, questions about the depiction of violence, of sex, of the representation of women, and of the representation of ethnic groups have received considerable attention. This is not unique to Australia, as the saga of Dan Quayle versus Murphy Brown in the lead-up to the 1992 U.S. presidential election demonstrated. While this debate addressed the issue of some perceived decline in American moral standards, a similar exchange between a federal minister and the central figure of a documentary about an upper-middle-class Sydney suburb called *Sylvania Waters* focused on excessive consumption of alcohol and tobacco. Despite the difference in subject matter, both debates concerned a perception that harmful effects may result from media representation.

In Australia considerable effort has been directed toward the exploration of assumed links between the depiction of violence in the media and violence in real life. In 1990 the ABT produced a comprehensive four-volume report, *TV Violence in Australia*. Although the terms of reference of the inquiry suggested the report would be a traditional media effects study, the ABT adopted a broader, qualitative approach. It monitored television programs, invited submissions, conducted forums, and commissioned specific cultural and textual research. The outcome of this process was not a new set of prescriptions about program content but rather a move toward self-regulation based on an industry-sanctioned code concerning such issues as reporting suicides, conducting grief-intrusive interviews, and depicting acts of graphic violence in news and drama. The aim was to increase awareness of the role of the media by severing the traditional nexus assumed between actual violence in the street and represented violence on the screen and by directing attention to the media as a forum for understanding violence.

A similar strategy has been adopted in attempting to reduce racism and sexism in Australian media. Just as the media are not viewed as a direct cause of violence but as a means to understanding its operation in society, so research about media representation of women and ethnic groups is directed toward understanding how audience attitudes are shaped. Out of this research, national agendas are being formulated to identify discriminatory representations and practices and replace them with responsible alternatives. These agendas involve the development of industry guidelines and codes of practice, the establishment of adequate complaints procedures, and the dissemination of educational packages to professional groups. One such package, *Women and Advertising*, is available from the Office for the Status of Women, a division of the prime minister's department, while another is being developed by the Office of Multicultural Affairs.

The rationale for these packages is that the media should be regarded as a forum for shaping understanding of social problems rather than as a cause of these problems. Such a view may lead media practitioners to reassess their role and take a different perspective on the representation of violence, ethnicity, and gender as they formulate codes of practice for their profession. Industry groups, government agencies, unions, pressure groups, and lobbies of various kinds, as well as academics and individual citizens, have the opportunity to contribute to these national agendas and to participate in shaping relevant codes of media practice. Although the issues in this debate are international, the process under way in Australia seems to be developing in a unique way. Only time will tell whether this diagnostic and democratic approach and the admittedly idealistic attitudes inscribed within it will enable the media to bring longer-term benefits to Australian society.

SELECTED BIBLIOGRAPHY

Australian Broadcasting Tribunal. *Broadcasting in Australia*, 4th ed. Sydney: Australian Broadcasting Tribunal, 1992.

Australian Broadcasting Tribunal. *TV Violence in Australia*, 4 vols. Canberra: Australian Government Publishing Service, 1992.

Bureau of Transport and Communications Economics. *Economic Aspects of Broadcasting Regulation*. Canberra: Australian Government Publishing Service, 1991.

Cunningham, Stuart. *Framing Culture: Criticism and Policy in Australia*. Sydney: Allen and Unwin, 1992.

Cunningham, Stuart, and Graeme Turner, eds. *Media in Australia: Industries, Texts, Audiences*. Sydney: Allen and Unwin, 1993.

Hall, Sandra. *Supertoy: Twenty Years of Australian Television*. Melbourne: Sun Books, 1976.

Hall, Sandra. "Broadcasting." In *The Australian Encyclopedia*, Vol. 2, 5th ed. Sydney: Australian Geographic, 1988.

Moran, Albert, ed. *Stay Tuned: An Australian Broadcasting Reader*. Sydney: Allen and Unwin, 1992.

Tulloch, John, and Graeme Turner. *Australian Television: Programs, Pleasures and Politics*. Sydney: Allen and Unwin, 1989.

Windschuttle, Keith. *The Media: A New Analysis of Press, Television, Radio and Advertising in Australia*, 3rd ed. Melbourne: Penguin, 1988.

The authors acknowledge the assistance provided by Associate Professor Stuart Cunningham and Dr. Errol Hodge of the School of Media and Journalism, Queensland University of Technology.

Epilogue

Whither the international world of electronic media? One point seems obvious: there is bound to be an increase in the importance of the electronic media throughout the world and an increase in the importance of world events to the further development of the electronic media. As the world heads toward an information superhighway, the scope of electronic media will grow. Not only will media encompass traditional entertainment and information, but they may include a vast variety of interactive services. Both radio and television are going to need to reconsider themselves in terms of added and altered services.

POLITICAL AND SOCIAL RAMIFICATIONS

In some areas of the world, communication has difficulty keeping up with the changing political and sociological climate. In Eastern Europe, for example, laws cannot be made quickly enough to handle the changes inherent in a switch from communism to democracy. Other areas of the world, such as Africa, have difficulty keeping up economically with the changes that are occurring within the communications structure. The growth of new, expensive technologies widens the gap between the haves and the have-nots, both on a country-by-country basis and on the basis of rich and poor within one particular country. Poorer countries may find they have greater access to information, but the information is biased in that it comes from richer, more powerful countries.

With the advent of satellites, it has become possible to program to the entire world simultaneously. This of course affects the speed with which information (both true and false) can be disseminated to everyone. It can also affect world unification, or lack thereof, as each nation is able to see the underpinnings of other nations. With satellite distribution individual cultures could be eradicated, or at least made to look inferior when compared with the "popular" cultures being transmitted over satellite. Such may already be happening in India and other Asian countries where STAR beams a great deal of Western programming.

Satellites also render censorship fairly ineffective. Although governments can legislate that their citizens not watch programming from other countries, enforcing the legislation is another matter. The ubiquity of videocassettes (legal and illegal) adds to the inability to control what people watch. Arab countries and former and present Communist countries find it harder and harder to shield their populaces from outside influences. With the communication technology that is presently available, it may be impossible for totalitarian governments to exist in the type of vacuums they could previously build around themselves.

CHANGES IN PROGRAM PRODUCTION

One of the effects of worldwide distribution and of increases in both quantity and quality of a number of the electronic media systems throughout the world is that programming product may come from a wider circle of producers. Long dominated by the United States, the international marketplace may soon feature other countries that can afford to program if they can realize profits from international distribution. Countries such as the Czech Republic, Egypt, and even Nepal may produce or coproduce programming for at least certain segments of the international audience. There are those who espouse that three major production centers be established in the world, one in Hollywood, one in an equally sunny part of Spain, and one in Australia near Brisbane, a city that has a climate not unlike that of Los Angeles.

Specialized production can flourish if it has an international audience. Channels devoted to model railroad collecting, Thai cooking, or wood carving could very well thrive if the worldwide audience were large enough. Even programs produced by amateurs with their camcorders might be economically viable. Of course, there are many factors mitigating against such specialized production. Language is certainly one of them. With the thousands of languages and dialects spoken throughout the world, it will be difficult, indeed, to program material to be understood internationally.

THE FUTURE OF EXTERNAL SERVICES

As worldwide broadcasting from satellites increases, there may be less need for the traditional external services that most countries presently operate. The points of view of the various countries can be merged with their international production—in a more subtle way than they can on radio transmission systems clearly designed for propagandistic purposes. Although there are still many tensions throughout the world, the disappearance of most of communism has already lessened the need for external broadcasting.

STRUCTURAL CHANGES

The structure of electronic media worldwide is also changing from one of benevolent government public systems to one of commercial private systems. Many of the older public systems are in danger of disappearing. Even the venerable BBC is under attack. This change could of course alter the cultural, uplifting focus that much of world broadcasting has previously had.

Related to the structural change is the question of the effects the commercials that appear on private TV will have worldwide. Will they spur economies? Will they cause unrest among the disadvantaged who cannot afford what is advertised? Will they make materialists out of the world's population?

Ratings take on an interesting focus in a worldwide market. How will advertisers know how many people are exposed to their messages? In Europe, for example, at least seven different methods are being employed to calculate audience levels. Rating points differ by as much as 30 percent from country to country, and media terminology also differs. In addition, exchange rates throughout the world make the calculation of ratings as related to advertising costs a nightmare.

Other issues revolve around the power of the media moguls. They have always been powerful in some parts of the world, such as South America. But as Murdoch, Berlusconi, and others increase their media holdings, will a few people wind up controlling what the rest of the world sees and hears? Will a few reap the economic benefits to the detriment of the many?

NEW TECHNICAL POSSIBILITIES

The question of a worldwide technical standard has been under discussion for decades. The adoption of one HDTV standard would improve pictures worldwide and help in the distribution of programming materials. However, technical solidarity is not as important as it once was. Mechanisms that "translate" from one set of technical parameters to another are becoming more common. Signals on satellites can be downconverted to satisfy a number of different needs. A bigger question involves the economics of technical change. If, indeed, people are coaxed (or forced) to buy new equipment in order to receive desired entertainment and important information, the companies and countries that are at the forefront of equipment development stand to profit handsomely.

The present forms of distribution have much to fear from the future. Terrestrial broadcasting is not as glamorous as it once was. The difficulties of transporting signals over mountains and into valleys are much less intense when distribution occurs from satellites. In a country such as the United States, local stations may no longer be needed because everyone will be able to set up small reception dishes that bring in signals directly from satellites. Cable TV, which is flourishing in some countries, floundering in others, and nonexistent in others, may be superseded by other distribution forms or may become the worldwide distribution method of choice. Will teletext take hold in countries that have not embraced it, or will it be buried by new forms that enter the information highway?

ETHICAL ISSUES

Worldwide electronic media will be involved in numerous ethical issues. Those wishing to broadcast the news first do not always get it right. Irresponsible reporting could unnecessarily upset international relations. Sex and violence on TV and in music lyrics broadcast on radio are already a major topic worldwide. Although most of the controversy centers around United States programming, other countries participate in the dissemination—Italian striptease game shows, Japanese violent cartoons. Worldwide understanding of the effects this can have on various cultures is needed.

Whatever the future of electronic media, the events are likely to be exciting and significant. If this book has led its readers to a better understanding of where the various media systems have come from and where they might be headed, then it has served its purpose of aiding those who may lead the future direction of the international world of electronic media.

Index

ABA (Australian Broadcasting Authority), 335–336, 339, 343
ABC (*see* American Broadcasting Company; Asahi Broadcasting Corporation; Australian Broadcasting Corporation)
ABCB (*see* Australian Broadcasting Control Board)
Abiola, M. K. O., 251
ABN (Asia Business News), 256
Aborigines, 321, 327, 331
ABT (*see* Australian Broadcasting Tribunal)
ABU (Asian Broadcasting Union), 271
Academy of Motion Picture Arts and Sciences, 173
  awards, 173, 284
Adenauer, Konrad, 129
Afghanistan, 2, 262, 264, 274
Africa, 241
Africa Media Review, 249
Africa News Service, 5
Africans, The, 241
Afrikaners, 230
AFRTS (Armed Forces Radio and Television Service), 220
Against the Wind, 338
AGB Research, 115
AIR (All India Radio), 262–266, 268–271, 273–276
Akashvani, 264, 270
Aktuelle Kamera, 142
Alawada, 243
Albania, 149, 152
Alf, 15
Algeria, 8, 195–196, 198
All India Radio (AIR), 263–266, 268–271, 273–276
All India Variety Program, 264, 269–270
Allende, Salvador, 56–57
Amchi Mati, Amchi Manse, 271
America (*see* United States)
American Broadcasting Company (ABC):
  beginnings, 33
  buying of, 38
  cable network ownership, 39
  David Brinkley's program on, 50
  formation, 33
  LATINO, 57
  and news, 5
  programming exports of, 5–7
  radio and TV fortunes, 35–36
  and Roots, 42
  vs. TV Globo, 83
  Venezuelan business interests, 55
American Public Radio (APR), 37
American Telephone and Telegraph (AT&T), 32
America's Funniest Home Videos, 10, 13
Amos 'n' Andy, 33
Ampex, 38, 50, 293
Angola, 227
Animal Farm, 121
Ansett, 333
Antenne, 2, 95
Antiope, 96
AP (Associated Press), 220, 291
Apartheid, 230–231
APR (American Public Radio), 37
Arabian American Oil Company (ARAMCO), 205, 210–211, 216, 218–219
Arabsat, 13, 201, 219
ARAMCO (*see* Arabian American Oil Company)
Arbeitsgemeinshaft der Rundfunkanstalten Deutschlands (ARD), 128–141, 143–144
Arbitron, 47, 189, 292
ARD (*see* Arbeitsgemeinshaft der Rundfunkanstalten Deutschlands)
Are You Being Served?, 243
Argentina, 15, 55–57, 71
Armed Forces Radio and Television Service (AFRTS), 220
Army Corps of Engineers (COE), 196, 206–210, 212, 218
Arnett, Peter, 7
ARTE, 139
Arts and Entertainment, 11, 39
Asahi Broadcasting Corporation (ABC), 302, 313
Asi, Morad, 218
Asia Business News (ABN), 256
Asian Broadcasting Union (ABU), 271
Asianet, 268
Asiasat, 13, 267
Associated Press (AP), 220, 291
Associated Redifussion (ATV), 103, 255
Astra, 94, 104–105, 117–120
A-Team, 230
AT&T (American Telephone and Telegraph), 32
ATN, 263

351

ATS-6, 265–266
ATV (Associated Redifussion), 103, 255
ATVI (Australian Television International), 344–345
Aussat, 335–336
Australia, 321–322
   as Australasian leader, 324
   Canadian programming, 25
   Empire Service, 237
   external services, 119
   news service, 5
   program exports of, 9–11, 294, 323, 349
   and Radio Prague, 172
   Rupert Murdoch, 16, 36
Australian Broadcasting Authority (ABA), 335–336, 339–343
Australian Broadcasting Company, 329, 337
Australian Broadcasting Control Board (ABCB), 330–332, 334, 339–340
Australian Broadcasting Corporation (ABC), 256, 329–339, 344–345
Australian Broadcasting Tribunal (ABT), 330, 333–335, 339–343
Australian Television International (ATVI), 344–345
Austria, 25, 92–94, 137, 158–159
Austro-Hungarian Empire, 158
Avengers, The, 243
AVEX, 159
AVRO, 94
Azcárraga, Emilio, 16, 26–27

Babangida, Ibrahim, 234, 240, 242, 245, 247, 251
Bahrain, 214
Baird, John Logie, 102
Banco Itaú, 70
Bandeirantes, 63–64, 69–70, 74, 79, 83
Bangladesh, 8, 257–258, 275
BARB (Broadcasters Audience Research Board), 115
Barris, Chuck, 1
Basic services, 37
Battista, Bobbie, 5
Bay Radio, Inc., 39
BBC (*see* British Broadcasting Corporation)
BBC Cymru, 107
BBC Wales, 107
BBDO (advertising agency), 15, 189
BCC (Broadcasting Complaints Commission), 116
Beijing Broadcasting Institute, 281–282
Beijing Television, 282
Belgium, 89, 91–94, 104, 225, 249
Benson and Hedges, 341
Berle, Milton, 34–35
Berlin Wall, 10, 124, 130, 142–143

Berlusconi, Silvio, 16, 96–97, 350
Bertelsmann, 134
BETA, 208
Better Life, 242
BFBS (British Forces Broadcasting Service), 220
Bharat, 262
Bhutan, 257–258, 262, 275
Bild Zeitung, 134
Black Entertainment Network, 250
Bloch, Adolfo, 69, 77
Blumlein, Alan, 102
Bodyline, 334
Boers, 230
Bohemia, 158
Bold and the Beautiful, The, 267, 274
Bond, Alan, 333, 336, 340
Bond Corporation, 340
Bop TV, 231, 239
Bophuthatswana, 231
Bosch, 144
BrasilSat, 65, 78, 82
Brazil, 61–85
   and Eastern Europe, 151
   export programs, 7
   influence in Latin America, 55–59
   and India, 272
   Tele-Monte Carlo, 16
Brazilian Association of Alternative Video Producers, 75
Brazilian Association of Community Antennas, 78
Brazilian Video Association, 66
Bredow, Hans, 126
Brezhnev, Leonid, 178–179
Brides of Christ, 338–339
Britain, 99–122
   and Africa, 226–227, 230–231, 234, 237, 243, 246
   and Asia, 257–258, 262, 264, 271, 273
   and Australia, 322, 324, 326, 331, 345
   cable TV, 93
   as colonial power, 195, 197, 198, 225
   on European continent, 89
   external broadcasting, 5
   franchising, 10
   and Middle East, 204, 213, 217, 219
   music from, 8
   as news provider, 5
   piracy in, 1, 14
   programming, 9, 13, 36, 74, 91, 94, 151
   radio, 32
   and Rupert Murdoch, 333
   and South America, 57, 81
   and U.S. companies, 16
   (*See also* England)
British Broadcasting Company, 101
British Broadcasting Corporation (BBC), 103–112

British Broadcasting Corporation (*Cont.*):
   and Africa, 225–227
   and Asia, 257
   audience measurement, 115–116
   and Australasia, 321, 323
   and Australia, 326, 328–329, 340, 344
   BBC Cymru, 107
   BBC Wales, 107
   and Canada, 23
   charter, 89
   and China, 283–284, 286, 290, 294
   and Eastern Europe, 172, 179, 181, 184
   external services, 105, 118–120
   formative years, 101
   and India, 263–264, 269
   and Japan, 315
   and Latin America, 57
   and Middle East, 196
   as model, 100
   and Nepal, 259
   as news provider, 5, 7
   and Nigeria, 235–237, 241, 248, 250
   and pirating, 102
   as program supplier, 7, 11
   regulation, 112–113
   and Saudi Arabia, 205, 217–220
   on STAR, 255, 267
   survival of, 121–122, 349
   transmission of, 116–117
British Cable and Wireless, 249
British Forces Broadcasting Service (BFBS), 220
British Information Service, 5
British Satellite Broadcasting (BSB), 104–105, 117–119
British Sky Broadcasting (BSkyB), 16, 105, 121, 256
   in Africa, 226
   in Britain, 105, 119, 121
   in Czechoslovakia, 163
   in Israel, 199
   in Nigeria, 239
Broadcasters Audience Research Board (BARB), 115
Broadcasting Complaints Commission (BCC), 116
Broadcasting and the People, 274
Broadcasting Standards Council (BSC), 116
Brock, Bazon, 135
Brown, Murphy, 346
Bryne, Gay, 111
BS-3, 304, 306, 314
BS-4, 305–306, 310, 312, 314–315
BSB (British Satellite Broadcasting), 104–105, 117–119
BSC (Broadcasting Standards Council), 116
BSkyB (*see* British Sky Broadcasting)
Buhari, Mohammadu, 247
Bulgaria, 149, 173
Buniyad, 272

Burkina Faso, 226–227
Burma, 262
Bush, George, 4, 5

CAAMA (Central Australian Aboriginal Media Association), 331
Cable News (China), 288
Cable News Network (CNN), 5–7
   in Africa, 226
   in Asia, 256
   in Bangladesh, 275
   in Brazil, 67
   on cable TV, 37, 40
   in China, 283–284
   CNN World Report, 6
   in Czechoslovakia, 163
   as external service, 50
   in Guatemala, 59
   and Gulf conflict, 134
   and India, 263, 267, 271
   in Israel, 199
   in Japan, 306
   in Latin America, 58
   in Nepal, 259
   news functions, 43
   in New Zealand, 323
   in Nigeria, 239, 241–242, 250
   popularity, 1, 10, 144
   in Russia, 181, 185
   satellite reception of, 31
   vs. teletext, 111
Cagney and Lacey, 231
Camcorder, 13–14
Cameroon, 226, 234
Canada, 23–25
   and Africa, 226
   and Australia, 336–337
   and China, 294
   Empire Service, 237
   and Japanese broadcasting, 315
   Marshall McLuhan, 1
   and New Zealand, 16, 323
   satellites of, 13
   South American investment, 55
Canadian Broadcasting Corporation (CBC), 24
Canadian Radio and Television Commission, 25
Canal France International, 163
Canal Horizon, 250
Canal Plus, 95
Canale 5, 96
CanWest, 336–337
Capital Cities, 5, 38, 256
Carlton, 115

Caruso, Enrico, 32
Castro, Fidel, 5, 56, 59
CBC (*see* Canadian Broadcasting Corporation; Chubu Nippon Broadcasting Company)
CBS (*see* Columbia Broadcasting System)
CCTV (China Central Television), 281–282, 284–287, 292, 297
Cellular telephones, 124
Central Australian Aboriginal Media Association (CAAMA), 331
Central News Organization, 264, 274
Central Television, 115
Česko, 159 (*see* Czech Republic)
CET-21, 162
CFI, 263
Chair for Our Guests, 168
Challenger, 267
Channel 1, 165, 167
Channel 2, 165
Channel 2 × 2, 181
Channel 3, 211
Channel Four, 104, 107–109, 111–113
  Channel Four News, 108
Channel 5, 16
Channel 6, 185
Channel 9, 332, 334
Channel 10, 332
Chaplin, Charlie, 151
Charlie's Angels, 243
Charter, 89, 100
Chase Enterprises, 153
Chateaubriand, Assis, 63–64
Chayefsky, Paddy, 169
Cherry pickers, 332
Chile, 16, 55–58, 75
China, 190, 258, 262–263, 277–298
  in Asia, 246–257
  and Australia, 327, 331, 344
  and Coca-Cola, 15
  external services of, 5
  external services to, 119–120
  and *Hunter*, 1
  music in, 8
  TV sets, 255
China Central Broadcasting, 282, 285
China Central Television (CCTV), 281–282, 284–287, 292, 297
China TV Play Production Center, 297
Chitrahar, 272
Chubu Nippon Broadcasting Company (CBC), 302
C.I.S. (Commonwealth of Independent States), 182–183, 191
Civita, Victor, 69
Classic FM, 106
Clay, Lucius, 128

Close Encounters of a Third Kind, 14
Closed captioning, 112, 115
CNN (*see* Cable News Network)
CNN World Report, 6
Coca-Cola, 15
Cock Crow at Dawn, 241
COE (Army Corps of Engineers), 196, 206–210, 212, 218
Colgate, 71
Columbia, 12, 16, 40, 316
Columbia Broadcasting System (CBS):
  beginnings of, 33
  in China, 284
  co-productions of, 11
  exporting programs, 5–7
  radio and TV operations, 35–36
  and *60 Minutes*, 43
  vs. TV Globo, 83
  Uruguan investments, 55
Columbia House, 11
Columbo, 151
Commonwealth of Independent States (C.I.S.), 182–183, 191
Communications Act of 1934, 33, 45–46
Compression, 17
Cook Islands, 321
Coproductions, 10–11
Copyguards, 14
Copyright, 14, 59, 93, 163, 185–186
Coronation Street, 109–110
Corporation for Public Broadcasting (CPB), 36, 89, 241
Cosby Show, The, 267
Costa Rica, 55–56
Country Practice, A, 345
CPB (Corporation for Public Broadcasting), 36, 89, 241
CPBS, 290, 292
Crawford Committee, 101, 117
Crocodile Dundee, 322, 338
Cronkite, Walter, 167
Crossfire, 271
Cross-media ownership, 56, 328, 330, 336–337, 340
CTV, 24
  CTV Kano, 241–243
Cuba, 4, 50, 55–56, 58–59, 71, 190
Cultural imperialism, 225–227, 242
Cultural Revolution, 278, 288
Curtin, John, 327
Czech Republic, 25, 94, 154, 157–174, 349
  (*See also* Czechoslovakia; Slovak Republic)
Czechoslovakia, 2, 149, 152, 157–174
Czechoslovakia II, 160

DAB (digital audio broadcasting), 49, 143, 304
Daily Times, 240

Dallas, 42, 96, 137, 230, 243
Danmarks Radio, 91
Dating Game, The, 1
Davidson, Basil, 241
DBS (*see* Direct broadcast satellite)
Death of a Princess, 217
Declaration of Talloires (France), 4
Defamation, 246
DeForest, Lee, 32
Deng Xiaoping, 279–280, 284, 288–289, 295
Denmark, 90–91, 93, 125
Deregulation, 9, 341
Desert Shield, 204, 220
Desert Storm, 204, 211
Deutsche Bundespost/Telecom, 125
Deutsche Rundfunkgesellschaft, 125
Deutsche Welle, 105, 133, 143–144, 163, 184
Deutscher Fernsehfunk (DFF), 134
Deutschland Fernseh GmbH, 129
Deutschlandfunk, 133, 143
Development programming, 228, 242, 251, 271
Devin, 160
DFF, 134
Dialogue, 49
Diana, Princess, 110
Diários e Emissoras Associadas, 63
Different Strokes, 243
Digital audio broadcasting (DAB), 49, 143, 304
Digital pail, 17
Digital technology, 343
Direct broadcast satellite (DBS):
    in Asia, 255
    in Brazil, 62–63, 66–67, 78, 82, 84
    in Britain, 104, 118–119, 121
    in Europe, 92
    in India, 273
    in Japan, 304
    in Nepal, 259
    and programming supply, 9
    in Russia, 191
    in United States, 30–31, 51
Discovery Channel, 256
Dismissal, The, 335
Disney cartoons and Latin cultures, 57
Disney Channel, The, 10, 38
Djibouti, 8
Doctor, The, 109
Dominican Republic, 55–56
Domsat, 249
Don Manua, 245
Donahue, Phil, 180
Doordarshan, 263, 265, 267–276
Dow Jones, 256
Drahtloser Dienst AG, 127
Drifter, The, 312

Duarte, L. G., 82
Dubai, 214
Dubček, Alexander, 162, 165, 167
Dutch (*see* Netherlands)
Dynasty, 42, 284

East Enders, 109
East Germany:
    audience research in, 141–142
    Berlin Wall, 10
    game show interest, 139
    reunification, 124–125, 129–130, 134, 149
    (*See also* German Democratic Republic; Germany)
Echo Moskvy, 184
Ecuador, 56
Editora Abril, 69–70, 77
EDTV II (extended-definition TV), 314–315
Educational Channel, 183
Educativa, 64
Edward VIII, 102
Egypt:
    and Middle East, 195, 197–201
    programming production, 349
    and STAR, 255
    and Saudi Arabia, 204–206, 208–209, 211–214, 216, 218, 222
Eilts, Hermann, 213
Ekene Umunwany, 245
Ekran, 179, 268
Eldorado, 109
Electronic churches, 44
Elizabeth II, 102
EMI, 102, 249
Empire Service, 119, 121, 237
England:
    and Australia, 327, 328, 334
    exporting programs, 11, 163
    and Germany, 127
    as industrialized country, 2
    music of, 41
    ownership of American companies, 39
    as part of United Kingdom, 99
English Garden, 151
English House, 151
ERT (*see* Greek Radio and Television)
Esperanto, 290
ESPN, 37–40, 43, 67, 256, 323
E. T., 1, 14
Ethiopia, 119, 227
Euromusic, 163
Europa Plus, 184, 190
European Telecommunications Satellite (Eutelsat), 13, 105, 118
Eurosport, 163, 239

Eurovision, 136, 173
Eutelsat (*see* European Telecommunications Satellite)
Evening Balance, 154
Excelsior, 64, 73
Extended-definition TV (EDTV II), 314–315

FAB (Fernsehen aus Berlin), 134
Face to Face, 188
FACTS (Federation of Australian Commercial Television Stations), 341
Fahd, king of Saudi Arabia, 5
Faisal, king of Saudi Arabia, 205, 207, 212–213, 218
Falcon Crest, 284, 286
Falklands War, 57
FAMU (Prague Film University), 169, 173
Fantástico, 74
FARB (Federation of Australian Radio Broadcasters), 329, 331
Farewell, My Concubine, 291
Fat Cats and Friends, 342
Fax machines, 328
FCC (*see* Federal Communications Commission)
Federal Communications Commission (FCC), 25, 33–36, 45–47, 51, 323
Federal Radio and Television Service Russia, 183
Federal Radio Corporation of Nigeria (FRCN), 234, 238–240, 245, 250
Federation of Australian Commercial Television Stations (FACTS), 341
Federation of Australian Radio Broadcasters (FARB), 329, 331
Fenic, Fero, 168
Fernsehen aus Berlin (FAB), 134
Fibber McGee and Molly, 33–34
Fiber optics, 328
Fielden, Lionel, 264
Fifth Program, 190
Fiji, 321–322
Film Studios Koliba, 169
Filmation, 16
Filmnet, 112, 163
Fine Romance, A, 11
Fininvest, 16, 97
Finland, 89–90, 93, 173
First Amendment, 3, 41, 46, 92
First Channel, 179, 181–183, 190, 209
First Program, 177, 182
Flintstones, The, 57
Flip Wilson Show, The, 243
Foley, John, 1
Foster, Stephen, 291
Four Corners, 339
Fourth Channel, 179, 182–183
Fourth Program, 178, 182

Fox, 16, 36
France, 89, 95–96, 104, 125
    Berlusconi involvement, 16
    and Brazil, 71, 81, 83
    as colonial power, 195–196, 225
    Declaration of Talloires, 4
    and Eastern Europe, 151, 163
    equipment, 190
    and Germany, 127
    and Luxembourg, 94
    and Middle East, 199, 204, 220
    and Nigeria, 249
    ownership of American companies, 39
    programming, 7, 9–12
    and SECAM, 17, 92, 218
    and South Africa, 230
    and South America, 55
France-Culture, 95
France-Musique, 95
France-Régions, 95
Franchising, 10
Franco, Francisco, 94
FRCN (Federal Radio Corporation of Nigeria), 234, 238–240, 245, 250
Free market, 279–280
Free Radio, 184
Friday the Thirteenth, 14
FR3, 95

Gabon, 250
Gabriela, 83
Gallup, 189
Gambia, 228
Gandhi, Indira, 269
Gandhi, Rajiv, 267
Gannett Company, 39
Gastil, Raymond, 248
GATT (General Agreement of Tariffs and Trade), 92
GDR (*see* German Democratic Republic)
GE (General Electric), 38–39, 249
General Agreement on Tariffs and Trade (GATT), 92
General Electric (GE), 38–39, 249
General Headquarters of the Allied Powers (GHQ), 302
General Motors (GM), 39
George VI, king of England, 102
Gere, Richard, 284
German Democratic Republic (GDR), 129–130, 141–142
    (*See also* East Germany)
Germany, 123–146
    Berlusconi in, 16
    Brazilian immigrants, 62
    as colonial power, 225
    Czech programming, 163

Germany (*Cont.*):
    and Czechoslovakia, 158, 160
    and Denmark, 93
    Deutsche Welle, 105
    and India, 274
    Israeli programming, 199
    and Luxembourg, 94, 104
    PAL, 17
    piracy, 14
    programming, 9–11
    and radio, 32
    and Russsia, 190
    and Slovak Republic, 159
    in South Africa, 230
    transmitters, 50
Gesselschaft für Kommunikations/Marktforschung (GfK), 141
Ghana, 228, 245
GHQ (General Headquarters of the Allied Powers), 302
Gilette, 15
Giwa, Dele, 247
Glasnost, 180
Glen Miller—Moonlight Serenade, 151
Global TV, 24
Globo, 16, 55, 63–70, 73–80
GloboSat, 67, 70, 78, 82
GM (General Motors), 39
Goebbels, Joseph, 127
Goncz, Arpad, 155
Good Night, Moscow, 182
Gorbachev, Mikhail, 118, 176, 180, 182, 184, 191, 284
Gostelradio, 176–185, 189
Goto, Shimpei, 301
Gowon, Yakubu, 249
Granada TV, 163
Great Soviet Encyclopedia, 176
Great Britain (*see* Britain; England)
Great Cultural Revolution, 278
Great Moravian Empire, 158
Greece, 89–91, 93–94, 327
Greek Radio and Television (ERT), 90
    ERA (1–4), 90
    ET (1–3), 90
Greenberg, Bradley, 79
Growth Rings, 150
Grupo Carvalho, 63
Grupos, 63
Grzimek, Bernard, 136
Guatemala, 31, 55–56, 59
Guyana, 59

Haiti, 55
Haley, Alex, 42, 231
Hallmark, 27
Happy Family, 258

Harden, Blaine, 251
Harlech Television (HTV), 104, 107
Harper Collins, 16
Hawke, Bob, 340
HBO (Home Box Office), 37–40, 56, 59, 152, 256
HDTV (*see* High-definition television)
Heimat, 139
Hello Mum, 150
Hi-Vision Promotion Association, 314
High-definition television (HDTV):
    in Australia, 343
    in Britain, 102
    future of, 350
    in Germany, 143
    Japan's involvement in, 17, 304–306, 313–316
    in United States, 49
Hirohito, emperor of Japan, 302
Hispansat, 13
Hitler, Adolf, 94, 124, 127–128, 158
Hlinka, Anton, 162
Home Box Office, 37–40, 56, 59, 152, 256
Home Service, 101–102
Home shopping, 44
Honduras, 56
Honecker, Erich, 130
Hong Kong:
    and Australasia, 324
    and China, 280, 289, 291–293
    external services to, 119
    and music, 291
    programming, 9, 236, 258
    and STAR, 12, 120, 255–256, 267, 283, 322
Horo do Brazil, 75
Hostile takeovers, 38–39
How to Read Donald Duck, 57
Hoyts Media, 337
HTV (Harlech Television), 104, 107
Hugenberf Press, 127
Huguenots, 230
Hum Log, 272
Hungary, 94, 149–154, 158–159, 173
Hunter, 1, 286
Hussein, Saddam, 196, 198
Hviezda, 160

I Love Lucy, 7, 35, 41
IBA (Independent Broadcasting Authority), 103–104, 106, 113, 119
IBOPE, 78, 82
Ilera, 242
Il Giornali, 97
Imperialist Ideology in the Disney Comic, 57
Imprensa, 77
Incredible Hulk, 15

Independent Broadcasting Authority (IBA), 103–104, 106, 113, 119
Independent Television (ITV), 103–116, 121
Independent Television Authority (ITA), 102, 106
Independent Television Commission (ITC), 100, 106, 111–112, 114–115, 117
Independent Television News (ITN), 5, 121, 181
India, 258, 261–276
   British influence, 257
   Empire Service, 237
   external services to, 119
   and *I Love Lucy*, 7, 12–13
   and Nigeria, 235–236
   and South Africa, 230
   and STAR, 12–13, 348
   and Zee-TV, 255
India Today, 263, 274
Indian Broadcasting Company, 263–264
Indian State Broadcasting System (ISBS), 263
Indonesia, 195, 219, 255–257, 344
INR, 106
Insat, 13, 267, 271, 274–276
Institute of Sociology of the Academy of Sciences, 189
Intelsat, 12–13
   in Bop TV, 231
   in Brazil, 65, 82
   in Middle East, 201
   in Saudi Arabia, 209, 219
Intendancy OK, 3, 163
Intendancy TA, 3, 163
International Commission for the Study of Communication Problems, 3
International Telecommunications Satellite Organization, 13
International Telecommunications Union (ITU), 12–13, 227
International Telegraph and Telephone (ITT), 205
Intersputnik, 13
Intervision Consortium, 172–173
Invizible Arts, 189
Iran, 195, 200
Iraq, 7, 196–198, 200–201, 204, 206, 218, 267
Ireland, 90, 94, 99, 111, 230, 327
ISBS (Indian State Broadcasting System), 263
Israel, 154, 195–201, 206, 267
Israeli Broadcasting Authority, 199
ITA (Independent Television Authority), 102, 106
Italy, 96–97
   and Australia, 327
   and Austria, 93
   and Brazil, 62, 83
   as colonial power, 195, 225
   and Latin America, 57
   programming of, 9, 350
   and radio, 32
   satellite programming, 12
   and Switzerland, 95
   during World War II, 119
   and Yugoslavia, 151–152
ITC (Independent Television Commission), 100, 106, 111–112, 114–115, 117
ITN (Independent Television News), 5, 121, 181
ITT (International Telegraph and Telephone), 205
ITU (International Telecommunications Union), 12–13, 227
ITV (Independent Television), 103–116, 121

Jack Benny Show, The, 33
Jackson, Michael, 1, 291
Jamaica, 55
Japan, 299–317
   and American companies, 16, 39
   in Asia, 258
   and Australasia, 321–322, 324
   and Australia, 327, 330, 344
   and Brazil, 62
   and China, 278, 280, 285, 292, 294–295
   as economic force, 255
   equipment, 50, 81, 117, 190, 343
   external services, 274
   and free flow of information, 2–3
   and Germany, 124, 143
   and HDTV, 17
   involvement in Asia, 256–257
   and Nigeria, 249
   programming, 9–11, 350
   and Saudi Arabia, 204
Japan News Network (JNN), 303
Japan Satellite Broadcasting (JSB), 304–305
JC SAT, 306
Jeffersons, The, 243
Jennings, Peter, 286
Jiang Zemin, 289
JNN (Japan News Network), 303
Johnson and Johnson, 186
Jordan, 195–196, 198–199, 206, 209, 211, 214, 218
Jornal do Brasil, 68
Jornal Nacional, 74
Jos Play of the Week, 243
JSB (Japan Satellite Broadcasting), 304–306

Kaddafi, Muammar, 5
Ka-shing, Li, 267
KDKA, 32
Keating, Paul, 326, 336
Kendras, 271
Kennedy, John F., 4, 294
Kenya, 241

INDEX

Kern, Jerome, 291
Kerr, John, 334
KGB, 176, 184
Khandaan, 272
Khazbulatov, Ruslan, 183
King, Martin Luther, 294
King, Michael, 10
King World, 10
Kodak, 186
Kojak, 151
Korea, 11, 257, 295, 343
Kottak, Conrad, 79
Kreslo pre host'a, 168
KRO, 94
Króner, Josef, 173
Kto je vinný, 168
Kume, Hiroshi, 310
Kuomintang, 278
Kurkova, Bella, 183
Kurosawa, Akira, 305
Kuwait, 195, 198, 200–201, 204, 208–209, 218
Kysuca, Kysuca, 167

LA Law, 345
La Cinq, 95
La Sept, 163
Länder, 125, 128–129
Landesrundfunkanstalten, 130
Laos, 257
Lapin, Sergei, 176, 179
Late, Late Show, The, 111
Latin American Television International Network Organization (LATINO), 57
Latvia, 176
Laugh-In, 58
League of Nations, 199
Lebanon, 195, 198, 200, 206, 209, 211, 213–214
Lee, Sophie, 343
Lenin, Vladimir, 161, 177
Lenin University of Millions, 179
Leningrad Committee on Television and Radio, 183
Leningrad Television, 183
Let the World Know China, 294
Li Ka-shing, 255–256
Libya, 195
Lifestyle, 163
Lifetime, 38
Light Programme, 101–102
Lighthouse, 177
Lindenstrasse, 137
Lintas, 39, 240
Lithuania, 176
LNB, 118
London Sun, 16

Look, 77
Loutsenko, Nikolai, 185
Lowenstein, Ralph, 248
L'udia, roky, udalosti, 167
Luxembourg, 91, 93–94, 104, 117

MAC, 117, 120
McArthur, Douglas, 302
MacBride, Sean, 3
MacBride report, 3–4
McCann-Erickson, 240
McLellan, Iain, 248
McLuhan, Marshall, 1, 7
MacNeil/Lehrer Newshour, 37, 50
Mad Max, 322, 338
Madame Butterfly, 126
Madonna, 1, 2
Magic World of Disney, The, 187
Magyar Radio, 154
Magyar Television (MTV), 150, 154
Mahabharata, 272, 274
Main Program, 197
Mainichi, 302
Malaysia, 14, 195, 255–258, 274, 344
Maldives, 258, 275
Malu Mujer, 74
Manchete, 64, 68–89, 74, 79, 83
Manchete, 77
Many Voices, One World, 3
Mao Zedong, 278–279, 284, 288, 294–296
Maoris, 321, 323
Marathon TV, 185
Marc et Sophie, 10
Marcomer Research Firm, 235
Marconi, Guglielmo, 23, 102, 119, 160
Marconi Company, 197
Marinho, Roberto, 56, 63, 68–70
Marplan, 78
Married . . . With Children, 36
Martin, L. John, 248
Marty, 169
Masani, Mehra, 274
Mass Communications in Africa, 248
Matsushita, 16, 38, 313, 316
Mattelart, Armand, 83
Mattelart, Michelle, 83
Mattos, Sérgio, 63
Maximum, 184
Mayak, 177, 182, 190
Mazrui, Ali, 241
MBC (Korean TV network), 11
MBC (Middle East Broadcasting Center), 222
MCA-Universal, 16
MCM (French TV programming), 163

Media Are American, The, 274
Mellor, David, 114
Menzies, Robert, 331
Merchandizing, 70
Merv Griffin Productions, 10
Mestre, Goar, 56
Mexican Television Cultural Network, 27
Mexico, 25–27
    and China, 292
    influence of, 16, 55–58
    interference with U.S. broadcasts, 12
    newscasts of, 5
    and North America, 23
    programming of, 272, 292
Middle East Broadcasting Centre (MBC), 222
Mind Your Language, 243
Minder, 345
Minichová, H., 169
Minitel, 96
MIP-TV, 9
Mitterand, François, 95
MMDS (*see* Multichannel multipoint distribution service)
M-Net, 231
Mongolia, 173, 257
Moravia, 158
Morocco, 195, 198
Moscow Global, 190
Moscow's Echo, 184
Moskva, 181–182
Moskva Globalnaya, 190
Motion Picture Association of America, 14
Motorola, 50, 315
Movie Channel, The, 38
M-6, 95
MTM, 16, 83
MTV (*see* Magyar Television; Music Television)
Multichannel multipoint distribution service (MMDS):
    in Brazil, 66, 75, 77, 82
    effects of, 9
    in Middle East, 201
    in Nigeria, 235, 239
    in New Zealand, 323
Multiple Sub-Nyquist Encoding (MUSE), 314, 316
Mundt, Carl, 303
Murdoch, Rupert:
    and Astra, 105, 119–121
    in Australia, 332–333, 345
    in Eastern Europe, 153
    and Fox, 36
    media holdings of, 16, 350
    and STAR, 255–256, 267, 283, 322
Murgaš, Josef, 160
Murphy Brown, 267
Musad, Faisal ibn, 207

Musad, Khalid ibn, 207
MUSE (Multiple Sub-Nyquist Encoding), 314, 316
Music Television (MTV), 163
    in Asia, 256
    beginnings, 41
    in Brazil, 66, 69, 81
    in Latin America, 56
    in India, 263
    in Nigeria, 239
    overseas popularity, 10
    satellite reception, 31
    on STAR, 255, 267
    as U.S. cable service, 37–38, 40
Mussolini, Benito, 119
My Brilliant Career, 322
My Brother's Children, 242
Myanmar, 262
Mytton, Graham, 248

Na aktuálnu tému, 168
Namaste America, 272
Namiesto výrobkov l'udia, 167
NAN (News Agency of Nigeria), 240, 244–245
NASA (National Aeronautics and Space Administration), 265–266
Nasser, Gamal Abdel, 197, 205
National Aeronautics and Space Administration (NASA), 265–266
National Broadcasting Company (NBC):
    airing material on, 9
    in Argentina, 55
    beginnings, 33
    buying of, 38–39
    as news provider, 5–7
    radio and TV operations, 35–36
    and TV Globo, 83
National Broadcasting Company International (NBCI), 206, 208, 212–213
National identity, 2–3, 12
National News, 74
National Programme, 101
National Public Radio (NPR), 36–37, 89
National Television Systems Committee (NTSC), 17–18, 49, 117, 219, 313–314
Nazis, 125, 127–128, 158, 178
NBC (*see* National Broadcasting Company; Nigerian Broadcasting Corporation)
NBCI (National Broadcasting Corporation International), 206, 208, 212–213
NBS (Nigerian Broadcasting Service), 237
NC9, 309
NCRV, 94
Neighbours, 11, 345
Nepal, 257–260, 262, 275, 349

INDEX **361**

Nepal Television (NTV), 258–259
Nestle, 272
NET, 303
Netherlands, 10, 12, 90–94, 230, 249, 257
Network-affiliate relationship, 33
New Adventures of Skippy, The, 342
New Caledonia, 230
New Guinea, 344
New Nigerian, 240
New World Information Order (NWIO), 3–4
New Zealand, 16, 25, 321–324, 334
New Zealand on Air, 323
News Agency of Nigeria (NAN), 240, 244–245
News Corporation, 16, 255, 332–333
News International Corporation, 105, 120
News Services Division (NSD), 264, 269, 274
News at Ten, 110
News Station, 309–310
Newswatch Magazine, 247
NHK (Nippon Hoso Kyokai), 302–305, 307–309, 311–313, 315–316
Nicaragua, 55–56
Nickelodeon, 38
Nielsen, 47–48, 189, 292, 313
Nigeria, 2, 225–226, 231, 233–252
Nigerian Broadcasting Corporation (NBC), 237–238
Nigerian Broadcasting Service (NBS), 237
Nigerian Television Authority (NTA), 234, 239–245, 248–250
Nightline, 13
NIKA TV, 185
Nine Network, 5, 337, 342
Nineteen Eighty Four, 121
Nipkow, Paul, 178
Nippon Electric, 249
Nippon Hoso Kyokai (NHK), 302–305, 307–309, 311–313, 315–316
Nippon Television (NTV), 303
NJB (Shin Nippon Broadcasting Company), 302
North and South, 155
North Korea, 257, 294–295
North Yemen, 6, 196
  (*See also* Yemen)
Northern Exposure, 345
Northern Ireland, 99
Norway, 89–91, 93
Nova, 162
Novosti News Agency, 184
Novotný, Antonín, 167
NPR (National Public Radio), 36–37, 89
NRK, 89
NSD (News Services Division), 264, 269, 274
NTA (Nigerian Television Authority), 234, 239–245, 248–250
NTSC, 17–18, 49, 117, 219, 313–314

N-TV, 134, 144–145
NTV (*see* Nepal Television; Nippon Television)
NWIO (New World Information Order), 3–4

Obshod na korze, 173
Ogilvy-Benson, 240
O Globo, 63
OK 3, 163
OKO, 168
Oman, 195, 196, 198
On Topicals, 168
One World, 290
OPEC (Organization of Petroleum Exporting Countries), 209, 234
Open University, 179, 289
Optus Communication, 335–336
ORF, 92, 159
Organization of African Unity, 227
Organization of Petroleum Exporting Countries (OPEC), 209, 234
Oriental TV, 284
Ortheus, 182
Orwell, George, 121
Oshin, 312
Otari, 293
Oyo State Television Service, 248

Packer, Kerry, 332, 334, 336–337, 345
Pakistan, 2, 219, 257–258, 262–264, 275
PAL (phase alternate line), 17–18
  in Australia, 333, 344
  in China, 293
  in Czechoslovakia, 163, 172
  in Eastern Europe, 152
  in Germany, 143
  vs. MAC, 117
  in Middle East, 196
  in Nigeria, 249
  in Russia, 190
  in Saudi Arabia, 218–219
  in Western Europe, 92–93
Palapa, 255, 344
Palestine Broadcasting Service, 199
Palestine Liberation Organization (PLO), 199
Panama, 14, 55–56
PanAmSat, 13
Panasonic, 293
Panorama, 109
Papua, 344
Paramount, 40, 256
Parker, Genero Delgado, 56
PBS (Public Broadcasting Service), 11, 36–37, 50, 89, 106–107
PCM (pulse code modulation), 301, 315

Peacock, Alan, 113
Peacock Report, The, 113
Pearson, 120
People Instead of Products, 167
People meters, 47, 79, 82, 313, 324, 341–342
People, Years, Events, 167
People's Daily, 288–289
Pepsi, 186
Perestroika, 186
Peru, 55–56
Phase Alternate Line (*see* PAL)
Philippines, 309
Philips, 117, 159, 249, 265
Pillarization, 94
Piracy, 14–15
　in China, 291
　in Czech and Slovak Republics, 163
　in Eastern Europe, 152
　in Russia, 185–186
　in Saudi Arabia, 209, 217
　in South America, 59
Pirates, 91–92, 95, 101–102, 120, 256
PKS-Programmgesellschaft, 134
Place for the Animals, A, 136
Platz für Tiere, Ein, 136
Playboy, 10, 38
PLO (Palestine Liberation Organization), 199
Poland, 125
　and Brazilian programming, 57
　CNN, 5
　in Eastern Europe, 149, 151–153, 155
　as Second World Country, 2
　and TV, 1
Political Discussion, 310
Polska Telewizja Kablowa, 153
Pope John Paul, 151–152
Poptsov, Oleg, 181
Portugal:
　and Brazil, 83
　cable TV and satellites, 93
　as colonial power, 225
　and Latin America, 55
　public broadcasting system in, 89
　rádionovelas, 71
　Roberto Marinho, 69
Posner, Vladimir, 180
Powerful Saturday, 311
Prague Film University (FAMU), 169, 173
Prague Spring, 162, 165, 167, 170
Pravda, 177, 182
Premiere, 163
Press Trust of India (PTI), 269
Prime Network, 255
Producer Choice, 122

Program exchange, 7–12
PTI (Press Trust of India), 269
PTT, 89, 96
Public access, 47, 321, 330, 336, 343
Public broadcasting, 321, 330–331
Public Broadcasting Act, 36
Public Broadcasting Service (PBS), 11, 36–37, 50, 89, 106–107
Public Radio International, 37
Puerto Rico, 27
Pulse code modulation (PCM), 301, 315
Putonghua, 281

Qatar, 195
Quayle, Dan, 346
Quotas, 9, 11, 23, 25, 330, 341
QVC, 105

Radio 1, 102, 182, 190
Radio 2, 102, 182, 190
Radio 3, 102
Radio 4, 102
Radio 5, 102
Radio Australia, 330, 344–345
Rádio Bandeirantes, 63–64
Radio Beijing, 290, 293
Radio Cairo, 197, 206, 220
Radio Caroline, 101
Radio Ceylon, 263
Radio Club of Calcutta, 263
Radio Corporation of America (RCA):
　David Sarnoff, 34, 102
　equipment, 50
　and NBC, 38
　in Saudi Arabia, 196, 206–207, 218
Radio Enugu, 245
Radio for All Society, 177
Radio France, 95
Radio France Internationale, 226–227
Radio Free Europe, 50, 162, 172
Rádio Globo, 63
Radio Japan, 315
Radio Joint Audience Research (RAJAR), 116
Rádio Jovem Pan, 66
Radio Kuwait, 220
Radio Liberty, 50
Radio London, 101
Radio Luxembourg, 101, 104, 134
Radio M, 184
Radio Marti, 50
Radio Mayak, 177, 182, 190
Radio Mecca, 205

Radio Monte Carlo, 196, 210, 218, 220
Radio Moscow, 190, 269
Rádio Nacional, 76
Radio Prague, 172
Radio Rocks, 184
Radio Russia, 181–182, 190
Radio Russia-Nostaligie, 184
Radio Tokyo, 309
Radio Vatican, 172
Radiodiffusion de France, 95
Radiodiffusion Télévision de France (RTF), 95
Radiokommissia, 177
Rádionovelas, 63, 71
Radiosoviet, 177
Radiotelevisione Italiana (RAI), 96–97
Rádiožurnál, 160
Rahman, M., 263
RAI (Radiotelevisione Italiana), 96–97
RAJAR (Radio Joint Audience Research), 116
Ramayana, 272, 274
RAN, 131
Rather, Dan, 167, 284
Ratings, 15, 47–49, 79, 324, 341–342, 349–350
RBS, 68
RCA (*see* Radio Corporation of America)
Record, 64
Red Versus White Singing Competition, 302
Reference Material, 288
Reference News, 288
Regional Programme, 101
Regional Radiocommunication Conferences (RRC), 13
Reichsrundfunk, 125
Reichssender, 127–128
Reith, John, 101, 119, 340
Request TV, 38
Reuters, 5, 269
Rich Also Cry, The, 27
Rights fees, 43, 283
Riviera, 10
Riyadh Domestic Service, 205
Rocky IV, 14
Rogers, Kenny, 291
Romania, 149
Roots, 42, 231
Rosing, B., 178
Royalties, 14
RRC (Regional Radiocommunication Conferences), 13
RSMB Television Research, 115
RTE, 111
RTF (Radiodiffusion Télévision de France), 95
RTL, 11, 134–135, 141, 163
RTO (Russia State Radio and Television Company Ostankino), 182–183, 185, 188, 190
RTP, 89

RTR (Russian State Radio and Television Company), 181–184, 186–190
Rubio, Maria, 26
Rumanovský, Ivan, 167
Runaway production, 25
Rundfunkgesetz, 126
Russia:
  in Asia, 268
  and China, 294, 295
  coup in, 153
  in Eastern Europe, 149
  and Germany, 127
  and Israel, 199
  radio in, 32
  telenovelas in, 27
  (*See also* Soviet Union)
Russian Media Monitor, 189
Russian State Television and Radio Company (RTR), 181–184, 186–190
Russian State Television and Radio Company Ostankino (RTO), 182–183, 185, 188, 190
Russian Universities Channel, 183
Rysher Entertainment, 11

Saad, 69
Saatchi and Saatchi, 15
Saban International, 11
SABC (South African Broadcasting Corporation), 230–231
Sadat, Anwar, 197
Saint, The, 243
St. Petersburg Russian State Television and Radio Company, 183
St. Petersburg Television, 183
Saklambac, 1
Salinas, Carlos, 26
Samoa, 321
Sanchez, Homero Icaza, 80
Sanford and Son, 243
Santa Barbara, 267, 274
Santos, Sílvio, 64, 69, 77
Sarabhai, Vikram, 265
Sarney, José, 77
Sarnoff, David, 34, 102
Sat.1, 131, 134–135, 141, 163
Satcom, 13
Satellite Instructional Television Experiment (SITE), 265–267, 275
Satellite master antenna television (SMATV), 9, 62–63, 67, 78, 82
Saud, Abdul Aziz ibn, 204
Saudi Arabia, 5, 13, 195–198, 201–222, 235–236
Sawyer, Diane, 286

SBS (Special Broadcasting Service), 327, 329, 331, 333, 335–339, 343
SBT, 64, 69–70, 74, 79
SCC, 306
Schnitzler, Eduard, 142
Schwarze Kanal, Der, 142
Scotland, 99, 111, 327
Screen Digest, 235–236
Screensport, 163
SECAM (Sequence Couleur à Memoire), 17–18
　in Belgium, 92
　in China, 293
　in Czechoslovakia, 172
　in Eastern Europe, 152
　in Middle East, 196
　in Russia, 190
　in Saudi Arabia, 218
Second Channel, 179–181, 190, 209–210
Second Program, 177, 197
Section 315, 46
Sedition, 246
Seiko, 303
Selassie, Haile, 227
Senegal, 250
SEPT, 95
Sequence Couleur à Memoire (*see* SECAM)
SES (Société Européenne de Satellites), 104
Sesame Street, 42, 57, 137, 151, 198, 242
Seven Network, 337
Sex, 342
S4C, 107–108, 114
Shagari, Shehu, 238
Shah, Neer Bikram, 258–260
Shanghai TV, 284
Shangri-La, 259, 275
Shin Nippon Broadcasting Company (NJB), 302
Shiokawa, Masajuro, 310
Ship-to-shore communications, 32
Shoenberg, Isaac, 102
Shoriki, Matsutaro, 303
Shortwave, 50
Show de auditório, 71, 73–74
Show of Life, The, 74
Showtime, 37–38, 40
Siemens, 144
Silicon Graphics, 293
Simpsons, The, 15, 36
Singapore, 255–256
SITE (Satellite Instructional Television Experiment), 265–267, 275
60 Minutes, 43, 150, 339
Skiffle Club, 101
Sky TV (New Zealand), 323
Slovak National Network, 160

Slovak Republic, 94, 154, 157–174
　(*See also* Czech Republic; Czechoslovakia)
Slovensko, 159
SMATV (satellite master antenna television), 9, 62–63, 67, 78, 82
Smile, Please, 10
Société d'Éditions de Programmes de Télévision, 95
Société Européenne de Satellites (SES), 104
Solidarity, 152
Sondhi, Krishan, 266
Sony:
　in China, 293
　and Columbia Pictures, 16, 316
　in Czechoslovakia, 172
　in Germany, 143
　leadership, 313
　in Nigeria, 249
　VCRs, 38
South Africa, 225–226, 230–231, 235, 239, 243
South African Broadcasting Corporation (SABC), 230–231
South Asian Association for Regional Cooperation, 258, 275
South Vietnam, 258
South Yemen, 6, 196
　(*See also* Yemen)
Southern TV, 104
Soviet Central Radio, 178, 180–181
Soviet Central Television, 178–181, 185, 190
Soviet Union, 176–187, 190–191
　and Africa, 229
　and China, 279–281, 284, 295
　as Communist model, 149–151, 152–154
　and Cuba, 56
　and Czechoslovakia, 158–159, 162, 170
　and East Germany, 128
　and Egypt, 197
　and Germany, 130
　and Intervision, 172
　programming, 7
　and Radio Liberty, 50
　satellite launch, 309
　as Second World leader, 2
　(*See also* Russia)
SpaceNet, 222
Spain:
　Berlusconi in, 16
　as colonial power, 225
　on European continent, 89
　government control of media, 94
　and Latin America, 55
　media financing, 91
　Olympics in, 272
　programming, 349

Spain (*Cont.*):
  rádionovelas in, 71
  and satellites, 93
  and TV Globo, 83
Spanish International Television, 74
Special Broadcasting Service (SBS), 327, 329, 331, 333, 335–339, 343
Spielberg, Steven, 1
Spies, 11
Sportkanal, 163
Sports News, 139
Sportschau, 131, 139
Springer, Axel, 134
Squandering of the Riches, The, 241
Sri Lanka, 256–258, 263, 275
Star, 160
STAR, 255–256
  in Asia, 348
  in Australasia, 322
  in China, 283
  in India, 12, 267–268, 275–276
  Murdoch interest in, 16, 120
  in Nepal, 259
Star Trek, 41
Startext, 112
STASI, 130
State Committee for Television and Radio (*see* Gostelradio)
Station representative, 39
Stephenson, Pamela, 342
Store on the Promenade, 173
Streets of San Francisco, The, 151
Sudan, 195, 198, 201
Sunday Morning, 310
Sunday Project, 310
Sunday Word, 139
Super Channel, 163
Sutekini Document, 313
Svobodnoye Radio, 184
Swaggert, Jimmy, 226
Swaziland, 226–227
Sweden, 91–93
Switzerland, 25, 83, 90, 93–95, 137, 249
Sylvania Waters, 346
Syria, 12, 196, 200, 206

Taiwan, 1, 256–258, 291–293, 343
Takayangi, Kenjiro, 302
Tama Cable Network, 307
Tantawi, Shayki Ali, 213
TA 3, 163
TBS (Tokyo Broadcasting System), 11, 301, 309–310
TBS (Turner Broadcasting System), 185, 256
TCI, 256
TCN Nine Sydney, 332
Tekst TV, 93
Telam, 58
Tele-Monte Carlo, 16
Telecasters North Queensland, 337
Telefunken, 144
Telegraph, 3
Telenovelas, 73–74
  in Brazil, 80
  Brazilian export of, 83–84
  development of, 64–65
  in Eastern Europe, 151
  in India, 272
  in Latin America, 58–59
  merchandizing of, 70
  in Mexico, 26
  popularity, 27
  production of, 77
Teletekst, 93
Teletext, 93, 96, 111–112, 323
Televisa, 16, 25–27
Television Broadcasts, 256
Télévision Française, 95
Television New Zealand, 256
Television University, 289
Televisor, 102
Televízne noviny, 166
Telsat, 13
Telstar I, 12
Ten Network, 332, 337
Terminator 2, 185
Terrorism, 4–5, 7
TESLA, 159
Texaco Star Theater, 34
TF1, 11, 95
Thaicom, 13
Thailand, 255
Thames Television, 104, 151
Thank You to Women, 245
Thatcher, Margaret, 5, 113–114
Third Channel, 179, 181
Third Program (Egypt), 197
Third Programme (United Kingdom), 89, 101–102
3rd Programs (Germany), 129, 131, 134, 139, 141–142
Third Reich, 124, 127
This Is My Town, 167
This Week with David Brinkley, 50
Thompson CSF, 249
Thomson Television, 117, 227, 293
Thunder in Paradise, 11
Tiananmen Square, 284–285, 288–289, 295
Tieta, 70
Time, 179

Time, Inc., 37
Time-Life, 55, 68, 70, 83
Time Warner, 37, 39, 134, 256, 345
Times of London, 16
TNT, 67
Tofa, Bashir, 251
Tokyo Broadcasting System (TBS), 11, 301, 309–310
Tokyo Rose, 315
Toll station, 32
Tonight Show, The, 13
Top Model, 70
Top of the Pops, 11
Toto je moje mesto, 167
Trinidad, 55
Tunisia, 195, 198, 201
Tunstall, Jeremy, 274
Tupi, 63–64, 77
Turkey, 1, 195, 199
Turksat, 13
Turner, Ted, 5, 50, 153, 185
Turner Broadcasting System (TBS), 185, 256
Tutti Frutti, 12
TV1, 139, 230–231
TV-5, 263
TVA, 66–67, 69, 70, 82
TV-AM, 113–114
TV Asahi, 303, 309–310
TV Bandeirantes, 64, 69–70, 74, 79, 83
TV Cultura, 64, 78
TV Educativa, 64
TV Excelsior, 64, 73
TV Globo, 16, 55, 63–70, 73–80, 83
TV Manchete, 64, 68–69, 74, 79, 83
TV News Features, 271
TV Ontario, 24
TV Record, 64
TV Rio, 64, 73
TV Tupi, 63–64, 77
TV Violence in Australia, 346
Twentieth Century Fox, 16
Twin Peaks, 243
TWW, 104
Týžden vo filme, 166

Uganda, 227
Ulema, 204, 212
UNESCO (U.N. Educational, Scientific, and Cultural Organization), 3, 235–236, 265
Unicap, 186
UNILAG Media Review, 249
Union of Soviet Socialist Republics (*see* Russia; Soviet Union)
Union of South Africa (*see* South Africa)

United Arab Emirates, 196, 198
United Arab Republic, 200
United Kingdom (*see* Britain; England)
United Nations, 12, 17, 199, 227
U.N. Educational, Scientific, and Cultural Organization (*see* UNESCO)
United Press International (UPI), 166, 211, 222, 269
United States, 23, 29–51
  advertising, 15
  and Africa, 226–227, 231
  and Australia, 321, 326–327, 331, 343, 345, 346
  and Brazil, 57, 59, 66–69, 71–76, 79, 81, 83–84
  and Britain, 100
  and Canada, 13–15
  and China, 280–282, 284–286, 290, 292, 294
  and CNN, 7
  companies in other countries, 16
  consultants, 10
  cross-ownership, 5
  and Czechoslovakia, 162–163, 166–167, 169, 172
  and Eastern Europe, 150–152, 155
  equipment, 343
  and France, 95
  and free flow of information, 2–3
  and Germany, 124, 127, 128, 130, 135, 139, 143–145
  and Guatemala, 59
  and India, 264–265, 271
  and Italy, 96–97
  and Japan, 299–301, 304, 306, 313–315
  and Mexico, 12, 26–27
  and Middle East, 195
  and New Zealand, 323
  and Nigeria, 235–236, 242, 245, 249–250
  patents, 160
  per capita income, 227
  piracy, 14
  programming, 5, 7–11, 14, 58, 316, 349–350
  public broadcasting, 89
  ratings, 189
  Rupert Murdoch, 333
  and Russia, 187, 190
  satellites, 13
  and Saudi Arabia, 204–205, 210–211, 213, 217
  and South America, 55
  and Soviet Union, 180
  technical standards, 17
  teletext, 111
  television development, 102
  UPI service, 222
  and Vietnam, 258
  Voice of America, 105
  and Western Europe, 90–91
U.S. Agency for International Development (*see* USAID)

U.S. Information Agency (see USIA)
Universal, 40, 316
Univision, 27
UPI (United Press International), 166, 211, 222, 269
Upjohn, 186
Upper Mongolia, 255
Uraguay, 55, 58
Us, You, Them, 150
USAID (U.S. Agency for International Development), 243, 245
USIA (U.S. Information Agency), 49, 218, 248
USSR (see C.I.S.; Russia; Soviet Union)

VARA, 94
Vargas, Getulio, 67, 69, 76
Vatican, 1
Veja, 77
Venezuela, 55, 75
Viacom, 256
Video on demand, 256
Video Research, 313
Videofilm, 185
Videotext, 93, 96
Vietnam, 4, 257
Village Headmaster, 243
Virgin Radio, 106
VISNEWS, 166
Vividh Bharati, 264, 269–270
VixNews, 5
Vltava, 160
Vlyarkovski, Vladislav, 187
VOA (see Voice of America)
Voice of America (VOA):
  in Africa, 226
  in Brazil, 82
  in China, 294
  in Czechoslovakia, 172
  on Eutelsat, 105
  in India, 269
  in Japan, 315
  in Middle East, 196
  news, 5
  in Nigeria, 250
  and Radio Australia, 344
  in Russia, 184, 190
  in Saudi Arabia, 220
  in South America, 58
  structure of, 49–50
Voice of Brazil, 82
Voice of Islam, 205, 208, 212
Voice of Nigeria (VON), 249–250
Voice of the Arabs, 197, 205–206
Volksempfänger, 127–128

VON (Voice of Nigeria), 249–250
VOX, 126
VPRO, 94
Vremya, 179–180, 187

Wada, Shoichi, 310
Wales, 99, 107–108, 111, 327
Walesa, Lech, 1
WARC (World Administrative Radio Conferences), 13, 17
Warner-Roadshow, 345
Washington Post, The, 251
Weather Channel, The, 37
Week in Film, 166
Weimar Republic, 127
Werich, Jan, 167
Wesgo, 337
West Germany, 124–125, 129–130, 133, 142, 249
  (See also Germany)
Westinghouse, 50
Westwood One, 39
WETA, 37
Wharf Cable, 256
What Is Your Name, 302
Wheel of Fortune, 10, 311
White, Vanna, 10
Whitlam, John Gough, 330, 334
Who Is Guilty?, 168
Williams, Don, 245
Winds of War, 155
Winfield, 341
WLBT, 45
WNTV, 238, 243
Women and Advertising, 347
World Administrative Radio Conferences (WARC), 13, 17
World in Action, 110
World Radio Television Handbook, 236
World Radiocommunication Conferences (WRC), 12–13
World Report, 250
World Service, 118–121
  in Africa, 226
  and Australia, 344
  in China, 284
  and CNN, 7
  on Eutelsat, 105
  in Middle East, 196
  in Nepal, 259
  in Saudi Arabia, 220
  on STAR, 255
World Television News, 5
World This Week, The, 271

Worldnet, 5, 49, 163
Wort zum Sonntag, 139
WRC (World Radiocommunication Conferences), 12–13
WST, 263
WSTV (World Service Television), 120

Xian Film Studio, 286
Xiaoping, Deng (*see* Deng Ziaoping)
Xinhua News Agency, 5, 282, 288, 291–292
Xuxa's Show, 83

Yamashita, Tokuo, 310
Yarase, 313
Yeltsin, Boris, 153, 181–183, 185, 189
Yemen, 205, 214
  (*See also* North Yemen; South Yemen)

YLE, 89
Yomiuri, 302
Yugoslavia, 97, 149, 150–152
Yuv Vani, 270

Zaire, 227
ZDF (Zweite Deutsche Fernsehen), 129–131, 133–141, 144
ZDF-Magazin, 142
Zedong, Mao (*see* Mao Zedong)
Zee-TV, 155, 259, 263, 268
Zimbabwe, 2, 226, 243
Zweite Deutsche Fernsehen (ZDF), 129–131, 133–141, 144
Zworykin, Vladimir, 102